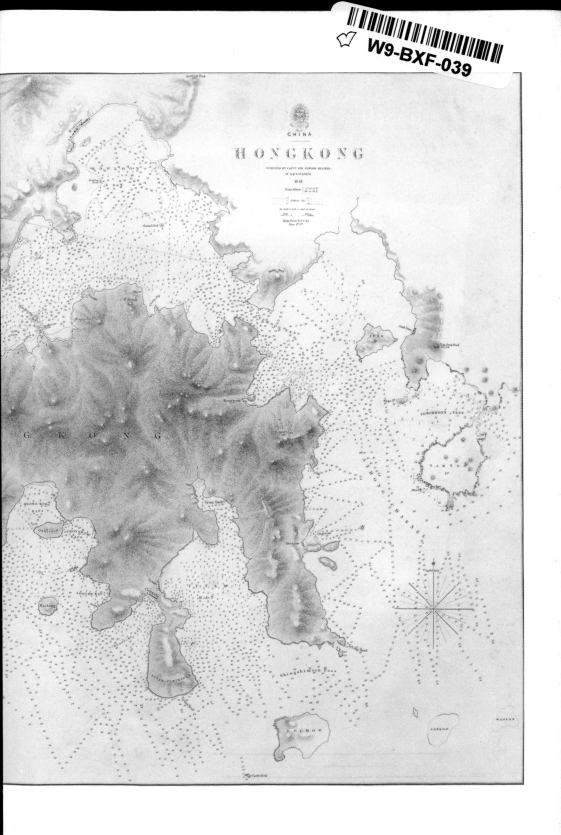

BOSTON
PUBLIC
LIBRARY

THE HISTORY OF HONG KONG

Frank Welsh

KODANSHA INTERNATIONAL
New York • Tokyo • London

Kodansha America, Inc.
114 Fifth Avenue, New York, New York 10011, U.S.A.

Kodansha International Ltd.
17-14 Otowa 1-chome, Bunkyo-ku, Tokyo 112, Japan

Published in 1993 by Kodansha America, Inc.

Printed in the United States of America

Endpaper of the Admiralty Chart of Hong Kong waters as surveyed
by Captain Sir Edward Belcher of H.M.S. *Sulphur* in 1841.
Reproduced courtesy of the trustees of
the National Maritime Museum, Greenwich, England.

93 94 95 96 97 6 5 4 3 2 1

Library of Congress Cataloging-in-Publication Data

Welsh, Frank.
A Borrowed place : the history of Hong Kong / Frank Welsh.
p.   cm.
Includes bibliographical references and index.
ISBN 1-56836-002-9
1. Hong Kong—History.   I. Title.
DS796.H757W45   1994
951.25—dc20   93-5017
                                                   CIP

The jacket was printed by
Phoenix Color Corporation,
Long Island City, New York.

Printed and bound by
R. R. Donnelley & Sons Company,
Harrisonburg, Virginia.

CONTENTS

MAPS

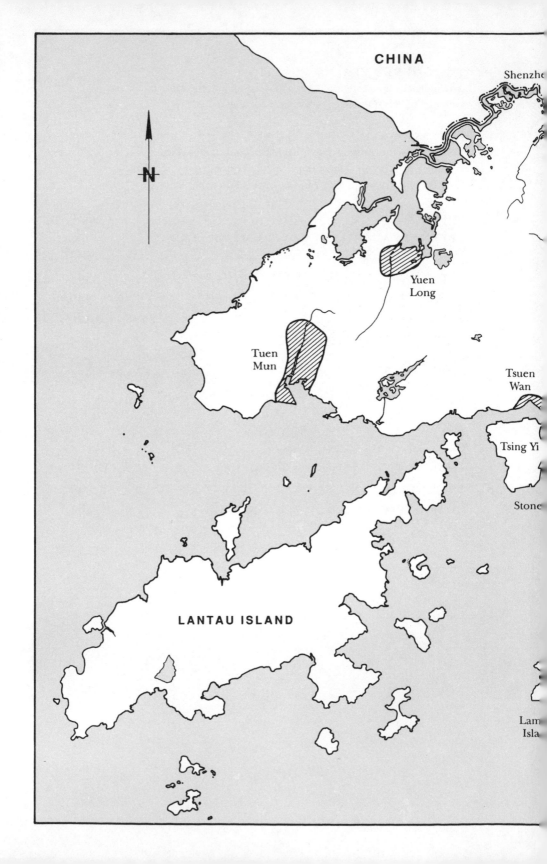

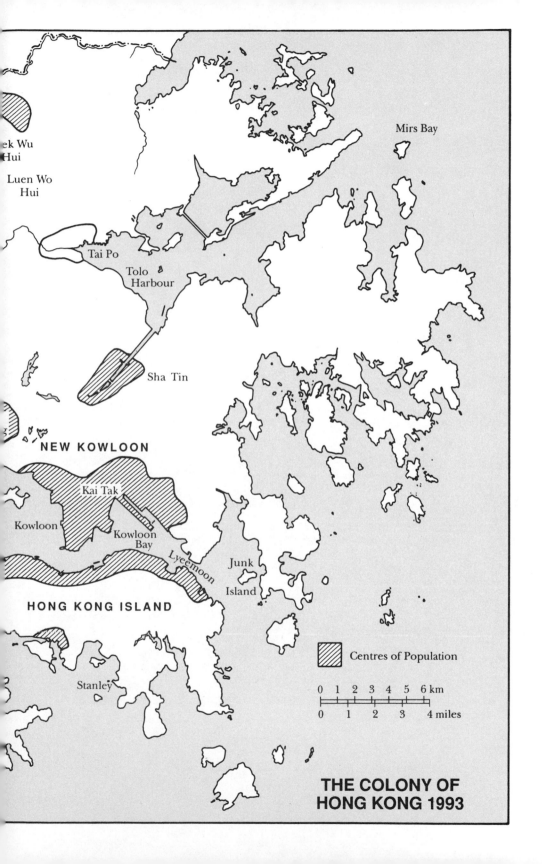

Mirs Bay

ek Wu
Hui

Luen Wo
Hui

Tai Po

Tolo
Harbour

Sha Tin

NEW KOWLOON

Kai Tak

Kowloon

Kowloon
Bay

Lyeemoon

Junk
Island

HONG KONG ISLAND

Stanley

Centres of Population

0 1 2 3 4 5 6 km

0   1   2   3   4 miles

**THE COLONY OF
HONG KONG 1993**

FOREWORD

My interest in Hong Kong was first aroused by a visit there in 1970, following the acquisition, by a London bank of which I was a director, of the Dao Hang Bank, one of the colony's larger Chinese banks.

Shortly afterwards, in 1972, my family bought Flass, the Westmorland house built in 1849 by the Dent brothers, Lancelot and Wilkinson, formerly merchants of Canton and Hong Kong. It was the Chinese authorities' threat to arrest Lancelot Dent that had, in 1839, set in motion the events that led to the first Anglo–Chinese war, commonly known as the 'Opium War' (commonly but erroneously, as I endeavour to prove in Chapter 3). As a result of that war Hong Kong was ceded to the British Crown, most of the Canton trade following the flag, and the firm of Dent's becoming one of the most influential in the new colony. Flass, together with its remaining furnishings (the Chinese bed in the Gulbenkian Museum of Oriental Art in Durham is worth a look), precisely reflected the tastes of those early Victorian 'merchant princes'. In some interesting details Flass also exemplified the differences that distinguished the Dents from their great rivals, the Jardines and Mathesons. Modest by comparison with the Highland palaces constructed by James and Alexander Matheson, Flass reflected the primmer, less flamboyant character of Lancelot Dent; its distinction lay in such details as the hand-painted wallpaper, the ivory door-furniture, and the Italian wrought-metal work. As the house was open to the public we put together, with the help of the Abbot Hall Museum in Kendal, a small exhibition illustrating the development of the China trade. In writing a short guide to this I took the first steps that later led to the present book being produced.

Some apologies need to be made in advance. Any history of an

Anglo–Chinese enterprise is unhappily likely to be both one-sided and patchy. One-sided since scholars equipped to deal with Manchu and Chinese official documents housed in the Historical Archives in Beijing may well not be alert to the nuances of nineteenth-century British politics and society; and any academic might find some difficulty in dealing with the sharply commercial aspects of the colony's history. A writer with no Chinese, on the other hand, has to rely on translations and selection from the great mass of available material, and as a result this work, in addition to its other defects, is inescapably Anglocentric. Dealing with so extensive a subject as the history of a society over the better part of two centuries in the compass of a single volume leads either to bland generalizations or to selections of episodes that seem to be revealing. In attempting to avoid the former I am sadly aware of omitting much relevant material, but trust that the bibliography may at least offer some access to this.

Events in Hong Kong move too fast for a book, constrained by the inevitable time-lag between writing and publication, to do justice to them. In the twenty-four months between March 1991 and March 1993 the Gross Domestic Product per capita of Hong Kong has exceeded that of Great Britain. By this, as by many other criteria, the colony has finally, probably permanently, and certainly unexpectedly quickly, overtaken the 'Mother Country'.

Political developments have also been rapid, and much more surprising. In October 1992 the Governor of Hong Kong decided to use Crown prerogative in a way that had rarely – if ever – been done before. By simple decree the composition of the Executive Council, and the balance between that and the Legislative Council, was changed. It was as if a Tudor monarch had used his absolute powers to alter the workings of his government. Although this initiative of Chris Patten underlined the plenitude of Crown powers, it diverted the course of constitutional development in Hong Kong, which had been moving towards the representation of elected Legislative Councillors on the Executive Council. The move was accompanied by proposals to extend the franchise, which aroused widespread consternation and great indignation from China. A minor consequence was that my description of Hong Kong's constitutional structure as it was before Mr Patten's arrival has had to be revised in an epilogue, to reflect these changes.

My consciousness of these defects leads to the acknowledgements to those generous people who have helped being more than usually heartfelt. A visit to Beijing, which was made possible by Laura Rivkin of the Great Britain–China Association, Tony Farrington of the India Office Library, and Feng Zizhi, Director General of the State Archives Bureau in Beijing, led to obtaining the help of Xu Yipu, Deputy Head of the First Historical Archives and Shen Lihua, Deputy Chief of the Foreign Affairs Division of the State Archives. Their unstinting and friendly assistance enabled us to identify some material which may give a new understanding of Anglo–Chinese relations in the 1840s. The most difficult task of translating from cursive classical Chinese was ably performed by Charles Aylmer, of the Cambridge University Library. In Hong Kong Dr Elizabeth Sinn and Dr (Chan Lau) Kit-ching patiently instructed me on several issues, and the inexhaustible hospitality of Dr John Cheong and Dr Priscilla Roberts was combined with guidance on subjects as diverse as the Canton trade and modern American history. To them, and to those other members of the History Department, especially Dr Adam Lui, who uncomplainingly put up with an uninvited guest, I am grateful. As I am also to the Vice Chancellor, Professor Wang Gungwu, Sir Albert Rodrigues, the Pro-Chancellor, Dr Norman Miners, Dr Peter Wesley Smith, the Master and Staff of Robert Black College. In Hong Kong I also owe thanks to Lord and Lady Wilson, Sir Piers Jacobs, Sir Jack Cater, Simon Murray, Gordon Wu, and especially to Clare Hollingworth and to Mark and Maurine Sabine. Nigel Cameron, Susanna Hoe and Alan Birch, all historians possessing much greater experience of Hong Kong than mine, were particularly kind. Mark Pinkstone and Shirley Wong of the Government Information Services Department, Dr Joseph S.P. Ting of the Hong Kong Museum of History, and Dr Thomas Lau of the Government Records Service provided much valuable material. To Mark and Lesley Henneker-Major, and to Philip and Mary Walker I owe introductions to many Hong Kong residents, including the Honourable Miriam Lau, Angus and Bibi Forsyth, and Peter and Tricia Carton.

In retrospect I realize how much instruction I have gathered from conversations over the years with such wise and knowledgeable men as Lord Gore-Booth, Sir Colin Crowe and Sir John Colville, whose experience in both foreign affairs and in the byways of Westminster was difficult to parallel. More recently I am also indebted to John Page Philips, the Revd. Elliott Kendall, John M. Scott, D.B. Ellison, Mrs M.J.F. Logan of the FCO, Robert Maxtone Graham, Yen Chung, Professor James Cassels, Jonathan Saville of the Rowley Gallery,

Shirley Hazzard (Mrs Francis Steegmuller), George and Ellie War-
burg, Mary Turnbull, and Leonard Rayner.

The staff of the libraries I have used, in Britain, Hong Kong, France
and America, were unfailingly patient to an inexperienced and barely
computer-literate researcher. I am especially grateful to John Yaxley,
the Hong Kong Commissioner in London, who went out of his way
to be helpful, and to the Commission's librarian, Ursula Price, as
well as the obliging staff of the National Maritime Museum's library.
Particular thanks are also due to Jardine Matheson for permission to
use their archives.

For permission to reproduce illustrative material I am obliged to the
Bibliothèque Nationale, Paris; Brigadier G.H. Cree and the Trustees
of the National Maritime Museum, Greenwich; the Hong Kong
Government Information Service; the Trustees of the British Museum;
the Wellcome Institute Library, London; the Royal Hong Kong Police;
and the *South China Morning Post*. The Martyn Gregory Gallery has
generously made available the painting which appears on the cover of
this book.

One problem facing any book on China is whether transliterations
from the Chinese should be according to the Wade-Giles system, the
most usually found in books published before about 1985, or in *pinyin*,
the method now adopted universally. Since most historical works in
English – including the magnificent *Science and Civilization in China*
of Dr Joseph Needham – that the reader might come across employ
Wade-Giles, or a variation of it, this has been used for all references
prior to the establishment of the People's Republic in 1950. Contemporary Chinese proper names, on the other hand, are given in *pinyin*.
Between the two classes are such names as those of Chiang Kai-Shek
and Mao Tse-tung, which still appear in the Western press in that
form. As well as avoiding 'a foolish consistency' this compromise, it is
suggested, will save a lot of trouble in referring to indexes; as a safeguard important historical names are introduced in both systems.

Hong Kong Cantonese names present a peculiar problem. Dr W.K.
Chan in Appendix III of his fine book *The Making of Hong Kong Society*
gives at least fifty-four different ways of presenting any such name in
English; add to this the use of Christian names as well as Chinese
names, and the difficulty in adopting a standard becomes apparent.

Another fruitful field of misunderstanding is that of the Hong Kong
unit of currency. The silver dollar was traditional in the Canton trade,

and therefore adopted as the currency of commerce by Hong Kong, although transactions were often recorded in taels, the Chinese ounce of silver. Early colonial accounts were prepared in sterling, but the Hong Kong dollar became the official unit for all purposes in 1862, its value fluctuating according to the price of silver. Since 1981 the Hong Kong dollar has been tied to the US dollar, at a rate of HK$7.80 = US$1. Unless US dollars are specified the Hong Kong dollar is used throughout this book. When comparisons are made with the UK, figures are also sometimes given in pounds sterling.

Explanations are also needed of the following measures:

tael = 1 Chinese ounce = 1⅓ oz avoirdupois
lakh = 100,000 (Indian accounts are prepared in lakhs: one million, one hundred and fifty thousand = 11,50,000)
mau or mou = approximately one-third of an acre

It should be noted that both the second-in-command in the Hong Kong administration and the Secretary of State for the Colonies in Whitehall are frequently referred to as the 'Colonial Secretary'.

INTRODUCTION

Unwilling parents

Hong Kong, that natural child of Victorian Britain and Ch'ing China, has been a source of embarrassment and annoyance to its progenitors since it first appeared on the international scene in 1842. Neither parent was initially prepared to recognize the infant: the British Foreign Secretary, Lord Palmerston, described it as 'a barren island, which will never be a mart of trade'. He would much have preferred more ready money, or the larger and more prosperous Chusan, and immediately sacked the envoy who had been responsible for negotiating the barren island's cession. Queen Victoria, however, was quite amused by the idea that her little daughter might be 'Princess of Hongkong'. For his part the Chinese Emperor Tao-kuang, forced into acknowledging the loss of this minuscule piece of his territory, hitherto almost certainly unknown to him, by the guns of the Royal Navy levelled at the walls of Nanking, was baffled. He concluded that 'these barbarians always look on trade as their chief occupation; and are wanting in any high purpose of striving for territorial acquisition . . . It is plain that they are not worth attending to.'[1]

Closely associated with a notorious drug-smuggling trade, the circumstances of the birth were disreputable. Ever since, Hong Kong has presented Britain with a series of irritations; scandals concerning opium, prostitution, gambling, flogging and corruption, together with quarrels between Governors, civil servants, government departments and the community, erupted and arrived in Whitehall – and have not yet ceased to arrive – with depressing frequency.

Nor was China much pleased with the loss of the island. Hong

Kong might be nothing more than an inconsiderable pimple on the great empire's extremity, but it has been and remains of symbolic significance to the rulers and the people of that empire. An even more insignificant foreign body, the Portuguese settlement at Macao, has been left unremoved for over four centuries, but the method by which Hong Kong was ceded to the British has been a continuing aggravation. It came as the result of the first armed clash between China and the West, from which China emerged decisively and rapidly as the loser. The cession of Hong Kong was followed by increasingly rapacious demands for territorial and commercial concessions from foreign governments which left China, by the end of the nineteenth century, defeated, indebted and humiliated. Many myths have become encrusted around this first foreign encroachment, and have invested the subject of Hong Kong with a powerful emotional charge. As the loss of Hong Kong initiated these depredations, its recovery in 1997 will, it is believed, mark the end. The history of the colony is therefore indissolubly linked with that of China's relations with the West, and with the development of the West's attitudes towards China.

At a time when colonialism and imperialism are seen as irredeemably wicked, and democracy as a panacea for all society's ills, it is perverse of Hong Kong, until recently a colony without any democratic institutions, to be both successful and an agreeable place in which to live. It might be expected that a small community would, in economic matters, out-perform China herself, hampered as that great country has been by a runaway increase in population and periods of erratically bad government, but Hong Kong also compares well with the other 'little Asian dragons' – South Korea, Taiwan and Singapore. Commercially it is as least as successful as any of these countries, and it enjoys better protection of personal freedoms. Hong Kong's corruption, compared with that of Taiwan or Korea, is kept within decent bounds, and the undemocratic Crown Colony does not have any of the pettifogging restrictions imposed by democratic Singapore (where long hair and chewing gum, for example, are statutorily banned).

Moreover, Hong Kong is more successful than Britain. Its growth rate in the last decade has been rapid – from about 50 per cent of British Gross Domestic Product per capita in 1980 to more than 85 per cent in 1990 – and as early as 1981 Hong Kong had actually bettered Britain in such important indices as the expectation of life at birth (72.4 and 71.1 years respectively for men, and 78.1 and 77.1 years for women).

It may be illuminating to compare progress in British-administered Hong Kong to that in an American-administered territory. Puerto Rico, with a comparable population – 4 million as against 6 million – has been under American control for the same period (since 1898) as the greater part of Hong Kong has been under British rule. Certainly Puerto Rico has more democratic institutions – an elected governor and administration – with the United States retaining control of such items as foreign and defence policy, but in most respects the people of Hong Kong have a better time of it. Infant mortality is sixteen per thousand in Puerto Rico, but below seven in Hong Kong (a better figure even than in the USA, where it is 10.1). Expectation of life at birth is today higher in Hong Kong than in Puerto Rico, at 78.3 years against 73.0 (and higher than in the USA, with an expectation of 74). Other indicators of a decent standard of living – absence of crime, pupil—teacher ratios, newspaper readership, illegitimate births, quality of public transport, free provision of health services – also show Hong Kong ahead of Puerto Rico, sometimes by a considerable margin, and in many instances again better than the United States. The murder rate in Hong Kong, for example, is 1.64 per 100,000 people; in the USA it is 7.91 per 100,000.[2]

Present-day Hong Kong shows little sign of a colonial presence, and even less of a colonial past. On the slopes of Victoria Peak, hidden behind overtopping skyscrapers, lies concealed what was once the centre of the colony. Government House, resembling nothing more than a Japanese railway station, St John's Cathedral, a banal piece of colonial Gothic architecture, the French Mission House, and Flagstaff House, formerly the elegant quarters of the General Officer Commanding, once looked proudly out on a harbour on which lay the sleek grey cruisers of the China Squadron. Today these remnants of empire look up into the bedrooms of the Hilton Hotel and the offices of the Bank of China. Government House was absurdly remodelled in the Japanese style – including the addition of an incongruous Shinto-esque tower – during the occupation in the Second World War, and has never been rebuilt; the cathedral was looted at the same time; Flagstaff House, the only intact survivor of the earliest days, is now devoted to a collection of teapots. Queen Victoria has vanished from Statue Square, where the only memorial is now – entirely appropriately for this temple of commerce – that of a bank manager. The spot where the Union flag was first raised in the colony, in Possession Street, is unmarked; the proposal to commemorate the

150th anniversary raised a vigorous protest from civil servants, and was allowed to drop.

No uniforms are to be seen in the streets except those of the police – almost invariably Chinese. The only British serviceman visible is the sailor on the gate of H.M.S Tamar, the Royal Navy base. He guards no ships of greater might than three motor patrol boats, except when those of some visitors call. Nor is economic imperialism much in evidence. In the car park of the Government Offices, which might reasonably be expected to contain at least some products of the colonial power, nothing can be seen but Toyotas and other Japanese vehicles; the senior civil servants are allowed Mercedes cars, and only the Governor himself is driven in a Rolls-Royce.

The obvious trappings of empire have been fading steadily since the end of the Second World War. In 1950 the British government dispatched a force equivalent to two fully equipped divisions to warn off the Chinese People's Liberation Army. By 1967 a single British soldier stood on guard at Government House while thousands of demonstrators massed outside. At that time Hong Kong still looked what it had been for a century – a colonial backwater, where the cricket pitch occupied the city centre, benignly guarded by Sir Aston Webb's Supreme Court, with the art deco building of the Hongkong and Shanghai Bank as a backdrop. On the waterfront the new Mandarin Hotel and the City Hall stood out well above the surrounding blocks; along at Wanchai the police station looked out directly over the harbour.

Today the court building survives, and houses the Legislative and Executive Councils, but the cricket pitch has vanished, and the Hongkong Bank's magnificent new inside-out headquarters shrinks beside that of the Bank of China, the dominating symbol of the People's Republic's presence. The Mandarin Hotel, now not what it was, and the City Hall, showing its age, are dwarfed by the office buildings that soar above them. At Wanchai reclamation has advanced the land by nearly a quarter of a mile, and the tallest building in Asia is rising. Seen from Kowloon the skyline of what was the city of Victoria now changes by the week, but continues to constitute the most spectacular of views, with the tightly-closed ranks of fine buildings rising from the harbour up the misty slopes of the Peak.

Inland from Kowloon, in the New Territories, the new towns hardly existed at all twenty-five years ago, the settlements at Tsuen Wan and Tuen Mun housing perhaps in all three hundred thousand people.

Today over two million live in the new towns, linked by the sparklingly clean and efficient Metro and the modernized railway. While the older communities remain uncompromising blocks of multi-storey housing, Sha Tin, the largest, has two universities, a new racecourse, concert halls, and all the amenities that might be expected of a city of half a million.

Hong Kong's skyline might be that of a more picturesque Manhattan, but at street level Hong Kong is evidently a Chinese city. Even in Central with its concentration of Western tourists and businessmen, and certainly in the new towns, where there is hardly a *gweilo* to be spotted, the crowds are as Chinese as those of Canton or Shanghai. But Hong Kong is uniquely diverse; apart from the well-established Indian and Portuguese communities, its population is mainly Cantonese, but with half a million others having come from all parts of China to this British colony in search of security and prosperity (conditions which are regarded with some pride in the rest of the country). Peasants from Shandong or Sichuan, visiting Beijing, take home postcards of the marvels of Hong Kong along with those of the Temple of Heaven. They can, however, only guess at the style, energy and ebullience of that remarkable fusion of cultures. That has to be experienced for itself, on the streets among the absorbed and bustling crowds, and in the offices of the enterprises which have placed Hong Kong among the most advanced economies in the world.

In order to explain the evolution of Hong Kong some reference to the political history of Britain, Europe and China during the last two centuries is needed, since events elsewhere have so decisively affected the colony's development. Contemporary writers in China have difficulties in analysing this sensitive period in their country's history. The achievements of Communist China in the last fifteen years, especially when compared with the previous chaos under the Kuomintang, have encouraged an always latent chauvinism; the fate of those who questioned the regime during the days of the 'Great Proletarian Cultural Revolution' has discouraged any inclined to be critical. Only very recently has a less engaged view become possible, and otherwise serious Chinese historians still condemn too close an attention to facts as 'undesirable pragmatism in historical study'.[3] Works published by the state-controlled Foreign Languages Press generally analyse the period in terms of imperialist exploitation.

There certainly was the most ruthless exploitation of China, but it came later in the nineteenth century, and the worst culprit was no

European power, but China's old feudatory, Japan. Nor was Britain, at the time of the acquisition of Hong Kong, an expansionist power in the mould of France or Germany. During the formative years of the colony British opinion and policy was in a stage of development, with frequent changes of governments in Westminster, often accompanied by realignments of parties as Tories developed into Conservatives and Whigs to Liberals.[4] Administrations were always at odds with large sections of public opinion, frequently disagreeing with the actions of their representatives in China, and invariably much more concerned with those domestic issues which would decide the next elections than with any colonial difficulties. Only towards the end of the century was public opinion to seem more bellicose and ready to support colonial wars with some degree of enthusiasm. Even this waned rapidly after the poor showing of the Imperial forces in the Boer War and the return of a Liberal government. A little later, after the end of the First World War, many senior men in the Foreign Office saw Hong Kong as an impediment to good relations with China, and pressed for the colony to be restored to Chinese rule, a sentiment which has never entirely dissipated.

The analyses of Communist apologists usually reflect Marxist theory rather than the evidence itself. Consider for example the Soviet Academician S.L. Tikhvinsky, editor of *The Modern History of China* (1972): 'In January 1840, Queen Victoria declared in her speech at the opening of Parliament that the British government was in sympathy with the actions of Captain Charles Elliot and the British merchants in China. Following the Queen's approval, Lord Palmerston no longer hesitated to start hostilities against China.' In fact almost everyone was annoyed with Elliot, the British representative in China, especially those merchants who considered him to have caved in to Chinese threats; and the idea of Lord Palmerston dithering until the twenty-year-old Queen, who at that time was still clinging nervously to Prime Minister Lord Melbourne's coat-tails, had signified her approval is absurd.

Only by exposing such fallacies, and describing political events in England, is the development of Hong Kong explicable. Take, for instance, the Napier mission of 1834, which, by its failure to reach a reasonable commercial agreement between Britain and China led to the war that brought the new colony. That unfortunate episode was due primarily to the confused arrogance of Lord Napier himself, who should never have been selected for so sensitive a responsibility. The question of why so unsuitable a choice was made has never been asked by historians of Hong Kong or China, but the answer is simple: the Whig government of Lord Grey had an obligation towards Napier for services rendered during the difficult passage of the 1832 Reform Bill, and Napier put in a claim for just such a post.

Or take the story of Sir John Bowring, surely the most remarkable man ever to be Governor of the colony. 'Quack Doctor' Bowring, as Palmerston called him, had been a Radical M.P., the closest friend and executor of Jeremy Bentham, editor, spy (according to the French), steelmaster, financial expert, hymn writer, and translator from Russian, Hungarian and Spanish. When appointed Governor of Hong Kong, and representative of Britain to the whole of China and Indo-China in 1854, Bowring, former Secretary of the Peace Society, precipitated the second Anglo–Chinese war. The results of this war were decisive for the future of all Asia: but how this proto-European with no Eastern or indeed any colonial experience came to be a prime mover in these great affairs has never been explained, or the details exposed of his conspiracy with Sir Harry Parkes, the British Consul at Canton, to force the opening of hostilities.

And why, root of the current problems, did the British government in 1898 only require a ninety-nine-year lease of the New Territories, rather than outright ownership, if it really was party to an unprincipled rush to dismember China?

The explanations, which are detailed in Chapters 3, 7 and 11, are to be found in the changing policies of British governments and the personalities of British Cabinet Ministers, the perennial need to reward faithful party supporters, and the pressures exerted by international rivalries, which can only be understood in the context of events in Britain and Europe.

The course of history in China must also be noted, for Hong Kong is a British colony only in a special sense (the British government do not even like to call it a colony: in official pronouncements Hong Kong is referred to as a 'territory', but this is more due to a desire to shuffle off responsibility than to semantic accuracy). Properly speaking, a colony is a settlement made by emigrants in a foreign land, with a degree of self-government: Australia and North America were colonies in this sense. Hong Kong is an animal of a different species: even before its official foundation, the austere and industrious Sir James Stephen, Under-Secretary for the Colonies – and grandfather of Virginia Woolf – noted that 'methods of proceeding unknown in other British colonies must be followed in Hongkong, and that the Rules and Regulations . . . must, in many regards, bend to exigencies beyond the contemplation of the framers of them'.[5] Other colonies, many a great deal smaller, have become independent nations, but Hong Kong remains a Crown Colony, one where the home government is responsible for the administration and where the inhabitants have only the most restricted representation. It would therefore be more accurate to describe Hong Kong as a Chinese colony that happens to be run by Britain.

This anomaly has led to an often considerable degree of insulation between the colony and the upheavals that have racked the mainland. Neither the Taiping rebellion of the 1850s, which devastated much of southern China, nor the Boxer disturbances at the turn of the century, which caused massacres of Europeans in the north and led to the occupation of Peking by foreign troops, brought more than ripples to Hong Kong, which for the first eighty years of its existence enjoyed a tranquillity unparalleled elsewhere in the region. While Britain remained the undisputed world power, attempting to keep on good terms with the Chinese authorities, this domesticated outpost of empire continued undisturbed. Only after 1898, when, in response to increasing pressures on China from other Western powers, the British acquired the lease of the New Territories, was the Hong Kong government pulled into closer contact with events on the mainland.

From the Chinese side, too, some clarifications are needed. Hong Kong was given a flying start by the immigration from Canton and Macao of almost all the foreign community, who flocked to the 'barren island' on the heels of the Royal Navy's first landing party. The colony's early history is therefore a continuation of that of the Canton trade, and some explanation of how that important branch of international commerce worked is essential. Some of the myths can also profitably be examined; was the 'Opium War' really about opium; did the valiant peasants of the village of San-yuan-li defeat British troops in 1841; was the Treaty settlement of 1842–43 unequal and unjust? The emotions aroused by these questions (and I suggest the answers are all in the negative) continue to bedevil exchanges between China and Britain. In spite of the twentieth-century's upheavals, the past of China is very much alive in the national consciousness, and historical continuity has by no means been broken. Jonathan Mirsky of the *Observer* has noted how the present leaders of China pride themselves, as did the Ch'ing mandarins, on being able to produce elegant calligraphy and correct verse. Alain Peyrefitte, who as a Minister under successive French governments has had excellent opportunities for studying modern China, commented: 'I was struck [in 1971] by the strange similarities between the Maoist state and the one Macartney [the British ambassador in 1793] had confronted. There was the same cult of the Emperor, Mao merely replacing Qianlong . . . the same concern for the rituals of protocol . . . the same adherence to a common set of references that provided the answer to everything . . .'[6] and so on for a total of thirteen parallels. Similarly Ssü-Yu Teng and John King Fairbank observed: 'In spite of all the furore of change in recent decades, the hold of the past is still curiously strong in present-day China. Not far below the surface lies the ancient civilization of the Middle Kingdom, a subsoil which limits and conditions the new growth.'[7]

In the same period Chinese institutions have changed radically, while those in Britain have remained apparently unaltered. The last Emperor of China died working as a gardener in Communist Beijing, while in London Queen Victoria's great-great-grand-daughter, successor to the last Emperor of India, still sits on the throne, with the Houses of Lords and Commons still forming the High Court of Parliament. Such continuity is deceptive. Since Lord Macartney, on behalf of the Honorable East India Company, first attempted to establish relations with China in 1793, the character and position of Britain in the world has undergone drastic changes. In that year Britain was a small agricultural country, recently deprived of its most important overseas possessions, the North American colonies, but with developing industries at home and an equivocal but rapidly consolidating position in India. Within only a few years the nation was transformed into a world imperial power, the inheritors of the Indian raj, with a chain of colonial acquisitions forced from the French, Dutch and Spaniards and domestic industries that made it 'the workshop of the world'. After less than a century of unprecedented power a slow decline began that brought Britain, from ruling one quarter of the world's population, to being one of the less prosperous Western European states. The massive social engineering needed to enable Britain to function as an imperial power transformed British society in the nineteenth century; it proved a good deal more successful than that subsequently required to adjust to the decline, and the history of Hong Kong reflects these uncomfortable changes.

The rise of the British Empire phased with the fall of the Chinese. In that same year of 1793 China felt secure within her extensive boundaries, the Middle Kingdom, centre of the civilized world. Power was entrusted to the Emperor, a figure of cosmic significance, the Heavenly Dragon, comparable to the Sun and the Pole Star, the fount of wisdom and justice: Most Powerful Monarch, Wisest Ruler, Exponent of Heaven's Law. Holding as he did the mandate of Heaven, the Emperor was himself accepted as personally divine, of greater religious significance than had been even the Byzantine Imperator, Supreme Augustus, Instinct with Divinity. He was both autocrat and high priest, entrusted by Heaven with the governance of China for the welfare and the glory of its people. The visible incarnation of the Han people, the Emperor personally presided over the great sacrifices in the Temple of Heaven in order to ensure good harvests and the blessings of the gods. In theory his divine attributes ensured that whatever the Emperor did must be correct and beneficent; when things began to go wrong this was taken as a sign that the mandate of Heaven had been forfeited, and that it was time for a change of dynasty. The responsibilities of godhead were taken more seriously than those of contemporary leaders; the last Ming Emperor, before he hanged himself (in 1644), apologized to his ancestors and to his people: 'Now I meet with Heaven's punishment above, sinking ignominiously below . . . May the bandits dismember my corpse and slaughter my officials, but let them not despoil the imperial tombs nor harm a single one of our people.'[8]

Chinese society was imbued, as it had been for nearly two millennia, with the principles of Confucius, and society fell into the categories prescribed by Confucian philosophy. In this hierarchy the peasantry were accorded second rank in the state, immediately below the rulers, and above the craftsmen; at the very lowest level, persons of the most meagre consideration, who contributed little to the welfare of the community, were the merchants. When eventually Western traders, who had no such conceptions of their humble condition ('the princes of the earth – the MERCHANTS,' according to one of the most famous of them, James Matheson[9]), met Chinese officials, a clash, at least of cultures, was inevitable. Given the supreme self-confidence of both parties it was almost equally certain that this would lead to armed conflict.

I

THE TWO EMPIRES

The last dynasty

A confrontation between China and the West became increasingly likely from the beginning of the nineteenth century, and when it came resulted in the cession of Chinese territory to the British. But why, when the choice was made, it fell upon the outstandingly unattractive island of Hong Kong requires a detailed explanation.

The rocky and precipitous island of Hong Kong is one of the hundreds scattered in the Pearl River estuary: not the largest, nor the most prominent, nor, at the time of its acquisition by the British in 1842, the most populous, and certainly not the most fertile. It was an unconsidered appendage of an isolated Chinese county to which no one had paid much attention, even though the Pearl River had been one of the most important commercial waterways, not only in China, but in the world, for a thousand years. That importance was due primarily to the weather systems of the South China Sea. From April to October a reliable south-west wind provides easy passage for ships coming from the west, while from November to April reciprocal north-easterlies facilitate the return voyage. To vessels making the dangerous passage from the west the Pearl River is the first safe haven in the Chinese Empire.

The first Europeans to visit the region, the Portuguese, in the sixteenth century, found an immediately available anchorage in the lee of the Macao peninsula, where they had been allowed to settle. No suggestion was made of a permanent alienation of Chinese territory; the Portuguese were confined within a strong wall, through which provisions were allowed to trickle, in quantities calculated from day to day. Some seventy miles upstream from Macao is the great commercial city of Canton, the sea-gateway to China and capital of the twin provinces of Kwantung and Kwangsi (Guangdong and Guangxi), which stretch for eight hundred miles across the south of China. The physical geography of rivers sometimes has profound effects on history – the expansion of London is largely due to its position as the lowest bridge point on the Thames, at the head of an estuary which narrows at Tilbury to an easily defensible point. Canton occupies a similar position, on an estuary notably easy of access. The *Admiralty Pilot* for 1864, the first published for those waters, described the approach as 'probably more safe than that of any other large river in the world'. Sheltered harbours abound near the islands of Lantao, Lamma, and, further upriver, Lintin. Dangers other than navigational, however, existed: the islands in the estuary, extending the coastline to hundreds of miles, gave shelter to a population which existed by fishing, piracy and smuggling. Piracy continued until well into modern times, but is now rare; fishing and smuggling still flourish.

In theory the Pearl River is as easily defensible as the Thames. About thirty miles above Macao the channel narrows to a few hundred yards into the strait known as the Bocca Tigris, the aptly named Tiger's Mouth, commonly known as the Bogue, or Humen, where the passage is commanded by the guns of the Ch'uen-pi and Ty-tok-to forts. Between Ch'uen-pi and the Second Bar, for rather less than twenty miles, a ship has to stick to the channel, never out of range of the shore. At the Bar a sea-going vessel has to wait for a tide to help it over the shallows: the First Bar, just below Whampoa, is even more restrictive. Whampoa, some seven miles below Canton, is therefore the limit for ocean-going ships of any size. Captain Richard Alsager[1] reported in 1829 that while six-hundred-ton ships could make Whampoa with ease it would not be prudent for a 1200-tonner, there not being more than twenty-five feet of water at best on the First Bar. Canton itself is accessible only by shallow-draught vessels. A hostile man-of-war, if it braved the gauntlet of the forts in the Tiger's Mouth, would in most conditions find herself stuck at Whampoa, unable to bring Canton within the range of her guns, with only the ship's boats able to penetrate further upriver.

Kwantung is an odd region, regarded by the rest of China with suspicion and disdain. The Sung emperors, who ruled China from

960 to 1279, were worried by reports of the great number of wizards and sorcerers in the city, and issued special edicts forbidding human sacrifices to be made to demons. In part this distrust is due to its remoteness, the better part of two thousand kilometres from Peking, and separated from the older capitals of China by mountain ranges crossed only by difficult and infrequent passes. The language spoken by the inhabitants is unintelligible to northern Chinese; their customs are looked upon with distaste. It seems Cantonese will eat *anything* – and it is not all that easy to find food unacceptable to Chinese cookery – bats, tortoises, raw monkey's brains and new-born rats, for example. This appearance of strangeness and remoteness was to be of some importance in the events that led to the establishment of Hong Kong. A Peking government would expect nothing but difficulties from the province, which after all was a very long way off; when in the eighth century A.D. Canton was sacked by Arab raiders Peking viewed the event with some equanimity. Little that went on in the remote and dubious south was likely to fret Peking unduly, but when barbarian warships showed up in the Bay of Chihli, as they did in the nineteenth century, alarm signals flashed in the Imperial palace.

Canton, in spite of its peculiarities, was acknowledged to be a great city, known throughout the Empire as 'the Provincial City'. At the beginning of the eighteenth century, when the East India Company eventually settled there to trade, a French visitor to Canton wrote: 'This city is larger than Paris, and almost as populous. The streets are narrow and paved . . . with large, level and very hard stones . . . The finest quarters are very like the rue de la Foire St Germain in Paris . . . there are many fine squares and magnificent triumphal arches'.[2] To this great centre the Portuguese settlement of Macao was nothing but an appendage, although at that time one of strategic commercial importance.

On Chinese maps of the Ch'ing period (1644–1911) Hong Kong is either omitted or unrecognizable; its first appearance is on a chart published in 1760, which shows only the west coast of the island. A slightly later chart prepared by Captain George Hayter of the East India Company's ship *York* is an eccentric production which, although giving soundings in what is now Victoria Harbour, indicates the anchorage as south of the Soko Islands, a very exposed spot. Incredibly, Hong Kong is depicted as two separate islands; clearly a botched job, but at least Captain Hayter recorded the now famous name. The larger of his two fictitious islands is named 'An-chin-cheo' or 'He-ong-Kong'.[3]

Like so much of the British Empire, Hong Kong was acquired almost by accident. The Emperor Tao-kuang (Daoguang) became, on his accession in 1820, the sixth emperor of the ninth dynasty to rule China over a period of two thousand years. He was the favourite grandson of the great Ch'ien-lung (Qianlong) Emperor (1736–96),[4] in whose long reign China had expanded to its greatest extent ever, and he inherited supreme control of six million square miles of territory, from the Karakorum mountains to the sea, and from the steppes of Siberia to the borders of Indo-China.

The Emperor was not himself Chinese, but a Tungu, Manchu or Tartar, a race of different language, customs and traditions, from the region between Korea and Russia. Many of his Chinese subjects were bitterly antagonistic to Manchu rule, and movements to restore a purely Chinese dynasty were endemic. His forebears inhabited Manchuria, the region beyond the Great Wall and north of Korea, towards the Amur River and the present Russian frontier. They were hunters and fishers, using reindeer and canoes, growing crops when it suited, but relying mainly on their considerable skills as horse- and bow-men. In 1607 the Tungu prince Nurhaci succeeded in forcibly uniting Manchuria and proclaimed himself as Great Khan. He reinforced his military victories by generous rewards to those prominent Chinese, Mongols and Koreans who surrendered, and was therefore able to create in Manchuria a state on a Chinese model, but one which remained characteristically Manchu. The royal family was in command of the field armies, organized in eight Banners or divisions of some eight thousand men each. The very names of the first Manchus – Dorgon, Jirgalang, and Manggultai, give a flavour of the un-Chineseness of them all.

Nurhaci turned his united Manchu state against Ming China in 1618, capturing Peking in 1644. When Nurhaci's son Abahai made the transition from Khan of Manchuria to Emperor of China, he took the reign name of T'ai-tsung and declared that his dynasty should be known as the Ch'ing. In his proclamation T'ai-tsung made a brutally frank statement of Manchu aims: 'By keeping peace inside and grabbing outside a great empire is rising.'[5] The dynastic tradition of the Ch'ing continued to be military: princes were brought up not only with a modest classical learning, but to excel in such warlike skills as archery and horsemanship. The Manchu standing army of bannermen was an impressive force, which in the eighteenth century proved itself capable of extended hard fighting as well as holding down enormous tracts of newly-conquered territory. The moral shock experienced by the dynasty in the following century when Manchu armies later crumbled under the assault of numerically much inferior Western forces was therefore great, in fact nearly terminal.

The pure Han Chinese found their new masters crude. Dutch traders were taken aback when they met in Peking one of the highest early Manchu officials, the President of the Board of Rites, guardian of the most sacred traditions, who 'sent for a piece of Pork to satisfy his appetite, which was half-raw, whereof he did eat most heartily, in a slovenly manner, that he looked more like a Butcher than a Prince'. They found Manchu ladies equally lacking in Chinese formality – one 'great Tartar Lady ... was very debonair and free ... she took the Embassador's hat, and put it on her own Head, and unbuttoned his doublet almost down to his Waste'.[6] In time the Manchus adapted more closely to Chinese manners, but they made sure that their individuality was retained by legislative measures. Intermarriage with Chinese was banned; the Manchu heartland was forbidden to Chinese, a willow pale marking the limit beyond which Chinese emigration was not allowed. An Imperial Clan court closely supervised the activities of all members of the Imperial family, largely distancing them from any real share in power, but ensuring their education, comforts and generally good behaviour.

The perspicacious Lord Macartney, who had ample opportunities for observing Chinese and Manchus during his embassy in 1793, recorded that: 'A series of two hundred years in the succession of eight or ten monarchs did not change the Mogul into a Hindu, nor has a century and a half made Ch'ien-lung [the Emperor] a Chinese. He remains, at this hour, in all his maxims of policy, as true a Tartar as any of his ancestors.'[7] A firm hold was kept by the Ch'ing on the army. All military communications, down to field orders, were written in Manchu, and therefore unintelligible even to an educated Chinese. Although the standing army, the bannermen, brigaded Manchus with Chinese and Mongols, the Manchus were considerably better paid (seven ounces of silver per month for a Tartar horseman, 3.3 ounces for a Chinese trooper: fifty *mou* of land for a Manchu, thirty-five for a Mongol, and twenty-five for a Chinese).

Scholars and gentlemen

While maintaining the Manchu character of the court and army, the Ch'ing dynasty wisely made use of the established Chinese administrative machine. The Chinese civil service had survived many changes of dynasty since it took its original shape during that of the Tang, who ruled from the seventh to the tenth century. Unlike that of other great empires, where administrators came usually from the ranks of the clergy, the army, or court favourites, the Chinese civil service was based upon recruitment through strictly controlled examinations. In assessing merit polished style was paramount: learning counted for something, but originality was positively discouraged. Examinations centred around the 'eight-legged' essay, of between 360 and 720 words, in prose and in verse, which had to be elegantly phrased and written in the finest calligraphy. The set topics were all from Confucian classics, and impeccable Confucian orthodoxy was expected. Three sets of preliminary examinations were needed before the successful candidate gained admission to the lowest rank of the 'gentry', that of *sheng-yuan*, at an average age of twenty-four. It took another ten years of dedicated study to reach the top, the *chin-shih* degree, the examinations for which were held under the personal aegis of the Emperor himself, and to which only an elite handful of scholars were admitted each year.

A *chin-shih* graduate would be typically about thirty-five, and would therefore have spent over twenty years treading and retreading the same intellectual mill. It is hardly surprising that successful candidates were 'stunned into submissiveness, and became cautious and meek officials of the court'. Undeniably, those who survived the rigours of unremitting competition had qualities of resilience and toughness, but the suppression of original thought often led to a crippling incapacity to react to new circumstances, which was to have serious effects. When faced with the baffling new problems imposed by the nineteenth-century barbarians demanding entrance to the Celestial Kingdom, even men of great personal ability such as Lin Tse-hsü could do little more than repeat previously successful responses and fall back on platitudes. It was more often the Manchu officials, less attached to intellectual formulae than were the Chinese scholar-governors, who showed signs of readiness to adapt to changing circumstances.

The *chin-shih* graduate was assured of a senior position: others had to take their chance, and chances could be improved, quite legitimately, by buying a step, but only at the lower end of the scale. Those who had passed intermediate examinations or were able to buy promotion joined the ranks of the 'gentry' or 'literati'. Gentry were allowed privileges which included the right to wear distinctive costumes and exemption from many legal requirements, taxes and services. Since examinations were open to all (all males, at least), a young man from the humblest of backgrounds, if talented and dedicated enough, could in theory reach the highest position in the administration. In practice, the odds were weighted in favour of those whose families could support them during the long apprenticeship, and who, having gained an official position, could then consolidate and perpetuate family fortunes. Such intimate links between gentry families and office holders ensured that there was always a large body of unofficial support available to supplement the efforts of the numerically very restricted official class. In this way their function was parallel to that of Justices of the Peace in English shires, assisting Lord Lieutenants in raising militia, settling local disputes, and encouraging accepted morality. Although Manchus, very much a minority – there being only two million of them – took a share in these tasks, they were more often found among the military or at court. The tradition of their race was one of military prowess rather than literary or administrative skills, and they retained a less formal and more open attitude to many subjects than the classically educated Chinese.

The Manchus' most lasting influence is seen on the present map of China: the boundaries of the People's Republic follow the limits established by the Ch'ing Empire, with the important exceptions of Formosa and Mongolia, now independent. It was the Emperor Ch'ien-lung who made the most imposing additions to the Empire, settling the western borders in a series of vigorous expeditions that brought Chinese Turkestan, now the autonomous region of Sinkiang, within it. Successful campaigns also forced the Gurkhas of Nepal, the Burmese, and most of Indo-China to acknowledge the Emperor as overlord. The conquest of Sinkiang had proved extremely expensive, and the costs of retaining the huge territory continued to deplete the Imperial treasury, but for much of his long reign Ch'ien-lung could rely upon the resources amassed by his predecessors, and China continued to enjoy tranquillity and prosperity. The population doubled, to something like three hundred million at the end of the eighteenth century, an expansion which was matched by a similar increase in agricultural production.

By the time Ch'ien-lung's successor came to the throne, however, the treasury had been further emptied by the depredations of the old Emperor's favourite, Ho-shen, who had amassed a huge fortune at public expense. The new Emperor, who took the reign name Chia-ch'ing (Jiaqin), was forced to cut expenses and raise income wherever possible. Although Chia-ch'ing was a man of sober, even frugal personal habits, dedicated to reform and retrenchment, his reign (1796–1820) was plagued by difficulties: the Yellow River overflowed its banks seventeen times, causing widespread famine; serious rebellions erupted and pirates devastated the coasts; and the Western barbarians, having insinuated themselves uncomfortably close to the boundaries of the Middle Kingdom, were beginning to be troublesome.

An empire acquired in a fit of absent-mindedness

The question of who owned the world, or at least that portion of it which had not as yet come to the attention of the Pope, should have been settled once and for all on 4 and 5 May 1493. Pope Alexander VI, who had, of course, divine authority to dispose of all lands inhabited only by the heathen, devoted those two days to adjudicating the division of all new discoveries equably between Spain and Portugal. All lands to the west of a line from the North to South Poles, at a distance of one hundred leagues west of the Azores and the Cape Verde Islands, were to become the property of Spain: the remainder was to be Portuguese. One of the Pope's reasons for wishing to oblige Spain was that the Vicar of Christ, after betrothing his daughter Lucrezia to two Spaniards in succession, was finally about to marry her to an Italian, Giovanni Sforza. If any problems remained as to who was entitled to what, they should have been clarified in 1580, when the crowns of Spain and Portugal were united.

This arrangement did not commend itself to the other European nations, especially those who had adopted the reformed faith, but during the sixteenth century their energies were occupied elsewhere. England, apart from an unsuccessful attempt to colonize Virginia, restricted herself to looting Spanish possessions and capturing Spanish ships; France was occupied with religious civil wars; Holland was just emerging as a nation, free from Spanish oppression. By 1600 things had changed, at least in England and Holland, although it was some years before France joined in the quest for new territories and foreign trade. Territorial expansion was confined to the New World, the British concentrating on North American settlements and the West Indian islands, and the Dutch on building a Brazilian empire. America, apart from the already conquered Spanish and Portuguese lands, was inhabited by aboriginals who could be driven out, absorbed or simply exterminated, but the East was partitioned between two great empires, the Moghul in India and the Chinese, with many other organized states forming powerful obstacles to would-be colonizers. The Dutch and English therefore confined their attention to expanding trade in the East rather than in attempts at conquest. At first the Dutch expended a much greater effort. Their United East India Company was founded in 1602 with a capital equivalent to over half a million pounds sterling; their British competitors, the Honorable East India Company, established two years earlier, had only a little over thirty thousand pounds; in the first decade the Dutch sent out sixty ships, the English seventeen.

Subsequent British voyages prospered, and the Company, although driven almost to extinction by the policies of Charles I, was placed on its feet again by a Cromwellian reorganization. Shortly afterwards its position in India was consolidated when Bombay was presented to the Crown as part of Charles II's wedding settlement with the Portuguese Princess Catherine of Braganza. When Bombay was then granted by the King to the Honorable East India Company a legally unquestioned and secure British base was for the first time established in the East, matching those already held by the Portuguese and Dutch, and eventual diversification into the China trade became again a possibility. By 1711, with the Ch'ing emperors firmly in control and willing to relax the restrictions on foreign trade, the Company was able to establish a trading post in Canton itself.

At this time the Indian subcontinent was still peripheral to European affairs, with British, French, Portuguese and Danish traders relying on the goodwill of native rulers. The Company was operating from three Indian centres; Bombay, a British possession, Madras and Calcutta, both leased from Indian princes. Its Indian trading concessions and permissions were granted by the Moghul Emperor in Delhi and by his at least nominally-subject rulers, a state of affairs all concerned found satisfactory. Two separate factors changed this; the Moghul Empire crumbled with astonishing speed under attacks by Persians, Afghans and Maharata Hindus, creating a power vacuum in north India, and the British and French became embroiled in the first wars to be fought on a global scale, between 1740 and 1758.

The upshot of this was that, after some extraordinary adventures, the Honorable East India Company emerged as undisputed masters of the richest province of India, Bengal, and the unchallenged European trading power. As holders of the *diwani*, or tax farm, the Company was entitled to collect all the revenues of Bengal, which before had been paid to the Moghul Emperor. They had, it was observed, 'acquired an empire in a fit of absence of mind'. Having thus become effectively a corporate Indian princely power, a trading company exercising sovereign rights over tens of millions of subjects, and disposing of considerable armed strength, the directors were driven into defending their interests against the dozens of other Indian rulers scrabbling to profit from the disintegrating Moghul Empire. This proved a costly business. Dividends suffered and the Company teetered on the brink of bankruptcy, forcing the British government to step in to assist.

In doing so ministers were motivated by pressing economic reasons. It was not only that the India merchants and stockholders were a rich source of patronage, which all eighteenth-century governments kept a lively eye upon, but that British governments, by the latter part of the century, were dependent upon the activities of the East India Company for a substantial part of their revenue. Or, more accurately, upon the Company's trade in China tea, which had become its most important source of profit as the British settled into their national addiction. Peter Mundy, who was probably the first Englishman to taste the stuff, had not been overimpressed by 'a certain Drinke called Chaa ... which is only water with a kind of herbe boyled in itt. It must bee Drancke warme and is accompted wholesome,'[8] but his descendants took to it with alacrity. In 1664 2lb 2oz of tea was imported into England. By 1783 this had risen to over 2600 tons. And this was the amount landed officially – tea was smuggled in great quantities (thought to have amounted to three times the amount legally imported) in order to avoid the high duties levied upon it. Even so, and after substantial reductions in the rate of duty the revenue on tea represented something like 10 per cent of the total British government income; and all the tea, lawful or illicit, came from a single source, Canton, for the cultivation of *Thea sinensis* outside China did not begin until 1832, in Assam. Such a valuable trade had to be safeguarded, and the East India Company was proving incapable of so doing.

By 1772 the Company was in dire trouble: it had increased its trade much beyond what was prudent, and outstripped its banking facilities so far as to be unable to meet debts falling due to the Bank of England and to the Customs and Excise. Proving for what was probably the first time in commercial history that if you owe enough money someone will be forced to bail you out, Lord North's government produced a loan of £1,400,000 for what would otherwise have been a bankrupt East India Company and insisted, in return for its money, on the passage of a Regulating Act (1773) which tightened controls on the Company.

Feelings ran so high that two successive governments fell on Indian reform issues before William Pitt the Younger was able, after fighting a general election on his policy, to bring in a definitive India Bill (1784) which settled the future pattern of Indian administration. Commercial control and the power of appointing to all political and military posts – subject to a government veto – remained in the hands of the Court of Directors of the Honorable East India Company, themselves elected by the Court of Proprietors – the stockholders. The government itself took 'the power of directing what political objects the Company's servants were to pursue, and recalling such as did not pay obedience to such directions'. Policy was to be defined by the Board of Control, a government body, the President of which afterwards became a Cabinet minister. Matters were settled for a limited term only, subject to the renewals of the Company's charter at regular intervals, the next review of which was due in 1793. It was the third of these reviews, in 1833, that led to the events which caused the first Chinese War and the cession of Hong Kong.

The oddity, to put it mildly, of vesting a commercial joint-stock company with powers to run what was then the equivalent of the largest European state, can be explained by English pragmatism – it worked, so leave it more or less alone, subject to keeping an eye on it – but also by the government's worries about patronage. There were so many lucrative offices within the gift of the rulers of India that no British government, however happy it would have been to use these to reward its own devoted supporters, would be willing to let them slip into the hands of the opposition when their turn came. The first President of the Board of Control, Henry Dundas, acknowledged this: 'No person wishing well to the interests of this country and the freedom of its constitution can soberly wish to see the patronage concentrated in the hands of any Administration.'[9]

The India Act of 1784 centralized power in India in the office of the Governor General, nominated by the Crown, and resident in

Calcutta, two Governors being responsible for the other Presidencies of Madras and Bombay. The first Governor-General appointed under the new Act, George, Lord Cornwallis (1786–94), effectively founded modern India. Under his rule Bengal was given a civil service, a system of law and a judiciary; merchants and administrators were clearly separated – administrators were salaried, forbidden to engage in trade, which was how their predecessors had made their fortunes, and their 'relaxed habits' tightened up. Bengal became the most modern and powerful Indian state, but was still only one among dozens disputing for territories and hegemony. The customs and practices of the people were left undisturbed, as they had been by the previous rulers, the Islamic Persian-speaking Moghuls, who would have seemed to a Hindu Bengali to be no less foreign than the British, and a good deal less efficient.

Cornwallis – who in 1781 had surrendered the British forces to the Americans at Yorktown – was a civilized and pleasant man who, although an able General, was pledged to non-aggression. Lord Wellesley, elder brother of the Duke of Wellington, initiated a very different policy on his appointment in 1797. This had the effect of bringing, within the following twenty years, the greater part of the subcontinent under the sway of what remained a trading company, even if one subject to the control of British governments.

The 1793 review took place without stimulating any but the most feeble interest in a House of Commons much more occupied with the war that had just begun with France. Few alterations were made to the Company's monopoly, which was, however, beginning to be seriously eroded from other quarters. Any British subject – including, of course, Indians themselves – was allowed to trade from India to anywhere in the world *except* Britain. This trade was generally known as the 'country' trade, and the ships engaged in it, often built in the East, as 'country' ships. Their operations were subject to licences from the Company, but these were freely issued. What concerned the government more was that a foreign clandestine trade, estimated at the equivalent of ten thousand tons of various merchandise a year, a considerable proportion of the total, had grown up, as nationals of other countries muscled in. And India was proving increasingly costly; the expansionist policy initiated by Lord Wellesley, and the resulting wars, were expensive, sending the political budget (that concerned with administration, the commercial affairs being accounted for separately) shooting up. At home, financing the titanic struggle against Napoleon was draining the

Treasury. Demand for Indian produce slumped; profits fell from 1799, moving into loss from 1809; by 1824 raw silk imports were altogether halted. Only the China trade remained profitable, thanks to the insatiable British thirst for tea, and it remained a Company monopoly, protected not only by the British government but by the Chinese insistence that all trade be carried out in Canton under strictly regulated control.

Not that the British government was much concerned with such matters after the final defeat of Napoleon in 1815. Britain came out of that period of turmoil having lost the most populous of its North American colonies, but gained a portfolio of formerly French and Dutch possessions scattered across the globe. Restoring, as far as possible, the status quo at home was the object of government, and anything suggesting change was deeply distrusted. Tory governments remained in power for fifteen years, although they became more liberal in attitude as younger men came to the fore. On most subjects the views of such politicians as Robert Peel, George Canning and William Huskisson would have been considered dangerously advanced by Continental administrations, and were at least as liberal as those of the Whig opposition. If anything the Whig leaders were more personally aristocratic than their Tory counterparts, from whom they differed most sharply on the subject of Parliamentary reform. The Whig Prime Minister Lord Grey, who forced through the 1832 Parliamentary Reform Bill, was a great landowning Earl, 'an aristocrat both by position and by nature' as he described himself: only four of his Cabinet were not with him in the House of Lords, and all of these were substantial landowners, with handles to their names; the sole exception was the President of the Board of Control of the East India Company, plain Charles Grant (and even he rapidly became a peer as Lord Glenelg).

What distinguished Whigs from Tories were the pressures to which they responded. Whigs were more ready to listen to Irish grievances, and usually enjoyed the support of most Irish M.P.s. Tories remained sensitive to the prejudices of the established Protestant Churches in England and Ireland, and fiercely protective of what they believed to be the interests of landowners. The Whigs, although their leaders shared such concerns, were much more subject to the influence of the increasingly important and prosperous classes of merchants and manufacturers. Their Reform Bill was much more a measure to transfer power from the countryside to the new industrial towns, than one to extend the right to vote. Whig ministers might not dine with Lancashire mill owners, but they were conscious of their economic power and their importance to the wealth of the nation in a way the Tories were not. This readiness of the Whigs to listen to manufacturers, traders and merchants was to have an important effect on affairs in China.

Listening did not imply personal regard. C.H. Philips, in his history of the East India Company, remarked: 'The ruling class in England in the late eighteenth and early nineteenth centuries seldom praised the Board without at the same time censuring the Directors – perhaps because the latter were closely associated with commerce and with the upstart Nabobs.' To the aristocratic politicians, Whig or Tory, the Directors of the Honorable East India Company were but 'those worthy cheesemongers', those 'mean-spirited men', those 'paltry shabroons'.[10] Neither Whigs nor Tories encouraged colonial expansion. Indeed, Whig statesmen were quite prepared to rid themselves of possessions which seemed to be a nuisance, of which Canada was deemed the 'most dangerous'. And colonists themselves were remarkably troublesome: West Indian planters mounted a rearguard action against the emancipation of slaves, which succeeded in driving up their own compensation to the staggering figure of £20 million, equivalent to a full year's government expenditure; Australia was proving not entirely satisfactory as a penal colony, and the free settlers there constantly agitated for political rights well in advance of any they might have expected in the home country; the South African Boers were perennially recalcitrant, and frequently rebellious.

India was a special case, a source of mingled pride and anxiety, but neither Indian nor colonial affairs attracted any attention outside specialist circles: debates were poorly attended, and, except when a dramatic war seized attention, public opinion voted all colonies a bore (colonial affairs are almost totally absent, for example, from Anthony Trollope's political novels).

In addition to the various points of view affecting British attitudes towards China, there was one man who for many years exercised the greatest influence. For thirty-five years British foreign policy was dominated by the opinionated, adventurous, highly conservative Liberal, Henry Temple, Lord Palmerston. Although he had held office since 1807, when, as a Tory, he became a Lord of the Admiralty straight from Cambridge, Palmerston first attained real power in 1830, as Foreign Secretary in the Whig government of Lord Grey. Even had he been a less powerful and effective politician his span of office would have given him enormous influence: between 1830 and 1865, while Britain was at her peak as the world power, there were only a few years when he was not occupying one of the highest offices of state, as Foreign Secretary, Home Secretary, or Prime Minister.

A cross and costly voyage

The two empires, British and Chinese, had their first confrontation in the seventeenth century, during the last days of the Ming dynasty. Sir William Courten, a rich London merchant, who had already to all intents and purposes acquired Barbados, persuaded King Charles I to give permission for a trading enterprise towards China, with the added intention of, if possible, discovering a north-east passage 'by California, on the backside of America'. It was hoped that the enterprise would be assisted by the Portuguese, ancient allies of England, who were the only European nation to enjoy even a limited trade with China. It was therefore at the Portuguese settlement of Macao that Courten's expedition, under the command of an aggressive Yorkshireman, Captain John Weddell, first called in June 1637.

Although Weddell and his ships were civilly enough received by the Portuguese, they were only moderately successful. In fact, the Portuguese had no intention of allowing the British to muscle in, and ensured that the Chinese authorities in Canton extended only a cool welcome. Weddell made matters worse by bluster and an attempt to use force. Six British merchants were detained by the Chinese in Canton, treated reasonably well, but only released when Weddell formally agreed to leave; a friendly Chinese admiral, Tsung-ping, admitted to one of his involuntary guests, Nathaniel Mountney, that 'he was sorry he could do noe more for them, beinge the plaine truth that the Portugalls had outbribed them'.[11]

Eventually, after 'a cross and costly voyage', Weddell's ships were able to collect a reasonable cargo, six hundred tons, mainly of sugar ('very good, smelling like roses'), but also green ginger, cloves, gold and porcelain, which was as much as he might have expected. To ensure continuing trade persistent negotiation over a number of seasons, accompanied by diligent, accurate and adequate bribery combined with a willingness to make a fuss if cheated too badly, would have been essential, and might have resulted in a compromise being reached with both Portuguese and Chinese. Such a long-term effort could only have been made if the British had been able to operate from a secure base somewhere conveniently near: it was certainly not possible to do so from England, half a world away. Even had the East India Company been willing to co-operate with what was a rival concern, their own first settlement in India, Fort St George (Madras), was only established in 1640, and remained for some time precarious.

Nor were the Chinese then able to take a long-term view; a change of policy towards trade with the foreign barbarians was out of the question, since a violent change of dynasty, with all the civil turmoil that portended, was imminent. Whole provinces were already in revolt: Szechuan, and the ancient heartland of Honan and Shensi, were in Manchu hands. Only four years after Weddell's departure the last Ming emperor hanged himself in Peking. The imposition of the Ch'ing dynasty's control over the whole of China took another generation, and the process brought an end to prospects of trade for many years: the East India factor at Surat reported: 'The Tartars overrun and waste all the inland country without settling any Government in the places which they overcome ... nor is there any certainty of trade in any part of China under the Tartar; who is an enemy to trade and hath depopulated all the vast quantityes of islands on the coaste of all maritime parts of Chyna and 8 leagues from the sea merely not to have a trade with any.'[12]

By 1711, when the East India Company were permitted to establish a post in Canton, they no longer needed to rely upon Portuguese goodwill. Macao had a bad time of it in the seventeenth century, after its trade to Japan had been cut off when that country closed its boundaries to foreigners in 1639. The population, 'mostly mongrels', was described in 1759 as being 'kept under servile Awe by the Chinese',[13] and at the end of the century Lord Macartney was no more complimentary: 'The Portuguese ... as a nation, have long been really exanimated and dead in this part of the world.'[14] The residual importance of Macao lay in its proximity to Canton, which soon became the only outlet for Western enterprise in China, as foreign trade was organized by the Manchu emperors. A series of edicts issued between 1685 and 1752 established the conditions under which this might be allowed. Traders could come only to Canton (in the early years some were allowed to visit Ningpo, and one or two other ports, but Canton was always much the most important, and, after a while, the only, centre). Tribute-bearing missions from foreign states were to proceed to Peking, but otherwise no access was allowed to the capital by foreigners (excepting the Russians, who, coming from overland, were not regarded in the same suspicious light).

For the greater part of the eighteenth century Canton acted much as does the venue for a modern trade fair, as an outlet for Chinese goods. Sugar was no longer in such demand, since nearer alternative sources had been established, of which the most important to Britain, oddly enough, was William Courten's island of Barbados. Silks, nankeen cottons, porcelain, paper, medical products such as rhubarb (sovereign against constipation) and spices were all in demand. Imports developed only slowly, and payment remained, as it had been for Weddell, strictly cash. Business was allowed on a strictly regulated basis. Private enterprise was banned: only a restricted range of goods could be bought or sold, and only by duly authorized persons, at the appointed season, and in accordance with multifarious rules. Authority was vested in the Hoppo (Cantonese *hoi poi*, an abbreviation of the Mandarin *yueh hai kuan pu*), superintendent of the South Sea Customs, an office which had existed since the eleventh century, but was now reformed and extended in power. The Hoppo was a medium-ranking official, now always a Manchu, appointed for three years and socially much inferior to the Viceroy or Governor-General (*tsung-tu*) of Kwantung and Kwangsi, one of the highest officials of the Chinese Empire, or even to the Governor of Canton City. But these distinguished gentlemen, usually traditional Chinese scholar-administrators, were only paid modest salaries (a contemporary calculation was that the ratio between the official remuneration of a Governor and that obtained – to put it politely – irregularly, was 7 per cent: 93 per cent) and therefore depended for their comfort on the exertions of the Hoppo. These were always forthcoming, for the Hoppo had paid a great deal for his appointment, and had to recoup it within the term of his office: his first year's emoluments paid off the purchase price, the second provided the wherewithal to satisfy the 'squeezes' demanded by superiors, leaving only the third year's income for himself.[15] In theory, Chinese customs duties were clearly specified: in practice as much as possible was collected, and as little as prudent remitted to Peking.

Under the Hoppo's aegis was the merchants' guild, the *Kung-hang*, or Cohong, which was progressively more tightly organized into the 'instrument by which he [the Hoppo] tapped the foreign trade to an extent . . . unparalleled since the palmy days of the Roman Empire'.[16] Only members of the Cohong were allowed to sell to foreigners, and every foreign ship coming to Canton was obliged to conduct its business through a guild member, who became the recognized sponsor for ship and crew, responsible for ensuring that all requirements were duly fulfilled by the captain and owners, and that crews behaved with propriety. In spite of the base position usually accorded to merchants in the Chinese hierarchy, the head of each Hong, or firm, was given official rank as mandarin of the lowest, ninth, degree, and entitled to append the honorific '*kuan*' to his name. It was an honour sometimes dearly bought, for given the enormous volume of trade that developed and their monopolistic position, the Cohong houses assumed great responsibilities. Eventually they 'not only settled prices, sold goods, guaranteed duties, restrained the foreigners, negotiated with them, controlled smuggling, and leased premises to them; they also had to manage all the aspects of a banking business, act as interpreting agencies, support the militia and educational institutions, and make all manner of presents and contributions to the authorities far and near'.[17]

Some of these nineteenth-century Hong merchants did extremely well for themselves; Howqua, the best known, estimated his net worth at $26 million, which would probably have made him the richest businessman in the world. But others, as is the way when business presents great opportunities and demands great risks, did badly, with both commercial and official repercussions. As failed merchants they were bankrupt, and as their failure entailed a loss – often a considerable one – to the Imperial exchequer, they were liable to exile to remote and uncomfortable parts. Some took their own lives rather than face the consequences.

Foreign traders were similarly regimented, not too unwillingly, into a comparably tight organization, under the supervision of the Honorable East India Company. 'Country traders' were allowed to ply between India and other eastern ports, but all other British ships were prevented by the Company's monopoly from making the passage to the East, while the emergent British sea-power ensured that Dutch, Spanish, Swedish, and later American merchants were content to accept the Company's hegemony. France made a great effort to obtain a share of the Eastern trade, but the Compagnie des Indes (which had a whole new city, L'Orient, provided for them as a base on the coast of Brittany) never made much of a showing in China. There was no question of foreign diplomatic representation at Canton, and accordingly it was the East India Company's officials who acted as consuls would otherwise have done in representing the foreign community to the Chinese. While each captain dealt with his own Hong guarantor, more serious difficulties could be sorted out by Company representatives, who themselves became formally organized into the Select Committee of Supra Cargoes, commonly known as the 'Select', and headed by a President. Originally 'Supra Cargo' – and always so, as far as the East India Company was concerned – the supercargo was a representative of the owners of the cargo, responsible for disposing of it profitably and buying whatever return merchandise he could find. In earlier days he was appointed, like the ship's officers, for a single voyage, but as trade became more regular supercargoes tended to become more permanent residents in Macao and Canton.

The most serious difficulties between the foreign community and the Ch'ing authorities arose from the coexistence of their different and incompatible ideas of justice. This clash became apparent in the famous case of the gunner of the *Lady Hughes* in 1784, when an unfortunate seaman accidentally caused the death of two Chinese while firing a salute. The Chinese insisted he be put on trial, and reinforced their demand by kidnapping one of the ship's officers. The Committee of Supra Cargoes, on the understanding that he would be given a fair trial and a lenient sentence, instructed the captain to surrender the accused man. This he did, writing a touching letter to the President: 'Pray Dear Smith take care of the Old Man, you had better leave something with Muqua [the Hong merchant] for the Old Man's maintenance, I hope the Chinese will not do harm to the poor Old Man as it was only a misfortune.'[18] It was not an unreasonable expectation, since Chinese law allowed for commutation in cases of accidental death; a previous incident in 1722 had been settled by a payment of 2000 taels. The captain's hopes were vain, however; the unhappy gunner was secretly executed, without anyone being present to put his case, and the supercargoes received a severe lecture from the Chinese Viceroy for having refused to hand him over in the first place. The question of 'extra-territoriality' – the right of foreigners to be tried by their own rather by than local laws – was at the root of many subsequent clashes, including the first Anglo–Chinese war of 1840–42.

Such grave events were rare, trouble usually being avoided by mutual consent and forbearance. Both sides relied upon the same pressure to avoid confrontations and to bring the other into line – the threat of suspending the mutually profitable trade, which was almost as serious to the Chinese as to the English. When in 1727 the supercargoes threatened to transfer their activities up the coast to the port of Amoy and to abandon Canton, the mandarins quickly conceded the point at issue. The remaining constraints, although irritating, were tolerated. Trade was allowed in Canton only during the summer; at the end of the season all business must be wound up, all debts settled, and all foreigners must leave Canton, either for home, or to spend the winter with the Portuguese at Macao. When in Canton they were restricted to a small area outside the city walls, but on the waterfront. Here 'factories' were built (the word signifies a place occupied by factors, or agents, from the Portuguese '*feitoria*'), crammed close together in the limited space allowed, each occupied by merchants of a single nation. The English factory was naturally the largest, a combination of warehouse, where goods were stored before being either sold or shipped, counting house and Oxbridge college, in which a small number of Britons lived in some style, attended by numerous Chinese servitors. Foreigners' movements outside the factory area were closely restricted: the authorities were anxious to avoid possible disturbances, and the populace of Canton was known to be hostile to and suspicious of foreigners. For the same reason such signs of ostentation as the use of sedan chairs (a prerogative of high Chinese officials) was banned. Above all, no foreign women were allowed at any time.

As always happens, the official regulations were modified by informal understandings. As long as the 'Select' managed matters without fuss, the Chinese were content to wink at minor infringements. Since all the merchants were in Canton with but one idea – to make as much money as quickly as possible before retiring to their own countries – they were willing to accept the restrictions. They were only in Canton for a few months every year, and in the intervals Macao could supply all the comforts of home, although in the first half of the eighteenth century, when communications were difficult, wives and families did not venture on the voyage east. If such enormous fortunes as had been made in eighteenth-century India were no longer available, it did not take long to amass a reasonable competence. Salaries were high, and the grant of free cargo space on the Company's ships was, as long as the monopoly continued, a valuable privilege.

In spite of occasional contretemps the system worked well throughout the eighteenth century and for some time thereafter. Michael Greenberg, its historian, wrote: 'The honesty and commercial integrity of the distant Hong merchants were a byword in the alleys of the City of London as in the bazaars of Bombay.'[19] An American merchant praised 'the facility of all dealings with the Chinese who were assigned to transact business with us, together with their proverbial honesty, combined with a sense of perfect security to person and property . . . In no part of the world could the authorities have exercised a more vigilant care over the personal safety of strangers, who . . . came to live in the midst of a population whose customs and prejudices were so opposed to everything foreign.'[20]

2

A STREAM OF SILVER

The plant of joy

Many circumstances combined to make the East India Company wish to liberate its Canton trade from some of the restrictions placed upon it – the rising costs of Indian administration, increasing competition, and a desire to find a market for British exports combined with a growing intolerance of extortion. In order to effect this, diplomatic contact was needed, along the well-tried lines of previous negotiations with Russians, Turks and Moghuls.

The first British embassy arrived in Peking in 1793, headed by a former Governor of Madras, George, Lord Macartney. Although carefully planned, plentifully staffed, and conveyed in a 64-gun man-of-war, all presenting a convincing picture of British power and wealth, the embassy was a failure, and a failure because of complete mutual misunderstanding. The old Emperor Ch'ien-Lung was perfectly prepared to be affable and welcoming to this latest consignment of barbarians, and ready to stretch a number of points in order to accommodate their peculiar prejudices, but had no idea of altering what seemed to be an entirely satisfactory system. Macartney was an ideal ambassador, an accomplished and agreeable man who had earlier headed a successful diplomatic mission to Russia and dealt amicably with that difficult lady, Catherine the Great; but he could not impress Ch'ien-lung.[1]

British requests for relaxation of the restrictions on trade were not even considered: the Emperor could hardly believe that they had been made seriously even by the princeling of a barbarian state. 'It may be,

O King,' he said in a letter to King George III, putting the blame for so gross a breach of decorum on Macartney, 'that your proposals have wantonly been made by your ambassador on his own responsibility.' Perhaps the most horrifying of these impertinences was the suggestion that the British were thinking of acquiring a little Chinese real estate. Macartney had been instructed to ask for 'a small unfortified island near Chusan for the residence of English traders, storage of goods, and outfitting of ships'. This was a subject that, in spite of the initial negative response, was not to be allowed to drop by the British.

What the Macartney embassy did achieve on its return was to quicken British interest in China and to extend knowledge of that country. Two members of the embassy, John Barrow, later famous as Secretary to the Admiralty, and Sir George Staunton, published detailed accounts which impressed 'the grandeur and extent of the Chinese Empire' on the British consciousness (and Sir George's ten-year-old-son, George Thomas, who accompanied his father, left a record of his painstaking Chinese characters in the Historical Archives of Peking).[2] For its part the Chinese Empire chose to stay completely uninterested in the affairs of the world outside its borders. The Emperor himself made this abundantly clear in the politely dismissive letter that Macartney bore back to George III; his 'genuine respect and friendliness' was appreciated, but as to his request 'to send one of your nationals to stay at the Celestial Court to take care of your country's trade with China', the King was told that 'this is not in harmony with the state system of our dynasty and will definitely not be permitted'.[3] Lord Macartney in his journal made an uncomplimentary but accurate assessment:

The Empire of China is an old, crazy, first rate man-of-war, which a fortunate succession of able and vigilant officers has contrived to keep afloat these one hundred and fifty years past, and to overawe their neighbours by her bulk and appearance, but whenever an insufficient man happens to have the command upon deck, adieu to the discipline and safety of the ship. She may perhaps not sink outright; she may drift some time as a wreck, and will then be dashed to pieces on the shore; but she can never be rebuilt on the old bottom.

Even while Macartney was in Peking, however, one development was obtruding itself. The new British administration in Bengal, bent on optimizing the revenues now accruing to the East India Company, recognized that the most profitable cash crop offered by their farmers was that useful drug, opium. Growers and processors were organized with brisk efficiency, and the finest and best opium began to reach the auctions of Calcutta. Something had appeared that could be offered to the Chinese in exchange for their tea.

Opium is the oldest recorded and best-documented of drugs.[4] Fourth millennium Sumerians called the poppy 'the plant of joy'; Egyptians prescribed opium in the sixteenth century B.C.; the Minoans had a poppy goddess; Homer knew it as nepenthe. When medicine was systematized by the Romans, opium took its place as the principal soporific. Dioscorides, an army surgeon under Nero, lists it in his *Materium Medica*; Galen, who set Western medicine and psychology in a mould which was not broken until the seventeenth century, relied upon it; Avicenna of Hamadan, centuries ahead of European physicians and philosophers in medical knowledge, is reputed to have died of an overdose in 1039. John Arderne, the fourteenth-century English physician, who left a detailed record of many of his prescriptions, used it at least locally, applying some compound so that the patient 'schal slepe so that he schal fele no kuttyng', but its main utility was as a soporific, to permit sleep to encourage natural healing.

In eighteenth-century Britain there was no feeling of disapproval towards opium; the popular demon remained for a long time alcohol. It was the time of Hogarth's Gin Lane – 'Drunk for a penny, dead drunk for tuppence.' Opium, on the other hand, had the blessing of no less respectable an institution than the Royal Society of Arts, which instituted an award of fifty guineas or a gold medal to anyone who could successfully cultivate the drug in Britain. Naturally enough many of the winners were medical men. Dr Crawley of Buckinghamshire produced over ten stones of opium from eleven acres of land. Even more surprisingly, Dr Howson and Mr Young, a surgeon, received gold medals for producing opium in Scotland, Mr Young producing a remarkable profit of £117 6s. an acre, which must have been a record for any crop.[5] These results were obtained not only from opium poppies, but from common white and garden red plants; Mr Young also collected opium in quantity from lettuces. If such results could be obtained in bleak North Britain, how much more could be expected in fertile Bengal? And so it proved: using the abundant labour resources of the province opium of great purity could be produced in quantities far too large for available outlets.

There was, to be sure, a steady medical demand, since alcoholic tincture of opium – laudanum – was the preferred drug for a wide range of conditions, not only as a narcotic but in reducing fevers. It was also used, most famously by De Quincey and Coleridge, as what would nowadays be called a recreational drug, and widely among the poor as a tranquillizer and an alternative to alcohol. Since opium remained legal in Britain until the twentieth century, and was subject for most of that time to only the loosest of controls, it is hardly surprising that the British-Indian authorities chose to see nothing morally indefensible in expanding opium production and organizing it as a Company monopoly.

China was an immediately attractive market, since smoking opium, sometimes mixed with tobacco, was already common. Edicts against both had indeed been issued since the early seventeenth century, with tobacco being considerably the more strictly condemned. Sales of opium for medicinal purposes had always been legal, and opium was regularly imported, and duty paid on it, throughout the eighteenth century; but decapitation was made the penalty in the 1630s for selling tobacco. Little attention had been paid to any of these prohibitions until an Imperial edict of 1729, which inveighed against young people being introduced to drugs, was taken seriously at least by the East India Company. Instructions were given to their captains that, since the penalty for being found with opium on board was confiscation of ship and cargo, 'Upon no consideration whatsoever, you are neither to carry, nor suffer any of it to be carry'd in your Ship to China, as you will answer the contrary to the Honorable Company on your peril.'[6] In other quarters the edict was largely ignored and opium continued to be consumed in considerable quantities; in the 1770s a French visitor noted that the Chinese had suddenly developed 'an unbelievable passion for this narcotic'.[7]

After the Company assumed responsibility for organizing production in 1781 they continued to avoid shipping the drug to China. Opium was sold in the Calcutta market by the Company to speculators, who shipped it to Canton for disposal through the private 'country' traders. In this way the Company was able to wash its collective hands and deny any responsibility for the drug reaching China. Before 1781 country ships had brought up to a thousand chests a year from India (a chest contained between 135 and 160 pounds of opium), but within nine years, by 1790, over four thousand chests were being imported. This was a large enough increase to attract attention, and resulted in an edict absolutely prohibiting all imports of opium, after which the trade became illegal and contraband. But only officially: 'There was no pretence of enforcing them [the prohibitory edicts] in the spirit, and the restrictions of their letter had only the effect of covering the traffic with a veil of decency ... The irregular dues levied over and above the official traffic were already heavy, but when it became necessary to pay for connivance in addition to ... complaisance, they became heavier; and they were distributed between the officials, Hoppo, Viceroy, Governor, Treasurer, and so on down the list.'[8]

The only visible difference was that instead of being offered openly for sale in Canton, the opium was kept on board ship at Whampoa. The Select Committee at Canton continued to ensure that the left hand remained in ignorance of the activities of the right: 'It was judged more advisable to avoid any public communication [with the private English] and merely advising the Traders ... that we perceived no impropriety in their bringing the Article to Market' (Opium Committee, 1804). At that time, and for thirty years after, the volume of opium sales remained static, and the matter was not regarded as one of strategic importance to British India. Among the instructions given to Lord Macartney had been the undertaking that the opium trade would, if the Chinese insisted, be given up: 'Useful as the opium revenue was to India, it was less to be desired than the China trade monopoly.'[9]

As it happened, this point was never raised, since the Chinese authorities refused to enter into negotiations with Macartney; it might therefore be said that the responsibility for subsequent events lay with the Chinese. Had they been willing to talk things out with Macartney, as the accredited representative of a foreign power, the opium trade could have been suppressed, and war avoided. Closing the trade would not have been unduly damaging to the Indian government; the revenue from Calcutta opium sales was a welcome, but hardly crucial, part of the Company's income. It was comforting to be able to rely upon opium sales: 'You will have observed with peculiar pleasure,' wrote Lord Mornington, the Governor-General, to Henry Dundas at the Board of Control, on 21 March 1799, 'that the revenue arising from the sale of opium has been completely restored ... the public is greatly indebted to Mr Fleming, second member of the medical board, for his careful inspection of the opium.'[10] Ten years later, when the excellent Mr Fleming's work had borne fruit, opium still accounted for only 6 per cent of the revenues of Bengal, ranking sixth in order of importance.[11]

Item	Current Rupees
Land taxes	3,32,85,671
Salt sales	1,82,69,505
Oude revenues	1,79,22,320
Conquered provinces revenues	1,22,68,014
Benares (pilgrim) revenues	61,55,472
Opium sales	59,56,354

The total revenue for the province was 9,83,83,516 Current Rupees. After allowing for the cost of collection (CRs 9,67,278), the net opium revenue was the equivalent of £498,908; a respectable sum, but hardly a *casus belli*, especially when the revenue from Fort St George (Madras) is added in to the total of the Indian income. This amounted to nearly half the Bengal income, and had no contribution from opium; nor did the relatively small Bombay income. Taking the provinces together, and ignoring the costs of collection, opium might account for 4 per cent of the gross revenue of the Company in India. All these figures relate only to internal Indian receipts, and do not include the Company's trading income, which is what enabled the dividends to be paid, at that time £875,000 annually. Nor had matters materially altered in the year 1817–18, when, in sterling terms, opium sales accounted for £873,599 of an Indian revenue of £18,322,547, still under 5 per cent. (Sources: East India Company annual accounts.)

For the first two decades of the nineteenth century there was little increase in production: the five-yearly averages during that period were:

Period	Chests sold
1797—1801	4,009
1802—06	3,700
1807—11	4,718
1812—17	4,135

Officials worried that perhaps they were failing the Chinese consumers in not providing more of the article, since 'altho' the sudden deprivation of the drug would almost certainly occasion great distress to those accustomed to the use of it, there is no moral obligation on Government to extend the manufacture'.

Profits from Indian opium during the first two decades of the nine-teenth century can therefore hardly be said to have been a major concern of the East India Company, nor, in spite of future growth, were they ever to assume dimensions critical to Indian prosperity. But it was in everyone's interest that the Canton trade continued uninter-rupted: the prosperity of Canton, the comforts of Peking, the livelihood of thousands of officials, and, through the duties levied on tea a sub-stantial part of the revenue of the British government, all depended on it.

Insolent, capricious, and vexatious procedures

Canton's contribution was particularly useful to the Chinese exchequer, since it concentrated extra burdens on a few merchants rather than irritating the populace. It was hardly surprising that, given a system 'beautifully suited to systematic exploitation', desperate officials had recourse to the easiest source of income by increasing the 'squeeze' on the Canton merchants. In 1807, for example, the unfortunate Cohong merchants were forced to pay, among other exac-tions, 127,500 taels for suppression of piracy and river control works, and 200,000 taels for 'sing-songs' (imported watches, clocks and mechanical toys). The danger of a Cohong merchant failing was meant to be covered by the existence of the Consoo fund, a sum accrued from annual percentages of profits and held, in theory, to cover insolvent debts, but official extortions began to eat voraciously into its assets.[12]

Strains appeared in the system as the foreigners in Canton objected. The British in particular were beginning to feel conscious of belonging to what was now a major world power rather than a company of mer-chants, and were no longer contented to accept so many undignified restrictions. Napoleon, who had only three years previously bound almost all Europe from Warsaw to the Pyrénées under French domi-nation, was defeated at Waterloo and exiled to a remote Atlantic island, the prisoner of none other than the East India Company, for St Helena was one of the Company's chain of victualling stations.

The contrast between the Company's position in India and in China was now vivid. An Indian griffin (cadet) could expect to be given, in a short time, an executive post in which he would act as the heir to the Moghul Empire, travelling with an imposing retinue, surrounded by deferential Indian servants and assistants, supported by well-trained soldiers who had repeatedly proved themselves masters of any other force the subcontinent could produce. He was the undisputed great man in his own territory, even if this was officially an independent princedom. He was required to speak the language of the country, and may well have learnt it at the Company's Hailebury College. Admittedly, now that he was barred from private trading the Company officer could not hope to amass the fortunes of previous nabobs, of whom Jos Sedley in Thackeray's *Vanity Fair* is a vivid portrait. He did, however, enjoy a very respectable standard of living, usually within reach of a centre of English civilization, with such amenities as pianos, ladies, billiard rooms and circulating libraries. Not least among his comforts was the constant availability of Himalayan ice, to cool his Bass's beer and soda water.

The young man posted to Canton as a 'writer' in the Company's factory was in a much less pleasant situation. Unlike his Indian cousin, he was no Imperial administrator, but a trader, the lowest form of Chinese life. He lived for more than half the year in the hot and soggy Cantonese climate, cramped in a narrow factory, his quarters a single modest room. He was not allowed even to walk outside the tiny European sector except on specified occasions. The populace was clearly hostile, even though relations with the Hong merchants might be civil, even sometimes friendly. Holidays in Macao were better, but the decidedly mixed society there, in which English women were rare, could not bear comparison with that of Calcutta, Madras or Bombay. The intellectual or studious writer could, with great difficulty, master enough Chinese to interest himself in the traditions and culture of the country, but few were inclined to make the effort.

The compensation should have been the prospect of making money by trade; this was indeed still possible in Canton, but becoming increasingly more difficult for the Company's staff when, in 1813, the monopoly of trade to India was revoked. The Court protested, but without avail, for the Company had become widely unpopular; one observer mentioned that 'If an additional article was proposed to cut off the heads of one or more of the Directors, the House would have voted it by a very great majority.'[13] And in Canton real money was demonstrably beginning to be made by the private traders, regarded by respectable

Company servants as quasi-piratical nobodies from nowhere, opium smugglers to a man, and not at all *comme il faut*.

After the 1793 revision of the Company's charter, which allowed outsiders to participate legally (they had been doing so unlawfully for some time) in the 'country' trade between India and China, British merchants established themselves in the Indian import-export trade, usually in Calcutta. This was not easy, as newcomers had to find a niche in the existing pattern. Raw cotton, the principal Indian export and one of the few to attract Chinese buyers, was kept in Company hands, and in Canton the Select Committee used its licensing powers to restrain interlopers from the staple trades, powers also reinforced by the Chinese, who restricted trade in the more important exports to the Company and to the Hong merchants.

One potential import was spring-driven products, one of the few fields in which Europe had been ahead of China since medieval times: watches, clocks, mechanical singing birds, cascading waterfalls, dancing figures, musical boxes and the like became eagerly sought after. The Chinese lust for such toys which, according to the President of the Select Committee in 1811 had 'now become the established vehicle of corruption between the officer [the Hoppo] and his superior at the Capital'[14] caused a number of squabbles. In an attempt to avoid these the Company limited their own imports of these aggravating articles, which gave such enterprising outsiders as James Cox of Cheapside the opportunity to muscle in. The firm that he founded, after many vicissitudes, eventually became that greatest of all China houses, Jardine Matheson. Cox also tested the market for other potential imports, of which sea-otter and seal skins from the 'backside' of America were the most successful, an immensely lucrative trade later taken over by John Jacob Astor. Other merchants employed their ingenuity in locating imports that might appeal to Chinese tastes and be substitutes for cash payment; metals, dyestuffs, ginseng, sandalwood, ivory, coral and amber, and such delicacies as sharks' fins and bird nests. Markets abroad for Chinese goods were similarly investigated; a London 'Drug Concern' was formed to import Chinese rhubarb, cassia and camphor.

The Company's directors did not take kindly to such competition, and made every effort to harass those unlicensed traders who were making their own fortunes at the Company's expense. The interlopers soon hit on a device to protect themselves; they became honorary consuls of foreign powers, legally foreign subjects to whom therefore, albeit regretfully, the Select found it 'improper to give ... any molestation'. Cockneys and Scots, poorly disguised as loyal Austrians, Prussians, Swedes, Poles, Hanoverians, Neapolitans and Genoese, were able legitimately to carry out their business at Canton under the disapproving gaze of the Select. For their part the Chinese officials made no objection, scarcely differentiating between different tribes of red-haired barbarians, as long as they behaved themselves, and contributed the usual 'squeezes'.

The private merchants found that the easiest and most profitable article to dispose of in Canton was, increasingly, opium. The Company had excluded itself from that trade, but remained anxious to dispose of the excellent opium it was now producing for the Calcutta markets. China was considerably the largest purchaser, and for sales there the Company had to rely on private merchants, thereby considerably reducing any disciplinary powers the Select Committee of Supra Cargoes might have. Their authority was further impaired by the growing weakness of their counterparts, the Cohong merchants, subject to ever more rapacious demands from Peking's representatives.

In 1816, in an attempt to find a remedy, the East India Company sent William Pitt Amherst, Lord Amherst, to Peking to try to persuade the Emperor to relax his restrictions and open more ports to trade: 'The CAUSES which in the opinion of the Company's Administration in China, of the Court of Directors, and of the Prince Regent's Government, have rendered a Mission from this country expedient are the insolent, capricious, vexatious procedures ... by which they [the local government of Canton] have obstructed trade.' Lord Amherst was even less successful than Macartney had been in 1793, but the British government was in no mood to press the Company's case, being much more concerned with events at home and in Europe.[15]

I never saw a chest of opium in my life

The only colonial issue of the time to raise political temperatures in Britain was slavery. Abolition of slavery, the future of the freed slaves, compensation for their owners and the suppression of the trade engaged successive governments. Apart from the stockholders of the East India Company no one concerned themselves with events in China. The trade to Canton continued satisfactorily, surviving both the appointment of a distinguished and incorrupt civil Governor-

General, Juan Yuan, and the succession, in 1820, of an energetic and conscientious Emperor.[16]

Tao-kuang (Daoguang), an active thirty-eight-year-old, had as a boy been close to the old Emperor Ch'ien-lung, and inherited his grandfather's view of the world: the Middle Kingdom might have its difficulties, but it was the only civilized society, surrounded by obstreperous and unpleasing barbarians, whose concerns were matters of little importance. In his policies Tao-kuang followed his father Chia-ch'ing's frugal example, to the point of wearing old and patched garments and eating simple food. On his death thirty years later he ordered that no laudatory tablets be placed on his tomb, thereby acknowledging his personal shortcomings and his failure to succour the empire.

It is impossible to read the Emperor's comments on the communications he received from his mandarins without being impressed by his personal decency and dedication to his arduous duty. Many of the corrupt mandarins had died or retired, and Tao-kuang was well served by some men of high character and ability, both Chinese and Manchu. The senior counsellor, Mu-chang-a, a close relative, attracted a permanent following, scattered all over the country. Having fewer of the ideological prejudices that hampered the more traditionalist Chinese, when disagreements with the foreigners arose Mu-chang-a's supporters advocated a policy of compromise, and were fiercely opposed by the advocates of resistance to foreign influence. All, however, Manchu and Chinese, and none more so than the Emperor himself, were dangerously restricted by their almost complete ignorance of the world outside.

When Juan Yuan's attention was drawn to the opium trade he immediately banned the drug from Whampoa or Macao, decreed severe penalties, and arrested a number of dealers and users in Canton. The trade responded, not by abandoning or even restricting the traffic, which was unthinkable, but by providing it with a more decent cover. The drug would be brought from India not to Whampoa, but only as far as Lintin island, a convenient anchorage in the estuary, where it would be transferred to permanently-moored receiving ships, owned and staffed by the private merchants. These would then negotiate with prospective Chinese buyers in Canton, and when a deal was reached, would arrange for the merchandise to be collected from the receiving ships. The 'drop' was made to small, fast galleys, owned and crewed by Chinese, picturesquely known as 'fast crabs' or 'scrambling dragons'.

Chinese coastal defence forces – there was nothing that could realistically be described as a navy – contented themselves with occasionally chasing these galleys and, once a year at the end of the trading season, pursuing the departing opium ships. This was done at a respectful distance and at the most deliberate pace, but with the maximum discharge of ordnance. Peking was then informed. 'A few days after this farce has been performed, a proclamation is issued to the whole nation, stating that "His Celestial Majesty's Imperial fleet, after a *desperate conflict*, has made the Fan-quis run before it." '[17] Upsets, of course, sometimes happened; in the 1820s a fire destroyed valuable stocks in the factories; an American seaman was delivered up to the Chinese authorities for strangulation (the Terranovia case); British seamen accused after a fight at Lintin were not (the *Topaze* case). But these untoward occurrences were swiftly put to rights, since all concerned were acutely aware that maintaining the system intact meant substantial profits. All goods taken to or from Lintin were free of duty, and even cargoes of perfectly legal merchandise soon switched from Whampoa to the estuary, the extra cost of carriage being more than compensated for by the saving of duty.

The opium trade continued to burgeon: imports rose steadily in quantity, although prices did not; the 4,770 chests bought in 1821 fetched $8,400,800, the 9,621 chests of the 1826 season only $7,608,205. Vigorous efforts to extend the market were begun, so effectively that by 1830 imports had nearly doubled again, to 18,760 chests, a far cry from the four thousand or so that had been the norm for the thirty years to 1820. By divorcing the legal trade from the smuggled business the British officials in Canton were able to disclaim all responsibility, and even any knowledge of it. A former President of the Select, John Francis Davis, who had served in Canton for seventeen years, was able to assert, when asked by a Committee of the House of Commons in 1829 whether the opium was stamped with the Company's mark, 'I never saw a chest of opium in my life; and therefore I cannot speak to it.' Davis was an honourable man, and this otherwise quite unbelievable statement has to be taken seriously, even with the reflection that he must have known very well where not to look, since almost every European in Canton, excepting the members of the Company's staff, was busily engaged in little else than in selling as much opium as possible to the Chinese. But Davis's claim is supported by the testimony given to the same committee by Dent's bookkeeper at

Canton, Mr Henry, that he too 'had never seen a chest of opium in his life'.[18]

Useful though the income from opium sales was to the Indian government, it did little for British exporters of other goods, whose chances to make sales in China were limited both by the superior attractions of the drug and the continuing East India Company monopoly there. Pressure from the merchants to be allowed to export direct from England was first manifested on 10 July 1820 in a petition presented to Parliament from 'several Merchants, Manufacturers and other Inhabitants of the Towns of *Manchester* and *Salford*, and the surrounding neighbourhood . . . requesting that general freedom of trade with the port of *Canton* in *China* may be granted . . . and that the Sovereignty of *Sincapore* may be retained, if not inconsistent with the good faith and honour of our country'. The Tory government of Lord Liverpool was at the time far too occupied with such matters as Queen Caroline's divorce from George IV and the aftermath of the Peterloo massacre, at which demonstrators protesting against agrarian hardship were fired upon by representatives of the law, to debate the Manchester men's petition, which was merely 'left on the table of the House'. Singapore did indeed become a British colony in 1824, but that decision was taken by the Governor General of India, who realizing the vital commercial importance of a station nearer to China, confirmed Stamford Raffles' purchase of the island five years earlier from the Sultan of Johore.

The 1820 petition was the earliest example of a delusion that was to persist for the rest of the century, and to have important effects on the future of China. As the industrialization of Britain speeded up, with the general application of steam power and the organization of factory production, the need for new markets became pressing. The process was headed by the Lancashire cotton industry, the harbinger of the Industrial Revolution. In 1820 the industry was still dominated by the hand-loom workers, but power looms were beginning rapidly to oust the individual workers; in 1813 there were only 2,400 power looms in England, a number which had risen to 55,000 by the end of the 1820s and a quarter of a million by 1850, producing one half of all British exports. The voracious demand for new markets was soon reinforced by the spread of factory production methods to other industries. As Europe and America began to catch up with Britain, and later to overtake it, British exporters became more agitated. The very size of China, by far the largest untapped source of demand available, excited them. If only, they urged at first, the Canton trade regulations were relaxed and the Company's monopoly ended; if only, then, other ports were opened; if only Britain had a port in her own possession; if only opium were legalized; if only navigation on the rivers were permitted; if only customs duties were lowered, then the Chinese masses would rejoice at being able to buy Staffordshire mugs, Birmingham trays and Lancashire frocks, all brought to them cheaply by British-built railways. British officials, sniffily distrustful of anything pertaining to trade, were reluctant to accede to these demands (rightly enough, as it turned out, for the Chinese market never developed as it was expected to, a disappointment that only served to prompt the industrialists to press for more concessions). These attitudes, already implicit in the 1820s, later became a source of constant disagreement between traders, often backed by the Hong Kong authorities, and the British government.

By the end of the decade the foreign residents at Canton had coalesced into a prototype of what became the first Hong Kong community. The Company men metamorphosed into colonial administrators, the private traders continued the impetus that put the new colony on its feet, and the missionaries assisted in establishing contact with the Chinese. Already by 1830 a future Governor of the colony, John Davis, had made a first career as a supercargo; the Morrisons, father and son, who were to be essential in bringing some measure of communication between British and Chinese negotiators, had established their credentials as interpreters; and the two British houses that formed the nucleus of the Hong Kong commercial world had become pre-eminent in Canton. These were Magniac & Co. (already Jardine Matheson in everything except name) and their implacable rivals Thomas Dent's.[19] Eighteen of the fifty-two-strong British community were employed by these two firms, which, since the Company staff accounted for another twenty, gives an indication of their relative importance.

Of the remainder of the Western community, the most colourful was the short and portly Rev. Charles Gutzlaff, something of a cross between missionary and merchant. Gutzlaff, formerly a staymaker's apprentice from Pyritz in Prussia, spoke several languages fluently if imperfectly, and was much sought after by the opium traders as an interpreter – 'I would give a thousand dollars for three days of Gutzlaff,' the independent merchant James Innes once wrote. Thrice married, Gutzlaff became one of the liveliest inhabitants of early Hong

Kong, playing an important part in the colony's affairs until his death in 1851. The score or so of Americans – New Englanders for the most part – included two missionaries, the Rev. E.C. Bridgman and Dr James Bradford, and one William Hunter, a merchant whose book of reminiscences, *The Fan Kwae in Canton*, is a lively record of daily life in the factories and at Macao. Between them the tiny community supported two periodicals, the *Chinese Repository*, edited by Bridgman, and the *Canton Miscellany*, put together mainly by Company staff, and two newspapers, the *Canton Register*, owned by Matheson, and the *Canton Press*, which took a strongly pro-Dent line.[20]

Apart from the missionaries and their pupils all the Europeans – and all Chinese without exception, for it was some time before any Chinese mastered English – could only communicate in pidgin. This lingua franca comprises a vocabulary of English, Chinese, Portuguese and Anglo-Indian words arranged according to Cantonese syntax; it uses, for example, measure words or classifiers such as the Chinese 'ge', translated as 'piece', as in 'three piece newspaper' (meaning three newspapers). Some pidgin words have passed into common usage, particularly in Hong Kong: for example 'shroff', originally assayer and money changer, 'chop', seal or permit, and 'godown', warehouse, are Anglo-Indian from the sixteenth century; 'joss', god or luck, and 'amah', nurse, are Portuguese; 'hong', factory or firm, 'taipan', 'junk' and 'chow' are Chinese. Pidgin was easily learnt and adequate for commercial purposes but formed an impenetrable barrier to any more than the most superficial understanding between Chinese and English-speakers. It became something of a joke to translate well-known pieces into pidgin:

> One young man walkee; no can stop.
> Maskee de snow; maskee de ice!
> He carry flag with chop so nice –
> Topside galow![21]

Both Anglo-Saxons and Chinese, always prone to consider foreigners as difficult children, were confirmed in their prejudices by such baby-language being their only means of communication. The Rev. Bridgman recorded the dangers: 'Hardly a foreigner devotes an hour to learn the language of the Chinese. The effect of an intercourse so circumscribed can never be otherwise than to keep the two parties totally separated from each other in all those offices of kindness, sympathy, regard, and friendship.'[22]

A set of popinjays

The trade shared between the Company and private traders, British and American, was of the first importance – nothing less than the largest long-distance trade in the world, amounting to nearly $50 million a year. Raw cotton, woollens, and, of course, opium, were the main elements of the import trade, with tea and silk being exported. Of these opium and tea were by far the most important:

Canton Trade 1831 ($ thousand)

Imports		Exports	
Woollens	2,496	Tea	12,188
Cotton Goods	984	Silk (raw & piece)	4,611
Raw cotton	4,933	Other (including c.$4 million in silver bullion)	6,968
Opium	13,029		
Other (mainly metals and Eastern products)	3,653		
Total	25,095		23,767

By 1831 the lion's share of this was no longer in Company, but in private hands, British and American – $20 million of the imports, mainly opium, and $14 million of the exports. The Company's share was respectively $3.7 million and $9 million – almost all the latter being tea, of which the Company still retained the British monopoly (the remainders being other-flag trade and port and other expenses). At the same time that the opium trade edged out the other Indian imports, the days of the Company's undoubted hegemony were drawing to a close, and the splendid self-confidence of the Select Committee of Supracargoes was declining, to be replaced by a nervous aggressiveness. The nervousness was exacerbated by the increasingly precarious situation of the Hong merchants as the legal trade, which provided them with an income, was driven out by the smuggled trade, which did not. The Select Committee reported to the Company's headquarters in Leadenhall Street that only three substantial Hong merchants remained, 'The Chinese Government by exactions and impositions [having] driven nearly all the foreign traders to resort to illicit traffic, by which public revenue was diminished, the trade of the Honorable Company was left to support almost unassisted, the heavy demands of the port.'[23]

In 1829 power on the Select passed into the hands of a more radical group, led by Supercargo William Baynes, who began an attempt to force new privileges from the Chinese, as Macartney and Amherst had failed to do. They were consistently but unsuccessfully opposed by the more conservative President of the Committee, William Plowden, a man steeped in Company traditions, who now found himself permanently in a minority. The activists presented a list of peremptory demands to the Viceroy and, in an endeavour to force his hand, ordered British ships to stay away from Canton, thereby avoiding payment of port and customs dues. In choosing alternative anchorages where business could still be transacted in security, it emerged that the favourite haven was 'the anchorage within the North-West Point of the Island of Hong-kong proceeding in an easterly direction towards the Lyee-moon Passage' – or just about where the Star Ferries now cross to Kowloon. When the news of the Committee's proceedings reached Leadenhall Street, together with Plowden's record of his unavailing remonstrances, the Court of Directors was furious. The adventurous Baynes and his colleagues were summarily recalled, and what it was hoped would prove a more conservative committee appointed. But before these decisions could be transmitted to Canton, Baynes had embarked upon another, more personal, indiscretion, by inviting his wife to join him in Canton.

It was clearly understood that European women were not allowed to go to Canton, and in the century and more of trade there this prohibition had never been contravened. Baynes, in addition to stopping the trade at Canton for six months, brought Mrs Baynes there not once, but twice, and in the company of other ladies. William Hunter recorded that she produced a sensation: 'She is the beauty of the party ... dressed in fine London style ... much admired by us.' Not all the foreigners approved: 'Three from number 2 Suy-Yong called on the ladies. Coats, gloves and cravats – such cravats! I heard one say when he returned "Thank God that is over!" and then call for a jacket and black neck-ribbon. He next lighted a cheroot, and looked as if a great burthen was off his mind.' When the Chinese officials objected

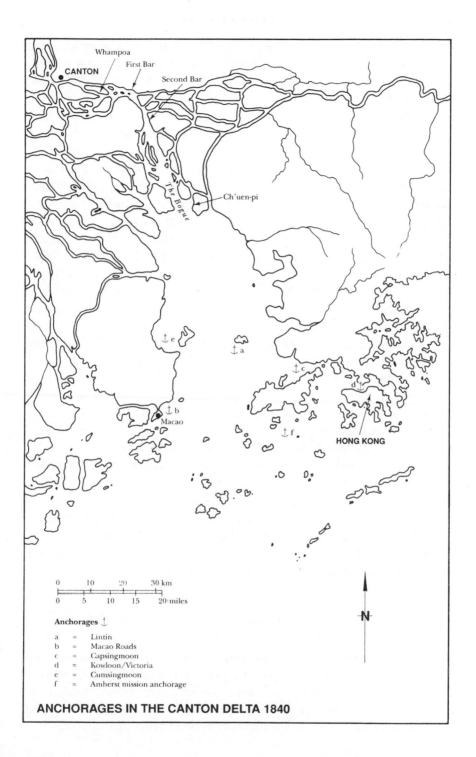

Whampoa
First Bar
CANTON
Second Bar

The Bogue
Ch'uen-pi

⚓ e
⚓ a
⚓ c
d ⚓
⚓ b
Macao
⚓ f
HONG KONG

0   10   20   30 km
0   5   10   15   20 miles

Anchorages ⚓

a = Lintin
b = Macao Roads
c = Capsingmoon
d = Kowloon/Victoria
e = Cumsingmoon
f = Amherst mission anchorage

N

ANCHORAGES IN THE CANTON DELTA 1840

to Mrs Baynes's first visit, she returned 'escorted by a train of ships' boats, each of the sailors being armed as if for combat. Some cannon from the Indiamen were mounted upon the roof of the factories.' And, in defiance of all custom the women had the effrontery to be carried about in sedan chairs.[24]

The Governor fulminated: 'How can the chief Baynes resist the prohibition and orders, and bring with him a barbarian woman to Canton! . . . The said foreigners, ignorant of how to be excited to gratitude, turn round, and because of the proclamation disallowing them to bring barbarian women to Canton, and sit in Sedan chairs, bring whining petitions . . . Exceedingly does it display refractory stupidity . . . if again, any dare to oppose or transgress . . . a severe scrutiny will be made, and punishment inflicted . . . tremble at this! Intensely are these commands given!' It was impolitic to do more than inveigh against the English, but the unfortunate Hing-tai, the Hong merchant who had sponsored Mrs Baynes's ship, was thrown into prison and heavily fined.[25]

Baynes's superiors were less dramatic, but were decisive: the Court of Directors, in recalling him, wrote: 'The commerce between Great Britain and China is too important to be put at hazard without the most urgent and imperious necessity, and on no account upon considerations of a personal nature.' The aristocratic interest was confirmed in its instinctive distrust of these socially deplorable tradesmen. Lord William Bentinck, Governor-General of Bengal, wrote to Lord Ellenborough at the India Office on 22 March 1830: 'We consider the proceedings of that Committee to be in the highest degree injudicious and hazardous . . . the possible effects of this state of things . . . cannot be contemplated without the utmost dismay.' Lord Ellenborough replied (23 September 1830): 'The wretched mismanagement at Canton (a set of popinjays) . . . have endangered the existence of the trade instead of being its protectors.'[26]

A snug business

In spite of disapproval in London and Calcutta, the 'popinjays' enjoyed the active support of many of the private traders of Canton, who, although they were up to their necks in an illegal traffic, wanted the laws amended in their own favour, and who were even more vehement in their demands. This was evinced in their petition of Christmas Eve

1830, probably drafted by James Matheson, who possessed a highly characteristic prose style, which reached Parliament on 28 July 1831. The petition complained of 'the authorities of Canton, a venal and corrupt class of persons, who, having purchased their appointments, study only the means of amassing wealth by extortion and injustice'. For 'British Subjects resorting to this Empire, Trade has been the sole object', as a result of which they had been subjected to 'privations and treatment to which it would be difficult to find a parallel in any part of the world'. Among these privations Matheson complained that: 'even the sacred ties of domestic life are disregarded, in the separation of husband and wife, parent and child; rendered unavoidable by a capricious prohibition against foreign ladies residing in Canton, for which there appears to be no known law, and no other authority than the plea of usage'.

At the very end of this prolix document, a remedy was suggested:

If unattainable by the course suggested, Your Petitioners indulge a hope that the Government of Great Britain, with the sanction of the Legislature, will adopt a resolution worthy of the Nation, and, by the acquisition of an insular possession near the coast of China, place British Commerce in this remote quarter of the globe beyond the reach of future despotism and oppression.

Although few had the bleak island in mind at the time, Hong Kong was to become that 'insular possession'.

Far from complying with the request for armed intervention and the taking of an island or two as its signatories conjured the government to do, Parliament did not react sympathetically. Lord Ellenborough, then in opposition, the Tories having split on the issue of treating Roman Catholics as second-class citizens and being replaced by the Whigs under Earl Grey, returned to the attack on the East India Company. The Directors ('those persons who ... have placed our interests in peril') 'should order the British merchants to obey the laws of the country in which they resided'. Chinese restrictions 'might be very absurd, but they were all imposed by the law of the country'. The emotional language employed by the merchants baffled some sympathizers in Britain, who could not see that they had much to complain about. The *Chinese Repository* attempted to explain: 'We have heard some of our most intelligent visitors inquire, – what are the grievances and oppressions of which we have heard so much, and seen

ıg? ... We reply, that we are discontented, because
ted than our remote predecessors with the rights and
... we feel our confinement to be a prison, and long
berty.'[27] The most awkward of the foreigners in Canton
James Innes, who was always ready to contest Chinese
ompany's regulations, often successfully. On one occasion
he ... ocket attack on the house of a mandarin who had offended
him, and received an apology. 'The Viceroy and the Hoppo,' reported
Innes, 'wrote very proper answers to me.'

The most famous of the private traders was Dr William Jardine, the
'Iron-Headed Old Rat',[28] founder with James Matheson of the greatest
of all the European Hongs, Jardine Matheson. Jardine had first come
East as the surgeon's mate of a Company vessel in 1802, and made
enough in 'privilege' trade to set up on his own, first in London, and
then in Bombay, before moving to Canton in 1822, when he established
a House of Agency. Agencies, which required little in the way of
capital, were the standard form of private business in Canton, and
continued to be so for the first years of the new colony of Hong Kong.
Canton agents confined themselves to acting for principals, usually
well-established private merchants in Calcutta and Bombay, buying,
selling and administering their affairs in China. Their services included
acting as executors, managing estates, collecting rents and debts,
freighting and chartering, but most importantly the sale and purchase
of goods. Remuneration was by a fixed scale of fees – 5 per cent
commission on everything except opium and precious stones, which,
being more easily disposed of, attracted only 3 per cent. Steady though
this business was, there were more tempting opportunities. At an early
date the Canton agencies developed banking and insurance facilities,
the earliest example of the latter, and one of the most striking examples
of initiative, being the establishment in 1805 of the Canton Insurance
Society. Run along the lines of the Corporation of Lloyds, with unlimited liability attaching to each of the members, this concern was managed alternately by the two great English houses of Davidson, which
became Dent's, and Magniac, which developed into Jardine Matheson.
The British firms had begun colloquially to be known also as hongs,
and their partners as 'taipans'; Jardine's were the Ewo Hong – the
upright and harmonious, Dent's the Pao-shun Hong – the precious
and compliant.

Banking was less co-operatively organized, each house making its
own arrangements with correspondents in India and in London. This

was made necessary by the length of time involved in transmitting cargo and remittances between Canton, India and London; up to twelve months had to be allowed for the round voyage. Remittances were a particular problem. The East India Company in Canton could be relied upon to sell bills to merchants wanting easily negotiated paper only to the amount needed for its own purchases. As private business burgeoned and the Company's share decreased this became totally inadequate. Recourse had to be made to a number of expedients, including American bills, but in the end it was often only by shipping bullion out of China that the merchants could effect transfers. This was totally illegal under Chinese law, and was a contributory factor in the anti-opium campaign dealt with in Chapter 3.

Fuelling the demand for money were the difficulties of the Cohong merchants. The constant raiding of the Consoo fund, which was intended to underwrite the Hongs' debts, had led in 1815 to the Company advancing the threatened Hongs a quarter of a million taels to enable them to pay the imperial duties (like debts to the Inland Revenue, these always took priority, and could not be postponed), while Cohong debts to private traders were placed in the hands of three foreign merchants as administrators. In this way the management of Chinese official merchants actually passed into European hands, with the full approval of all. Since the Hong merchants, even when solvent, were always ready to pay high interest rates – 15 per cent was regarded as very reasonable, at a time when half that was thought extortionate in Europe – it became common for investors to leave their money with the agencies in Canton rather than repatriate it.

Modest men might be content to remain as agencies, earning high fees with little risk from this 'snug business' (as James Matheson called it), but most sought to maximize profits by diversifying. In a small community where few rules were generally enforced, this called for high standards of commercial conduct: dog could not eat hungry dog. As a result, in spite of the fiercest rivalry, the word of a Canton merchant was his bond, and the Agency houses went to considerable lengths not to let down their principals. Jardine himself, a cynical venturer, given to sailing as close to the wind as any, never had his personal probity called into question. 'The vast commercial operations of Mr Jardine seemed to be conducted with sagacity and judgment,' wrote Dr C.T. Downing in *The Fan-Qui in China*. 'He was a gentleman of great strength of character and of unbounded generosity.'[29] Jardine's letters show a rather gruff person – he only kept one chair in his office, discouraging visitors from staying, which is odd behaviour in an agent; not too well-educated – he seems never, for example, to have read Byron, since he rarely managed to spell the name of his own schooner *Hellas* aright, and his handwriting is laboured; and personally frugal – his order to 'Mr Scacht, fashioner', in London was for but 'one blue coat, one black coat, and one cashmere, of a dark colour'.[30] His younger partner Matheson was more fashionable and cultivated – a gentleman of great suavity of manner and the impersonation of benevolence, according to Downing – but had a somewhat chequered history.

Matheson, who was not the son of a baronet, as stated in some histories,[31] although from an old Highland family, came to India as a young man in 1819, after a brief stay at Edinburgh University and an apprenticeship in London. More sociably inclined than Jardine, as well as better connected, he joined the counting house of his uncle's firm in Calcutta, MacIntosh & Co., one of the great India Houses (it was to fail a little later for two and a half million pounds, an enormous sum at the time), but soon left for Canton to establish an opium-dealing business with one Robert Taylor. On Taylor's death in 1820 the business folded, and Matheson was left in Canton, at the age of twenty-six, looking for something to do. The answer came through MacIntosh's, who had many contacts throughout southern Asia. One of these was with a Spanish firm, originally from Manila, who had established a Calcutta agency: a partner in this agency, Xavier Yrissari, decided to move to Canton and joined Matheson in the new firm of Yrissari and Co. Matheson was delighted: Yrissari would bring business of 'an unexampled magnitude . . . with which he will enable us to commence our Establishment far exceeding the most sanguine hopes I could have formed'. After five years' adventurous speculations in opium, which included unprecedented sales voyages up the Chinese coast and an attempt to corner the market, Yrissari died, and left Matheson once more responsible for winding up a venture.

He bounced back remarkably quickly, coming out of the partnership with at least a quarter of a million dollars, while claiming that Yrissari's share was only $17,000. Dr John Cheong, in his study of the firm, found this 'incredibly small', and the tone of Matheson's letter to the joint executor of his partner's Estate in Spain certainly sounds 'outrageously fierce': 'Yrissari did not put a single dollar of capital in the house of his name with me, apart from his share of the property gained, less the costs arising from liberal living during the period of some five years during which our association lasted, and that is the only good thing I can report to his sister.' After a flirtation with the rival firm of Dent, probably never meant to be taken seriously, but more for the purpose of placating his uncle's firm, who were engaged with Dent's through their London bank, Matheson took the money he had amassed through his association with Yrissari to Jardine, with whom he had already established friendly relations.[32]

The Jardine—Dent rivalry might well have been exacerbated by the fact that the Dents were English Borderers, from Westmorland, who have traditionally had unfriendly views about the Scots. The two companies' house flags reflected this division, that of the Jardines incorporating the St Andrew cross, Dent's that of St George. The initial cause of their rivalry is suggested by Dr Cheong to have been the Dents' using their influence in London to have a Jardine bill dishonoured. Matters cannot have been improved when a confidence trickster, one Nisbett, having failed to deceive Dent's, succeeded in extracting money from Matheson.[33]

The Dent generation contemporary with Matheson, the brothers Lancelot and Wilkinson, lacked the panache of the Scots, but were regarded as perhaps more respectable and worthy: Lancelot was an almost painfully correct and precise man. In a letter detailing in his meticulously clear hand the disposal of articles acquired at a bankruptcy sale – many of which he gave away – he concluded: 'do not think I have a single sin of omission or commission in this matter – unless there may be some Dollars – more than 2 or 3 but under 10 . . . if so they must be claimed and paid for on my ac. Yet again – the small lamp in Beale's dressing room I gave away, and I purchased and am debited for a Watercloset purchased from Mr Aquino.'[34] Certainly the Select Committee, who were hot against the conduct of Jardine Matheson ('So great has been the desire of Messrs. Jardine, Matheson & Co., and of Captain Grant as commanding their Opium Ships, to erect themselves into an authority independent of the Committee . . .' and referring to a letter from the firm as being 'as objectionable in its tone as devoid of truth in its statements'[35]) went out of their way to make it clear that there were no grounds for complaints against the Dents or their ships; and Robert Inglis, writer of the Company's factory, left them to join Dent's. Sir John Davis, President of the Select, Chief Superintendent of Trade, and Governor of Hong Kong, who despised most private traders, described the Dents as the 'more respectable' part of the British community, at a time when he was contrasting them with the Jardine faction, and equally complaints of aggressions against the Chinese were less frequently levied against the Dent employees. It is also noteworthy that the former senior partner of the Davidson-Dent form, W.S. Davidson, had forecast to the 1829 Select Committee of the House that the withdrawal of the East India Company's power would lead 'sooner or later, to a war . . . accompanied by widespread ruin',[36] a view contrasting strongly with the bellicose sentiments of the Jardine supporters.

But Thomas Dent, at any rate, was not liked, and Matheson was. One reason for this was surely his generosity of spirit, as revealed in a letter from him to one John White, whose deceased brother had been one of Matheson's customers, and who had left in Macao a 'female pensioner' unprovided for. Matheson suggested that White should 'continue some allowance to her, the want of which would reduce her to a state of misery that would be extremely distressing to the deceased's friends who respect his memory. She is of a superior class of women in her situation, being educated and having become a Christian at Macao, she is, of course, an outcast from her people.'[37] Taking such trouble for someone else's Chinese mistress shows remarkable thoughtfulness on the part of a very busy man.

Jardine and Matheson usually took the initiative in developing new business, as in 1832 when the Canton market for opium appeared to be saturated. In that year they dispatched two expeditions up the coast as far north as Tientsin, an unprecedented extension of their usual market area, but which produced encouraging results. From then onwards opium sales were regularly made at convenient points all along the coast with little interference from the authorities.

Among the more notorious of the Jardine Matheson masters working up the coast were Captains Parry and Grant. Parry, Captain of the *Hercules*, was sometimes too much even for the liberal Matheson, who had to report to Jardine, then in England, 'news of an unfortunate nature . . . Parry had a jollification on the Queen's birthday, and nothing would satisfy him after dinner' but to fire off one of his guns, to test its range, and in doing so hitting a Chinese official junk, which caused a 'great sensation'. Charles Grant, who had also commanded *Hercules* previously, was officially described as having 'rendered himself and the *Hercules* notorious for acts of aggression and violence against the Chinese . . . from beginning to end, there has been pursued by Captain Grant a series of unjustifiable acts, amounting we might almost say to piratical conduct, which render him altogether unworthy of the command of any British vessel.'[38]

Who can desire a war with China?

A few years previously the Select Committee of Supracargoes would have cracked down on such enterprises, which were directly contrary to all previously understood usages. But the Select had changed with the times, and become restless in their turn. Charles Marjoribanks, who had replaced the disgraced Baynes as Chairman in 1829, soon proved equally independent, ordering an illegal expedition up the coast to explore the market potential. The conscientious captain of the *Lady Amherst* refused to obey Marjoribanks' orders, as 'at Variance with my instructions, and the Regulations of the Service, and equally illegal in the eyes of the Law',[39] but the voyage went ahead with a more compliant commander. The Court of Directors deplored the enterprise, and the following year Marjoribanks was in turn recalled, although the private traders regretted such 'cruel and inconsiderate measures', and felt that the Chairman's action had been 'very judicious'.[40] Marjoribanks cannot have been much worried by his demotion, since all the East India Company officials knew that their time as traders was approaching an end; the current charter under which they operated was due for review in 1833, and a decision on their future would be made by an unsympathetic government. After strikes and agrarian uprisings – nine hanged, 250 transported – riots in Nottingham, Derby and Bristol, the Mansion House sacked, cavalry charges in London, cholera epidemics, financial crises, and a constitutional crisis lasting over a year, the Great Reform Bill had been forced through a reluctant House of Lords and passed by a disapproving William IV in December 1832. The new reformed Whig government of Lord Grey had then to cope with agitation for factory legislation, a new Poor Law, the emancipation of slaves and the usual troubles with Ireland. Had it been possible to postpone consideration of the East India Company's charter the hard-pressed administration would doubtless have been grateful: but it was not. The charter had been renewed for only twenty years in 1813, and legislation was inevitable.

There was little doubt what this should be: the East India Company must effectively be wound up as a commercial concern. It had developed into an imperial power in its own right, ruling over a population much greater than that of the home country, and deploying a standing army and navy that made it the equal of many great states: such a role was quite incompatible with that of a trading company, and one or the other must be terminated. The alternative would have been for the British government to assume responsibility for ruling its Indian territories directly. Any other European country would have done this with alacrity, but Whigs were not empire-builders, and did not even regard India as a permanent possession. Macaulay thought the British Raj would not end in his lifetime (he died in 1853): Ram Mohun Roy, the Brahmin scholar and reformer, believed (in 1830) it would continue 'for at least forty or fifty years'.[41] In the meantime the Company was doing a reasonable job of looking after the place, and even the politicians were conscious of the temptations for corruption and place-seeking if 'an absolute despotism, the British Parliament' was allowed to get its hands on the wealth of India. (Not that the party in power, whichever one that might be, would countenance such a thing; nevertheless, could one ever be entirely sure of the intentions of one's opponents?)

The real questions at issue resolved themselves into the future of the Canton trade, and the great point of how stockholders might be compensated for giving up their commercial activities. Whatever the Court of Directors might plead, there was never any real possibility of the Company being allowed to retain an unfettered monopoly of the China trade. Monopolies had been out of fashion for years. As early as 1820 a Committee of the House of Commons had reported that 'The time when monopolies could be successfully supported, or would be patiently endured . . . seems to have passed away.' Thirteen years later even the arch-Tory *Quarterly Review* had to admit that 'From the moment, indeed, that the FREETRADE mania became the order of the day, the China monopoly received its death-blow.'[42]

The free-traders had indeed made themselves felt: the previous Prime Minister, the Duke of Wellington, had been overwhelmed by petitions from such sources as the merchants of Plymouth, Sunderland, Leeds, Kidderminster, Cockermouth, Lancaster, Limerick, the Corporation of Cutlers and the Corporation of Traffickers of Leith. The most vociferous of all the anti-Company propaganda came from the merchants of Canton, conscious of the opportunity to rid themselves of the restrictions imposed by the Select, and give themselves a free hand to exploit the Chinese. J. Crawfurd, parliamentary agent for the Canton private traders in their carefully planned and well-funded campaign, published a pamphlet in 1830 which began with a quotation from Edward Gibbon: 'The Spirit of Monopolists is narrow, lazy, and oppressive,' and rumbustiously attacked arguments 'replete with error, or foolery, or bad reasoning'.[43]

Many Company stockholders, and some of the Court of Directors, were not minded to take the attacks lying down, and argued for the retention, if not of the monopoly, at least of a share of the China trade, and the continuance of the Select Committee's supervision. Some powerful arguments could be advanced for this: the idea of free trade was unintelligible to Chinese imperial officials; the private traders were a disreputable and unruly bunch, certain to upset the even tenor of commerce if left to themselves; and any interruptions to trade would cost the British Exchequer some £3 million of annual duties on tea. A spirited defence along these lines was advanced by Sir Charles Forbes, formerly chairman of the largest private traders in Bombay and M.P. for Malmesbury. Forbes was a die-hard Tory who stigmatized the Reform Bill as 'the vile Reform Bill, that hideous monster, the most frightful that ever showed its face in the House'.[44] Less crusty Tories advanced the more reasonable argument that, after all, things had not gone too badly under the supercargoes' aegis: 'The facility and quietness with which the whole commerce of the port [Canton] is now conducted is admirable.' But the private traders would have none of it: they wanted the East India Company and their too-gentlemanly supercargoes out, and replaced by someone prepared to take a firm line.

If this was the voice of a new economic imperialism there were others advocating a milder policy. The former Governor of Bombay Sir John Malcolm, speaking in the stockholders' debate, pointed out that however arrogant the Chinese might be, 'there was no other nation which assumed pretensions to be above the laws and usages of other countries in a greater degree than the English' (Hear, hear, and laughter). Malcolm was, of course, Scottish. Besides, he asked, how were the Chinese to be persuaded to change their ways? The Whig government might argue, as good Benthamites, that the inexorable laws of the market economy, once allowed free play, would inevitably ensure the best and most profitable solution, but he remained sceptical. 'Political economists treated a question of human rule like one of arithmetic: and he would no more expect success from the application of their general principles ... than he would find the application of the wonderful machine of the ingenious Mr Babbage.' The Chinese were likely to be difficult to convince, and should they remain obdurate the alternative was war, which 'would be a war waged for mere interest. But who can desire a war with China, for the sake of forcing the trade?'[45]

Malcolm was outspokenly against any idea of coercion, which he saw as the inflated fantasy of civilians: 'It was a fine thing to talk of the insulted honour of England; but if assistance was to be given by this country to the merchants trading to China in every little quarrel . . . consequences of the most serious nature would be produced.' Even Sir Charles Forbes agreed: 'so wild an idea as the conquest of China, never could have entered the mind of any person in that Court, or in the British dominions; although it appeared to have been entertained by some of the wise men in Canton.' But at that point in Sir Charles's speech 'a show of impatience' was noted: the new men were losing patience with the outmoded decencies of the old.

To some extent the discussion was academic. Charles Grant, President of the Board of Control, made his intentions unequivocally clear: 'Whatever may be the decision of the Company, I must repeat, that it is not the intention of the government to recommend to Parliament the renewal of the Company's exclusive trade to China.' He spelt out what would happen if the Company did not agree: their property would simply be confiscated, subject to litigation; and then, where, 'it may be asked, are the East India stock-holders? From what funds are the dividends to be paid?'[46] With a little oiling of wheels – Grant had some personal ambitions for posts in India which would not have been helped by a public quarrel with the Court of Directors – an agreement was reached. All the Company's commercial activities were to cease, in India and in China, 'with all convenient speed'; all 'merchandise, stores and effects, at home and abroad', were to be sold. In return the stockholders were to receive an annuity of £630,000 redeemable at a rate of 5 per cent.

The debate in the House of Commons on 26 July 1833 was perfunctory, but two members combined to make the same significant point. Sir Robert Inglis, a staunch old-fashioned Tory, feared that 'the continuance of the trade itself might be risked by the want of a just authority over the Europeans'. From the other side of the House he was supported by Sir George Staunton, Member for South Hampshire, and that same George Thomas who had as a boy accompanied his father on the Macartney embassy, and chatted to the old Emperor Ch'ien-lung in Chinese. He forecast inevitable conflict between with the Chinese authorities and the foreign merchants 'unless some higher power – some public representative – were sent there to control both parties'. In this he was absolutely right, but his warning fell on deaf ears; only a handful of Members came to listen, and in the absence of a quorum his speech was forced to conclude.

Charles Grant impatiently agreed: 'I need hardly state that ... it would be necessary that there should be stationed at Canton by the appointment of the Crown, some officer or officers invested by law with adequate power over supervision over all British subjects', and the Bill was duly passed by a lethargic House of Commons. Macaulay commented: 'The House had neither the time, nor the knowledge, nor the inclination ... several of the members present were asleep, or appeared to be so.'

Even the Canton traders, inspired by Matheson's ebullient prose, agreed on the need for a British representative – not in order to control their own activities, but to force the Chinese away from their restrictive practices into methods more in keeping with modern ways. 'We must,' insisted Jardine, 'have a commercial code with these celestial barbarians ... We have the right to demand an equitable commercial treaty.'[47] This was not how they saw things in Whitehall, which led the exasperated Jardine, hearing that a naval officer had been arrested by the Chinese and put in irons, to 'wish most sincerely H. M. Ministers were in irons with him'.[48]

3

THE HUMILIATION OF
LORD NAPIER

The epitaph drear: 'A fool lies here
Who tried to hustle the East.'

Rudyard Kipling, 'Naulahka'

While negotiations were being pursued in London, the situation in Canton was developing. There had been a brawl at Lintin between the crews of the merchant ships and the inhabitants, blamed by the Viceroy on 'the stationary demon Magniac' (Matheson), but on 16 June 1833 James Matheson was able to record: 'We have nothing new here – everything going on quietly and the viceroy appears to have made up his mind to keep Foreigners in a good humour if possible.'[1] The Chinese authorities at Canton were aware that changes were taking place among the foreign traders. Through a process unfathomable to the Chinese mind, it was clear that political vicissitudes at home were occasioning personnel changes in the traders' camp. Who might be chosen to represent the foreigners was a matter of absolute indifference to the mandarins; but it must be clearly understood that negotiations with any such persons could only be on the existing, established basis.

Even though the ebullient and often aggressive Lord Palmerston was Foreign Secretary and responsible for the new mission, there was no question of any attempt being made to coerce China as the Canton merchants demanded. The mission that was appointed, in December 1833, to take over from the Select Committee was instructed in the most emollient of terms; the members, who were to be known as Superintendents of Trade, were 'to cautiously abstain from all unnecessary use of menacing language ... to study by all practicable methods to maintain the good and friendly understanding, and to ensure that all British subjects understood their duty to obey the laws and usages of the Chinese empire'.[2] Anything less imperialistic could hardly be imagined. They were to 'avoid any conduct, language, or demeanour, which should excite jealousy or distrust among the Chinese people or government or to revolt their opinions or prejudices'. They were to proceed to Canton, and to stick to the established and customary methods of communication. Critics of British policy towards China in the nineteenth century might acknowledge that at least it began with the best of intentions.

Good intentions, however, sometimes lead to proverbially undesirable destinations. One of the more important tasks of the Superintendents was to monitor the activities of British traders, and in order to do this they were vested with the power to hold a court having both criminal and Admiralty jurisdiction, either at Canton, or on board any British ship. Two unlikely assumptions were made: that the Chinese would tolerate such an assumption of jurisdiction within their own country, and that the recalcitrant British subjects there would accept it. The Duke of Wellington disapproved: it would be 'a mistake if they supposed they had any right to appoint commissioners', and Sir Charles Forbes was scathing; 'He was very much mistaken if his celestial majesty would submit to this presumptuous conduct on the part of the BARBARIANS,' and ridiculed the appointment of Superintendents of trade, 'to be invested with unheard-of powers ... to punish every offence (EXCEPT SMUGGLING, OF COURSE!)'.[3] Attempting to have his cake and eat it, Palmerston had the power to establish courts published by Orders in Council (which were public), but in his private instructions warned the Chief Superintendent that he should not act upon these Orders in Council 'until he had given the matter his most serious consideration'.[4]

The two years of dissension and unrest needed to force through the Reform Bill of 1832 left the Whigs with many obligations to their supporters in both Houses of Parliament, and especially to those in the Lords, with its substantial and vociferous Tory majority. Once the Bill became law, the markers began to be called in, and one of these was that of William John, the eighth Lord Napier, previously best known as author of 'A Treatise on Practical Store farming as applicable to the Mountainous Region of Etterick Forest and the Pastoral District of Scotland in General'.

Napier had rendered good service in the House of Lords all through the difficult passage of the Reform Bill, but did not hold a permanent seat there through hereditary right. He was not a peer of the United Kingdom, but only of Scotland, and subject therefore to election by the other Scottish noblemen as one of their representatives, since peers of Scotland and Ireland had only the right to select sixteen representatives from each kingdom to every Parliament. Peers not so selected were able to contest seats in the lower House.[5] Lord Palmerston, for example, was a peer only of Ireland, and was therefore able to sit in the Commons for some sixty years. Napier had been a Scottish representative peer since 1824, providing a reliable Whig vote, but in 1832 the Scottish peers – mostly Tories – decided not to re-elect him for the following Parliament. Propriety demanded that the party Lord Napier had supported found an adequately rewarding position for him.

To an unprejudiced observer Napier's previous career had not marked him very clearly as suitable for a diplomatic posting. Before devoting himself to oviculture he had been a naval officer, serving at Trafalgar as a midshipman and as Lieutenant under the adventurous Thomas Cochrane, Lord Dundonald, whose exploits served as a model for those of the fictional heroes Hornblower and Jack Aubrey, and into whose family Napier later married. This continuing influence was a poor preparation for diplomacy, since Cochrane, although a splendid fighting sailor, was a most difficult, awkward, opinionated individual. Lord Napier was also brusque in manner and reputedly devoutly Presbyterian, neither desirable qualities in dealing with the worldly and sophisticated Chinese; he certainly had no experience of trade, diplomacy or Asiatic affairs, but was confident that a few broadsides were the best possible argument that could be brought to bear in any negotiation. To cap it all Lord Napier was red-headed, and red hair was to Chinese 'a particular and diabolical abomination', according to Dr Downing, who was present at the time of the mission to Canton.[6]

But to one person at least there was no doubt that Lord Napier had all the qualities necessary for the post of His Majesty's Chief Superintendent of Trade in China, at a salary of £6,000 a year, and that was the gentleman himself. This was made clear in a speech he gave in the House of Lords on the Navy Bill on 23 May 1832, in which he advanced the claim that officers of the armed services, no matter what their lack of experience, were especially suitable for any public post, of whatever description: 'Men of that character formed much more able and effective men of business than others, and would do more in ten minutes than any noble Lord, who had been brought up in public offices, would do as in as many hours . . . the regard to personal character was quite sufficient to ensure the proper discharge of the duties of any office.'[7] Not everyone agreed, the Tory *Morning Post* being particularly vitriolic about his appointment: Lord Napier, it felt, 'can know as much of the port of Canton, and the very difficult duties to be performed there, as does an orang outang'. His appointment was 'an insult and a gross injustice to the experienced and highly respectable gentlemen over whose head this popinjay lord has been so shamefully placed'.

In order to provide the tedious command of detail needed by the mission Lord Napier was given two colleagues, John Francis Davis and Sir George Best Robinson, as Second and Third Superintendents. Davis was already in post at Canton, as the about-to-be superseded President of the Select Committee of Supracargoes. Later to play an important part, as Chief Superintendent and Governor of the new colony of Hong Kong, he had advanced rapidly, aided by his family connections in the Company's service – 'deeply connected with the Court of Directors' – and with Lord Palmerston, who had known him as a boy.[8] After serving on the Amherst mission to Peking he became a member of the Select Committee in 1827, and in 1832 its Chairman. A proficient linguist, and with a rare first-hand knowledge of Chinese Imperial diplomacy, as well as twenty years of commercial experience, Davis had impressed the 1829 Select Committee of the House of Commons on the China Trade. His evidence to this body had emphasized the important role played by the supercargoes in maintaining stability and the need to ensure an effective replacement, with qualities very like those that he himself possessed, including a command of Chinese, a point which he stressed. The Chinese, who considered 'all nations wearing hats and coats to belong to the general class, of which they certainly acknowledge the English to be the head', would look to the British government to send a mission led by some person of authority experienced in sorting out any difficulties that might arise, and capable of dealing with mandarins in their own language.[9]

With his appointment as Second Superintendent (at a salary of £3,000, which he considered inadequate), Davis must have felt that his was to be the real guiding hand of the mission, for the Third Superintendent was a lightweight. Sir George Robinson had admittedly been a supercargo, although a junior one, and only for a short time, but had done little in Canton except to annoy his superiors. But although both timid and bumptious, Robinson was a Baronet, and grandson (even if on the wrong side of the blanket) of an Earl, neither negligible qualifications in England of the 1830s. Furthermore, his father had also been a Director of the East India Company, and the family connection with the East dated back to the foundation of Calcutta.

The Superintendents were provided with a considerable staff, including a Secretary, a Chinese Secretary, chaplain and surgeons. Very few of the other selections had been made without an eye to patronage. The Secretary, J.H. Astell, twenty-seven at the time, was the son of William Astell, who had been a Director of the East India Company for the record period of forty-seven years. At first Astell senior had opposed the government's proposals in the charter renewal debate, but eventually he changed his mind: some reward was therefore in order. Alexander Johnston, a cousin of the Chief Superintendent, became Napier's private secretary. Johnston (later known as Campbell-Johnston) was also the modestly talented offspring of a distinguished and influential father, who constantly exercised himself on his son's behalf. Sir Alexander Johnston had been a steady supporter of the Whigs, who made him a Privy Councillor in 1832. Sir Alexander badgered Palmerston on such matters as the ceremonial uniform young Alexander was entitled to wear, and sent the Duke of Wellington himself some 'Heads of Instruction for the Guidance of the Chinese Superintendent'.

The most blatantly nepotistic of the mission's appointments might have seemed that of Captain Charles Elliot R.N., as Master Attendant, the naval officer in charge of shipping, a comparatively junior post commanding a salary higher than that of the 'Clerk of a superior class' but the same as the assistant surgeon. The Elliots were in financial straits at the time, and Charles only accepted the appointment since it was made clear that it was the only post on offer: 'If I did not choose to go to China as Master Attendant, a category acknowledged inadequate, I am to expect their [the Admiralty's] displeasure.'[10] Elliot had hoped for something better, both because of his previously success-ful record and the fact that he came from a very influential family indeed, and one higher in the pecking order of British society than the Napiers. Preparing for the voyage out, Clara Elliot, who accom-panied her husband, was annoyed at being condescended to by Lady Napier's 'Canton etiquette'. On 25 March 1834 she wrote to her sister,

Lady Hislop, complaining, but pulled herself up: 'I mustn't go on, or you'll say that I am angry and to be angry at such a wherefore, would assuredly be somewhat vulgar.' And Elliots were too aristocratic to be vulgar; but they were also known to be good at looking after their own. Charles's cousin, Lord Minto, was a staunch Whig peer whose career as First Lord of the Admiralty was distinguished, as one commentator put it, 'only by the outcry raised at the number of Elliots who found places in the naval service'.[11] When, later, a naval task force was sent to Canton, it was commanded by another of Charles's cousins, Admiral Sir George Elliot. Charles's father, Hugh, brother of the first Lord Minto, had been educated in France by the rationalist philosopher David Hume and had become a friend of the revolutionary Mirabeau. After a promising start in the diplomatic service he blotted his copy-book when Ambassador to Naples, and had to be found another re-munerative job. He was accordingly made Governor first of the Leeward Islands in the West Indies, and then of Madras;[12] and, which came in useful later, the Elliots were kinsmen of Lord Auckland, Governor-General of India when the first war with China began in 1840.

Family influence had protected young Charles by securing a posting to the West Indies squadron, where he had work any young naval officer would have dreamed of, in command of schooners and sloops of war engaged in anti-slavery missions. A post-captain at the early age of twenty-seven, he was then given the position of Protector of Slaves in British Guinea. His experiences there did nothing to develop his admiration for the British expatriate commercials, but did win him praise in London. Lord Howick (later Earl Grey, at that time Under Secretary of State for the Colonies) wrote on 2 March 1833 that 'His Majesty's Government are indebted to him [for services] far beyond what the functions of his office required of him ... not only for a zealous and effective execution of the duties of his office, but for communications of peculiar value and importance.'[13] Howick was attempting to persuade the Treasury to authorize a payment to Elliot, but in spite of both merit and influence this was not forthcoming, and the Elliots perforce had to accept what work was available. That better things might be in store was however hinted at by Davis's commen-dation of Elliot to the Foreign Office: 'The talents, information, and temper of that gentleman would render him eminently suited to the chief station in this country.'

A matter of national prestige

Admirable though the instructions given to the Napier mission were, its success was fatally compromised, not only by the irresponsibility of its chief, but by a single paragraph of his brief. Palmerston's otherwise correct and conciliatory letter of instruction contained one sentence which would lead to disaster: 'Your Lordship will announce your arrival at Canton by letter to the viceroy.' Those few words were to cause two wars and much travail.

The Foreign Office had correctly appreciated that commercial relations must be picked up where they were to be left off, at Canton, where there should be no risk of a rebuff such as had been given to Macartney and Amherst at Peking. And it was surely no more than common courtesy that a visiting officer of His Majesty, and a peer, should present his respects to the local representative of the Emperor? But the Chinese did not see it like that; their protocol permitted only two possibilities. Either Napier came as a tribute-bearing envoy, in which case he should present himself with due formalities at Peking, or he was a taipan, in which case he must seek admission to Canton and discuss matters in the usual way with Hong merchants and Hoppo, communicating only in the form of a petition. No merchant, however senior and dignified he might claim to be, could presume to approach the Viceroy of Kwantung and Kwangsi, Mandarin of the First Grade, Junior Guardian of the Heir Apparent, entitled to wear the double-eyed peacock feather: but that was exactly what Napier had been instructed to do.

The Napier mission arrived at Macao on 15 July 1834 in the frigate *Andromache*, a suitable form of transport for an ambassador, but hardly for a taipan: the Chinese took note. Any impressive effect was however marred by the fact that *Andromache* drew too much water to proceed to Canton, and the deputation, when it left, had to make its slow journey upstream in small boats. But before that could be done there were important questions to be settled at Macao, where the mission was joined by Davis, who had been in post at Canton as last President of the Select Committee. His successor there as the Company's representative (the Company was retaining an office in Canton, to assist with finance for the trade) was to be paid £5,000 a year: as some compensation, could Davis's own salary start from the time the *Andromache* sailed, as though he had been on board? And there was the Company's furniture to be valued, and their cutter *Louisa*, which was to become famous in the river, bought into the royal service.

These matters being speedily arranged, Lord Napier lost not a minute in Macao before taking himself off to Canton, in spite of Chinese protests, and leaving his 'minder' Davis, with Robinson, in Macao. This was shockingly precipitate: the correct action would have been to notify the Hong merchants, from Macao, that the new headman had arrived. They would then, in suitably humble terms, petition the Viceroy to allow the barbarians access. Until such permission had been issued, the mission must wait at Macao. Arriving in Canton on 25 July 1834, only ten days after he reached Macao, Napier took up residence at a house offered to him by William Jardine. A worried Hoppo reported to the Viceroy the 'arrival of a ship's boat at Canton, about midnight, bringing four English devils, who went into the English factories to reside ... We think that such coming as this is manifestly clandestine stealing into Canton.'[14] The next day the two Scots dined together, and found they had much in common. Jardine had growled to Matheson when he found that two of the three Superintendents were old Company men: 'You will, no doubt, be surprised to find the 2nd and 3rd superintendents nominated from the factory. I believe that Canton community are unanimous in condemning the mix of King and Company ... I disapprove, but am silent, from a feeling that the arrangement is only a temporary one,'[15] but he hoped that the Chief Superintendent at least, with the prestige and force of the Royal Navy behind him, would browbeat the Chinese into altering their terms of trade.

This was a role that Napier proved happy to accept, in spite of the clear instructions he had received from the British government. Without consulting his colleagues Davis and Robinson, whom he had left cooling their heels in Macao, and within two days of his arrival in Canton, Napier 'had transgressed the Chinese regulations in six ways: he had proceeded to Canton without a pass, taken up residence there without a permit, attempted to communicate with the governor-general by letter instead of by petition, used Chinese instead of English, had his letter presented by more than two persons, and tried to communicate directly with a mandarin instead of through the medium of the Hong merchants'.[16]

The Viceroy, Lu K'un, was a tough old soldier who had acquired a formidable reputation during the Sinkiang wars of the 1820s. He was puzzled rather than angry, and wrote to the Emperor: 'Whether the foreign chief Napier has any official title we are not in a position to find out. Even if he is an official of his country, he cannot claim equality with an important guardian of the territory of the Celestial Dynasty. This is a matter of national prestige.' In spite of his belief that 'it is clear that his aim is to challenge us and violate our laws', the Viceroy was prepared to be conciliatory: 'although the English barbarians are beyond the bounds of civilization, yet having come to the inner country to trade, they should immediately give implicit obedience to the established laws. If even England has laws, how much more the Celestial Empire . . . But, in tender consideration of his being a newcomer strict investigation will not be made.'[17]

Tender consideration was wasted on Lord Napier, who continued to add insults to the original offences of riding roughshod through the Chinese regulations. When the Viceroy sent representatives to a conference he met them with a 'severe reprimand' for not having arrived at the appointed time, their delay being characterized as an 'insult to His Britannic Majesty', and made it clear that he was perfectly prepared for war if necessary. The one man who might have saved the situation was the missionary Robert Morrison, who had accepted the responsible position of Chinese Secretary to the Superintendency, at the salary of £1,300. For such a restrained man, Morrison showed considerable excitement about his new post: 'I am to wear a Vice-Consul's coat with King's buttons . . . A Vice-Consul's uniform instead of a preaching gown!'[18] But he did not live long to enjoy the coat. After only two days' work with Napier, Morrison was taken mortally ill, and within the week was dead. Napier thus lost the only man in Canton who had enough knowledge, influence and prestige possibly to have diverted him from his headstrong course of action.

In accordance with his original remit, Napier had been given no force to bolster his intendedly pacific mission, but as accident had it the *Andromache*, which was still lying at Macao, had been joined by another frigate, *Imogene*, part of the regular patrolling force of the East India squadron. Thrashing about for some way of impressing the Chinese, while sending angry dispatches to London demanding armed intervention, the Chief Superintendent persuaded the senior naval officer, Captain Blackwood, to bring his vessels upriver to Whampoa, 'and if their presence there was not sufficient protection, to anchor under the walls of the town' – which, in fact, they could not reach. It should have been impossible for two sailing ships to force their way, against the current, up a narrow channel under the hundreds of fortress guns, but the frigates managed this without much difficulty, although they took casualties. The action – the Battle of the Bogue, as the English press called it – was the only creditable-sounding piece of news to emerge from Napier's mission, and was made much of in the British newspapers.

The Viceroy's answer to this ill-advised adventure was simply to announce a boycott of the British, suspending all trade with the rebellious barbarians. This was almost immediately effective. Soldiers were sent to see that no Chinese servant approached the English factory, and Chinese were forbidden on pain of death to sell provisions to the British. Dispatched at great expense to secure the China trade, Lord Napier had succeeded only in having it stopped; the other foreign merchants, who had been suspicious of the Jardine—Napier axis, rebelled and petitioned the Hoppo to allow trade to be resumed.

Napier found himself completely powerless. He could not even further disregard his instructions and attempt to force his way back to Macao through the Chinese lines, as the frigates had returned to Macao, and the river between Whampoa and Canton was now completely blocked even to small boats. Within three weeks Napier and his staff, having had to beg for permission to leave Canton, were jostled off downriver to Macao, running a gauntlet of jeering Chinese; inside five weeks, on 11 October, Napier was dead of a fever. The trade at Canton, this irritant having been removed, was peacefully resumed.

Although Lord Napier failed in his mission, he should be given the credit for having first suggested taking possession of Hong Kong, at least on a temporary basis (although someone else, probably Jardine, must have told him of it, since the Superintendent had no opportunity of visiting the harbour himself). In a dispatch of 14 August Napier recommended the occupation of 'the island of Hong Kong, in the entrance of the Canton River, which is admirably adapted for every purpose'.

Not to lose the enjoyment of what we have got

Nothing could have been more deplorably ineffectual than the 'Napier Fizzle', as it speedily became known, but when the news of it reached England there was little of the righteous indignation that might have been expected at hearing that a diplomatic mission had been shamefully rebuffed. To some extent this was due to the fact that Palmerston, who would have been furious at the débâcle, was temporarily out of office, as a result of an odd constitutional interlude.

The diarist Charles Greville reported that, on 16 November 1834, 'the town was electrified by the news that Melbourne's Government was at an end. Nobody had the slightest suspicion of such an impending catastrophe.'[19] William IV, who hated the Whigs, had seized upon a trivial excuse to accept Melbourne's resignation, and, instead of appointing another man from the same party, as constitutional convention demanded, had summoned the Tory Robert Peel. It was therefore the Duke of Wellington, acting as Foreign Secretary, rather than Palmerston, who received the news of Napier's failure from China, and reacted to it in his inimitable manner: he expressed not a word of regret for Napier, who had disobeyed orders, but enjoyed the opportunity to put much of the blame on the Whigs: 'it is quite obvious that the attempt made to force upon the Chinese authorities at Canton, an unaccustomed mode of communication . . . had completely failed . . . it is obvious that such an attempt must invariably fail, and lead again to national disgrace'. He tersely analysed what was wrong with Palmerston's brief to the Superintendents, and how it should be amended:

> They are instructed to proceed to and reside at the port of Canton.
> The port of Canton is described as being in the Bocca Tigris, to which point it is stated that H.M.'s ships are not to go.
> The Superintendents are therefore required to go to, and reside at, the place to which the Chinese authorities will not allow them to go, and at which they will not allow them to reside.
> This and other matters require alteration . . .

The Duke summed up future policy in a particularly pragmatic one-liner. 'That which we require now is, not to lose the enjoyment of what we have got.' To this there was general agreement: only King William remained 'mightily indignant at Lord Napier's affair at Canton, and wants to go to war with China. He writes in this strain to the Duke, who is obliged to write long answers, very respectfully telling him what an old fool he is.'[20]

The Chinese government was equally content to let the matter rest, having some cause for satisfaction in the outcome. True, the forcing of the Bogue by *Imogene* and *Andromache* was reprehensible: Viceroy Lu was accordingly stripped of his honorific button and peacock feather, and required to remain in post, but when the presumptuous headman had been humiliatingly banished Lu's decorations were restored. There were also more pressing items on the Peking agenda, which although thousands of miles from Canton, were to have their effects on the problems there. Troubles on the western frontier of China were as endemic as those of the north-west frontier of India, and for the same reasons. The restless Moslem tribesmen of that region were just as foreign in race, religion and language to the Chinese raj as were Pathans and Ghazis to the British. The pacification of southern Sinkiang by Tao-kuang's grandfather had been secured by a chain of forts protecting the trade routes over the Pamirs to what is now Afghanistan, Pakistan (Gilgit) and to Kokand, on the old silk road to Tashkent, Samarkand and Bokhara. Just as the British bought off the Pathan tribesmen after the war with Afghanistan in the 1840s, the Chinese had stabilized their border by subsidies to the Khan of Kokand for keeping the border quiet. The Khan however stepped up his demands, and fomented an insurrection in Chinese Kashgar followed by an invasion. It took five years before that was settled by a treaty in 1835, which provided that the Khan should have a political agent at Kashgar, and commercial representation in five other cities, his officials to have extra-territorial powers, both judicial and police, over foreign residents, and a favourable tax regime.[21] These conditions were similar to those embodied only seven years later in the British Treaty of Nanking, which is still regarded by the Chinese as an unequal treaty forced upon China by foreign aggression, rather than as something for which ample and recent precedent existed in Ch'ing diplomacy.

It is difficult to imagine a less aggressive, more pacific response to what could be interpreted as a national disgrace (and was, especially by the Jardine faction) than that offered by the Tory government to the result of Lord Napier's mission, but this was also to be the policy of the Whigs when in April 1835 Lord Palmerston got back his old desk in the Foreign Office.

John Davis, whose views had been ignored by Napier, was content to let things in Canton continue quietly as they had done when he had been President of the Select. In his dispatch telling the Foreign Secretary of Napier's death, Davis recommended that 'a state of absolute silence and quiescence on our part seems the most eligible course'. The new Chief Superintendent did however make one decision of future importance. On Napier's death, Johnston, bereft of his protector, applied to be appointed as Secretary to the Superintendency. Davis had already taken Johnston's measure, and was reluctant to agree to the promotion; he examined Johnston's personal file, and found that the experience he claimed did not quite match the records. In due course, when Davis resigned, Johnston was to get his promotion, but now Charles Elliot was given the post, and began his rise up the Superintendency. For the rest, Davis was relieved at being able to revert to Palmerston's original instructions, and urged the British merchants to 'avoid giving the Chinese any just cause for complaint'.

This was optimistic of him. 'Absolute silence and quiescence' could never recommend themselves to so enterprising a group. They resented the fact that Davis, whom they regarded as a left-over of the Company's, was now in charge ('one brought up in the late School of Monopoly can never therefore be a fit Representative and Controller of free traders', objected the *Canton Register*). Jardine took himself off to England to stir things up at home, escorting the widowed Lady Napier, while the Canton Chamber of Commerce sent a strongly-worded petition to the King, which advocated sending another representative, accompanied by an armed force, who was to be allowed no discretion 'to swerve in the smallest degree from a direct course of calm and dispassionate, but determined, maintenance of the true rank of your Majesty's empire'. Above all, the new envoy should be in no way connected, or tainted by association with, the distrusted East India Company.

Davis found all this very trying: the petition, he reported, was 'crude and ill-digested', from only 'a *portion* of the English traders at Canton (for some of the most reputable houses declined signing it)' – he meant the Dents – and is said to have been drawn up by a casual visitor from India, totally unacquainted with the country'.[22] In effect Davis's ground had been cut from under him by the failure of the mission, and there was nothing to keep him in a community most members of which he despised with true John Company *hauteur*. He therefore resigned the Superintendency and returned to England in January 1835, presumably never thinking to see the Pearl River again. But nine years later he was back, not only as Superintendent, but Governor of Hong Kong, Plenipotentiary, and Baronet.

Davis was replaced by the former Third Superintendent, Sir George Robinson. As Davis's resignation was followed by that of the Secretary, Astell, the posts of Second and Third Superintendents were allotted to Elliot and Johnston respectively. Robinson adopted the supine position with enthusiasm, refusing to stir an inch in any direction; literally so, for he took up his headquarters on the little cutter *Louisa*, anchored at Lintin, safely out of everyone's way. Safely, but uncomfortably, his staff being terribly cramped on the eighty-ton boat, which was nothing more than an armed yacht. Immune to their dissatisfaction, Robinson remained on board for two years, maintaining the lowest of profiles, but sending a steady stream of self-abasing dispatches to Palmerston: 'I trust it is not necessary for me to add anything like an assurance of the most profound deference and respect with which I shall implicitly obey and execute the very spirit of such instructions as I may have the honour to receive, on this or any other point. Strict undeviating obedience to the orders and directions of which I may be in possession . . . is the foundation on which I build . . .'

Charles Elliot had distrusted Robinson from the beginning. Although he was delighted by his own promotion, which, he wrote to his wife on 19 January 1835, would clear their debts if he could hold it for only six months, 'on the whole I would rather he [Davis] had not gone for he leaves a sad foolish fellow to replace him'.[23] Robinson's performance in office fortified Elliot's misgivings; he could not stomach Robinson's weak-kneed attitude to what Elliot perceived as flagrant violations by the private merchants. In particular he deprecated the ineffable James Innes (a madman, who ought to be caught and hanged, said the American trader Bennett Forbes, who had every opportunity of observing him), who had announced his intention of personally starting an individual war against China unless the customs officers surrendered some goods they had confiscated. Robinson cringed and wrung his hands, but avoided taking firm action either with Innes or the Chinese. This was too much for Captain Elliot, who as Second Superintendent was permitted to correspond with Whitehall independently of Robinson. Elliot persuaded Johnston to join him in a remonstrance to Palmerston, in which they condemned 'the mode of proceeding on the part of Sir G.B. Robinson; and concur in the opinion that steps should be taken to compel Mr Innes to forgo his hostile intentions'. It was also too much for Palmerston, who wrote back saying that what Innes proposed constituted nothing less than piracy, and that if he went ahead the Royal Navy would deal with him, but that if he had right on his side the Superintendents should take up his case with the authorities. That was the end of the road for Robinson, who was curtly dismissed, to be succeeded by Elliot.

Your most humble and obedient servant

Hong Kong has no Stamford Raffles, no single undisputed founder commemorated in place names, monuments or even hotels. The man who should be so remembered, Charles Elliot, is ignored. In December 1836, two years after coming to Canton in the relatively junior post of Master Attendant, Elliot found himself in charge (although at a salary considerably less than that of his predecessors) of Great Britain's relations with the Chinese Empire, with only young Alexander Johnston having any share in the responsibilities. It was not an enviable position, since Elliot's powers, either to control the British merchants or to communicate with the Chinese authorities, were lamentably ill-defined, and Palmerston failed to give him any decisive lead. The Foreign Secretary certainly wrote vigorously condemning such 'piratical' actions as Innes's, but at the same time warned Elliot against any attempt to exert his authority. There was 'no effective power to the Superintendent to remove or punish anyone', Palmerston wrote on 8 November 1836[24] – this in spite of the Order in Council setting up a court. The Superintendent had to be 'very careful not to assume a greater degree of authority over British subjects in China than that which you in reality possess' (22 July 1836[25]): at the same time he was to 'do all that lies in your power to avoid giving just cause of offence to the Chinese authorities'. Since the behaviour of the British merchants itself formed 'the chief cause of offence' this was difficult. Elliot attempted to explain that Canton was now 'filled . . . with a class of people who can never be left to their own devices among the natives of this country'; he went on to note 'evidence of a growing dislike upon the part of the common people to our countrymen. It is the fashion of the young men particularly to treat the Chinese with the utmost wanton insult and contumely.'

James Matheson followed Jardine to England in 1836, in order to commission a monument to Lord Napier and to encourage another, stronger approach to China, which he attempted to do in a vituperative book, *The Present Position and Prospects of the British Trade with China.* God Himself is not immune from blame: 'It has pleased Providence to assign to the Chinese – a people characterized by a marvellous degree of imbecility, avarice, conceit and obstinacy – the possession of a vast portion of the most desirable parts of the earth, and a population estimated as amounting to nearly one-third of the human race.' These creatures subjected innocent foreigners to 'injuries and insults not merely of a harassing, but even of a horrible, description'; 'the laws of nature were outraged' (by not allowing Mrs Baynes to come to Canton!), making British merchants in China 'worse off than even our West Indian slaves'. The East India Company had been shamefully weak; their policy was that 'the Chinese are a great, powerful and peculiar people with whom it is purely optional to continue or refuse permission for us to continue our intercourse, since they are not, nor ever will be, bound by any treaty; that, in the absence of any treaty, the law of nations prohibits any attempt to enforce our supposed claims upon the Chinese'. That this statement pretty accurately reflected the views of the Duke of Wellington, Lord Palmerston, and almost every other politician or administrator was of no significance; the matter would be corrected by 'those "princes of the earth" – the MER-CHANTS' who would 'overcome this feeling of indifference and repugnance. A spirit of noble and persevering enterprise led them to dare all dangers, to despise all difficulties.'

The way forward was made clear in Matheson's breathless prose: 'We must resolve upon vindicating our insulted honour as a nation, and protecting the injured interests of our commerce – or . . . humble ourselves . . . in ignominious submission, at the feet of the most insolent, the most ungrateful, the most pusillanimous people upon earth.' If the Chinese did not immediately accede, the remedy of taking a spot of their territory was available. Not Macao, however easy that might be, because of its poor harbour and unfavourable location: 'If any island is taken possession of, it should be in a central part of China – Chusan, for example'. Hong Kong was still far from people's minds. Others, led by the Dents, took a less belligerent view. Elliot wrote: 'There are "two houses" here, and they are so desperately angry with each other that their feuds colour their opinions on every subject under the sun . . . I wish I could add that the moderate party were the stronger, but . . . the ardent gentlemen have it hollow in point of numbers.'[26]

Notwithstanding all Matheson's expressions of discontent, free trade at Canton continued to be only moderately successful. In the years following the Company's withdrawal raw cotton imports doubled, as did silk exports: tea exports increased, but quality declined – as the Company had forecast – and markets became both saturated and fractious, making for difficult sales. Optimistic newcomers, hoping for a free-for-all expansion of trade, rushed to Canton, but it was only that staple, opium, for which demand remained strong. From the modest four to five thousand chests of the early years of the century, annual imports of the drug had risen to about twelve thousand chests in the late twenties. By 1834 this had shot up to twenty thousand, and from then on the rise was steep, to over thirty thousand in 1835, and forty thousand in 1838.

So sharp an increase began to cause alarm; since all opium was imported illegally, no duties were paid, all exactions going to the middlemen and mandarins' private accounts. As smuggling opium was so widespread, traders saw little reason to import even legitimate cargoes through the Canton customs; they might just as well also be offloaded in the estuary and the customs duty saved. And since all illegal imports had to be paid for in bullion, the strain on China's reserves was considerable.

It is difficult to use the term 'smuggling', with its connotations of surreptitiousness, to describe so very blatant an operation on so large a scale. Elliot regretted his lack of power to control his fellow-countrymen, and pressed 'for active intervention on the part of Her Majesty's Government', which 'cannot be deferred without great hazard'.[27] Elliot's difficulties were exacerbated by Palmerston's insistence that his communications should be direct to the Viceroy and not through the established medium of the Hong merchants. In particular the Foreign Secretary objected to such letters being styled 'petitions', a matter of essential good form to the Chinese (although Palmerston saw nothing odd in himself signing a stiff reprimand as 'your most humble and obedient servant', he had little patience for other countries' protocol). Doing his best to follow what he called Palmerston's 'tight-rope instructions', the Chief Superintendent did succeed in establishing reasonable relations with the new Viceroy, Teng T'ing-chen.

In default of a coherent and workable British policy it was the Chinese who took the initiative. If the opium trade was becoming intolerable, there were two possibilities: either legalize it or suppress it, and a debate on the subject was formally initiated at Peking early in 1836. There was much to be said for legitimizing the trade; while this would cut off their illicit income, the mandarins and their subordinates could still squeeze the Hong merchants for a percentage of greater official profits; better than nothing. The public revenue could be greatly increased, and the retail price fixed at a level that would discourage abuse. The Canton officials were unanimous that the trade should be legalized. Hsü Nai-tsi, who had been senior judge there, took this line; his supporters, from Viceroy Teng down to the Hong merchants, made the natural proviso that opium imports should be strictly restricted to Canton, and the vile trade up the coast severely prohibited! The policy was supported by the venerable scholar Juan Yuan and, it was reported, by the Empress. Hsü's memorial was translated and published in the *Canton Register* of 12 July 1836, and both Europeans and Chinese there took legalization pretty much for granted. Elliot reported on 27 July: 'The formal and final orders [for legalization] will probably be here in the course of a month or six weeks,' and on 6 August he described the expected move as 'undoubtedly the most remarkable measure ... in respect of the Foreign Trade since the accession of the dynasty'. Matheson was not happy, writing on 12 July: 'I do not think well of the plan as far as our interests are concerned – tho' it has already enhanced prices.'[28] Six months later, in February 1837, nothing had happened, but Jardine was still writing: 'sooner or later this article will be admitted and when admitted the consumption will be increased'.[29] In October that year his partner was of the opposite opinion: 'The legalization of the trade is no longer to be thought of and the government is evidently making a strong effort for its entire suppression. In this, of course, they will be unable to succeed.'[30]

Matheson was proved right; as early as August 1837 a crackdown was taking place. The Jardine Matheson day-book clerk recorded on the thirteenth: 'The smuggling boats are again prevented from running and the brokers have absconded. There is consequently no inquiry after the drug.'[31] It soon became inescapably clear in Canton that, far from legalizing the drug, the Chinese authorities had resolved on its absolute and final suppression, and that in the most rigorous form. The Emperor had made his decision that the drug was not to be allowed, and that the only question was how best to put an end to the trade.

The War of Lancelot Dent's Collar

Was the first Anglo-Chinese war (1840—42), which led to the foundation of the colony of Hong Kong, really caused by the unscrupulous British flooding China with illicit opium, as the conventional view has it? Opinions differed at the time: *The Times* was the first, on 25 April 1840, to give the conflict the name of an 'Opium War'; Gladstone, then a member of the Tory opposition, had no doubts, but Gladstone rarely harboured doubt: 'A war more unjust in its origins, a war more calculated in its progress to cover this country with permanent disgrace, I do not know, and have not read of.' Macaulay, as Secretary of War, took an exactly opposite view: 'The liberties and lives of Englishmen are at stake . . . there will be, as respects China, no change of measures . . . I . . . have only to express my fervent hope that this most righteous quarrel may be prosecuted to a speedy and triumphant close.'[32] The former US President John Quincy Adams, in the *New York Herald*, took an unexpected stand: 'Who has the righteous cause? You will be surprised to hear me answer – Britain! The opium question is not the cause of the war . . . the cause of the war is the Kotou [kowtow]! The arrogant and unacceptable pretensions of the Chinese',[33] the Chinese seizure of the opium held at Canton being 'a mere incident in the dispute';[34] the French were, as ever, sure that perfidious Albion was to blame.

Distance has hardly lent clarity to the view; writers from the People's Republic of China have no doubts on the subject: 'To protect her lucrative opium trade, England had been preparing for war against China for some time before 1840 . . . Despite the courageous resistance of the people and the patriotic officers and men, the war ended with defeat for China because of the Qing court's domestic policy of hostility to the people and its foreign policy of compromise with and capitulation to the invaders'[35]; 'marauding capitalist aggressors, exploiting the trade in opium began to invade China'.[36] Western scholars are not so sure of the case: 'Historians have repeatedly laid to rest the ghost of fighting a war to force opium on the Chinese, but with singular persistence it appears in anti-opium pamphlets and undergraduate text books . . . Palmerston . . . made it amply clear that to the government the opium question was incidental';[37] 'It would be called an opium war because opium was the article of commerce that had caused it. But the war would not be fought over opium; it would be fought over trade, the urgent desire of a capitalist, industrial, progressive country to force a Confucian, agricultural and stagnant one to trade with it'.[38] The doyen of historians of the period, John King Fairbank, is scathing: 'The opium war of 1839–42, all agree, was a classic iniquity . . . What's wrong with this picture? Only that it is the afterthought of slightly guilt-ridden individuals . . . or of Marxist-minded patriots (who have to live with the fact that the Chinese were the opium distributors within China and soon became the principal producers).'[39] Chinese writing in the West often agree: 'In retrospect, it is apparent that opium was the immediate, but not the ultimate cause of the war';[40] 'In the broad sense the Opium War was a clash between two cultures . . . But the vital force that brought on the cultural conflict was Britain's commercial expansion . . . The opium trade was an indispensable vehicle for facilitating this expansion and the two could not be separated. Had there been an effective alternative to opium, say molasses or rice, the conflict might have been called the Molasses War, or the Rice War. The only difference would have been a matter of time.'[41] Given these widely differing opinions, and since the legitimacy of Britain's occupation of Hong Kong is still challenged on moral grounds, the remainder of this chapter attempts a clarification of the 'Opium War' debate.

When suppression of the opium trade was decided upon, suggestions on how this might be done were submitted to the Emperor. Huang Chueh-tzu, from the Board of Rites, wanted extreme measures: 'I understand that according to Red Hair country's law, smokers are hung on high poles for public exhibition and then shot into the sea by cannon. China should do better than these foreign barbarians.'[42] Ch'i-shan and Mu-chang-a, both sensible Manchus, preferred to cut off supplies by a blockade of Canton, and wisely pointed out that severe laws were useless unless they commanded general respect. They were supported by the majority of the respondents, but the arguments that swept the board were those of Lin Tse-hsü (Lin Zexu), who proposed a programme for the rehabilitation of addicts combined with increasingly severe punishments for suppliers, leading to a total interdiction of the drug. The Emperor wholeheartedly agreed, adding many vermilion endorsements to the manuscript.

In accord with bureaucratic tradition everywhere, the man who had submitted the best memorandum was given the job of putting it into practice. Lin seemed more suited for the role than most civil servants might have been. Aged fifty-three, and a native of Foochow, in Fukien, he was brought up in a coastal trading community. His career had been remarkably swift and unblemished, earning him the nickname of Lin Ch'ing-t'ien – Lin the Clear Sky, the incorruptible. Not only was Lin trustworthy, methodical and intellectually brilliant, but he enjoyed a 'hands-on' method of dealing with problems, even in risky situations. He is today perceived, and with some justification, as a hero of the Chinese people, a scholar-statesman in the finest Confucian tradition, courageous in his resistance to foreign encroachments.

Lin much resembled that seventeenth-century Englishman, Samuel

Pepys. Both were renowned administrators who kept diaries and were curious and analytical observers of all they saw: both were amateurs of the arts, both had a close circle of friends that included the greatest scholars of their day, and both also took an interest in more fleshly pleasures. Like Lin, Pepys enjoyed the absolute trust of his sovereigns; and, by the standards of the day, Pepys was similarly honourable. Even the descriptions of Lin sound not unlike those of Pepys: 'Lin is short, but of a compact make . . . with a fine intelligent forehead and a rather pleasing expression of countenance, enlivened by small dark piercing eyes, and possessing a voice strong, clear and sonorous. In dress he is plain [perhaps not a Pepysian characteristic], while in his manners he can be courteous, but is more generally rather abrupt'; 'a dignified air . . . a bland and vivacious character without a trace of the fanatics . . . rather stout, with a full round face . . . and a keen black eye'.[43]

Where Pepys and Lin differed was in their knowledge of the world outside. Pepys had visited Europe and North Africa, and was in daily contact with mariners who had touched in all quarters of the globe including China; the affairs of Bombay became just as much part of his routine as those of Portsmouth. Lin, although he took a lively intellectual interest in what was known of the barbarian world, remained in almost total ignorance of life outside the Middle Kingdom. The British, he believed, could not exist without regular supplies of rhubarb and tea: 'If China cuts off these benefits with no sympathy for those who are to suffer what can the barbarians rely upon to keep themselves alive?'[44] There was, he felt, no real possibility of conflict – how could the barbarians hope to challenge the might of the Celestial Dynasty? Their troops could never fight on shore, since their legs were too tightly bound to permit them to box or wrestle. Their ships might be large, but were helpless in shallow waters. Above all, Lin was convinced that Britain came to China as a suppliant, as did all barbarians: 'The kings of your honourable country', he wrote to Queen Victoria, 'have always been noted for their politeness and submissiveness'; and therefore remonstrated with them in the reasonable tones of a superior civilization.

If it was difficult for Lin to evaluate the capabilities of barbarians, it was not much easier for his counterpart Charles Elliot to comprehend Lin's strategy. He had the advantage of having passed five years in China, but without learning the language or having anything but the most superficial contact with the people, and none at all with the administrator-scholars who held the reins of power. In spite of these obstacles it should have been possible for two such reasonable men as Lin and Elliot, both of whom were antipathetic to the whole idea of opium smuggling, to have managed things between them. What Lin was proposing was after all nothing except the effectual administration of his country's own laws, laws which Elliot was both in duty and inclination ready to support. The responsibility for the situation developing into open war has to be shared between the British government, who refused to allow Elliot proper powers, and the conscientious Lin, led into a blunder by his ignorance of the West.

Even before Lin's appointment, measures against Chinese opium dealers had been intensified. On 3 December 1838 the Jardine Matheson clerk recorded: '. . . many idle reports are afloat – such as the Viceroy having made up his mind to strangle one of the offenders in front of the foreign factories, as an example to the others – and to seize . . . all the Chinese comparadores, servants and coolies in the service of foreign merchants – such reports we do not believe.'[45]

He was wrong not to believe the rumours; an attempt was indeed made to execute a Chinese opium dealer in front of the factories, which so enraged the Westerners as to lead to a riot. Although this hanging was prevented, many others followed: 'The Governor General,' Jardine wrote, 'has been seizing, trying, and strangling poor devils without mercy . . . We have never seen so serious a persecution, nor one so general.'[46] Superintendent Elliot issued more stern admonitions to the recalcitrant British, warning 'owners of such . . . craft engaged in the said illicit opium traffic . . . that Her Majesty's Government will in no way interpose if the Chinese Government shall think fit to seize [them]'. And if any smuggler caused the death of a Chinese in the course of his activities, he must expect to be liable to capital punishment himself. Elliot's energetic approach was rewarded by the reopening of trade, a circumstance in which he took great satisfaction.

In an effort to add weight to his already severe warning, Elliot asked Governor-General Teng for his support, even, as he afterwards told his wife Clara, offering to bring the little cutter *Louisa*, a Queen's vessel, to assist in rounding up any offenders, a remarkable gesture from a Royal Navy officer: 'I had already offered the *Louisa* to do the will of the Emperor and was perfectly ready to have ordered officers of our own establishment to accompany their officers on board any of the ships that he saw fit.' The American traders saw the writing on the wall; Russell's, the largest house, decided to 'discontinue all connection with the opium trade in China', a business that was fast becoming 'as dangerous as it was disreputable'. The British traders, with more at stake, and with a residual expectation that if the worst came to the worst they would be bailed out by the Royal Navy, awaited the coming of Commissioner Lin with only moderate unease.

Armed with full authority from the Emperor as Imperial Commissioner, the incorruptible Lin set out from Peking on 8 January 1839. The news of his appointment left the cynical Jardine unmoved. Writing from Macao on his way back to England on the twenty-ninth of that month he reported: 'A special envoy has been appointed, and is soon expected to enforce the prohibitory laws, with authority entirely independent of the Viceroy, who was so alarmed at learning the intelligence that he fell into a swoon of an hour's duration . . . In order to make a parade of zeal he and the Foo Yuen [the Governor] have just issued a long proclamation.'[47] But as a precaution, Jardine suggested that deliveries of opium and piece goods should be diverted to Hong Kong and up the coast, which would indicate that some trade was already taking place in the island's waters. Some months later Jardine's partner Matheson claimed that he had considered sending the opium ships away, but that the project had been aborted owing to 'Mr Dent's usual dilatoriness'.[48]

Lin did not arrive in Canton until 10 March 1839, when Elliot was in Macao, leaving Johnston in charge in Canton. Instructions had been sent ahead by Lin for the Canton authorities to arrest nearly sixty Chinese identified as active in the opium trade, who were to be tried over the next few months; at least four of these were sentenced to death. Information had also been laid before the Commissioner as to the identity of the chief foreign smugglers; in Jardine's absence Lancelot Dent was, correctly, named as their head. But Lin made it clear that his targets were the Chinese. As long as the foreigners obeyed the law, and refrained from smuggling, they would not be harmed but, on the contrary, benevolently treated as they had been in the past: the legitimate trade was important, and must be protected. On 18 March the Commissioner laid down his conditions: all opium stocks must be surrendered and the foreigners must pledge themselves never again to deal in the drug. If these conditions were not met, the Hong merchants would suffer imprisonment, expropriation and decapitation. Nor would the foreigners be spared: if they refused or reneged on their undertakings 'it will become requisite to include you also in the severe punishment prescribed by the new law'.[49] Three days were given for compliance, and in the meantime the foreigners were to be confined to their factories.

The foreigners, who had heard all this sort of thing before in the periodic purges, were not unduly perturbed, and at a meeting of the Chamber of Commerce on 21 March contented themselves with bland assurances that they too greatly deplored the opium traffic and, as a gesture, agreed to surrender a small quantity, just over a thousand chests. This was a grave misjudgement of Lin, who was furious at what he recognized as blatant procrastination, and immediately issued an order for Lancelot Dent's arrest. To lend weight to this, on 23 March he sent the two senior Hong merchants, Howqua and Mowqua, to the factories in chains, with a warning that if Dent did not present himself they would be decapitated that very night. Dent, relying on his good relations with the Chinese, was willing to surrender himself, and the other merchants were content to let him, until Matheson intervened. He considered the whole thing to be 'the most complete exhibition of humbug'. It was 'almost amusing to witness the forced gravity which Howqua and the younger Mowqua tried to assume in their chains, which, however, did not prevent them from occasionally chatting about business or news with any friend who happened to be near'. He was able to dissuade Dent from complying 'which was of course a matter of no great difficulty',[50] as Matheson, always willing to be sarcastic about the Dents, remarked.

Whether Dent stood in real peril or not has been the subject of some debate. In a memorial to the Emperor of 2 May 1839 Lin suggested that 'the said barbarians are from a far-off country' and should therefore be treated leniently, and that 'our policy is to be rigorous without resorting to any offensive action'. Opinions differed among the British as to Lin's seriousness. Dent's partner, Robert Inglis, did not believe him to be in grave danger when the following year he described the incident to a Select Committee of the House of Commons: 'Mr Dent was probably the most popular man amongst all the foreigners with the Chinese. It was not from any enmity to him that he was selected; quite the contrary . . . it was hoped to work upon his feelings.' Lancelot's brother Wilkinson was not so sure, and 'was in a great state of excitement . . . if he went to the city he was sure he would be put to death'. Jardine pooh-poohed the whole business: 'if there had been more resistance, the measures would have been less severe than they were';[51] but Jardine was not present at the time.

Help however was at hand, and in a dramatic fashion. The American resident Gideon Nye recorded: 'nor were visions of the "Black Hole" wholly dispelled until the conciliatory but intrepid Elliot, sword in hand, made his way in his cutter from Macao, and by dint of great exertions reached the British factory.'[52] Mrs Elliot described how when the news of the threat to Dent reached Macao, 'Charles, much to my horror, dashed off to Canton in a most gallant style. He had to push his way through hundreds of war junks in a small boat (his four-oared gig). Happily he had on his uniform coat which probably saved him ... he landed in safety among the chaos of his countrymen.' Even the cynical Matheson was affected by the scene: 'It was an arresting sight about 6 p.m. [on 24 March] to descry from our terrace a small foreign boat with a sitter in a cocked hat, pulling up – crowds of Chinese boats in chase. It proved to be Charles Elliot who managed to effect a landing as a barrier of boats was closing in to intercept. In a moment the flag was hoisted.'[53] It was only the small boat's flag, the official Union flag having been mislaid, but its flying over the Superintendent's residence indicated that the foreign community was under British protection and that the confrontation was now an official dispute between the British and Chinese governments.

Not that the British were able to offer any but moral protection, the only force available being the four-man crew of Elliot's gig. Lin, from a position of considerable strength, having a good proportion of the foreigners in China cooped up inside the few acres of the Canton factories, but completely unaware of the furore he had started, was insisting on three demands: 1) The surrender of all the opium in the port and on the river; 2) The agreement of all merchants to an undertaking not to deal in opium in the future; 3) The surrender of Lancelot Dent. Until at least the first of these conditions was fulfilled, the factories would be blockaded, all trade would cease, and all Chinese would leave the factories. Once the opium was delivered conditions would be relaxed and the question of Dent's arrest would fall away.

Agreeing not to import more opium presented little problem: being made under duress, it could be argued that such promises were not binding. Certainly Matheson expressed himself very ready to sign: 'As far as regards JM & Co we had resolutely determined to abide by the cession made', but at the same time he wrote to his correspondents that they should send their opium to Alexander Matheson at Macao, who would be happy to continue to dispose of it:[54] the distinction between the company and one of its staff acting as an individual was not likely to commend itself to the Commissioner. It is also probable that the merchants might have been persuaded to surrender all their opium – for Lin had accurately calculated the quantity in hand – hoping that the Chinese might later be cajoled or coerced into paying for it. But Elliot solved any difficulty by 'enjoining and instructing', on behalf of the British government, the surrender of the drug. Since this clear order meant that opium which had looked to be unsaleable was now, at least in theory, replaced by a British government obligation to compensate them, the traders were delighted. Even Matheson was brought to admit: 'Though at the time and long after I had doubts as to the judiciousness of what Captain Elliot has done, now that I am able to view its progress ... I am inclined to regard it as a large and statesmanlike measure more especially since the Chinese have fallen into the snare of rendering themselves directly liable to the British Crown ... Captain Elliot is desirous to make his receipts as complete as they can possibly be rendered ... the only point left for adjustment is the rate of compensation.'[55]

The receipts were as complete as could be wished, since the merchants scoured out every ounce of opium they could find, even sending to the ships up the coast and on their way from India for whatever they had to supply. The astonishing quantity of 2,613,879 pounds of opium was delivered – more than one thousand tons, making it surely the largest drug haul ever collected – and burned in Lin's presence at a specially constructed site by the banks of the Pearl River.

If Lin had left off at this point matters would probably have arranged themselves. There would certainly have been controversy about who was to pay for the surrendered opium, valued at over £2 million. Elliot would have found himself in deep trouble with the Treasury, and years of painful negotiations would have ensued, but an expensive war might have been avoided. It was not as if the Chinese government could not easily afford to make such a sum available. The much larger amount – more than three times the original sum – finally agreed three years later was paid on the nail, and (as cynics in Britain pointed out) could be recovered whenever the Chinese wished by putting a modest tax on exports of tea, of which China still had a monopoly, and making the British consumer thereby foot the bill.

The plausibility of this theory is reinforced by events then taking place in Britain. Things were not going well for the government: on 21 March, as the Canton Chamber of Commerce was worrying over Lin's ultimatum, Lord Melbourne's Whig administration had suffered a Parliamentary defeat – over, as so often at the time, the Irish question.

Since the vote had been only in the House of Lords the government was not immediately threatened, but two months later, as the collection and destruction of the opium at Canton was in full swing, the government came within five votes of losing a motion in the House of Commons and felt obliged to resign. This came as a great shock to the nineteen-year-old Queen, who had succeeded her uncle William IV two years previously. Victoria was distraught at the idea of losing the guidance of Lord Melbourne, for whom she felt the tenderest affection. She gave full vent to her distress in a letter to him: 'The Queen thinks Lord Melbourne may possibly wish to know how she is this morning . . . she was in a wretched state till nine o'clock last night, when she tried to occupy herself and try to think less gloomily of this dreadful change . . . she couldn't touch a morsel of food last night, nor can she this morning.'[56] The Opposition leader, Sir Robert Peel, had to be sent for to form a government, but the young Queen was spoiling for a fight. Peel was not in a strong position – he might well have been defeated in the House on the first vote – and a constitutional crisis ensued which ended up with Melbourne and the Whigs back in office, and Palmerston continuing, although precariously, as Foreign Secretary.

It was not until August that reports of the Canton troubles reached London. Communications were improving, but the service from Canton to London was still unreliable, and took up to four months. Elliot's news was another burden to a wretchedly harassed government. At home Chartist riots, demanding an extension to the franchise and electoral reform, were beginning; abroad the French were being difficult in the Middle East, where their protégé Mehemet Ali was enthusiastically dismembering the Turkish Empire: and here was Minto's nephew demanding an expensive expedition – 'a swift and heavy blow unprefaced by one word of written communication' – and him already £2 million sterling in hock to British merchants.

To Clausewitz, war was diplomacy by other means: to British governments it seemed more a department of accountancy. There could be – although the suggestion was canvassed – no question of repaying the merchants out of public funds for the opium surrendered at Elliot's behest. There simply was not the money, for the expense of the new Penny Post was adding to an already unbalanced budget, and increased taxation would practically ensure a Tory victory. Theoretically, it would have been possible to repudiate Elliot and the debt together, but this would have been equally certain political suicide for the government, given the notoriety of the Elliot family as furious Whigs – two cousins of Captain Charles, Minto and Auckland, in the Cabinet, and the Home Secretary, Lord John Russell, in love with Minto's daughter Fanny. Probably the most sensible course would have been to let the merchants stew in their own juice until the government's finances were stronger, and then make a negotiated settlement at well under the initial figure. (As it turned out, within a couple of years trading profits had more than recouped the loss.)

But at the time this looked impossible, since all trade at Canton was reported as stopped, and Palmerston had some powerful figures at his elbow urging the merchants' case. One suggestion tendered to the Foreign Secretary is vital to an understanding of British aims. The London East India and China Association were asked for their advice, which they gave in a long letter of 2 November 1839. It was essential, they considered, that any British representative be allowed direct access to the Chinese authorities, upon equal terms, and specified ports in addition to Canton must be opened for trade. If this was not allowed, then 'the cession, by purchase or otherwise, of an island [should] be obtained'.[57] The Association was ready to accept that British subjects in China be subject to Chinese laws, but on the principle 'each man for his own – the innocent not being confounded with the guilty', which would have been tantamount to leaving the opium trade to the adventurous fringe. An appendix was attached detailing precisely what forces would be needed to bring the Chinese Empire to the negotiating table: two line-of-battle ships, two large and two small frigates, some smaller vessels, including steamers, with 2,540 sailors and marines.

Perhaps the most important part of the Association's memorandum was that dealing with opium. Quite simply it accepted that if the Chinese government seriously wished to suppress the trade, this decision must be complied with: 'we have no desire that it should for one instant be supposed, that we are advocating the continuance of a trade against which the Chinese Government formally protest. We are quite prepared to admit, should the Chinese persist in prohibiting the import of opium that henceforth the British merchants trading to China, must obey the laws of that country in respect to that article, and that the Crown of Great Britain cannot be called upon to interfere in any manner in support of its subjects who violate them.' The suggestions of the Association were adopted in their entirety by Lord Palmerston – clear proof that continuation of the opium trade was not a part of British policy.

This memorandum was supplemented by a delegation from the Association led by John Abel Smith, Whig M.P. and banker, who acted for Jardine Matheson. Its most important member was the Iron-Headed Old Rat himself, William Jardine, shortly to become Whig Member for Ashburton. He was accompanied by Alexander Matheson and Hugh Lindsay, who had been Supercargo on the *Lady Amherst*'s voyage, sent out from China to second their cause. Although the deputation could not persuade Lord Palmerston to yield an inch on the question of the government's paying, then and there, for the surrendered opium, he was brought to accept that the Chinese could be forced, without too much difficulty, to pay up instead. They added practical advice on how this should be done. Jardine gave a detailed account of the background to the current situation, and added some very specific recommendations, to which the Foreign Secretary paid close attention. Three years later, on the successful conclusion of peace, Palmerston acknowledged the debt in a letter to John Abel Smith (28 November 1842): 'for to the assistance and information which you and Mr Jardine so handsomely afforded to us, it was mainly owing to them we were able to give to our affairs, Naval, Military, and Diplomatic, in China those detailed instructions which have led to these satisfactory results . . . There is no doubt that this event, which will form an epoch in the progress of the civilization of the human races, must be attended with most important advantages to the commercial interests of England.'[58]

Palmerston experienced little difficulty in convincing the rest of the Cabinet of the need to dispatch an expedition to China, to be organized by the government of India and the Admiralty, although they took their time – after all it was the summer, when no business was allowed to be too pressing. At the crucial meeting Russell, the Home Secretary, appeared to be dozing, and Melbourne, by that time a very tired man, left things to Palmerston and Macaulay, newly appointed as Secretary of War. John Cam Hobhouse, in charge of India as President of the Board of Control, commented: 'The charges made against us of idleness could hardly be maintained: for at the first Cabinet which he [Macaulay] had attended we had resolved on a war with the master of Syria and Egypt [Mehemet Ali] backed by France, and also on a war with the master of one-third of the human race.'[59]

Hobhouse was making a wry joke, since it was hardly a war that was envisaged either with Mehemet Ali or with China. Britain simply did not have the resources to carry out such an intention. The Royal Navy, which had to be the key to success in a coastal blockade half the world away, was reduced to less than thirty thousand officers and men, compared with four times that number during the Napoleonic wars twenty-five years before. Some three thousand soldiers were initially considered sufficient to subdue a third of the human race; they, being provided by the government of India, consisted for the most part of Indian sepoys, with units from three British regiments. Such a force, operating three thousand miles from its Indian base, could be intended for nothing more than an armed demonstration designed to bring some realism into the negotiations with the Chinese. The news of this expeditionary force's formation – carried by a Jardine Matheson clipper rather than a ship of the Royal Navy – was not to reach Elliot until February 1840, nearly a year after the troubles at Canton had begun: and by then events had reached the point where something more like a full-scale war was inevitable.

Flushed with pride at his great victory over the barbarians, Lin proceeded to work through his list of demands. As promised, the foreigners were released from their confinement and allowed to resume trading, providing always that they had fulfilled his first requirement by signing the undertaking that their ships did not contain opium. This Elliot refused to allow British ships to do, not out of any sympathy with the trade, but because Lin's bond was a singularly unsatisfactory document that might allow any interpretation. It was drafted in the primitive English that was the best that Lin's linguists could manage:

A Truly and Willing Bond

. . . I, with my officer, and the whole crew are all dreadfully obey the new laws of the Chinese Majesty, that they dare not bring any opium; if one little bit of opium was found out in any part of my ship by examination, I am willingly deliver up the transgressor, and he shall be punish to death according to the correctness law of the Government of Heavenly Dynasty . . .[60]

The Pandora's box of troubles that this document might cause with the Chinese was one that Elliot could not permit to be opened. The possibilities included mistaken identity, which had already happened (the wrong ship was seized by the Chinese, which action then formed another item in British demands for reparation); squeezing on the part of officials who had made sure that opium would be found on a ship by previously depositing it there; as well as sheer intransigence, could all result in British subjects, whom Elliot was in duty bound to protect, being delivered into very uncertain Chinese jurisdiction. For his part Lin was persistent; the barbarians, he explained to the Emperor, attached much importance to promises, which, once given, were strictly adhered to: 'They never break an agreement, or even fail to keep an appointment.' The general undertaking they had given in March – and which might, just, have been honoured – was not enough, but if the foreigners could be coerced into signing a formal bond ('a very serious matter . . . as they look at it'), they could be trusted not to break it.[61]

Elliot took the only action he believed possible: he issued an instruction banning any British vessel from trading with the Chinese, and withdrew the community from Canton to Macao, leaving the Americans to look after affairs at the factories. At Macao, considering that they had been released from their undertaking to cease trading by Lin's insistence on a bond, the opium merchants took their business in hand once more. Although it was prosecuted with even more than usual vigour, a degree of surreptitiousness was now needed. Code words were used, disguising grades of opium as cotton piece-goods; ships had their names changed; deliveries were made not to the estuary but to Manila, and transhipped to the east coast of China in the usual fashion. On 10 June Matheson wrote to a client in Bombay 'We have, under the rose, sent the *Hayes* back to her former situation,' and to Jardine, on the same date, 'The coast trade promises fair. Rees and his gang are at work as before.' By the twenty-seventh Matheson informed his partner, 'in all my commercial experience I have never been so severely fagged as in the month since our arrival at Macao . . . Your friends [Captains] Rees, Jauncey, Baylis, Strachan and Hall are now at their old work again . . . Jauncey on his way to surrender to Elliot made a few sales . . .' The Dents were again actively competing: when he learned that Lancelot, freed from captivity, had already bought a house in Manila, intending to use that port as an alternative centre for his opium distribution, Matheson warned Jardine 'we should take care not to be behindhand in this respect'.[62]

When that letter was written, on 24 August, it was not from the comfortable Jardine Matheson office in Macao, but from the firm's schooner *Maria* at anchor off the port. Putting pressure on the Portuguese Governor, Lin had succeeded in driving the English from Macao, as he had from Canton. His determination to harry the British into submission was no longer, however, based upon the anti-opium campaign, but on what was to be the most important cause of the war, the old question of extra-territoriality – who should have jurisdiction over crimes committed by foreigners. On 7 July a party of drunken sailors, certainly British, probably with some Americans among them, got into a fight on shore at Tsim-sha-tsui, in what is now the commercial centre of Kowloon. One Chinese, Lin Wei-hsi, died as a result of his injuries. Elliot, who was furious at this new provocation to the Chinese, immediately started an inquiry, offered rewards and paid compensation to the family of Lin, who then – as they were expected to do – acknowledged that the death had been accidental, and therefore was properly settled by a money payment.[63] As a result of the inquiry it was found, as might have been thought highly likely under the circumstances, impossible to discover which man had struck the blow which proved to be fatal, but five suspect sailors were arraigned before a court constituted under the 1833 regulations, the first court to be so summoned; by doing so Elliot was certainly going beyond the limits of his authority, but this was the only action open to him. The Superintendent could not accede to Lin's demand to have a culprit brought to Chinese trial, but he did his best to ensure that justice could be seen to be done. 'I can deliver no man into their hands, which they have required me to do; but I have invited their officers to be present at as impartial a trial (according to our own forms of law) for the grave offences charged against British subjects, as if those offences had been committed upon our own countrymen, upon our own shores.'

The charge of murder was dismissed by the jury – it is hard to see how they could have done otherwise, in the absence of any proof as to who struck the fatal blow, and in what circumstances – but the men were found guilty of 'riotously, unlawfully, and injuriously entering certain dwelling houses . . . and there riotously assaulting the inhabitants, men and women, cutting, beating, and otherwise dangerously ill-using them'. For this they were sentenced to fines and short terms of imprisonment, subsequently suspended.

The result went no way towards satisfying the Commissioner. In accordance with Chinese practice he demanded the surrender of a culprit – it did not matter much which culprit, but one had to be provided. Elliot could not possibly do so, but Lin attempted to coerce him by having the British expelled from their refuge in Macao. In a letter which unconsciously reveals how closely the foreign community had been united by Lin's pressure, Clara Elliot wrote home that: 'Because Charles could not either prove the murder or give anyone of us up we were on the 15 August turned out of our houses.' The whole British community, several hundred in number, including women and children, transferred to ships which anchored in the harbour of Hong Kong, and all settled down on board as best they might. Lin reported to the Emperor that although the British refugees must have some dried food, 'they will very soon find themselves without the heavy, greasy meat dishes for which they have such a passion'.[64] The final step was to make sure, therefore, that fresh food and water should be denied them, and edicts were sent to the villagers around Kowloon to inform them of this. Elliot, always ready to take a personal hand, went on shore in an attempt to persuade the Kowloon authorities to relent. In this he was partly successful: some provision boats loaded and set off towards the British, only to be intercepted by Chinese war-junks. This was too much for Elliot, who opened fire on the junks with the little guns of the *Louisa*, supported by an armed schooner and a small boat.

These, the first shots of what eventually turned into a war, were fired on 4 September 1839, but further conflict was by no means then inevitable. Elliot had chosen, at considerable risk, to confine the action against the junks to his own small boats. He had the alternative, for the first time since the dispute began, of calling up heavier metal, for a few days before a British man-of-war, the twenty-six-gun frigate *Volage*, had arrived and was standing by. Her Captain Smith was itching to teach the Chinese a lesson, and could have sunk the junks and disabled the shore batteries with the greatest of ease. Elliot restrained him, although with some difficulty. His dispatch of the following day indicates what was to be his constant policy of restraint, carried usually to the point of greatly irritating his subordinates.

> I conferred with Captain Smith, and he acceded to my recommen-
> dation not to proceed in the morning and destroy the three junks,
> and above all not to land men for the purpose of attack upon the
> battery, a measure which would probably lead to the destruction
> of the village and great injury and irritation to the inhabitants . . .
> it did not appear to me to be judicious, or indeed, becoming to
> recommend the employment of Her Majesty's ship in the destruc-
> tion of three junks, already checked by my own smaller vessel.

The Superintendent had by no means given up hope of a negotiated settlement with Lin. The affair at Kowloon, which Lin proudly reported to the Emperor as a Chinese victory, was allowed to pass, and the supply of provisions resumed. Elliot was ready to agree that those foreigners nominated as undesirable by the Chinese should be removed, including Donald Matheson, but stood firm against the demand to surrender a culprit in the Lin Wei-hsi matter. It looked at one point as if the opportunity to comply, and to save face all round, was presented to him on a plate. A convenient drowned corpse had been found, which the Commissioner would have been happy to accept as a veritable murderer, drowned in a fit of remorse. Elliot, inconveniently standing by the law as he understood it, refused to accept this inviting opportunity, and the chance slipped away. In spite of this stubborn conscience, by 20 October it seemed as though peace was in sight. Lin had written politely to Elliot: 'Captain Elliot has stated that he must await his sovereign's commands. It is enquired when the dispatch left, and when a reply may be expected? And then a modified arrangement will not be difficult to determine upon, if Captain Elliot acts obediently . . .' Captain Elliot was ready to do much, and more than his instructions permitted him to do: he agreed to ban all ships containing opium from the fleet at Hong Kong, to allow the Chinese to search any suspected vessel, and to obtain from every British firm an undertaking not to deal in the drug: he would even mount another investigation, jointly with the Chinese, into the death of Lin Wei-hsi; but he would never be prepared either to surrender a possibly innocent man or to allow any British subject to sign a bond making them subject to Chinese jurisdiction in capital matters.

No Chinese corroboration has been found, but Elliot claimed to have 'an agreement under the signets of the High Commissioner and Governor', and Commissioner Lin seemed at least tacitly to have accepted the conditions. On 20 October, more than three months after the death of Lin Wei-hsi, Elliot felt able to issue a public notice announcing that trade could be resumed with China. It would not be at Canton, but at Ch'uen-pi, although upon the terms and conditions that had formerly applied at Whampoa; and it appeared that all might yet be well. The English began to go back to their homes in Macao, and the Hong merchants, who had taken refuge there, to return to Canton.

Then the unexpected happened. Clara Elliot described it thus:

On the 19th October I was in high spirits for Charles had just achieved a triumph in gaining the Commissioner's consent that pending orders from home the trade should once more be opened, and carried on 'Outside' instead of 'Inside' the Bogue as had been customary – This was an immense object gained as Outside there was no danger of being locked up, as on a former occasion ... After securing this promise ... Charles recommended the return of the English community to Macao to their homes ... You will not believe me when I tell you the Commissioner has again broken faith – A wretched merchant vessel *Thomas Coutts* lately arriving from England had in defiance of Charles' injunctions gone 'Inside' the Bogue ... the Commissioner has declared that if one ship can go in all must do likewise. His promise is whistled to the wind. Charles with Captain Smith of the *Volage* (26 guns) and Captain Warren of the *Hyacinth* (18 guns) went up a few days since to the Bogue and sent in a letter to request that we might remain in Macao unmolested and be provided with provisions etc. The letter was returned unanswered and a fleet of 29 junks sent to turn them back or to destroy them. *Volage* and *Hyacinth* upon this were forced (in self-defence) to give them a severe lesson – In less than two hours the 29 ships were put hors-de-combat. *Volage* sailed here as fast as possible to advise the English once more to embark.

Clara was an accurate reporter – the *Thomas Coutts*, the master of which believed that Elliot had exceeded his authority in forbidding British ships to accept Lin's bond, did just that, and was allowed by the Chinese to take his ship to Canton. It now appeared clear to Lin that the British front was cracking, and that if he persisted he might after all manage to get his bond accepted. The *Thomas Coutts* having arrived at Canton, Lin immediately tore up his agreement with Elliot and reverted to his previous tone of ferocity, threatening 'measures of extermination' and immediate destruction of all ships that would not either leave or accept his bond. Elliot's hopes for a peaceful settlement were shattered, and on 26 October, after receiving Lin's ultimatum, he had to warn all British ships to leave Hong Kong, 'the high commissioner and the governor of these provinces having this day violated their engagements, made under their signets, to conduct the trade outside the port of Canton ... under menaces of destruction'.

As Clara had mentioned, Elliot's fleet had been augmented by the arrival of the sloop *Hyacinth*; the fighting may have been touched off by a warning shot she fired across the bows of a British ship, *Royal*

Saxon, which was emulating the *Thomas Coutts*, and the Chinese ships then attempting to protect her. The junks advanced, and *Volage* opened fire. In less than an hour four war-junks were destroyed, at the cost of a single British sailor wounded. On 3 November 1839, after months of negotiations which had seemed to be finally successful, the war was on.

Not that anything very dramatic happened, or even that the British government accepted that a state of war existed. Lin announced a scale of rewards for capturing British ships and taking British servicemen, dead or alive, but preferably the latter; nobody grew rich on this. Potentially more damagingly, the Commissioner banned 'forever' the British from Canton, with the result that the Americans, who had remained in the factories, simply took the trade over on their cousins' behalf. The vital tea exports continued, and legitimate British imports went through as normal. Even opium continued to be sold through the ports up the coast, and Jardine Matheson rapidly began to recover the profits they had lost on the confiscated drug. Lord Palmerston wrote to Elliot informing him that a naval force, and probably a small army detachment, would arrive about the end of March the following year and occupy some suitable island – probably Chusan, off the mouth of the Yangtse, 'to serve as a rendezvous and a basis for operations for our expedition, and afterwards as a secure basis for our commercial establishment – it being our intention to retain personal possession of some such station'. This force was to be in the command of Elliot's cousin, Admiral George Elliot, as Commander-in-Chief and Joint Plenipotentiary, acting with, but senior to, the Captain.

Opium and whisky

But did subsequent events constitute an 'opium war'? As far as the immediate events that led up to *Volage*'s broadsides are concerned there can be little dispute. The immediate cause of the hostilities was an attempt by Elliot to enforce his legitimate demands on British shipping by stopping the *Royal Saxon*; this had been preceded by his refusal to surrender a British subject to the processes of Chinese law, especially as it had not been possible to identify a guilty party; the British community had been forced into living on board ship, and the Chinese had threatened the destruction of these vessels, a threat which was interpreted by the British commander as imminent. This situation had arisen since the Chinese were insisting upon a bond so extreme in character that it was impossible for the British authorities to accept.

Both Lin and Elliot were doing their utmost to interpret the wishes of their governments and to manage things in a reasonable and equitable manner, although each according to his own, substantially different, standards. Elliot was in a particularly difficult situation owing to the procrastination of his masters in London, who would have much preferred to forget all about China. When the Whigs returned after the short-lived Peel government of 1834–5 the Napier débâcle must have caused Palmerston considerable embarrassment: an inquiry into his conduct of Chinese affairs, when all the facts had come to light, very nearly brought down his government. All the official documents originating in Britain on the matter – and there are not too many of them – breathe a strong desire that sleeping dogs should be left to lie. There were also more pressing matters to be dealt with in Europe and the Near East, so that the emerging problems in China were simply not addressed by the British government.

Inevitably, the Chinese stepped into the power gap. And by the 1830s China was no longer the force it had been under Ch'ien-lung two generations earlier; a consciousness of decline was beginning to be expressed. A contemporary Chinese scholar, Kung Tzu-chen, lamented: 'There are no talented chief ministers nor talented historians to assist the ruler. There are no talented generals in the army; there are no talented scholars in the schools . . . what is more, there are no talented petty thieves roaming the alleyways, no talented scoundrels in the markets, and no talented bandits in the marshes.'[65] Most Chinese, though, continued to see their country as it had once been, but was no longer. Lord Amherst had been turned away with contumely; the misguided Napier had received the dusty answers he provoked, and the more patient Elliot's efforts to establish reasonable communications ran into exactly the same bland refusal to accept anything like equality.

But opium was surely the root cause of the trouble? Lin might have based his policy upon a mistaken idea of barbarian power, but he would not have been charged with his task had not the illegal import of opium existed. This is undeniable, but the responsibility for allowing the trade to continue for thirty years, with the minimum of molestation, has to be shared between the rapacious merchants, who saw nothing indefensible in disregarding completely the laws of the country in which they chose to live, and the irresponsible officials, who protected the trade while taking huge sums of money from it. Certainly the British government at that time was not concerned to insist on the opium trade, as Palmerston made clear in his letter of 20 February 1840 to 'The Minister of the Emperor of China':

> ... the British Government would not have complained, if the Government of China, after giving due notice of its altered intentions [to enforce the laws against opium, instead of allowing them to continue 'a dead letter'] had proceeded to execute the Law of the Empire, and had seized and confiscated all the opium which they could find within the Chinese territory ... The Chinese Government had a right to do so, by means of its own officers, and within its own territory. But for some reason or other known only to the Government of China, the Government did not think proper to do this. But it determined to seize peaceable British Merchants, instead of seizing the contraband opium ...

What politicians say in public is perhaps an unreliable source of information on their real intentions, but in his private instructions to Elliot of the same date Palmerston makes it clear that he has no objection to the Chinese enforcing their own laws: the treaty Elliot is to negotiate should stipulate that 'if any British Subject shall introduce into China, Commodities which are prohibited by the Law of China, such Commodities may be seized and confiscated by the Officers of the Chinese Government'. But he must insist that 'in no case shall the Persons of British Subjects be molested on account of the importation or the exportation of Goods'. The Chinese must leave it to the British Superintendent's own court to adjudicate on any charges brought against British Subjects: that remained, as it had since the *Lady Hughes* case in 1784, the bitterest cause of dissension.

A year later, on 26 February 1841, Palmerston had changed his ground, and wanted Elliot to point out that life would be much simpler if opium was legalized: 'You will state that the admission of opium into China as an article of legal trade, is not one of the demands which you have been instructed to make upon the Chinese Government ... But you will point out that it is scarcely possible that a permanent good understanding can be maintained if the opium trade be allowed to remain upon its present footing.'[66]

The best proof that the trade in opium was not a primary concern of the British is to be found in the Parliamentary debates on the war, held between April and July 1840, after all the dispatches and papers were produced. The Tories had scented blood, knowing that the Whig government could barely summon a majority in the House of Commons, that Ministers had lost control, and that Melbourne himself was anxious only for retirement. A 'cry' that looked likely to 'dish the Whigs' was to be welcomed, and the conduct of affairs in China seemed to offer a real opportunity for winning a vote of censure. 'God, if it's carried they will go!' exclaimed the Duke of Wellington at a meeting of the party leaders on 18 March.[67] Anything that would contribute to this most important of ends would suffice; the near-victory that had precipitated the previous year's crisis had been over the suspension of the Jamaican constitution – 'Jamaica had been a good hare to start,' was Peel's comment when the votes were counted. The new opportunity was seized with equal cynicism, few Tories caring any more about the rights of China than those of Jamaica. If there had existed a general feeling against opium the Tories would have doubtless used it, but their attack was instead, and with a sound political instinct, based upon the mishandling by Palmerston of affairs in China, and in particular his failure to give adequate instructions to his man on the spot. The vote was a near thing, but the Whigs were able to fight off the motion with a majority, albeit of only nine votes. In so doing the 'War of Jenkins' Ear' of the previous century was referred to; in the same strain this conflict, begun by an attempt to arrest a British merchant, might have been named the 'War of Lancelot Dent's Collar'.

But whatever the immediate causes of the conflict, the awkward moral question arose of whether it was right for Britain to insist on forcing its view of how nations ought to conduct their affairs on China. *The Times* of 6 November 1840 put the case clearly: 'The fact is, that these overbearing pretences, by which we would summarily justify our interference, really mean . . . that civilized nations are so far higher in the scale of being than their uninstructed fellow-creatures, that they are privileged to make these latter mere instruments for the production of tea and crockery, and to cannonade them if they begin to slacken in their work.'

4

UNJUST TREATIES?

A protecting joss

The first stage of the conflict which, unintentionally and to general disappointment, culminated in the British acquisition of Hong Kong was supervised by Charles Elliot, as the representative of the British government with plenipotentiary powers. Officially, he had been joined with his cousin Admiral George – 'a good fellow, but I have no notion of his capacity . . . frightened to death of responsibility', Charles told his wife Clara – but Admiral George, constantly ill, left everything to young Charles, who was convinced that peace must be achieved as soon as possible, and on terms that would secure the future, with the use of the minimum possible force. Since he had undertaken to ensure that the merchants were paid for the opium they had surrendered, Elliot had to obtain an indemnity for at least that sum from the Chinese, but he was not willing to trade more lives for more money. And he was well aware that lost income could soon be recovered by the resumption of trade, which was therefore always a prime objective.

By his instructions to Elliot on 20 February 1840 Lord Palmerston had made it clear that he was thinking of a naval show of strength sufficient to impress the Chinese rather than anything in the nature of war. The small number – not much more than three thousand – of troops initially allocated would have been impossibly inadequate for anything more. These modest forces were in practice commanded by Commodore Sir Gordon Bremer, who had at his disposal three seventy-four-gun third rates, useful for engaging shore batteries, but unwieldy in narrow waters (two of them were quickly put out of action by a grounding at Chusan), two big frigates and a number of smaller vessels including some of the East India Company's armed steamers. There was no army officer of higher rank than Colonel Oglander, of the Cameronians, who died en route, and was replaced by an incompetent, Burrel of the 18th Foot (the Royal Irish), described by Jardine's interpreter Robert Thom as a 'haverel'.

Palmerston had ordered the expedition first to blockade the Pearl River, then 'to occupy the Tchusan Islands, and to blockade the Estuary opposite to those Islands; the Mouth of the Yang-Tse river, and the Mouth of the Yellow River' – which amounted to nothing less than a blockade of all China's major rivers. Finally, they were to go north to the Peiho River, at the approaches to Peking, and wait for an answer to Palmerston's demands. Since this programme could well be attempted without much in the way of bloodshed, which Elliot knew would prejudice future relations with China, the orders were faithfully obeyed. In June, leaving one frigate and some sloops to watch Canton, the rest of the force moved to Chusan. Here the fort which commanded Tinghai, the main town, surrendered after a preliminary bombardment of exactly nine minutes, the town itself being taken the next day without casualties on either side.

After securing Chusan, leaving the administration of justice in the dubious hands of Gutzlaff – 'a perfect farce' – the expedition sailed to the mouth of the Peiho river, or, to be more exact, as near to its mouth as it could get, which was some miles off. Palmerston had not appreciated that the Bay of Chihli, a shallow, muddy bight, is hardly a suitable place for a demonstration of naval power. Deep water is found only six miles out to sea from the estuary, at which distance the low-lying land is scarcely visible. The river is protected by a bar, and is navigable only by shallow-draft vessels. Elliot reconnoitred the entrance himself, in a ship's boat, and found that only the East India Company's steamer *Madagascar*, drawing twelve feet, could be used, as nothing larger could cross the bar. The naval squadron might have made a fine spectacle, but there was no one on land who could see it, and nothing for the guns to shoot at. Peking itself was over a hundred miles away, near enough to be irritated, but too far away to feel over-awed, by a small and invisible fleet.

In spite of the disadvantages, this demonstration was not without success, as a comparison of the dates of events and Imperial marginalia reveal. On 8 August Emperor Tao-kuang was issuing instructions to prosecute vigorously actions on all fronts against the British; from the ninth, when the British fleet appeared in the bay, a different tone appears. An Imperial kinsman of the highest rank, Ch'i-san (Kishen), a hereditary Marquis, Governor of Chihli province, was appointed to soothe the barbarians. When Palmerston's note was handed to Ch'i-san on the fifteenth the Emperor had already instructed him to receive it, in spite of any discourtesies the communication might contain. On the twenty-first, when the Emperor had received at least a sanitized version, he dashed off a furious reprimand to Lin in Canton: 'You are just making excuses with empty words – nothing has been accomplished but many troubles have been created. Thinking of these things I cannot contain my rage. What do you have to say now?'[1] Hitherto the Emperor had believed in Lin's reports of a succession of victories, and had supported his aggressive plans. Now, it seemed, all he had done was to irritate these inconveniently-close-at-hand barbarians. For the time being, to allow Peking to collect its thoughts, Ch'i-san was instructed to persuade Elliot to leave the sensitive north, and to return to Canton for further negotiations. Lin was to be replaced by Ch'i-san, who would take over in Canton in order to finalize an agreement. Since there was clearly little point in staying in Chihli, Elliot was prepared to comply. At Canton the forces he had would be in one place, apart from those left to garrison Chusan, of whom a worrying number had fallen ill, and could be deployed to the maximum advantage.

The four months' absence in Chihli had seen a rearrangement of the players on the Canton scene. Lin, although dismissed, was ordered to stay on at Canton to assist Ch'i-san. Admiral Elliot's health had finally failed, and he was forced to resign, leaving cousin Charles in command of the expedition and all British interests in China as sole Plenipotentiary. Bremer was temporarily absent in Calcutta, the naval command devolving on Captain Sir Humphrey le Fleming Senhouse. For the first time a competent general officer, Sir Hugh Gough, was appointed, but he would not arrive until February. When Ch'i-san reached Canton, ostensibly to conclude the negotiations he had begun at Chihli, it was clear that he had been told to play for time, and had been given little authority to negotiate. Neither, for that matter, had Elliot, but he did not intend that to impede a peaceful solution: he admitted to Lord Auckland, Governor-General of India and another of Elliot's cousins, that he proposed stopping 'far short of the demands of the government', but by doing so would avoid disrupting the trade, and the 'protraction of hostilities, with its certain consequence of deep hatred'.

By November the expeditionary force was regrouped on the Pearl

River, without some hundreds who had succumbed to malaria while in Chusan, but with six hundred sepoys of the 37th Madras Native Infantry and the steamer *Nemesis* added to their strength. *Nemesis* was the predecessor of the gunboats that were to follow, and a remarkable vessel. Designed to draw only six feet of water, she could penetrate the previously inaccessible shallow waterways, and carried a reasonable armament – two thirty-two-pounders and a rocket launcher, together with several lighter pieces. While this was only a fraction of the fire-power of the smallest man-of-war, *Nemesis* could sail anywhere a junk might go, and offer close support to landing parties. It is useful to remember that no senior Chinese official had yet seen at first hand what the Royal Navy could do. Deliberately or not, Lin had misreported the previous year's engagement at Ch'uen-pi as a Chinese victory; the restricted cannonad˄ at Chusan had been a local affair; and no one had seen more than the topmasts of the fleet at the Peiho. Even the peaceable Elliot realized that unmistakable proof of British power had to be given if Ch'i-san was to be persuaded to a settlement. He there-fore proposed to force the entrance to the Bogue, blocked by a massive chain, and destroy the forts that guarded it.

The operation took exactly one day, 7 January 1841, with no British killed. It was made possible by a rapid flanking attack on the forts, with three field guns being manhandled into position, and a simultaneous bombardment from the river, in which *Nemesis* played a crucial part. Delighted by the easy success over what should have been a strong position, and eager to go on to the forts next upstream, the sailors were disconcerted when Elliot – 'full of compunctious feelings, perhaps not unnatural'[2] – announced that that was to be as far as things would go. Ch'i-san appeared willing to settle, and Elliot was anxious to stop the one-sided fight as soon as possible. On 28 January 1841 the Pleni-potentiary felt able to announce the terms of preliminary arrangements, which became known as the Convention of Ch'uen-pi. As Elliot was well aware, the terms fell far short of those he had been instructed to demand. The first item was 'the cession of the island and harbour of Hong Kong to the British crown', but with a provision that duties should continue to be paid to the Chinese authorities. This was to be followed by arrangements for the payment of a $6 million indemnity, in six annual instalments, and 'direct official intercourse to be upon equal footing and the port of Canton opened'. There was no mention of opening other ports for trade, and, a point that later formed a serious charge against Elliot, the British were to evacuate Chusan.

Losing no time about at least making sure of Hong Kong, the British flag was hoisted there at 8.15 a.m. on 26 January 1841 by Captain Edward Belcher, R.N., of the *Sulphur*, and the Queen's health drunk with three hearty cheers. Elliot, from on board H.M.S. *Wellesley*, proclaimed that Hong Kong was now part of Her Majesty's dominions, and that he himself was exercising for the time being the government of the island.

Why did Captain Elliot, who was fully aware of Palmerston's likely hostile reaction to the Convention of Ch'uen-pi, specify that Hong Kong, of all places, should be ceded to the British? Certainly an 'insular station' of some sort had been considered a useful acquisition: it had to be, it was agreed, an island, which would present no problems of frontier pressures and inevitable further entanglements, and would be capable of protection by the Navy. No one cared to dispute Lord Macartney's judgement that 'The prospect of territory on the Continent of China . . . is too wild to be seriously mentioned.' One Indian empire was quite enough for a British government to have to worry about.

But what island was open to debate. Formosa was a favoured candidate, not only with British merchants, but later with the Americans, who cast covetous eyes upon it; and Captain Elliot expressed some enthusiasm for the Bonin Islands, more than a thousand miles away, between Japan and the Mariannas, but already, since 1827, a British possession. Palmerston had in mind Chusan or Ningpo, both well known and considerable ports at a time when the only community on Hong Kong was an insignificant fishing village. William Jardine advised the Foreign Secretary that possession should be taken of 'three or four islands, say Formosa, Quemoy and Amoy . . . also the great Chusan island', in order to force China into a treaty. It was the treaty, which would open ports other than Canton – Jardine suggested 'Ningpo, Shanghai and also Kiachow if we can get it' – that was important; the islands were only to be used for the purposes of negotiation.[3] Never a mention of Hong Kong, nor a suggestion that any captured territory should be permanently retained. Jardine and his fellow merchants were businessmen, not empire builders.

Only in the context of warlike operations on the Pearl River did Hong Kong become relevant: 'Should it be deemed necessary to possess ourselves of an island or harbour near Canton, the island of Hongkong might be taken,' but Jardine suggested that Formosa was really to be preferred. Even then Hong Kong was only one of many possibilities mentioned by Jardine; a spot nearer Canton might be better – Ch'uen-pi or Lintin. Other commercial opinion differed, being against, often vehemently against, territorial expansion. 'In a political or commercial point of view,' pontificated the *Chinese Repository*, 'no advantage would be gained from it whatever . . . Puerile indeed does appear the idea of influencing a great empire by the seizure of one of their petty islands: it has been fledged under leaden wings, and scarcely rises above the atmosphere of Boetian dullness.'⁴

Elliot, a career naval officer, saw things in a different perspective; it was the magnificent harbour, in which he had sheltered from the Chinese, that attracted him, as it had attracted Sir John Barrow, now Secretary to the Admiralty, on his voyage with Macartney. Barrow had available to him a recent survey which reported that 'Lycemoon [Lei Yu Mun, or Lyeemon, properly only the eastern entrance to Hong Kong harbour, but at that time used to describe the whole harbour] was . . . an excellent harbour for ships of any size, which might be defended against a superior force in time of war.'⁵ Accordingly, in November 1839 Barrow set out the reasons why Hong Kong was selected as a naval centre: 'It would be prudent, in the first instance, to confine the operation to Canton, to take possession of the island of Hong Kong, which is outside the Bocca Tigris, has a good road-stead for the anchorage of a multitude of ships, and plenty of fresh water. Here a few guns mounted, and men to work them, with a ship of war, would afford protection to merchant shipping.' Barrow also rather acidly pointed out that, should the Foreign Office not have noticed, 'Formosa was rather larger than Ireland', and might therefore be some-what troublesome to take and hold.⁶

But in his instructions to Elliot of 20 February 1840 Palmerston sketched a draft treaty which made it clear that the cession of an island was not essential: if the Chinese were willing to guarantee 'security and freedom of commerce to Her Majesty's subjects resident in China' and nominate ports where British subjects could live and trade without molestation, the British government would 'forgo the permanent pos-session of any Island'. The open ports should probably include 'Canton, Amoy, Fou-Tchow-Foo, Shang-Hae-Heen [Shanghai] and Ningpo'. A commercial treaty with China, which settled those points on which complaints had been raised, and opened more ports to trade, would be all that was needed. A colonial possession was a bother to look after, always likely to be seized in times of trouble by the jealous French or Americans, and would need expensively defending.

A year later, Palmerston was beginning to appreciate the merits of Barrow's advice, since his envoys, after having occupied Chusan, bombarded Amoy, and penetrated to the mouth of the Peiho, had been persuaded to return to Canton: in his letter to Elliot of 3 February 1841 he first mentions the suggestion that 'an Island at the Mouth of the Canton River, such as might serve as a depot and base for further operations . . . should be declared to be permanently annexed to the British Dominion, and placed under the protection of the British Crown'.

But Palmerston mentioned the suggestion only to disagree with it. If there had to be an 'Insular Station', 'it seems to Her Majesty's Government that an Island, somewhere on the Eastern Coast, and either in the Chusan Group, or not far from it, would, for all commercial purposes, be by far the best, because it would afford to British traders an opening to the wealthy and populous cities of the central part of the East Coast of China, and would give to British Commodities an easy access to the interior of the Chinese Empire'. Therefore, 'although it might be convenient also to have some secure Station at the Mouth of the Canton River, the main point to be gained is a position off the East Coast'. But it was up to the envoys themselves to choose whatever island they wished, and not to be fobbed off with what the Chinese chose to give them.

When Captain Elliot, after all these insistent demands for Chusan, or some other island off the east coast, came up with Hong Kong, Palmerston was furious, and the government thrown into confusion. Lord Ellenborough, for the opposition, took advantage. Did the government really intend to ratify the Ch'uen-pi agreement? Lord Melbourne said not. But had Hong Kong 'been taken possession of under the Treaty'? Lord Melbourne believed it had. And had Chusan been evacuated? Lord Melbourne did not know.[7] The Foreign Secretary took it out on Elliot; his angry report on the Plenipotentiary's misdeeds made to the Queen on 10 April 1841 stated: 'Viscount Palmerston has felt greatly mortified and disappointed at this result of the expedition to China . . . Captain Elliot seems to have wholly disregarded the instructions which had been sent to him, and even when, by the entire success of the operations of the Fleet, he was in a condition to dictate his own terms, he seems to have agreed to very inadequate conditions.'

The Queen transmitted Palmerston's feelings, with her usual profusion of emphases, to Uncle Leopold, King of the Belgians: 'The

Chinese business vexes us much, and Palmerston is deeply mortified at it. *All* we wanted might have been got, if it had not been for the unaccountably strange conduct of Charles Elliot (*not Admiral* Elliot, for he was obliged to come away from ill-health), who completely disobeyed his instructions and *tried* to get the *lowest* terms he could.' But there was a brighter side: 'The attack and storming of the Chorempee [Ch'uen-pi] Forts . . . was very gallantly done by the Marines, and immense destruction of the Chinese took place . . . Albert is so much amused at my having got the island of Hong Kong, and we think Victoria ought to be called Princess of Hong Kong in addition to Princess Royal.'[8]

Elliot had to go, and in a stiff letter of 21 April 1841 announcing his supersession, Palmerston was ironically dismissive about Hong Kong: 'You have obtained the Cession of Hong Kong, a barren island with hardly a house on it . . . Now it seems obvious that Hong Kong will not be a Mart of Trade . . . our Commercial Transactions, will be carried on as heretofore at Canton; but they [the British residents] will be able to go and build Houses to retire to, in the desert island of Hong Kong.'[9]

Both Palmerston in London and Elliot on the Pearl River had reasonable cases. The British government, in the delicate condition in which it found itself, needed both a visible success and its expenses reimbursed. With his long experience of negotiations the Foreign Secretary knew that in holding so large and strategic an island as Chusan he had a trump card to play in forcing an agreement out of the Chinese. By discarding his trump, Elliot had lost his chance of getting the money and the concessions; all he had to show for it was Hong Kong. Two years later, having recovered his equanimity, Lord Palmerston made this clear to Elliot. In a revealing document, previously unpublished, Elliot gave his account of the interview. Palmerston spoke in the most civil of terms: 'he spontaneously assured me of the deep regret it had occasioned him to recall me . . . He told me that he certainly should not have done so if I had not consented to restore to the Chinese, the island of Chusan which, according to his judgement, should have been held as a guarantee . . . I observed that I had not given up Chusan without taking a much more sufficient material guarantee in the steady possession of the Island of Hong Kong and the completely prostrate position of the City of Canton . . .'[10]

In the same interview Elliot explained why he, no politician but an experienced naval officer, had not wished to hold on to Chusan: 'Personal experience of Chusan had convinced me contrary to my previous predilections that it was a totally unsuitable position for our objects in China. The navigation . . . was perilous, and indeed almost impossible by any other than powerful steam vessels with reliability.' On the contrary, as he told Palmerston's successor at the Foreign Office, Lord Aberdeen, in his long report of 25 January 1842, a port such as Hong Kong had 'the advantages of a large and safe harbour, abundance of fresh water, ease of protection by Maritime ascendancy, and no more extent of Territory or Population than may be necessary for our convenience'.[11]

If Elliot could push ahead and establish a community there, satisfy the military and naval commanders that the island would make a suitable base, in the face of their preference for one nearer the Yangtse, and above all convince the merchants to invest there, the wisdom of his choice would be proved. But there was very little time left. Something like six months would be needed before London reacted – almost certainly angrily – to the news of his agreement with Ch'i-san at Ch'uen-pi. This was, therefore, the period the Plenipotentiary had available to establish a colony, during which he must also continue action against the Chinese. One precaution he took was to enlist the support of his kinsman Lord Auckland in India, writing from Macao a full explanation of his policy on 21 June 1841:

> I take the liberty to record my opinion, that a treaty which consigns British Merchants and Ships to the Ports of Amoy, Ning Po and Shang Hai Heen, will do no more than place very valuable hostages in the hands of an irritated Government, with what may be taken to be a certainty, that the impatience of our own Merchants, and the perfidy of the Chinese, will rapidly produce new troubles . . . It seems very plain to me . . . that Her Majesty's Government must keep the island of Hong Kong . . . and the immediate organization of the settlement upon a very firm and comprehensive footing, is not a question but in strictest terms a necessity . . .

But before the reaction from London arrived there was more fighting to be done. If the British government was likely to be annoyed with the Ch'uen-pi arrangements, the Chinese were certain to repudiate them, as Elliot later explained: 'Fully sensible of the possibility, not to say the probability, that Kishen would be disavowed by his court, I had taken good care to collect the whole force at Canton.' It quickly became apparent that the Chinese were going to renew hostilities as soon as possible. Forts were being manned, new batteries built, and barricades across the river prepared. By the end of February Elliot accepted that Ch'i-san was not going to be able to deliver his part of the Ch'uen-pi agreement, and that further encouragement would be needed. Chusan had been evacuated as promised (a move that much puzzled the Chinese, who could only see it as an enforced retreat), but the British forces available were still, allowing for those sick and in garrison, not many more than two thousand, supported now by two ships of the line, deadly against any enemy they could reach but incapable of penetrating to Canton. This would have to be done by the smaller craft, including the redoubtable *Nemesis*. The initial stages were straightforward; once more the Bogue was forced, and within thirty-six hours, in spite of the fortifications, the smaller warships had reached Whampoa. This must have been something of a shock for Lin, who was still at Canton, and had just written complacently in his diary that the English had been beaten off.

After a delay of some days, waiting unavailingly for the arrival of someone with whom to negotiate – Ch'i-san had been, as Elliot had expected, packed off to Peking in chains – the expedition pushed on, with the small craft, to Canton itself. There the English flag was raised once more over the factories and, yet again, the trade was opened. For three months business flourished, with the willing co-operation of the local authorities, and much to Elliot's satisfaction. Tea, in enormous quantities – more than half a million pounds a day – was loaded, the duties on which would in due course bring considerable income to the British Treasury, a consideration which Elliot kept always very much in mind. Little could be done to further negotiations since Ch'i-san's replacement, Yang-fang, 'did nothing but refer back to Peking the questions which had been referred from Peking for settlement at Canton'.

With legitimate trade, opium made its reappearance. Elliot made a vain effort to stop the inflow of the drug, asking the senior naval officer for help in so doing. This Sir Humphrey Senhouse indignantly refused. It was asking him 'to act as head of the Chinese revenue and river police', he complained to his absent colleague Bremer. Senhouse was justified in this by Palmerston's doctrine that the Navy had no authority to interfere with a perfectly legitimate – in British law – item of commerce, and if the Chinese wanted to stop it, that was their business.

British forces would not protect the smugglers, but neither would they interfere with them.

This state of affairs could not last for long, since Chinese reinforcements were on their way with instructions to attack the foreigners now so conveniently assembled within the Tiger's Mouth, and to 'cut off their rear, close in all sides, and recover Hong Kong'; the Emperor awaited 'the news of victory with the greatest impatience'. The attack came on 21 May, and very nearly succeeded, as fireships descended on the moored warships and masked batteries opened fire. Once again *Nemesis*, with her mobility and firepower, was invaluable in saving the situation; the few casualties included the New York harbourmaster's son, captured and murdered near the factories. A swift advance on the city itself was then ordered.

It is worth noting that with a force of 2,395 – sepoys, soldiers, Marines and bluejackets – the army commander, Major-General Sir Hugh Gough, who had during forty-six years' service fought his way right through the Peninsular War and therefore knew what he was about, was confident of being able to subdue a city of a million or so inhabitants, defended by at least twenty thousand troops and a militia numbering tens of thousands. He had already – it took only a few minutes and cost the British one man killed and the Chinese, who left precipitately, very few more – stormed the outlying forts, and was in position on the city wall itself when, to the absolute fury of the British commanders, the action was suddenly brought to an end. 'At dawn, the ominous white flag was again displayed, and for some hours there had been repeated cries of "Elliot, Elliot" as if he had been their protecting joss.'[12] Once again Captain Elliot had, or thought he had, reached a settlement.

This time Elliot's terms were rather more onerous, but still well below those he had been instructed to obtain: the $6 million was to be paid on the nail, plus compensation for further damages. Elliot's motives at this critical time were complex. Uppermost, with the humanity he always showed, was the desire to avoid bloodshed. This he made clear in his instructions to his exasperated and uncomprehending commanders: 'the protection of the people of Canton, and the encouragement of their goodwill towards us, are perhaps our chief political duties in this country'. He may also have been, as Gough certainly was not, apprehensive about holding a presumably rebellious city against a turbulent countryside and an advancing Imperial army. Chinese writers have made much of the only occasion when armed villagers attacked a British force, and the battle of San-yuan-li is found in all Chinese textbooks. In fact, all that happened was that on 29 May 1841 a company of some sixty Indian sepoys with three British officers was cut off outside Canton and surrounded. For some time they fought off several hundred attackers, losing one killed and some wounded, until they were rescued by two companies of Royal Marines. General Gough commended the sepoys, and remained confident that there would be no serious trouble from the Chinese, regulars or irregulars.[13]

The crucial factor limiting Elliot's choices may well have been the depth of the Pearl River. It took the powerful threat of a battleship's guns trained on Nanking to force a settlement in the following year, but a ship of the line could not get near Canton. In 1841, with only small craft able to offer support, an occupying army in Canton would have been perhaps dangerously exposed; by 1857, with the new gunboats able to steam right up to the city and all around the West River channels, the situation had changed.

Captain Elliot has been much criticized by military historians for his readiness to call a halt to offensive actions, but whatever the merits of his policies in the spring and summer of 1841, his recall had already been decided upon. Lord Auckland's sister, Emily Eden, had observed to her brother that cousin Charles 'means to show the world &c. how right he has been. I foresee a long life of pamphlets don't you?'[14] But Captain Elliot was no pamphleteer. He left Hong Kong on the S.S. *Clyde* on 10 August, with a cordial message from James Matheson, enclosing an official address of thanks from the Chamber of Commerce: 'It is, however, a satisfaction to us, to give vent to the feelings at the moment of your departure . . . I still intend seeing you off [from Macao].'[15] And at Bombay another testimonial was waiting from Jeejeebhoy, which showed how Elliot's qualities of restraint and consideration had been appreciated in some quarters: 'How greatly does it redound to your Honour that you have always been on the side of Mercy, and have sought rather to lead and reason with the Chinese people, than crush and overwhelm them by the Power of British Arms.'[16]

Once back in London the Captain set about establishing his case with the new government; Lord Melbourne's Whigs had been replaced by the Tories under Peel. Elliot's conscience was clear, public opinion was largely on his side, and he appeared quite relaxed. Greville's description of him does not sound like that of a man seeking to justify his actions; he was 'animated, energetic, and vivacious, clever, eager,

high-spirited and gay'. The diarist recorded that Elliot 'was very amusing with his accounts of China . . . I am inclined to think that he will
be able to vindicate his latest exploit at Canton . . . He puts as much
blame on the Admiral and General as they on him . . . he treats them,
and their notions . . . with great contempt. He also disapproves of the
course we are meditating and says that we are wrong to think of waging
war with China in any way but by our ships, and, above all, should
wish to establish diplomatic relations with her.'[17]

It was to be expected that the Tories would back Elliot; they had,
after all, made the point that it was Palmerston who had let down his
man on the spot, who had himself behaved with admirable firmness.
Sir Robert Peel stated in Parliament that he 'reposed the highest confidence in [Elliot's] integrity and reliability'. Even the defeated Whigs
were understanding; Charles Villiers (later Lord Clarendon) wrote:
'Melbourne praised Elliot in a very becoming manner.' Sir John Barrow
approved, and the Directors of the East India Company awarded a
nomination to one of Elliot's sons. Elliot thought of also enlisting the
help of Lord Ripon, then President of the Board of Control, 'but he
would just grin like a seal, and bob about from leg to leg, and dismiss
the whole matter'. Such support was hardly needed, for Villiers went
on to record the award to Captain Elliot of the ultimate accolade: 'the
Duke of Wellington upheld his character and conduct, and took a
review of his difficulties in a far higher and more masterly tone than
has yet been done either in or out of Parliament. Upon such matters
he is the authority of the country and Elliot may henceforth laugh at
his detractors.'[18]

Elliot was obliged to stay in London in order to tidy up his opium
accounts with the Treasury. That department, never famous for speed,
did eventually – in 1846 – agree that Elliot had properly, even admirably, prepared his accounts. Even if opinions differed on his actions
in China, Elliot's record during his next position, as chargé d'affaires in
the Republic of Texas, indicates his engaging combination of personal
charm and courage. He quickly won the respect of both Samuel Houston and Anson Jones, Presidents of the Republic.[19] After Texas Elliot
dropped out of public attention. He was given a series of second-rank
colonial appointments, as Governor of Bermuda, Trinidad and
St Helena before retiring in modest glory, an admiral and a knight.
The last word could be left to his old antagonist Ch'i-san, who had
also survived the wrath of his employers, and had likewise been posted
to the most distant part of the Chinese empire. A French traveller,

the Abbé Huc, came across Ch'i-san in Lhasa, in Tibet. They talked
of the war; Ch'i-san supposed the British had cut off Elliot's head: 'A
dreadful fate that of poor Elut; he was a good man.'[20]

Guns at the Porcelain Tower

Breathing flames of wrath at Elliot, Palmerston looked for a man less
troubled by a tender conscience or undue regard for Chinese susceptibilities, who could be relied upon briskly to finish the job. He found
Sir Henry Pottinger, formerly political agent of the East India Company
in Sind, ready to hand in London. Pottinger was an Ulsterman, energetic, handsome, amorous, with a thick Irish brogue, fond of having
his own way and not suffering much in the way of disagreement. He
was quick to make friends and enemies; his affection for the Manchu
negotiator Ch'i-ying, and his distaste for the British trading community, both became noteworthy. The commanders who had to work
with him, although they appreciated his combativeness after Elliot's
humanitarian hesitations, had occasion to complain about his fondness
for 'extraordinary powers and salutes'. Neither Gough nor Admiral
Parker, who commanded the naval force after Senhouse's death, were
particularly difficult to work with, and their complaints were tactfully
worded, but revealing. Parker recorded: 'Sir Henry Pottinger is an
able diplomat, whose decision and firmness has been well calculated
for his functions here, but from his long services in India, he has
possibly acquired the habit of exercising his authority in a manner to
which we are unaccustomed in Europe.'[21] Pottinger had been in the
Company's army since 1804, but since 1825 had been in the political
service, first as Resident and later as Agent in Sind, the region of the
lower Indus Valley, not then part of British India. As Political Agent
Pottinger had forcefully represented British interests, and had been
particularly successful in browbeating the native rulers into allowing
passage to a British army en route for an invasion of Afghanistan. For
these services he was rewarded with a baronetcy on his retirement
from India in 1840.

Lord Melbourne, telling Queen Victoria of Elliot's recall and Pottinger's appointment on 3 May 1841, described Pottinger as being 'distinguished in the recent operations in Afghanistan',[22] a country where
Sir Henry had never set foot, although his nephew, Eldred Pottinger,
had recently made himself famous there. In spite of that, Henry was

RIGHT: The French were in no doubt of the malevolent intentions of the Royal Navy in forcing opium upon the Chinese.

BELOW: The Dent schooner-rigged clipper *Eamont*. A 64-lb long gun was carried between the masts, together with smaller ordnance. The Dent house flag is also flown on the brigantine-rigged vessel in the background, probably *Eamont* herself, differently sparred.

FOOT: The first part of a scroll, probably printed in London from sketches made on the spot, purports to show Pottinger's first expedition leaving Hong Kong in August 1842. The artist may have had some guidance as to the hills above Victoria, but the buildings, and the quay, are entirely imaginary.

Chief Justice Hulme, 'anything but grave, flinging his long skinny legs, encased in breeches and black silk stockings, in all directions... having anything but a judge-like appearance', sketched by Surgeon Edward Cree dancing a hornpipe with Tung, 'a Manchu Tartar'.

Jardine Matheson's establishment at East Point, c.1845. The original shoreline has long been lost under successive reclamation schemes.

Ch'i-ing's formal reception in Hong Kong, November 1845. The portly Gutzlaff is interpreting before Ch'i-ing and Sir John Davis, who is dwarfed by the substantial Commissioner. Frederick Bruce is on the left, with Caine in front. General d'Aguilar is on Ch'i-ing's right, and the naval officer to the left of Davis is Admiral Sir Thomas Cochrane, who succeeded Parker in command. Appointed Captain at the age of seventeen, Cochrane had benefited by one of the most flagrant examples of naval nepotism.

RIGHT: The always-soldierly
Colonel Caine, towards the
end of his career.

BELOW: A satirical comment on
the loans raised to fund the
Greek War of Independence in
1826. Bowring, as Secretary to
the London Committee, was
involved in some very dubious
personal transactions connected
with the loan.
Left to right: Joseph Hume M.P.,
Bowring, Edward Ellice M.P.,
Sir Francis Burdett M.P.,
John Cam Hobhouse M.P., and
Alexander Galloway, the
incompetent engineer whose
steam vessels never managed to
reach the new Greek navy.

ABOVE: Chinese merchants' lorchas. The *Arrow* was one of these interesting vessels, the forerunners of modern junk-rigged yachts.

BELOW: This *Punch* cartoon of August 1848 shows Thomas Chisholm Anstey, then M.P. for Youghal, as father of innumerable parliamentary bills, motions and amendments which stood little chance of success.

probably the right Pottinger – since it was Palmerston, advised by Lord Auckland, rather than the Prime Minister who had made the choice, it was probable that the confusion existed only in Melbourne's mind, never noted for its grasp of detail. For the purposes of speedily finishing off the war Palmerston had found the right man. In 1834 Lord William Bentinck had been taken aback by Pottinger's fiery dispatches from Sind, as he bullied the Princes into submission, and exhorted the Indian government to 'carry Fire and Sword throughout Afghanistan' – a task easier to recommend than to achieve. Bentinck felt that a warning note was required, and recommended 'the natural fitness at all times, when a strong and enlightened power has to do with a weak and ignorant one, to forbear rather to a fault and only to put forth the effective argument of your strength as the very last resource'.[23]

As far as China was concerned Pottinger had no intention of accepting this advice – although he might well have thought that an expeditionary force, even if one now increased to eight thousand effectives, was hardly excessive to subdue a nation of some three hundred millions. Putting forth 'the effective argument' of whatever strength was available right from the start was, however, just what Palmerston wanted, and Pottinger did not disappoint him.

This time there was to be no shilly-shallying, no tender-hearted avoidance of casualties. Emily Eden commented that 'The Chinese news is already better since Charles [Elliot] and Sir Gordon [Bremer] came away. Sir H. Pottinger began in the right way . . . The Chinese by their proclamations seem thoroughly frightened. The General and all the Navy people seem to be in ecstasies at having somebody who will not stop all their fighting, and I should not be surprised if Sir H. Pottinger finished it all in six months, by merely making war in a common straightforward manner.'[24] It took ten rather than six months, but otherwise Miss Eden's forecasts were correct. But, even before Pottinger reached Hong Kong on his first visit, on 21 August 1841, pausing only for a few hours on his way to attend to affairs in the north, a new government had taken office in London. Twelve years of Whig rule, broken only by the Wellington—Peel entr'acte of 1835, had been brought to an end by a general election in June decisively won by the Tories.

Melbourne's Cabinet had been showing symptoms of terminal decay – 'so melancholy a picture of indecision, weakness and pusillanimity', Greville called it – and finances were getting worse, the 1841–2 budget calling for a million and a half pounds more in expenditure than for the previous year. After several defeats on minor matters the government lost on a motion of confidence, and was forced to go to the country. Its subsequent defeat was something of a relief to Lord Melbourne, who had by then almost given up any pretence of leading his party. Sir Robert Peel was asked to take over, and this time there were no difficulties with the Queen, who now had Prince Albert to give her a new confidence.

Lord Aberdeen, the new Foreign Secretary, was not one of the more scintillating figures of nineteenth-century politics, and is today remembered mainly for the mismanagement of the Crimean War that took place under his premiership in the following decade. Gladstone was deeply attached to Aberdeen, but others were less generous. He was said to have 'a sneering tone' in debate; Palmerston referred to the 'antiquated imbecility of his principles'; Disraeli, never the most charitable of men, wrote of him that 'his temper, naturally morose, has become licentiously peevish . . . with the crabbed malice of a maundering witch'.[25] If that description was ever accurate, it was not so in 1841, but it has to be admitted that Aberdeen lacked many of the qualities possessed by his predecessor. He was almost a direct opposite of Palmerston – reserved, studious, conciliatory to the point of dithering: being preoccupied with the usual troubles with France, he adopted a policy of judicious inaction towards China, leaving the conduct of affairs there to the Indian authorities. The new Secretary for War and the Colonies, Lord Stanley, had the qualities of easy charm that Aberdeen lacked, but remained chiefly interested in Ireland, bothering himself little about Chinese affairs.

Since it took some months for Pottinger to learn of the change of government, he proceeded energetically to ensure that Lord Palmerston's demands were unequivocally enforced. The new Plenipotentiary's wholehearted acceptance of these instructions is shown in his report to the Foreign Office before the final move on Nanking in April 1842. Pottinger wrote in full-blown imperial style: 'The time strikes me to be fast approaching when the Chinese must bend or break. In the latter case it will rest with the Queen of England to pronounce what ports, or portion of the sea coast of China shall be added to Her Majesty's dominions.'[26]

From the military point of view the 1841–2 expedition was impeccable, a textbook example of how a small expeditionary force, backed by sea-power, can subjugate an empire. And this time there was no compassionate Plenipotentiary to call a halt to operations just as they were about to become decisive: in fact the military had to restrain the fiery Sir Henry from giving the order to loot the town of Ningpo, when it seemed that some resistance might be offered: 'The most annoying thing you could do,' advised the sagacious Gough, 'is to prove to the people by our moderation and our justice that our characters are foully belied.' Parker sided with Pottinger, and wrote privately to Lord Aberdeen on 5 February 1842: 'It causes me great regret to have to allude to any difference of opinion with either of my colleagues . . . but H.G. disagrees with H.P. and myself on seizing Private Merchandise as Ransom or Impost . . . I suspect that the General is disinclined to force payment from individuals.'[27]

The details of the campaign are peripheral to the history of Hong Kong, although the treaties that ended it are of the first importance. The fighting was generally much fiercer than that under Elliot, but while the Manchu forces fought desperately, they were badly led, and never committed in sufficient numbers. Perhaps twenty thousand regulars, and many more militia, were available, but only a few thousand were ever deployed in an action: they inevitably took heavy casualties, and their defeat was a grave blow to Chinese confidence. The critical factor was the arrival of the *Cornwallis*, towed with great effort up the Yangtse, which moored in the river off Nanking on 4 August 1842. Only a third-rate, and obsolescent at that, her firepower was nevertheless, by the standards of any land army in the world at that time, tremendous; unassailably blocking the great river, and the Grand Canal to Peking, she cut off the most important communications of the Empire.

The lessons of this conflict were then, and have always since been, misunderstood by the Chinese. Seeking for an explanation of British successes, spies gathered information from some unlikely sources. One of the first reports was that of an agent to Ch'i-san's agents, who had been told by an English lady that the British ships were strongly constructed of hard woods such as oak or teak, and the guns they carried were made of brass, weighed eight thousand pounds and fired thirty-two-pound shot. He added that apparently the British were ruled by a woman, that twenty families were related to her, that women found their own husbands, and that the barbarians were completely lacking in ritual or discipline. Emperor Tao-kuang was impressed, and noted approvingly 'Very clear and detailed.'[28] Since that time it has been almost invariably assumed that the Western victories were simply due to superior hardware, and that once China had mastered these specific techniques that temporary disadvantage would disappear. This is only true in part, and misunderstanding the facts led to much wasted effort and recriminations by later Chinese governments.

In naval matters British superiority was undeniable, although it should be realized that, with the exception of the little steamers, which were used mainly as tugs, transports and army support vessels, neither British warships nor their guns had changed much since Charles I built the 100-gun *Sovereign of the Seas* in 1637. But they had developed in a specifically Atlantic shipbuilding tradition, very different from those of the China seas. Chinese shipbuilding techniques had evolved to suit local factors, of which the most limiting was the scarcity of timber. Junks were therefore constructed, although along sophisticated and highly developed lines, but without the very strong scantlings needed to support a battery of heavy guns (not, as it happened, of brass, but of iron). It should have been possible however for Chinese shore batteries to inflict devastating damage on unarmoured wooden vessels, as indeed they were to do on one occasion (the action off the Taku forts in 1859, when a squadron of steam gunboats was decisively repulsed). Chinese gun manufacture was well established, and capable of producing excellent weapons of great size, such as the nine-ton, twenty-seven-inch brass mortar brought to Woolwich in 1845. These fortress pieces were smooth-bore muzzle-loaders operating on exactly the same principles as Western weapons.

On land the superiority was not so evident. In 1842 the opposing cavalry and infantry fought with similar weapons, which would in a few years be obsolete. Most of the British infantry were armed with the flintlock smooth-bore muzzle-loading musket of .753 bore, essentially the same weapon as that used at the Battle of Blenheim in 1704. A minority – the Marines and some of the British regiments – had the same weapon fitted with percussion ignition, which made for easier use in wet weather, although the rate of fire and the range (at best two hundred yards) were unchanged. Chinese infantry relied on matchlocks, as had Cromwell's, but their greatest deficiency was in mobile artillery, their field-pieces, the gingalls, being considerably smaller than the British six-pounders. Even so, much of the fighting was done with the simplest of weapons on both sides – bayonets, swords and pikes.

The most important differences between the armies lay in training, discipline and communications. It might well be said that the most significant items of British military hardware were not weapons, but such items as the signal flag, the pocket watch and the level. Whereas

British operations were planned in some detail, and accurately synchronized, only the most senior Chinese carried a watch, and their timings were of the vaguest. Wherever a British ship or an Engineer officer went accurate maps and charts were made: Chinese commanders had to rely on local opinion. But training and discipline, which in spite of reports to the contrary the barbarians possessed in abundance, were decisive. In emergencies junior British officers and NCOs knew where they were expected to be and what they were expected to do; difficulties were contained, and not allowed to develop into disasters.

An example of how devastating simple disciplined action could be is given by Lieutenant Ouchterlony, describing how the Chinese attack on Ningpo on 9 March 1842 was repelled after an artillery piece had been brought into action:

> It had only been fired three times ... the infantry party had resumed their platoon fire, the front rank, after discharging their pieces, filing off to the rear right and left to load and form again in the rear, their places being filled by the next rank, and so on; by which means ... in a short time the street was chocked up, and when, for want of a living mark, the men were ordered to advance, their steps fell upon a closely packed mass of dead and dying of fully fifteen yards.[29]

Even had the discrepancies in arms (which must have been countered to some extent by the superior Chinese numbers) been evened out, it is highly probable that similar results would have been obtained; the troops of Oliver Cromwell or Gustavus Adolphus, armed only with the weapons of their time, but well-trained and disciplined, would have been, in similar circumstances, equally successful.

A further error made by the Chinese was to assume that peasant levies might do better than regular forces, and the legend of San-yuan-li was invented to justify this belief. Since the Red Army, which developed into the People's Liberation Army, was originally itself a peasant-based force, and was successful against the more professionally led Kuomintang armies, the legend has become part of accepted orthodoxy, although it has repeatedly proved to be a dangerous illusion – most recently by the heavy casualties sustained during the unsuccessful border war with Vietnam in the 1980s.

The Poppy War is ended

H.M.S. *Cornwallis* never needed to fire her guns, for, faced with what would have been the certain destruction of Nanking, the Chinese were obliged to negotiate. 'How completely abominable!' the Emperor had exclaimed when Pottinger's demands for an envoy with plenipotentiary powers was received on 9 July 1842, but on consideration Tao-kuang agreed to send two mandarins of high rank to Nanking, empowered to agree on compensation, diplomatic equality, and the opening of further ports to trade. Yilipu (I-li-pu) was the senior of the two, but was in such poor health and spirits that most of the work was left to his colleague. Ch'i-ing (Keying in contemporary British documents, Qiying in pinyin) was a close friend and near relative of the Emperor, a descendant of Nurhaci, a hereditary Marquis and a central figure in nineteenth-century Chinese history. He has been reviled by genera-tions of Chinese writers as one who sold out to the British in the selfish interests of the dynasty, but in fact the realistic and personable Manchu ably negotiated a settlement, or more accurately a series of settlements, which might well have lasted for longer than it did, and was nothing like the one-sided arrangement so often portrayed. From his first appearance Ch'i-ing impressed the foreigners: 'graceful, digni-fied in carriage . . . a stout, hale, good-humoured looking old gentle-man with a firm step and an upright carriage'.[30]

At Nanking, with the British forces having demonstrated their power to occupy the two greatest cities in the Empire after Peking, there was little choice for the Chinese negotiators but to accede to Pottinger's demands. Ch'i-ing explained the situation to the Emperor: 'We are governed at every hand by the inevitable . . . what we have been doing is to choose between danger and safety, not between right and wrong . . . But the spirit of the invaders is running high. They occupy our important cities.'[31] The British terms were those set out originally by Palmerston: the cession of Hong Kong (this on Sir Henry's own initiat-ive, and against his latest orders from Lord Aberdeen) and the opening of five ports to foreign trade – Amoy, Foochow, Ningpo and Shanghai, as well as Canton, where consuls were to be appointed, responsible for controlling trade and their own citizens, who would be subject to consular rather than Chinese law. All future correspondence was to be as between equal powers, and a much larger sum of compensation than the $6 million required by Elliot was demanded – $21 million, an amount far exceeding the costs of the expeditions, the Hong debts, and the surrendered opium put together. It had been decided in White-hall that the $6 million already collected by Elliot was a ransom for Canton, and accordingly accrued as a windfall to the British Treasury.

Whether the final assessment could be calculated in quite such clear accountancy terms is less clear. Elliot had obtained $6 million and Hong Kong at the cost of a dozen or so British lives – not counting those who died of cholera or malaria – and perhaps two thousand Chinese. The extra $15 million was purchased at the cost of hundreds of British and many more thousands of Chinese dead, the result of Pottinger's obedience to Palmerston's instructions, and left a legacy of resentment that has not yet been dissipated. Of the vexed opium question there was not the slightest mention in the treaty agreement: 'Such omission may perhaps provoke the trite remark of its resemblance to performing the Tragedy of Hamlet and leaving out the part of the Prince', the *Friend of China* tartly commented.

When the Nanking agreement is taken in conjunction with the sup-plementary treaty negotiated the following year between Pottinger and Ch'i-ing the facts seem not to support the terms as particularly unjust or exorbitant. The British commanders were concerned not to appear in the light of an invading army; they had not only not been obstructed by the populace during the move to Nanking, but had found it easy to recruit assistance. When souvenir-hunting servicemen chipped pieces off Nanking's famous Porcelain Tower 'a fine row was made' about 'the serious public effect that must result from these outrages, to say nothing of the regret that all reflecting persons must feel at the wanton destruction of a building of such celebrity'.[32] An armed guard was set, and compensation of $4,000 paid.[33] (Fifteen years later the tower was indeed 'wantonly destroyed', but by the Chinese in the course of the Taiping rebellion.) The discussions themselves struck a cheerful note;[34] Hope Grant, Lord Saltoun's Brigade Major, observed that the 'high and mighty Chinese commissioners seemed to relish the maraschino, noyau and cherry brandy wonderfully – so much that one of them took Mr Gutzlaff our interpreter, a great broad-faced Pole, and with drunken endearment kissed him heartily.'[35] A naval observer recorded that 'Old K [Ch'i-ing] must have taken fifty large glasses of wine at least', and sang a song. 'What do you think of that, the Emperor's uncle singing a song?' But when Pottinger expressed a desire to visit Nanking 'the Chinese refused, and Sir Henry Pottinger naturally yielded'.

The final ceremony that took place on 29 August 1842, in the great cabin on the *Cornwallis*, was amicable enough, as observed by the young Harry Parkes – who was in fourteen years' time to be responsible, with John Bowring, for starting another, more damaging, war. Having been given Sir Hugh Gough's 'terrible large cocked hat and feathers' to look after, the fourteen-year-old Parkes described how Ilipu, the aged and ailing Chinese negotiator 'was met at the gangway by Sir Henry, the Admiral, and the General, who partly carried and partly supported him into the after cabin, where he was laid on a sofa'. When the Treaty was signed, 'they all sat down to tiffin . . . Each party seemed satisfied and pleased with each other.'[36] Surgeon Edward Cree admired the Tartar guard, 'fine, dark, weatherbeaten men with foxes' or squirrels' tails in their caps and every fifth man an officer with a banner'.[37]

News of the Treaty was received without much enthusiasm in England. It suffered by arriving, on 22 November, in the same mail as reports from Afghanistan that the Khyber Pass had been forced, Kabul taken and its Great Bazaar burnt. Nanking was much less exciting, and Lord Stanley, forwarding the dispatches to the Queen, although getting in a dig at the Whigs for having started the war, was forced into bathos: 'In China a termination has been put to the effusion of blood by the signature of a treaty . . . which has opened to British enterprise the commerce of China to an extent which it is almost impossible to anticipate. It may interest your Majesty to hear that already enquiries are made in the city for superintendents of ships to trade to Ningpo direct.'[38] *Punch* observed, wryly and prophetically:

The poppy war is ended . . . The war, 'bequeathed by the Whigs' to Sir ROBERT PEEL, returns to the minister . . . a very handsome profit on the ball and powder expended in this great moral lesson on the uneducated Chinese . . . The dollars, however, are a minor advantage. John BULL, having expended so much powder and ball, and applied so much cold iron, to the Chinese, is in future to be treated like a gentleman. He has washed out the 'barbarian' in the blood of two or three thousand bipeds . . . Besides the dollars and civility, we are to have five Chinese ports open to English commerce. Politicians and bagmen may exult at this, and in the anticipative eye of profit, already see the Emperor of China clothed in a Manchester shirt, and his wives in Manchester cotton, and the whole of his court handling Sheffield knives and forks.[39]

Peel's new government had been reluctant to decide what might be done about Hong Kong until the war was settled. Pressed on the subject in the House of Commons by Mr R. J. Blewitt, Whig Member for Monmouth, the Prime Minister tetchily answered: 'Really, during the progress of hostilities in China, I must decline to answer such a question' (15 March 1842). Lord Aberdeen blew hot and cold over the future of the island: in his letter to Pottinger of 4 November 1841 the Foreign Secretary had envisaged Hong Kong, as well as Chusan, only as temporary bases, the surrender of which might be used to gain concessions from the Chinese:

> Her Majesty's Government do not feel disposed to regard any such acquisitions in the light of a permanent conquest. It would rather be their desire that the commercial intercourse of Her Majesty's subjects with the Chinese Empire should be secured by means of a Treaty granting permission to trade with four or five of the principal towns on the East Coast of China . . .
> In addition to the Island of Hong Kong, it is probable that Chusan will again have been occupied by Her Majesty's forces . . . But the permanent retention of these possessions under the dominion of the Crown, would be attended with great and certain expense . . . It would also tend to bring us more in contact politically with the Chinese than is at all desirable; and might ultimately lead, perhaps unavoidably, to our taking part in the contest and changes which at no distant period may occur among this singular people, and in the Government of the Empire.

Lord Aberdeen went on to establish a principle which subsequent British governments continued to observe: 'A secure and well regulated trade is all we desire; and you will constantly bear in mind that we seek for no exclusive advantages, and demand nothing that we shall not willingly see enjoyed by the Subjects of all other States.' The corollary of this was that Britain would expect to share equally in any advantages offered to other countries – the 'most-favoured nation' clause that became a feature of all such treaties.[40]

This was neither pure altruism nor economic imperialism, but an example of the almost religious fervour with which most British politicians of either party believed in the doctrine of free trade. Unfettered international commerce, it was believed, would advantage all countries alike, lead to universal prosperity and better understanding and go far to abolish disputes and war. Since Britain was by some way the largest trading nation it might benefit most, but only as long as it could hold its own in fair competition. Later British administrations only deviated from this doctrine in the 1890s, when it became apparent that other nations were not playing the game by the same set of rules, and when, British industries being overtaken by others, the advantages of protection were clearer.

Aberdeen's instructions were amplified in January 1842. Hong Kong was not to be thought of as a permanent British possession, but only as a bargaining counter, 'a place militarily occupied, and liable to be restored to the Chinese Government on the attainment of the objects which Her Majesty's Government seek from China'. Therefore the island 'should be considered a mere military position and . . . all buildings and constructions not required in that light should be immediately discontinued'. Aberdeen was nervous lest the Chinese should find a settlement at Hong Kong a cause for future aggression, since 'not only commercial establishments, but the necessary permanent garrison, would be a constant provocation and temptation'. If trade, which was the important point, could be secured without the expense and trouble of a colony, so much the better.

At this stage Hong Kong might well have been allowed to revert to China, but Pottinger had been converted to Elliot's point of view: 'The retention of Hong Kong is the only single point in which I intentionally exceeded my modified instructions [those of 4 November 1841] but every hour I passed in this superb country has convinced me of the necessity and desirability of our possessing such a settlement.'[41] Some, both Chinese and British, found this inexplicable. Sir James Urmston, former President of the Select and later Chairman of the Court, continued to press the case for Chusan, and complained that Hong Kong 'has been most unaccountably . . . praised and puffed-up . . . it is not only, in its present state and condition, an utterly useless island to us, in a commercial point of view, but it is hopeless to imagine or expect, that it can ever be rendered capable of becoming an emporium'.[42] The Chinese were indeed in no position to object to the cession of a more desirable spot; when the British demands were presented the Chinese negotiators merely remarked – and not ironically – 'Is that all?'

It was not until 4 January 1843 that the British government decided to keep Hong Kong. In his letter to Pottinger of that date acknowledging the receipt of the Treaty of Nanking, Aberdeen conceded that, 'as soon after the exchange of the Ratifications as may be convenient, you will assume the Government of the Island of Hong Kong, then become a Possession of the British Crown . . . You will thenceforward administer the Government of the Island and make all arrangements for its defence against foreign aggression.' The ratification did not reach Hong Kong until June, and the formal exchange took place on the twenty-sixth of that month.

An umpire between the empires

Before Sir Henry's diplomatic task was over all the loose ends left in the Treaty of Nanking needed to be tidied up. There were no fewer than four supplementary instruments in the peace settlement: a declaration on transit duties, amplifying Article II; on Free Trade, amplifying Article X; the General Regulations of Trade; and the Supplementary Treaty. It took many months for these to be completed; negotiations started in the New Year of 1843 and continued until 8 October, when the Supplementary Treaty, commonly known as the Treaty of the Bogue, was signed. Chinese opinion, deeply resentful of later humiliations imposed by foreigners, has classed the Treaty of Nanking together with other agreements as an 'unequal treaty', unjust and unapproved of by the people, and with no validity. The argument is doubtful in international law, and successive Chinese governments, while maintaining this stand, have in practice conscientiously fulfilled treaty obligations. Foreign governments, the beneficiaries of these agreements, have gradually renegotiated their terms so that by the end of World War II all foreign leases and concessions had been revoked, apart from that of the Kowloon New Territories on the mainland.

Whatever might be said of the later (1860 and 1898) Conventions of Peking, which gave Kowloon and the New Territories to the British, it is not easy to argue that the Treaty of Nanking, when taken with the Supplementary Treaty, was unequal or unreasonable. Wang Tseng-tsai, writing from Taiwan in 1972, agreed that so far as treaty-making procedures were concerned, the Treaty of Nanking conformed well to present-day diplomatic practice.[43] Nevertheless both Taiwan and Beijing maintain that all three sections that make up the territory of Hong Kong are rightfully integral parts of China, that happen to be administered by the British, and not a British colony.

The British government certainly wanted, in 1843, a secure and lasting settlement with China. Lord Brougham, for the opposition, had asked that 'every pain might be taken . . . to restore not a nominal peace, but a real and cordial good understanding with that great and powerful empire', which Lord Haddington, First Lord of the Admiralty, assured him would be the case.[44] The agreements reached at the Bogue, which gave substance to the Nanking terms, were the result of serious and protracted discussions carried on in a cool and reasonable fashion, which brought benefits to both sides. The outburst of indignant criticism from British merchants is a good indication that the terms were not one-sided, and even a brief examination of the points at issue indicates that orderly discussions, which resulted in real compromises, were customary. Pottinger made his own position clear at the outset, on 10 December 1842: 'I consider myself to stand as it were in the light of an Umpire between the Empires . . . all commercial arrangements shall be reciprocal as far as it is possible to make them'.

At Nanking Sir Henry had simply stood firm upon his instructions (except in the matter of Hong Kong) and refused any concessions of substance, although he conceded in the interests of saving Chinese face some points which proved to be of greater significance than he appreciated. The most important of these was the failure to ensure representation in Peking, which taken in conjunction with the Chinese refusal to allow access to the city of Canton, was to cause the second Anglo—Chinese War in 1856. At the Bogue Sir Henry had a much more complex task, and was faced with a team headed by that accomplished diplomat Ch'i-ing, assisted by the Chinese Treasurer of Canton, Huang En-t'ung (Huang Entong), who had a solid background of financial expertise, as well as the Viceroy Ch'i Kung (Qi Gong) and the Hoppo, Wen Feng. Pottinger was perhaps not the right man to negotiate a technical agreement on trade with such able and sophisticated opposites. He had made his own ignorance of the subject manifest in a letter to John Morrison in December 1841: 'I must commence by saying, that although I am Chief Superintendent of it, I know nothing about *Trade*, or proper duties.'[45] His contributions were therefore those of a practical man with a military background, looking above all for a permanent and orderly structure.

This showed in his insistence that the collection of customs duties should be placed on a regular basis, and at a fair rate, ensuring a reasonable return to the Chinese government. British consuls in the treaty ports would see to it that 'the duties and other charges are regularly paid, that abuses do not creep in, and that smuggling be entirely prevented'.[46] When they became aware of the consequences of this – Chinese customs cruisers and, later, unbribable officers – British merchants, who had looked for a much looser control, regarded it as a betrayal of their interests, and agitated for revision over the next two generations.

Any negotiations begin with a more-or-less clearly defined set of aims; in the progress of talks these are altered by the personal predilections of the negotiators and their success or failure in gaining their objectives. Further complications set in when the various groups report to their principals, naturally putting the most favourable gloss on their results. When this process is further confused by misunderstandings in translation the outcome is bound to be unsatisfactory in some respects. This was certainly so in the Nanking—Bogue settlements, and on the most important point of the status of Hong Kong. At Nanking it was stated that:

> It being obviously necessary and desirable that British subjects should have some port whereat they may careen and refit their ships when required and keep stores for the purpose, the Emperor of China cedes to the Queen of Great Britain &c. the island of Hong Kong to be possessed in perpetuity.

Nothing was said about naval bases or trade, which was specifically confined to the five treaty ports, although Pottinger made it clear that he intended to develop the island for both purposes. The drafting of the treaties had been done, with the tacit understanding of both sides, in such a way as to save the Emperor's face. Enlightenment had to be both tactful and gradual. By the time Ch'i-ing visited Hong Kong for the ratification of the Treaty of Nanking in June 1843 the development of Hong Kong was obvious, and the Emperor was informed accordingly:

> In recent years . . . these [British] barbarians have levelled hills and constructed roads, and at a place called Qundailu [Skirt Sash Road] more than a hundred foreign edifices have been built and gradually brought to completion. Moreover, destitute riff-raff and Tankas [boat-dwellers] from eastern Guangdong have erected shacks at the same place, and subsist by selling comestibles. The number of barbarian merchants is estimated at no more than a few hundred, but already several thousand Chinese are trading

with or working for them . . . For over three hundred years, since the former Ming Dynasty, all manner of barbarians have congregated in Macao, where they have peacefully engaged in trade without causing trouble, and there has been no significant evasion of transit dues. Hong Kong is in a comparable situation, and unless regulations are clearly defined and strictly enforced, smuggling and tax evasion will multiply a hundredfold, and collection of the full duty may be prevented.[47]

This was a cause of some concern to the court; when the details of the Bogue settlement reached Peking it was discussed at the Grand Council. The critical point was not the fact that Hong Kong (a 'barren island comprising many rocky peaks . . . isolated in the sea some one hundred li from the chief town of Xia'n County . . . formerly a lair for pirates and almost uninhabited, save for a few dozen scattered families of poor fisher folk at a place known as Chizhuwan'[48]) had been given to Britain. What really concerned the court was future income, and Ch'i-ing was instructed accordingly:

The matter of opening Hong Kong to trade is of crucial importance. If it were to become an important trading centre it could determine whether Our excise revenues are in surplus or deficit. If import and export certificates are only issued by the Deputy Magistrate of Kowloon Sub-District, who will carry out his checks in conjunction with a British official, the procedure is certain to be lax, and revenues will inevitably be lost through evasion and fraud. Let Qiying and others once more fully apply their minds to the question of ensuring strict controls, and let them memorialize Us when they have devised a satisfactory solution. Let strict instructions be given to civil and military officials at all ports to conduct physical inspections of all vessels putting to sea. As to the five trading ports, let all provincial authorities in whose jurisdiction they lie pay increased attention to defensive measures, and prevent merchant vessels from coming and going at will. Thus by preventing leaks and evasions shall Our revenues be augmented.[49]

This memorial, which was not received by Ch'i-ing until early December 1843, placed him in an uncomfortable dilemma, since he could not alter the agreements he had already reached. His explanation to the Emperor was long and involved, and gave a fictitious account of the reasons why the cession of Hong Kong had been demanded:

> Barbarian merchants, arriving at Canton after a long voyage, are ignorant of the state of the market, but unlike Chinese merchants, are unable to avail themselves of the services of the 'establishments', and they have a limited time available to them before they must return. As the saying goes, their goods are 'dead on arrival', so they have no choice but to obey the instructions of the Hong merchants, sell their goods as soon as they can and buy whatever they can find. Chafing thus under manifold and egregious impositions, they asked for Hong Kong island as somewhere they could reside, their sole purpose being to follow the state of the market in Canton so they can move their goods at a time of their choosing and do business with the 'establishments' like the Chinese merchants.

The fact of Hong Kong being a free port was neatly avoided.

> However, it is by no means certain that Hong Kong will become a trading centre, or that our profits will suddenly vanish to the outside. Kowloon lies directly opposite the barbarian settlement and the anchorage for all ships arriving at or leaving Hong Kong. My investigations reveal that this place is ideally situated for our purposes. A ship bound for Hong Kong with goods for export must pay duty first at the point of export, and an export certificate will be issued. On arrival at Hong Kong, the certificate will be examined, and any ship importing goods into Hong Kong will have to pay duty at the point of import. These procedures are in conformity with the regulations laid down; their effectiveness depends not on the seniority of the inspectors but on the thoroughness with which the inspections are made.[50]

While such a system would work for exports, there was no possibility of Britain allowing the Kowloon customs to examine British merchants' cargoes or to levy dues. But the pass system would secure payment of duty by Chinese vessels, since duplicated passes could be sent to the Hoppo at Canton. The Emperor professed himself satisfied with Ch'i-ing's explanation, and in his vermilion endorsement instructed the officials at the treaty ports to make the necessary arrangements.

More trouble lay ahead in Article XIII of the Treaty. In part this was due to incompetent translation. The invaluable John Morrison having died on 29 August, it was left to Robert Thom, at best a reasonable commercial interpreter, to collate the English and Chinese versions, which he signally failed to do. This had the effect, as far as the Chinese were concerned, of putting it within their power to cut off any trade between Hong Kong and any other Chinese port (the English version was not much better, as it made trade between Hong Kong and the treaty ports subject to Chinese permission). One omission from the signed protocol was the question of jurisdiction over Chinese residents in Hong Kong. It was not accepted at the time, as it was later to be, that residents in Hong Kong might be British citizens (except when inconvenient to Britain, as in the 1981 Immigration Act). Pottinger's first, unworkable, proposal was that the British should be responsible for policing Hong Kong, but hand Chinese offenders over to a Chinese magistrate for trial under Chinese law. When Whitehall pointed out that this would prove, at the very least, extremely difficult, Sir Henry found himself in the embarrassing position of having already agreed it with Ch'i-ing: 'It seems,' dryly commented Sir James Stephen, Permanent Under-Secretary at the Colonial Office, 'that the Chinese High Commissioner has the best of the argument.' Since the matter could not be settled in time to allow the other items to be effected, it was allowed to drop.

What was to become the most significant privilege of Western nations in China, and the source of the fiercest resentment, that of extra-territorial jurisdiction, was originally conceived as a compromise. Extra-territoriality had been the direct cause of the war – first in Lin's attempt to arrest Dent, and then in his later demand for someone to be delivered to account for the murder of Lin Wei-hsi. The Annex concerning the General Regulations of Trade at the Treaty Ports stipulates that disputes between foreigners and Chinese should be 'arranged by arbitration and diplomacy', and that 'Regarding the punishment of English criminals the English Government will enact the laws necessary to attain that end, and the consul will be empowered to put them into force . . . Chinese criminals will be tried and punished by their own laws.' This was primarily a concession to the Chinese, made in order to impose much-needed discipline on unruly British crews, who had previously caused such trouble in Canton. In their treaty of July 1844 the Americans went nearer to the point; 'Citizens of the US . . . shall be subject to be tried and punished only by the consul.' The French expressed the principle most clearly in their Treaty of Whampoa (October 1844): 'In all circumstances ... the principle being that ... the French shall be subject to the law of France.'

The narrative of those serious and intensive discussions, 'argued back and forth and considered ... time and time again, and having done all that seemed proper to do', the detailed reports of the negotiators to their principals, and the many compromises reached, make it clear that the Supplementary Treaty was a legitimate international instrument, doubtless with ambiguities and defects, but not with more than most such, and certainly not a simple dictation of terms by a victorious power to a suppliant. Ch'i-ing was a man of great personal charm, able to out-blarney Sir Henry, and won a good deal of genuine regard from his British counterparts. Pottinger might not have officially, as requested by Ch'i-ing, christened his son Frederick Keying,[51] but he did present the Commissioner with portraits of the child and his mother, and reported 'with a touch of awe' to Lord Aberdeen that his 'yin-te-me-t'e' (intimate) friend had 'thrown a perfectly new light on the character and habits' of the Chinese authorities.

It is also true that many of the Nanking provisions were foreshadowed in the agreements made between Britain and the Khan of Khokand in the previous decade, which also allowed for fixed tariffs, and consular representation with judicial powers – agreements never regarded as unjust, unequal or one-sided, although equally forced upon the Ch'ing by outsiders. Subsequent efforts to ensure that the Treaty worked properly, and that remaining contentious items were arranged by mutual negotiation, reinforce this argument. Professor Fairbank's judgement is that although the arrangements were 'expressions of a new order imposed upon the Chinese by British power', they were also 'by and large, compromises. British desires had to be modified. Sir Henry Pottinger finally settled for what was feasible.'[52]

5

A BARREN ISLAND

A free and inexpensive asylum

The initial phase of Hong Kong's history was the uncertain and provisional period beginning with Elliot's proclamation that Hong Kong was part of Her Majesty's dominions on 26 January 1841, and ending on 1 February 1842, when Sir Henry Pottinger returned from the first part of the Northern campaign to determine what should be done with the island. On his first visit the previous August, Pottinger, in a tearing hurry to get to the scene of action, had remained only a few hours which he spent in a tent on the foreshore, conferring with Elliot's former deputy Alexander Johnston, who had come out in the train of Lord Napier seven years before. Johnston now found himself, unexpectedly and not at all comfortably, at the head of things in Hong Kong while the Plenipotentiary was forcing the Chinese to a settlement on the Yangtse.

Left to his own devices by both Elliot and Pottinger, Johnston might have sat on his hands and done nothing beyond co-operating with the service chiefs. Instead of this he displayed great energy, pressing ahead with the infrastructure of the colony, and in doing so presented his superiors, when they came to consider what should be done about Hong Kong, with something of a *fait accompli*. Johnston was perfectly happy to assume responsibility for running Hong Kong; indeed he liked the idea so much that he described himself in later life as 'sometime Deputy governor of Hong Kong',[1] and did not hesitate to take responsibility for decision-making upon himself.

Elliot had been kept busy with settling affairs in Canton until the beginning of June 1841, limiting the time he had to spend on Hong Kong. In fact, he never had much of an opportunity to inspect the 'insular station' he had acquired for the Queen: except for one trip round the island in the *Nemesis*, and some brief visits in April and July, he remained with his staff at Macao. Apart from Johnston, the only resident official was Captain William Caine, late of the 26th Regiment of Foot, the Cameronians, who had been appointed Chief Magistrate on 30 April. They were later joined by the First Lieutenant of the *Nemesis*, William Pedder, as Harbour Master, shortly before Elliot was superseded. Caine was a soldier of the old school. He had been in the service since 1804, and was a firm believer in discipline reinforced by frequent floggings. As Chief Magistrate and later Lieutenant-Governor, Caine was to be a key figure in the colony for the next eighteen years.

Local opinions about the future were reserved. Jardine, back in England, was all in favour of reviving the trade at Canton, a place he knew well and in which his firm had made substantial capital investments, but he had not been personally subjected to the inconveniences – and dangers – to which the foreign community on the spot had in the course of the past two years been exposed. Similarly, the Americans, who had remained at Canton during the time when the British had been expelled, were unwilling to give up their comfortable residence there until matters were very much clearer. Even if Hong Kong was to be a permanent possession of the Crown, foreign businesses especially would wish to be informed on the regulations, terms of land tenure and suchlike before making investments.

But to the British, especially the opium traders, it seemed well worth while at least to run up some temporary stores for their products, which they had perforce left on their ships for two years: what was spent on property could speedily be saved on insurance and demurrage. Stocks were beginning to build up again, since the East India Company back in Bengal was producing its customary quantities of opium. Elliot explained this in a letter to Lord Auckland: 'It is the peculiar and prodigious difficulty of operations in China, that property of immense amount is constantly pouring in upon our hands ... At the very date of this dispatch a vast amount of tonnage is again accumulating, but the erection of Warehouses is commencing at Hong Kong, with a spirit which will I trust enable us to clear the Ships.'[2]

Jardine's and Dent's, responsible for millions of dollars' worth of opium and other goods, were anxious to get them landed and under guard. Deprived of their Canton base, and restricted in Macao, they also urgently needed office and domestic accommodation. With their customary energy they worked fast.

As early as February 1841 sites were being bought direct from their Chinese owners in order to erect temporary matshed godowns and labourers' huts. Lindsay's were said to have been the first house on the scene, but Jardine Matheson were certainly not far behind. And, of course, Chinese tradesmen immediately crossed from Kowloon ready to provide any form of service. Within weeks a rash of buildings gave Hong Kong the air of a Gold Rush town. Land was bought from Chinese owners with often the vaguest of legal titles, and transferred without much thought as to its final use.

Selection of appropriate sites was governed by the lie of the land and by the submarine contours. Deep-water moorings in Hong Kong harbour are found towards Kowloon, and off the northern shores of the island only to the west of the present site of the Macao Ferry Terminal. The forty-foot submarine contour lay as much as a mile off this coast, which prevented off-shore mooring for sea-going ships, but was to favour later land reclamation projects. The contours of the land follow similar patterns on the island, rising less sharply, especially towards Happy Valley. Possession Point, where the flag was raised by Captain Belcher on 26 January 1841, has deep water inshore, but the first settlements were further to the east, taking advantage of the flatter ground to be found there.

Ships coming from the west were limited in draught by a bar in the approaches to the Sulphur Channel, which lies close inshore of Kennedy Town, deep-draught vessels usually making an approach from the east through the Lyeemoon (Lei Yue Mun) passage, a narrow entrance which, surrounded by steep hills, very effectively protects the harbour from the prevailing easterlies. North of Lyeemoon the bottom shelves rapidly, and much of this area is today occupied by the airport's runways. For this reason deep-water berths are now found in the lee created by the Kowloon peninsula. Warehouses convenient for this deep-water traffic, and also away from the more expensive central area, were likely to be more economical, which is why Jardine's were content with their site at East Point. From East to West Point, which marked the boundaries of the first settlement, is a distance of nearly four miles, and the construction of a road was the first essential. This was Queen's Road, which followed the high-water mark at a distance of some one hundred feet, leaving a reasonable space for the erection of buildings benefiting from both water and road frontage.

It could be argued, as later Johnston did argue, that at least a modicum of development at Hong Kong would have been needed even if possession was to be strictly temporary. Barracks, hospitals and storage facilities would be essential for the use of the expeditionary forces then in the north, batteries would be needed to protect the installations, and some attention to roads, waterfront and piers would have to be paid even if Hong Kong, like Chusan, were eventually to be handed back to the Chinese. But Elliot was anxious that Hong Kong should be much more than a mere military depot. Attempting to enlist the support of Lord Auckland in India, he again showed his concern for justice:

> But, My Lord, if the preservation of Hong Kong is of such first-rate importance for our own trade and interests, it is to the full as much so, as an act of justice and protection to the Native population upon which we have been so long dependent for assistance and supply. Indescribably dreadful instances of the hostility between these people and the Government are within our certain knowledge; and they cannot be abandoned without the most fatal consequences.

If Captain Elliot's choice was to be justified his island must become a new Canton. He therefore pressed ahead with development, putting up for sale as much of the available land as possible. The strip, nearly two miles long, roughly between the present sites of the Central Market and the Ruttonjee Sanatorium, was divided into marine lots, each with a hundred feet of road and harbour frontage, the depths varying with the contours. It was intended that one hundred marine and the same number of 'suburban' sites, not having water frontage, were to be offered, but Elliot was impatient to press ahead, and waited only until fifty of the sites were marked out before they were offered for sale by auction on 14 June 1841. The Superintendent's haste led to ambiguities which were to be the source of much future annoyance.

Plots were advertised for sale at a 'quit rent', on conditions which Elliot attempted to make clear to his old acquaintances Matheson and Dent, as the chief representatives of the British community, on 17 July:

I am of opinion that I shall be consulting the interests of the
establishment in making immediate public declaration of my proposal to move Her Majesty's government either to pass the lands
in fee simple for one or two years purchase at the late rates, or
to charge them in future with no more than a nominal quit rent.
May I request you, gentlemen, to circulate this letter.

In other words, the land would be transferred freehold (fee simple)
for the sum of at most two years' rent, or on long lease at a peppercorn.[3]

Prices obtained at the sale were regarded as satisfactory, averaging
some ten shillings per foot of harbour frontage, £20 per acre for town
lots, and £2 for 'suburban' lots. Sites in the bazaar area opposite the
Central Market, which was set aside for Chinese, fetched the high
rent of £1 for a lot of forty by twenty feet. These were allocated first
to 'those persons who against every obstacle settled down in Hong
Kong, and have on various occasions supplied the Fleet when it could
not otherwise obtain provisions'– the Chinese shopkeepers, without
whose enthusiastic support the colony could never have survived. The
most important waterfront site, a double lot, was snapped up by the
Dents: Jardine Matheson had intended to buy an even larger site, but
this was compulsorily acquired by the Services, and Jardine's were
compensated with the land around East Point, a good deal further off.
Government and the armed services naturally enjoyed the privilege of
first choice, the Navy settling upon what is still the Royal Navy dockyard off Harcourt Road, the Army preferring the higher ground away
from the waterfront for both batteries and hospital. The Government
Offices in Lower Albert Road, and the Anglican cathedral, are on the
site of the Murray battery and guardhouse, while Flagstaff House
opposite was originally chosen as the location for the General Officer
Commanding's house by Lord Saltoun. For more than a century
official Hong Kong was able to look down upon the commercial classes
below, but the case has been altered since; a present-day Governor's
guests taking their pleasure on his lawns are viewed from thousands
of hotel and office windows.

Allowing the Services first choice led to the new town being nipped
in two, as it still very nearly is, by government developments, a constric-
tion that soon caused planning difficulties. For some time buildings
were nothing more than matting or wood, perhaps on a stone base:
the merchants had too much outstanding in the way of potential losses
on Lin's opium and the Hong debts to be enthusiastic about sinking

large sums in fixed resources. Certainly when Pottinger paid his brief visit in August 1841, the fact that he was received in a tent speaks for the paucity of accommodation. Later, Johnston, who was rather given to complaining, described conditions at the time in a letter pleading with the British government for more adequate recognition of his services: 'I received no instructions [from Elliot] as to what I was to do when I arrived and did take charge . . . There was no difference between Hong Kong and the numerous islands situated all along the coasts of China . . . the only inhabitants were of a migratory character, and principally engaged in fishing . . . to induce the first one hundred labourers to leave Macao and Canton cost me some trouble.' The 'respectable Chinese' were suspicious of the new administration: 'They viewed me in the light of an imitator of Commissioner Lin.' In spite of this Johnston claimed to have constructed six forts at Kowloon, each with accommodation for an officer and forty men, placed guns on Kellet's Island, built two barracks, a storehouse, three batteries and connecting roads, 'all with no reward and no increase in pay'.[4]

One of the first acts of Johnston's term of office was to make a census, and on 15 May 1841 the island's population was said to have been 4,350, with another two thousand fishermen living on their boats, eight hundred – presumably immigrant merchants – in the bazaar, and three hundred labourers from Kowloon. But, as Elliot had pointed out to Lord Auckland, the sparseness of the population, and its distribution, were exactly the reasons why the British could take over the island without objections being raised by the Chinese on the spot: had Hong Kong been as populous, thriving and well-known as Chusan this would certainly not have been so, and the British would have assumed the character of usurpers rather than virtual founders. The largest settlement was Chek-chu (now Stanley), 'The Capital, a large town', with a population of two thousand according to the census. Chek-chu would not have much changed when a few months later it was described in the *Canton Press* as 'the resort of large fleets of fishing boats, and the site of a considerable town . . . having a very good bazaar, an extensive rope-walk, and shops well-stocked to supply the wants of the Chinese sea-faring people'.

Since almost the only attraction of the north coast of the island was the deep-water harbour, it is not surprising that there were few Chinese to be incommoded by the new developments. On 15 May 1841 the *Canton Press* had been ironic on the subject: 'The site of the principal town has been selected with the judgement which is characteristic of the English authorities in China: and we may mention in proof of this that every street will be perfectly sheltered from the south wind, which will be an immense comfort during the approaching hot season. There are abundant supplies of granite and cold water.' But by the following March the *Friend of China* was able to enthuse: 'It is a matter of astonishment that our neighbours of the sister settlement [Macao] continue to invest large sums in building . . . Hong Kong has advanced with a rapidity of movement unexampled in the annals of colonization, and offers A FREE AND INEXPENSIVE ASYLUM, WITH AMPLE PROTECTION, FOR PERSONS AND PROPERTY.'

Elliot's initial proclamation on 26 January 1841, together with a supplementary issued the following week, was made on his own initiative, without much time for thought, and reflects his own concerns. There were to be two codes of law, English and Chinese; Chinese law and customs were to be interfered with as little as possible, except that 'all forms of torture' were banned; all were to be protected 'against all enemies whatsoever and they are further secured in the free exercise of their religious rites, ceremonies and social customs, and the enjoyment of their lawful property and interests.' This was followed, on 7 June, by a declaration that Hong Kong was to be a free port, with 'no charges . . . payable to the British Government'. Apart from maintaining two separate codes of law, all Elliot's good intentions have been well fulfilled by his successors.

It took the eye of faith, when Captain Elliot left China in August 1841, to see the future 'vast emporium' in the few scattered sheds that lined the foreshore of the island. Matters had not been improved by an outbreak of a fever, which was to be for some years a devastating annual visitant, followed by a typhoon which nearly claimed the lives of both Elliot and Sir Gordon Bremer, returned from his visit to India, since it struck while they were sailing *Louisa* across to Macao. Disease and tempest were succeeded by a devastating fire on 12 August which destroyed most of the temporary structures. In the face of these discouragements Hong Kong, had it become a permanent British possession, might well have remained only as a naval base and fortified camp, with the trade reverting to Canton and social life to Macao. The Chinese themselves ensured this did not occur by looting and destroying the Canton factories in December 1841. If rebuilding had to be done, then there was a good case for incurring the expense in the relative safety of Hong Kong rather than in Canton. The danger of the island being handed back to the Chinese, although it discouraged the Americans, does not seem to have disturbed the British merchants, who could not conceive of 'the lion surrendering anything on which its paw had once been placed'.[5]

In spite of the fact that Pottinger, during his brief conference with Johnston, had ordered all land sales and civilian building to be stopped, he returned from the north in February 1842 to find that his instructions had been disregarded and that, in place of matsheds and tents, there was at Victoria (as it was to be officially known from June 1843) a community of over fifteen thousand, of whom more than twelve thousand were Chinese. A wide metalled road, laid out by the Royal Engineers, ran nearly four miles along the shore, the initial public building plots had been developed with permanent structures – houses, godowns, land-, police- and post-offices, and a commodious jail, to say nothing of the naval and military installations. Some of the houses were of stone, and one of these belonged to Johnston himself. Many others were in course of building, their owners meanwhile roughing it in matshed or bamboo huts. It was however the less respectable institutions that struck 'the noble and distinguished author' of an article, 'Hong Kong and the Hong Kongians', published in the *Canton Register* on 14 January 1842. It appears that many of the facilities enjoyed in Hong Kong today were already available:

> The shops on either side of the grand road present an animated scene of bustle and activity. On the brow of the hill stands the phlegmatic Sheik Modeen . . . opposite is the smiling Chonqua, who is an English tailor of the first class, though of Chinese extraction. Here is the newly-built hotel 'The Victoria' . . . the celebrated Chinese physician . . . the cookshop . . . and there is the abode of the fallen of the fair sex – beautiful, and full of wickedness . . . In fine the scene is exhilarating, novel, and interesting . . . but the magnificence of the gambling house threw us into a labyrinth of amazement . . . built after the approved Hongkongian style of architecture, Venetian in its moist exterior – in the interior, decidedly *Attic*. On either side there are ten or a dozen well-lighted tables . . . At the South extremity a species of banqueting room . . . to the North is the abode of the owner, the Crockford of the place.

Theatrical entertainment was also available; an Australian touring company visited that year, followed by a programme staged by an Italian impresario; and there were rumours that actresses whose 'beauties and talents are only to be surpassed by their spotless virtues' were to be imported by a Mr Gaston Dutronquoy. A rather more credible attraction was soon to be found at the Victoria Theatre (at that time nothing more than the upper floor of a two-storey godown in Wanchai), where the 'Wonder of Wonders' could be seen daily 'from 12 o'clock to 1 o'clock, the great ORANG OUTANG named Gertrude . . . taking her dinner, sitting on a chair at a table, using spoons, knives and forks, wiping her mouth with a towel, she will open a bottle of wine and drink to the health of the spectators, she will after smoke a cigar'.[6]

Hong Kong very early had a newspaper of its own. That lively institution, the Hong Kong press, started early with the publication of the *Friend of China* on 24 March 1842. The paper, edited by the American Baptist minister Lewis Shuck and James White (who had been a City of London Alderman and came east to recover his fortune, which he apparently did), took an anti-opium stance ('that fascinating vice'). The *Friend of China* was joined in Hong Kong the following year by the *Canton Register*, which had been moved to Macao during the 1839 disturbances. Being funded by the Matheson family, the *Register* did not agree with the *Friend* on the subject of opium, and tended to be less on the side of the angels, often appearing to be anti-Chinese and critical of missionary endeavours. Since Dent's had interests in the *China Mail* (1845), the colony's three hundred English-speakers were thus provided with an interesting choice of reading.[7] The *Friend of China* was enthusiastic about the new settlement's prospects; in one of its early issues (26 May 1842) Shuck pontificated: 'We believe that Hong Kong is destined, by the uncontrollable force of circumstances, to become the base of naval and military operations, which sooner or later, must revolutionize, or subvert, the existing state of things in China. Meanwhile we suppose we must be content with a policy, which Napoleon must have appreciated, when he called us a nation of shopkeepers.' One hundred and fifty years later the fear that Hong Kong may 'revolutionize, or subvert, the existing state of things in China' is still a powerful factor.

All this development had been sanctioned by Johnston in contravention of Pottinger's instructions that things should be left as they were until a policy directive was obtained. But Pottinger took it upon himself, as had Elliot, to decide that the settlement should be given its chance to survive. He therefore confirmed Johnston's actions and authorized arrangements for a land registry, announcing on 22 March 1842, 'pending the Queen's royal and gracious commands, that the proprietory of the soil is rested in and appertains solely to the Crown'. Not unnaturally, everyone on the spot took this to mean that it was settled that Hong Kong should permanently remain British.

Pottinger's bold action was taken within days of the indecisive debate in the House of Commons on the future of Hong Kong. Justifying himself later, Sir Henry wrote to Lord Ellenborough, who had succeeded Auckland as Governor-General of India: 'I have done as much as I could to retard, without injuring this settlement, but the disposition to colonize under our protection is so strong that I behold a large and wealthy City springing up under my temporizing measures, and the chief difficulty I now have is the provision of locations for the respectable and opulent Chinese Traders who are flocking to this island.'[8] The last clause was unfortunately a great exaggeration; the paucity of respectable and wealthy Chinese was to be for many years a source of considerable worry.

When, only a fortnight afterwards, just before he left to join the renewed campaign on the Yangtse, Pottinger received Aberdeen's dispatch calling for all works 'of a permanent character' to be 'immediately discontinued', he found himself in a dilemma. On 20 May a long exculpatory and at times incoherent letter was sent to London. Quoting Elliot, Johnston and the General Officer Commanding, Lord Saltoun, Sir Henry enthused over

> the extraordinary, and, as I believe, unequalled progress which this settlement has made . . . aided by the subsequent proceedings which Mr Johnston has adopted . . .
>
> I found when I arrived in China that it was even then impossible supposing that it had accorded with my first impressions to set aside all that Captain Elliot had done regarding Hong Kong . . . the General Commanding had pointed out and recommended extensive and still I think very judicious improvements on the Island . . . including a Fort or Fixed Work and Barracks on the opposite Mainland . . .
>
> I will only add my solemn and unprejudiced opinion that . . . the Settlement has already advanced too far to admit of its being restored to the authority of the Empire consistently with the Honour and advantages of Her Majesty's Crown and subjects.

Sir Henry covered his rear by letting the Hong Kong public know that they should blame Johnston if anything went wrong. At the same time as sending his enthusiastic dispatch he issued a memorandum: 'A year has now elapsed since Captain Elliot made arrangements for establishing a Civil Government on this Island . . . Measures . . . taken subsequently adopted during my absence by Mr Johnston have tended to confirm the impression, that the Island would, in due time, become a British Colony.' These measures, and in particular the quite clear indications that Elliot had given regarding the tenure of land sold at auction, Pottinger refused to sanction. When approached by residents wanting to build a church, he replied that although he was willing to confirm the choice of site, and to undertake that any private subscriptions raised for the purchase would be matched from public funds, 'it is advisable to defer commencing the Building, or incurring any expense about it'.

Such reservations were kept from Whitehall, and, faced with the enthusiasm manifested in Sir Henry's dispatches, the British government accepted the cession of Hong Kong with tolerably good grace. Pottinger was generously permitted to do most of the things – building barracks, letting off parcels of land, and encouraging developments – that he had already authorized. Poor Johnston attempted to justify his actions in a formal memorandum to Sir Henry, complaining that he had been

> left in charge of this Government with no instructions to guide me . . . I considered that I was doing no more than carrying out the measures, in progress, of the late Plenipotentiary, which I understood, from Your Excellency's Notification of 12th August, you did not wish to interfere with until Her Majesty's gracious pleasure was known. I also felt that my situation here was one in which I was obliged to take upon myself great responsibilities for the good and welfare of the Society under my charge . . . the approach to some regularity and order in buildings, and the laying out of proper thoroughfares through them.[9]

He got few thanks for it, then or later, but it is largely due to Johnston's initiative that Hong Kong was allowed to develop.

Methods of proceeding unknown in other British colonies

Only when the settlement at the Bogue was finalized could Sir Henry turn his full attention to his other responsibilities. As Plenipotentiary he was responsible for diplomatic relations with China, in respect of which he reported to the Foreign Secretary. In his capacity as Superintendent of Trade the organization of a consular service and the functioning of consular courts was another set of tasks, overseen this time by the Secretary of Colonies and War, with the Board of Trade expecting to be kept informed, and the law officers of the Crown giving their views. For military or naval assistance he had to call upon the Governor General of India, but the commanders in the field, as well as taking the Plenipotentiary's instructions, reported to the Admiralty and the Horse Guards. Only the governorship of Hong Kong was a relatively straightforward matter, and fell within the ambit of the Colonial Office.

Modern management theory would immediately identify such an arrangement as absurd: responsibilities so arbitrarily divided could never be expected to function even reasonably well. More importantly, the qualities required by the diverse posts were often mutually exclusive. A colonial governor needs patience, tact, commonsense and charm; supervision of consular courts and the avoidance of clashes with the domestic authorities demand ready authority and a good working knowledge of local customs, language and trading practices; while diplomatic representation calls for cunning, histrionic gifts and the ability to scent the slightest whiff of a potential compromise, together with negotiating skills of the highest order. No single person could be expected to possess more than a fraction of these qualities. Deficiencies on the spot could not be repaired by skilful direction from London, as the communications gap meant that emergencies had to be dealt with through the Governor General of India, or the army and navy commanders on the spot. Since only the Cabinet in London could issue orders to the Plenipotentiary-Governor-Superintendent, which orders could not arrive for a considerable time (only gradually reducing: by the 1850s the journey out was down to six weeks), the element of central control remained feeble. During the Peel government of 1841—46 this caused few difficulties, since their interest in China was minimal, but once Palmerston regained office sparks might be expected to fly.

Pottinger returned to Hong Kong from Nanking on 2 December

1842, to the acclamations of the *Friend of China*: 'We are nearly bewildered at the magnificence of the prosperous career which seems now before us' – an enthusiasm which was soon modified. Two weeks later the expeditionary force sailed back to India, leaving a garrison of only some seven hundred men. As the officers, who were a sociable lot and of good family for the most part, had contributed enormously to the general liveliness, their departure much reduced the attractions of Hong Kong society. This now consisted only of a few dozen merchants and a handful of officials, since non-commissioned officers, private soldiers, shopkeepers and those Portuguese who had come over from Macao did not, of course, exist for social purposes. The Chinese, respectable or not, were regarded as best left to their own devices.

It was a curiously mixed and top-heavy society. Most of the old Canton taipans were gone: James Innes was dead, William Jardine a respectable M.P. for Ashburton, Devon[10] (but not for long, as he died in 1843). Lancelot Dent and James Matheson soon left, James being succeeded by his nephew, the less agreeable Alexander, a 'lonely and ill-tempered . . . crabby' individual.[11] John Morrison, the able and diligent son of Robert, died in the 1843 outbreak of fever. By the end of 1844 all the relics of the earlier age had gone, either dead, or to set themselves up in Britain as gentlemen. Lancelot and Wilkinson Dent, laden with tributes to their 'splendid hospitality . . . unwavering integrity, charitable munificence and uniform kindness' rebuilt their unassuming ancestral home in Westmorland in a majestic Tuscan style replete with every modern convenience, including central heating and no fewer than two bathrooms, and added a chapel to the parish church. James Matheson did better, buying the island of Lewis and building a magnificent castle thereon. The profitability of the opium trade may be judged by the fact that he was able to spend over half a million pounds on buying and developing the island, and that Alexander Matheson, when he retired, was able to spend £773,020 on buying a fair slice of the county of Inverness, as well as £300,000 on acquisitions in Ross-shire.

Their successors were, in common with early Victorians at home, consumed by an awareness of social distinctions. This was the time when the English passion for class stratification took shape. The more relaxed society of Regency England, which had been faithfully reproduced in Canton and Macao, had given place to a self-conscious striving for gentility. A change can be seen in the character of Britain's statesmen; the uninhibitedly aristocratic manners of the Whigs (Melbourne

habitually used language that would have scandalized any subsequent audience) had been succeeded by the respectability of Sir
Robert Peel. Visitors to England were often astounded by 'the system
of ranks, as absolute as an oriental caste ... galling, clogging and
unhealthy'.[12] Thackeray, Dickens, Trollope and Surtees all accurately
chronicle the obsession of the 1840s, when 'gentility is the death and
destruction of social happiness among the middle classes in England'.[13]
So it was to be, and even more so, in Hong Kong. There the problem
was exacerbated by the small numbers: the three hundred or so British
residents were perhaps equivalent to the population of a large English
village, but comprised the social distinctions of a county.

At first the unquestioned top dog was not the Governor, but the
General Officer Commanding, Lord Saltoun, the sixteenth Baron, and
a Major-General of the Grenadier Guards. Saltoun was a man of
personal charm and cultivation, an accomplished musician and a
remarkable soldier, once described by Wellington himself as 'a pattern
to the army both as a man and a soldier'. It was Saltoun who at
Waterloo commanded the detachment of the Guards which held out
in the garden of Hougoumont against everything the French could
bring against them, and who personally received Cambronne's sword
when he surrendered the Imperial Guard. The General was permanently in Hong Kong, whereas the Governor was obliged to move about
on diplomatic business: and although Pottinger as Plenipotentiary was
theoretically senior, in every other respect, whether of rank, record,
or personal abilities, he was less distinguished than Saltoun.

Below Governor and Commander there were exactly forty-three
residents who counted themselves as gentlemen. This figure can be
accurately measured since it is the number of magistrates that Pottinger
felt it necessary to appoint, with powers to sit in judgement on 'all
British subjects resorting to the Dominions of the Emperor of China'.
Such an excessive number was due to the fact that any of them would
have been mortally offended at being excluded. To be a Justice of the
Peace, to sit upon the local bench, was a privilege and responsibility
of the squirearchy, conferring the right to be called 'Esquire', thus
differentiating the Magistrate from the mere tradesman. Not to be a
J.P. in Hong Kong was therefore to stamp one as being of the 'polloi':
''E sells 'ams, and I sells 'ats, so what's the difference?' complained one
aggrieved colonist. Much satirical indignation was aroused, especially
among those not appointed: 'Will it be believed in England that the
first act of our Governor was to create a body of Justices of the Peace

(none of them, by the way ... of the slightest use in Hong Kong) exceeding in number by one-third the whole constabulary force?' read a letter printed in the *Friend of China* of 1 July 1843 (needless to say, journalists were not regarded as gentlemen). The ridiculous situation did not last, and the magistrates were soon quietly relieved of their posts.

Pottinger had little patience with such polite distinctions. He had spent his life in the East, dealing only with Indians, soldiers, and company officials, and had no experience of commercial gentlemen. Like Elliot, he found many of the merchants disagreeable and distasteful, but unlike Elliot he was irascible and impatient. Sir Henry was not pleased to be faced with an outbreak of the Jardine Matheson— Dent hostilities when, immediately on his return, he received a letter from Matheson asking him to intercede in an affair that had taken place five years before his appointment. The trouble had arisen over the settlement of the Hing-tai Hong debts. This Canton firm was one of the more dubious Hongs, formed in the 1820s: it been heavily and imprudently backed by Jardine's, to the extent of nearly $3 million. When it collapsed in 1835, a committee of Hong merchants had been established specifically 'to examine the claims of the Hing-tai Hong and Messrs Jardine Matheson'. With what seems like either great want of tact or positive malice, Lancelot Dent was appointed as chairman, 'arbitrarily selected', as he explained, 'to supply the requisite knowledge of foreign languages and accounts'. Dent's committee had agreed that the principal was due to Jardine Matheson, but disallowed three years' interest, amounting to the considerable sum of $432,543. Matheson was furious, and wrote to Dent that his 'interference with the interest, or balance of that account, was an officious interference as unjust as the decision was absurd'. Dent was, in fact, acting reasonably and within his terms of reference, but the incident had added fuel to the rivalry that already existed. Now that the Treaty of Nanking allowed for the payment of the insolvent Hong debts, Jardine's raised the question once more, and Pottinger was asked to intervene. He could get nothing from Dent beyond an explanation of how the committee had been established and a dignified refusal to reopen the now five-year-old question.[14]

On 8 March 1842 Pottinger, finding the whole business incomprehensible, pushed the papers off to London. Although both Davis and Elliot had found Dent's the more acceptable house, Sir Henry had been close to Jardine in London, and made a point of visiting Alexander

Matheson as soon as he arrived in Hong Kong. By now however he had been offended by both the great Hongs: Dent's made difficulties about honouring a bill drawn in favour of the administration, which led to a pained letter from the Governor ('I am sorry to express myself in these terms with regard to any British merchants, and especially those whom it has always been my wish and duty to uphold'[15]). Jardine's interfered with his mail: 'The *Mor* arrived at Hong Kong three days ago but I have not got our letters. She lay off and sent Mr Matheson's packets on shore which they got on the morning of the 20th! This is an infamous and disgraceful system.' And now that he had settled compensation with the Chinese, all the traders were out for whatever they could get from government: 'I understand that some of the honest British Merchants have been exulting at the idea of having more than they claimed, while others are inventing claims under the pleasing impression that $3,000,000 must be got rid of amongst them.'[16]

Pottinger had no intention of having such persons interfere with orderly government. Hong Kong became a Crown Colony, governed by a Charter, on 26 June 1843. It was a sparse document, drafted by London in some haste and without benefit of any consultation with the new Governor, who was accordingly given wide discretionary power. He was to appoint a Legislative Council, which was to have no effective powers, even though his appointees were dismissible by the Governor at any time. Any real powers – and there were very few – were vested in an Executive Council whose members were all to be Crown servants, meeting only when the Governor required them, and to discuss only those matters which the Governor tabled. The only redress available to the members if they felt the Governor was acting wrongly was the right to communicate directly with the Secretary of State, a right rendered considerably less valuable by the time that was needed to effect communications. Hong Kong, from the beginning, was fated to be anomalous, as James Stephen at the Colonial Office regretfully acknowledged: 'methods of proceeding unknown in other British Colonies must be followed in Hong Kong, and . . . the Rules and Regulations . . . must, in many regards, bend to exigencies beyond the contemplation of the framers of them'.

As things turned out Pottinger – who had come out to settle accounts with the Chinese Empire, not to act as Governor of a colony which he regarded as consisting of a couple of hundred Europeans, very few of whom he would wish to give the time of day to – contrived to avoid most of the gubernatorial work. He avoided the place altogether for as long as possible, occupying the old Superintendency House in Macao until late in 1843. When finally established in Hong Kong, Pottinger announced that he would hold himself available at specified times for interviews with gentlemen requiring them, but it does not seem that much advantage was taken of this offer, and it was his successor, Sir John Davis, who was responsible for running in the Constitution. Government was simplified by Pottinger appointing the same three individuals – the minimum – to each council. All three, naturally, were paid officials – Johnston, Caine and Morrison.

When, in August 1843, John Morrison died, his loss was irreparable. A man of calm capacity, and the only senior member of the administration to speak Chinese, Pottinger had relied on him heavily, writing to him almost daily when absent from the colony: his death, said Pottinger, was 'nothing less than a national tragedy'. After Morrison died, and Johnston went on sick leave, Pottinger was able to do very much as he wished, issuing notifications which had the force of law, often without prior discussion. There could be no effective interference from the trading community, even though many of his actions were vehemently objected to by the merchants, who believed he was deliberately acting against their interests. This impression was reinforced by the high-handed attitude he took towards them. His letters were written in a tone that might have been accepted by a village grocer, but was regarded as intolerably insulting by the senior merchants, whose wealth entitled them, in their opinion, to a high degree of consideration, even from Plenipotentiaries. Take for example Pottinger's letter of December 1842 to the British merchants in Canton, who had asked for some force to be retained there, if only the steamer *Proserpine*. The Governor demanded of them

collectively and individually whether you, to whom this letter is particularly addressed . . . have in any single iota or circumstance striven to aid me in my arrangements as the humble but zealous instrument of the Government whose protection has been extended to you in an unparalleled degree, and which, I may add, you are always ready to claim and expect . . . I may even ask whether you have not thrown serious difficulties and obstacles, if not positive risk, in the way of the very arrangements and measures which you so earnestly desire to see perfected?[17]

The most important cause for dissension lay in the complex story of the land settlements. Elliot's original land disposal had not been welcomed by the home government. Lord Aberdeen had begun by rejecting Hong Kong, and even when the Treaty of Nanking was accepted he still dithered about what should be done about land sales and tenure. His instructions to Pottinger on the subject, sent on 4 January 1843, are full of hesitant suggestions, and lack any clear guidelines:

> The principal source from which revenue is to be looked for is the Land; and if by the liberality of the Commercial regulations enforced in the Island, foreigners as well as British Subjects are tempted to establish themselves on it, and thus to make it a great mercantile Entrepot, with very limited dimensions, Her Majesty's Government conceive that they would be fully justified in securing to the Crown all the benefits to be expected from the increased value which such a state of things would confer upon the Land. Her Majesty's Government would therefore caution you against the permanent alienation of any portion of the land, and they would prefer that Parties should hold land under Leases from the Crown, the terms of which might be sufficiently long to warrant the holders in building upon their several allotments.

Aberdeen concluded by dropping all responsibility back in Pottinger's lap:

> It would probably be advantageous also that the portions of land should be let by auction; but of the expediency of resorting to this process you will of course be best able to judge on the spot.

In the two years between Elliot's sales of land and the receipt of Lord Aberdeen's cautious warnings, much development had taken place. The palm mat houses were being replaced by elegant stone structures, and prefabricated wooden houses brought from Singapore. Almost the whole of the waterfront from Wanchai to the market was faced either with naval and military installations or with substantial two- and three-storey stone warehouses, with offices and living accommodation over, near-replicas of the Canton factories. Jardine Matheson were developing their own independent fiefdom at East Point, and official buildings – the first and largest being the commodious jail built to house William (now promoted to Major) Caine's culprits – were appearing on the lower slopes of the peak. Less essential structures – the theatre, churches and mosque – remained in temporary accommodation. One early planning error was made apparent as expansion westwards became limited by the thriving bazaar opposite the Central Market: this had to be dealt with, at the cost of infinite trouble, by rehousing the leaseholders further westward in what became the Chinese quarter of Tai-ping-shan.

Commercial development had been funded on the assumption that Elliot's original titles would be convertible to freehold. The leaseholders were very cross when Pottinger, subsequent to Lord Aberdeen's tentative instructions, limited their tenures to seventy-five-year leases. Enough confusion and uncertainty were generated to discourage anyone from investing in new projects when it might take years to establish whether they were going to be allowed to continue. The opium traders, in spite of the enormous profits they were making, were also angry that the payment of their compensation claims was delayed. Hugh Lindsay, formerly of the Select Committee in Canton, procured a debate in the House of Commons on the subject on 17 March 1842, in the course of which William Jardine made one of his rare speeches, demanding quick payment: 'nothing was clearer than that the merchants ought to be compensated before the expenses of the expedition were taken into consideration'.

Pottinger was finding Hong Kong a tedious place: his accommodation, a newly built small bungalow, although grandly named as Government House, was absurdly mean beside the palace he could expect back in India; his task in bringing the Chinese to a settlement had been completed, and he had not the taste for the detailed task of organization, which once again devolved upon the industrious Johnston and the disciplinarian Caine. They were much helped by the non-functioning of the constitutional councils, which enabled government ordinances to be issued without debate, by simple notifications. In the absence of any professional assistance these were loosely drafted and elicited disapproving noises from the Colonial Office. Nor were they popular with the community, since this seemed much too authoritarian a procedure. The British traders demanded – as they were to continue to demand for the next century or so – an active part in the island's government: although of course they had no intention of allowing the much larger Chinese population any say in things whatsoever.

Just as soon, therefore, as Sir Henry was able to settle the terms of the Treaty of the Bogue, he sent off his resignation to Lord Aberdeen. But it was to be nearly a year before his replacement arrived. In the meantime Pottinger appears to have solaced himself with the company of 'pretty Mrs Morgan, fair, fat and forty'.[18] Certainly during his sojourn at the Cape of Good Hope, after leaving Hong Kong in June 1845, Pottinger made a name for himself as one who 'enjoyed his glass and his lass, smoked his cigar, and took things easy'.[19] A less charitable writer claimed: 'No other governor of the [Cape] Colony ever lived in such open licentiousness as he. His amours would have been inexcusable in a young man: in one approaching his sixtieth year they were scandalous.'[20]

By the time of his departure it was arguable whether the British in Hong Kong disliked Sir Henry more than Sir Henry disliked them, but the antipathy was mutual. What might serve as a valedictory was published in the *Friend of China* on 4 March 1844:

> The many instances which the mercantile community has been annoyed and oppressed: we need not specially notice the spirit of liberality and generosity they have ever exhibited towards government . . . the ten extraordinary ordinances already passed by a military legislator . . . these documents contain more that is objectionable, illegal, and unconstitutional than all similar ordinances passed in our numerous colonies in the past twenty years . . . If elderly Gentlemen will have their hobby horse we have no objection, so long as they ride quietly, and the animal is not vicious.

The missionary and scholar James Legge described Hong Kong in Pottinger's day. The few European houses were quickly enumerated: Edger's, Gibb's, Livingston's, Johnston's, the 'small bungalow where Sir Henry Pottinger and after him Sir John Davis held court', Gemmel's, Fletcher's, Lindsay's and of course the 'imposing flat-roofed house' of Dent's and the Jardine establishment at East Point. Although Legge was 'charmed by the general appearance of the place, and the energy that was manifest in laying out the ground and pushing on building', he found 'many of the residents oppressed with gloom because of its unhealthiness. 1843 was, no doubt, a very sickly year . . . the drains were for the time all open . . . an atmosphere of disease, which only the strongest constitutions and prudent living were able to resist'.[21]

Respectable and opulent Chinese

Once the initial reluctance which Johnston had described was overcome, Hong Kong quickly proved popular with enterprising Chinese,
especially those who had previous experience of dealing with the barbarians. British settlements in Malacca and Singapore had already
encouraged Chinese to learn the foreigners' language and adapt to
their customs, and well over a century of trading to the Pearl River
had produced merchants capable of satisfying their requirements. Such
a one was Loo Aqui (also referred to as Lu Agui, Loo King and
Sz-man-king), who had worked his way up through the hierarchy of
pirates to make a fortune provisioning the opium traders. This he
invested in Hong Kong property, including a number of brothels and
opium divans, a gambling hall, and Aqui's Theatre, where the first
amateur production in the colony was staged in December 1845. Tam
Achoy (Tan Acai or Tam A-tsoi) had been a foreman in the Singapore
dockyards before setting up as a contractor and property speculator in
Hong Kong. Together Loo and Tam founded, in 1847, the Man-Mo
temple in Hollywood Road, dedicated to the Gods of Literature and
War, which soon became a recognized centre among the immigrant
Chinese. As leaders such as Loo and Tam were accepted by the
Chinese community, an alternative to the incomprehensible forms of
British administration emerged: the temple became a court of arbi-
tration and communal deliberation, a substitute for the clan and gentry
organization left behind in their native villages.[22]

The original inhabitants of Hong Kong, soon very much in the
minority, were at a disadvantage by comparison with the newcomers,
who brought to the colony the experience of generations of catering
for barbarian tastes, and quickly became the most prominent among
the Chinese community, acting as building contractors, shopkeepers
and domestic servants, as well as supplying the essential manual labour.
Some contemporary Hong Kong people can trace their ancestry before
1842, but those who were there when the British came were largely
submerged among the newcomers, and probably continued with their
original occupations as fishermen and gardeners.

Most of the newcomers were single men, recruited by labour contractors, who had no intention of settling in Hong Kong. The contractors themselves were men of substance, capable of executing 'extensive
works . . . as well as they could be in England'.[23] While the majority
of their men were peaceable, anxiously avoiding contact with the

foreigners, others – Triad organizers and pirates looking for new opportunities – who rapidly attracted the unfavourable attention of the British authorities, also flocked to the island. Less noticeably, a new class of English-speaking Chinese who had to some degree rejected their traditions and accepted Western values was emerging.

The most famous of these spent only a few years in Hong Kong, between 1842 and 1847. Yung Wing (Rong Hong or Yung Hong) had been a pupil at the Morrison Education Society's School in Macao before it moved to Hong Kong in 1842. Funded by local businessmen under the patronage of Lancelot Dent, the school did not long survive the departure of its headmaster, the Revd. Samuel Brown, a Yale man, in 1847. Brown took Yung back to America with him, where in due course he became the first Chinese to graduate from an American university. Returning to China, Yung was recruited by Tseng Kuo-fan (Zeng Guofan) to develop the Ch'ing government's armaments industry. The careers of the two men span the transition between scholar-gentry and modern methods, between the eighteenth and the twentieth centuries. Tseng was a respected Confucian scholar and senior official, who was to raise, train and equip armies to suppress the Taiping rebellion which devastated southern China in the 1850s, selecting and organizing his men on the best traditional lines. Yung married an American woman, sent his children to Yale, and was as much at home in English as in Chinese. He bought and equipped the new arsenals with the latest European and American machine tools, negotiating on equal terms with international companies.[24]

Others who were educated in Hong Kong remained in the colony and joined forces with the colonial authorities. This was a gradual process, and it took another generation before Hong Kong Chinese were equipped to participate in the complex game of colonial politics. Perhaps the most famous such family was that of the Revd. Ho Fuk Tong, the son of a Singapore government worker, whose own son became the redoubtable Sir Ch'i Ho-Ch'i;[25] Ho Fuk's son-in-law, Ng Choy, was the first Chinese called to the British bar. Both Ho-Ch'i and Ng Choy became members of the Legislative Council in the 1880s. Only at that time, forty years on, was there any representation of Chinese opinion in government, and even then on most issues prominent Chinese tended to agree with the European businessmen.

Similarly developing in the early years of the colony was the power of the compradores, Chinese members of the European Hongs, who acted as a link between their principals and the Chinese business community, and as guides through the complex network of relationships within that community. Introducing European business practices and technical skills into China, the compradores' influence took, like that of their political brothers, a generation to come to maturity. Nor, for some time, was there any mechanism for the transmission of more traditional Chinese views. Until self-generated institutions, originating in the temples and trade associations, began to act as a conduit for these, the earliest 'respectable' Chinese in Hong Kong had little alternative but to accept the colonial structure, and attempt to foster their own prosperity, keeping a prudent distance from both the authorities and the more raffish elements of society.

6

THE DAVIS RAID

A negro streaked with leprosy

The Chinese expedition safely out of the way, and a satisfactory treaty ratified, Sir Robert Peel's government had better things to do than worry about Hong Kong. Sir Charles Napier was taking another huge slice of India in the Sind campaign, France was being pugnacious in Tahiti, income taxes were causing trouble, repeal of the Corn Laws was being tackled, and the Irish were agitating for the restoration of their own parliament. When Whitehall finally got around to seeking a replacement for Pottinger, which they did much later than Sir Henry would have liked, they not unnaturally looked more for an experienced and peaceable administrator, and one who knew something of trade, than a forceful and belligerent personality. Being Tories, they shied away from consulting those private merchants who had clearly identified themselves with the Whigs.

The choice of John Davis, veteran of the Amherst mission, sometime President of the Select Committee and, for a short time, Chief Superintendent of Trade in succession to Lord Napier, was regarded as a party political appointment and a direct affront by a Tory government to the private merchants. They expected the worst from the return of Davis, a man 'altogether identified with the ideas of mingled senility, autocracy and monopoly as exemplified in the history of that Company', and were not disappointed. 'Governor Davis is, we must report, a delusion. He has neither dignity, nor temper . . . he cannot get rid of his old John Company notions . . . the sooner he is recalled the better for our prospects in China,' wrote the *Friend of China*.[1] Alexander

Matheson was slightly less damning: he found Davis 'very frank and affable, but his mind is most contracted'. Still, he felt the merchants would 'be able to bully him into adopting their views'.[2]

Nor was Pottinger pleased at having been kept cooling his heels for the better part of a year in awaiting his replacement. 'Sir Henry Pottinger is much annoyed at being kept here against his will, that he has ceased to take any interest in Hong Kong,' Alexander Matheson wrote.[3] When eventually he was relieved in May 1845, ten months after he had resigned, Sir Henry was not promoted to the governorship of Madras, as Palmerston had promised him, but shunted off to South Africa, as Governor of Cape Colony, to wait for the return of the Whigs before being given his reward. Furthermore, he was not awarded a peerage, even an Irish one, as might have been thought his due after negotiating the Treaty of Nanking, an event which even Peel thought ought to be the occasion for 'fireworks and Feux de joie'. On the contrary, when, in 1843, it was suggested that a vote of the House of Commons be given thanking Sir Henry Pottinger for his services Peel coldly rejected it, a refusal which the *Illustrated London News* of 7 April 1845 called 'one of the most singular ever broached'. Before Pottinger died, in Malta in 1856, he was visited by Lord Granville, the Leader of the House of Lords, who reported that he had 'just seen Sir H. Pottinger, living in retirement and bearing, in addition to a load of infirmities, the most painful burden of soreness and mortification at the neglect of his services'.[4]

Sir John Davis arrived in Hong Kong in May 1844, armed with what Lord Aberdeen described as 'a degree of authority more comprehensive in extent and unusual in character than is ordinarily imparted to any servant of the Crown'.[5] He had not only a new colony to govern, but as Superintendent of Trade he was required to visit each of the new treaty ports annually, and as Plenipotentiary to conduct negotiations with other powers. It was now accepted that discussions with China would not be through Peking, but via Canton, where Pottinger's old friend Ch'i-ing was established as both Governor-General and Imperial Commissioner. For the next twelve years Ch'i-ing and his successors acted virtually as Foreign Secretaries in negotiations with Western powers, reporting as required to the Emperor. The main item remaining on the Anglo–Chinese agenda was access to the city of Canton, which the British believed to be provided for in the Treaty of Nanking. The Chinese did not agree, and the subject was to be productive of much dissension.

The new Governor was accompanied by a suite of colonial officials, intended to provide both an appropriate government for the colony and the means of administering the treaty port foreigners. It was an ill-assorted and poorly qualified team. Frederick Bruce, the younger brother of that Lord Elgin who was to take over as Plenipotentiary thirteen years later, came as Chief Secretary, the second-in-command of the colony. He was soon promoted away, but William Mercer, Davis's twenty-two-year-old nephew, a 'gentlemanly scholarly man', very much like Davis himself, remained for twenty-three years and became an essential prop of successive administrations. For a total period of three years Mercer was left in charge of the colony in the intervals between Governors, and did nothing worse than write some bad verse, as this, to a Chinese skull:

> O Chow, or Wong, or by whatever names
> Men called thee, or the Gods do call thee now . . .

Charles Cleverly, who became Surveyor General and designed Government House, was another newcomer who stayed for more than twenty years, but the other new arrivals proved less satisfactory. A.E. Shelley, the Auditor General, was unfortunate in his business speculations and was accused of fraud. Five barristers had refused the post of Chief Justice before it was accepted by John Walter Hulme, who had the reputation of being reliable on law, but was without judicial experience. From the start it was apparent that his relations with the Governor were likely to be difficult – they quarrelled on the boat coming out – but it took three years for them to rupture completely.

The Colonial Treasurer, Robert Montgomery Martin, reacted more quickly, deciding within weeks of his arrival that Hong Kong was impossible, and should be abandoned. Martin's claim to a colonial appointment was based on no qualification or administrative experience (he had apparently taken a year or two of medical studies), but he had written a number of very long books, starting in 1840 with the *History of the British Colonies*, in five volumes. He was able to assert, in 1840, that he had 'printed and published fifty thousand volumes on India and the Colonies', which included such diverse topics as an 'Analysis of the Bible', a 'History of the Antiquities of Eastern India', and 'Ireland as it was, is, and ought to be'. Perhaps predictably, once arrived in Hong Kong, he neglected his immediate responsibilities and settled down to justify in prolix and passionate prose his condemnation of the colony:

> ... the straggling town of Victoria, which stretches along the water's edge for nearly four miles, although only comprising about sixty European Houses, and several Chinese huts and bazaars ... the rugged, broken, and abrupt precipices, and deep rocky ravines, will ever effectually prevent the formation at Victoria of any concentrated town adapted for mutual protection, cleanliness, and comfort ...

Nothing could be said for the landscape either:

> ... the hills assume somewhat of a greenish hue, like a decayed Stilton cheese ... [the mainland hills] presenting the appearance of a negro streaked with leprosy ... the granite is rotten and passing, like dead animal and vegetable substances, into a putrescent state ...

The effects of the sun were unparalleled:

> Even at Macao, only forty miles west ... Europeans may walk about the whole day in the month of July, when to do so at Hong Kong would be attended with almost certain death.

Nor was there any prospect of matters improving:

> There is no trade of any noticeable extent in Hong Kong ... The principal mercantile firms are those engaged in the opium trade ... which they frankly admit is the only trade Hong Kong will ever possess ... There is scarcely a firm in the island but would ... be glad to get back half the money they have expended in the colony, and retire from the place ... There does not appear the slightest probability that, under any circumstances, Hong Kong will ever become a place of trade ... it is worse than folly to persist in a course begun in error, and which, if continued, must eventually end in disappointment and in national loss and degradation.

Martin laid the blame for this at Pottinger's feet, for his encouragement of 'absurd and ruinous projects', which 'none but the wildest theorists could have projected or entertained'.[6]

Probably not too distressed by this trenchant criticism of his predecessor, which would prove a useful justification if things went badly, Davis forwarded Martin's report to the Colonial Office on 20 August 1844 with only the mildest of disclaimers: 'It is fair, however, to Mr Martin to observe that his remarks were written after only a few weeks' residence ... I could easily point out errors in regard to facts and conclusions (did I deem it necessary to dwell upon the subject) ... I cannot give the sanction of my opinion of its general tenor.'

This put the cat among the pigeons in Whitehall. Aberdeen had never been happy about the colony, and was, in the climate of financial stringency obtaining in London, very willing to consider its suppression. It would be easy enough, and not without political attractions, to blame the Whigs for having foisted Hong Kong upon the British Empire, and to negotiate its return to China – with appropriate compensation. And to a government committed to reducing taxation, and at the same time achieving large budget surpluses, any suggestion of waste was anathema. A justification from Davis was therefore demanded, which, if Hong Kong were to survive as a British colony, had better be a good one. The Secretary of State for the Colonies, Lord Stanley (later Prime Minister, as the Earl of Derby), accordingly wrote to Davis on 17 December 1844: 'It is evident that unless that gentleman's [Martin's] views be altogether incorrect, they afford ample motive for deliberation before Her Majesty's Government authorize incurring the very large civil and military expenditure which has been proposed in contemplation of Hong Kong becoming a permanent British settlement, the resort of a large population, both European and Asiatic, and the centre and principal seat of an extensive and valuable commerce.'

Once more the colony's future hung in the balance, but, by the time Stanley's dispatch reached Hong Kong, Davis was able to reply in a more optimistic tone, demolishing Martin's case in a skilfully worded dispatch: 'Mr Martin wrote under a feeling of strong prejudice, founded in apprehensions for his personal health, regarding which he is remarkably sensitive, and on account of which he has had more leave of absence than any individual in the service.' Mortality, although still a cause for serious concern, had decreased somewhat: of over 350 government employees and prisoners on the sick list, only nine had died in the previous six months, one of these by violence. A programme of building barracks had been put in hand, and was already proving beneficial to the health of the military – although a mortality of over 15 per cent from illness was still no advertisement for the colony's salubrity, however strongly Davis defended it. The climate of Hong Kong was 'precisely that of Macao . . . where for many years I and a number of others enjoyed as good health as in England'. As for Chusan, which Martin assiduously canvassed as an alternative settlement, 'if the Chinese fulfil their engagements, I do not see how this is now to be done'. In conclusion, nothing was so bad that an able and experienced administrator – such as Davis – could not put it right: 'Time alone is required for the development of this colony, and for the correction of some evils which may have hindered its early progress.'

Lord Aberdeen was not entirely convinced by the Governor's arguments, especially when it was rumoured that the French intended to take Chusan. Many would have agreed with Martin's description of that island's superior qualities, which made the rumour 'particularly irritating since the Government were well aware that they would have done better to have obtained Chusan, rather than Hong Kong'. Aberdeen complained on 21 October 1845: 'Anything would be better than ridicule so overwhelming' as would result if the French succeeded.[7] Davis's assurances were therefore accepted by London only with several pinches of salt, and when Martin's attacks continued, sufficient concern was aroused to make a House of Commons inquiry necessary.

However unsatisfactory some of Davis's aides might be, the task of constructing a colonial administration had to be attempted, since the simplistic direct rule adopted by Pottinger could not be allowed to continue (in fact, owing to lack of a quorum, neither the Legislative nor the Executive Council met before the arrival of Davis). The intention of the Colonial Office was that a pattern for Crown Colony government already developed in such colonies as Ceylon should be adapted for use in Hong Kong. According to this model the Governor was assisted by an Executive Council, acting as a Privy Council or cabinet, composed of his own departmental heads. It had only consultative powers, and was subordinate to the Governor: its only power was to have requests recorded in the minutes, and to oblige the Governor to explain himself to London if he should act against the advice of a majority of the Council.

The other arm of government, the Legislative Council, was initially responsible for issuing regulations not only for the colony but for 'all

British subjects with in the Dominions of the Emperor of China and within any ship or vessel . . . not more than 100 miles from the coast of China'. Only after 1853 was the Legislative Council's responsibility confined to Hong Kong. The British community in the colony expected to be allowed an active participation in the Legislative Council, as was the custom in those settlement colonies where the white population soon became a majority, such as New Zealand and the Canadian and Australian states, or where the non-whites could be simply ignored, as in South Africa. There was never any prospect in Hong Kong of the Europeans – under pressure the Hong Kong British were prepared to extend representation to Indians and to other Europeans – being anything but a tiny minority, and no British government was willing to rely upon the disinterestedness of that community towards the Chinese majority. The alternative of allowing the Chinese to participate was not even considered: the reins of power were to be kept in Whitehall's hands, and delegated only to the Governor and his colleagues; it was not until 1850 that any non-officials were allowed Legislative Council membership – and then they were, and so remained until very recently, extremely carefully selected. Hong Kong was to continue as authoritarian an administration as any Chinese government, but the final authority was to be the law, rather than individual whim.

The dreadful sight of an Englishman being hanged

Martin doubtless exaggerated the hardships of life in the colony, but some disillusionment on the part of the merchants in Hong Kong was justified. The possibility of trading at the newly opened treaty ports was, initially, more seductive, and it soon became apparent that Shanghai was considerably the most likely to warrant a diversification of effort. (One benefit of the Treaty of Nanking for the Chinese government was the regular collection of customs, the records of which afford a measure for determining the flow of trade. In 1844–5 Shanghai was already the largest of the new ports, but was collecting only 5 per cent of the revenues of Canton: within six years this had risen to 80 per cent.) Both silk and tea sold better there than in Hong Kong, while the import trade rose from forty-four foreign vessels in 1844 to over four hundred ten years later. Tea, which had been the mainstay of the Canton export trade, failed to come to Hong Kong, either remaining at Canton or moving to those northern ports nearer the growing areas.

At Hong Kong the provisions of Article XIII of the Bogue Treaty, which discouraged the junk trade, were biting, and imports remained sluggish: 189,257 of tonnage entering in 1844, rising to only 229,465 three years later.[8]

Conditions at the time were described in the gloomiest terms:

> This remote and completely unimportant settlement ... derives its importance only from its being a Diplomatic and Military Station ... mercantile houses now reduced to ten or twelve ... buildings unoccupied ... Canton and Shanghai are the principal (almost the exclusive) Marts in China for Imports from Europe and India, as well as for Exports from China ... the sad mistake committed by Sir Henry Pottinger in choosing for a British Settlement an island as barren as HongKong.[9]

Gutzlaff was instructed to enquire into the reasons for the unsatisfactory growth rate, and identified piracy as the most important. Certainly pirates were numerous and daring: in 1844 a military convoy was ambushed at Stanley and members of the British Army escort killed in a successful payroll robbery. Intelligence of such likely hauls was easily available since pirates, many of whom doubled as fishermen and traders, were able to pick up information, at a modest price, from government servants in the port. The Royal Navy was at that time disinclined to seek out pirates (this policy later changed, partly at least due to generous arrangements in respect of prize money), citing lack of suitable craft, the difficulty of distinguishing potential pirates from marginally more lawful traders, and the subsequent possibility of clashes with mandarin boats. Davis commissioned an armed ship to control piracy, which did some useful work, although only scratching at the surface of the problem. When pirates were caught they were sternly dealt with; James Legge, who came to the colony in 1843, found 'the most wretched experience' of his life was 'visiting pirates and other murderers under sentence of death'.[10]

Nor had things much improved in Victoria, which Legge found with 'next to no police guardianship'. All the traders set armed guards in their premises, and Europeans went about at night carrying pistols. Reporting later to a Select Committee of the House of Commons Alexander Matheson described the situation as it then was: 'I have seen thirty, forty, or even fifty men come armed; I have seen two men shot at our own premises. We shot two men one night there.'[11] At a

more domestic level one Mary Anne Le Foy had a narrow escape
when she found 'fifty Chinamen in her bedroom. She jumped out of
bed and without dressing ran down . . . to fetch the guard. But before
she got back the robbers had decamped . . . Poor Mary Anne lost the
clothes she was going to put on – but they had a great fright. These
affairs are constantly occurring at Hong Kong where the Chinese are
most expert and daring robbers.'[12]

Robert Montgomery Martin is not the most reliable of witnesses,
but his description of the Chinese community is supported from more
unbiased sources: 'It is literally true, that after three years and a half
of uninterrupted settlement, there is not one respectable Chinese
inhabitant . . . There is in fact, a continual shifting of a Bedouin sort
of population, whose migratory, predatory, gambling, and dissolute
habits, utterly unfit them for continuous industry, and render them
not only useless but highly injurious subjects in the attempt to form a
new colony. There are no other inhabitants.' Gutzlaff concurred: 'The
most numerous class are from Whampoa: many of them are of the
worst characters, and ready to commit any atrocity . . . It is very natural
that depraved, idle and bad characters . . . should flock to the colony
where money can be made . . . The moral standard of the people . . .
is of the lowest description.'[13] Bishop George Smith, asked whether
'the population of Hong Kong [was] much lower in character than the
population upon the Coast', answered, 'Yes. They are the refuse of
the population.'[14] The reliable and knowledgeable Samuel Fearon[15]
explained: 'The shelter and protection afforded by the presence of our
fleet soon made our shores the resort of outlaws, opium smugglers,
and, indeed, of all persons who had made themselves obnoxious to
the Chinese laws.'

In an attempt to counteract this Davis attempted to attract 'more
respectable Chinese', and granted some East Point lots to 'men of
substance' from Fukien. On mature consideration of the potential of
Hong Kong these gentlemen declined. Fearon blamed the Hakkas,
immigrants from the north (the name has the same meaning as the
German *Fremde* – both visitor and foreigner), for the crimes: they
wandered, 'unrespected, wherever gain may call them. The unsettled
state of the colony, and the vast amount of crime during its infancy
afford abundant proofs of the demoralizing effects of their presence.'
He added that 'Hong Kong has been invested by numbers of the Triad
Society, the members of which . . . perpetrate the grossest enor-
mities.'[16]

A distinct atmosphere of the Wild West prevailed during the formative years of the colony. One Chinese shot after dark, presumably engaged in some malfeasance, was laconically noted as 'dead of a pistol shot': case closed. And in 1845 the census showed that there were twenty-six brothels compared to only twenty-five families. Major – now promoted to Lieutenant-Colonel – Caine, who had been given the post of Colonial Secretary when Frederick Bruce left in 1846, was succeeded as Magistrate by Charles Batten Hillier, previously mate of a merchant ship, whom Caine 'treated like a son'. Hillier was, as Caine had been, 'a noted flogger', but a British administration faced real difficulties in dealing with Chinese crime. Davis was able to recruit a Inspector of the Metropolitan police, Charles May, to organize a Hong Kong police, but the shortage of funds resulted in an under-strength force of very dubious quality. Since most of the police were either European or Indian, Chinese being recruited only in 1847, and then in small numbers, the language difficulty made effective policing even more problematical. Those few interpreters available had now to be spread among the treaty ports – Thom, for example, went to Amoy. Fearon only spent a few months as Registrar-General before being appointed Professor of Chinese at King's College, London, at the very early age of twenty-six. Gutzlaff was the only experienced Chinese interpreter in Hong Kong, although from 1844 he was joined by Daniel Caldwell, the Assistant Superintendent of Police. And Gutzlaff was not the most reliable of men: when he eventually did leave China, Forth Rouen, the French Consul at Macao, wrote to the Quai d'Orsay to warn that he was bound for Paris, where it was hoped that he would not be taken seriously, since he, 'in enumerating his many evangelical works in China, and requesting pecuniary assistance . . . is a man of considerable inventiveness, who has always sought to enrich himself . . . I regret to say that there is not a word of truth in the tales of this Sinologue.'[17]

In his initial proclamation Charles Elliot had announced that the Chinese in Hong Kong would be governed by the laws and customs of China. At Nanking Pottinger had, in principle, agreed both to this and to the Hong Kong Chinese coming under the jurisdiction of a district magistrate in Kowloon. This was not a policy to which London would assent: Hong Kong having been ceded to Britain, its inhabitants could not be allowed to remain under the jurisdiction of China. It was however acknowledged that English laws and customs should not immediately be imposed upon the Chinese inhabitants. Similar difficulties had been experienced in India, where it had taken decades to abolish even such objectionable practices as suttee. In minor matters it was at least tacitly agreed to let the Chinese manage things themselves, with some attempts at formalization. Within quite broad limits, legislation was therefore left to the men on the spot, and specifically to the Governor.

Suitable selection of punishments presented a particular problem. Incarceration, with regular meals and without torture, was thought to be no discouragement to Chinese malefactors. Ordinance No. 10 of 1844 therefore provided that the courts 'may sentence anyone of Chinese origin to undergo such punishment in conformity with the usages of China as has hitherto been usually inflicted on natives of China committing offences in the colony'. These traditional punishments were generally a fine of $15 or twenty strokes with the rattan, also, admitted Mr Hawes, defending the ordinance on behalf of the Foreign Office in the House of Commons on 25 January 1847, 'the loss of their tails' – considered a great humiliation. But 'the most ingenious barbarities that could be devised', characteristic of Chinese law, were not allowed. In other colonies such punishments, which were not in accordance with the laws of England and which were carried out in public, would not have been permitted, but the Colonial Office had reluctantly conceded that this was a special case, 'one of those insoluble problems that flow out of the anomalous position of Hong Kong' to which 'no sagacity can discover a path to which plausible and well-founded objections may not be raised'.[18]

The foreign community hardly presented a good example to the Chinese population: 'A Resident', commenting on the calm of Hong Kong evenings in 1845, wrote: 'probably also the nature of the pursuits of most, have a tendency to encourage seclusion. Our military gentlemen are the same all over the world.' Bishop Smith was more forthright, and described 'the frequent spectacle of European irreligion . . . scenes frequently occur in the public streets, and in the interior of houses, which are calculated to place the countrymen of Missionaries in an unfavourable aspect before the native mind', but he did not consider that the police treatment of Chinese helped matters. They were 'treated as a degraded race of people . . . not permitted to go out into the public streets after a certain hour in the evening, without a lantern and a written note from their European employer'. Insensitivity amounting sometimes to brutality towards the Chinese population remained common in Hong Kong, but the rule of law prevailed to an extent unknown elsewhere in Asia. In capital cases the laws and the penalties were equal for all. Europeans were tried, flogged and even hanged, in public, in the same way and for the same offences as Chinese. The first such execution to provide 'the dreadful sight of an Englishman being hanged in Hongkong' was carried out on Charles Ingwood, a seaman from H.M.S. *Driver*, on 3 July 1845, for the murder of a baker named Wilkinson. To make matters worse, Ingwood suffered 'the further indignity of being hanged with the Chinaman Chun Afoon', which did not, however, seem to worry Ingwood unduly. American observers were particularly impressed by the even-handedness of colonial law in capital cases, which was strongly in contrast to the habits particularly of the Southern states of the Union: 'It is only in the colonies of Hong Kong and Macao that a European would be executed for the murder of a Chinese,' one commented.[19]

It was the less serious cases that caused the problems. Davis's previous experience on the Select Committee at Canton had amply proved to him the difficulty of controlling the European private merchants there, and things were now further complicated by the dispersion of the merchants throughout the treaty ports. Under the terms of the colonial constitution such persons were equally subject to the jurisdiction of the courts of Hong Kong and bound by the ordinances issued by the Governor in his capacity as Superintendent of Trade; but no police were available at the treaty ports to enforce such regulations. The most obstreperous troublemakers were naturally the crews of the opium-smuggling ships. Temple Layton, the Consul at Amoy, described their ships as 'the resort of Thieves, Robbers, Pimps and Prostitutes with few exceptions . . . there is a close connection between the vilest of the vile Chinese population and our opium ships'.[20]

The threat of misbehaving British subjects was taken so seriously that Pottinger, not a nervous man, had a warship stationed at each of the ports. This was not to protect British interests, but in order that 'evil disposed subjects of her Majesty shall be effectively restrained from riotous and disorderly conduct'.[21] The system was not generally effective, but what the presence of the warships did provide, however, was a something-more-than-moral force to the arguments of the consuls with the local Chinese authorities. The lightly armed gunboats enabled consular officers both to coerce the mandarins and to offer them substantial support in suppressing disorders. These comparatively pacific local settlements were the origin of the unduly maligned 'gunboat diplomacy', which was often successful in preventing far worse troubles. Gunboats were however no substitute for regular policing, as the Compton case (pp. 178–9) proved. Lord Aberdeen had piously trusted that the normal British respect for law would go at least some way to remedy this deficiency, but 'nothing but the extreme hazard of exempting our fellow subjects in China from an effective local control would justify such an innovation'.[22]

Sulphur, pitch, beer or porter – and opium

Far more worrying to Lord Aberdeen's colleagues was the likely cost of their new colony, estimated by Mr Martin, whose views as Colonial Treasurer had to be taken reasonably seriously however intemperately expressed, at upwards of half a million pounds a year – an alarming figure, though it proved to be grossly exaggerated. While some allowance might be made for the colony's serving as a depot and centre for support of trade throughout China, the greater part of its costs must be matched by local revenue, and any attempt to do this was certain to encounter bitter resistance. Davis had admitted the difficulties of raising income in his April 1845 dispatch, citing piracy and Article XIII of the Bogue Treaty ('an injury that nothing but a fresh convention can remedy'). He had been able to contradict Martin's prediction 'in his peculiar province of treasurer' only by instancing a rise from his estimate of £5,000 to an actual sum of £13,000 – hardly significant in the context of Martin's figures – in that most important source of revenue, the sale of land. Although Sir John believed the prospects of the colony to be good ('The progress made during the last winter is quite striking ... the capabilities of the place, with all its natural difficulties, will altogether surpass the first expectation'), the income from land had shrunk as the general disillusionment had grown.

The merchants did not share their Governor's optimism, being thoroughly discontented. They had come to Hong Kong for one reason only, to make money, and they were not doing so. A deputation informed the Colonial Secretary on 29 August 1845: 'Hong Kong has no trade at all and is the mere place of residence of the Government and its officers with a few British merchants and a very scanty poor population.' The *Economist* of 8 August 1846 agreed: 'Hong Kong is nothing but a depot for a few opium smugglers, soldiers, officers and men-of-war's men.' Piracy and crime might contribute to the poor level of profitability, but the root cause was the overblown expectations of the merchants themselves.

When at last China was opened for trade by the Treaty of Nanking, enthusiastic exporters, primarily in Britain, but also in America and Australia, began flooding the market with their products, not all of which succeeded in finding ready buyers. Mr John Ford, of Holyrood Glassworks in Edinburgh, sent out a large speculative consignment of glassware, which languished in Jardine's godown for years. It would eventually be sold, Alexander Matheson assured Mr Ford, but 'The total absence of demand arising from the smallness of the community and the custom of sending home for supplies' would make it a slow business. Boulcotts of Wellington, early New Zealand exporters, fared no better: 'We are sorry the slates and soap are still on hand, the former being quite unsuitable for Eastern houses, which are so much exposed to Hurricanes, and the stock of the latter in this place being much greater than can be used for years!' Oddly enough, considering the accusations of drunkenness that were to be thrown around, wines and spirits were in only moderate demand. There was some success with sherry, but Marsala was, as it were, a drug on the market: even the military refused it. Mr Jameson Hunter of Fenchurch Street had to be advised that 'Everything in our power has been done to get rid of it [the wine], even so much as tendering it to the commissariat, but all in vain . . . We have for years past urged on our friends the impolicy of sending out large quantities of Wines and such articles to a country like this, where no demand exists for them beyond the few hundred individuals composing the foreign community . . . These remarks will prepare you for our dissuading you in the strongest terms from sending out here such goods as Brandy, Currants, Macaroni, Sulphur, Pitch, Beer or Porter.'[23]

Those traders, like Matheson, who had bought land at the first sales on the assumption that it was to be on either a long lease or freehold, had spent large sums on building, and when leases were fixed at only seventy-five years they found themselves left with an expensive investment. They had paid what were considered full prices for the land: one firm of merchants at the Select Committee of 1847 testified that they had sent a partner from Macao to the first sale advertised by Captain Elliott: 'We thought that for a sea lot 50 or 60 $ ground rent would be quite ample: but when it went up to the price that it did, we gave up all notion of having land there' (Item 1352). Alexander Matheson suggested that they would be satisfied with the present rent if a

999-year lease were granted, but 'no British merchant would spend £10,000 on a house if the ground lease was only for seventy-five years' (Item 2175). It was true that large sums of private money had been disbursed: Lieutenant Bernard Collinson of the Sappers, who in 1845 produced the first, very fine, map of Hong Kong, and probably did most of the work in designing Flagstaff House, wrote to his parents in England on 26 January of that year: 'If you leave Hong Kong for a month, where you left a rock you find a drawing room in the height of Indian luxury – and a road where there was 20 feet of water.'[24] Captain Arthur Conynghame wrote at the same time: 'The town itself is long and straggling . . . It would be difficult to state its limits, as it is daily increasing in a most surprising manner; what, on my first arrival, was scarcely more than a crowd of bamboo huts, has now become a substantially built town . . . The buildings, which cannot fail to attract the attention of the most casual observer, as being far more magnificent . . . are the . . . "godowns" of Messrs Matheson and Jardine, the merchant princes of the Far East. Immediately above them are two handsome bungalows, or summer residences, belonging to the same proprietors.'[25]

As well as making maps, the Royal Engineers had been busy on roads, drains, harbour facilities and public buildings, not to everyone's pleasure: 'The innovators . . . dig drains, lay out streets and give names to places, establish London[?] from A—Z, keep lamplighters and lamps to light, and won't look at the old warriors at all [who vow] that everything was perfect before the "Queen's people", as they call them, came.'[26]. But facilities were still few by comparison with those of Canton and Macao, and Conynghame did not much like the colony: 'The climate of Hong Kong for nine months of the year, is hot and oppressive . . . the want of substantial buildings, libraries, billiard rooms, or other places of resort, render a residence there, to a person who has not constant employment, an extremely monotonous existence.'

Until the dissatisfaction with the leases could be remedied, which it eventually was in 1848, there was little likelihood of a buoyant income from land rents or auctions. Local unhappiness was increased by the high cost of living: the *Canton*, now the *Hong Kong*, *Register* reported that the only British hotel in Victoria 'is conducted on a small but respectable scale . . . prices are necessarily high: board and lodging for a single person without wines or beer is $2 per diem'. Conynghame complained that 'the rent of a house of four rooms is there constantly known to be 60 or 70 $ per month . . . and the price of anything like luxuries equally high'. He instanced an advertisement: 'The gentry of Hong Kong . . . can be furnished with fine English mutton (at one half dollar per pound), by sending their orders to "The Briton's Boast".'

Nothing in John Davis's character or experience helped him conciliate the disappointed colonists: cool and aloof, short and personally undistinguished, he lacked Pottinger's bravura. His interest in Chinese literature, and his ability to write passably good Latin verse ('Hic, in remotis sol ubi rupibus Frondes per altas mollius incidit . . .'), did little to commend him to so raw a community, which 'considered Rupees and dollars of a great deal more consequence'. Alexander Matheson complained of cronyism: 'I am disgusted beyond measure just now at finding from Cleverly that Davis has named all the streets in Victoria after his personal friends . . . and not even a lane has been named after a merchant . . . Just fancy "Shelley St." named after a swindler etc. etc. How much more natural Jardine St., Dent St., Gibbs St., etc. would have sounded. No! the devil of a dollar shall I lay out in Hong Kong except for the sake of a profitable investment.'[27]

Sir John began his term inauspiciously by having 'a row with everyone and is therefore not generally popular'.[28] In an effort to establish some degree of control in the colony, Davis, using the wide powers he had been given, issued an ordinance which was announced (in October 1844) only a fortnight before it was due to go into effect, prescribing compulsory registration for all residents – even the British. This was immediately the object of furious attack: 'a poll tax was to be levied not only on Chinese vagabonds but on all the inhabitants without exception . . . The only distinction between a British merchant and a Chinese coolie was the enactment that the former should pay five dollars and the latter one dollar a year.' If Eitel, forty years later, still found the suggestion horrifying, the reaction of the Europeans at the time was hysterical: 'They rose up like one man in wrathful indignation, feeling their self-respect, their national honour, the liberty of the subject trampled underfoot.'[29]

Remonstrances against 'a measure unexampled in modern British legislation, fraught with great and certain mischief . . . which, if forced into operation, will reduce apparently the Island of Hong Kong to the level of a Penal Settlement'[30] poured in upon the Governor, to be answered by accusations that the merchants had 'by unworthy practices, tampered with an ignorant and unfortunate Chinese population by instigating them to passive resistance'. It might be that this was true, since notices were posted by the compradores of the European Hongs urging resistance to the proposal, but the Chinese needed little persuasion. In the first action of a sort that was later to prove most effective, they simply downed tools and went on strike, some three thousand actually leaving the colony.

These reactions proved that although the Governor's authority was in theory unlimited, the European and Chinese communities had it in their power to prevent his taking any measure of which they disapproved sufficiently strongly. The ordinance was accordingly amended, exempting everyone from registration who might complain ('all civil, military and naval employees, all members of the learned professions, merchants, shopkeepers, householders, tenants of Crown Property and persons having an income of $500 a year' – which can have left few Europeans exposed), and cancelling the tax on the Chinese. This was not enough to satisfy the editor of the *Friend of China*, who wrote on 25 January 1845, when the worst of the tumult was over: 'Whatever may be the opinion of His Excellency on the point, we fear that the registration ordinance will call forth a rebuke from the colonial office, which, from a proud man, will at once demand an immediate resignation.'

In an attempt to make up for the disappointing returns from land, Davis had to scratch around for other taxes of almost any kind, which eventually included duties on auctions, marriages, funerals, carriages, billiard tables, alcohol and tobacco and domestic rates. These, especially the last, drove the colonists to complain to the Secretary of State, William Gladstone, of 'harassing taxation' being 'arbitrarily' levied without representation – a time-honoured cry. They demanded a municipal council, which Gladstone refused on the grounds that 'the English minority could hardly be entrusted' with the powers that this would give them over the Chinese. The Hong Kong residents argued that Britain had taken the place as a strategic base, and the Services ought therefore to pay the expenses of running it; Gladstone rejected that too, insisting, not quite accurately, that Hong Kong had been acquired 'solely and exclusively with a view to commercial interest'.[31]

The subjects of registration and taxation refused to go away, and remained persistent bones of contention between the merchants and the home government. The merchants had better success with their objection to Davis's proposed duty on imported wines and spirits, which was unanimously opposed by the Legislative Council (all officials), who persisted in carrying their opposition to the Colonial

Secretary. Gladstone upheld their objections, and the Governor had
to withdraw the proposal.

A similar row followed Davis's decision to subcontract the right to
deal in opium for consumption in Hong Kong, the 'opium farm' which
Montgomery Martin was bitterly opposed to and made a resigning
issue. Davis had overcome the distaste for the drug he had shown to
the Select Committee ten years previously, and raised money first by
selling the sole right to distribute opium in the colony, and later by a
system of licensing premises and retailers. Whitehall on this occasion
supported him, but the experiment was only moderately successful,
and aroused the particular ire of the drug importers. Opium sales in
the rest of China, however, were rising rapidly.

Immediately upon his arrival Davis had been introduced by Pottinger
to Ch'i-ing, and had at once raised 'the important and at the same
time delicate question of legalizing the opium trade, repeating that
such a wise and happy measure would remove every existing chance
of unpleasant discussion . . . provide an ample revenue for the Empire,
and check to the same extent the consumption of a commodity which
at present was absolutely untaxed'. He appealed to psychology: 'The
disposition of men attaches value to what is difficult of attainment . . .
In China, since opium was prohibited, it has greedily been purchased
. . . In England, where it has always been lawful . . . men generally
dislike it.' But arguments were in vain; it was not that Ch'i-ing was
averse to finding a solution, since he had earlier suggested a lump
payment in lieu of duty on the drug, which Pottinger had found impracticable. Ch'i-ing now had to turn down Davis's proposals flat, saying
that 'he dared not originate such a discussion'. Reporting this to Lord
Aberdeen on 13 June 1844, Davis expressed the hope that he might
yet succeed: 'Were it my good fortune at some future period to
announce to your Lordship that the trade had been legalized, I should
consider myself amply repaid for my present residence in this
country.'[32] But some arrangement had to be made. An understanding
was accordingly reached, which although informal was none the less
well understood.

The campaign against the use of opium had always been patchy,
with very occasional savage sorties punctuating peaceful periods of
blind-eye-turning. The latter now became the rule, and prosecutions
'a pretense'.[33] Throughout the whole of China in 1843 only twenty-
four drug offenders – mostly users – were remanded for trial; in 1845
sixty were convicted, but sentencing was held over; in 1846 nine cases

were held for trial: in 1848 eight, of which seven were from Peking. Confiscations, when they were made, were measured in ounces. This was at a time when the opium imports from India alone, according to W.H. Mitchell, who reported on the trade in December 1850, averaged over forty thousand chests a year – between three and four thousand tons, to which must be added the Turkish and the home-grown opium, about which only guesses can be made.

Needless to say there was therefore no attempt on the part of the Chinese authorities to suppress imports; this was actually agreed in writing by Ch'i-ing in 1842: 'Whether the merchant vessels of the various countries bring opium or not, China will not need to enquire, or to take any proceedings with regard to it'[34] – than which it is difficult to get closer to legalization. Thoughtful Chinese were saddened by what they appreciated was a condemnation of their own society:

> For the past several years, we have wanted to stop the people from smoking opium. But the people have not complied. This is an age in which servants adamantly squat on their haunches . . . while descendants beat their grandfathers. Even if the English neither encroached upon nor rebelled against us, but rather anxiously sought to submit and pay tribute, China would still be disgraced and miserable.[35]

For his part, Pottinger had agreed to ban British ships from all but the ports opened by the Treaty, and from sailing beyond latitude 32 degrees North (just north of Shanghai). In order to reinforce his proclamation the Foreign Office secured an Order in Council to this effect. Pottinger believed that this was no less than what was 'due to the China government to enforce the prohibition', but the cynical James Matheson wrote that the ban was not intended to be taken seriously, but was considered 'a great joke', something to keep 'the Saints' at home content.

But the Royal Navy did not 'for a moment suppose that a British Minister would issue proclamations without the intention to act upon them', and in April 1843 Captain Charles Hope, commanding at Chusan, arrested a Jardine Matheson ship, *Vixen*. The opium traders remonstrated vigorously to Pottinger in a most extraordinary communication, graciously conceding that 'they would be always ready to obey, *as far as their duty to their constituents and they themselves will admit* [my italics] any legal regulations that may be laid down'.[36] If ever mercantile arrogance deserved one of Sir Henry's fizzers, this surely did, but nothing of the sort ensued. He knew too well the value of the opium income to India, and the implications of the agreement with Ch'i-ing. The unfortunate Captain Hope was therefore disowned and sent back to England. The Services protested, but even Wellington's backing could not alter matters: the opium interest was too strong for any government, British or Chinese, to oppose. Pottinger did feel that Hope was entitled to an explanation, and wrote a revealing letter (secret and confidential) to Admiral Parker, copied to Hope. The Plenipotentiary explained that he had 'constantly' raised the opium question with 'His Excellency the Viceroy [of Fukien] who roundly admitted I was quite right, but said, as it pleased the Emperor to disallow the traffic', he could do no more than promise 'that the Chinese Authorities should not trouble themselves to inquire what Vessels brought opium or which did not: and that their business would be to see that the Soldiery, and the People of China, did not purchase the drug'.[37]

After this hiccup things settled down. No officials, British or Chinese, would interfere with the opium traders, but neither would the smugglers benefit from official protection. Their ships were banned from entry into the ports under consular control, which only incommoded them insofar as they were therefore more exposed to pirate attacks. Their habitual mooring stations were however openly recognized, described in sailing directions, and even occasionally moved to comply with the advice of the local mandarins. The legal traders and the smugglers were strictly separated; different vessels had to be used for legitimate and contraband cargoes, since a ship carrying even a small quantity of opium would not be allowed into a treaty port.

One effect of this was to give added strength to the richer merchants, of whom there were by 1844 effectually only two, Jardine Matheson and Dent. For them Hong Kong was invaluable. Opium could be imported and left in store under British protection until one of the clippers was ready to take it up the coast. If smaller fry attempted to muscle in, the duopoly would simply combine to undercut them. The previous rivalry was shelved, Jardine Matheson and Dent opium ships operating in pairs at all of the most important of the unofficially recognized clearing anchorages. This did not help the economy of Hong Kong, since if Jardine Matheson and Dent kept the opium in their own hands, selling only up the coast, there was no incentive for anyone else to come to Hong Kong. The 1850 Mitchell Report described the situation thus:

Really it is a matter of immense surprise to me how Hong Kong has any trade of any kind whatever. Here we have these two powerful Houses making heavy pecuniary sacrifices every other month, to *beat back to the Coast*, any trade which may try to force its way down to this Colony, and thereby utterly shutting out the sugars and coarse drugs, such as Camphor and Alum and similar stuffs, which the native coasters would otherwise bring down to us. This in itself would be hard enough for any young Colony to contend with. But, when in addition to this, our Treaty with China limits all Junk traffic with this port to Junks clearing out of the Five Ports, and places even these under the most vexatious restrictions – my repeated wonder is that the Colony has any trade at all.[38]

If they attack our people, they will be shot

Many writers have assumed that the Chinese government, smarting under the humiliation of the Treaty of Nanking, had no intention of observing its provisions any longer than necessary, and of taking the first opportunity of revenge. Quite apart from the fact that Chinese governments, Imperial, Republican, or Communist, have a rather better record of fulfilling international obligations than those of many Western nations, the evidence of the Historical Archives in Beijing is that the Emperor Tao-kuang ratified the Treaty in the best of faith, and personally went to some lengths to ensure that his subordinates followed its provisions. In April 1844 Ch'i-ing advised the Emperor that French and American ships were now coming to Canton, and that the populace there had been warned to behave themselves. Acknowledging this, the Emperor commented in the same month in response to a memorandum from Liu Yun-k'o, Governor of Fukien, that the treaty arrangements were 'just, practical, strict and clear'. Four months later this was reinforced by a vermilion note ordering that 'everything in relation to the foreigners should be done well and carefully, so as not to lose face for the state and make trouble for ourselves. This point must be recognized.'[39]

A corps of officials who made a real effort to accommodate themselves to the British, without losing sight of the interests of the Empire, emerged. The most distinguished of these was Hsü Chi-yü (Xu Jiyu),

Financial Commissioner and subsequently Governor of Fukien, later member of the Tsungli (Zongli) Yamen, the bureau for foreign affairs established in 1861 at Peking, and author of the world survey published in 1850 that 'was destined to become the leading world atlas for a whole generation of Chinese literati'.[40] The Hsü family have been at the forefront of modern Chinese history: Hsü's grandson was the famous civil war general Xu Xiangqian, early colleague of Mao and Commander-in-Chief of the Fourth Front Red Army, who later sided with Chou En-lai in attempting to halt the Cultural Revolution. 'We want more people like Hsü,' wrote his superior, Liu Yun-k'o, 'flexible, knowing their business, capable of weighing the pros and cons and acquainted with the manners of the foreigners.' Again the Emperor approved – 'Very sincere: let it be so.'[41]

Although Pottinger's communications were also described by the Emperor as 'very sincere', his brand of bluster was not appreciated by the Chinese with whom he had to deal. 'Impolite, demanding, knitting his brows – I had to argue till my mouth was burning,' complained Ch'i-ing to the Emperor when reporting the negotiations at the Bogue: 'low taxes, light punishments, permission to buy books, to run Hong Kong freely, build houses, churches and cemeteries, free access for missionaries – all were demanded'.[42] At first the bland Davis made a welcome change from his brusquer predecessor. On his visit of inspection to the treaty ports he omitted the customary gun salutes, which always worried the Chinese. Hsü was pleased to find the new barbarian head 'subservient, removing his hat, always polite'.[43] For his part Davis enjoyed making use of his considerable knowledge of the Chinese language and customs to smooth relations.

In spite of Imperial support, Davis's experience and the considerable good will that Ch'i-ing invariably extended, the city of Canton continued to be a focus of trouble for the British. It might have been that the population of Canton was more hostile to foreigners than that of other ports, where relations developed satisfactorily, or that the stirrings of unrest that were to lead to the Taiping revolt were becoming apparent.

This complex and fascinating movement began in a similar way and at much the same time as that of the Mormons in the United States. A partly-educated young man, Hung Hsiu-ch'uan (Hong Xiuqan), was granted a heavenly vision, as a result of which an idiosyncratic version of Christianity developed, leading in turn to the foundation of a theocracy, the Heavenly Kingdom of Eternal Peace, the T'ai-ping t'ien-kuo.

Hung came from a peasant family of Hakka descent (the Hakkas being seventeenth-century and later immigrants from further north, whose dialect and customs differentiated them from the Cantonese). Beginning his missionary work in 1843, within six years he had attracted some ten thousand followers. In 1852 an anti-Confucian, anti-gentry, anti-Manchu crusade was launched. By March of the following year the Tai-pings, as they were known, had marched 1,300 miles to capture Nanking, which was to be their capital for eleven years. Canton itself was held for the Manchus against the rebels only by violent repression, assisted by the dislike of many Cantonese for what seemed a Hakka enterprise, and one with unpleasant connotations of Western influence.

Bishop George Smith, who travelled extensively in China in the 1840s, had noted 'a wide and marked difference between the friendly and peaceable demeanour of the people in the more northerly cities, and the arrogant turbulence of spirit which still forms the discriminating characteristic of the Canton mob'. Defiant wall-newspapers took 'the place of the press, and being anonymous, their language is unrestrained, generally provocative, and often scurrilous'. These were deployed to incite the populace to discontent: 'The wild barbarians must be destroyed,' and the people must determine 'first to decapitate and exterminate the odious race and then burn and destroy their habitations'.[44]

Ch'i-ing, in his capacity as Imperial Commissioner, endeavoured to keep relations on a friendly basis, but never succeeded in establishing the same close friendship with Davis that he had so successfully forged with Pottinger. He did pay a state visit to Hong Kong, which Collinson described (23 November 1845) as three days of 'reviews, dances, balls and levees, all in honour of Sir Henry Pottinger's friend Keying, Governor General of the Two Quangs, Imperial Commissioner, Member of the Royal Family etc. etc. He came down in the *Vixen* from Canton on Thursday and whatever his special business may be he has had very little time for it, for he has been eating and drinking with very little intermission ever since he landed ... He is however a very intelligent Chinaman, but as fat as a pig.'

Attacks on foreigners were severely discouraged and appropriately punished by Ch'i-ing, but the arrogant behaviour of some of the British exacerbated matters. British officials, since the days of the Select Committee, had deplored the manners of their compatriots, which had not apparently improved. It was one of the much-distrusted private traders who sparked off the worst disturbances, with the most serious effects.

On 4 April 1846 one Charles Compton, a British merchant based in Canton and said to be known as 'a hectoring sort of man, noted for his repeated acts of violence towards the Chinese', became annoyed with a Chinese fruit vendor, whom he thought too noisy, and knocked over his stall. Three days later he attacked the man, dragging him into the foreign quarter and beating him. There was an immediate riot. Placards appeared demanding the death of the British: 'It is only you English, who, to gratify your wolf-like hearts, unbridled and without fear . . . are truly detestable.' The merchants appealed for the protection of a warship; Francis Macgregor, the British Consul, tried his best to smooth things over, and had the case brought before the consular court.

Davis, acting as Chief Superintendent of Trade, anxious to preserve good relations with Ch'i-ing and seeing in Compton another Innes up to his tricks, found Compton guilty, and fined him $200. Compton appealed to the Supreme Court, where Chief Justice Hulme found that 'the whole proceedings were so irregular as to render all that had occurred a perfect nullity', accompanying his judgement with some severe reflections on the Governor's actions, which were 'unjust, excessive and illegal . . . evincing a total disregard for all forms of law and for the law itself'. Davis, taking the decision as a direct insult and a challenge to his authority, appealed to London.[45]

Back in Whitehall, the government had changed once more, and with the Whigs back in power, different attitudes towards the colonies emerged. Sir Robert Peel's Tory government had grasped the nettle of Corn Law repeal, but in doing so had bitterly alienated the right wing of the party. After a defeat – again over Ireland – Lord John Russell was given his opportunity, in July 1846, to form a Whig administration, with Palmerston back at the Foreign Office and Lord Grey, son of the Reform Bill Earl, as Secretary of State for the Colonies. Grey did not approve of Palmerston, and needed to be cajoled into sitting in the same Cabinet as him, so Davis had to report to difficult masters. Palmerston, very much in charge of matters insofar as they affected relations with China, vigorously set about all concerned. Compton was sent a departmental dispatch on 11 March 1847, regretting that 'in consequence of the irregular manner in which those proceedings were conducted, you have escaped the penalty you would otherwise have incurred'. This was accompanied by a letter from Palmerston himself, of the same date, warning Compton that he could be prosecuted for murder under British law if any deaths resulted from his actions in China: 'Her Majesty's Government are determined . . . that no injury shall arise to peace and good order in China from the concession which has been made to Her Majesty of exclusive jurisdiction over British subjects in China.'

But already the Compton case had been succeeded by another, in which the Chinese seemed to be the aggressors. Two British sailors had been badly injured in a disturbance in Canton, and Davis had dealt with the case by fining their captain for allowing them to enter the city. Palmerston, when he heard of this, was furious, and took Davis to task on 12 January 1847: the obligation to behave properly was reciprocal, and British subjects must be guaranteed 'freedom from molestation': 'I have to instruct you to demand the punishment of the parties guilty of this outrage . . . and that, if the Chinese Authorities will not by the exercise of their own authority punish and prevent such outrages, the British Government will be obliged to take the matter into their own hands.' Rather more civilly, but spelling out the facts of life as seen by the Foreign Secretary, he added: 'We shall lose all vantage ground we have gained . . . if we take a low tone . . . Of course we ought, and by we I mean all the English in China, to abstain from giving the Chinese any ground for complaint, and much more from anything like provocation and affront; but . . . we must make them all clearly understand, though in the civillest terms, that our Treaty rights must be respected . . . The Chinese must learn and be convinced that if they attack our people and our factories, they will be shot.'

It was probably the receipt of Palmerston's sharp note that spurred Davis to take the precipitate action that he did, and his official correspondence shows signs of rising hysteria. A minor incident on 12 March 1847, when some visitors to Fatshan, near Canton, had stones thrown at them, led to increasingly high-pitched letters from Davis to Ch'i-ing: 'It is my duty to inform you that you will bring down calamity upon the Chinese people . . . there is no remedy but to proceed to Canton with a force and demand reparation on the spot.' The force then available was commanded by Major-General Charles D'Aguilar. Originally a rifleman, commissioned into the 86th (Royal Irish Rifles) in 1799, he had seen a good deal of action with his regiment in India, but since 1810 had been a successful staff officer, mainly in the Adjutant-Generals' departments, although including one mission to the famous Ali Pasha of Janina. A cultivated and humane man, although prone to tetchiness, D'Aguilar had been horrified by the illness he found among the army in Hong Kong: 'The 4th Madras Sepoys are destroyed and quite useless . . . so many walking skeletons.' Acting on his own responsibility, he took the initiative of sending an entire regiment back to India in a successful effort to halt the spread of disease. He threw himself into the task of building healthier barracks, and had the satisfaction of seeing the health of the troops rapidly improve.

When the agitated Davis approached him, suitably enough on 1 April 1847, with the prospect of a punitive expedition to Canton, D'Aguilar could call upon less than a thousand available men, but he enthusiastically agreed to the proposal. Both Pottinger and Davis had previously been forced to restrain the General's lust for action: D'Aguilar had written in his diary in September 1845: 'I have no diplomatic or political authority and they must settle it their way,' but added prophetically: 'It will be strange if they don't want my assistance later.'[46] Now it appeared 'they' did, and the following day Governor and General set off with their forces, comprising some men of the 18th Foot, the Royal Irish, and sepoys of the 42nd Madras, in four steamships. It was these small vessels that made the adventure possible, being of shallow enough draft to penetrate right up to the city. Somehow, against all sensible expectations, they managed to sail right through the defences of the Bogue. D'Aguilar was able to report that 'in a sudden promenade' he had 'assaulted and taken all the principal forts at the Bogue, and in the Canton river, and, after destroying the gateways and blowing up the magazines, spiked 827 pieces of cannon'.[47] Having suffered no casualties worth mentioning, the tiny force was confidently preparing to storm the city, when Ch'i-ing, luckily for all concerned, smoothed things over. Foreigners, he promised, would indeed be allowed access to Canton, but only in two years' time, when he was sure popular unrest would have subsided (and by which time neither he nor Davis expected to be in their respective posts). The foreign community, who had been flabbergasted by Davis's sudden eruption, were relieved but unconvinced. The old Canton hand Gideon Nye wrote: 'His Excellency's action in 1847 was restrained by two influences: one, a want of force; the other the want of unanimity among the leading merchants.' It was also, he rightly observed, completely ineffective, since the point at issue, the immediate right of entry to Canton, had not been conceded: 'And thus his administration of affairs, like that of Sir Henry Pottinger, left Canton without its suffering chastisement for accumulated wrongs.'[48]

Nevertheless, Lord Palmerston found this bit of bloodless sabre-rattling, generally known as the 'buccaneering expedition', very much

to his taste, and congratulated all concerned. But the already disgruntled Chinese population's fury was exacerbated, and only a few
months later six young Englishmen were murdered in a village outside
Canton, in the worst incident so far experienced.

By then Davis had shot his bolt, and could do nothing but expostu-
late to Ch'i-ing: 'You either cannot or will not protect the lives of
British subjects . . . It is now time for the British Government to
require not only satisfaction for the past, but security for the future.'
He demanded that the whole village should be punished if the culprits
could not be identified and executed, and received in return a dignified
remonstrance on 17 December 1847: 'as in any debt there is a debtor,
so in all wrongs there are chief culprits. Now, the number of people
in the village in question is great, and if a whole village is destroyed
without distinction of good and bad . . . how could the azure heaven
above . . . possibly endure such an excessive implication of the innocent? In the whole world there is no such principle of reason as this,
and your Excellency's country must itself have no such punishment.'
Ch'i-ing did succeed in bringing those chiefly concerned in the mur-
ders to justice, but no further progress was made on the immediate
question of admitting foreigners within the city.

Davis had already decided to go, thoroughly disgusted by the atmosphere of the colony. Although payment was eventually, in 1846, made
by the Treasury for the opium commandeered by Captain Elliot, this
had not appeased the more extreme among the merchants, who pressed
for the conquest of whole provinces of China, so that 'the degenerate
natives would be supplanted by Saxon races transplanted, mature and
fresh'. General D'Aguilar contributed to the fractiousness, for being a
gentleman of sometimes uneven temper he had offended the civilians.
Not only did he object to 'furious riding', but a jollification in one Mr
Welch's house had been interrupted by a sergeant sent on behalf of
the General, 'to whose gentle ear the rude sound of civilian hilarity
was particularly obnoxious'. Welch offered to throw the General out
if he came himself, and the local press, attempting to explain this
'eccentric conduct' of the General's, 'supposed he had passed his life
among Helots and knew little of the manly independence of a British
community'.[49]

Sir John embroiled himself in a spot of bother with more drastic
consequences – this time in his capacity as Governor rather than as
Plenipotentiary. Relations with Hulme, the Chief Justice, culminating
in his stinging criticisms of the Governor over the Compton case, had

deteriorated to the point where, in a desperate effort to get rid of him, Davis had written to Lord Grey asking for his removal on the grounds that he was habitually drunk in public. Hulme was certainly a jovial and sociable creature, whose conduct at a ball given by Admiral Cochrane is sympathetically described by the surgeon E.H. Cree: 'Tung ['a merry fellow . . . husband of an Imperial Princess'] spoils a quadrille by dancing a hornpipe with the Chief Justice, both having partaken too freely of simkin. It was a laughable exhibition; Tung fat . . . and capering about like an elephant, and the Judge anything but grave, flinging his long skinny legs, encased in breeches and black silk stockings, in all directions, his long visage and protuberant nose, his bushy head and broad grin, having anything but a judge-like appearance.'[50] An accusation of habitual drunkenness, however, made in a letter from the Governor to the Secretary of State, was a serious matter – more serious than Davis, who had dashed off the letter in a fit of exasperation with the world in general, and with Hulme in particular (there had been a dispute as to whether Hulme could properly be addressed as 'His Lordship'), had expected. An inquiry was held by the Executive Council, against the opposition of General D'Aguilar, who could well see whither the affair would lead. Evidence was given that while the Chief Justice had certainly been seen the better for drink, a condition not entirely unknown even among the highest ranks of the judiciary, he was by no means a habitual drunkard, unfit for his post. Davis had however painted himself into a corner and, in the face of the evidence, suspended Hulme from his functions and sent him back to England. Hong Kong society, unanimously supporting Hulme, was furious against the Governor, and was immensely satisfied when London eventually decided that the whole proceedings had been wrongly conducted, and the Chief Justice was reinstated. It was also felt in Whitehall that troubles in Hong Kong were becoming too frequent, and a Select Committee of the House of Commons was appointed to investigate the affairs of the colony and to recommend on its future.

By then it was too late for Davis, who had already resigned, and was to leave the colony in March 1848 for forty-seven years of retirement. As on the previous occasion, his departure from the China Coast was not lamented. Eitel recorded: 'the community, with stolid apathy, watched from a distance the salutes fired, the faint cheer of a few devoted friends . . . there was no public address, no banquet, no popular farewell. The leading paper of the colony gave voice to the feelings of the public by stating that Sir John "was . . . unfit for a Colonial

Government by his personal demeanour and disposition".'[51] The more generous Legge wrote: 'How it came about, I hardly know; but of all our governors he left his office under the greatest cloud of popular dissatisfaction.'[52]

7

RETRENCHMENT

Houses of bad fame, billiard rooms and boats

Montgomery Martin's attacks, the squabble between Hulme and Davis and the complaints of the residents had made an investigation into the affairs of Hong Kong and the China trade essential, and a Select Committee of the House of Commons was accordingly appointed to do this in March 1847. Its senior figure was Francis Baring, Chancellor of the Exchequer in the previous Whig administration. Commercial experience was provided by the old China hands James Matheson, now Member for Ashburton in succession to Jardine, together with his banker John Abel Smith and Sir George Staunton. Among the other members were Edward Cardwell, William Ewart and Benjamin Hawes, all sensible reformers; and Dr John Bowring, a radical reformer of varied experience, but often seen as something of a figure of fun by reason of his immense learning and singular lack of tact.

The Committee offered the Hong Kong traders who had clamoured for it an opportunity to present their points of view, and the most telling evidence came from Alexander Matheson. Hong Kong, he submitted, had begun well enough:

Hong Kong possesses one of the best harbours in China . . . When the first Europeans settled at Hong Kong, the Chinese showed every disposition to frequent the place, and there was a fair prospect of its becoming a place of considerable trade . . . There were no restrictions of any kind, people went and came as they chose . . . Had the same unrestricted freedom of trade gone on, Hong Kong would inevitably have become a place of great trade. It would have been in time the emporium of China.

But the rot had set in with Davis – although Matheson was careful not to condemn the Governor personally.

In 1843 however, peace was proclaimed; Hong Kong was regularly ceded to us. A formal government was established, great expenses were incurred, and it became almost the exclusive study of the government to raise as large a revenue as possible, to meet the expenses of the place . . . From this time may be dated the reverses of Hong Kong.

The junk trade had, under the supplementary provisions of the Treaty of Nanking, been 'exterminated'. The iniquities of the police ('composed of Chinese of the most abandoned character') and the opium farmers had 'completely extinguished the trade of Hong Kong', which had taken itself off to Cumsingmoon, where

since 1844 a considerable native town has sprung up, with a population of from 3,000 to 4,000 composed entirely of petty traders and junk-men, who have deserted Hong Kong. They have built houses, and pay almost no ground rent. There is an European hotel and billiard room [containing what was formerly the East India Company's billiard table] on shore . . . The place is rapidly increasing under Chinese rule, while Hong Kong, under British sway, is entirely without trade, and daily abandoned by some portion of its population.

But Matheson's highest indignation was reserved for the exorbitant demands of the government for land sales and rents. Short leases and high ground rents, he insisted, must be abandoned, and replaced by perpetual leases at moderate prices. If this were done, together with the

abolition of all the farms now in existence, as well as the discontinuance of all the wretched taxes now levied; such as on houses of bad fame, billiard rooms, boats &c. Also the registration of Chinese, which is extremely repugnant to their feelings . . . I feel convinced that in the course of a few years, Hong Kong will take a new turn, and become one of our most flourishing, as well as valuable possessions.[1]

Alexander Matheson's views were reinforced by a more independent witness, Colonel Malcolm, who had acted as Pottinger's aide. The initiative in questioning Colonel Malcolm was taken by Dr John Bowring, who asked some leading questions:

> Bowring: Then are the committee to understand that your opinion is that a revenue from the sales of land, and a police rate, for the purposes of protecting persons and property, are the only reasonable and proper sources of revenue in the colony?
> Malcolm: I think so. I think a greater revenue would be raised by the land rent, so if the island were perfectly free from all petty taxations, I think that much more land would be let, and that the colony would thrive much better if all those were taken off.
> Bowring: The removal of the petty vexations would be a great encouragement to settling in the island?
> Malcolm: Yes; the Chinese are a peculiar people, and they do not like being interfered with. They do not understand us; they cannot understand our ways: and when they are told that they are to do first one thing and then another, they get frightened and will not come to us.

Hong Kong's problems received only a moderate degree of attention from the Committee in its brief and sober report. Seven of its ten pages presented arguments for a reduction in the duties on tea, citing the rapid rise in the British consumption of coffee (from something over 7 million pounds in 1821 to over 36 million in 1846, carrying duty of four pence a pound) to show that total government income would not necessarily be decreased by a reduction in the percentage rate of duty. Proving that it was, as always, the British revenues from tea rather than opium that concerned Whitehall, the latter subject was dismissed disapprovingly, and almost out of hand: 'The Opium trade, however, already flourishes at Foochowfoo with its usual demoralizing influences on the population, and embarrassing effects upon the monetary condition of the place. The latter would be diminished by the legalization of the traffic; the former, we are afraid, are incontestable, and inseparable from its existence.'

Hong Kong was the final item to be dealt with, in just over a page, which took account of the complaints of 'a highly respectable body of merchants resident at Hong Kong ... that good faith had not been kept in conveying to purchasers no more than a limited tenure of seventy-five years, in lieu of the more permanent interest which they allege to have been held out'.

The Committee sympathized: 'We think it right that the burden of maintaining that which is rather a post for general influence and the protection of the general trade in the China Seas than a colony in the ordinary sense, should be thrown in any great degree on the merchants or other persons who may be resident upon it.'

The 'whole system' needed revision, since 'the Establishment of the Settlement ... has been placed on a footing of needless expense.' They pointed out the difficulties of the Governor's position: 'As Governor of a Colony, he is responsible to the Colonial Office; as in a manner representative of the Crown to a Foreign Court and Superintendent of Trade, to the Foreign Office. It would be well if this relation could be simplified.' An effort must be made to improve communications: 'Facilities should also be given in Hong Kong for the acquisition of the Chinese language and encouragement to schools for the Chinese; and the study of the Chinese language should be encouraged in the Consular officers.'

But there was, the Committee felt, every indication that with good will on both sides, relations should develop peacefully:

> The provisions of the Treaties negotiated by Sir H. Pottinger appear to have been honestly carried out by the Chinese authorities, except at Canton; and even there the difficulties which have been experienced seem to have arisen more from the turbulent character and hostile disposition of the populace ... than from any ill-will or want of good faith on the part of the ruling power. Indeed any other supposition would be totally inconsistent with the conciliatory course of policy pursued in the other ports, and more especially with the character of that distinguished statesman, Keying, who presides over the Government of Canton, and who has on all occasions shown himself not less the friend of peaceful intercourse than the enlightened supporter of his country's interests.

In Hong Kong the report was welcomed, and the major point of the residents' complaints rectified by the substitution, in the following year, of 999-year leases for those of seventy-five years. In due course land sales would provide a revenue income for future Hong Kong administrations, but such income would take time to develop, and the government was adamant that subsidies to Hong Kong must stop. It was a time of financial stringency in Britain. The Irish famine and the collapse of railway speculation had brought extra expense and damaged confidence: commercial failures multiplied; as a crisis measure the Bank Act had to be suspended. Defence spending increased as tension with France grew, and Peel's income tax, meant as a temporary measure, had to be – with great reluctance – extended.

In such a climate there was little prospect of the home government permitting any increase of colonial expenditure, and if there had been Hong Kong would not have been among the favourites. The new Colonial Secretary, the austere Lord Grey, made this clear in his report to the Prime Minister, Lord John Russell: 'the chief object we had to consider . . . was that of the very heavy expenses which [Hong Kong] occasioned'. Very probably the whole venture had been a mistake: 'If the exceedingly large amount of that expense, and the limited use of which the place has proved to our commerce, could have been foreseen, it may well be doubted whether it would have been thought worthwhile that it should be taken possession of.' That, however, could be blamed on their Tory predecessors: 'This had however been done long prior to the formation of your administration; and there only remained for us to endeavour to reduce the expense of the establishment.'[2] Davis's successor as Governor was therefore to carry through a policy of drastic retrenchment. A necessary corollary was that he must refrain from any trouble with the Chinese which would lead to extra expense. This was to be made easier by the fact that China was beginning to experience the worst disruption of the dynasty.

When the Emperor Tao-kuang died in 1850, the 'crazy first-rate man-of-war' was left without a 'sufficient' man at the helm, and, as Macartney had forecast, things rapidly went to pieces. The new Emperor, Hsien-feng (Xian Feng), was only twenty, unreliable, wayward, and much under the influence of his favourite concubine Tz'u-hsi (Cixi), later the famous Dowager Empress, who held the reins of power in China intermittently from 1856 to 1908.[3] Hsien-feng's inheritance was in such a terrible state – on the verge of disintegration, and menaced by famine, flood and war – that it would have daunted a much abler and more experienced man. In 1845 the Yellow River shifted its course to flow north of the Shantung peninsula, causing widespread death and destitution; three years later the Grand Canal, that engineering masterpiece of the Ming linking the Yangtse with northern China, had been rendered impassable; and within months of Hsien-feng's accession the Taiping revolt, which in the next four-teen years was to claim more victims than the Second World War – twenty million is a moderate estimate – had begun its devastating course.

Marxist historians tend to see the Western powers as responsible for much of this, and the Taipings as 'glorious' revolutionaries, whose 'magnificent struggles and historic achievements will always be remembered for propelling the forward advance of history and stimu-lating the revolutionary will of the Chinese people'.[4] What certainly did occur was that the Chinese people themselves, led by traditionalist Confucian gentry, were organized, not unwillingly, into new model armies, and the Western powers decided that stability was best ensured by supporting the Ch'ing central government. Two important develop-ments eventually resulted; the empire's financial resources were better ordered by the establishment of a professional customs service, and a nucleus of conservative reformers willing to avail themselves of Western methods was encouraged. On the debit side, the expan-sion of the lower gentry and their takeover of local administration, together with the formation of regional armies independent, in some degree, of Peking, led to the phenomena of oppressive landlordism and irresponsible warlords that ruined the prospects of Chinese repub-licanism.

Contemporary events in England were less dramatic than those in China, although more than usually complicated in the years following the fall of Peel's government in 1846. Succeeding governments found themselves permanently on the knife-edge of precarious Parliamentary majorities, often indeed without a majority. Party loyalties were stretched by personal antipathies, and parties themselves shifted between being Whigs, conservative-liberals, liberal-conservatives, con-servative progressives and Peelites before evolving into simply Liberals and Conservatives: and on the sidelines stood a permanent block of Irish votes, usually allied with the Whigs as the least unresponsive to Irish demands, but ever on the lookout for tactical opportunities. Lord John Russell's government hung on until February 1852 as a minority administration, surviving an election in 1847 and a Parliamentary defeat in 1851 simply because no grouping of the opposition could be formed to replace it.

Like Pottinger and Davis, Sir George Bonham, who took post as
Governor in March 1848, was an East India Company servant, but
one with considerable experience of colonial administration. At the
early age of thirty-four he had been appointed Governor of Prince of
Wales Island (Penang), Singapore and Malacca, subsequently known
as the Straits Settlements. Although this was a considerably larger
colony than Hong Kong (with a population of 140,000, compared to
Hong Kong's thirty thousand), Bonham's new responsibilities were
greater. In the Straits he had been responsible to the Bengal Presidency, one of three administrative units in India, and was therefore at
two removes from London. In Hong Kong, as Plenipotentiary and
Superintendent of Trade as well as Governor, he was directly responsible to the Cabinet for British relations with the Chinese Empire.
This was not a position for which Sir George was well-fitted, since
he had become imbued with a deep distrust of the Chinese, to the
extent that he refused to countenance the promotion of Chinese-
speakers in the Consular Service; the logic was that they were too
sympathetic to the Chinese. But, as Governor, Sir George was a good
choice. Palmerston commented that Bonham's practical common sense
was the chief cause of his appointment, and during the six years of his
tenure of office Hong Kong was unprecedentedly sedate. Sir George's
attitudes much resembled those of the British merchants, with whom,
unlike his predecessors, he maintained civil relations. This was helped
by the fact – a sign of the more settled times – that he was accompanied
by his pleasant wife. As Governor he placated the merchants by removing most of the annoying small taxes levied by Davis and by ensuring
that they were extensively consulted on all domestic issues. Consultation was formalized by the admission of two civilians to the Legislative
Council in June 1850, in accordance with Grey's policy of ensuring
that every colonial legislature was brought 'more under the influence
of the opinion of the intelligent and educated inhabitants', and that
the councils should become more closely involved with colonial
finances. The first civilians – 'unofficials' – to become members were
David Jardine and John Edger; from that time until after the end of
the First World War it was understood that the Legislative Council
should include a member of Jardine Matheson's.

There was not much that could be done about the state of trade.
James Legge described it as being 'in a dead-alive state during all
[Bonham's] time', and W.H. Mitchell commented regretfully in his
1852 report to Bonham: 'It seems a strange result after ten years of

open trade with this great country . . . that China should not consume half so much of our manufactures as Holland.'

The business community believed that trade could be revived only by opening the interior of China to foreign commerce, so avoiding what was thought to be deliberate official obstructionism outside the treaty ports. The London East India and China Association (the East India part of the title was soon dropped, and the reborn 'China Association' became a powerful lobby representing British business interests in Chinese questions) found a willing listener in Lord Palmerston, who by 1850 was beginning to cast about for some excuse to extort more concessions from China.

When his term of office began, Bonham saw no prospect of a serious clash with the Chinese. Legge had asked the new Governor if he was going to insist that the city of Canton should be opened as agreed on 1 April 1849. 'How can I?' Bonham replied. 'My instructions are to keep the peace, and by no means bring on another war with China.' But sentiments in Britain were changing. The revolutionary upheavals of 1848 in Europe produced in Britain only a minor spasm, of which the most typical symptom was the presentation of a 'monster' petition to Parliament by the Chartists, but when Palmerston was made to leave the government in December 1851 (he had been prematurely enthusiastic in congratulating Louis Napoleon on his coup d'état of that month, and Russell had lost patience with the Foreign Secretary's 'tracasseries') the government's fall was inevitable. Palmerston was out of office for only three months before he brought down his former colleagues in what he triumphantly called his 'tit-for-tat with John Russell'. The succeeding government of Lord Derby lasted only another nine months before being replaced by a coalition of Peelite conservatives and Whig-liberals with Lord Aberdeen as Prime Minister, Russell as Foreign Secretary and Palmerston, still not trusted with that post, as Home Secretary. When Russell resigned in 1853 he was replaced at the Foreign Office by George Villiers, now Lord Clarendon, who ensured that Palmerston's views were represented there. The misconduct of the Crimean War led to the coalition being defeated and Palmerston, for the first time in his long career, being given the opportunity of forming his own Cabinet in February 1855, with Lord Clarendon continuing as Foreign Secretary. The Colonial Office, never the most popular of posts, had a record number of five incumbents in a single year: Sir George Grey, Sidney Herbert, Lord John Russell, Sir William Molesworth and Henry Labouchere.

Quack Doctor Bowring

The personalities of Davis and Bonham, as with those of most of their successors, had only limited effects on the development of Hong Kong. Governors had their enthusiasms and dislikes, and these were reflected in their conduct of affairs, but their limited freedom of movement, caught as they were between the upper millstone of Whitehall and the nether of the colonists, together with their relatively short tenure of office, restricted their personal impact. Also, it must be said, few Governors were men of outstanding capacity. Only Sir Matthew Nathan (1904–7) and Sir Frederick Lugard (1907–10) made any subsequent contribution to British national life (and that of Nathan was less than uniformly successful), and men of notable talent, such as Sir Cecil Clementi (1925–30), were regarded in the colony with some dismay. From the small pool of those wishing to make a career in China the consular service, diplomacy, and the Chinese Maritime Custom Service attracted many of the more able. But Dr John Bowring was a man of European reputation (even if not an entirely creditable one) when he was appointed to the Consulship of Canton in 1849, and his influence on the future of Hong Kong was to be decisive.

The period of Whig ascendancy naturally brought with it opportunities for party supporters to be rewarded, and one of these beneficiaries was that same Bowring who had questioned witnesses to the Select Committee of 1847, and had been a well-known figure for twenty-five years before that. A radical intellectual of great gifts, enormous energy, but uncertain judgement, Bowring had been the literary executor and close friend of the utilitarian reformer Jeremy Bentham, who died in his arms: in the 1820s, as Secretary of the London Greek Committee, arranging assistance for the Greek War of Independence, he had been involved in somewhat shady dealings in Greek bonds – and incidentally received delivery of the mortal remains of Lord Byron, in a puncheon of rum.[5] Various Ministers, from Canning in 1826 onwards, found it worthwhile to employ this man, who possessed almost every gift but that of common sense, who was at home in almost every European language, and who had manifold connections in Spain, Turkey, Egypt and above all France. In 1827 he had been arrested as a spy by the French and had been lucky to escape; five years later he was negotiating a trade treaty with them. As well as being a radical M.P. (for Bolton and Kilmarnock), Bowring was editor of the *Westminster Review*, and therefore moved in London's literary circles. He tried his own hand at verse, writing at least one hymn that is still sung – 'In the cross of Christ I glory/Tow'ring o'er the wrecks of time', and translated poetry from the Hungarian.

Some exalted personages had low opinions of Bowring. Melbourne detested him: 'Bowring, damn him, why, he collared a Prime Minister!' (Bowring had, in fact, so treated Thiers, the French Prime Minister, but this was at least partly in fun); and Palmerston, while willing to use his talents, sneered at the 'Quack Doctor Bowring' (he was an honorary Doctor of Letters of Groningen University in Holland); but he received honours from the monarchs of Belgium, Portugal, Spain, Siam, Austria, Sweden, Russia and Holland, and was not without powerful supporters at home. Of these the most influential was Lord Clarendon, Whig and Liberal Colonial Secretary and Foreign Secretary, a considerable figure in national politics for many years. Bowring and Villiers had produced the First Report on Commercial Relations between France and Great Britain, presented to Parliament in 1834. This was the weightiest of the commercial investigations made by Bowring, and Villiers afterwards retained a sincere admiration for the multi-talented radical.

Emily Eden, the sister of Lord Auckland, Governor General of India, provided the best character sketch of Bowring in one of her lively letters to Lord Clarendon:

I think you will allow that the first beginning – *le premier abord* – the rudiments of an acquaintance with Bowring – are hard to get over. He began by flinging himself at full length upon the sofa, saying – 'Well! What have you been doing in the sketching line?' I was actually awed by his audacity into giving him my book. 'Ah – very good – very good. Well now, this is the result of travelling. I like a *result*. Always look for the result!' . . . I behaved no worse to Bowring than by contradicting every assertion he made – on subjects of which I knew nothing. I actually argued myself black in the face about Spanish proverbs, Dutch fisheries and Belgian tariffs, knowing nothing about the language or the fish or the trade. I do not think our acquaintance was long enough for him to detect my ignorance, because he argued to the last just as if I were a reasonable creature, and, thank Heaven, after two days' wrangling I had the last word. He most politely saw us on board our steamboat at Antwerp, and did everything to make us comfortable, and, just as he left the deck, I contradicted him flat on a point of geography. *You* know that my geography is – worse than nothing – so that he must have been right, which made it the more necessary to take the contrary opinion. However, I must say that, barring his detestable manner ... there is a great deal to like in him. He is so intelligent and quick; and then, with such a fund of vanity that it must be mortified ten times a day, he never lets the mortification fall on his temper, but is always good-humoured and obliging.[6]

In his capacity as a Member of Parliament Bowring had already evinced an interest in Hong Kong when in 1846 he had drawn the attention of the House to the 'frequent application of flogging for petty offences ... no less than fifty-four persons [were] so punished on Saturday 25 April last for not having obtained tickets of registration'. The flogging debate continued for years, with a division between the middle-class Hong Kong population (in favour) and the home government (cautiously against), with most governors, except Sir John Pope-Hennessy (1877–82), backing the floggers.

As economic experts often do, Bowring handled his own affairs badly: after the Greek episode an investment in an ironworks went awry, and in 1847 he was forced to look for paid employment. Since this occurred when his friends were in power, some provision for him was found in the Consulship at Canton. The office of China Consul was no plum – it was the least profitable of those that Dickens in *Little Dorrit* imagined the Barnacle family disposing of, and was usually reserved for younger sons and cousins of moderately important people.[7] Bowring, in spite of his financial embarrassments, would have been reluctant to accept it unless the prospect of something better was held out. Before leaving to take up his post the new Consul had a personal interview with the Foreign Secretary – an unusual privilege – in which he was given some moderate encouragement.

Palmerston clearly expected developments in Bowring's new sphere, since he wrote on 29 September 1850:

I clearly see that the Time is fast coming when we shall be obliged to strike another Blow in China ... These half civilized Governments, such as those of China Portugal Spanish America require a Dressing every eight or Ten years to keep them in order. Their Minds are too shallow to receive an Impression that will last longer than some such Period, and warning is of little use. They care

little for words and they must not only see the Stick but actually
feel it on their Shoulders before they yield to that only argument
which to them brings conviction, the *argumentum Baculinum*.[8]

A former President of the Peace Society might not have seemed the
ideal man to administer a taste of the rod, but Bowring accepted the
task with some alacrity. It was entirely typical that as soon as he
assumed his appointment, Bowring took it upon himself on 17 April
1849 to send a bumptious autograph letter to Louis Napoleon, the
President of France, in oddly imperfect French for a famous linguist:

> Mon cher President,
>   Je m'attendait a l'honneur de vous voir, avant mon départ
> pour la Chine. Le départ a été precipité, car le gouverne-
> ment voulut que j'arrivais ici dans la Cité de Canton suivant
> a la Traité de 1847. Cette question a été tranché tres nette-
> ment par les Chinois. Ils ne veulent pas reconnaitre les
> stipulations du Traité. C'est un Casus belli . . . Je ne vois
> qu'un avenir pour nous – pour vous – pour tout le monde
> . . . Ni vous – ni nous – nous ne pouvons accepter la position
> humiliante ou on nous place. Le traité obtenu par M. Lag-
> rené [the Franco—Chinese Treaty of Whampoa] est une
> lettre morte.[9]

This hitherto unpublished letter, as well as indicating Bowring's
capacity for pushiness, shows that from the start of his career in China
he was assuming that a conflict would inevitably occur. It is possible,
although with Bowring's capacity for self-dramatization nothing is ever
very clear, that the next seven years were spent waiting for a colourable
pretext for beginning a second, decisive, conflict.

   Canton was recognized as the potential flashpoint of any such outbreak, and April 1849, when Bowring arrived there, was the date that
had been agreed between Ch'i-ing and Davis as when the right of
foreigners to take up residence in Canton should be exercised. But
Davis had been replaced by the more emollient Bonham, and the
reliable old Manchu Ch'i-ing's place at Canton had been taken by the
Chinese Hsü (Xu) Kuang-chu, Imperial Commissioner for Foreign
Affairs from February 1848. When the due date came, and the British
began to press their case, Hsü proceeded to score easy points off Sir
George Bonham, who was hampered by his instructions to avoid

causing trouble. Hsü stalled, as had his predecessors, claiming that the hostility of the populace still made it too dangerous for foreigners to be allowed out of their own quarters, and succeeded after some months in getting Bonham to drop the matter – permanently, Hsü claimed, a claim which rested on Gutzlaff's translation into Chinese of Bonham's definition of the result of the abortive talks.[10]

The point hinged around a single phrase: 'the question at issue rests where it was, and must remain in abeyance'. When he saw this phrase in Bonham's dispatch Palmerston pounced on it, writing on 8 October 1850: 'it might, without much straining, be made, by translation into a foreign language, to bear the meaning which the Chinese have attached to it; namely, that Her Majesty's Government had entirely abandoned all discussions connected with their right of entry into the city of Canton.' The never entirely reliable Gutzlaff was by then touring France on his fund-raising exercise, and Bonham had to rely on his other interpreters to exculpate himself. Their efforts were not impressive. The phrasing in English is less than precise, and one of the interpreters did not succeed in even reproducing the original English correctly. 'Abeyance' is equivalent to dormancy, and Chinese believe in letting sleeping dogs lie. Moreover, an informed recent analyst, J.Y. Wong, has criticized Gutzlaff's translation, claiming that it reads that the issue 'must not be discussed' and that therefore Hsü was perfectly correct in his assumption that the British had dropped their claim.[11]

The discussions terminated in the frustrated Bonham attempting once more to appeal to Peking over the heads of the Canton officials. By that time he had become convinced of the necessity for a show of force, which Palmerston was willing enough to sanction, if a convenient pretext could be found. The Foreign Secretary was advised that the right of entry to Canton was the only possibility, but before much progress could be made Palmerston had been forced out of office. During these exciting diplomatic manoeuvres Bowring had been left on a sideline, obliged to content himself with tedious consular work. Finding little else to occupy his lively mind at Canton, he occupied himself in adding Chinese to the score or so languages he already possessed.

Meanwhile Sir George at Hong Kong continued to pare away the colony's expenses, to the gratification of Earl Grey, who was able to report that expenditure had been reduced from £49,000 in 1846 and £36,900 the following year to only £15,500 in 1851, while the military expenditure had been more than halved, from £115,100 in 1847 to

£51,900.[12] Sir George may have been encouraged in his retrenchment policy by a pamphlet published in 1850 which found the 'present establishment of Hong Kong' was being 'conducted on a much larger and more expensive scale' than justified by what was nothing more than a 'municipal body under the supervision of a very petty mandarin, of the rank of Police Inspector'.[13]

The *Economist* took the opportunity to report, in its issue of 8 March 1851, on: 'One of the latest, if not the latest, additions to that huge conglomerate, our Colonial Empire . . . the hilly, stony island of Hong Kong with its excellent harbour.' That feature of the colony was the only one to win unqualified approval: 'So bright were the visions, that Sir Henry Pottinger spoke of Hong Kong as a new Carthage . . . ten years have elapsed . . . for four or five years hope was nourished . . . but it has gradually become known and avowed that these bright prospects were the delusions of fancy . . . few merchants go there to reside.' The only successful houses were those of Jardine Matheson and Dent, pursuing their accustomed trade – of which the *Economist* thoroughly approved: 'The island is a kind of bonded warehouse . . . for the opium trade . . . the principal part of this trade is carried out by two firms . . . to these two firms Hong Kong must be quite a Californian mine.' It was, just, possible that things would improve: 'there is some prospect of Hong Kong becoming a useful settlement. It is, at any rate, a refuge for our China trade . . .'

More lively developments were foreshadowed in January 1852, when Bonham took a year's leave of absence and Bowring was appointed to act as Superintendent and Plenipotentiary in his place. The appointment was made with some hesitation; Gladstone later said that Bowring was given the post in the hope that his Consular experience had fitted him for the responsibility. A severe – and abundantly justified to anyone knowing Bowring – warning came from Lord Granville, who had replaced Palmerston as Foreign Secretary the previous month: '. . . it is the anxious desire of her Majesty's Government to avoid all irritating discussions with that of China . . . you will not push argument on doubtful points in a manner to fetter the free action of your Government; and you will not resort to measures of force without previous reference home'. Bowring's appointment had come just in time, before Palmerston's tit-for-tat led to the defeat of the Whigs and their replacement by Lord Derby's Conservative government in February 1852. In reply to his letter of appointment Bowring wrote a long dispatch, giving the government the benefit of the acting Plenipotentiary's advice. He recommended that the Chinese should be 'peremptorily urged' to allow entrance to Canton, that negotiations be held to establish an embassy in Peking, and announced his intention of visiting the treaty ports. In reply he received a curt, three-sentence, letter from Lord Derby's new Foreign Secretary, Lord Malmesbury: '. . . It is the intention of Her Majesty's Government that you should strictly adhere to the instructions given to you by Earl Granville . . . you will abstain from mooting the question of the right of British subjects to enter into the city of Canton . . . you were enjoined . . . to take up your residence at Hong Kong . . . consequently you will not be authorized to visit the various ports of China, as you seem to intimate your intention to do, and you will therefore abstain from so doing.'

Due to the delays in transmitting mail Bowring had not received this stiff letter before he followed his first dispatch with a second, enclosing copies of his correspondence with Hsü; this provoked another bleak missive on 21 July 1852: '. . . considering that your tenure of office is only temporary, and that it will terminate on Sir George Bonham's return to China at the end of the year . . . I have to repeat to you the injunction . . . not to press to be received . . . I have further to enjoin you not to raise any question as to the admission of British subjects in to the city of Canton . . . Any undue interference on your part may be productive of much inconvenience.' This reminder of Bowring's precarious position, and the clear indication that the former radical had nothing to hope for from a Tory government, elicited the humble response on 8 September that 'I beg to assure your Lordship that the instructions therein contained shall be most implicitly obeyed.'

But Bowring's star was in the ascendant. The Conservative government only lasted a few months before being replaced in December by Lord Aberdeen's coalition, in which Bowring's old friend and supporter Lord Clarendon speedily became Foreign Secretary (in February 1853). By good fortune Bowring was in London on leave after Bonham's return to Hong Kong, and was able first to make sure that he would indeed succeed Sir George, who was due to retire after completing six years in post, and to have many discussions with the Foreign Office before returning to China. From being the heavily criticized Consul at one of the treaty ports Bowring, now Sir John, with one bound officially became on 13 April 1854 Plenipotentiary, Superintendent, Governor, 'accredited not to Peking alone, but to Japan, Siam, China and Corea, I believe to a greater number of human beings (indeed no less than one-third of the human race), than any individual . . . before', as he himself characteristically put it.

Bowring's predecessor, although only fifty-one when he left Hong Kong, does not appear to have looked for further employment. Bonham had been fortunate in receiving unusually clear instructions, thanks to the single-minded Lord Grey and the terms of reference outlined in the House of Commons Select Committee Report. These instructions he fulfilled well, and, unlike Davis or Bowring, Bonham succeeded in avoiding trouble either with the Chinese authorities or the Hong Kong merchants.

Chinese 2: Plenipotentiary 1

Whatever his defects of character, Bowring had it in him to be an efficient diplomat, as his trade agreements with France (never the easiest of countries with which to reach an accommodation), negotiated together with George Villiers in the 1830s, had indicated. He proved this in his new capacity by becoming, in 1855, the first Western representative to conclude a treaty with the kingdom of Siam. Bowring was accompanied there by his secretary, the same young Harry Parkes who had been present at the signing of the Treaty of Nanking. Although only twenty-seven at the time of the embassy to Siam, Parkes was already an experienced China hand, having been sent out in 1841 as a protégé of Gutzlaff, and attached to John Morrison in order to learn Chinese. Within two years he had mastered enough Chinese to serve as chief interpreter to Rutherford Alcock, then Consul at Amoy: 'Mr Alcock came over in a very flash style. Full uniform . . . no less than six Spanish orders of knighthood and chivalry.' Parkes became interpreter at Canton, where he worked under Bowring, and was acting Consul there between June 1856 and September 1858.

In Bangkok Bowring confronted a court more arbitrary and less exposed to the modern world than even that of Peking: 'The king was accustomed to see all his courtiers, clothed chiefly in orange paint, crawling on all fours in his august presence, and it took all the doctor's learned eloquence to explain that Ministers' and Naval Officers' swords were just as much part of their dress as the turmeric with which Siamese aristocrats decorated their skins.'[14] Both the United States' emissaries and those of the Governor-General of India had been refused access to the court, and even Sir James Brooke, the 'White

Rajah' of Sarawak, had been forced out of the country by hostile demonstrations. Bowring's success, however comic he must have appeared (he donned his Groningen academic robes in order to be more imposing), has to be acknowledged as a personal triumph.

But before going to Siam Bowring had the opportunity of dealing with affairs in China, which he had been itching to set straight for so long. He was at last permitted to make the journey up the coast to the other treaty ports, in the course of which he helped to initiate what was to be the most significant development in relations between China and the outside world, the inauguration of the Imperial Maritime Customs Service. At Shanghai the British Consul was Parkes's 'very flash' Rutherford Alcock, an original and colourful figure, later to become the British Minister at Peking. Shanghai had succumbed to the Taipings in their great sweep north in 1852–3, during which they sacked Nanking, massacring some forty thousand or so of its Manchu inhabitants and establishing the Taiping capital there, where it remained for the next eleven years. Events at Shanghai were less violent, the Chinese town being taken by a well-organized rising on 7 September 1853, in which Canton-based Triad members played leading parts. Although the foreign settlement remained untouched by the Taipings, the Imperial officials had fled, and in their absence Alcock was left to cope with the question of what should be done about the collection of customs.

The foreign merchants were in no doubt about it; Shanghai, abandoned by the Chinese government, should be declared a free port, with no dues being charged. Alcock took a different view, arguing that merely because the Chinese government was unable, presumably temporarily, to assert its control locally, it should not therefore be deprived of its rightful dues under the Treaty of Nanking. Almost immediately after the rising Alcock published a notification to foreign merchants warning them that 'the capture of an isolated sea-port on the coast of a vast Empire can in no sense abrogate a solemn treaty entered into between the two Sovereigns of Britain and China. The obligations continue to exist on either side.' Alcock intended to carry out what he believed to be his duty by collecting the revenues on behalf of the Imperial government during the enforced absence of its officials. He was followed in this, somewhat reluctantly, by the American Commissioner, one Humphrey Marshall, 'a big, coarse, headstrong man, has never been out of Kentucky before he came here', according to Bonham. Marshall was equally anxious to do justice to the Chinese, but deeply suspicious of British motives.

Grumbling at not being allowed a free port, and complaining that the disturbed conditions of the country had made trade difficult, most of the merchants nevertheless complied, issuing promissory notes for the customs due. Over a period of six months Alcock succeeded in collecting more than $1 million of such notes, a sum considerably greater than that which the Imperial customs officials would have expected under their own methods (or rather, a sum that would have been greater had it all been paid; when it came to the crunch only some of the Americans and none of the British redeemed their notes).

Sir George Bonham, as Superintendent of Trade, and much influenced by local opinion in Hong Kong, had tended to side with the Shanghai merchants, but this changed with Bowring's arrival. He had been champing at the bit during his stay first as Consul in Canton and then as temporary Governor at Hong Kong, forbidden to interfere in diplomatic matters, and saw in the Shanghai situation a chance of making a breakthrough in diplomatic relations. When Alcock produced a formal plan for the establishment in Shanghai of a 'Foreign Inspector of Customs', nominated jointly by the three Treaty powers (Britain, France, and the USA) and the Taotai (senior local mandarin), which 'could scarcely fail to furnish a most effective check upon the venality and supineness of the Custom House Officials',[15] Bowring seized on the suggestion with enthusiasm. He was backed by the new American Minister, Robert McLane, and by Admiral Sir James Stirling, commanding the East India and China squadron. McLane arranged to see the Provincial Governor-General, I-liang, and obtained his agreement to talks with the Taotai, Wu Chien-chang. In very short order Wu agreed, and the new service accordingly began on 12 July 1854. It was to develop, under the leadership of Sir Robert Hart, into the Maritime Customs Service, described by Fairbank as 'a chief financial pillar of the Chinese government': the customs commissioners became 'the trusted councillors of Chinese officialdom . . . They supplied at first some of the functions of a diplomatic service . . . But above all the Customs set a standard of incorrupt public service and of devotion to the central administration which has been of incalculable value to the Chinese government of the twentieth century.'[16] It was also to become a source of constant aggravation to the trading community and to the government of Hong Kong.

But the Canton question remained as a perpetual irritation. On his second appointment Bowring, rendered uncharacteristically cautious by Malmesbury's stern memorandum, had taken the precaution of

clearing in writing with Lord Clarendon, on 25 April 1854, what policies he was to be expected to follow:

> It cannot be denied that we are entitled to demand redress of
> grievances that we have suffered from violations and disregard of
> Treaty obligations . . . as among the most prominent:
>> Non-admission into Canton city;
>> Difficulty of obtaining personal intercourse with the Chinese
>> authorities.

In order to obtain redress Bowring proposed to attempt, if necessary
in conjunction with the Americans and the French, a journey to the
court of Peking in order to protest against the complete refusal of the
Canton Commissioner even to meet him. But: 'As a general rule of
conduct in China I intend to demand nothing which I am not prepared
to enforce.' Clarendon's reply on 5 July 1854, although approving
Bowring's proposals carried the warning: 'you will use every precaution
for ascertaining beforehand that you will not meet with any indignity
that will require to be avenged, and this more particularly at a moment
when the aid of the British naval force in the Chinese Seas might not
be available for that purpose'. The unwritten corollary was that an
indignity would necessarily require revenge.

An excuse for increasing pressure on the Chinese immediately presented itself, since it could be argued that 1854 was the due date for
revising the Treaty of Nanking (the somewhat specious case rested
upon applying the most-favoured-nation clause to the terms of the
American treaty, which provided for a revision of the treaty after twelve
years). Although Clarendon was cautious, Palmerston was not averse
to some action, especially after 1855, when he was freed from the
restraints imposed by the coalition government. It was hardly a propitious time for diplomacy. Palmerston's previous attempts to reopen
negotiations with Peking via Bonham had arrived just as the Emperor
Hsien-feng, who was greatly offended by them, had taken over. Even
Tao-kuang, perhaps justifiably wrath at Davis's raid on Canton and
Palmerston's bluster, had adopted a tougher attitude towards the
foreigners in the last years of his reign, and the young Emperor quickly
replaced the experienced Manchu negotiators, now habituated to the
arts of barbarian management, by more intransigent Chinese. The
prudent councillor Mu-chang-a, who had acted almost as Prime Minis-

ter to Tao-kuang, was dismissed. Ch'i-ing was exiled, and the more extreme of the new men were selected to confront the foreigners at Canton: first Hsü Kuang-chu, followed by Yeh Ming-ch'en, who became a particular *bête noire* of Bowring's. Professor Fairbank characterized Yeh as 'a stubborn die-hard xenophobe',[17] but facing down the barbarians was by no means the most important of Yeh's responsibilities; the Taiping movement had begun in Kwantung-Kwangsi, and Yeh was energetically stamping it out there, an operation he achieved by executing tens of thousands of rebels and suspects. His success in so doing won him the full support of the thoroughly frightened young Emperor, so that in the intervals between his exertions in pacification he had little inclination to oblige the British and full authority from Peking to be uncompromising.

Matters began civilly enough. Although Bowring's first letter to Yeh went unanswered, he maintained a diplomatic tone, but with an implied warning: 'Nothing could be more painful to me than irritating and unfriendly discussions, the consequences of which might be deplorable. Nothing more gratifying than the amicable arrangement of any point of difference, and the establishment of a durable harmony.' Yeh's answer on 25 April 1854 was short but equally polite: '. . . it would gratify me exceedingly to meet your Excellency, that we might demonstrate publicly our friendly sentiments . . .', but he was much occupied with military affairs. The implication was that meeting Bowring was a mere courteous formality, which could be deferred. After that things got crosser: pressed, Yeh proposed a meeting, in a tone which was meant to be insulting, 'at the Jinsin Packhouse on the Canton river'. Bowring could not accept this, and insisted on an official reception at the Governor General's office. Yeh then took to arguing, on 22 May, that there was nothing to settle, since Bonham had already agreed to forgo the right of entry to Canton, having written to Hsü: 'Henceforth, moreover, this matter must not be again discussed.' At this Bowring, who badly wanted to be off on his tour of the treaty ports, gave up for the time being, hoping to do better with the mandarins nearer Peking.

In his discussions with the authorities in Fukien and Nanking he was no more successful, merely being referred back, very urbanely, to Yeh. For a moment it seemed as though Yeh's attitude had changed, as in December Bowring received a request for assistance in 'destroying and seizing' the 'river thieves' who had become so 'strong and troublesome'. Yeh's letter, which must have been prompted by real anxieties on his part, presented Bowring with the opportunity to steam upriver to Canton, accompanied by units of the Royal and United States Navies, to demonstrate how useful the Powers might be. But the crisis passed, and Yeh resumed his intransigence: Bowring could do nothing except take his leave, although not without, on 27 December, 'again formally advising your Excellency that the state of our intercourse is most unsatisfactory and intolerable; that many great grievances remain wholly unredressed; and that Her Britannic Majesty's Government . . . will be further advised . . . in order that such measures may be adopted as in its judgment become the dignity of a great nation.'

At this point it seemed that the score was Chinese 2: Bowring 1 – the Plenipotentiary's point being the settlement of customs at Shanghai. In his original self-defined tasks – securing the right of entry into Canton and obtaining personal contact with Chinese officials – Sir John had completely failed. It should not have been the cause for much surprise when, in October 1856, the seizure by Chinese officials of a small coasting schooner, the lorcha *Arrow*, Chinese-owned but carrying the British flag, was grasped by Bowring as a pretext for action. It was not much of a pretext – the ship and crew were delivered unharmed a few days later, and the ship was not at the time actually entitled to wear British colours – but it was eagerly welcomed by both Parkes and Bowring: their excited correspondence records the escalation day by day and almost hour by hour. Bowring writes from Hong Kong to congratulate Parkes on his obduracy in demanding apologies from Yeh: 'I am very pleased with the manner in which you have done this work . . . I am determined on obtaining redress . . . cannot we use this opportunity to carry the City Question? If so I will come up with the whole Fleet.' Was the legal situation obscure and perhaps not as strong as might be wished? Then 'The delay and annoyance to which the *Arrow* has been subjected will induce me to look more favourably to his having failed to comply with the conditions' (17 October). Would the armed forces back the belligerent pair? 'I have just seen the Admiral. It will be necessary to be very cautious as we shall not obtain the aid of the Naval Authorities beyond a certain limit. I do not think the Admiral will make war' (20 October). 'You may well believe that we wait the development of events with extreme anxiety. I doubt not the success of the attack on the Forts if Yeh's obstinacy compel that measure and it is almost to be hoped that he will . . . as we are so strong and so right'(21 October). And if there were still complaints from the navy or from London that the *casus belli* was trivial, then it must be made clear that 'the *Arrow* affair is a subordinate one in the present state of affairs' (one of three notes dated 1 November).[18]

London was of course given only a doctored account of the proceedings, but whatever the British government thought of them – and there were many reservations – Clarendon was in no position to complain, since Bowring had hitherto been meticulous in securing the Foreign Secretary's assent to the increasingly severe warnings he had sent to Yeh. The war that developed out of the case of the lorcha *Arrow* has only limited relevance to Hong Kong, and is dealt with elsewhere, most interestingly by the British Foreign Secretary at the time of writing, Douglas Hurd. It began with a bombardment of Canton on 27 October 1856, an action made possible by the navy's new shallow-draught gunboats, and developed into a full-scale conflict in 1858. Immediately, however, the state of hostilities made for tension in Hong Kong, as Yeh replied with fulminations and offers of reward for barbarian heads.

When the news of the *Arrow* incident and the bombardment of Canton reached London, intense excitement was provoked in Parliamentary circles. Once more it seemed that Palmerston's man in China had presented the Tories with an opportunity. A caucus meeting was held, with Gladstone, at that time still a Tory, raring to condemn British aggression in China, and Lord Derby insisting that all his colleagues fall behind the party line. Disraeli alone was reluctant, 'throwing cold water on the China question',[19] believing that although the government might be defeated in Parliament, the electorate would take a different view. He was supported in this, had he known, by the Queen, who wrote to her uncle Leopold, King of the Belgians, when the result of the debate was known: 'The Opposition have played their cards most foolishly, and the result is that *all* the old Tories say they will certainly *not* support them; they very truly say Lord Derby's party – that is those who want to get into office *coute qui coute* – wanted to get in under *false colours*' (24 March 1857).[20]

But the chance to dish the Whigs, after a period of eleven years in which there had only been a few months of Tory government, seemed too good to miss. An odd alliance of the pacifist section of the radicals, led by Richard Cobden and John Bright, the Peelites and traditional Tories, with even Lord John Russell taking the opportunity to level scores with Palmerston, attacked the government in debates which continued for four days in the House of Commons and two in the Lords. Poor Bowring was subjected to some quite unjustified personal

attacks, constantly being referred to ironically as 'Dr Bowring' – Gladstone called him a 'metamorphosed consul'; Malmesbury, his former
chief, spoke of his 'colleague and competitor in folly, Parkes'.
Bowring's own side was hardly enthusiastically supportive. Lord Grey,
then moving rapidly to the right, condemned the 'unjust war . . . waged
in China . . . carried on with a fearful destruction of the lives and
properties of the people'. Lord Granville, the Liberal leader in the
Lords, spoke publicly on Bowring's behalf, but wrote privately on 10
March to his friend and political ally Stratford Canning, Ambassador
at Istanbul: 'You will probably think the opposition right in their estimate of the Doctor's proceedings at Canton, but you will also judge
that they have acted very foolishly, and have contrived to help
Palmerston over a very difficult session.' Canning, the most distinguished British diplomat of his day, replied on 4 May: 'I thought your
speech very good indeed. I should not like to have had to make it.
The subject would not have been *simpatico*. I think we [English] were
wrong about the lorcha and right about the entrance to Canton, but
that Bowring's presumption in swelling the small case to the great on
his own hook was indefensible. I quite think that there was nothing to
do but uphold him – or rather the war – and that makes the awkwardness of the question.'[21] Behind the scenes at the Colonial Office
Under-Secretary Frederic Rogers worried about 'the Chinese War,
which seems to me one of the greatest iniquities of our time . . . I was
half alarmed . . . lest I be found responsible for it, by allowing to pass
the Colonial Ordinance [concerning the registration of ships] under
which Sir John Bowring has made such a fool of himself.'[22]

The alliance between Tories hungry for office and Manchester
reformers deprecating foreign aggression was indeed successful in
defeating the government in the House of Commons, but Palmerston,
like Disraeli having an accurate feeling for the sentiments of his
countrymen, chose then to ask for a dissolution of Parliament and a
general election in March 1857. Pointing out, correctly enough, that
the China issue had been adopted by the opposition 'as a question on
which to try the strength of the parties' rather than a principled stand,
he went to the country with a full-blooded appeal to nationalistic sentiment. His own constituents at Tiverton were told that Yeh was 'an
insolent barbarian, who unites in his person all the obstinacy, perfidy
and cruelty ever collected in a single man', and that he had violated
the British flag. Once again the Tories had miscalculated, and a triumph ensued: Yeh had become too much of a bogeyman for the

voters to appear to defend him, and the Whigs were returned with an increased majority in what was seen as an unprecedented personal triumph for Palmerston (Prince Albert described it as 'an instance in our Parliamentary history without parallel'[23]). Gladstone was mortified, and 'fully conscious of the new awkwardness of his public position'.[24] Cobden, Bright and most of the reformers even lost their seats.

But Bowring was too much discredited to be allowed to continue as Plenipotentiary, and was relegated in July 1857 to the less important post of Governor of Hong Kong, while James Bruce, the 8th Lord Elgin, was appointed in his stead. It is unfortunate that two successive Earls of Elgin should be best remembered for having committed what are often regarded as crimes of vandalism. The 7th Earl spent much of the family's assets in, as he saw it, rescuing the Parthenon marbles from Turkish hands: his actions were attacked at the time, and have been ever since. His son's destruction of the Imperial Summer Palace at Peking in 1860 as a reprisal is not so easy to justify; but Elgin himself, however great the act of vandalism he may have ordered (in British terms it might be compared with the destruction of Greenwich or Blenheim), was an almost painfully moral man, much more sensitive than others of his time to the suffering his actions caused. Three years in China, it may be supposed, did something to harden him.

The Elgin family fortunes had been sadly impaired by the 7th Earl, and his son had to make his own way, which he did with great success. A Fellow of Merton College Oxford at twenty-one, he became Member of Parliament for Southampton in 1841, voting with the Tories, and in 1847 was appointed by Peel to the post of Governor General of Canada, where he performed brilliantly in difficult circumstances.

The task now assigned to him, that of pulling Bowring's irons out of the fire and concluding a satisfactory settlement with China, was not one he greatly relished. It was much the same work as that done in the previous decade by Sir Henry Pottinger, but unlike Pottinger, Elgin had no responsibility for Hong Kong, nor did he want to have anything to do with the Colony. He did not trust Bowring; he deplored the power of the merchants ('the Hong Kong Chamber of Commerce is run almost as a department of Jardine Matheson and Company'); and he anathematized the expatriate British: 'I did not know what brutes – lying – sanguinary – cheating – oppressive to the weak crouching before the strong ... [were] these smooth-faced country men of ours'. (But Elgin at some time or other loathed almost everyone – Admiral Seymour was 'a perfect driveller', Reid, the American Minister, a 'sneaking scoundrel'.[25]) He called at Hong Kong as little as possible, and when there preferred to stay on board the flagship in the harbour.

In part because the forces to do more were not available, Canton was dealt with first, although this was not attempted until December 1857. By this time France had decided to join in the enterprise, inspired to do so by the execution in Kwangsi, in gruesome circumstances, of a French missionary, the Abbé Chapdelaine. After a preliminary bombardment the walls of Canton were taken by an Anglo-French force, at a cost of perhaps six hundred Chinese casualties and ten allied dead. The city itself paid no attention, Yeh continuing to cut off rebel heads – seven hundred of them one morning – until after a week the allies lost patience and entered the hostile town. Harry Parkes was given the satisfaction of doing this at the head of a hundred British sailors, a force that proved quite capable of making its way unharmed into the centre and capturing Yeh. Interestingly enough, in view of all the previous insistence on the hostility of the Canton population, there was little popular resistance and Canton enjoyed what was probably the most tranquil period of its existence. S. Lane-Poole, the biographer of Sir Harry Parkes, recorded:

A remarkable proof of the feeling that has been maintained between the allied troops and the people may be seen in the fact that during the 3 years and 10 months that the occupation continued, only two instances occurred in which attempts to take life were committed by the Chinese upon our men ... the two offenders in the instances above mentioned were the only Chinese who suffered capital punishment at our hands during the period of the occupation ... the occupation has at least proved that most of the professedly popular opposition which we encountered prior to its capture was the result of official instigation.[26]

A city of a million inhabitants was policed only by an additional three hundred allied servicemen, and foreigners – including Lord Elgin – were able to walk about the town without molestation.

Although the conduct of the war is peripheral to the history of Hong Kong, the consequences of the peace were to be important, resulting in the first expansion of the island colony to the mainland. Palmerston's government gave place in February 1858 to a Conservative administration headed by Lord Derby; proving that the previous opposition to the conduct of affairs in China had been essentially a party political manoeuvre, the new government followed exactly the same line as their predecessors. A series of treaties was agreed with Britain, France, Russia and the United States in June 1858 after the Anglo-French forces had moved north and taken the forts at Taku (Dagu) guarding the town of Tientsin and the approaches to Peking. This was made possible by the new classes of gunboats developed during the Crimean War: the 'Clowns', little craft armed with two heavy guns but drawing only four feet of water, and capable therefore of steaming right up the Peiho, were best suited for actions in China.

Lord Elgin, considering his task complete with the treaties signed, left China in August, calling at Japan on his way home to conclude a treaty there. He left the conduct of affairs in China to his brother Frederick Bruce, formerly Colonial Secretary in Hong Kong under Davis, and later to be the first British Minister in Peking. Before he left Shanghai on his way to sign the Treaty of Tientsin in March 1858, Elgin was presented with an address from Jardine's, Dent's, and the other British merchants in the port which spoke of their trust that 'the elevating influences of a higher civilization ... might be extended among the Chinese people'. Lord Elgin replied, barely concealing his disdain for such narrowness: 'The Christian civilization of the West will find itself face to face not with barbarism but with an ancient civilization in many respects effete and imperfect but in others not without claims on our sympathy and respect.'[27]

Much to his annoyance, Elgin was soon back in China. In conjunction with Admiral Hope, Frederick Bruce mismanaged the ratification of the treaty, and involved the British forces in a repulse at Taku. Lord Elgin, by then enjoying a seat in the restored Palmerston Cabinet of June 1859, had to be reluctantly sent out again. At the end of 1860 peace was finalized and the terms of the Treaties of Tientsin ratified by the Convention of Peking. Foreign embassies were at last allowed in the Imperial city and Prince Kung, the abler brother of the Emperor, took charge of foreign relations, with support grudgingly accorded by the more conservative courtiers. The new office, the Tsungli Yamen, developed into the Ch'ing equivalent of the Foreign Office, although the direction of foreign policy continued to be strongly influenced by Tz'u-hsi, Dowager Empress after the death of her husband in 1861, and the ultimate power after her *coup d'état* in November that year suppressed the Regency Council.

With direct inter-government relations now established in Peking,

Hong Kong ceased to be the centre of British diplomacy. Governors who attempted direct contact with their Chinese opposites were warned off by the Foreign Office; it was that department's business, through the consular officers, to deal with the Chinese, and the Governors should please get on with the domestic affairs of their little colony. The new diplomatic exchanges developed only slowly, the Tsungli Yamen's task being complicated by the fact that the more chauvinist Chinese regarded all contact with the foreigner as reprehensible, branding those who conducted it as 'traitors'. While this was unhelpful, since the alternative of armed resistance was impracticable, such attitudes are understandable. The Convention of Peking was a very different agreement from those concluded earlier at Nanking and the Bogue. In 1843 the foreigners had retreated to the seclusion of the treaty port settlements and to the island of Hong Kong, but in 1860 they were allowed to travel anywhere in China, to preach Christianity, to establish an embassy in Peking, and to trade up the Yangtse to Hankow, which was, with nine others, designated as a treaty port. Not only were the barbarians now to be very much in evidence, but to the humiliation of the Summer Palace's destruction was added that of an Imperial apology. In the context of such painful forced concessions, the loss of another scrap of Chinese territory, a few hundred acres of wasteland looking south to Hong Kong, passed almost unnoticed.

8

THE TUMULT AND THE
SHOUTING DIES

A reckless spirit of hostility

In London the conclusion of the war was unanimously welcomed. It had never been a popular cause, and its ending enabled a penny to be taken off the income tax. In Hong Kong Sir John Bowring, stripped of his more resounding titles as Plenipotentiary and Superintendent of Trade, settled down to the relatively restricted responsibilities of a colonial Governor. It was not a task for which he was well fitted. Some of his social superiors were prepared to be amused by his braggadocio and to admire his intellectual gifts, but to the conservatively inclined, inward-looking and conventional Hong Kong community, officials and businessmen alike, this Governor was incomprehensible. On his first appointment London had been aware that this might be so. The Colonial Office at that time – during the coalition government led by Lord Aberdeen – was in the charge of the Duke of Newcastle, no fan of Bowring's, who wanted to limit his powers as much as possible. A Lieutenant-Governor, old Colonel William Caine, was therefore to act as chief executive of the colony, and Bowring was instructed to hold aloof from strictly colonial matters, although with the powers to intervene in an emergency. This idea of a '*gouverneur fainéant*' very quickly fell apart, but in February 1855 the Whigs were back in power, with Palmerston as Prime Minister for the first time. Bowring had no difficulty in persuading him and the Foreign Secretary, Lord Clarendon, that the separation of responsibilities was an 'administrative solecism', and complete powers were immediately restored to him.

Fate did not serve Sir John kindly by sending out as Attorney

General in 1854 the appalling Thomas Chisholm Anstey, acknowledged as the biggest bore in Britain. Anstey had been a Member of
Parliament for only five years, between 1847 and 1852, but had established himself as the scourge of governments, speaking for up to six
hours on topics of not the slightest interest to the rest of the House.
Punch's 1848 alphabet began 'A is for ANSTEY, who talks the House
blind', and parodied *The Rime of the Ancient Mariner*:

> With speech uncheer'd, to benches clear'd,
> Without a pause or stop
> He rav'd away, though all did pray
> He would the subject drop.[1]

A fanatic Roman Catholic convert, Anstey was violently critical of
Palmerston, chicory growers, customs officers and anything else that
aroused his fertile disapproval. His posting to Hong Kong is best
explained by a strong desire to have him as far away from London as
possible.

The move was only moderately successful. Anstey remained in Hong
Kong for less than three years before returning to England, to publicize
his grievances in what must have been the longest ever letter to *The
Times* – 116 pages, when published (for of course *The Times* declined
to print it) as a pamphlet, 'Reasons for an Enquiry, into the Disgraces
brought on the British Name in China, by the Present Hong Kong
Government'.[2] Deprived of chicory and Palmerston, Anstey lambasted
almost every official in Hong Kong with indiscriminate enthusiasm.
The Chief Justice – the reinstated Hulme – the Chief Magistrate
Charles Batten Hillier and the Governor were all attacked, but his
main target was Daniel Caldwell, Registrar General, responsible for
Chinese affairs. Caldwell was married to a Chinese Christian (which
fact caused more than a few raised eyebrows: Chinese mistresses were
acceptable – the irreproachable Sir Robert Hart, Inspector-General
of the Imperial Customs, had a long and respectable liaison with a
Chinese lady – but a Chinese wife posed almost insuperable social
problems), and was an excellent colloquial linguist. He was quickly
accused by Anstey of, among many other offences, keeping brothels,
consorting with pirates and taking bribes.

At least some of the charges were almost certainly justified, for
Caldwell embodied in his own person many of the difficulties which
still afflict the maintenance of law and order in Hong Kong. There

was no doubt that in his previous post as Assistant-Superintendent of Police Caldwell had been very effective in thief-catching, and in assisting with the suppression of piracy, having often been commended by the Royal Navy captains with whom he had worked. Bonham himself had reported to Lord Grey on 3 November 1849 that the senior naval officer, Commander Hay, 'speaks in the highest terms of Mr Daniel Richard Caldwell . . . states without his services he does not think that he could have succeeded', and asked that some recognition should be given since 'the duties of Mr Caldwell have been of a most important and responsible nature, and totally unconnected with his ordinary official avocations'. But Caldwell had laid himself open to criticism: he relied for much of his success on the cultivation of a network of informers, which in turn demanded, there being no one to whom he could delegate the task, an absorption in the Hong Kong underworld, to say nothing of a flow of funds which could hardly be officially obtained.

Anstey found Caldwell particularly distasteful, for reasons that tell one much about Anstey: 'Mr Caldwell himself is a native of St Helena, and apparently of mixed blood. His father, a common soldier in a local militia corps, brought him to Pulo Penang, where, and at Singapore, his youth was passed in various inferior occupations ashore and afloat.' As Attorney-General, Anstey was able to amass enough evidence to have Caldwell brought before a committee of inquiry, which found that only four of the nineteen charges preferred against him, and those the least important, could be proved. But others were shown to be more culpable, including the Acting Colonial Secretary, Dr W.T. Bridges, who almost certainly burnt some papers which would otherwise have implicated Caldwell – 'a contemptible, damnable trick', according to Anstey.

The very violence of Anstey's attacks – 'the reckless spirit of hostility . . . gross disrespect', as the Colonial Office described it, made it impossible to take him seriously, however correct his suspicions may have been. And a subsequent inquiry, carried out in 1861 by Bowring's successor, Sir Hercules Robinson, did conclude that Anstey was right, as the Duke of Newcastle admitted himself: 'the truth of the charges, of which you were the principal author, brought against Mr Caldwell . . . has been substantially established'.[3] But the peaceable members of the Chinese community were supporters of Caldwell to a man, for however shady some of his activities may have been, he was indisputably effective on the side of the law. When finally dismissed in 1862, after the Robinson inquiry, Caldwell still had to be recognized as indispensable, 'the one person on whom the authorities are dependent': he was recalled in 1868 to advise the next Governor, Sir Richard MacDonnell, on licensing gaming establishments and establishing a Chinese detective force, at the 'monstrous' salary of $25,000 a year.

Hong Kong needed someone of Caldwell's peculiar talents, for criminal behaviour, which had decreased under Bonham, became more worrying with the influx of refugees from the Taipings. Lieutenant C.A. Newman of the King's Dragoon Guards described Victoria as 'the fearfullest hole in the world, for I might say it is inhabited by a den of thieves; for instance, if anyone were walking down a street with a medal on his breast they would come and snatch it off . . . I never was in such a place before and never wish to go into another like it.'[4] Yeh's calls to obliterate the barbarians exacerbated feelings: local papers carried 'a daily Chronicle of Chinese atrocities', which included, in the space of two weeks, the 'shooting of four men with fireballs upon them; temporary stupefaction of three Europeans after eating poisoned soup; discovery of a headless body; firing matsheds in Queen's Road Central'.[5]

The gravest incident was an alleged attempt at mass poisoning on 15 January 1857, thought to be caused by a bakery putting large quantities of arsenic in the bread: 'the excitement was of course most intense. The medical men of the colony, whilst personally in agonies through the effects of the poison, were hurrying from house to house, interrupted at every step by frantic summons . . . Emetics were in urgent request.'[6] The symptoms were nausea rather than anything worse, though there were later said to be long-term fatalities, of whom Lady Bowring was one. Public reaction amounted to hysteria: local papers seriously urged the Governor 'to have the whole of the poisoning crew of E-sing's bakery strung up in front of the shop'. But the rule of law once more took its course; a jury acquitted the bakers, since it could not be determined who poisoned the bread – it was exactly the same strange British system of demanding clear evidence of guilt that had so annoyed Commissioner Lin in 1839 in the Lin Wei-hsi case. Augustus Heard Junior, an American merchant, reflected gloomily that this was what might have been expected of British justice; 'Alum [Cheung Alum, the owner of the bakery] was tried in an English court with the advantages of English technicality, and, as we feared would be the case, he could not be proved to have mixed the arsenic with the bread, and was acquitted.'[7]

This was not quite as praiseworthy as it seemed. In an episode that illustrates the contradictions still inherent in Hong Kong, the whole of the bakery workforce was indeed thrown into jail, and confined, forty-two of them, in a room fifteen feet square. This satisfied indignant feelings but provoked quick protests, most noticeably from the very doctors who had been treating the poisoned victims. Charles May, a London policeman who had been brought out in 1845 to take charge of the police force, claimed that 'the door of the room opens on Queen's Road, and as I am informed and credibly believe, this door was frequently open', as well as offering the conventional excuse of other 'pressing and arduous duties' in the 'peculiar circumstances of the time', which made it not 'a matter of surprise . . . that every arrangement was not carried out with the usual regularity'.[8]

Resisting the more absurd proposals from the British inhabitants for persecuting the whole Chinese population, Bowring did introduce emergency measures providing that 'Any Chinaman found at large . . . elsewhere than in his own Habitation . . . not having a Pass . . . shall be summarily punished by any Justice of the Peace by [Fine or Imprisonment] or by Public Whipping, and Public Exposure in the Stocks.' Vigilantes were encouraged: 'Every Person lawfully acting as Sentry or Patrol is hereby authorized . . . to fire upon with intent or effect to kill', and 'No Act done or attempted in pursuance of this Ordinance shall be questioned in any Court.'[9] A delay in issuing the necessary passes to the Chinese led to the morning papers not being delivered in time for breakfast, an inconvenience the locals were quick to resent. The *Friend of China* talked of 'moonshine anent "security"', and jeered at the prospect of Bowring's 'Tabbies at the next Exeter Hall meeting' (the headquarters of the Peace Society and all similar good causes) when faced with their former hero's lapse into rough justice, 'when no Court may afterwards take cognizance of the act, however California-like the cause of death'.

Outside observers however noticed a marked improvement in life in Hong Kong under Bowring. Lieutenant Henry Ellis, R.N., had described in 1855 'a bleakness of life and prisoner like sensation . . . arising in great measure from the difficulty experienced in moving more than a mile or two on either side of the town of Victoria, partly from want of practicable roads and partly from the unscrupulous treachery of the Chinese'. The British community, although 'all more or less rowing the same boat i.e. striving to amass as many dollars as opportunity would admit of . . . were absurdly snobbish', displaying 'much nonsensical narrow-mindedness and unsociability'. Three years later, Ellis qualified this description: 'This, be it remembered was written as things were in 1855, since which time . . . there has been a vast improvement in every way.'[10]

Bowring was certainly reluctant to take arbitrary measures, since he remained a convinced democrat and reformer, ready to seize an initiative in any direction that offered prospects of moving Hong Kong towards a more liberal society. His most radical endeavour was an attempt to introduce an element of properly representative government, that would include the Chinese population. Like many of Sir John's efforts it met with failure, partly due to his own lack of tact in not winning the co-operation of his second-in-command, the Colonial Secretary William Mercer, who presented argumentative counter-proposals. More seriously, the ethos of the Whig government of the day was not in favour of electoral reform. The 1832 Reform Act had left the British franchise very limited; less than one in five of the adult male population had the vote. Lord Palmerston lacked interest in further reform; his own constituency of Tiverton, with a population of 11,143, had a conveniently small electorate of only 508. Only 193 of the 3,432 inhabitants of Ashburton, now almost the proprietary seat of the China interest, were entitled to vote. Lord John Russell, the only enthusiast for reform among the principal Whigs, had resigned his post as Colonial Secretary, so Bowring's proposals, first advanced in his dispatch no. 110 of 2 August 1855, fell upon deaf ears in Whitehall.

He had suggested that there should be three new unofficial members of the Legislative Council, to be directly elected by all persons, irrespective of race, in possession of land worth £10 per annum, to hold office for three years. The new Colonial Secretary, Henry Labouchere, could not agree. Labouchere, later Lord Taunton, was a thoughtful statesman and a humane liberal, not to be confused with his more entertaining and flamboyant nephew of the same name, a politician and journalist who had worked in a circus and lived with Red Indians. In his dispatch no. 82 of 29 July 1856 Labouchere set out his reasons for restricting the representative element in Hong Kong's government. This is a document of great importance to the understanding of all subsequent British governments' attitudes to the question of democracy in Hong Kong. The Colonial Secretary wrote:

I believe that the present is the first proposal that has been made for introducing those institutions amongst an Asiatic population, containing but a very small proportion of British or even European residents: I have, therefore, thought it the more necessary to weigh carefully the reasons for and against it.

Elections, he decided, were impossible: the population of Hong Kong was unruly, unbalanced and transient, and looked unlikely soon to improve:

> The testimony of those best acquainted with them represent the Chinese race as endowed with much intelligence, but as very deficient in the most essential elements of morality. The Chinese population of Hongkong is, with perhaps a few honourable exceptions, admitted to stand very low in this respect.

Nor could there be any question of entrusting power to the small British community, presumably not so 'deficient in the most essential elements of morality':

> Few if any of the British residents in Hong Kong are persons who go to establish themselves and their descendants permanently in that place; they merely sojourn there during a limited time, engaged in commercial or professional pursuits, but intending to quit the colony as soon as circumstances will permit.
>
> To whatever extent the control of local affairs might be conferred on this class by the partial introduction of representative Government, the effect would be, to give power over the permanent population to temporary settlers, differing from them in race, language and religion, and not influenced by their opinions. However respectable the character of the residents may be, I cannot believe that such an arrangement could work satisfactorily.

But the Colonial Secretary held out some hope for the future: 'If you should hereafter be able to select from the Chinese inhabitants persons deserving of confidence, whom you may think fit to hold this or any other administrative office, I should be willing to assent to such appointments.' There was no need for elections to such offices, since 'for the simple purpose of discerning the persons most competent . . . the judgement of the officer administering the Government seems to me quite as good a test . . . as public election.'[11]

Bowring's first attempt having failed, it was another century and a quarter before any element of democracy, and even then a much less radical one, was introduced into the Hong Kong legislature, although slow and hesitant steps were taken to ensure that the Chinese were to have an increasing share of influence and responsibility. Bowring contrived at least some progress in improving opportunities for the Chinese inhabitants. Since Labouchere had indicated that Chinese could be made Magistrates, the first step was to allow them access to the legal profession, which Bowring duly did. Finding considerable difficulty in filling consular and other posts with even reasonably suitable men – most of the early appointments were the result of political patronage, and Bonham's distrust of Chinese-speakers had not helped – Sir John also initiated a recruitment and training scheme for official posts. This made use of the newly formed Chinese department at King's College, London, also seeking candidates from Irish universities. The programme was only moderately successful at first – Bowring thought the departmental head at King's, James Summers, formerly headmaster of St Paul's College in Hong Kong, was ignorant and useless – but later it became more effective.

Bowring also made an effort to control the worst aspects of the Chinese coolie emigration trade. With the opening of the Californian gold fields in 1848, a demand for unskilled labour had rapidly developed. This was a commodity of which China had a large reserve, and coolies were ready to undertake the long voyage for the sake of higher wages. The trade was organized by labour contractors, who engaged the coolies and delivered them to the ports to await shipment in barracoons, where the unfortunate emigrants were confined in deplorable conditions, each man allotted only eight square feet. Conditions on board ships in the 'Pig Trade' were worse even than those on slavers; on one voyage 128 emigrants out of 332 who embarked committed suicide – this in spite of a bonus to the crew of $400 for every one landed alive. Bowring insisted on minimum standards, which included the provision of hospital accommodation and a surgeon, but he was not helped by the verdict of a Hong Kong court which, having found an Englishman and five Chinese guilty of imprisoning emigrants, sentenced the Chinese to prison but only fined the Englishman $5. Whitehall commented that the sentences did not 'do credit to British authority or increase respect for British justice', but a stricter application of the Chinese Passengers Act of March 1855 only had the effect of driving the trade from Hong Kong to more compliant ports.[12]

During Bowring's term of office, Hong Kong gradually assumed a rather more civilized aspect than in its earlier, wilder, days, an improvement assisted by the practice of Governors bringing their wives to Government House and the arrival of the first bishop in 1850. Until that time the only representative of the Church of England had been the Colonial Chaplain, the Revd. Victor Stanton. Missionary initiative in Hong Kong had been seized by the Non-conformists and the Roman Catholics, based on Singapore and Macao respectively. The American Baptists had opened chapels in both Victoria and Stanley as early as 1842, closely followed by the Catholics. The protean Gutzlaff, acting as a missionary, was instrumental in founding a Basel Missionary Society chapel in 1844. British Protestants were uncomfortably divided between the established Church of England and a group which included the Non-conformist sects and the Church of Scotland. As the state Church, the Church of England naturally became the official Church of Hong Kong as soon as colonial status was defined, but until then it was somewhat hampered. Although the Protestant missionaries often worked together, even extending some toleration to the Catholics – 'the professors of a corrupted form of Christianity', according to the first Anglican Bishop – their differences were still marked. It had been suggested that they might share a temporary chapel, but this ecumenical step had been specifically forbidden by Whitehall. A similar rivalry was reflected between the Church Missionary Society, an Anglican body, and the London Missionary Society, run by Non-conformists. Fortunately most of the early missionaries were men of considerable ability and generosity of spirit, who, together with their wives, gave a much needed tincture of civility to Hong Kong society.

The Stantons were particularly liked, and Victor, who had earlier undergone the uncomfortable experience of being kidnapped by the Chinese, was instrumental in starting both St Paul's College, which began to train Chinese as teachers and clergy in 1849, and the first school for English children. Sir John Davis spoke highly of the 'liberality and absence of sectarian feeling' found in this school, which gives an idea of conditions in other establishments. The first headmaster of St Paul's, James Summers, typified the narrow and prejudiced view too often found. On a visit to Macao in June 1849, Summers was asked to remove his hat as the Corpus Christi procession passed. As a protest against such papistical extravagance, he refused, and was promptly arrested. Captain Henry Keppel, the senior naval officer, who happened to be on the spot, peremptorily, but unsuccessfully, demanded his release. Keppel thereupon sent a raiding party which stormed the prison, killing a warder, and freed Summers. A full-scale international row ensued, which resulted in Lord Palmerston having to make a formal apology and to censure Keppel. This does not appear to have done the unrepentant Captain any harm, since he died Admiral of the Fleet at the age of ninety-four. Summers went on to the chair of Chinese Literature at King's College, London.[13]

Formally established religion arrived with the appointment in 1850 of George Smith as the first Bishop of Victoria. It was at a time when the Church of England was deeply split by the Tractarian movement, which caused vitriolic ill-will between the High and Low elements. Smith, although fervently Low Church, was primarily a missionary, who had spent three years exploring China on behalf on the Church Missionary Society. He returned to England in 1847, believing 'that this country has been honoured by God as the chosen instrument for diffusing the pure light of Protestant Christianity throughout the world'. Such complacent pomposity was entirely typical of the new Bishop, and of the increasing respectability of the colony; the old, more raffish, order lost one of its most picturesque supporters with Gutzlaff's death in 1851. Even then a scandal ensued, since the Bishop's chaplain fell for Gutzlaff's widow, and was sent home for unbecoming conduct.

Some Hong Kong missionary efforts were more successful than others; the Diocesan Native Female Training School was obliged to wind up when it was discovered to be a little too successful. According to Eitel, who can be regarded as an authority since he married one of the teachers, almost all its successful Chinese girls, having been trained in Western ways and being able to speak English, found comfortable situations as the mistresses of resident foreigners.[14] However useful a contribution this might have made to the pleasantness of life in Hong Kong, it was not quite what the school's founders had envisaged. Bishop Smith attempted to persuade the British government to finance a college to train 'Native Interpreters' who 'by the efficiency gained from a European education and by the principles of moral integrity instilled during the progress of Christian instruction' might manage to 'repay the debt of gratitude in some subordinate official trust', and help in 'leavening with the influence of Christian loyalty the whole mass of Native Society'.[15] It went without saying, of course, that 'the management of such an institution might be undertaken by the ecclesiastic representatives of the Church of England in the Colony'. In the inflamed climate of religious opinion in England no government was going to risk the opprobrium of spending public money on such a project. Nor did the sceptical Unitarian Bowring think much to the alumni of St Paul's, none of whom had been of the slightest use in the government service, and he preferred to concentrate on the state sector of education. A beginning had been attempted in 1848 when modest grants ($10 a month – about £2) were made to the existing Chinese schools, which were then to be supervised by an education committee, but the reforming Governor found it 'quite monstrous' that only £120 was spent on educating, as against £8620 on policing, the populace. Of perhaps nine thousand children of school age in the colony only 150 were in government schools (there were also a number of private, unsupervised, Chinese schools). Bowring managed to increase the school population to 873 boys and sixty-four girls, to secure an annual budget of £1200, and to appoint an Inspector of Schools, but it was only after Bishop Smith left in 1864 that it proved possible to establish a well-organized state system.[16] But Bowring did have the satisfaction of worsting Smith over a day of fasting and humiliation, which the Bishop demanded and the Governor, with the backing of the Colonial Office, refused.

Bowring, urbane, cultivated and good-tempered, was like most of his fellow radicals out of touch with the majority opinion of his day, and incapable of mixing easily with persons of different interests – although he did manage to fall off one of Matheson's racehorses, which may have endeared him to the more sporting. He had much need of an even temper for, in addition to domestic upsets (Lady Bowring's poisoning was followed by their daughter's decision to become a nun) and the impossible Anstey, the Governor was inflicted with James Keenan, a Kentucky Colonel who had served in the Mexican War and been given the post of US Consul in Hong Kong as his dubious reward. Keenan was quarrelsome either sober or, as he frequently was, drunk. He had a very cross correspondence with the senior US naval officer, Captain Cadwalader Ringgold, who found it necessary to remind the Consul of the difference between 'pirates' and 'pilots' and recommended that he read a few good books. There were persistent difficulties with British deserters who were encouraged to abscond by US whalers in the port. The Hong Kong Colonial Secretary William Mercer complained to Keenan that 'about fifty men' from the 59th Foot (East Lancs) had deserted in the first three months of 1856, and asked for his co-operation in controlling the problem. Almost certainly this was not forthcoming, since Keenan was permanently irate, as were many of his countrymen, at the British use of Sikh policemen, always referred to in his correspondence as 'Negroes' or 'Blacks'. One incident in 1855, when the steamer *River Bird* was boarded in a search, was picked up by the *New York Times* with banner headlines: 'Outrage. An American Vessel boarded by Blacks. American Consul Dragged through the Streets.' Keenan, who had been charged with obstructing the course of justice, wrote a bitter letter to the US Secretary of State William Marcy complaining of British methods of law enforcement and crying for vengeance:

> I now have most earnestly to request that such steps will be taken by our Government, as will not only prevent a recurrence of such conduct, but also effect the removal of all the officials engaged in these outrages. The immediate recall of Sir John Bowring, governor of the Colony and the removal of Charles B. Hillier, W.J. Mitchell (Assistant Magistrate) and Charles May (Superintendent of Police).
>
> If prompt and energetic measures are not taken to punish the audacity and arrogance of these violators of international law . . . the American name will . . . become a byword and a reproach.

Consul Keenan went on to protest in increasingly hysterical tones against: 'The illegal proceedings of a mob calling themselves a Magistrate's Court and a Police Force . . . the Chinamen and the Negro Musulmen who are brought to sustain him . . . this growing hostility of English officials . . . this British gangrene . . . must meet with a speedy remedy.'

Sir John deployed his 'restraining influence' to mollify Keenan, who found an outlet for his aggressive energies in accompanying the American Navy to the taking of Canton, where he got into trouble for allegedly raising the American flag on the wall, since the United States was not taking part in the proceedings. In spite of his vehement denials Keenan was dismissed by the American minister, Dr Parker, which led to another major row, eventually settled by President Buchanan himself dismissing the unrepentant Consul.[17]

Bowring too had to go; he had been too radical for his countrymen, and left in May 1859, amid the execrations of a large portion of the European community, with venomous epistles and libellous accusations continuously hurled at him. The Chinese, on the other hand, presented their retiring Governor with most magnificent testimonials of their 'genuine esteem', recognizing that Bowring had been the first Governor to take Chinese interests to heart. His wife's death, a shipwreck on the way home that left Sir John stranded with his fellow passengers on a coral reef, and a severe illness, did not impair his fondness for giving other people advice. Palmerston forgave Bowring enough to send him off to Italy to counsel the new government of King Victor Emmanuel on economic policy, and not very long before he died in 1872 at the age of eighty, Sir John could be found lecturing an audience of three thousand in his native town of Exeter.

Kowloon

One unlooked-for benefit of the *Arrow* war to the colony was the acquisition of the Kowloon peninsula, some three square miles of the Chinese mainland opposite Victoria. British interest in the northern shore of the peninsula had been manifested as early as 27 July 1844, when a government notification was inserted in the *Gazette* to the effect that 'houses and buildings of a permanent nature' had appeared there and that 'the British Government would not interfere, should the Chinese Government proceed to remove such erections'. Davis had pointed out to Ch'i-ing that these incursions – which were made by Americans as well as British – had been effected without his permission; the intruders were subsequently expelled, and 'for some years the Kowloong Peninsula was occupied solely by some half dozen insignificant hamlets tenanted by stonecutters and limeburners'. The situation in June 1859 was summarized by William Mercer:

> It was as nearly as my memory serves to fix it, about the summer of 1853 that the present village began to arise at Teem-cha-tsuy and has ever since been well known as a place of reception for stolen goods of all kinds. It has largely increased in the last two years and its character is by no means improved.
>
> The shipping having moved over to that side of the harbour for the Tai-foong [typhoon] months will probably tend to promote still further the growth of this objectionable settlement.

Mercer took a look himself, with the escort of a party of police, to confirm the disreputable habits and appearance of the population. He decided it would be an act of kindness, as well as a strategic move, to take over this noisome spot, and set out the advantages of so doing: 'I would class as foremost the prevention of the occupation of Kowloong by another foreign power, or, which is still more to be feared, by irregular settlers acknowledging no order, obeying no rule, and setting the Chinese jurisdiction at defiance.' Which indeed was almost the present circumstance, since what authority existed had been deposed by 'a gang of Hakka bandits'. The limits of the harbour area of Hong Kong, now indistinct, would be defined, and the inhabitants of 'this overcrowded and expensive city' provided with 'occasional change of air and scene, and an escape such as it is from the monotony of this dreary hill side'.[18]

There were, however, more pressing reasons for taking over Kowloon. The proximity of the mainland to Hong Kong had worried naval and military men from the earliest days. Any forts on Kowloon held the island within easy cannon shot; a 24-pounder was reasonably accurate at two thousand yards, which would enable guns at Tsim sha Tsui to cover most of the new settlement's shoreline. Elliot had immediately spotted the danger and suggested that the existing Chinese batteries should be dismounted, even though they were described by one military observer as 'honeycombed rusty old pieces of iron', which 'if anyone attempted to discharge them with shot, the Gunners would stand a good chance of being killed'.[19] In times of war, however, military men could indulge themselves, and accordingly areas of Kowloon were temporarily taken over in 1842, and again when hostilities broke out in 1857. This was done in a reasonably amicable manner, without objections from local officials or populace. As an indication of the informality of relations, when Sir John Bowring was upset by the actions of the military mandarin at Kowloon he simply arranged for him to be kidnapped, brought to Government House on the island, duly scolded and returned.

By that time technical developments were bringing a change in attitudes. The effective range and power of guns had greatly increased with the introduction of rifled cannon. The French had used them in their Italian campaign of 1859, and William Armstrong, a Newcastle solicitor, had developed his new rifled field-piece, which allowed a higher charge and greater range in a lighter gun; his breech loaders gave an impressively high rate of fire (they were used to equip the new *Warrior* of 1860, and some can still be seen on her at Portsmouth). Other powers were beginning to take an acquisitive interest in China. Kowloon in relatively friendly and ineffective Chinese hands might be tolerable, but what if the French or Russians should install themselves there with a few batteries of the new guns commanding the harbour and the city of Victoria? Britain had just concluded the costly Crimean War against Russia, and conflict with France, even though the two countries were at the moment allied, was permanently possible. Major General van Straubenzee, in command of the Hong Kong garrison, and Captain Hall, late of the *Nemesis* but now commanding the line-of-battle ship H.M.S. *Calcutta*, made these points forcefully to Bowring, who was persuaded to press the British government to acquire at least the Kowloon peninsula – essential for cavalry exercise – and Stonecutters Island, a mile or so offshore, which General van Straubenzee was particularly anxious to have for gunnery purposes. When the expeditionary force reached Hong Kong General Sir Hope Grant, in China once more, found Kowloon to be 'essential to the defence of Hong Kong harbour and the town of Victoria', and 'a spot of which I was most anxious to gain immediate possession'. Reluctantly, however, Grant appreciated that 'the forcible seizure of the promontory would not have been quite legal'.[20]

Although both the Plenipotentiary, Lord Elgin, and his brother Frederick Bruce appreciated the military arguments, they too were perturbed by pangs of conscience, which deprecated forcible demands for more Chinese territory, and by the bad example this might set to other European powers, as well as by the fact that the 1858 Treaty of Tientsin had been agreed, and was only waiting for ratification from Peking. Bruce suggested that a separate agreement on the subject of Kowloon might be made at Canton, perhaps accompanied by the remission of all or part of the previously negotiated Canton indemnity. Lord John Russell was especially worried that the French would be upset by Britain gaining territory as a result of joint Anglo—French action, and would demand a quid pro quo.

It was left to that stirrer-up of events, Harry Parkes, to find a solution. He settled the whole thing personally with Governor General Lau at Canton on 19 March 1859, and produced draft proposals for General Hope Grant's consideration. Parkes reported the meeting thus:

Got up to the Heights with said draft at 1 o'clock, and at once saw General Grant, who fully approved the letter. I also talked with him about the police etc., and got him at once to authorize the formation of a strong mounted corps, to be raised from 30 men, as at present, to 70 or 80, if 100 could not be given. Took tiffin with the two Generals, their respective ladyships, and staffs, and back to office. In the afternoon to Lau, with my letter in my pocket, and got him to agree to the whole of the scheme whereat I felt jolly in mind though seedy in body.

The next day Parkes 'had to draw up a deed of lease and a proclamation relative to Kowloon and in a word to carry into execution the arrangement of yesterday, but I was rewarded in the evening by signing, sealing and delivering, I to Lau and Lau to me, the desired deed of lease which settled the Kowloon question, until the peninsula can altogether be ceded to us, which will be the next step, I doubt not.'[21]

In this casual way, at a cost of 500 taels, was Kowloon ceded by one senior Ch'ing official to a British Consul during a period when the two countries were at war. Bruce approved, although without much enthusiasm: 'This arrangement is an imperfect one, but I thought it would be inadvisable to delay acquiring even this much title to a district'. Clearly perturbed that a junior consular official – Parkes was thirty-one at the time – had appropriated a slice of Chinese territory in his own name, the Secretary of State for the Colonies, the Duke of Newcastle, suggested that 'it was advisable to send out an intimation of the wishes of Her Majesty's Government to Mr Parkes to whom the lease appears to have been made'. Lord John Russell accordingly acquainted Parkes that Her Majesty 'would gladly acquire possession of the Cowloon Peninsula' – at, presumably, any time that Mr Parkes found it convenient to surrender his title.

Some more official confirmation of the area's permanent cession from the Emperor of China was also needed, and Bruce tiptoed delicately around the subject, attempting to fix the responsibility on someone else. He wrote, havering, to van Straubenzee on 19 February 1860:

Her Majesty's Government has expressed itself desirous of obtaining a cession of that part of the Kowloon Peninsula which is necessary to the security of the harbour, and to the maintenance of order among the population . . . I can offer no opinion as to the probability of the Chinese agreeing to cede it to us, but it would be a step gained were it to be occupied . . . Should Your Excellency deem such a measure advisable, you will see that I do not think it is politically open to objection . . .

On 6 March he wrote to Sir Hercules Robinson, Bowring's successor: 'I wish to state to you, as the person most interested, the position, diplomatically speaking, of the question, leaving it up to you to decide ... But I need not say that acting as we are with others, there may be grave political objections to mooting the subject of territorial acquisition.'

It fell again to Parkes to make this possible, although involuntarily and in a very uncomfortable fashion. With his command of spoken Chinese and his eighteen years' experience of Chinese diplomatic methods, Parkes was an obvious choice to accompany Lord Elgin on his second expedition north in August 1860. While negotiating with the Chinese Parkes, with a small party that included Elgin's private secretary, Henry Loch, and Thomas Bowlby, the *Times* correspondent, were seized by the Manchu general Seng-ko-lin-ch'ing. After some days of brutal treatment Loch and Parkes were released just before the Emperor's order for their immediate execution was received, but the other members of their party, including Bowlby, and many of their small escort died in a particularly unpleasant fashion.[22] The incident immediately brought negotiations to an end. Either the Chinese accepted every British demand or Peking would risk destruction, assuring the collapse of the dynasty. As it was the Summer Palace, in which the captives had been imprisoned, was looted and destroyed in what Elgin, after much heart-searching, believed was a suitable reprisal; not as drastic as the sack of Peking would have been, but a severe enough warning. The absolute cession of Kowloon then became nothing more than a trifling addition to the allied requirements, and was granted without demur.

There remained to be settled the future use of the new area, whether it should be employed for civil or military purposes. Sidney Herbert, Secretary for War, who had helped Florence Nightingale in her campaign to improve standards of care in the army, warned General Grant to 'look carefully at Kowloon. There is a strong feeling among the Hong Kong civilians that all the advantages of the acquisition should be reserved for them. I have urged on the Colonial Office that merchants go out to Hong Kong or elsewhere at their own risk for their own good; but the soldier is sent out to protect the merchant ... and the duty of the Government is to give them the best chance of health and comfort.'[23] Sir Hercules Robinson, on behalf of the colonists, claimed that the idea of appropriating the peninsula was theirs, and that the Peking Convention expressly declared it to be ceded as 'a

Dependency of the Colony of Hong Kong'. The General won, leaving Dr Eitel indignant that the colonists' 'incontrovertible arguments . . . were brushed aside by the simple fiat of the Imperial Government. The wants, the welfare and the development of the Colony were mercilessly sacrificed to Imperial military interests.'[24] It was some time before Kowloon became anything more than a useful appendage to Victoria, with only wharfs, godowns and some summer houses supplementing the military installations.

With the signature of the Treaty of Tientsin Hong Kong entered upon a period of relative obscurity. Ten new treaty ports had been added to the five already existing, which not only opened the coast as far north as Manchuria to international trade, but also the Yangtse, although the establishment of facilities there had to await the suppression of the Taipings. Once the question of access to Canton was resolved, it began to compete more seriously, and a new international settlement, considerably larger than the old, was created on the reclaimed island of Shameen, close to the old factory area. With the appointment of a British Minister at Peking, Hong Kong was no longer the sole centre of British interests in China, and its Governor became a Colonial Service officer, under the direct control of a single Whitehall department, the Colonial Office; and new forces were at work even in that institution.

> 'What a land is this; with its subject continents and islands,
> hardly able to maintain the peace in Ireland, and yet
> conquering nations on the Indus, and the Emperor of the
> third part of the human race at Amoy and Chusan.'
> Sir James Stephen[25]

Since Virginia was founded at the beginning of the seventeenth century British colonies had proliferated. In addition to the original settlements in North America, numerous and widely scattered parts of the world had found themselves, in the course of a couple of centuries, attached to the British Crown. In 1843, when Hong Kong was added to the list, it joined Singapore, Malacca, Prince of Wales Island, Labuan, the Seychelles, Mauritius, Ceylon, Cape Colony, Gambia and Sierra Leone, St Helena and the Falkland Islands, Aden, the numerous Caribbean possessions, Gibraltar and Heligoland. In Australia the original convict settlements were developing into properly constituted colonies, as were New Zealand and the later Australian states (India was never regarded as a colonial possession, but treated separately under the Board of Control and the India Office).

Any attempt to manage centrally the affairs of so geographically scattered and diverse a group of dependencies, at a time when communications were limited by the time it took dispatches to travel by the fastest sailing ship (steamers of that period were still being outstripped under most conditions by sail), was beset by impossibilities. The residents of numbers 13 and 14 Downing Street, where the Colonial Office was uncomfortably housed, wisely did not attempt to do this, relying on colonial Governors to take most decisions. This habit of leaving things to the man on the spot was to stay with the Colonial Office long after telegrams, telephones and jet travel had rendered it less imperative.

Neither assistance nor much interference was offered by the officials' political masters. The post of Secretary of State for the Colonies (until 1854 also the Secretary for War, although the departments themselves were quite separate) was never a plum job. At the end of the Napoleonic wars the Whigs had even wanted to wind the department up, amalgamating it with the Home Office. Sometimes held by able young men on their way to better things, but often by second-rankers, the Colonial Office was rarely a place to linger (in 1855 the post changed hands four times). With the exception of Edward Cardwell (1864–66), the army reformer, the occupants of the post in the twenty years or so after the *Arrow* affair, although all decent gentlemen, were not distinguished by great talent. Of the Duke of Newcastle, the Earl of Carnarvon ('Twitters'), Lord Granville and Lord Kimberley, only the last took colonial administration seriously, and none displayed any interest in Hong Kong unless forced by circumstances to do so. The House of Commons considered colonial affairs to be unutterably tedious, and often found difficulty in mustering a quorum for the infrequent debates on the subject.

By contrast the senior civil servants at that time, and for thirty years thereafter, were men of considerable distinction, who held their jobs for long enough to give form and continuity to colonial policy. Sir James Stephen was the initiator. A widely-learned (he later become Regius Professor of Modern History at Oxford), conscientious, evangelically religious man, he held the post of Permanent Under-Secretary from 1836 to 1847. His personal abilities, combined with an immense capacity for work, established a system of clear channels of communication and defined responsibilities within the department. When Stephen retired, under considerable nervous stress, three posts had to be created to cope with the workload he had managed alone: Herman Merivale succeeded as Permanent Under-Secretary, Frederick Elliot, another of that ubiquitous family, as Assistant Under-Secretary, and Sir Frederic Rogers, later Lord Blachford, as legal adviser. All three of these were men of outstanding talents; Merivale, the only man in his time to be compared to Macaulay for the breadth of his learning, had been a Fellow of Balliol at twenty-two and became Professor of Political Economy at Oxford; Rogers, who in turn succeeded Merivale in 1860, had been a Fellow of Oriel. Colonial Secretaries came and went, but these men continued to wield the real power; 'The colonies', an Australian journalist acidly remarked, 'have been really governed during the whole of the last fifteen years by a person named Rogers.'

When Rogers retired in 1872 the office of Permanent Under-Secretary had therefore been in only three pairs of hands since 1836. A recognizable 'house style' had emerged, which might be defined as liberal, with a strong bias towards observing the rule of law, a high degree of conscientiousness towards the subject races already in their charge, and a strong disinclination to add to their number. The subordinate clerks – the senior clerks were in fact highly-placed civil servants, who would today be described as Deputy Under-Secretaries – were sometimes equally eminent. Sir Henry Taylor was a literary lion, as was James Spedding, both friends of Tennyson; Spedding was in fact offered the Under-Secretaryship when Stephen retired, but declined the post, preferring to get on with his monumental edition of the works of Francis Bacon. Selection of clerks was on the basis of personal introduction from prominent friends, and almost all came from the upper-middle classes, the gentry rather than the aristocracy, who preferred the less earnest atmosphere of the Foreign Office.

Breezes of change in the system were discernible, originated by Lord Macaulay, who proposed in 1854 a system of admission to the East India Company's service by competitive examination. His criteria were not dissimilar from those of the Chinese bureaucracy: 'Skill in Greek and Latin versification has indeed no direct tendency to form a judge, financier or diplomatist. But the youth who does best what all the ablest and most ambitious youths about him are trying to do well, will generally prove a superior man.'[26] (The Scotch, he admitted, were 'very little cultivated' in 'the art of metrical composition in the ancient languages', and ought to be allowed to excel in more mundane subjects.) Macaulay's ideas were embodied in the Northcote Trevelyan Report of 1853, which recommended the foundation of a Civil Service Commission to superintend a selection system. In 1855 this was done, and by 1873 extended even to the Foreign Office. In practice this made little difference to the type of candidates who, a century later, were still coming from very similar backgrounds, in spite of many efforts to broaden the entry. It did, however, something to weed out the totally incompetent, and much to further the somewhat complacent attitudes of superiority that characterized the successful.

The great achievement of Sir Hercules Robinson, who replaced Bowring in September 1859, was to establish a similar system for the recruitment and training of future Hong Kong administrators, along the lines earlier suggested by Bowring. Some such programme was urgently needed, since on Robinson's arrival there were only four men in the government service acquainted with Cantonese, and of these only one, the court interpreter, had even an imperfect knowledge of the written language. The 'cadets', selected by competitive examination, made their first appearance in 1862, and speedily began to make themselves felt; within two years Cecil Clementi Smith had become Registrar General, responsible for all Chinese affairs. From that time, instead of having to rely on the scratch assortment of locals and those who could be persuaded to leave England, Hong Kong began to be staffed by professionals who created a competent administration, although a great gulf still separated them from the powerful mandarins of Whitehall. Cadets tended to come from modest middle-class families, to have attended 'minor public and obscure private schools', and nearly half were from provincial universities, at a time when admission to the Home and Foreign Services was very much an Oxford and Cambridge preserve.[27]

For some time, however, the old methods of selection had to be employed by the Colonial Office, and the Hong Kong government officials continued to constitute a mixed, although improving, bag. Robinson himself would not have passed any competitive examination. He came from a remarkable Anglo-Irish family, the Robinsons of Rosmead, Westmeath. The new Governor's father, Admiral Hercules, had served with Collingwood, keeping in, so he said, with the surviving victor of Trafalgar by petting his dog Bounce; his brother Bryan spent half a century as a judge in Newfoundland. Two of the Admiral's sons became colonial governors; William – who was also a well-known composer – of Western Australia, South Australia and Queensland, and Hercules of New South Wales, Ceylon and South Africa as well as Hong Kong. After a short military career (commissioned into the Royal Irish Fusiliers in 1843 at the age of nineteen, resigning three years later), Hercules served as an Irish civil servant, concerned for the most part with Poor Law administration and famine relief before becoming Governor of the little West Indian islands of Montserrat and St Kitts. Only thirty-five when appointed to Hong Kong, Robinson enjoyed a long career in the Colonial Service, being recalled in 1895, after his retirement, to his previous post in Cape Town when things there began to look difficult. Robinson was a professionally affable Irishman, with a young and attractive wife, together described as 'projecting an image of healthy sociality'. Late in life, in New South Wales, he made a name for himself as the winner of the colonial Derby and St Leger, and was extremely popular. The joviality was superficial, though, the real Robinson being described as 'cold and calculating, very cautious, without any personal ties or friendships or hatreds. His first interest was to secure his safety.' Joseph Chamberlain complained of his performance in South Africa that 'I wish he would show his teeth occasionally.'

But a somewhat bland personality was what Hong Kong needed after the excitements of Bowring's tenure of office. Sorting these out occupied much of Robinson's time during his early years in office. When on 16 December 1861, more than two years after his arrival in the colony, Robinson was able to forward to the Duke of Newcastle the Minutes of the Civil Service Abuses Inquiry, it was hoped that this would prove to be the final report on the Caldwell case and that official life would begin a more even tenor. The Inquiry found Caldwell guilty of a 'long and intimate connexion with the pirate, Machow-Wong', and his dismissal from the public service was recommended. On 10 April 1862 this was confirmed by the Duke, although it took him rather longer to silence Anstey, who had proved at least one of his points by what he described in characteristic terms in a letter of 4 June 1862 as 'this late . . . partial, mutilated and ex parte inquiry'.

As well as Caldwell, others connected with the stormy past left the scene; that survivor of the Napier mission, Alexander Johnston, had gone in 1852; William Caine and John Hulme retired in 1859, leaving the discontented Mercer as the only remaining member of the original colonial administration. New appointments were of safer men, not for the most part of much distinction – although one, Julian Pauncefote,

Attorney General later in the decade, was to become deservedly renowned – but competent and honest. Fixed salaries were agreed, ranging from £5000 for the Governor and £2500 for the Chief Justice to about £1000 for departmental heads. These included a Postmaster General, since the colony was now given its own postal service, and, as another indication of Hong Kong's growing freedom from London controls, its own coinage. This was not to be sterling, as in other newly founded colonies, but the dollars traditional in China. From 1862 the colony's accounts were published in dollars.

Not too Scotch

Although Robinson himself had not much to do with it, it was during his period of office that the Hongkong and Shanghai Bank was established. This institution, usually referred to in Hong Kong as 'the Bank', as the Bank of England is known in the City of London, became the leading financial house in China in a remarkably short time, and remains an important international bank, of major significance in the colony.[28] The credit for its foundation should go to Thomas Sutherland, agent in Hong Kong for the Peninsular & Oriental Steam Navigation Company. Sutherland was a self-made man of impressive ability; by the age of twenty-eight he had been made superintendent of the company's China and Japan agencies and a member of the Legislative Council. F.W. Kendall, who later became Chief General Manager of P. & O. under Sutherland as Chairman, wrote in 1862 from India: 'Sutherland passed through. He went home rather under a cloud, I think, but had come out with full authority, and is to be Superintendent at Hong Kong. We have few men with better heads and more enlightened and refined ideas than Sutherland has. He had mixed more in society . . . and is a thorough man of business without being too Scotch.'[29]

In July 1864 Sutherland discovered that Bombay financiers were planning to float a 'Bank of China', as a majority Indian-owned financial house, intended to mop up the profits of the China trade. On hearing of this plan to glean what he believed to be the rightful pickings of firms resident on the China coast, he set off with great speed to put together an alternative concern. Within five days he had prepared a prospectus and obtained the backing of the Dents, through whom the prospectus was issued. Given the state of relations between the two Hongs this automatically excluded Jardine Matheson, which since Sir James Matheson had been chairman of P. & O. until six years previously, must have been a cause of some annoyance. A Provisional Committee under Francis Chomley of Dent's allocated shares – eight thousand each to Hong Kong and Shanghai, two thousand to India, and two thousand for Japan, Manila and the rest of the world. Since no shareholder was to be allowed to subscribe for more than 2.5 per cent of the total, a wide shareholding was ensured, and the considerable sum of $2.5 million pledged.

An interesting parallel to the flotation of the Hongkong (always one word) and Shanghae (later Shanghai) Bank is that of the National Bank of India in Calcutta at almost the same time. This had similar aims – to enable local investors to profit from the banking services engendered by their own activities – and was similarly successful in raising an important capital: 50 lakhs of rupees, or £500,000. The National Bank of India soon became London-based, while Hongkong and Shanghai remained a Hong Kong-registered Bank, although many of its shares were owned outside the colony. Another interesting contrast is that while the National Bank of India had from its foundation Indian directors, a practice it continued until its final absorption in 1985 by the Australia and New Zealand Bank, it took the Hongkong Bank a century to elect its first Chinese to the Board.[30]

Sutherland had tapped an existing vein of enthusiasm, as the prospectus – which was in fact hardly more than an initial statement of interest – indicated in its first sentence: 'The Scheme of a Local Bank for this Colony, with Branches at the most important places in China, has been in contemplation for a very long period.' The prospectus, in an optimistic tone, knocking the competition, contained some sweeping claims of the sort that would today horrify the New Issues department of the Stock Exchange, but which in the event were to be fully implemented:

> The Banks now in China being only branches of Corporations, whose headquarters are in England or India . . . are scarcely in a position to deal satisfactorily with the local trade which has become so much more extensive and varied than in former years. This deficiency the Hongkong and Shanghae Banking Company will supply . . . For the anticipated success of this enterprise there are therefore ample grounds . . . The Bank will commence operations simultaneously in Hongkong and Shanghae.

Jardine Matheson, who saw no reason to encourage any Dent project, endeavoured to put a spoke in their rival's wheel by using their influence on the Legislative Council, but since both Sutherland and Chomley were members, the necessary ordinance was pushed through, and the bank began trading on 3 March 1865.

With hindsight, this must have seemed the worst possible time for such an enterprise, for scarcely a year later the financial world was rocked by the collapse of the London discount house Overend and Gurney. In the wake of its failure there was a run on the banks which brought down many other businesses. On the China coast Jardine's just avoided closure by negotiating a capital sale, and lease-back, of their extensive property portfolio, but Dent's had to shut their doors, bringing to a close the history of one of the two original great hongs.[31] Their place in Hong Kong, and the seat which it had become customary to allot them on the Legislative Council, passed to Gibb Livingston, another of the original Canton hongs. But the British firms were rapidly declining in importance relative to the Chinese. Within fifteen years of Dent's closure only Jardine Matheson remained listed among Hong Kong's eighteen largest ratepayers; all the remainder were Chinese.

Jardine's also managed to withdraw their balances from at least one of the failing banks by taking advantage of the speed of their ships, one of which raced the mail steamer bringing the news from Calcutta, 'to the thunder of our paddles and the hiss of our steam pipes . . . until I would have thought every bearing was at melting point'. Jardine's won by an hour, and managed to empty their accounts and cash all outstanding notes, getting away with 'A boatload of specie, mostly English gold', before any one else on Hong Kong heard the news.[32] Their old rivals having left the scene Jardine's were able to take their place in the Hongkong Bank, and thereafter played a leading role in the direction of the Bank's business.

The Hongkong Bank's survival in those dangerous times, when the colony's banks were reduced in number from ten to four, was due to its youth. More established banks had built up balance sheets and lending books which produced good profits in years of boom, when as much as 14 per cent could be charged on loans fully secured by government paper, but placed a great strain on the quick assets needed in order to survive a sharp run. Newly formed banks, not having developed their business to the same extent, had preserved more of their original liquidity: not only the Hongkong Bank's survival, but the even more dramatic instance of the new National Bank of India's continuing when nearly all the older Indian banks collapsed, prove the advantages enjoyed by the newcomers.

After the crash a clearer field was left to the Hongkong Bank, of which the directors were quick to take advantage. Within a decade branches and bank agencies had been opened in Japan, India, Saigon, Manila and San Francisco, in addition to the Chinese branches. Competition was never unduly threatening. The biggest British bank in the East, the Oriental, closed in 1884; and an attempt by the National Bank of India to establish itself in Hong Kong between 1869 and 1880 ended in losses and recriminations. In 1872 the Bank became bankers to the Hong Kong government. The then Governor, Sir Richard Mac-Donnell, wrote to the Duke of Buckingham: 'I have not been slow to enter into an agreement with the Hongkong and Shanghai Banking Corporation . . . the Executive Council were firmly of the opinion that the opportunity of obtaining the more favourable terms of the HKSB should be seized without delay, and as that Bank stands on a sound basis, and is accounted so highly in commercial circles, I had no hesitation in agreeing.'[33] Two years later the Bank was given the Peking Legation business, and from then was considered indisputably the leading bank in China and a great asset to the colony in which it was based.

Unlawful games

As Hong Kong ceased to be the centre of interest in Anglo—Chinese relations, the colony turned inward to address domestic issues. On these there was often a difference in perception between the men on the spot and the civil servants in Whitehall, perennially conscious that at any time their political masters might be ambushed by some colonial issue which had been overlooked. There were few questions raised on colonial affairs and even fewer debates, but Hong Kong attracted attention on particularly embarrassing topics – prostitution, slavery, flogging and gambling being especially noticeable, and always sure of an extensive coverage in the press.

Gambling was the first of these to cause trouble. In Britain gambling was controlled by laws of considerable complexity; diversions ranging from backgammon, bagatelle, billiards, boat races and bowls to whist and wrestling were under certain circumstances permissible; others, such as dice, faro, boulet or roly-poly were absolutely unlawful; boxing was dubious. The rich, who placed their bets in such private clubs as White's or Tattersalls might lose as much money as they pleased; the poor, who had to frequent common gaming houses – unlawful institutions – or place their bets on the streets – equally illegal – were in effect banned from betting. Originally these laws had been enacted because 'crafty persons' had enticed honest men 'to play at the tables, tennis, dice, cards, bowls, clash, coyting, loggeting' and sundry unlawful games, 'by reason whercof archery is sore decayed . . . and divers bowyers and fletchers, for lack of work, gone and inhabit themselves in Scotland.' Therefore, it was stated, 'no manner of artificer or craftsman, husbandman, mariners, fishermen, watermen, or any serving man' might so indulge themselves, 'except it be in their masters' house over Christmas'.[34] Although the decay of archery was no longer a matter of pressing concern, this class-based legislation suited the mid-Victorians, anxious to remove temptations from the lower orders, admirably: but its enforcement in Hong Kong was unthinkable.

Something for nothing is universally popular, but the Chinese addiction to gambling is a cultural phenomenon. Closely related to the Confucian world-view, which stresses the importance of propitiating the gods in order to secure favours, the search for luck was embedded in every part of national life, from the Emperor sacrificing in the Temple of Heaven in order to ensure a good harvest, to the coolies betting at fan-tan on the number of pebbles remaining in a pile. Anything could be made the subject of bets, from horse-racing to thimblerig, and although officially illegal in Imperial China, betting flourished everywhere. When the pragmatic Bowring came to consider the question he saw no merit in laws that could not be enforced, and proposed the legalization of gaming, under strict supervision, after a model recently, and successfully, introduced by the Portuguese colonial administration in Macao. But Bowring's proposals fell upon stony ground: the older Whigs might still carry about themselves a flavour of the hard-playing Foxites, who won and lost fortunes on the tables, but the party was evolving into the respectable Non-conformist Liberal party led by the ultra-respectable Gladstone: there were no votes to be gained in permitting gambling, even somewhere as distant as Hong Kong.

It was not until Sir Richard MacDonnell took the initiative in 1867 that anything was done. Sir Richard had little to lose: unlike his predecessors he was nearing the end of a long career – Hong Kong was his last posting before retirement – having already been governor of the

Gambia, St Lucia, St Vincent and South Australia, and received the appropriate order of knighthood, and had therefore no reason to avoid controversy with Whitehall. He was naturally authoritative, fond of adventure – he made some pioneering explorations in Australia – and intolerant of idleness and humbug. He habitually addressed the grandees of the Colonial Office in terms not ordinarily used by colonial Governors – which particularly irritated the aristocratic and urbane Earl Granville – and did not hesitate to intervene in matters which the Foreign and Consular Services considered their own business; an indignant Rutherford Alcock described MacDonnell as 'coarse, bumptious and exceptionally inconsiderate and uncourteous'. A qualified barrister, who had acted as a colonial chief justice, MacDonnell knew his law, and his West African experience, which involved some fighting, proved his willingness to take risks. His dispatches are lively, penetrating, and ready to take on the Colonial Office on contentious issues.

As might be expected of someone of MacDonnell's character, he ran Hong Kong personally, even dictatorially, not relying on his staff or caring overmuch for public opinion. Right or wrong, he pulled the colony, Chinese and Europeans, together as a working unit in a way no previous Governor had done. After four months' investigation he proceeded to brisk action covering taxation, registration of local craft, the suppression of piracy, and the criminal justice system, all of which he pushed against sometimes bitter opposition. The most controversial of MacDonnell's innovations was his licensing of gaming establishments. The combination of irrepressible habits and formal interdiction had inevitably led to widespread corruption. An underpaid and ill-trained police force was taking huge sums from the proprietors of illegal gambling houses: and even such drastic steps as replacing English by Scottish constables, as being less bribeable, had failed. Sir Richard persuaded a reluctant Colonial Office that a licensing system was admissible. He was fortunate that the Colonial Secretary at the time, Lord Carnarvon, was young and open-minded (he even supported women's suffrage), with a seat in the House of Lords that made his personal position secure. Carnarvon was therefore willing to take potentially unpopular decisions, which his successors, nervous of precedent, were unwilling lightly to overturn.

In September 1867 eleven public gaming houses were opened, to an outcry from the missionaries, which in turn stimulated indignant broadsides from the reform-minded Social Science Association in London, who were very sarcastic on the subject of 'local authorities' who had 'taken it upon themselves to pass an "Ordinance"' which had brought 'great discredit . . . upon the British name at home and abroad'. MacDonnell fought back, with added acerbity since he was himself a member of the Association. From somewhere, he observed, the Association had got hold of the very odd idea that gambling had been 'entirely suppressed' in China. It might be possible, he admitted tongue in cheek, to suppress gambling for a short time, by methods such as had been used in China; by 'razing houses to the ground and torturing the landlords, measures to which it was true this government has never yet resorted'.[35]

Legal measures had been tried in Hong Kong, with such pussy-footing punishments as British justice allowed, but had resulted only in increased corruption and crime. Sir Richard 'declined to bear a part voluntarily in continuing the sham which the committee unwittingly recommend', and rhetorically asked if they would prefer 'a style of "ad captandum" legislation, tinselled and varnished to catch the applause of vapid declaimers, but ill fitted to win the approval of earnest men, thoroughly understanding the question, and filled with a conscientious sense of their responsibility?'

It was possible that Sir Richard might have succeeded in his fight for good sense but for one factor: the former black sheep, Daniel Caldwell.

MacDonnell's licensing policy worked only too well, in that the proprietors of the gaming houses, who were making a great deal of money, were anxious to appear whiter than white. The Governor wanted foreigners excluded? Very well, so they should be, in spite of the loss of profits. Suspicious characters and known villains should be picked up? So they were, in considerable quantities. The instrument of this amelioration was none other than the dubious but effective Daniel Caldwell. Now employed by the licensees, at a salary of $20,000, which was nearly as high as that of the Governor himself, Caldwell undertook to assist them in keeping on the right side of the law. To some effect; when a survey was made of the arrests of 'Illegal Gamblers and Dangerous Characters' it was found that in one month (15 January–14 February 1869) twenty-one of the twenty-four subsequently jailed had been apprehended by 'Mr Caldwell's detective'. Caldwell's worth was appreciated by the Governor, who wrote to Lord Granville (who succeeded Lord Carnarvon and the Duke of Buckingham as Colonial Secretary – there were four different Colonial Secretaries to be dealt with during MacDonnell's time of office):

Mr Caldwell is a person who stands well in the opinion of the Chinese community, and possesses great personal influence amongst them, which, I think, is on the whole deserved. Moreover his present position in the foreign community may be estimated by the strong expression of feeling on the part of the Legislative Council in his favour, which was publicly given on the 15 August 1866, with a full knowledge of all his antecedents as well as of his conduct during recent years.

But the tide of Victorian morality was sweeping too strongly for Sir Richard. What stuck in the home politicians' gullets were the licence fees paid by the gaming-house operators to the Hong Kong Treasury, which amounted to embarrassingly large sums. Nervous of being accused of using 'the profits of vice' to supplement colonial finances, Whitehall refused to sanction the release of the fees, except to cover one or two specific items of police expenditure. They were reinforced in this attitude by the view of Sir John Smale, Chief Justice of the colony, who was waging a fierce campaign to revoke the licences. In 1870, when MacDonnell was away on leave, Smale began sending messages to the Hong Kong Colonial Secretary and General Whitfield, acting Governor, claiming that 'the evil results of gaming in this Colony are to an appalling extent never hitherto fully appreciated . . . the fearful consequences of gaming . . . the trustworthiness of the police . . . was never so low as at present'. Fortunately for MacDonnell, the Attorney General in Hong Kong at that time was the remarkable Julian Pauncefote, who later became a distinguished diplomat, Britain's first ambassador to the United States, and was instrumental in founding what became the International Court of Justice at the Hague. Pauncefote tore into Smale, using the bluntest of language:

I cannot admit the accuracy of the facts which he urges as the ground for his opposition to the system . . . On the contrary, I maintain that, since the establishment of the licensed gaming houses, there has been a vast decrease of crime . . . In conclusion, I venture to express a hope that the Chief Justice [will] abstain from attacking the policy of the government from the bench, as there can be no doubt that he thereby encourages . . . every kind of falsehood which can bring odium on this Colony, in relation to the system of licensing gaming houses.[36]

Even so forthright a rebuttal was not enough to save the day at the Colonial Office. The Hong Kong merchants, whose gaming in their clubs was not interrupted, joined with Smale, and the licensing system was abolished. Eitel, who was there at the time, wrote in 1895 after events had ample time to develop: 'no positive gain resulted from the abolition of the gaming houses. Gambling and police corruption continued thenceforth unchecked. The government thereafter simply ignored the problem which is still waiting for a master hand to solve it.'[37]

Sir Richard's cavalier way with his official masters in Whitehall was exemplified by his fight over the Hong Kong seal. This quaint device had been put together in something of a hurry in 1842, and depicted an Englishman and a Chinese in commercial congress on a beach amid tea chests, with an island in the background which might charitably have been identified as Hong Kong. In 1869 this was converted into a badge for the colony's new flag. MacDonnell did not approve of the result, and wrote indignantly to Lord Granville on 3 July: 'the design seems to have been compiled by an oilman at Wapping for about £3'. He proposed, 'in lieu of the gentleman in an evening coat who is purchasing tea on the beach at Kowloon, an unusual place for such a transaction . . . the well-known figure of Britannia and the British lion'.

Governors were not meant to address Earls and Cabinet Ministers in so ironic a fashion, and MacDonnell's letter was particularly hurtful as the badge had indeed been designed by Messrs Thomson & Co., a respectable painters' suppliers of Wapping; the badge therefore remained unaltered. Many years later, the scholarly Governor Cecil Clementi had another try when he suggested in 1926 that the badge should include the Chinese characters for Hong Kong surmounted by a royal crown. This was turned down by the Legislative Council, one member of which, C.H. Ross of Jardine's, commented that there were not 'ten Europeans in the Colony who could tell you what those characters were'. Clementi was indignant, and caustically observed that 'the community has at last educated itself up to the Wapping standards of fine art'. In spite of the criticisms the badge remained, with minor alterations, until 1958, when the then Governor, Sir Robert Black, asked for a new design to be prepared; the Hong Kong Police insisted on retaining the old device, which is still to be seen on the sides of their Land-Rovers.[38]

MacDonnell was very much at home in prosecuting the war against piracy, although he was not much helped either by the Foreign Office or the Admiralty, both reluctant to take action outside colonial waters without the permission of the Chinese government. The Governor solved this by arming two junks (one of which he christened the *Preposterous*), and taking the Kowloon magistrate on board to add some legality to the enterprise. In spite of the lack of sympathy from Whitehall it seems that after MacDonnell's treatment the industry of piracy never regained its former prosperity.

A royal visit

The war with China brought a lift to Hong Kong society and trade, as agreeable officers were temporarily added to the community and the support services for the expeditionary force developed. Bowring and Robinson, with their wives, were welcoming and hospitable, and modestly favourable accounts of life in the colony began to be received at home. Albert Smith, the London impresario whose entertainments at the Egyptian Hall in Piccadilly were a great success in the 1850s, decided to base one of his pieces on China, and made a journey for the purpose of collecting material in 1857. Smith was what might later have been called a 'card': a medical man – just – and the quintessential Bohemian, he was a leading light of the Garrick Club circle to which both Dickens and Thackeray belonged, and a great friend of the former, although he fell out with Thackeray. He was said to have inspired Dickens to start his enormously successful public readings, but Smith's own line was a little less elevated – his duet with his hand 'made up like an old woman, which I used to do in the scene of Baden Fair' was a great success with the Chinese girls. In the monotony of Hong Kong's social existence Smith's visit was a welcome break. He was looked after by Captain Twiss of the Gunners, who took him to 'an American Bar where we had some excellent sherry cobblers'. John Dent gave him dinner, 'one of the best I ever sat down to, in London or Paris', cooked by his French chef. The conversation was on horses, bets and yachts. Smith was impressed by 'many people out in carriages, and some Yankees in light iron 4 wheel trotting gigs; also a string of Mr Jardine's horses, led out for airing by black grooms'.

Sir John Bowring was civil, and spoke learnedly of the trees and plants in the Botanic Gardens which he had established. Smith dined convivially at Government House with Sir John, General van

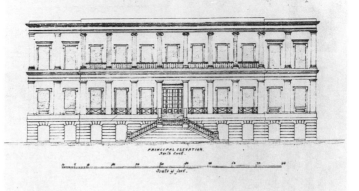

ABOVE: This 1857 view is taken from the present site of Chater Gardens, at that time the foreshore. The barracks are on the left, with the band of the 59th Foot performing on the parade-ground. The accompanying text from the *Illustrated London News* of 15 August 1857 describes the scene: 'Here a fortune-teller; further on a juggler (when the police is not there); charming maidens, three-and-three, two-and-two; white-attired soldiers; dashing European carriages, some with Chinese drivers, some without; coolies carrying ladies and lazy gentlemen; Chinamen on horseback; sepoys in undress, looking as if they had jumped out of bed in a hurry and put on their sheets and anything they could get; snobs in black hats – such is a mild description of a band evening at Hong-Kong.'

BELOW: The Sepoy barracks in 1857. The drawing shows the method of building matsheds, the temporary buildings that served many purposes, from godowns to churches and theatres.

RIGHT: This *Punch* cartoon, published in November 1860, refers to the destruction of the Summer Palace, which Lord Elgin judged to be the proper retribution for the imprisonment and killing of British envoys.

NEW ELGIN MARBLES.

ELGIN TO EMPEROR. "COME, KNUCKLE DOWN! NO CHEATING THIS TIME!"

BELOW: The sandy wastes of Kowloon Peninsula in the 1860s – acquired by Consul Harry Parkes for $500 in March 1859.

'Reputable' and 'disreputable' Chinese, c.1860

LEFT: A Chinese tea-room.

BELOW: Opium smokers – a photograph previously in the possession of the Dent family.

Straubenzee and Charles Jardine, when 'we had great fun about some wine that Sir John had received from Japan, than which nothing could be nastier'. Gifts for the Piccadilly show were generously forthcoming (they included Yeh's fur-lined coat and the execution crosses on which he had victims sliced, as well as some sketches by George Chinnery from Dent), but in spite of the genuine hospitality, Smith found the place plain and dull. Crime was still commonplace, although without its previous dramatic character. Smith had his pocket picked, and found that one friend always carried a hand spike and kept a 'sharp dog'. The British knew little of the Chinese, and did not seem to wish to: 'From the majority it was difficult to get any practical hints respecting the native habits of the people themselves – those small prominent traits about which the public most care.' But they knew a great deal about each other's affairs. 'A peculiar feature in the society of Hong Kong, is that everybody pitches into everybody else, and says the other will be of no use to me.' After the excitements of Piccadilly, colonial life seemed tedious:

> The young men in the different large houses have a sad mind-mouldering time of it. Tea-tasting, considered as an occupation, does not call for any great employment of the intellect: and I never saw one of the young clerks with a book in his hand. They loaf about the balconies of their houses, or lie in long bamboo chairs; smoke a great deal; play billiards at the Club, where the click of the ball never ceases, from earliest morning: and glance vacantly over their local papers. These journals are mostly filled with the most uninterestingly unimportant local squabbles, in which the names of Mr Anstey, Mr Bridges, Ma-chow-wang, Sir John Bowring, and Mr Caldwell, are pitched about here and there, to the confusion of the stranger, who wonders at the importance attached to these storms in tea-cups.[39]

Alfred Weatherhead, a government clerk who lived in Hong Kong between 1856 and 1859, found much the same, although his view was perhaps coloured by his own modest station in colonial society:

> Of social amusement there is but little of any kind in Hong Kong. No Literary and Scientific Institution, Mutual Admiration Societies &c. A branch of the Royal Asiatic Society exists, or rather languishes there but is confined to a select few. There is, to be

sure, a Library and Reading Room, supported by subscription at
the high figure of $2 per month – where the members might meet
to play at chess, practise music and get up lectures, soirees, and
classes if they liked. But they don't. In the first place such proceedings would involve people belonging to different circles meeting
each other, which would be highly improper and objectionable
. . . At the Club House, that paradise of the select, and temple
of colonial gentility, they rejoice greatly in billiards.[40]

Low life was more amusing. Sergeant James Bodell of the 59th Regiment (East Lancs) was posted to Hong Kong in 1850. At first he found
conditions appalling; the soldiers were made to drill for hours a day
in full uniform, with leather stocks; morbidity and mortality rates were
alarming; the Colonel fled to England, and no replacement could be
found until Major H.H. Graham was promoted. Then things got
better; cricket, football, boxing and skittles replaced excessive drill,
and Jardine's gave the soldiers several good pulling boats. Bodell acted
as a stage manager in the garrison theatricals, and was entertained by
the other participants: 'In hot weather . . . they would keep bottles of
Ale, gin &c in a basket down a well to keep it cool. These drinks
would be very soothing and acceptable.' Another useful friend was
Dent's groom, who had come out with two racehorses from England,
and took Bodell to the races where 'you could get more Chinese ladies
in one day at the Races than you could in five years in the City of
Victoria Hong Kong', although there were there 'more Houses of bad
repute kept by Chinese women than any place I have ever seen with
the same population'.
  Pirate hunting was also fun: H.M.S. *Reynard* was particularly successful, since she could lower her masts and funnel, and with after-
burners suppressing her smoke, could steal undetected up the rivers.
Bodell 'saw the pirates brought in, tied together with their queues,
and later executed hanged in three rows of three'. The attractions of
a young lady to whom he was 'paying advances in the love line' seduced
Bodell from army life, and in October 1854 he married one Sarah
Mackinay, with the regimental band in attendance and general
rejoicing.[41]
  Hong Kong's first royal visitor arrived on 31 October 1869 with
H.M.S. *Galatea*, a steam frigate, under the command of Prince Alfred,
the Duke of Edinburgh. 'Affie' was the Queen's second son and everyone's favourite; his 'very manly good temper' was contrasted sadly with

his elder brother's wayward disposition. He had been fortunate in having been allowed to choose a career in the Royal Navy, unlike the Prince of Wales who was denied any important occupation. By 1869 Affie was only twenty-five but had already been shot by an Irish terrorist (he survived) and elected King of Greece by an overwhelmingly favourable plebiscite (he declined). The Duke's talent to charm was immediately demonstrated to Hong Kong when he found that his old commander Henry Keppel – of the Summers incident, and now an Admiral – was about to leave the colony just before the Duke was officially to arrive. Affie immediately made arrangements to replace the crew of the admiral's barge with his own officers, who then rowed Keppel off from the pier to his ship, the Duke himself pulling stroke.

The character of the entertainment arranged for the Duke indicated how far Hong Kong had developed as a respectable colony. As well as the usual balls, fireworks and banquets, Affie was entertained by the Amateur Dramatic Corps (with a selection from Shakespeare given by Mr York) and the German choir at the new City Hall Theatre (illuminated by gas). He conducted another concert (he was a competent violinist), attended a Chinese theatre, played cricket (the cricket club had been founded as early as 1851) and bowls (at the Oriental Bowling Alley), and laid the foundation stone of the new cathedral chancel. The extra space thus afforded eliminated the troubles experienced three years previously when Mr Vaucher and Captain Thomsett, R.N., fell out over a rearrangement of the seating. The question of who was entitled to the sixth pew 'although the said sixth pew is 2'6" nearer the pulpit than the 6th pew originally was' had to be sent to Whitehall for settlement, where it was decided in favour of the Captain, since 'Parishioners have a claim to be seated according to their rank and station.' The rule at the Hong Kong Club, whose new clubhouse had been opened in 1860 – 'the interior arrangements are very elegant and reflect great credit on the Architect (Mr S. Strachan)' – that naval officers were not allowed credit might well have been waived for the ward room of Galatea. Certainly no such difficulties would have been experienced at the Masonic Lodge, of which the Governor was a member.[42]

At least one day of the Duke's visit was devoted to Chinese receptions and entertainments, which underlined the fact that the Chinese population of Hong Kong was beginning to be accorded a measure of recognition, although nothing in proportion to its importance. MacDonnell's instructions, drafted by the authority of the Liberal reformer

Edward Cardwell, had specified that no legislation could be passed by the colony without the consent of Whitehall 'whereby persons of African or Asiatic birth may be subjected . . . to any liabilities to which persons of European birth or descent are not also subjected'. MacDonnell did not let this stop him from taking actions resented by many Chinese, but only as a result of his willingness to offend anyone in the interests of getting things done rather than from any prejudice against the Chinese community, which was in fact rapidly developing a new cohesion and sophistication.[43]

One benefit of the Taiping upheaval had been to bring to Hong Kong its first considerable influx of 'respectable' Chinese, driven from secure and prosperous backgrounds on the mainland by the continuing violence. Unlike the coolies who had flocked to Hong Kong in the early days, the newcomers brought their families with them. Legge felt that this was 'the turning point in the progress of Hong Kong. As Canton was threatened the families of means hastened to leave it and many flocked to the colony.' In 1844 the ratio between men and women had been 5:1. By 1869 this had settled at 2.7:1, at around which it remained for the rest of the century. In 1845 there were only seventy-eight family houses, while by 1867 the number had risen to 1,775. Many of the migrants were indeed people of substance and enterprise: by 1859 sixty-five Chinese firms were large enough to be registered as 'Hongs', representing a considerable accumulation of capital. Some of these were comparable to the great British firms; Kwok Acheong, Compradore of P. & O., organized a management buy-out of P. & O.'s engineering division and established his own steamship line; by 1876 he was the third-largest rate-payer in the colony.

By 1869 the second generation of missionary-trained Hong Kong Chinese was also emerging, men who had not only learnt fluent English but who had experienced Western methods of business and politics. They had been educated not by bigots like Summers, but by Bridgeman and Legge, who combined liberal views with a knowledge of China and sympathy with Chinese aspirations, and formed a closely knit group able to exercise a growing influence in the colony. Tso Aon worked for the Superintendency of Trade from its inception until 1857; his nephew, Tso Seen Wan, became a member of the Legislative Council and his grandson, Tso See Kai, Rector of St Paul's church. In 1871 the Revd. Ho Fuk Tong died, leaving $150,000, the fruit of successful property speculations. Two years later his son, Ho Ch'i, left for England to begin his legal studies, at much the same time as his cousin-in-law, Ng Choy, who had married Fuk Tong's daughter. In 1880 Ng became the first Chinese member of the Legislative Council; his successor there was Wong Shing, who had earlier accompanied Yung Wing to America; his son-in-law, Wei Yuk, became a member of the same Council in 1896.

Paralleling this penetration of the government by the second-generation Chinese colonists, an attempt was made to recreate in the changed environment something of the infrastructure of a traditional Chinese community. The colonial authorities were cautious; such Chinese institutions as the Triad societies were viewed suspiciously, and with good reason; some others, including the trade guilds, with no justification at all. Yet others were, in varying degrees, encouraged. The first of these to achieve official recognition was the District Watch Force, recognized by MacDonnell, against considerable opposition, as an auxiliary police force deployed in Chinese areas to supplement the deficiencies of the regular police. Membership of the District Watch Committee became acknowledged as the anteroom to a political career, which might lead to the Legislative Council and British Imperial honours. More traditional societies centred around the temples, especially the new Man Mo temple in Hollywood Road, which had become a forum where grievances were aired and disputes settled in surroundings and in a language with which the Chinese were familiar. Such procedures were altogether less alarming than those of the new British courts, however sincerely these attempted to accommodate Chinese practices, for even if British justice was less arbitrary and ferocious than that of Imperial China, it was thought infinitely preferable to settle things among oneselves. In the eight years after the temple was founded no case involving only Chinese appeared before the British courts.

Representation on the temple committee – a parish council is a possible comparison – was through neighbourhood associations, or kaifongs. Members of the temple committees soon assumed more extensive responsibilities than those of a parish council; they 'secretly controlled native affairs, acted as commercial arbitrators, arranged for the due reception of Mandarins passing through the colony, negotiated for the sale of official titles, and formed an informal link between the Chinese residents of Hong Kong and Canton authorities'. Although kaifongs did not at first seek to represent the interests of the Chinese community to the Hong Kong government, their very existence led to government officials, when it suited them, consulting these emergent associations.

The colonial government looked on Chinese associations with some sympathy, especially those concerned with trade and policing, both areas of mutual concern, but British officials found great difficulty in understanding Chinese concepts of hygiene and medicine. Chinese medical theory and practice had remained for centuries at a similar stage to that of Imperial Rome – which had itself remained almost unchanged until the Renaissance. It was – and continues to be – based on a theory of 'humours' and balance not unlike those of Galen. Anatomical knowledge was almost non-existent, and surgical techniques were on a level with those in Europe before Paré. There was, however, a powerful pharmacopoeia, even more extensive than that of medieval Islam, and an awareness of some aspects of physiology that Western medicine has still to accommodate (acupuncture, exercise and breathing techniques are perhaps the most widely recognized).

Inevitably, the latest advances in Western practice, which had been coming thick and fast in the nineteenth century, had not reached China. Anaesthesia and asepsis had revolutionized surgery, but public health control had done much more to reduce mortality. With enormous energy mid-Victorian Britain had cleaned up its cities, which only a generation previously had been every bit as disgusting as Dickens described them, and brought the enthusiastic conviction of the newly converted to the problems of Hong Kong. Chinese culture recoiled from these invasive fields of medical activity with shocked distaste. Surgery of any kind was regarded with fear and abomination, and the unfamiliar discipline of Western hospital life was disturbing. In particular the enforcement of sanitary measures disrupted domestic privacy, and infringed many of the most cherished aspects of Chinese tradition which were concerned with death, interment and reverence for the remains of the dead.

In such a community as Hong Kong, where very few of the population were native, and through which a stream of emigrants passed, a demand quickly developed for the provision of an 'I Ts'z' – a death house or hospice, where bodies could await return to their own villages, and a communal ancestral hall, where memorial tablets could be kept. Since the act of dying was considered with peculiar revulsion, necessitating expensive and bothersome ceremonies and rendering the house in which it took place unclean, the Hong Kong I Ts'z also became a place where the moribund could be left without incommoding others. Nothing more calculated to horrify Victorian medical and moral standards could easily be imagined. Conditions in the I Ts'z were described by one of the first cadet officers, Alfred Lister, in 1869:

> Another room contained a boarding on which lay two poor creatures half-dead, and one corpse, while the floor, which was of earth, was covered with pools of urine. The next room contained what the attendants asserted to be alive ... and other rooms contained miserable and emaciated creations, unable to speak or move, whose rags had apparently never been changed since their admission, and whom the necessities of nature had reduced to an inexpressibly sickening condition.

MacDonnell, perhaps embarrassed by the existence of such deplorable conditions in his territory, but certainly displaying the vigorous practical approach that distinguished all his acts, closed the I Ts'z and produced plans for something better. This was the suggestion, initiated by some Chinese in the government service, of a hospital to be funded and managed by the Chinese community itself, to provide traditional Chinese treatment and accommodate the terminally ill, and which would be subject to official inspection. The proposal was accepted with alacrity in Hong Kong and agreed in London, where the Colonial Office was at the time more occupied with disturbances in New Zealand and Canada. Chinese leaders readily formed an organizing committee and produced generous funds: MacDonnell was allowed to give a subsidy from his politically embarrassing surplus from gambling licences. The Tung Wah Hospital emerged as an original and imaginative fusion of Western and Chinese ideas. In what was the most significant acknowledgement so far that Chinese views, even when these appeared to be 'prejudice and superstition', should be treated considerately, traditional Chinese medicine was afforded official recognition.

The governing body of the new hospital, composed of the richest and therefore – there being no Imperial scholar-administrators or clan gentry – the most influential Chinese in Hong Kong, almost immediately became the focus of Chinese power in the colony, intimately linked with the kaifongs and the merchant guilds. Leung On, the Compradore of Gibb Livingston, was the Chairman of the organizing committee, and was joined by such influential figures as the compradores of the P. & O., the Hongkong Bank, Gilmans, and the Chartered Mercantile Bank. These, acting together in the Tung Wah Committee as a recognized body, were able to exert pressure on the government, which, politely, they lost no time in doing.

The committee of the Tung Wah was a conservative group, with a keen attachment to status, many members having purchased Ch'ing Imperial ranks and honours, by that time freely on sale. Among them however were representatives of the new generation, including Ng Choy and the Revd. Ho Fuk Tong, although the hospital's Board of Directors was composed only of merchants, representatives of the guilds. Of these the most influential was that of the compradores. Playing a part not dissimilar to that of the Hong merchants in Canton, Chinese compradores were an essential component of any foreign business. Chinese language and customs, together with the complex system of influence and obligations that characterized Chinese society, made it almost impossible for a foreigner to transact business without an intermediary. Originally a humble major-domo or house-steward figure, the compradore had evolved into an official at once the servant and the partner of the foreign businessman, of considerable importance, whose services were eagerly competed for.

Chinese nationalist historians have often displayed their distaste for compradores, a class considered as traitors, running dogs of the foreigners. As a matter of course compradores had to possess a reasonable command of English, and they became well-versed in Western business methods. Allying to these Chinese sophistication and enterprise, some compradores based in Hong Kong and the treaty ports became powerful instruments of economic development and contributed greatly to what economic progress China enjoyed in the nineteenth century.[44] Compradore shareholdings in early Chinese industrial developments were significant, sometimes critically so. One young compradore, Cheng Kuan-ying, had a significant influence on Chinese political thought. While employed by the Dents, Cheng published a book which, under various titles and in different editions, was in print for over thirty years, and was apparently avidly studied by the young Mao Tse-tung. Cheng appreciated that Western strength lay not in military technology, but in commerce, industry and social structure: 'The reason why China is poor and weak whereas the West is rich and strong lies in their different social customs.' It was not the soldiers' muskets, but their firing discipline, that enabled them methodically to mow down the bannermen at Ningpo.

With the thoughts of such men as Cheng and Ho leavening their attachment to tradition, the committee of the Tung Wah Hospital developed into something approaching an alternative, if limited, Chinese administration. And the colonial authorities, for the first time, had a reliable means of canvassing collective Chinese opinion.

9

SOME DISTASTEFUL TOPICS

The evils of sewage flushing

'Affie's' visit in 1869 might be taken as signalling the start of Hong Kong's period of colonial respectability. The eccentricities of Bowring, who fancied himself as a figure of worldwide significance, had been submerged by the more domestic concerns of his successors, the affable Robinson and brisk MacDonnell. Nor was Sir Arthur Kennedy, who succeeded MacDonnell, faced with any international complications. Ch'ing rule had been restored in China after the Taiping rebellion had been repressed in an exceedingly bloody fashion, it being not uncommon for Imperial troops, having gained the upper hand, to slaughter every Taiping, man, woman and child. Such methods were applied with equal vigour in suppressing the later troubles that emerged in the 1860s – Muslim revolts in Sinkiang and Szechuan, and the persistent Nian rebellion in Shantung. In the course of ten years' campaigning the nucleus of at least one effective and disciplined Chinese army had been formed, and an outstanding leader, Li Hung-chang (Li Hongzhang) had emerged. For the next forty years Li functioned as the leading figure in the 'self-strengthening' policy, and was an indispensable representative of China to the rest of the world. At that time it seemed possible that with such men as Li and Prince Kong at her head, a united China, willing to accept Western support, might well find its place among the powers without further troubles.

MacDonnell had been the type of tough and forthright Governor Hong Kong appreciated, and both Europeans and Chinese regretted his departure, after seven years, on 11 April 1872. With his wide experience of colonial administration he had recognized that circumstances in Hong Kong were 'so entirely exceptional' that Colonial Office precedents were useless. The staff at the Colonial Office, more interested in Oxford than the Far East (at that date no senior member had penetrated further east than the Mediterranean), remained unconvinced.

Sir Arthur Kennedy, who arrived a week after MacDonnell left, was, at the age of sixty-three, near the end of his colonial career, and anxious for a peaceful existence. He was readily persuaded to second the business community's complaints, and was popular enough to be allowed such eccentricities as inviting Chinese on special occasions to Government House and increasing the number of Chinese in the police force, using the Sikhs who had so provoked Consul Keenan as prison guards.

The population of Hong Kong seemed to have stabilized at a little over 120,000:

Year	Non Chinese	Chinese	Total
1862	3,034	120,477	123,511
1865	4,007	121,497	125,504

After 1867 the proportion of foreigners increased somewhat:

1869	7,699	114,280	121,979

but thereafter declined:

1895	10,828	237,670	248,498

After which the European total remained in the region of twenty thousand while the Chinese population continued to increase.

It was this great disproportion between the races that gave rise to the most awkward problems. Chinese customs and culture were too strongly marked and deeply ingrained to adapt easily to those of the British. Infanticide and piracy evoked unanimous disapproval and were indeed gradually suppressed, but footbinding, gambling, opium smoking, child marriage and concubinage were not so easily dealt with. Prostitution, although it might perhaps exist (there were probably 250,000 women in London alone who earned their living at the trade), must certainly not be officially recognized. Even the punishments apparently accepted by the Chinese community were disapproved of by an increasingly sensitive electorate in Britain: branding (which, it was often explained, was in fact tattooing with Indian ink, with a broad arrow on the ear, and said to be quite painless) was un-English; flogging might be reasonable enough (it was only abolished in the British army in 1880, and was still in use in prisons until after the First World War), but had to be kept within bounds.

All these issues gave rise to the gravest concern in the Colonial Office, perpetually nervous lest they should be harried by a morally outraged electorate, but the Hong Kong administration saw things in another perspective. Being at the sharp end, as it were, they were all too conscious of the near-impossibility of changing Chinese habits, and not entirely convinced of the desirability of doing so. Skills in procrastination were developed which allowed some practices, such as that of *mui-tsai* (indentured girls), which shaded off into child slavery and concubinage, to persist until the 1930s in the face of shocked British opinion.

Chinese medical practice had been tolerated, and institutionalized under Tung Wah direction, but all Westerners were united in deploring Chinese ideas of sanitation. Personally clean and fastidious as they were, it seemed that the Chinese had no concept of public hygiene. They could crowd together in the most insanitary conditions, almost as a matter of course keeping a family of pigs under the bed (172 were found in a single tenement block), and disposing of their sewage in buckets to refuse collectors whose business it was to transport the mess to Cantonese farms for use as manure. Anything that could not command a price was consigned to stormwater drains, which therefore became public sewers. Cattle were rarer members of households than pigs, but an investigation in 1875 found calves reared in houses so small that when grown they had to be butchered on the spot. These conditions were not the result of any proclivities of the unhappy residents, but due to their exploitation by landlords, usually Chinese themselves, who crammed hundreds of families into minuscule tenements and charged extortionately high rents. As long as these nuisances were confined to Chinese areas the foreigners were prepared to tolerate them – especially if they happened to be landowners anxious to benefit by building high-density housing – but as they began to encroach on the expatriates' own houses patience evaporated. Strict segregation between European and Chinese types of housing was enforced, but pressure on space forced these into contiguity. The energetic newly appointed Colonial Surgeon Dr Phineas Ayres made an inspection in 1874 of the Chinese districts, where he found fearful conditions: 'Many and many a time have I come out of the houses to vomit in the street', and forecast some 'fearful epidemic if matters were not improved'.[1]

A destructive typhoon later that year, the worst that Hong Kong had experienced, exacerbated the already vile conditions. Eitel, who was there at the time, described it: 'the town looked as if it had undergone a terrific bombardment. Rows of houses were unroofed, hundreds of European and Chinese dwellings were in ruins, large trees were torn out by their roots . . . in every direction dead bodies were seen floating about or scattered among the ruins . . . thirty-five foreign vessels, trusting in their anchors, were wrecked or badly injured'.[2]

There were, as ever in Hong Kong, economic considerations. Believing that paper was cheaper than concrete, and might be as effective a building material, the administration issued a series of admirable sanitary regulations, but did little to improve sewerage systems. Dr Ayres formed an effective partnership with J.M. Price, appointed as Surveyor-General at the same time, in attempting to provide an effective sewerage system. For some time they were frustrated by foot-dragging at the Colonial Office, which put an effective stop not only to new projects but even to essential repairs. The hospital, badly damaged in the storm, took three years to replace, and the proposals of Ayres and Price to provide a comprehensive sewerage scheme were constantly stalled, criticized, and reduced in scope. These delaying tactics worked effectively in that 1877 saw the appointment of a Governor who set his face steadfastly against such modern fads as water closets, and from whom little progress on sanitary matters might be expected.

It might have been possible to find a man more unsuited to be a colonial Governor than John Pope Hennessy, but it would not have been easy. A diminutive and arrogant Irishman, Hennessy had great charm, and an innate sympathy for what he believed to be the underdog, but an almost complete lack of common sense, method, reliability, tact, or management skills. His was a purely political appointment, awarded by a Tory government to a former Tory M.P. as a consolation prize. Hennessy had been not just a Tory M.P., but that rarest of creatures, a Tory Irish nationalist, and a Catholic to boot. Something had to be done for him since, deprived of Parliamentary immunity after a defeat in only his second election, Hennessy found himself deep in debt and saddled with a pair of illegitimate children. He was saved by the Tory victory in 1866, when Disraeli, an admirer of Hennessy's undoubted panache, promised to find him a 'lucrative but quiet governorship'.[3]

Labuan, the smallest and least desirable of colonies, an island off the coast of Borneo with a white population of less than a hundred, was chosen as a suitable place, and Hennessy, muttering furiously at what he regarded as an insult, packed off there in 1867. In the succeeding years, as Governor of Labuan, the Gold Coast, and the Windward Islands, he blazed a trail through colonies, leaving unhappy civil servants in Whitehall and disgruntled colonists behind. The permanent officials were sometimes close to despair, as their comments in the memoranda reveal: 'backbiting'; 'waspish, petty and spiteful'; 'So many instances of Mr Hennessy's intrigues'; 'Mr Hennessy has grossly mismanaged every Government he has been entrusted with'.[4]

In view of such decidedly unfavourable opinions, it seems incredible that in 1877 the Colonial Office should have promoted Pope Hennessy to the important governorship of Hong Kong. Again, this was a party political gesture, and would never have come about if Disraeli had not returned to power in 1874, with titbits once more available for distribution among the party followers. The permanent staff in the Colonial Office were understandably nervous: 'I hope this restless spirit may quiet down,' one among them noted. The Colonial Secretary, Lord Kimberley, eventually saw the error of his ways, and recorded: 'I was unfortunate in removing Sir Arthur Kennedy to Hong Kong ... I was still more unfortunate in appointing Pope Hennessy ... A man of quick intelligence and considerable abilities, he is vain, unscrupulous, wanting in sound judgement and common sense, and prone to quarrel with his subordinates.'[5] On the other hand Sir Robert Hart, no poor judge of his fellows, found Hennessy 'essentially a fair man, and is also pro-Chinese and pro-Customs' – identical qualities, in Sir Robert's mind.

Sir John was certainly not lacking in imagination, flair, and genuine humanity, but these gifts were almost completely stultified by a continued failure to sustain reasonable relations with his colleagues. These relations deteriorated almost to the extent of making effective communication impossible, and were not much helped by Hennessy's policy of always consulting Chinese interests and, as disgruntled officials saw it, falling in with Chinese predilections. He claimed: 'I have often taken counsel with my Chinese friends as to what would be the best course to adopt for this colony.' Although admirable, this practice was not welcomed by the foreign community. Another of the new Governor's eccentricities was a rooted objection to what he termed 'The evils of house sewage flushing', and a preference for earth closets or simple buckets. In an angry memorandum to the Secretary of State, who must have been taken aback at its contents, Hennessy reported that the underhand Price had 'made an effort . . . to get the Government to sanction water-closets in the new hospital', that '182 water closets have unfortunately been constructed from time to time in Hong Kong', and asked for permission to insist that these pernicious devices should be replaced by earth privies. Both Price and Ayres protested, but the objections of Colonial Surgeon and Surveyor General were in vain. Ayres' 'annual philippica', as Eitel termed them, were not only ignored, but suppressed by the Governor, who actually went so far as to cancel some of the health ordinances and instruct Eitel, as Inspector of Schools, to draw up a new list, which he wisely seems not to have attempted. Price was driven to write to the Colonial Office on 15 August 1881 protesting against 'officially sanctioned . . . fever dens . . . abominable human rabbit warrens', and the 'official support of foul sewers' which had forced him 'to abandon further attempts in despair'.[6]

But help was at hand, for early in 1881 the Deputy Surgeon-General, Dr McKinnon, worried that the increasing insanitariness might affect the health of the troops, protested to the War Office, who sent a medical inspector to report. A stiff letter was sent to the Governor from Lord Kimberley, pointing out 'that in opposing the measures, which had been thought necessary by the sanitary officers of the colony, and were approved by your predecessor, you have incurred grave responsibility', and announcing the appointment of 'an officer of professional experience to decide, investigate, and report upon the actual state of affairs'.[7] The officer appointed was Osbert Chadwick, son of the famous Sir Edwin Chadwick, former colleague and collaborator of both Bentham and Bowring, who had from the early 1830s been the moving force behind the thorough programme of municipal reform carried out by successive Whig governments.

Chadwick could speak with authority, but it was perhaps just as well that his report was only published after Hennessy had left. It demolished any idea of earth closets, although admitting that 'slopping out' must continue until a proper system of water-borne sewerage could be installed, and pointing out that 'in advocating the system of *water-carriage* I do *not* advocate the use of the ordinary *water-closet* (mahogany seat and brass handle)'. But he used strong words to condemn the existing system:

> . . . the dwellings of the Chinese working classes are inconvenient, filthy and unwholesome. Accumulations of filth occur in and around them . . . Above all the water supply is miserable. It is unjust to condemn them as a hopelessly filthy race till they have been provided with reasonable means for cleanliness. I conceive that it is the duty of the Government to see that these means are provided and applied.[8]

Almost as dear to Victorian hearts as sanitation was corporal punishment, which was another of Governor Pope Hennessy's hobby horses. The early settlement was placed under an almost military discipline as far as the Chinese were concerned, conducted by the redoubtable Colonel Caine. The Europeans were left pretty much to themselves until a colonial court was established in 1844 under Chief Justice Hulme. Caine had very considerable powers; he could order up to three months' imprisonment, fines to a maximum of $400, or up to a hundred lashes. Since few Chinese had much in the way of ready money, and prison accommodation was limited, corporal punishment was freely administered. After Dr Bowring's intervention in 1846 public floggings were suspended, but they were resumed after a brief interval, much to the satisfaction of the European community, convinced that only rigid discipline and sharp punishments protected them from the evilly-disposed Chinese. The sight of an Englishman being lashed in public was naturally more contentious, and after 1866 Europeans were flogged in decent privacy.

Sir Richard MacDonnell shared the colonists' predilection for corporal punishment, and substituted for the rattan cane previously used, and judged too mild a punishment, the cat-of-nine-tails at that time still standard in the British services. He also introduced an ingenious system of offering convicted criminals the option of being deported, after branding (or tattooing). If they accepted their sentence was remitted, but if thereafter they should return to the colony and be identified by the brand, they would be liable to serve their original sentence, with a flogging in addition. Entirely illegal though it was under British law, this practice won the approval of the European community in Hong Kong, and seemed to be justified by the results, in that both the crime rate and the number of those sentenced to prison were very nearly halved. The Colonial Office was worried about MacDonnell's methods but, after an interval, allowed themselves to be convinced.

Only one case caused some controversy. In 1866 Colonel William Henry Sykes, Liberal M.P. for Aberdeen, an ancient campaigner and notorious House of Commons bore, complained that Mo-Wong, a man who had claimed political asylum in the colony, had been handed back to the Imperial authorities in Canton, who had him executed by the death of a thousand cuts, and concluded the performance by eating his heart. William Mercer, that invaluable source of continuity, acting as Governor in the interim between Robinson and MacDonnell, was able to demolish Sykes's story point by point, concluding that he had 'rarely met with a statement containing so many errors in so brief a space'.[9]

Pope Hennessy arrived in the colony in 1877, ready to make an issue of corporal punishment, and immediately ordered an investigation. It appeared that floggings were inflicted for the most trifling misdemeanours – 'committing a nuisance . . . general idleness . . . singing in solitary confinement . . . plucking fruit' – as well as for such grave matters as 'unnatural offences'. Some of the victims were very severely punished: one Lee-a-Yee twice received ninety lashes on convictions, and subsequently when in prison one flogging of thirty-six lashes and two of twelve, making 240 in all over a period of four years. Public floggings in particular horrified Pope Hennessy: 'The ostentatious marching of the prisoners half naked through the crowded streets, and the public exhibition of an English turnkey flogging with a vigorous arm the speedily bleeding body of a Chinese.' He sounded rather disappointed on discovering that floggings in public were rarer than he had believed: 'I was not at all prepared to find out of these floggings so small a percentage (55 of about 1,150) had been administered in public. Indeed I was under the impression that a public flogging was a very frequent exhibition,'[10] and had little difficulty in convincing the officials that the practice of public flogging could be safely terminated, as it was in 1880, even for Chinese.

The British in Hong Kong were less enthusiastic, having been loyal attenders at both public floggings and public executions, but no one was so radical as to suggest that corporal punishment should be abolished altogether. How it should be administered was a matter of great interest, and the Governor ordered an inquiry into the best methods of flogging, to be carried out jointly by Doctors O'Brien and Wells. Wells had served as a surgeon in the Royal Navy for thirty-three years, which had 'afforded him opportunities of judging the effects of flogging with the cat on the back and the breech'. In spite of the 'many ill consequences likely to follow severe wounds, such as are caused by the cat', the doctors found it preferable to the rattan, which they described as 'too heavy a weapon, and its effects are very likely to go deep into the cellular and muscular tissues, probably producing loss of substance by sloughing and thus for a long time delaying the healing of the wounds'. (Wells had never seen more than forty-eight lashes inflicted at any one time while in the Navy, which indicates something of the severity of Lee-a-Yee's treatment.) Much better to rely on the well-tried cat, with 'care being taken by means of a thick canvas collar that the neck is not injured and that the loins be protected in a similar way'. For those between thirteen and eighteen years of age 'flogging on the breech with the six tails of the cat' was recommended to be enough, and that the '"Birch" be used for any offenders of more tender years'.[11]

Hennessy's genuine sympathy for the underdog, which led him to consult Chinese interests, took him in similar directions to those pursued by Bowring on utilitarian grounds. Labouchere had written twenty years earlier in response to Bowring's suggestions: 'If you should hereafter be able to select from the Chinese inhabitants persons deserving of confidence, whom you may think fit to hold this [the position of magistrate] or any other administrative office, I should be willing to assent to such appointments.' He went on to suggest that 'The experiment should be very cautiously made.'[12] Since English was the only language of debate and legislation, and British nationality was a requisite for any Crown post, it would have been impossible to find any qualified candidates at that time.

Only when the second generation of Hong Kong Chinese had emerged could an appointment be made, and even then the field was extremely limited, there being in 1880 only one professional British-educated Chinese in the colony. This was Ng Choy, born a British subject in Singapore, and the first Chinese to be called to the British Bar three years previously. Hennessy accordingly appointed Ng a temporary stipendiary magistrate and a member of the Legislative Council, again on a temporary basis. The appointment was reluctantly sanctioned by Whitehall, even though the Colonial Secretary at the time, Sir Michael Hicks Beach, had a reputation as a liberally-minded Conservative. It is probable that London's lack of enthusiasm was due more to the deep distrust of Hennessy, and the assumption that anything advanced by him was likely to be wrong, than to a reluctance to admit Chinese. Certainly Beach's successor, the Liberal Lord Kimberley, when refusing to make Ng Choy's appointment permanent, minuted: 'Tell Hennessy's successor that it is desirable to have a Chinese on the Legislative Council' – but not, presumably, one of Hennessy's choice. As it turned out, Ng Choy resigned from the Council in April 1883, following financial difficulties, and joined the Ch'ing service, rising to become an adviser to Li Hung-chang and the first Chinese Ambassador to the United States.[13]

The Commissioners do not appear to appreciate that syphilis is only communicable by contact

For the British soldiers and sailors sent to Hong Kong the chief compensations for a hot, tedious and sticky life were cheap booze and sex. Statistics seem to indicate that the British soldier was either considerably more demanding or greatly more careless than his Continental comrades in pursuit of the latter, since as many as a quarter of them could be down with the 'Havana 'flu' at any one time.

Per 1000 unfit for duty with venereal disease[14]

Year	German	French	Austrian	British Home	British India
1876	28.8	57.0	65.8	146.5	203.5
1878	36.0	59.7	75.4	175.5	291.6
1880	34.9	65.8	75.7	245.9	249.0

Disease had always been by far the biggest killer of troops in foreign parts, and sexually transmitted disease was one against which effective preventative measures could be taken. In the early days of Hong Kong the incidence of disease was quite as high as in India. During 1853 one-third of the crew of H.M.S. *Winchester* got themselves infected. In 1856 the Colonial Surgeon reported that 'The police, both European and native, labour under the disease in the most frightful form'; the following year he noted that 'among the police and sailors of Hong Kong, some of the worst forms of the venereal disease are to be seen ... I have had under my care female prostitutes (picked up by the police in the streets, and evidently turned out by the brothel-keepers for the purpose) suffering from the disease in the most shocking form I ever beheld. Death at last put an end to their sufferings.' Even Colonel Caine, with his long experience of the East, spoke of 'ravages too fearful to detail'.[15]

Bowring, that unregenerate utilitarian, had tackled the problem in classic Benthamite fashion by registering those brothels used by servicemen and providing both for regular medical inspection and compulsory treatment. Compulsion was also used on some of the clients, since merchant seamen could be subjected to examination and treatment at the request of their captains. Reluctantly, the home government admitted the logic of Bowring's actions, but Labouchere, like all good liberals sensitive to any connotations of servitude, pointed out that:

> The Colonial Government has not, I think, attached sufficient weight to the very grave fact, that in a British Colony large numbers of women should be held in practical slavery for the purposes of prostitution . . . and allowed . . . to perish miserably of disease . . . for the gain of those to whom they suppose themselves to belong. A class of persons, who by no choice of their own are subjected to such treatment, have an urgent claim on the active protection of Government.[16]

In 1867 the British government, as part of the reforms both in the armed services and in public health, passed a Contagious Disease Act, providing for the compulsory medical inspection of prostitutes in garrison towns and designated seaports. Hong Kong adopted a variation of the Act by licensing all approved brothels but only continuing the inspection of establishments intended for the use of foreigners, and not those frequented by the Chinese. The idea of a Chinese woman being forced to undergo intimate medical examination and possibly removal for treatment in a Western institution was so repellent to Chinese sentiment that enforcement would hardly have been possible. Red light areas were formally established for both Chinese and foreigners. Since the police were allotted the task of searching out unregistered, or 'sly', brothels, it is hardly surprising that the rate of venereal disease among the force was extraordinarily high – 16.6 per cent of all police sickness in 1869 was caused by syphilis, compared with just under 7 per cent for servicemen.

Apart from that predictable discrepancy, Hong Kong's methods of control were everything that a Victorian social engineer could have wished. Rates of infection were halved, and the Colonial Surgeon reported: 'So completely satisfied am I of the incalculable benefit that has resulted to the Colony . . . that I shall be glad to see the provisions extended to both the so-called purely Chinese houses and to that still more fertile source of infection, the boat population. Both Military and Naval Officers concur with me in estimating very highly the advantages of the Ordinance as affecting the health of their men.'[17] The US Fleet Surgeon, Dr Maccoun, was agreeably surprised at the way in which the men of the U.S.S. *Delaware* had remained free from infection after their visits to Hong Kong; things were much worse in Japan, and he congratulated the Colonial Surgeon on 'the success with which . . . his labours in the cause of humanity . . . have been crowned'.

These arguments held no appeal for Governor Pope Hennessy. His personal history – a Roman Catholic west of Ireland childhood, a pensioned mistress, two illegitimate children and a beautiful young Creole wife – led to a peculiar sensitivity on sexual matters (he described a catalogue of the National Museum of Naples as 'obscene'). He therefore initiated a scathing attack on the system of registration, which turned out to be a typical Hennessy muddle.[18] A Commission of Inquiry of only three members was appointed, and they were told what answers were expected from them. Lord Carnarvon, Colonial Secretary at the time the Commission's findings came through, raised his eyebrows: 'I presume that you had a good reason for appointing this Commission, since I need scarcely point out that it is a somewhat unusual course to institute a Commission of private persons to inquire into the administration of an important Department of Government . . . you have adopted an unusual course in anticipating the conclusions of the Commission.'[19]

Not only did the Commission, when it began its operations in November 1877, fail to take evidence from any Europeans, apart from the officials, who had their own cases to make, but one member – William Keswick of Jardine's – disagreed with most of the conclusions of the other two, a disagreement the Governor attempted to gloss over. The inquiry did however result in a thorough report from the Naval Inspector of Certified (venereal) Hospitals, one Dr W.H. Sloggett. His report typifies the difficulty even experienced home-based officials found in comprehending the peculiar institutions of Hong Kong. Although Sloggett recommended the withdrawal of licensing, which he agreed was equivalent to granting formal permission to commit in Hong Kong what in England was an offence, he wanted all brothels, whether for Chinese or not, registered and controlled. He could not understand why Chinese brothels were exempt from control, and queried 'the extreme tenderness shown by the Commissioners for the feelings, and prejudices of the Chinese brothel-keepers and prostitutes so long as the latter are supposed to reserve themselves for the use of Chinamen only'. He also found it strange that 'very unnecessary delicacy and forbearance' had been shown to '"protected" prostitutes who use their premises as brothels for unregistered prostitutes'.

Sloggett dismissed the suggestion made by the Commission that there was no evidence for the effect of the laws on limiting venereal disease as 'contrary to all opinions of all medical authorities, civil, naval, and military'. His contempt for the Commission was made clear in one devastating comment: 'There is one fact in the history and pathology of syphilis which the Commissioners do not appear to appreciate, viz., that it is only communicable by contact, and that so long as an infected woman is prevented from having contact with other persons, she cannot communicate the disease.'[20]

But attitudes in Britain were changing, and rigidly utilitarian standards of legislation were being subjected to moral scrutiny on the grounds that the greatest good of the greatest number did not justify all intrusions on personal liberty, and that, as Sloggett suggested, the public recognition of 'vice' (which had only a single meaning) was immoral. In particular the right of magistrates and senior police officers under the Contagious Diseases Act to enforce medical examination was attacked, the opposition being led by the remarkable Josephine Butler. The British public were quickly impressed by both arguments, especially when an entirely innocent young woman (who proved to be a virgin) was forcibly examined as a suspected prostitute. In 1883 the Acts were suspended, to be repealed three years later.

It was inevitable that colonial legislatures should take similar action, however different they might consider their circumstances to be. Hong Kong procrastinated for as long as possible, forwarding to London appeals to the Governor from respectable brothel-keepers, and the girls themselves, that the law might be retained. This delayed action for a couple of years, but eventually the repeal had to be forced through a dissenting Legislative Council by the use of the official majority.

The result of the repeal of the Contagious Diseases Act on servicemen overseas was exactly what might have been expected; rates of

infection shot up to unprecedented heights, as the figures for British
soldiers in India demonstrate.

Year	State of law (all forms) Contagious Diseases Acts in Force	Admissions per 1000
1880	Acts in Force	249
1881		259.6
1882		265.5
1883		271.3
1884	Partial Suspension	293.5
1885		342.6
1886		385.8
1887		361.4
1888	Total Suspension	372.2
1889		481.5
1890		503.6

At which time over half the army in India was infected.

Hong Kong avoided the worst results by the simple method of behav-
ing as though the legislation was still in force: establishments remained
classified as either European or Chinese, the girls in the former continuing to present themselves for examination, the latter not. Even this
was scotched by the London authorities, and in 1890 the Legislative
Council, protesting bitterly, was obliged to dismantle the whole apparatus of control. This time there was no escaping the consequences:
the Chinese members (by then two) of the Legislative Council complained of the proliferation of 'sly' brothels; the China Association
produced statistics to show the 'persistent improvement' which followed the first regulations imposed by Bowring, compared to the
'immediate revulsion and deterioration which ensued upon their
recision'. The figures were impressive enough; both the ratio of admissions and the number of sick doubled, to the point that in the first
four months of 1897 the number of admissions per thousand of the
Hong Kong garrison reached 499.29, and of these 213.29 were for
syphilis. Within three years half of the Hong Kong garrison was being
treated for venereal disease.

Something clearly had to be done, and an ingenious solution was
found. Public opinion in England would not allow brothels to be permitted; but there was no objection to brothels *not* being permitted.

The Colonial Office and the Hong Kong administration therefore agreed that magistrates should be empowered to close down any brothel to which the police drew their attention; applause from the moralists. The police then did not draw to the magistrates' attention any brothel that continued to allow the girls to be examined. All were content, and this simple system continued to flourish for many years.

Young Rudyard Kipling was responsible for some of the British public's concern when he published his account of a visit to a Hong Kong brothel in 1889. He did not much enjoy it; Corinthian Kate frightened him, and he found the girls, 'who had been to Leadville, Denver, and the wilds of the Wider West, who had acted in minor companies and who . . . generally misconducted themselves in a hundred weary ways' disquieting.[21]

I have had my eyes on those junks for a quarter of a century

Absorbing as were the topics of sewerage, drugs, brothels and flogging, these were not the only sources of contention between the European population of Hong Kong and the government departments in Whitehall. With Hong Kong now clearly a dependency within the ambit of the Colonial Office, other ministries whose interests were sometimes opposed to those of the Colonial Office developed antagonistic positions. Of these the most prominent was the Foreign Office; both then and for many years after the rivalry between those two departments of state was notorious. The Foreign Secretary was one of the three great ministries, held by the most senior of politicians, while the position of Secretary of State for the Colonies, although officially ranking close behind, was regarded as something of a backwater, a fitting post for meritorious second-rankers or bright young men on their way up. The staff reflected these distinctions; elegant ambassadorial figures at the Foreign Office, groomed to embellish the chanceries of Paris and Vienna, looked down on members of the Colonial Office, whom they regarded as doubtless worthy and capable of dealing with horny-handed colonists, but essentially unsophisticated; these attitudes were countered in the Colonial Office by passive resistance and lack of co-operation.

The Board of Trade was even less decorative, but shared with the other departments a distrust of anyone actually in trade; and all civil servants, whatever their departments, were deeply suspicious of the British businessmen on the China Coast. Sir Louis Mallet, Permanent Under-Secretary at the Board of Trade, gave his views in 1863:

> The paramount difficulty and danger to be avoided in our dealings with China, is all unnecessary contact between British traders and Natives. The class of Britons who press into this new and untrodden field of enterprise is mainly composed of reckless and unscrupulous adventurers who seek nothing but enormous profits on particular transactions and care little for the permanent interests of commerce – still less for the principles of truth and justice. These men always cloak their injustices under the guise of patriotism and civilization.[22]

No merchant in Hong Kong would of course, then as now, recognize himself in such a description, but the colony was a particularly fruitful ground for such misunderstandings to develop. Colonists, Governor and Colonial Office were all concerned with the well-being of the colony, although they often had very different ideas as to how this should be achieved: relations with China were dealt with only through the Foreign Office, operating through the Minister in Peking and the Consuls who reported to him; and contacts between the colony and Chinese had therefore to be referred to the Foreign Office through the machinery of Whitehall. So too must any matters be processed which involved other departments, such as the Board of Trade and the Treasury. Much frustration was thereby created; and even in purely colonial matters the Governor's independence of action was becoming more restricted.

In 1869 the Suez Canal was opened, and a submarine telegraph link between Britain and Hong Kong was established in the following year. In theory this should have enabled London to exercise almost day-to-day control, but the practice remained to leave things to the man on the spot, even when his actions, as those of Hennessy, proved worrisome. Nevertheless, compared with the palmy days of the forties and fifties, when the Governor of Hong Kong was himself Minister, Superintendent and Plenipotentiary, and immediately available to be got at by the merchants, the new state of affairs proved a source of irritation to the colonists. Their frustration was aggravated by the fact that the Foreign Office considered maintenance of good relations with

China to be of greater importance than the domestic concerns of Hong Kong, or even, for much of the time, the united pressure of the China trade lobby (a reluctance to appreciate that this is still so, and that the well-being of Hong Kong is an object of real, but only secondary, importance to any British government and of very little interest at all to the mass of the electorate, explains much of the discontent and frustration still experienced in Hong Kong).

A particular acerbity often entered into the relations between the Governor of Hong Kong and the Consul-General in Canton. Governors, unduly influenced by businessmen, attempted clumsy interventions and 'failed to see the difference between governing and negotiating; their legalism was not suited to China', complained Sir Brooke Robertson, Consul-General in Canton.[23] There were also times when Governor and Colonial Office clashed, as MacDonnell and Whitehall did over the gaming house licensing; and when Governor and colonists failed to agree, as perennially on the question of taxation, and on almost all questions in the peculiar circumstances of Pope Hennessy's administration. But on what came to be known as the Chinese Customs Blockade, which engaged the attention of the colonists for twenty years, businessmen, Governor and Colonial Office developed a united front against the Foreign Office and its officials.

This controversy had begun with the establishment in Bowring's time of the Shanghai Inspectorate of Customs, which evolved into the Maritime Customs Service. From the beginning this was opposed by all the foreign traders, who were not at all anxious to see an incorruptible and efficient revenue collection service, forwarding its receipts intact to Peking. As Jardine Matheson commented in 1861: 'the country is in a state of desolation ... duties now collected at the foreign custom house are being applied to Imperial and not provincial wants'.[24] In spite of this, and of opposition from the more conservative Imperial officials, the new service, under the energetic leadership of the Inspector-General Sir Robert Hart from 1861 until 1906 (officially from 1863 to 1908), became the most important institution in the Chinese economy. From the beginning Hart made it clear in his instructions to the staff of the Customs Service that they were, as he was, part of the Chinese government's civil service: 'In the first place, it is to be distinctly and constantly kept in mind, that the Inspectorate of Customs is a Chinese and not a Foreign Service.' However badly other foreigners might behave, and in language that revealed the near-

contempt he felt for many of his compatriots, Hart left his own men
in no doubt as to what was expected of them:

> Whatever other Foreigners resident in this country may deem
> themselves entitled to do, whether from their position, or fancied
> superiority to the Chinese, or in the way of showing their superior
> enlightenment by riding rough-shod over prejudices . . . it is to
> be expected from those who take the pay, and who are the servants
> of the Chinese Government, that they, at least, will so act as to
> neither offend susceptibilities, nor excite jealousies, suspicion, or
> dislike. In dealings with native officials, and in intercourse with the
> people [they should remember] that they are the brother officers of
> the one, and that they have, to some extent, accepted certain
> obligations and responsibilities by becoming, in a sense, the
> countrymen of the others.[25]

Hart realized that a service so motivated could hardly expect much
sympathy from the foreign merchants. 'Most of the merchants are said
to entertain a deep-rooted dislike for the Inspectorate; many of them
are at no pains to conceal that dislike; and all of them equally will
cry out whenever regulations are enforced to their prejudice.' He
concluded by stressing that all staff, from the Inspector-General
down, were paid servants of the Imperial government of China: 'The
Inspector-General is responsible to the Chinese Government . . .
and he is liable to be dismissed from his post at a moment's notice,
in the event of his services . . . being deemed unsatisfactory by the
Government.'

The Inspector-General's expectations of opposition from the foreign
merchants were more than fulfilled, especially from those taipans in
Hong Kong who had been accustomed for so long to arranging their
own law. Jardine Matheson appealed to their friends in London: 'The
entire foreign custom house system has become such an obstruction
to business . . . the sooner foreigners cease to uphold it the better and
it is much to be desired that influential persons at home connected
with the trade would make a move in this direction.' Their newspaper,
the *Shanghae Recorder*, advocated that all duties and restrictions be
removed, Imperial officers ignored, and trade be conducted by personal
arrangements made on the spot and backed, as in former days, by
private armed vessels. The Hong Kong Chamber of Commerce early
took the lead in protesting against the monstrous idea of actually

imposing the law of the land. Their annoyance was aggravated by a strong, although not often publicly expressed, feeling that by helping the Chinese, and what was worse by doing so effectively, Hart's British staff were in some way betraying their own race.[26]

In their pursuit of the best interests of China the Customs Service had not only to cope with recalcitrant foreigners, often backed by the Hong Kong government, but also with the immemorial corruption and inefficiency of the rest of the Imperial administration. Hart's organization was concerned only with international trade; the coastal trade remained under the supervision of the traditional Imperial authorities who usually enforced their rule by armed sailing junks, 'pull-away gigs, snake boats and hak-kows', whose crews did not necessarily adhere to the same high standards as those of the steam revenue-cruisers, and smuggling therefore continued popular. Although opium was now legal, even the 5 per cent duty was considered worth evading, and a few dozen balls of the drug were easily concealed. Salt took up more room, but since duties on this Chinese state monopoly commodity were higher, smuggling it still presented profitable opportunities.

Canton remained a centre of this trade, legal and illegal, as it had done in former times, and under the jurisdiction of the same official, the Hoppo, who continued to administer it with a eye to the private profit of himself and his friends. In order to maximize his income the Hoppo maintained a chain of customs posts and, as he was entitled to, patrolled Chinese waters right up to the boundaries of the colony. Hart was well aware of the problems this might cause, and would have been happy if the Hoppo's duties could have been assumed either by the Chinese Viceroy or by his own service, but he was aware of the 'anomalous character' and 'angularities' of his position.[27]

At that time the colonial waters consisted only of those surrounding the island itself and the three square miles of the Kowloon peninsula; all the islands and bays of what became the New Territories, which afforded perfect cover for the illegally-minded, were then Chinese territory, and in places only half a mile distant from Hong Kong. Revenue patrols were therefore often conspicuous, and the steamships among them were, as men-of-war under international law, able to use Hong Kong Harbour's facilities themselves. Hart defined the situation for the benefit of his Commissioner at Canton, E.C. Bowra:

1. The collection of revenue from goods carried in Chinese ships in Chinese waters is a matter in which China is competent to legislate and take action without consulting any one.

2. The British government has declared that, so long as China does not take action in Hongkong and does respect what can fairly be styled British waters, the colonial authorities cannot interfere with the proceedings of the Canton officials.

3. Neither the governor at Hong Kong nor consul at Canton will be supported in any steps they may take, to suppress the opium stations, against the wish of the Chinese officials.

Bowra had previously been told by Hart, on 7 March 1871, that 'Mr Wade [who had succeeded Alcock as Minister at Peking] is with us, the Board of Trade is with us, the Foreign Office is with us, and we may safely infer that they [the Hong Kong authorities] cannot do much against us.'[28]

But they tried hard. Irregularities of greater or less importance in the controls exercised by the Chinese inevitably occurred, and were seized on by the Hong Kong merchants in their perennial struggle to avoid regulations of every sort. They believed Hong Kong to be a foreign port, a free port, and one at which all trade should be subject to the minimum of regulations. This individualistic interpretation was reflected in the statistics produced by the Harbour Master: all vessels coming to Hong Kong, even from Chinese ports only a few miles off, or from Macao, were adjudged 'foreign', which enabled the figures to be grossly inflated. By 1906, it was proudly proclaimed, Hong Kong was the largest port in the world: 22,453,007 tons of shipping had been entered and cleared, more than either London or New York (both about 20 million tons). But in fact the greater proportion of this was coasting trade, and that coming from genuinely foreign ports was only 8,812,827 tons, which puts the international position of Hong Kong in a clearer perspective.

An opportunity was handed to the Hong Kong traders in 1867 when the ten-year date for the revision of the Treaty of Tientsin approached. In language reminiscent of that which had so irritated Pottinger twenty-odd years before, they demanded Chinese 'compliance with both the spirit and the letter of the evaded and unfulfilled provisions', and denied 'the right claimed by employees of the Chinese maritime customs to adjudicate in cases of contravention of the revenue laws' – which was tantamount to denying the Chinese government jurisdiction within its own laws. Neither the Consuls, the British Minister at Peking, nor the Foreign Office were prepared to put up with this brand of arrogance, and the Colonial Office found itself uncomfortably caught in the crossfire.

In this instance the merchants prevailed, mustering sufficient support in Britain to persuade the Gladstone government to uphold their dubious case. Sir Rutherford Alcock, former chief of Harry Parkes, who succeeded Bruce as British Minister at Peking in 1865, had agreed terms for an update of the Tientsin Treaty with the Tsungli Yamen, allowing more ports to be opened and a modest increase in tariffs. These reasonable terms were vehemently opposed by the mercantile community, who continued to press for complete freedom of trade and residence. The revision, which had been amicably and painstakingly negotiated between the British and Chinese officials in Peking, should have marked a new stage in China's emergence into the comity of nations, but the business interest prevailed against it. Led from Hong Kong, the traders succeeded in convincing the British government not to ratify Alcock's arrangements. This was the more surprising in that the President of the Board of Trade at the time was the painfully upright radical John Bright; yet the Board's approval of non-ratification contained the devious suggestion that it 'should not be publicly attributed to mercantile opposition. Such a course could hardly fail to create an impression on the Chinese government that the merchants, whose attitude towards them had been so often of an unfriendly character, are strong enough to overrule the Government even in a case in which their own convictions are opposed to mercantile views' – which was, of course, exactly what had happened. If there was an occasion in the nineteenth century when the British government and British traders were united in exploiting their power to the detriment of China, it was this. Alcock was deeply disappointed, and complained bitterly about the conduct of his countrymen to the Tsungli Yamen, where Wen Hse-ang sympathized: 'I, too, am accused of being a renegade and only wearing Chinese clothes.'[29]

Disappointed too were the officials at the Foreign Office, who would much rather have backed Alcock. The government's surrender was announced in the strangest terms, 'with much regret', but they had 'determined to defer to the wishes expressed by the Commercial bodies who have so urgently appealed to them', in spite of their judgement that 'great immediate, and still greater prospective advantages' would have been obtained by ratification. Rarely can a weaker decision have been taken by a strong government, with a substantial majority; the only excuse was that the Gladstone Cabinet was, as usual, preoccupied with the much more important subject of Irish Land Tenure.

The recovery in trade after the crises of 1866–67 did not continue. Another slump began in 1873, and continued for some years, to be followed by an even more serious crisis in 1882–86, activated by the collapse of the great French bank Union Générale. The effects of the first caused an unpleasant shock in Hong Kong; company collapses, which included that of the old Canton firm Augustus Heard, proliferated; the Hongkong and Shanghai Bank, which had backed many of these enterprises, took heavy losses and had to pass their dividend; even Jardine's had some nervous moments. British exports to China fell, and remained long after below the level of the years 1869–72. Looking for a scapegoat, the Hong Kong merchants, as usual, blamed the Chinese authorities.

A Hong Kong commission of inquiry drawn from the merchants, the very people who had been complaining, predictably discovered that 'a most vexatious system of blockading is kept up . . . The confines of these waters are . . . infested with cruizers of every description'.[30] Wounded comments were made on the attitude of Sir Brooke Robertson, whose 'remarks seem peculiar as coming from a British officer, protecting British interests'. Diplomacy might be tried to remedy this sad state of affairs, but if that failed recourse should be made to gunboats operating against the Chinese customs vessels 'who now prey without let or hindrance on the trade of the Colony'. To bolster these arguments a petition was sent to the Governor purporting to come from some Chinese merchants, but which turned out to be an attempt by some of the English to disguise their own interest, written in 'almost unintelligible Chinese', and contrived by the firm of Caldwell and Brereton, the Caldwell in question being the untrustworthy son of Daniel, later deported from the colony.

At first Kennedy took these complaints with a pinch of salt, but increasing indignation spurred him to action. A public meeting on 14 September 1874 spoke of 'A flagrant and unparalleled breach of international usage . . . the impending annihilation of [Hong Kong's] trade'. Brooke Robertson did his best to expose the dubious arguments presented by the Chamber of Commerce in a long and carefully argued dispatch to the Foreign Office of 1 December 1874, which pointed out that smuggling remained at the root of the difficulties, a fact which the Hong Kongers were reluctant to admit. MacDonnell, ironic as usual, had described the establishment of the Chinese customs as 'a blow to the prosperity of the Colony, which unquestionably it was – that is, to the smuggling prosperity'. There was not the least evidence of any desire on the part of the Chinese to interfere with the legitimate trade, and far from this happening there had been a steady increase in the junk trade. Even in the last two years, when conditions generally had deteriorated, the junk-carried coastal tonnage had fallen only from 1,817,810 to 1,789,598, which was hardly annihilation. James Whittall, the senior partner of Jardine's, agreed; he had not heard a single grievance from a legitimate Chinese trader. The Chinese were simply collecting the dues to which they were entitled; there was no blockade of the port, and any diminution of trade had quite other causes. Robertson unequivocally backed the Viceroy at Canton and sympathized with his government's difficulties, which were great. 'They can not only obtain no assistance from Hong Kong, but are subject to complaints against the only plan they can devise to prevent smuggling ... At Hong Kong the Chamber of Commerce, and the merchants generally, with some exceptions, denounce the blockade system and call for its removal, but fail to point out any substitute for it. It is this unreasoning attitude that adds to the difficulty.'

In London Kennedy's pleas went to Lord Carnarvon and the officials at the Colonial Office, and Robertson's elegant rebuttals to Lord Derby at the Foreign Office: the Minister at Peking, now Sir Harry Parkes himself, with thirty-four years' experience of China, agreed with Robertson. The upshot was that on 22 March 1875, nearly a year after Kennedy's first approach, Lord Carnarvon replied. Although sympathetic in tone, the dispatch rejected the merchants' case: 'The right of the Chinese Government to search its national vessels on the high seas or within its own territorial waters cannot be disputed ... the exercise by the Chinese Government of the right of search complained of ... does not affect the freedom of the port, and affords no valid grounds for diplomatic remonstrance.' An ill-concealed reprimand was delivered to those who allowed 'a state of things which exposes the Colony to the imputation of giving protection and encouragement to a contraband trade', and they were warned that British assistance would only be given 'consistent with those principles of international law and justice which have ever been maintained by Her Majesty's Government'.

Lord Carnarvon's reply was not well received in the colony. International law did not figure too highly in the minds of the businessmen of Hong Kong: 'In some technical manner' a contention of Robertson's 'may possibly be true', the unofficial members of the Legislative Council admitted, and the Chamber of Commerce regretted, on 10 February 1876, that the British government had decided to adhere to the mere letter of the law: 'it is most unfortunate that the Government have thought fit to accord to the vessels in question the status of men-of-war, to which they are in no respect entitled, the only warfare they carry on being against the commerce of the colony'.

The whole round of communications began anew; Governor Kennedy, now thoroughly converted to the colonists' cause, attacked Consul Robertson: 'I am amazed at the unwarrantable claims and pretensions of the Canton authorities – claims and pretensions, too, which receive not only the acquiescence of Her Majesty's Consul at Canton, but his active support,' he wrote on 13 July 1876. The Chamber of Commerce discovered a new bugbear: a Mr Brown, of Canton (Thomas Brown, of the Maritime Customs Service), was actually seeking information on smugglers in the territory of the colony itself! 'Often . . . informers report that some junk . . . had opium concealed, and the *Peng Chai Hoi* [the Maritime Customs gunboat] follows and captures her. A search is made . . . and if any contraband goods are found, the junk is taken to Canton' (Police Magistrate's report, 3 May 1876). These proceedings, which sound like a classic piece of good intelligence work, were astonishingly characterized by the Hong Kong legal authorities as 'an organized system of espionage and secret detectivism carried on in this Colony in the interest of the Chinese Customs' (Acting Attorney General, 6 June 1876) and 'a species of terrorism practised by low officers in the service of the Chinese Government tending greatly to disturb peaceable Chinese residents in this Colony' (Chief Justice, 13 June 1876). It is hardly surprising that the exasperated Robertson wrote: 'I care very little for the opinion of the governor of Hong Kong or his subjects and know the position better than they do.'[31]

Some progress towards a solution was made in the Chefoo Convention of September 1876, which – among many other more pressing matters – appointed an independent commission to examine the question and warned the Hong Kong merchants that the Chinese would not alter their methods until 'the colony devised some scheme by which the Chinese government could collect the revenue fairly due to them'. When the commission eventually met, which was not until 1886, there having taken place another unconscionable bit of

foot-dragging on the part of the British government, some difficult
negotiation followed, mainly between Hart, representing the Chinese
government, and the Hong Kong authorities. At one point Hart, aggravated by the Hong Kong government 'funking the opium smuggling
interest', threatened resignation, but eventually it was agreed that the
opium trade should be exclusively carried out by the authorized government agent, and that all the junk trade, whether for opium or not, was
to be removed from the jurisdiction of the Hoppo and placed in the
reliable hands of Hart's Maritime Customs Officers. Sir Robert was
glad to get away from Hong Kong ('the place is very stupid for an old
fogey'[32]), but was delighted with the outcome of the talks, writing to
his American colleague Edward Drew, the Senior Commissioner, on
10 August 1887: 'we have put another nail in the coffin of the Hoppoate
. . . I have had my eye on those junks for a quarter of a century, I may
say, and now at last we have got hold of them. The twisting and turning
of the old gentlemen who wanted to retain the junks was at once
amusing and aggravating: I pity them, but we can't let abuse stand in
the way of reform.'[33]

Travellers' tales

Sea travel in the 1870s and eighties became altogether safer and more
reliable as shipbuilding techniques evolved. Compound engines, twin
screws, watertight bulkheads and the increased size of ships, combined
with the opening of the Suez Canal, made the voyage East less of an
adventure. Many tourists however remained anxious to press on to the
exotic sights and spent only a short time in the colony, enjoying the
amenities of civilization after their long voyage. Fresh butter particularly appealed to Prince Henry of Prussia, younger brother of the
future Kaiser Wilhelm II, who stayed at Government House in 1880.
Pope Hennessy recorded that the Prince played lawn tennis 'with great
vigour, in fact he strikes the ball too hard, though we have a very long
court'. The next year his two cousins followed, Princes Albert Victor
and George, later King George V, both midshipmen on HMS
Bacchante making a three-year cruise around the Empire to which
Albert Victor was heir-expectant. The Governor wanted to make a
great fuss of them, claiming that he had the 'special command of Her
Majesty to do so', but was suppressed by the princes' commanding
officer, and the midshipmen were received quietly. The princes were

particularly struck by a Japanese screen which showed the first Portuguese landings, recording that 'the people on board have enormous baggy breeches'. When it was discovered that Sir John had spent £800 on photographs taken during the visit the Colonial Office was furious.[34] General Ulysses S. Grant, former President of the United States, called in 1879, and was able to exchange pleasantries with the American Consul, his old opponent John Singleton Mosby, the Confederate cavalry leader.[35]

Reports of official personages were necessarily blander than those of private visitors. One of these was Isabella Bird (Mrs John Bishop), an indefatigable and well-known traveller. Miss Bird was an earnest evangelical, suspicious of the 'Romish' Church, who very suitably stayed with the Bishop. She liked and admired Victoria, 'moored to England by the electric cable, and replete with all the magnificent enterprises and luxuries of England', but had reservations about its society, with 'its cliques, its boundless hospitalities, its extravagances in living, its quarrels, its gaieties, its picnics, balls, regattas, races, dinner parties, lawn tennis parties, amateur theatricals, afternoon teas, and all its other modes of creating a whirl which passes for pleasure'. In private she was more critical: 'I believe that half the people don't speak to the other half – none of the missionaries except two are on speaking terms . . . The Governor [Pope Hennessy] . . . is believed to be . . . the tool of the Portuguese Bishop Raimondi [the Roman Catholic Bishop of Hong Kong].' She did not think much to the Governor, who was 'much overdressed . . . with a mouth which smiles perpetually and sinister eyes which never smile', and who manifested an 'obviously diseased . . . sympathy with criminals'.[36]

By something of a coincidence Mrs Gordon Cumming arrived at the same time as Isabella Bird – December 1878 – but saw a different side of Hong Kong life, and seems to have enjoyed herself a good deal more. Mrs Cumming first stayed with her friend Mrs Louisa Coxon, wife of Atwell Coxon, a broker. They went to the races together, Mrs Coxon rather daringly driving in her pony carriage, 'the only wheeled vehicle in that vast assemblage'. Mrs Cumming's hostess was, if not quite fast, at least a trifle bold; suitably concealed under a stage name she had appeared in the first performance of the Amateur Dramatic Corps to cast ladies; the 1879 production was, appropriately, *The School for Scandal*. Mrs Coxon was also a founder member of the Ladies Recreation Club, where ladies could play lawn tennis. A rather different aspect of society was shown by Mrs Cumming's other hostesses, Mrs Snowden, wife of the Attorney General, and Mrs Lowcock, whose husband was an unofficial member of the Legislative Council.[37]

Lady Brassey had no need to stay with friends since she arrived with her husband, Sir Thomas, on their yacht *Sunbeam*. It was a sign of the times that when Sir Thomas was invited to dinner with 'some Chinese gentlemen' he found their 'command of English, fully equal to the best educated Englishman'. He was fed with a variety of dishes, including 'duck's paws, fish brains, birdsnest soup', which afterwards made him rather ill. Sir Thomas, an Opium Commissioner, had come on an official mission charged with the investigation of trade. He visited one Hong Kong factory where he found a startling contrast between 'this accumulation of property, and the low scale of pay for the employees', which varied between one penny and fourpence per day.[38]

Few visitors had much complimentary to say about European society in Hong Kong. The open-handed hospitality of the great taipans no longer featured so prominently in their accounts, and many critical comments on the narrow and querulous attitudes of the colonists appeared. In the mid-1870s the distinguished photographer James Thomson was struck by the 'expensive style' of the Europeans, who lived 'much more expensively, I would think, than they need to', and especially by the way in which English assistants were housed, and 'the luxurious way in which they were indulged'. He concluded that Americans and Germans were not only more modest in their mode of life, but took trouble, unlike the English, to learn the language.[39]

This last complaint was frequently heard, and evidenced the increasing smugness and complacency that was doing so much to lose the industrial and commercial lead that Britain had previously enjoyed. Many visitors were shocked at the casually brutal treatment afforded to Chinese: 'You cannot be two minutes in Hong Kong without seeing Europeans striking coolies with their canes or umbrellas,' complained Miss Bird. Lord Ronald Gower deplored the way subalterns of the 74th Regiment (the Highland Light Infantry) treated Chinese 'as a very inferior race of animals to themselves. No wonder that we English are so cordially disliked wherever we go.'[40] The young Robert Hart, newly arrived from Ulster in 1854, was 'rather surprised' to see how his superior 'treated the Chinese – pitching their goods into the water and touching them up with his cane'.[41] One of the earliest Chinese missionaries, Dr Wong Fun, who had taken his medical degree at Edinburgh University, complained that his work was made more difficult by 'a strong prejudice against Englishmen for what they [the Chinese] think the high-handed way in which they carry everything'.

James Thomson was discreet about the low life of Hong Kong, although he reported that there were 180 'music halls', and found that those dealing with the police had discovered 'something of the security and dignified silence procurable by a judicious use of the coin of the realm'. Rudyard Kipling, less discreet about the underworld, was also revealing on many aspects of the island. His account of a meeting with 'the biggest Taipan on the island, and the nicest', summarizes the essential Hong Kong as it was then and remains today. Kipling asked: 'How is it that everybody here smells of money?' and was told: 'It is because the island is going ahead mightily. Because everything pays.' He was invited to look at the share list, all items on which were selling at a premium. 'Everything pays, from the Dairy Farm upwards.'[42] (The Dairy Farm was an imaginative innovation of Dr Patrick Manson, founder of the Hong Kong College of Medicine, who wanted to provide fresh milk for the European children; in Hong Kong even that modest venture could not help becoming a paying proposition.)

Kipling on Hong Kong as a colony is equally telling: 'There is something very pathetic in the trustful clinging attitude of the Colonies, who ought to have been soured and mistrustful long ago.' That was in 1889; Hong Kong may no longer be 'clinging', and is perhaps becoming 'soured', but it has still not appreciated quite how mistrustful of the 'Mother Country' it is prudent to be.

10

FORTRESS HONG KONG

The defence of greater Britain

In 1865 Lord Palmerston had died: and with his death an era was ended. He had first taken office fifty-six years before, in 1809, the year of the Battle of Jena. Three years after Palmerston's death Lord John Russell, his colleague and rival, finally retired, having been in Parliament since 1814 (he was able to impart some instruction to his young grandson, Bertrand, who survived to give Prime Ministers Eden and Macmillan some hard times in the 1950s and sixties). Palmerston and Russell had begun their political careers in a world dominated by Napoleon (whom Russell once met), and ended them in one over-shadowed by Bismarck.[1] For much of this time it had appeared that Britain was indeed a European power, but the limited ability of their country to control the course of events in Europe was better grasped by 'the two old boys' than by most of their contemporaries. When Austria and Prussia invaded Denmark in 1864, British public opinion was strongly pro-Danish. Intervention was demanded, and proposals made for a squadron to be sent to the Baltic. But Palmerston, always a realist, appreciated that Britain could do nothing on her own on the continent of Europe.

British resources were too few and too thinly stretched to allow for an independent European policy, as Bismarck made brutally clear when he said that if a British army landed in Prussia he would send a policeman to arrest it. Six years later the message was thrust home when, in the summer of 1870, it took less than three months for the Prussian army to crush the French in a war for which one million men were mobilized. Had Britain wished to intervene it would have been entirely powerless to do so. Sir Robert Morier, the Foreign Office German expert, declared that the war could have been prevented if for twenty-four hours the British public had been furnished with a backbone. 'What the hell is the use of a backbone without an army, which we have not got!' was the explosive comment of the Duke of Cambridge, Commander-in-Chief at the Horse Guards.[2] At that time the entire land forces of Britain, including the volunteers, were not much more than 100,000 men, and only with the greatest difficulty could an expeditionary force of ten thousand have been raised.

The Palmerston—Russell administration was succeeded by an interlude of Tory rule, first under Lord Derby and then Disraeli, between 1866 and 1868. Thereafter, for sixteen years, power passed between Gladstone and Disraeli – two periods of five years for the Liberals, and one of Conservative rule, during which the whole structure of Europe, and almost of the world, changed. A united Germany and Italy, a revived Austria-Hungary, Russia emerging as a modern power and France licking the wounds of war, manoeuvred for position. All, together with Holland, Belgium and the United States, made industrial expansion a priority and provided extensive government support by financing industrial developments, building railways, docks and canals, and adopting protective tariffs. Britain began to lose her previously undisputed position as the world's workshop: in 1870 more than half the world supply of pig iron and nearly half of steel production originated in Britain; within twenty years the United States was producing more of both than Britain.

	Britain		USA		Germany		World	
Year	iron*	steel	iron	steel	iron	steel	iron	steel
1870	5964	292	1665	69	1369	–	11900	629
1880	7749	1375	3835	1247	2685	728	17950	4205
1890	7904	3679	9203	4277	4583	2127	27157	11902
1899	9302	5001	13621	10639	7900	6189	39752	26685

*(,000 tons³)

World markets were little affected by the emergence of the USA as the leading industrial power, since the rapid expansion of the American domestic market speedily mopped up this capacity, but by the turn of the century Germany, a late starter which had shown a phenomenal increase, was also producing more steel than Britain. And German steel products, unlike those of America, quickly found their way on to markets where previously Britain had enjoyed a commanding lead. Some of these looked extremely difficult to penetrate – the settlement colonies and India – but others offered virgin territory to German exporters, and foremost among these were Africa and China.

Although other countries were taking the lead in modern industries, British pre-eminence in world trade continued. In 1870 British and British colonial trade was greater than that of France, Germany and the United States combined (£675 million as against £604 million); twenty years later the same situation prevailed (£1,038 million compared to £997 million). This was in part due to an unparalleled outflow of capital to foreign and colonial investments, investments which, although handsomely profitable, deprived home industry of the capital needed to keep pace with the new competition. There was considerable variance according to patterns of world trade: British money invested abroad frequently totalled at least half that invested at home, and often more – in the decade 1881–90 it rose to almost three-quarters of domestic investment. By the beginning of the Second World War British investment in foreign commercial and industrial companies amounted to as much as 75 per cent of that invested in domestic concerns. Returns, even when adjusted for risk, were comfortably higher than those obtainable at home, and the wealth of banking and trading experience available in the City of London made for easy identification of opportunities.

So huge a proportion of the national wealth had to be protected, and, just as the governments of Imperial Germany were influenced by their manufacturers towards an aggressive policy of securing new markets by colonial expansion, British administrations were under pressure to retain the investments already made and the outlets already developed. In order to protect these a strong navy was essential, but a large army unnecessary.

Edward Cardwell, Gladstone's War Minister, initiated an extensive reorganization of the army between 1869 and 1874, against the determined resistance of the Duke of Cambridge. Succeeding governments, Conservative and Liberal, carried through an impressively wide range of much-needed measures: abolishing the purchase of commissions; improving conditions and equipment (a breech-loading rifle was at last introduced, although the generals refused to accept anything but muzzle loaders for artillery); reorganizing the regimental system; even – and the Duke of Cambridge was near apoplexy at the idea – clothing the troops fighting in the Egyptian desert in khaki rather than red serge. With modestly increased numbers, the reformed army was one designed to protect existing interests abroad by fighting quick colonial campaigns, rather than engaging in pitched battles on a European scale. Even limited wars were regarded with suspicion. Colonists were expected to avoid confrontations and to see to their own defence should this be needed.

Cardwell's expansion of the home army had been achieved at the cost of repatriating some twenty thousand troops from the self-governing colonies, leaving the colonists to arrange their own defence, and Gladstone was permanently distrustful of any colonial entanglements that might lead to extra expense. Looking about, as ever, for an excuse to 'dish the Whigs', Disraeli seized upon the Liberals' anxiety to avoid Imperial commitments. His speech of 24 June 1872 is often taken as marking a turning point in Britain's selection of a world, rather than a European, role. He jeered that the utilitarian Whigs had no feeling for the glories of empire:

> It has been shown with precise, with mathematical demonstration that there never was a jewel in the Crown of England that was so truly costly as the possession of India. How often has it been suggested that we should at once emancipate ourselves from this incubus! They [the Whig–Liberals] looked upon the colonies of England, looked even upon the connexion with India, as a burden upon this country, viewing everything in a financial aspect and totally passing by those moral and political considerations which make nations great, and by the influence of which alone men are distinguished from animals.[4]

Disraeli's opportunity to put his views into action came early in 1874 when Gladstone, some months after having been defeated in the House of Commons (again over Ireland, as was almost inevitable), called a general election which produced a substantial Conservative majority. Apart from his nine months in office in 1868, this was Disraeli's only solid stint as Prime Minister. His policy for 'making nations great' was signified by the new title arranged for Queen Victoria: 'Empress of India'. While this was nothing more than an inexpensive piece of symbolism (although it gratified the Queen a good deal), the purchase of a 7/16th interest in the Suez Canal shares was a genuine stroke of policy. The route to India was secured, albeit at the cost of being drawn into continuous squabbles with the French and some expensive Egyptian complications, which brought down a British Prime Minister as long after as 1956.[5]

The division between Conservatives and Liberals on colonial affairs was more apparent than real. However anxious they might be to resist involvement, Gladstone's administrations were pushed into Imperial commitments. The Boers of the Transvaal, who were annexed unwillingly into the British Empire by Disraeli in 1877, assumed that Gladstone would restore their freedom: had he not described the annexation as 'almost insane', and said that he would repudiate it as being 'obtained by means dishonourable to this country'? Not a bit of it; on coming into office in 1880 the Liberal government chose coercion, and only the Boers' defeat of the British army saved the independence that Gladstone had promised to restore. Likewise in Egypt it was a Liberal, and not a Conservative, government that in 1882 authorized the bombardment of Alexandria and the suppression of the Arabi Pasha revolt, a genuine nationalist uprising that had promised to give Egypt its first independent and responsible government.

The truth of the matter was that whatever the political rhetoric, any British government was inevitably drawn into colonial disputes by matters outside its control: either the preservation of existing interests, as in the Transvaal and Burma (in 1885), or by the need to react to other European powers' increasingly aggressive policies. Since the permanent staff at the Colonial Office remained opposed to any additions to their responsibilities, and Ministers followed a course of reducing colonial expenditure whenever remotely possible, the effect was that something not unlike a bipartisan policy towards the colonies was quietly established, which lasted at least until the beginning of the Second Boer War at the end of the century. Bipartisanship did not always extend between departments of state, and the Foreign and Colonial Offices remained at odds over Hong Kong, with the Foreign Office continuing to insist that the interests of the colony must be subordinated to those of British relations with the Chinese Empire, while the Colonial Office transmitted, not always enthusiastically, the sentiments of the colonists.

Nor did the Admiralty and the War Office see things in the same light as the Colonial Office. Admiral Sir John Colomb had been reporting to the Admiralty on defence strategy for some time, but his publications on 'Colonial Defence' in 1877 and on the 'Defence of Great and Greater Britain' in 1879 were decisive.[6] Colomb described

how the defence of both motherland and colo
effected by a strong navy, capable of deterring a
navy was dependent upon a secure chain of fue
repair stations; the career of the Confederate com
during the American Civil War had shown how c
was on such ports, and how shipping was the
predictable routes. Although Colomb believed ꜱ᷂ᷤᷤ᷾
be more important than Hong Kong, the Admiralty, while acᴄᴇᴘ
his principles, was not convinced of Fiji. The strategic importance of
Hong Kong – although secondary to that of Singapore – was henceforth established. Hong Kong was to be not only a useful centre of
trade, but an essential link in Imperial defence. The question of who
should pay for this – colonists or British taxpayers – remained unre-
solved and contentious.

Gladstone and his successors were less interested in European and
colonial than in domestic matters – the Irish question, which eventually
destroyed the Liberal Party, being the most important among them. It
seemed indeed that a period of stability on the Continent was likely,
and this was at least partly true. Disraeli's swan song was his participation in the Treaty of Berlin (1878) which, ostensibly called in order
to end the renewed conflict between Russia and Turkey, turned out
to provide the mould into which European affairs settled until the eve
of the First World War. With no inseparable rivalries left engaging
them in Europe, the powers, for differing reasons, turned their attention to colonial expansion.

In search of la gloire

Between 1790 and 1852 there had been in France nine different forms
of government – three monarchies, two republics, two empires, a consulate and a directory – the changes of which had been habitually
accompanied by violence. As a result all French administrations were
twitchily nervous of public opinion, acutely conscious that their continuance in power, and even their personal survival (one Prime Minister
was nearly lynched as late as 1885 – as a consequence of events in
China) depended on their not unduly irritating the populace; and one
source of irritation was the continuously sinister behaviour of the English, most suspicious when seemingly inoffensive. National policy after
1815 inexorably dictated co-operation with Britain, as the only other

tutional, unautocratic European power, but only a secure and
fident ruler could afford to offend the powerful, sometimes hysteri-
al, Anglophobic lobby. At no time was French public opinion more
inflamed that in 1839–40. The Orléans monarchy reinforced its mundane appeal with Napoleonic sentiment when in 1840 Napoleon's body
was brought back to Paris from St Helena amid extraordinary scenes
of emotive pageantry; it seemed that Thiers, the Prime Minister, might
have so managed things in the Levant that French domination there
was secure; rearmament was enthusiastically embraced, and a war with
England was hopefully expected: 'a shudder of rage agitated the entire
country ... and France took its sword in hand'.[7] But the realistic
King Louis Philippe, who had made co-operation with England a
cornerstone of his policy, sacked Thiers, and accepted the Treaty of
London, which settled matters with Britain but greatly disappointed
the French people.

Casting around for something else to engage his subjects' attention,
the King turned to the East. At that time there was little reason for
the French to concern themselves with China. A nation of coffee- and
wine-drinkers, they did not rely on the revenue from duties on tea to
the extent that did Britain: they had their own well-protected silk
industry, and, shorn of most of their Indian possessions (by the infamous British!), had no need to find markets for cotton or opium.
Nevertheless, French governments remained anxious to keep informed
of events in the Chinese Empire, and in 1839 a secret agent was
dispatched to Canton.

M. Mallet de Bassilan, of Dieppe, sent by Louis Philippe's government on an undercover mission, does not seem to have been the most
judicious of spies. He was given a convivial welcome by the British
merchants, who clearly enjoyed misleading the credulous Frenchman,
convincing him that the East India Company still held power in Canton
– 'le nom seul est changé' – and that a cunning plot existed to take over
the whole of China. This was to begin with the removal of 'l'empereur
Tartare Mongol' and his replacement by another Chinese, or possibly
a suitable Englishman, none other than young Robert Thom of
Jardine's.[8]

Whether these flights of fancy were believed or not, a formal mission
was dispatched two years later, led by Adolphe-Philibert Dubois de
Jancigny, who had made a name for himself in India, and was anxious
to do the same thing in China. French and Chinese accounts of de
Jancigny's mission differ considerably. Officially he was there to show

the flag; unofficially he asked for the French to be given land for a settlement as the English had been given Hong Kong, which he suggested should be at Humen – Ch'uen-pi, at the entrance to the Bogue. Ch'i-ing dismissed this with polite derision; French trade was not nearly large enough to justify equal treatment with Britain, and Humen, the Tiger's Mouth, was a strategic site, the very gateway to China, quite unlike Hong Kong, which was regarded as an outer island of minimal importance.

To confuse things further, Captain Cécille of the French frigate *Erigone* pursued an independent course, and presented himself at Shanghai in August 1843 – an episode which still needs explanation.[9] It was put to the Chinese that the French had no quarrel with China, but were hereditary enemies of the English, and would therefore help China in her struggle with the British. With French aid, the Chinese would learn to build ships and cannon and to fight at sea. Again, Ch'i-ing was unconvinced: he was in the process of coming to an agreement with the British, whom he felt he could understand and rely upon, and whose power was all too obvious, whereas the French were an unknown quantity (and he had certainly been told of Trafalgar!).[10]

All this behind-the-scenes work bore no immediate fruit. When a formal delegation was sent out in 1844 under Théodore-Marie-Melchior-Joseph de Lagrené, an experienced diplomat who had been at the Congress of Vienna and sat at the feet of the super-diplomatist Talleyrand, it was found that the French Consul at Canton had already been accorded the most-favoured-nation status specified by the Treaty of Nanking, and there should have been no need for de Lagrené's accomplished diplomacy. His instructions also however included a very odd request, and one that foreshadowed future French strategy: he had been ordered to seek another strategic site for a French outpost, this time the small island of Basilan, off Mindanao in the Philippines. This territory, being in Spanish occupation, was hardly China's to give, unless France was looking for a pretext for a quarrel with Spain. Needless to say, no progress was made on this question.

Probably in order to save face, for otherwise the expensive French delegation would return without having achieved anything not already accorded, de Lagrené decided to specify toleration for missionaries as a French demand. Since he had been sent by the conservative Guizot ministry, which had been making efforts to win the support of the Catholic Church, large sections of which were hostile to the Orléans monarchy, this could be presented at Paris as a politically useful concession. The request was readily acceded to, and in future was to afford the French opportunities for creating a *casus belli* when the need was felt.

It was left to the next regime but one, the Second Empire of Louis Napoleon, to take advantage of the provision of their original treaty, reinforced after the Anglo–French expedition of 1858–60, which firmly specified that 'members of all Christian communities should enjoy entire security for their persons and property, and the free exercise of their religious practices' (Article XIII). At that point Mallet de Bassilan came back into the picture, with a series of documents formally presented to the French government between February 1857 and December 1859. Although charged with Anglophobia and hysterical overtones – 'They will attempt anything against the Empire, and it is *only* the Empire that can stop them' – de Bassilan produced some evidence to reinforce his thesis: 'It is clear to me from the disturbances in Egypt, that the English . . . wish to occupy it one day,' and forecast that Tibet would inevitably be interfered with by the British (both of which eventualities did in fact transpire). He also pointed out the importance of the south China rivers, which soon after became the preferred French route for expansion into China.[11]

For some time the small scale of French commercial interest in China left French and British able to co-operate. A change came after the catastrophes of French defeat in the Franco—Prussian War of 1870, and the humiliating Paris Commune of the following year. Emasculated in Europe, with no prospect of restoring the lost provinces of Alsace and Lorraine, now held by Germany, the Third Republic looked for foreign success in compensation. She came out of the war with her colonies intact, in spite of German industrialists lobbying Bismarck to have French possessions seized as war reparations. It was a repetition, although of greatly aggravated severity, of the situation after Waterloo, when the restored Bourbon Charles X had begun the conquest of Algiers, consolidated during the following reign of Louis Philippe. Successive governments had made forays into Mexico, Tahiti, and Egypt; the acquisition of Madagascar was openly intended as part of an anti-British strategy. De Lanessan, Radical Deputy and Navy Minister, pointed out in his book *L'Expansion coloniale de la France* that French fleets based in Madagascar and in Indo-China would 'put an end to all commercial relations between England and Singapore, Hong Kong and China and even menace India itself'.[12]

Whether consciously influenced by the suggestion of de Bassilan or not, the government of Louis Napoleon had turned to Indo-China as a potential field for expansion and a counterbalance to British India. By 1862 a foothold in Saigon was secured, promptly countered by the British annexation of Lower Burma. Within another five years, France had obtained all the Mekong River basin. The trouble with the Mekong delta, which became the French province of Cochin China, was that the Mekong led nowhere of commercial interest. Only the Red River, in the north of what is now Vietnam, offered access from the sea to Hanoi, and on to the Chinese province of Yunnan. But the Red River lay in the territory of the province of Tonking, part of the ancient empire of Annam, and Annam was, theoretically at least, numbered among the feudatories of China. The Annamese Emperors were racial Chinese, and the administration was partly staffed by Chinese scholar-officials.

Feudatory obligations were not necessarily observed by the Chinese – it was, for instance, judged prudent not to insist on traditional rights when the Japanese occupied the Ryuku (Liu-chi) islands in 1879 – but in this instance an appeal from Annam was recognized by China. Quite possibly China might not have thought it worthwhile bothering about Annam itself, but Tonking was useful as a buffer zone between the Middle Kingdom and the predatory French. It was therefore decided to intervene, at least to the extent of sending irregular but effective forces – the Black Flags – to counter French aggressions. Li Hung-chang, the most prominent of the Chinese reformers, who understood too clearly the limitations of his country's military and naval strength, attempted to avoid a clash, but the Dowager Empress's party were spoiling for a fight.

The French decision to expand this modest imperial success into what was, within a single generation, to become the second-largest Western colonial empire, was not taken quickly or unanimously. The French army was organized for large European rather than small colonial operations, and there were many who resented any diversion of effort from the preparation for '*revanche*' – the next victorious war with Germany that would restore to France her lost provinces. Among the left-wingers the curious idea that even the dissemination of French culture did not justify foreign adventures was beginning to spread. Nor was there the continuity of government that might encourage a settled policy. The 1870s and eighties were one of those periods when ministries succeeded ministries with breathtaking speed: between February

1879 and February 1883 there were no fewer than eight governments – Waddington, Fréycinet, Ferry, Gambetta, Fréycinet again, Duclerc, Fallière and Ferry once more. It was not until Jules Ferry's return, with a programme of anti-clerical education and colonial expansion, that progress was made.

In August 1884 China stumbled into a war with France for which neither country was prepared. Admiral Courbet earned some easy successes, destroying at Foochow (Fuzhou) a very inadequately modernized Chinese fleet, but the land forces had a more mixed record. A French expedition to Formosa got itself bottled up in the port of Keelung (Ch'i-lung), unable to break through the ring of Chinese defences, and in February 1885 a defeat at Langson, near the Sino— Tonkinese border, led to the downfall of Ferry's government: Ferry himself was lucky to escape with his life from an infuriated Paris mob (the Chinese forces contributed to this by returning the French dead with their helmets neatly sewn on, but without their heads). But in spite of nearly losing the war, the French won the subsequent peace. In the treaty arranged in Paris with Robert Hart's assistance, French sovereignty over the territories of the empire of Annam, Tonkin and Cochin China was recognized and direct French rule was imposed, while the areas of the Siamese empire, now Laos and Cambodia, were brought within the French sphere of influence: a slice of the world equivalent in size to France itself, stretching a thousand miles south from the border with China, had passed under French control. Some French politicians wanted more; the influential publicist Joseph Chailley-Bert thought that Siam, Macao and part of China proper ought to be allowed to benefit from France's 'mission civilisatrice'.[13]

What seemed to be an explosion of French colonial ambitions, reaching to the borders of both the Indian Empire and southern China, caused major concern in Whitehall. An indecisive and largely theoretical Chinese presence had been replaced by a predatory French one, intent on expansion into Yunnan. Insofar as the British government considered Chinese interests, it was with a benign neutrality. Having established diplomatic relations and secured the lion's share of the trade, Britain had accepted China as part of her 'informal empire'. French activity, on the other hand, was always an object of suspicion.

The bombardment of Foochow in August 1884, in which some three thousand civilians were killed, provoked widespread disgust; Harry Parkes called it 'little less than treacherous'. Questions were asked in the House of Commons; Mr Ashmead Bartlett, Tory Member for Eye, demanded on 28 October 1884 that 'The British admiral stop these piratical proceedings'. When the French announced a blockade of the Chinese coast, and added that they would consider rice to be a contraband of war, Britain responded indignantly, and hinted at the Navy being called upon to resist. One observer described the action as 'electrifying the civilized world', and in the House of Lords the French actions were described as 'barbarous'; Lord Bury said that it was well known that the country was in a position in which it might at any moment be involved in war; and Colonel Gordon, celebrated as 'Chinese' Gordon for his role in assisting in the suppression of the Taipings, wrote that 'humanly speaking, China going to war with France, must entail our following suit'.

The Chinese reaction to the French attack was fierce and immediate. For the first time the electric telegraph and steam-powered press enabled the news of the bombardment of Foochow and the destruction of the Chinese fleet to be speedily disseminated. The whole country was outraged, and the Viceroy of Canton issued a proclamation calling on all Chinese to sink French ships and to sell poisoned provisions to their forces. In Hong Kong this was received with some consternation by the authorities, but was acted on only to the extent of anti-French demonstrations and a refusal by port workers to service French vessels. It was the first manifestation in the colony of a spontaneous, grass-roots nationalism, distinct from the old generalized xenophobia, and directed against one specific nation. Not recognizing this, the colonial government acted with clumsy authoritarianism. The strikers were ordered to return to work and fined; the Buffs had to be called out to suppress the disturbances which followed, and an emergency ordinance was rushed through the Legislative Council giving extensive powers to the government. These actions were widely criticized, as considerable British sympathy for the Chinese protest was expressed. Sir John Hay, M.P. for Wigton, an Admiral who had seen service in China, defended the strikers, and asked that the Hong Kong authorities 'be directed to refrain from enforcing any contract to labour . . . which for patriotic reasons may reasonably object to such enforcement'. A Hong Kong court rejected the administration's attempt to prosecute the newspaper editor who had published the Viceroy's original proclamation.[14]

The results of the war were widespread. Although the settlement had conceded little to the French that damaged Chinese interests, the Ch'ing claims on Indo-China being largely theoretical, the conflict had destroyed any hopes of stability that had developed in the quarter century after the Convention of Peking. The other European powers, alerted to French ambitions in China, were determined not to be left behind in any division of the spoils that might be subsequently offered, and Britain had been made aware of Hong Kong's vulnerability to French or any other aggression. Naval strategists everywhere noted how easily China's new fleet had been overwhelmed, nowhere more so than in Japan, where modernization was proceeding swiftly and efficiently. Any illusions China might have had about the reliability of Western protection were shattered. Neither Britain nor the United States, generally counted as allies of China, had intervened. But the French had not had it all their own way, and a militant Chinese nationalism had begun to make itself felt.

General Sargent's guns

At a time of international tension and crisis, Hong Kong had to put up with a weak and nervous Governor. Sir George Bowen was a polished example of smooth pomposity, who had glided swiftly through the ranks of colonial administration. A brilliant Oxford career – scholar of Trinity, a first in Classics, twice President of the Union, a Fellow of Balliol – he was appointed Rector of the Ionian University of Corfu (which had slipped under British administration as a result of the Napoleonic wars) in 1847, at the age of twenty-six, and became Political Secretary to the government of the Ionian Islands. An adventurous journey to Hungary in 1849, where he was instrumental in rescuing the revolutionary hero Louis Kossuth, and a number of books – including *Murray's Guide to Greece* – kept Bowen in the public eye. Aptly described in the *Australian Dictionary of Biography* as 'self-opinionated, obstinate, and long-winded', he was much given to name-dropping, and fond of retailing anecdotes of the great and famous, but it was his friendship with Gladstone that got him the post of the first Governor of Queensland in 1859, at the age of thirty-eight.

Already a KCMG at thirty-four, Bowen was made GCMG[15] on this appointment, and looked set for higher posts, for underneath the pompous and time-serving veneer real abilities lurked. But the Antipodes were too much for him, as they might well have been for anyone who saw the sheep-runs of Australia as 'exactly the *dromoi eurees* of Homer', the squatter question as 'a revival of the strife between the patricians and the plebeians for the *ager publicus*', and was reminded by the Darling Downs of Horace's '*Larissae campus opimae*'.[16] Although Bowen's colonial career lasted for over twenty years – and was not without successes, especially in New Zealand, where he succeeded the pugnacious Sir George Grey as Governor in 1867, and persuaded the colonists, aggrieved at their treatment by Whitehall, that they should refrain from asking to become part of the United States instead – he came to grief in Victoria, to which state he was appointed Governor in 1872. There was a tremendous row over the budget proposals in 1877 between the elected Assembly and the Council, whose members had life tenure: 'a sort of political madness . . . some members of the Council talked of hiring and arming Irish mobs . . . while some members of the Assembly advocated violent and revolutionary measures'. Bowen failed to smooth things out, and wrote that he had 'damaged my . . . reputation and my career to a degree that I shall never recover'.[17] In this he was right; after three years in Mauritius, he was sent to Hong Kong for his last posting in 1882, being seen by the Colonial Office as likely to be a soothing influence after the turbulent Pope Hennessy. Sir George was happy to co-operate if that would assist in making his own life there as easy as possible.

By the time Bowen reached Hong Kong in 1883 he had developed into a consummate bore, idle, inordinately pleased with his lofty acquaintances and immensely conceited. His superiors viewed him with scorn. Lord Granville described him as a 'pompous donkey'; Kimberley noted his 'ridiculous egoism'. W.R. Malcolm, an Assistant Under-Secretary, revealed to Lord Ripon: 'Bowen has served a long time, and officially we say with distinction. But in truth he is nothing but a wind bag and has only been preserved during a long career by Lady Bowen's tact and popularity and by the great personal friendship of Herbert [Sir Robert Herbert, Permanent Under-Secretary at the Colonial Office, who had served under Bowen in Australia] which he has requited with the most violent abuses.'[18] Bowen's successor, William Des Voeux, described a dinner at Lord Carnarvon's which had also been attended by Hennessy, Bowen's predecessor. Bowen was talking 'according to his wont, in a somewhat loud voice. After a remark had fallen rather flat to the effect that he had had an interview on the same day with the Pope, Victor Emmanuel and Garibaldi, he shortly afterwards said, apropos of nothing: "Very extraordinary thing, very extraordinary; I was asked to dine the same day with the Prime Minister and the Archbishop of Canterbury."' Which was followed by a sharp putdown from 'little Pope Hennessy'.[19]

Bowen's expectation of an agreeably lazy sojourn in Hong Kong should have been amply justified, for, as he remarked: 'the routine and absolutely necessary work of Hong Kong administration seemed to me from the first to be much lighter than that of any Crown Colony which I had previously governed'. This was due mainly to the services of the officers who had passed through the cadet recruitment scheme, set up twenty years before. Such men as James Stewart Lockhart (Assistant Colonial Secretary in 1883), Alfred Lister (Colonial Treasurer), Walter Deane (Superintendent of Police) and Sir James Russell (Police Magistrate), had all passed the stringent examinations and developed a good working knowledge of the Chinese and their language. The Colonial Secretary, Sir William Marsh, proved his capacity for carrying out the Governor's post on his own by administering the government for considerable periods both before and after Bowen's appointment. But it was Bowen's misfortune to arrive in the colony at a time when wars and rumours of wars abounded, and the responsibility for defence lay in the hands of a particularly active and irascible soldier, Lieutenant-General J.N. Sargent.

It was Sargent's third tour of duty in the Far East, his first having been in 1860. Since that time there had been another major advance in gunnery, with the general introduction of very heavy steel pieces, with improved propellants, giving greatly improved range and accuracy. Even the wrought-iron rifled cannon developed during the American Civil war had a range of well over three miles, and more modern guns were capable of much more. French battleships of the 'Hoche' class onwards (1876) carried 13.4" seventy-five-ton guns in their main armament – more than capable of devastating Victoria from far beyond the range of the existing fortress batteries. Nor were these proof even against small-arms fire, since some of the most strategically placed were mounted in the open, *en barbette*, and therefore protected from direct but not from dropping fire. Sargent was acutely aware of this, and made sure that the War Office knew of his views. In spite of seventy years of Anglo—French co-operation both he and the Horse Guards in Whitehall remained nervous of France as a potential aggressor, and the tension over French expansionism in the East confirmed them in their apprehensions.

From being a colonial backwater, Hong Kong had been pushed into the foreground of international confrontation. The distinguished military engineer, later M.P. for Portsmouth, Sir William Crossman had visited Hong Kong in 1881 and designed suitable fortifications, but work on these had not been put in hand. Sir Andrew Clarke, Quarter-Master General, agreed with General Sargent that Hong Kong's 'defences were then far inferior in armament to those of many of the Chinese ports, and that in the event of war, it would be possible for the French with a preponderating force of six ironclads to destroy the capital and shipping of Hong Kong'. As an immediate measure it was recommended that the garrison be massively strengthened by the addition of three more Indian regiments, two first-class torpedo boats, and additional heavy guns and quick-firing pieces. Lord Derby was sufficiently concerned to authorize the immediate dispatch, 'in hot haste', of guns for the purpose, diverted from a new fort at Plymouth.

Sir Andrew Clarke had also written to Bowen: 'At present, against an ironclad, Hong Kong is almost defenceless, so if war broke out immediately suddenly I expect to see you a prisoner.' Bowen was only too well aware of the dangers, and had protested to the Colonial Office on 8 March 1884 that 'if four or five thousand soldiers of any Foreign Power were landed at the back of this island they could, of course, march into town (a distance of only four miles) without effective opposition from our small garrison'. Sir Andrew's letter had the effect of throwing Bowen into a major funk, and he cannot have been much pleased either by the curt telegraphic notification from Lord Derby on 13 September 1884 that the colony was expected to pay for Sargent's howitzers: 'full details by post . . . In the meantime advance to General Officer Commanding amount required.' 'To what,' Bowen plaintively enquired of the General, 'does the "advance" refer?' Two days later he took himself off to the safety of Japan, on the doubtful excuse that his rheumatism was playing up.

Sargent was furious, and wrote to Bowen: 'these are times when men circumstanced as we are must have no thought of their own lives, and should prefer death to dishonour'. The colonial press was derisory, the *Hong Kong Telegraph* writing on 13 September:

His Excellency calmly deserts his post on a frivolous pretence, at what is unquestionably the most critical period in the history of the colony since the last Chinese war. No amount of sham sophistry, no shallow explanations as to ill-health, no twisting of the truth, not one of the dozen stale pretences . . . can disguise the fact that Governor BOWEN . . . makes an easily obtained medical certificate a sufficient reason for . . . taking himself off to the baths in Japan for a pleasant holiday . . . Great Britain's

supremacy could not long be maintained if there were many
responsible officers in the service of the Crown of the calibre of
Sir GEORGE BOWEN.[20]

Sargent got his howitzers, although, as Lord Carnarvon complained
five years later, they were still of too small a calibre, but lost his job.
Sir George Bowen had enough friends in high places to procure the
General's recall, which prompted Sargent to write an entire book on
the iniquities of Sir George and of the Duke of Cambridge.[21] But the
new guns alone, which were speedily mounted, were not enough to
ensure the colony's safety. General Sargent had personally reconnoitred the numerous bays in which an enemy could shelter, and the
commanding heights on the north side of the harbour which would
enable him to threaten the colony, and had come to the conclusion
that nothing less than the occupation of these key points would suffice:
'The possession by the Chinese of the North Shore of the harbour is
a source of inconvenience and of insecurity . . . but should this territory
pass into the hands of any foreign Power, other than Great Britain, the
consequences would be disastrous.' These points of strategic weakness
must be, if not acquired, at least neutralized. It was, Sargent wrote,
'of the most vital importance for us to be in time to prevent either of
those two European Powers [France and Russia] seizing or in any other
way acquiring possession of the Chinese territory which commands the
entrance to the harbour of Hong Kong, as well as the harbour itself'.
Sargent was not necessarily thinking in terms of the whole of the area
now known as the New Territories, but only 'the land . . . absolutely
necessary to our defence'. He wrote energetic dispatches to Lord
Hartington, the Secretary of State for War, which Bowen countered
through the Colonial Office. The message was received, but the time
was not ripe for Britain to be seen to lay hands on more Chinese
territory.

Colonial officials who had suffered under Bowen's ineffective rule
were sorry to see Sargent go. James Stewart Lockhart expressed his
serious regrets – the colony needed 'leaders of a strong, vigorous and
fearless character'; Cecil Clementi Smith wrote: 'I am extremely sorry
that you are leaving this command for we shall never have another
General with who we shall get on so well.' Bowen himself did not stay
for long, leaving in December 1885 after a period in office of thirty-two
months, of which he had spent only fifteen in the colony. A 'leading
merchant' wrote to Sargent: 'I do not think anyone will regret his

departure. He is a vain, silly old man, with an egotism so obtrusive as to be disgusting. No arrangements were being made for any farewell entertainment, and he sent for Mr Ryrie and asked him to organize a demonstration of some kind, but that gentleman declined.'[22]

The politics of plague

Whether the credit should be given to Bowen or to his excellent staff, some useful things were done in his time. Perhaps the most significant was the reconstruction of the Legislative Council, which included the first Chinese sitting as of right, in succession to the temporarily-appointed Ng Choy. In discussions between Bowen, representing the views of the more prominent colonists, and the Colonial Office, it was decided that, as Kimberley had recommended, at least one unofficial member of the Legislative Council should always be Chinese. At the same time an element of representation was introduced by authorizing the Justices of the Peace and the Chamber of Commerce each to elect a member, a form of indirect election that still subsists. There were to be five 'unofficial' places in all, and therefore in theory the Legislative Council would be able to fulfil its function of representing community opinion considerably better than before. The difficulty was the preponderance of mercantile influence.

Both the Chamber of Commerce and the Justices were predominantly British. The Chamber had twenty British members and six other Europeans, three Jews, two Chinese, one Parsee and one American. Of the seventy-nine Justices sixty-two were British, seven Chinese, seven Parsee or American, and three Jewish. Only the sixty non-stipendiary 'unofficials' voted; all these were required to hold British citizenship, and they included all the Chinese. (Hong Kong Chinese could apply for British citizenship, but were not obliged to do so. Complete freedom for any Chinese to travel to, and live in, the colony was retained until the Second World War.)

The Justices elected David Sassoon, from the great Bombay Jewish family. This was done in a conscious effort to widen the non-Anglo-Saxon element on the Council (Sassoon was succeeded by Sir Paul Chater, an Armenian, in a continuation of the tradition). The Chamber of Commerce elected Thomas Jackson, the Chief Manager and undoubted Taipan of the Hongkong and Shanghai Bank.

Since one of the two remaining members was always a member of

Jardine Mathesons, the Legislative Council's opinions were usually both unequivocal and predictable. The system remained essentially unchanged for exactly a century, until 1985, when an element of election – albeit an extremely indirect one – was introduced.

Uninhibited comment was, however, not lacking in Hong Kong, for the colony enjoyed a free – sometimes free to the bounds of scurrility – press. Nor had Bowen any intention of muzzling criticism; Australia and New Zealand had habituated him to it. He arranged for the Council minutes and departmental reports to be distributed, and for the formation of a standing committee system with unofficial representation. The most important of these, the Finance Committee, was given the responsibility of commenting on budget proposals before these were referred to Whitehall, which at least gave it a useful psychological leverage. These reforms were accomplished with minimal opposition from colonists relieved at no longer having to cope with Sir John Pope Hennessy. When Bowen left the colony Phineas Ryrie, the senior member of the Legislative Council, was able to say that 'whereas a certain amount of friction and asperity of feelings between the official and unofficial elements' had existed previously, there was 'nothing of the sort now'.

Some progress towards institutional development was also made in Bowen's successor Sir William Des Voeux's term of office, which began in October 1887. In the interim of nearly two years after Bowen's departure the Acting Governor Sir William Marsh carried on running things as he had done since his appointment as Colonial Secretary in 1879, under the impossible Pope Hennessy and the ineffectual Bowen. Des Voeux had learnt from personal experience the truth of Talleyrand's advice to young diplomats, 'Surtout, pas trop de zèle.' At the age of twenty-nine, having taken a degree at the University of Toronto – an unusual background for a colonial governor – he had been sent in 1863 as a magistrate to Charles Elliot's old territory, British Guiana, and, like Elliot, had protested about the way the planters treated their labourers. Although these were not, as in Elliot's time, black slaves, but indentured Chinese coolies, their standards had apparently not been much improved. Des Voeux's protests, described by *The Times* as 'the severest impeachment of public officers' since Warren Hastings was tried for alleged offences in India seventy-five years before, led to the appointment of a Royal Commission. Some of his criticisms were declared to be exaggerated, and Des Voeux thereafter was considerably more restrained. In part this may have been due to his ill-health, which necessitated frequent vacations. F.H. May, Sir William's Private Secretary in Hong Kong, did most of the work, as the Governor was happy to acknowledge, although he still found it necessary to make the painful journey from the summer residence, Mountain Lodge, to Government Offices, 'once or twice a week'. Bowen's institution of regular Council meetings encroached too severely upon the Governor's leisure time, and was therefore abolished.

Sir William reserved his energies for visiting celebrities. The Comte de Bardi occupied a great deal of his attention. Hardly a figure of international importance, the count was nevertheless a Bourbon, and owner of the Château de Chambord, to which return invitations would be welcome. The Grand Duke Alexander Michael of Russia and the Tsarevitch, later Tsar Nicholas, also stayed at Government House in 1891, and went on that perennially favourite occupation of visitors to Hong Kong, a shopping trip. This was made incognito, the future Tsar heavily disguised in a billycock hat and tan shoes. Young George Curzon, already making a name for himself in Parliament and in society, was small beer by comparison, but within a comparatively short time was to have an important influence on the future of the colony. He was rather too enthusiastic for credibility, being enraptured by 'the Elysian graces' of Victoria.

It was a considerable sadness for Sir William to be absent on one of his extended leaves during the visit of Affie's younger brother, the Queen's favourite son, the Duke of Connaught, in 1889. The Duke's visit marked the official initiation of Des Voeux and Connaught Roads, the start of a new reclamation scheme which was to advance the waterfront to Connaught Road and provide valuable land in the heart of the central district. The original shoreline had been extended and protected by a sea wall and some reclamation done by 1862, but work had since been desultory. The new scheme provided, when complete (which was not for another seventeen years), space for a new clubhouse, the Supreme Court building, a cricket pitch, and the tramlines, all much appreciated additions to the city.

Sir William was however forced to give his attention to a less attractive subject – public health. Osbert Chadwick's 1882 report had been consigned to another new committee, the Sanitary Board, but before the Board could implement any of its recommendations, one of Chadwick's and Ayres' prognostications was realized. Neglect of sanitary conditions throughout Hennessy's obstructive tenure of office had constituted a time-bomb, which exploded in the form of a cholera epidemic in 1883. The new Board had its work cut out in coping with the immediate consequences of the epidemic, and when they were able to find time to produce plans for the future they ran into strident opposition. Chadwick's waterworks were indeed built at Tai Tam, and helped with sewage disposal, and his recommendations for food handling, the control of markets and the reorganization of garbage disposal were implemented, but nothing was done about the desperate overcrowding which made the spread of disease inevitable. There was, after all, no money in it, always a powerful argument in Hong Kong, and the two thousand Europeans were adequately, if not luxuriously, housed; in the 1890s all hotel bedrooms advertised in the *Hong Kong Guide* had bathrooms attached. Gross overcrowding was limited to the Chinese quarters – there were instances presented of more than a thousand to the acre – and meant high rents with consequent profits to landlords; compulsory clearances, the only effective remedy, were certain to lead to trouble.

Chadwick wanted three hundred cubic feet of space per person – a room about twelve foot square for a family of four – and at least one window per room, but even this modest standard was too much for Hong Kong landlords. The opposition was led by Ho Ch'i (rather strangely himself a qualified physician), and in an effort to move things forward he was invited to join the Board. An extraordinary man, Ho Ch'i (or Ho Kai), son of that Revd. Ho Fuk who was among the founders of the Tung Wah Hospital, embodied all the virtues and contradictions that form Hong Kong, and over the next thirty years he was to be the most considerable political figure in the colony.[23] Ho had spent ten years in England, where he studied medicine and law, becoming a member both of the Royal College of Surgeons and of Lincoln's Inn, and taking an English wife before returning to the colony enthusiastic about British constitutional and social ideas, but dedicated to presenting a Chinese point of view. He had been suggested as a member of the Legislative Council at the early age of twenty-five, and was only thirty-one when appointed in 1890. But for the moment, in spite of the Board also having as a member Dr Manson, the distinguished parasitologist, founder of the London School of Tropical Medicine, who had already identified the causes of elephantiasis and was to pioneer the research into those of malaria, very little was done. It seemed that the Chinese themselves would prefer to live in insanitary conditions, rather than pay higher rents and face inspections: certainly forty-seven of them petitioned against any form of regulation.

In 1879 Mrs Cumming had been horrified by the primitive standards of hygiene in the colony, writing that

> no sort of effective drains or sewers have been provided ... whatever sewerage finds its way [into rain-water conduits] is simply deposited along the whole harbour front, thus poisoning what else might be a pleasant situation ... as regards all that is generally understood by the term 'sanitary arrangements' ... all such necessary matters are provided for in a manner primitive in the extreme; and the arrangements for the daily (or among the poorer classes only bi-weekly!) removal of nuisances from every house (for subsequent conveyance to the mainland as an article of agricultural commerce) form a very unpleasant page in the sanitary statistics of Her Majesty's empire.[24]

It was not until 1889, seven years after the Chadwick report, that even the most basic action was taken to amend sanitation, and then only at the instigation of the Colonial Office. The Crown Lands Resumption Ordinance of that year gave powers of compulsory purchase in order 'to facilitate a contemplated experiment having for its object a permanent improvement in the sanitary condition of the town. A large part of the population is densely crowded in houses which are without yards or windows at the back, and which as regards five-sixths of the rooms are in perpetual and complete darkness.' But even if the experiment was not successful, Des Voeux felt there was no real need for concern:

> It is hoped that the cost of reconstruction and the loss of building area from the provision of 'back-yards' will be largely compensated by demand for the improved dwellings. If the event should prove otherwise the project need not be pushed further; but I apprehend that it would be worth some cost to the public to get rid of a grave scandal and a serious danger to the public health by the only method yet suggested which would not cause widespread distrust and discontent among the Chinese population.

At all events the Europeans were safe, for in the previous year the European District Reservation Ordinance had been published. A petition from foreign residents had characterized as a 'crying evil which demands instant removal' that 'such a concourse of Natives should be allowed to collect in such close propinquity to European Residents'.[25]

The evil was remedied by the Ordinance reserving the higher central part of the town 'not for exclusively European occupation, but for houses built according to European models'. This somewhat shame-faced attempt at racial segregation was hedged about with numerous explanations: 'No opposition was offered . . . on the part of the Chinese, possibly because they themselves prefer to be segregated from Europeans.' It was for the good of the Chinese themselves that Europeans should live in Hong Kong, 'For, though possessed of many valuable characteristics, [they] are still, and likely to be for a long time to come, lacking in some of the qualities that are essential for true progress.' They were used to 'close packing in houses . . . the normal condition of all classes among them'. They 'have, probably by a long process of natural selection, become inured and insensible to the con-ditions inseparable from extreme density of population'. And, after all, if they wanted to live in European areas, 'there is nothing in the Ordi-nance to prevent them from doing so'.[26]

But Nemesis was at hand. In 1894 plague struck Hong Kong, part of a great pandemic that swept through Asia. It had been preceded by a violent outbreak in Canton, when more than a hundred thousand were reported to have died. The onset of the plague found Hong Kong a society deeply divided between traditional Chinese and modern British, with only a very few of the Western-educated Chinese begin-ning to appreciate the advantages of a scientific approach to public health. At that time the causes of plague were only beginning to be understood, but by an ironical coincidence the *bacillus pestis* was identi-fied that year in Hong Kong by the Japanese doctors Aoyama and Kitasato. Japan had already begun to make important scientific dis-coveries at a time when Chinese science was still half a millennium behind the times.

Although rats were suspected, but not proven, to be the carriers of the disease, what was certain was that insanitary overcrowding was highly conducive to its quick spread, and that Hong Kong offered some of the best possible examples of such conditions. If they had done little to prevent the outbreak, the Hong Kong government set about dealing with it briskly enough, in the best traditions of paternal-istic colonial rule. Volunteer parties of soldiers, some of whom were to die from the plague, went to the worst areas to remove corpses and to disinfect and whitewash affected houses; emergency isolation hospitals, including a floating hospital ship, were prepared, and every-thing possible was done to control the disease. 'Unfortunately, how-

ever,' as the Governor reported, 'the Chinese do not see things with
European eyes,' and neither Des Voeux nor his officials made any
attempt to see things through Chinese eyes.[27] Des Voeux left Hong
Kong in May 1891 – for eighteen years of pleasant retirement, which
suggests that his frequent ill-health cannot have been too serious.

His successor, Sir William Robinson, showed every indication of
outright hostility to Chinese customs and ideas. Robinson had come
to this, his last post, the hard way. He joined the Colonial Service as
a boy clerk – not having been to university – and made the rare
transition to Colonial Governor. His career had been passed in London
and the West Indies, and he had no experience or knowledge of China.
Throughout his stay in Hong Kong he displayed a formidable insensitivity; the tone of his dispatches indicates the assumption of European
superiority which was to characterize his period in office. Sir William
explained the Chinese reluctance to co-operate with his preventative
measures:

> Educated to insanitary habits, and accustomed from infancy to
> herd together, they were unable to grasp the necessity of segre-
> gation; they were quite content to die like sheep, spreading disease
> around them as long as they were left undisturbed ... These
> feelings, no doubt the result of blind prejudice and superstition,
> naturally prompted concealment which eventually necessitated the
> organization of search parties and a system of house-to-house
> visitation. Harrowing tales are told of how, upon a search party
> entering a house in which there were cases of sickness, every
> possible means of evasion and concealment was hurriedly devised
> ... Never was Chinese ingenuity put to so sore a test, or exercised
> in such a pitiable cause.'[28]

Nor did the Chinese have any confidence in the government's hospital
treatment, preferring traditional Chinese remedies, which were almost
entirely useless. Not that Western medicine had discovered an effective
treatment for the plague, as opposed to preventative measures, but 82
per cent of infected Chinese died, compared to only 18 per cent of
Europeans. In this crisis of conflicting cultures the Tung Wah Hospital
Committee was able to intervene. Since its inception in 1872 the Committee had been too successful for its own popularity. With the encouragement of Sir John Pope Hennessy it had almost assumed the
functions of the Registrar-General, who was also Protector of the

Chinese. Hennessy, with a good deal of logic, saw the absurdity of having a single official (who did not, as it then happened, even understand the language) entrusted with the welfare of the great majority of the population, which ought to be the most pressing concern of the whole administration. But Hennessy announcing that the Tung Wah hall was a place where he had 'often taken counsel with my Chinese friends as to what would be the best course to adopt for this colony' was enough to ensure a surly response from the European community, who saw this as none of the Tung Wah's business; they had 'taken over the responsibilities that the Registrar-General was meant to fulfil' and were acting as 'Advisor-General' to the government. When Hennessy left William Marsh, who had been at daggers drawn with the Governor, succeeded in reinstating the office of Registrar-General, and appointing a cadet officer with good Cantonese to the post.

Again with Hennessy's support, the Hospital Committee had established a sister-organization, the Po Leung Kuk, the 'Protect Virtue Association'. Its purpose was to protect women and children from being kidnapped for sale, usually into prostitution, and it quickly became something very like an alternative legal system: 'the Po Leung Kuk directors aspired for mandarin costumes, wearing long gowns and hats with imperial feathers . . . The directors judged cases in the same manner as Qing mandarins did in imperial courts, but they took place mostly at night, with at least two directors present. Before the hearing started, all concerned would be escorted into the Kuk by the Kuk detectives.'[29] Only after the directors had recorded their verdict was the case passed on to the Registrar-General for action. Such a system was far more likely to be effective in difficult cases than the British courts, but was not popular with the British community, who appreciated nothing of the frustrations of their Chinese fellow-colonists.

The Governor and his senior officials inevitably spent most of their time in the company of a small number of the most prominent European citizens, at receptions, garden parties, the races, the club, cricket matches and games of lawn-tennis, musical and theatrical performances, and all the tea- and dinner-parties that made up colonial social life. No Chinese was encountered in this restricted society (and few lower-class British, for that matter). The Hongkong Club, the Jockey Club (founded in 1884), the Victoria Recreation Club (1872) and the Amateur Dramatic Corps (1844) had not a single Chinese member between them; even the Freemasons, supposedly dedicated to promoting the brotherhood of man, originally set their faces against admitting

Chinese. Under these circumstances there was not much chance of any official being left in ignorance of the European community's sentiments, but contacts with the Chinese were much more limited, and were almost entirely confined to matters of business, on which the interests of all races were likely to be identical. The Chinese members of the Legislative Council should have been able to present a Chinese view, but since such men as Ho Ch'i were themselves deeply concerned in business they tended to follow the same line as their European counterparts.

In such circumstances it was only reluctantly that Robinson co-operated with the Tung Wah Committee on controlling the plague. The Governor would not back down on house-to-house visitation, which was indeed absolutely necessary, as the more reasonable Tung Wah members agreed, but devised a plan

> which, however undesirable it may have been from a medical point of view, was fully justified by the urgency of the occasion and by circumstances generally. I allude to the establishment of a temporary plague hospital under the management of Chinese doctors belonging to the staff of the Tung Wa native hospital . . . The Chinese sick had now the choice of European or native treatment, and although many elected in favour of the former, the vast majority preferred to be attended by their own countrymen.

But little could be done about other injured susceptibilities; with so great a number of deaths 'the burying parties had to dispose of the dead by burying the coffins in trenches . . . a great shock to the feelings of a people whose chief form of religion consists in the rites and ceremonies of burial, and in the annual worship of the dead'. Robinson found it impossible to understand the horror with which this prospect was viewed. Most of the Chinese population were born outside the colony, and desperately wanted to return home to die in the bosom of their ancestors; the Governor saw this only as a sure method of spreading the plague further. Restrictions of movement had been the only method of control since medieval times; the strict quarantine of the lazaretto was still enforced, on pain of death, in those Mediterranean countries where plague was to be expected. Since Canton was quite as badly affected as Hong Kong such restrictions might have seemed unnecessary, but Robinson believed the Chinese request for plague victims to be allowed to leave the colony 'a most preposterous demand,

and all the more so seeing that it was made by a deputation of Chinese gentlemen who should have known better than to make it'. Sir J.F. Brenan, the Consul-General at Canton, 'incensed' at Robinson's attitude, attempted to argue the Chinese case in vain: 'The attitude in Hong Kong seemed to be that any deference to Chinese sentiment was a reflection on Western medical science . . . and as usual the Hong Kong press had stigmatized any tenderness towards Chinese feelings or religious conviction as selling the British birthright in Hong Kong.'[30]

But Robinson's hand was forced: he recorded that, on being refused permission to go, 'the Chinese retaliated by leaving the colony en masse. Compradores, contractors, shroffs, tradesmen, domestic servants, and coolies all joined together in a general exodus altogether numbering some 100,000 persons.' The refugees made their way to Canton, where anti-foreign hysteria was rampant: doctors were accused of removing the eyes from newly born children to make plague medicines, and placards were displayed 'accusing the Government of every kind of atrocity and inciting the people to take vengeance on the foreigners'. A controlled evacuation had therefore to be arranged, under medical supervision, with specially equipped junks taking plague sufferers to Canton, where it was piously trusted they would be confined in isolation hospitals.

In these anxious exchanges the Tung Wah Committee found itself caught in the crossfire. Not only the colonial administration but the scientifically-informed Chinese accused them of appeasing 'the angry, ignorant and riotous mobs composed of the coolie classes', and pandering to 'ignorance, fanaticism and ridiculous jealousy'. From the other side the Chinese masses, ready to believe anything of the foreigners (including their removal of plague corpses in order to be ground up for medicine for the British royal family), attempted to lynch the Committee's chairman when he admitted the necessity for some sanitary control.

With the cooler weather of autumn the plague subsided, only to recur with varying levels of intensity in the succeeding years. The worst-affected spot, Tai-ping-shan, was compulsorily purchased for redevelopment, at the considerable cost of $821,000, but trouble was created when the Sanitary Board attempted further reforms.[31] Four years previously, in 1891, byelaws had been passed requiring lodging houses, which were much used by immigrant coolies, to be registered so that some degree of sanitary control could be exercised. Registration of any sort was anathema to the Chinese, who saw it as an inevitable preliminary to taxes, squeezes and other interferences. So many objections had consequently been raised by the Chinese community, led by Ho Ch'i, that the byelaws had been quietly shelved. This policy of peace at any price had been drastically amended by the plague, and it was announced that the regulations were to be once again enforced.

One lesson of the plague had been learnt, and three months were therefore spent explaining the purposes of registration, and attempting to convince suspicious coolies that no wicked plot was afoot. In spite of these efforts, no registrations were forthcoming, and when it was decided 'to enforce the law without further parley', the response was a strike in the harbour. This quickly developed into a full-blown stoppage, involving over twenty thousand workers and bringing the movement of goods to a halt. Unlike the previous harbour strike, directed against French interests, or attempts to improve pay, this was the first large-scale example of action clearly aimed at influencing the Hong Kong government to change its policies. Governor Robinson correctly, if over-excitedly, described it: 'It was perfectly clear that the strike was not an economical one, but was in fact nothing short of a rebellion against the law and the Government.' The Chamber of Commerce was alarmed: 'the Chinese, no doubt, are children. But parents do not discuss with children; they simply say that this or that is to be done, and they insist on it being done.' Nevertheless they attempted to negotiate directly with the strikers, but the confident Robinson refused to accept their proposed compromise, and pushed for complete victory, which was achieved by the simple expedient of engaging other coolies – always plentiful on the mainland – at slightly increased wages. He complacently reported that 'the strikers, the coolie class, who were beginning to think that they held the reins of power, have received an object lesson which, it may be hoped, they will not forget.'

The whole episode had two informative features; it typified the British approach to multi-cultural problems, and marked a stage in the emergence of popular sentiment as a factor in Hong Kong politics. A thorough-going cultural imperialism would have ridden roughshod over what could be seen, with justification, as irrational objections to unquestionably improved practices: it is not easy to imagine a French, American or German administration showing the same tolerance, weary and superior as it undoubtedly was. But the British administrators had learnt in India that other people's sensibilities were only offended at a cost: a British officer accused of disrespect towards a

Muslim ceremony could be (and was) cashiered. As previously the
mandarins at Canton would go out of their way to avoid an upset, so
Colonial Secretaries and Governors would know when blind eyes
needed to be turned. At the same time it was felt that the Chinese
really should not be allowed to conduct their lives according to 'blind
prejudice and superstition', and that standards of education in the
English language and Western methods must be improved.

A vital step in this direction was taken by Dr Manson when in 1887
he founded the College of Medicine. This had been made possible by
the opening that year of Ho Ch'i's Alice Memorial Hospital, from
whose staff the instructors were drawn and where the facilities for
clinical study were provided. Manson had no illusions about the primitive state of Chinese medicine, but he had the sensitivity, so noticeably
lacking in the British officials, to appreciate that this could not be
remedied by attitudes of sneering superiority. It may have been true
that in Chinese medicine:

> The notions on Anatomy and Physiology are absurd; there is no
> Surgery worthy of the name; medicines they have in abundance
> but there is no knowledge of their action or of the diagnosis or
> pathology of disease ... there is nowadays nothing like original
> observation and thought ... but a persistent effort to make facts
> tally with fancies.

But Westerners could hardly expect an attentive audience for instruction when they so often committed

> the vulgar folly of confounding ignorance with folly, knowledge
> with wisdom ... We swagger before them and by word and
> manner say to the Chinese we would have follow us – 'You are
> a pack of fools. All these things you revere are arrant humbug;
> your ancestral worship, your literature, your talk of filial piety,
> your paternal Government ... are mere foolishness, superstition
> and vain words. Whereas, look at us – our steamships, our iron-
> clads, our railways, electric telegraphs, industrial machines, parlia-
> mentary government, free press and what not ... Are we not
> Gods and you a kind of idiots.[32]

Manson's college was a deserved success, and one of its earliest graduates was the first President of the Chinese Republic, Dr Sun Yat-sen.

Another move in the right direction, in which both Ho Ch'i and
Manson were involved, was made the following year with the introduc-
tion of an elective element into the Sanitary Board. This institution,
ineffective and limited in powers as it was, did constitute the first Hong
Kong official body to include some democratically elected members.
The first electorate, in June 1888, consisted of all ratepayers on the
jury rolls, 'all good and sufficient persons . . . not ignorant of the
English language', whatever their race: inevitably this included some
Chinese. The first two elections were lively, and although the first
produced a disappointing turnout – 187 from a list of 669 voted – in
the second, in 1891, 492 votes were cast from an electorate that cannot
have exceeded 738. It seemed as though a genuinely democratic (within
the British interpretation of local franchise, which was then similarly
confined to ratepayers) municipal authority might emerge. But however
limited the franchise, it was probable that it would not be long before
the number of Chinese electors outnumbered the British. At that time
there was no absolute restriction for the franchise on grounds of race
in British colonies (apartheid came later, and there were easier
methods of retaining control): Jamaica, Honduras and Mauritius all
had black voters with the same rights as whites.

Hong Kong, however, it was once again agreed, was different. Sir
Cecil Clementi, Governor in the 1920s, was to say: 'This colony is so
small and compact that it is in effect a large township, and the Government of Hong Kong is and must always be mainly concerned with
municipal affairs. I regard myself as being in effect Mayor of Hong
Kong.'[33] Sir George Bowen, like Margaret Thatcher a century later,
compared the task of governing Hong Kong to that of running a county
council; but it would have been a county council poised on the per-
imeter of a vast and potentially hostile empire, to which the great
majority of the voters owed some form of allegiance.

The European members of the community continued however to
press for a higher degree of self-government, with the support from
London of the successor to the East India and China Association, the
China Association. This body, chiefly composed of those who had
returned from Hong Kong and Shanghai, emerged as the most powerful lobby dedicated to persuading British governments to support what
were considered to be the British commercial interests in China. In
Hong Kong terms the Association was remarkable in that it marked
the end of a long feud. Alfred Dent, who as a junior in the old Dent
Hong had been forced to leave Shanghai after the collapse of 1866,

had found his way to the top as Sir Alfred Dent, Chairman of the British North Borneo Company, and sat amicably together on the Board of the China Association with the Jardine Taipans. These were then, and remain, the Keswick family, descendants of Jean Jardine, sister of the founder, Dr William. The message of the London China lobby, and of the Shanghai and Hong Kong Chambers of Commerce, had not changed much in half a century, in spite of the disappointing British exports to China between 1875 and 1895:

Year	£,000
1875	6,340
1880	6,382
1885	6,396
1890	6,357
1895	5,518

These astonishingly static results hid an increase in dollar terms, due to the variations in exchange, but the incontrovertible fact remained that China still took less than one third of the amount of British exports as Holland. The remedy, according to the manufacturers and merchants, remained the same – only do away with all restrictions and trade would boom. They did not explain how, during the same period, Japan had managed to increase her sales to China from £746,000 to £2,794,000.

They had to admit that Hong Kong itself was not doing badly, but claimed that the colony was suffering at the hands of a British government which did not understand its peculiar problems (it was not the last time that this complaint was to be heard!). Hong Kong, it was argued, was essential to the success of foreign trade in China, and as such should be regarded as an asset of the Empire, to be paid for by the Imperial government. Instead, locals were mulcted to the general benefit without having any real voice, and certainly without being able to take effective action. An annual contribution of £20,000 towards the colony's defence costs had been agreed as far back as 1863, but this was unilaterally increased by £56,000 in 1884 and £60,375 in the following year in order to pay for Sargent's new fortifications. In order to meet these costs the Hong Kong government had to float a loan, which it was forced to do in sterling, although its income was in dollars. This came at a bad time from Hong Kong's point of view, for the rate of exchange between the dollar and sterling had worsened significantly with a drop in silver prices. Then in 1889 London decided that the annual contribution should be doubled, pointing out that this represented only 17 per cent of the increased colonial revenue, and therefore restored the original value, which had been fixed at 16 per cent of annual revenue. The colonists, led by Thomas Whitehead, manager of the Hong Kong branch of the Chartered Bank, did not think much to this argument, and accepted the proposal only on certain conditions. These included the reinforcement of the garrison by British troops; in the event Indian sepoys were sent. Even Sir Francis Fleming, caretaker Governor in Des Voeux's absence, felt that Whitehall was being neither frank nor open. Great indignation ensued, and the unofficial members of the Legislative Council were unanimous in opposing the increases, voting to reduce the official's salaries as a measure of their discontent.

On the question of what might be done the unanimity was less complete. When a petition was dispatched to London it was supported by Whitehead, Ho Ch'i and Chater, but not by the two other unofficial members, Jardine's James Keswick and E.R. Belilios, the foremost opium trader in the colony. The petition referred to 'the common right of Englishmen' to manage their local affairs and control the expenditure of the colony where imperial considerations were not involved – thus revealing the inconsistencies in the colonists' arguments. The unfortunate facts were that the latest census indicated a population of 221,400, of whom 211,000 were Chinese. Of the remainder only 1450 were British, and of these only eight hundred would have been entitled to a vote on the basis of adult male suffrage. There was no possibility of a British government allowing the destinies of nearly a quarter of a million people to be decided by so small an oligarchy; Hong Kong would be much better off, decided the Colonial Secretary, Lord Ripon, as a Crown Colony, 'under which, as far as possible no distinction is made of rank or race, than by a representation which would leave the bulk of the population wholly unrepresented'.[34]

Ripon had addressed the petition with some care, observing that under the protection of the British government Hong Kong had become a Chinese rather than a British community, and was rapidly becoming more so. He did agree that unofficial representation on the Executive Council would be justified, but warned the petitioners that they should not necessarily expect that this should be European. In fact in a letter to Robinson, the Colonial Secretary suggested that there should be two members, one of whom should be Chinese. Robinson shied away in horror from this; the Chinese did not understand representative government, and no suitable candidates existed. Before finality could be reached, Ripon had been replaced by Joseph Chamberlain, who decided that there should be another unofficial member of the Legislative Council, dropping a strong hint that he should be Chinese, and that two unofficial members should be appointed to the Executive Council, to be chosen purely on merit, without regard to class or race. Not surprisingly, they turned out to be Mr Bell-Irving of Jardine's, and Paul Chater.

II

A SLIGHT EXTENSION TO THE
COLONY OF HONG KONG

A suitable occasion for action

The island of Hong Kong and the peninsula of Kowloon had both been ceded outright by China and were, at least as far as the British were concerned, a permanent part of the possessions of the Crown. The third constituent part of the colony, that much larger area known as the New Territories, was granted in 1898 only on a ninety-nine-year lease, a fact which has complicated, and which continues to complicate, the subsequent history of Hong Kong.

Historians are unanimous in their condemnation of Western countries' behaviour in China towards the end of the nineteenth century,[1] but the view from Hong Kong was rather different. At the start of 1894 it seemed as though China might once more be set on the road to stability. After the suppression of the Taipings there had been thirty years of something approaching normality; the internal reformers loosely grouped around Li Hung-chang – 'the Chinese Bismarck', according to his admirers – had brought about some steps towards a modern economy, with railways, cotton mills, steamship lines and a fleet which, on paper, was capable of standing against any likely aggressor; the Emperor's brother Prince Kung had established normal channels of diplomatic communication between the Tsungli Yamen and foreign governments; and Sir Robert Hart had made the Customs Service into an incorruptible and reliable source of government revenue. Apart from the Russian seizure in the 1870s of the border province of Ili, from which they were only dislodged after much negotiation, including the cession of a considerable extent of not-very-valuable territory, and the payment of an indemnity, Chinese borders had remained essentially intact. The Ryuku Islands were annexed by the Japanese in 1879, but the Chinese claim to the archipelago had never been convincing. The Portuguese gained official recognition of their occupation of Macao, which after 350 years of *de facto* presence was hardly a matter of great moment; and the French conquests in Indo-China and the British annexation of Upper Burma were theoretical rather than practical intrusions on Chinese sovereignty, being in reality the transfer of a vassalage from a Chinese suzerain who did not exercise his powers to French and Indian ones who did. Britain, although not much use in fending off French aggressions, had sided with the Ch'ing in discouraging foreign depredations, having secured a commanding position in the China trade which weighed British interests on the side of maintaining stability. Tseng Chi-tse, the Marquis Tseng, on his retirement from the post of Chinese Minister in Britain, felt able to write in 1886: 'Each encounter [with the French] and especially the last has, in teaching China her weakness, also discovered her strength,' and to forecast that China would soon be able to 'denounce' those treaties which referred to 'the alienation of Sovereign dominion over that part of the territory comprised in foreign settlements at the treaty ports, as well as in some other respects'.[2]

But such confidence was misplaced; the reactionary Dowager Empress still held power, acting as regent first for her son, T'ung-chi (Tongzhi), then for her nephew, Kuang-hsu (Guangxu). Huge sums were diverted from defence projects into the expenses of the Imperial Court, including the building of a new and lavish Summer Palace outside Peking; except in Hart's domain bribery and corruption continued to flourish – Li was said to have made an immense illegal fortune – and reformers were outnumbered by conservatives, complacent in times of relative quiet and hysterical when things began to go amiss.

Across the Strait of Korea the changes were much more real. Japan had undergone a similar uncomfortable exposure to Western pressures; treaties had been agreed, but not ratified, foreigners murdered, retaliations made, indemnities levied, and a strenuous rearguard action against Western encroachments fought by the Imperial Court. But it took only a decade after the first American treaty was signed for final agreements to be reached with Japan, after the collapse of the Tokugawa Shogunate and the accession of the young Emperor Mutsihito. The new reign, the Meiji, the Enlightened Government, transformed

Japan from a feudal to a modern state in a single generation, and a modern state as bent on expansion as any European power.

A foretaste of what was to come was given in 1874, when the Japanese occupied Formosa, from which they were dislodged after the protests of the British Minister at Peking, Sir Thomas Wade. Twenty years later, after a number of Sino–Japanese incidents in the independent kingdom of Korea, Japan manufactured a suitable pretext, not to declare war, but to open hostilities without that formality by sinking a British ship carrying Chinese troops to Korea. When, in spite of attempts by the Western powers to avert it, war ensued, the result was sharp and decisive. Within a matter of months the Ch'ing naval and military forces were decisively defeated, a defeat to a fair extent due to the siphoning off of defence monies to private corruption. Hart discovered that 36 million taels had been thus diverted, with the result that the navy 'have no shells for the Krupps, and no powder for the Armstrongs'.[3]

It was Li, who had benefited richly himself from such corrupt activities, who was left to discuss matters with the Japanese Prince Ito Hirobumi. Their recorded conversation on 20 March 1895 is revealing: Li suggested that China and Japan 'ought vigorously to maintain the general stability of Asia, and establish perpetual peace and harmony between ourselves, so that our Asiatic yellow race will not be encroached upon by the white race of Europe'. But Ito queried why China had been slow to modernize: 'Ten years ago, when I was at Tientsin, I talked about reform with the Grand Secretary [Li]. Why is it that up to now not a single thing had been changed or reformed? This I deeply regret.'[4] Li could hardly answer this satisfactorily, and Ito was too much of a gentleman to recall that, as a young samurai, he had condescended to take a berth before the mast on a British ship from Japan to London, where he had learnt the language and customs of the West.

Such an action would have been unthinkable to a Chinese of similar rank, and goes a long way towards explaining why Japan had adapted so much more effectively than China. By 1895 Japan had so progressed in achieving an acceptable rule of law that the British volunteered to cancel the extra-territorial privileges that had been written into the earlier treaties: it was to be another thirty-five years before this was done in China.

The Treaty of Shimonoseki (April 1895), which Li and Ito negotiated, was extremely harsh, making far greater demands on China than any of the Western powers had formerly exacted. All of Formosa, the Pescadore Islands and the Liautung peninsula of Manchuria were ceded to Japan and an indemnity of 230 million taels demanded – more than ten times that paid to Britain in the terms of the Treaty of Nanking. Great indignation was aroused in China by the treaty, which was felt as a gross humiliation. In particular Liautung was a part of the Imperial heartland, and not much more than a hundred miles across the bay from the Peking province of Chihli. In all probability its loss would have meant the downfall of the dynasty, but this was averted by the intervention of the Russians, who had their own eyes on the territory. With the assistance of France and Germany, Japan was persuaded, in return for an extra indemnity, to concede that Liautung should remain Chinese: but there was a price expected for this helpful intercession.

This was the first occasion on which Germany had taken an active interest in Far Eastern affairs. Bismarck, who powerfully influenced German policies until 1890, was not particularly enthusiastic about colonies, but when the inexperienced, ebullient and slightly deranged young Emperor, Kaiser Wilhelm II, dropped the pilot and took over erratically personal control of policy, colonial expansion was the order of the day, and China was seen as presenting exciting opportunities for the new German *Weltpolitik*.

It was however Russia which was the prime mover in extorting concessions from the Ch'ing government. The rapid expansion eastwards of the Russian Empire in the nineteenth century reached the Amur River, where the town of Nicholaievsk was founded in 1850. Eight years later, as part of the settlements reached at Tientsin, Russia gained a huge area running seven hundred miles from the Amur to the new city of Vladivostok ('Lord of the East'), which brought Russia to the borders of both Korea and Japan. The ultimate prize, an ice-free port, which had eluded the Russians in Europe, was gained as the price for their promised assistance to China against the Japanese. The agreement reached between Li and the Russians Prince Lobanov and Count Witte on 3 June 1896 was meant to be secret, but was widely leaked at the time. It provided for common action to be taken against Japan should there be an attack on either Russia or China (including Korea), and allowed Russian ships to use any Chinese port; immediate permission was given for the Russians to extend their railway, which had followed their advance from Moscow, to Vladivostok.

Russia's success stimulated a German initiative. Admiral Tirpitz, closely following the progress of the Sino–Japanese War, had already been convinced of the need for a coaling and victualling station, and identified Kiau-chou Bay and Mirs Bay as suitable. The latter, only fifteen miles north-east of Kowloon, was too close to Hong Kong to be acceptable, and Kiau-chou, with the town of Tsingtao, was selected as a suitable German foothold. The German Minister in Peking was instructed in November 1896 'to direct his special attention to bring about a suitable occasion for action'.[5] This was not too long in coming, since the convenient murder of a pair of missionaries the following November provided the pretext for dispatching a German fleet on 18 December 1897 with instructions from the Kaiser to demand recompense, 'if necessary, with the most brutal ruthlessness'. The hyperbole that accompanied the ultimatum indicated the magnitude of German ambitions: 'The German Michael has planted his shield with the device of the German eagle upon the soil of China,' the Kaiser declared, to be answered by the Admiral, Prince Henry (who had so much enjoyed Sir John Pope Hennessy's butter seventeen years before): 'The aim that draws me on, is to declare in foreign lands the gospel of your Majesty's hallowed person, to preach to everyone who will hear it, and also to those who will not hear it.'[6]

This was the signal for all the other powers to move in; Count Witte of Russia saw it as 'a favourable opportunity for us to seize one of the Chinese ports, notably Port Arthur [Lüshun]', and agreed with the French not to object to their own demand for Kwang-chou. Both Port Arthur, with the nearby commercial port of Talien-wan, and Tsingtao were promptly seized by Russia and Germany respectively. Subsequent negotiations led to these areas being granted by China on leases, and it was the terms of these which were used as precedents for the British expansion of Hong Kong. The land granted to Germany included the whole area of Kiau-chou Bay, together with the adjacent islands, for ninety-nine years. In addition a fifty-kilometre zone was established which was to remain under Chinese sovereignty, but to be garrisoned by German troops and to be governed with German approval. The Russian lease was for only twenty-five years, but restricted access to Port Arthur to Russian and Chinese ships only, although Talien-wan (also known as Lüda, Dalien or Dalny), was to be open to all. A similar security zone was established which remained Chinese, but under Russian control.

Both these agreements were reached in March 1898, and in the following month the French were able to announce that they had secured a lease of Kwang-chou Bay as a naval station. Once again this was for a period of ninety-nine years, and extended for a distance of thirty-five nautical miles from the port.

None of this was at all to the liking of the British government, which saw these armed interventions as gravely threatening the stability of the region. Gladstone, discouraged by the implacable opposition of the House of Lords to his proposals for Irish Home Rule, had been succeeded as Prime Minister in 1894 by Lord Rosebery, who struggled on against the opposition of the peers until defeated on a vote of confidence on the very secondary topic of cordite supplies. In 1895 a Conservative administration took office which was to hold power, first under Lord Salisbury and then Arthur Balfour, for the next eleven years. For the first nine of these the post of Colonial Secretary was held by Joseph Chamberlain, who proved to be the most influential politician ever to hold that office, and who exercised an influence far beyond the usual confines of the post. In other parts of the world, notably Africa, Chamberlain's policy was aggressively expansionist, but in China the Conservative government could reasonably claim to have no territorial ambitions.

What was believed to be of importance remained the potential China trade. As developing industrial countries sheltered their products by tariffs, British exports met with increasing resistance. Iron and steel exports increased only modestly (from £32 million to £38 million) in the twenty years between 1880 and 1900, while textiles, which still represented considerably the most important sector, actually fell (from c.£104 million to c.£97 million) in the same period, at a time when other countries' production was forging ahead. In China a free market still existed, and one in which Britain had a commanding lead, being by far the biggest of China's trading partners: in 1898 56.4 per cent of the customs revenue came from duties levied on British goods, while Russia contributed 1.63 per cent and France 2.49 per cent: of a total foreign trade of 378 million taels, 234 million was with Britain, the rest of Europe's share, including both France and Germany, being only 35 million. Only Japan and the United States were beginning to increase their share of the market in any significant quantities.

To put that market's economic importance to Britain in perspective, however, in 1898 only about 1.5 per cent of all British exports went to China. Even when the total of Chinese imports from all British possessions, including Hong Kong, was included – and opium still formed a respectable proportion of these – China still took a smaller value of British exports than did Holland; the total value had hardly increased in a quarter of a century. The China Association, however, argued, as it had done for all that period, that the potential was enormous; at a time when Argentina had more than six thousand miles of railways, China had only 340. Growing increasingly agitated at the success of foreign governments in forcing concessions from China, the Association's members in London and abroad badgered their own administration with a series of intemperate recommendations. Mr Keswick, of Jardine's, said that all the maritime provinces of China should be claimed as a British sphere: 'we had the might, therefore we had the right'. Thomas Whitehead, of the Chartered Bank and a member of the Legislative Council, wanted to send a telegram to the Foreign Office: 'Growing unrest seething mass discontent throughout China, impossible indefinitely avert serious outbreaks, position urgently requires the presence of a mobile column of British troops in Weihaiwei [in Shantung province] or Hong Kong,' but what would really be preferable was the occupation of the entire Yangtse valley, working alongside the local authorities and ignoring the Peking government. Those members who had seats in the House of Commons proposed that 'if necessary Great Britain should be prepared to go to war in order to maintain her predominant position in China'.

There were pressing economic reasons for this near-hysteria, for King Cotton was declining, and the heartland of the industrial revolution moving into recession. Exports of cotton goods fell from £75,564,000 in 1880, to £69,751,000 in 1900: European countries, which had formerly processed less than two-thirds of the quantity of raw cotton imported into Britain, had increased their intake to more than double that of Britain. Only India and China remained predominantly British markets, and, ominously, China had opened her first cotton mill in 1891. An official letter embodying the Association's anxiety was sent to the government on 13 July. R.S. Gundry, the Association's Secretary, privately attempting to persuade F.L. Bertie of the Foreign Office to adopt a more belligerent attitude, put forward the interesting suggestion that 'the best way would be to find a Ming claimant and set him up "counter" at Nanking'.[7]

There was never any possibility that a British government would take these proposals seriously. Bertie, later Lord Bertie of Thame and British Ambassador to France throughout the First World War, unequivocally rebutted such reckless and irresponsible ideas: 'Never,' he reported, 'would the Government consent to such action.' Little encouragement had ever been given to suppose they might. Arthur Balfour, then leader in the Commons, in a speech made in January 1898 specified that 'our interests in China are not territorial: they are commercial . . . territory, insofar as it is not necessary to supply a base for possible warlike operations, is a disadvantage rather than an advantage'. Sir Michael Hicks Beach, Chancellor of the Exchequer, followed that within a week by proclaiming a 'Monroe Doctrine for China': 'We do not regard China as a place for conquest or acquisition by any European Power. We look upon it as a place, the most hopeful place, of the future for the commerce of our country and the commerce of the world at large.' A debate was held in the House of Commons in March of that year on the proposal 'That it is of vital importance for British commerce and influence that the independence of Chinese territory should be maintained.' Replying for the government, George Curzon, the Under-Secretary of State for Foreign Affairs, stated that 'The Government have no difficulty in accepting the motion . . . the integrity and independence of China . . . may be considered to be the cardinal bases of our policy . . . We are opposed to the alienation of any portion of Chinese territory, or the sacrifice of any part of Chinese independence.'[8]

All this hardly betokened much enthusiasm for imperialist expansion on the part of Britain, but even as Curzon was speaking the actions of other European powers in China were forcing the pace, and the Under-Secretary was obliged to warn the House that if circumstances changed another policy might be needed, although it remained the case that 'the seizure of Chinese territory, the alienation of Chinese territory, the usurpation of Chinese sovereignty, is not primarily part of British policy'. In short order this proved to be so, when in spite of Curzon's words the British felt themselves forced to reply to what was perceived as a Russian threat. Lord Salisbury, doubling as Prime Minister and Foreign Secretary, took charge of the negotiations himself, and handled them blunderingly. He failed to reach agreement with any of the other powers, and could not persuade China to withdraw the concessions made to Germany, France or Russia. Last in the queue, therefore, the British looked for some titbits to balance the advantages gained by the others.[9] The Chinese suggested that Britain might consider Weihaiwei, not far from the Germans in Kiau-chou. At first Salisbury declined, on the grounds that it was not British policy to accept the alienation of Chinese territory, but when it became clear that the other European powers were not going to be moved, the offer was unenthusiastically accepted, 'for a period as long as Port Arthur shall remain in the possession of Russia'. At the same time China was asked to agree to an extension of the boundaries of Hong Kong.

The lease hath all too short a date

Arguments in favour of this had first been advanced by General Sargent in 1884, but were turned down in London, the feeling being that if trouble did break out any territory that was needed for defence could be acquired without difficulty by the simple expedient of taking it, since the fighting would either be with the Chinese, or, more likely, on their behalf. It was only when Japan proved how quickly Chinese forces could be defeated, and the European powers began to show their predatory intentions, that any urgency was felt. The General Officer Commanding, General Digby Barker, advised Sir William Robinson in 1894 that for the purpose of defence Hong Kong's boundaries should be extended to a line running from Deep Bay to Mirs Bay, including the islands within three miles from Hong Kong (approximately those eventually obtained, with the addition of Lantau island).

These considerations were reinforced by Sir Paul Chater, the remarkable Armenian financier who occupied a seat on either the Legislative or Executive Councils between 1887 and 1926. Chater had promoted the land reclamation in Central Victoria and had his eye, as had many others, on the property development potential of an expanded Kowloon. He pointed out that although China had been humiliated and defeated by Japan, 'that Empire is too intrinsically strong, too full of resources, too patient and persevering ever to remain for any length of time in her present condition', and that a move ought therefore to be made while China was still weak. Although Robinson enthusiastically pressed the case for extension, going to the lengths of suggesting that the troublesome Dr Sun Yat-sen might be surrendered to the Chinese in return – and getting his knuckles rapped for his pains – London was unresponsive. It was entirely against British policy that British territory should be increased by taking advantage of Chinese weakness; it would be immoral, and a poor example to the lesser breeds without the law. Only when the lesser breeds began throwing their weight about as aggressively as had Germany was it appreciated that things had changed, and the War Office agreed to request an extension. The British Minister at Peking, Sir Claude Mac-Donald was therefore told to approach the Tsungli Yamen to ask for compensating concessions.

Sir Claude became the object of the world's attention two years later when he organized the defence of the legations in Peking against the Boxer assault. Such bold strokes were meat and drink to Sir Claude, but as a diplomat he caused some misgivings. He had gone straight to Peking after twenty-four years in the army, rising only to the rank of major, during which he had served for nine years as a Consul-General in West Africa. That was the sum total of his diplomatic experience, while his knowledge of China was of course minimal. When the question arose of appointing him, the hero of Peking, to be the first British Ambassador to Japan, the Foreign Office was decidedly dubious. MacDonald's handling of the negotiations over the boundary extension was typically military and brisk.

He was dealing with the Tsungli Yamen at a weak point in that never terribly strong body's development. The defeat by the Japanese in 1895 had stimulated both the conservatives and the reformers at court to press their very different programmes. In June 1898 the reformers gained, for a brief period, the upper hand as the Emperor Kuang-hsu decided to exert his power and began a short-lived bid for constitutional reform. This abortive effort, which might have saved at least the bloodshed of the Boxer rebellion, and the consequent huge indemnities demanded by the foreign powers, was betrayed by the Deputy Minister of War, Yüan Shi-kai, and pitilessly crushed after only three months by the Dowager Empress. Nevertheless, the settlement reached over the Kowloon extension was not a walk-over for the British: stipulations were made by the Chinese, and accepted by the British, in a series of meetings and negotiations. On the British side, Lord Salisbury, having shot his bolt, left matters in the hands of Arthur Balfour, as leader of the House of Commons. Three major points of agreement were needed; the extent of the territory, the terms on which it was to be granted, and the question of jurisdiction within it.

From the start it was clear that the sticking point would be Kowloon city. An unsavoury collection of gaming houses, brothels and shops known as Kau Lung Gai formed the suburbs of the walled city of Kowloon, which was the fortified administrative centre of Chinese authority in the region. The Hong Kong authorities were anxious to suppress the nefarious activities in the suburbs, in which the Chinese would probably have concurred, but the walled city itself, constructed in 1847 as a counter-measure to the British in Hong Kong, was a symbol of Chinese authority, and Peking was anxious to preserve it intact.

MacDonald made it clear at the outset, on 26 April 1898, that 'negotiations would be much assisted if we grant the continuation of Chinese jurisdiction in the city of Kowloon', but Balfour insisted (28 April) that 'However much we limit our demands the town is necessary to us.'[10] The precedents were hardly helpful to the British case, since in all other leases with Western powers Chinese sovereignty had been preserved in the *cordon sanitaire*; even in Weihaiwei the Imperial officials were allowed to remain. Some fudge on the issue was needed if both Balfour and the Chinese were to be satisfied.

The extent of the land requested surprised the Tsungli Yamen, who had 'in contemplation only such a limited extension as would enable the British authorities to fortify both sides of Hong Kong Harbour and to defend the hills overlooking it'. Two sets of arguments justifying the extension had been proposed, but only one was advanced. Sir Claude did not hide his amusement at the parochialism of Hong Kong's case in his dispatch no. 225 to Lord Salisbury of 27 May 1898. The Acting Governor had sent papers containing 'sundry arguments in favour of an extension of Hong Kong territory, such as the necessity for a new rifle-range and for exercise ground for the troops, the inadequacy of cemetery accommodation at Hong Kong and the like; but in view of the fact that, as far as I could estimate, the area demanded amounted to some 200 square miles, I did not think it desirable to put forward these considerations . . . to the Yamen, for they would have met me with offers to give us all territory required for the purposes named'.

The rationale for the boundaries requested was that of the technical advances recently made in gunnery. Alfred Nobel's work on explosives, which had led to the adoption of cordite for use in British shells – as well as, indirectly, the downfall of the Liberal government – combined with developments in heavy steel forgings, had resulted in much more powerful guns (the 1893 model 9.4 Woolwich gun had a range of just under thirty thousand yards, with considerable accuracy). Construction of the railway line then under discussion between Canton and Kowloon – whether terminating in British or Chinese territory – would enable such heavy artillery easily to be transported within range. Any defensive line would therefore need to be sited much further back than the Chinese had envisaged, covering the reverse slope of the Lam Tsuen hills and the waters of Deep Bay and Tolo harbour. At the time it was not entirely clear what the British proposals were, MacDonald not having been given an agreed map, and there being confusion about the sea boundaries, but it was at least evident that the British wanted more than the Chinese expected to have to give. This comprised the mainland and islands – one of which, Lantau, was considerably larger than Hong Kong itself – within a radius of some twenty miles of Victoria Harbour, creating a land boundary of about ten miles with Imperial China.

Any cession of so large an extent of territory the Tsungli Yamen were very reluctant to agree, arguing that the British lease of Weihaiwei had already been agreed as a counter to the other foreign concessions. But Sir Claude made the point – and it is one that illustrates the essentially defensive nature of the British demands – that Weihaiwei had 'been leased to us as much in their interests as our own, and that we would give it up tomorrow if Russia would leave Port Arthur', and that as far as Hong Kong was concerned 'we should, long before this, have invited China to make over to us what was necessary for the Colony's safety had we not been afraid of setting an example to other Powers'. MacDonald also pointed out that the Germans, for very similar reasons, had been given an equally large area for the defence of their new territory of Tsingtao, and might have added that the French had demanded the same.

MacDonald had informed the British government on 28 April that 'the arrangements for the acquisition of the territory desired must be in the nature of a lease', but added what appears to be a suggestion that the arrangement might later be made more permanent: 'and it may be pointed out that British Kowloon was originally acquired by a lease'. Balfour did not demur, but hoped that the lease might be for an indefinite period, 'determinable by mutual agreement', but if this could not be managed a ninety-nine-year term 'as in the case of Kiao-chou' would be acceptable. There was a strong feeling that if an outline agreement in principle was reached the detail could be settled later; but the devil is in the details.

In the end concessions were made by the British which went some way towards satisfying the Yamen's main concerns, but aroused strong criticism from Hong Kong. The walled city of Kowloon was to remain within Chinese jurisdiction and the Kowloon landing stage was to be reserved for the use of Chinese ships, including men-of-war, which were also to be allowed to use Deep Bay and Mirs Bay. MacDonald was conscious of the fact that these concessions would not be popular in the colony, and pressed the need for the helpful co-operation of the authorities there, asking that 'every effort be made by the Hong Kong authorities to work smoothly with Chinese officials'. He also seconded Sir Robert Hart's efforts to persuade Hong Kong to be more helpful in controlling smuggling, suggesting that the colonial authorities should sign a pledge to 'take proper measures for the policing of Mirs Bay, and the other territory placed under their control, and for the prevention of smuggling'.

Hong Kong opinion was duly indignantly expressed; the Chamber of Commerce described the retention of Chinese jurisdiction in the walled city as 'tantamount to having a foreign authority exercise jurisdiction in British territory . . . absolutely without precedent'. Eyebrows were also raised in the House of Lords on 13 June when Lord Camperdown protested that a treaty had been signed, 'the effect of which was considerably to extend the boundaries of the colony of Hong-kong', without any official notice having been given to either House, the Members learning of it only from the columns of *The Times*. Lord Salisbury himself replied, with great portentousness: 'his noble Friend's discontent was due to the novel state of things brought about by the existence of the telegraph' (it had been connecting London and Hong Kong for twenty-seven years, but the House of Lords does not move quickly). As soon as the text of the agreement was available it would be communicated to Parliament, but he did 'not know that the details of this matter are of any general interest, although they are of strategic importance', and went on to talk of 'a slight extension to the colony of Hong-kong'. Hampered by knowing very little about the subject, the Prime Minister took refuge in verbosity: all that had been done was to act 'in conformity with the ordinary rules of military prudence that all strategical considerations should be so revised that if an accident we cannot foresee takes place we should not be exposed to any danger or disadvantage'. For their part the Chinese government 'value the solicitude that is displayed by us', and 'met us very frankly and freely in the matter . . . I do not know that there is anything else I can explain to the noble Lord.'

Although the agreement between the governments was ratified on 6 August 1898, much remained to be settled before the British could take over the area which has remained known as the New Territories. One complication was that the American navy was at that time using Mirs Bay as its base during the Spanish—American war, and an occupation by the British would disturb the Americans' right to stay. This the British government was reluctant to do, since relations with the USA, which in 1895 had been brought to their nadir by US Secretary of State Olney's claim that the USA was 'practically sovereign' over the American continent, were in the process of being repaired. It was also necessary to define the future of the Chinese customs stations in the territory, Sir Robert Hart having been left with only words of comfort from MacDonald that Chinese revenues would not be adversely affected. The Tsungli Yamen, encouraged by Hart, and permanently suspicious of the colonial administration, remained concerned about the collection of customs. Sir Robert conceded on 10 November that 'China has no objection to offer against anything that makes for the defence of Hong Kong and cannot but assist any means of that sort strenuously', but wanted to retain his customs stations in the leased territories. The Hong Kong Chamber of Commerce found this bitterly objectionable: 'If there was one benefit we hoped to derive from the accession of territory, more acceptable than another, it was the prospect of getting rid of these stations.' They found the Chinese requests 'wholly inadmissible . . . they should be most vigorously opposed in the interests not merely of trade, but of the position and prestige of Great Britain in Hong Kong and China'.[11]

It would have seemed logical to settle the boundaries definitively, but partly owing to the absence of a proper survey this was not done, and in fact arguments about details continued for many years; even in 1967 discrepancies were observable in official publications. The Canton Viceroy proved reluctant to accede to Peking's concessions, and advanced demands that his own regulations should be incorporated in the statutes of the leased area. This may have been plain uncooperativeness, or it may have reflected a genuine misunderstanding as to the status of the lease, but Lord Salisbury correctly assessed the Viceroy's demands as 'an attempt to treat the leased territory as if it were a settlement at a treaty port', and turned them down out of hand. The intervening period did however allow the Hong Kong Colonial Secretary, James Stewart Lockhart, the opportunity to make a thorough study of the territory and its people, which later proved of great advantage and formed the basis for the major decisions on the area's future.

Delayed by these various arguments, possession was not taken until the following year, after some complaints: 'We are told that the Kowloon hinterland now belongs to us, though we have as yet seen no sign of it being taken over' (Hong Kong Telegraph, 19 January 1899). In the interim period of uncertainty some inhabitants of the New Territories, who had not been consulted as to their future, formulated a resistance to the occupation. Claims were made that this opposition was due to Triad *agents provocateurs*, or to the agitation of the gentry and clan-leaders, who feared their own squeezes would be interfered with – as indeed they were – but many of the villagers seemed too well-organized for spontaneous resistance. It seems likely that there had been a change of heart by the Ch'ing government, since only a few weeks after the ratification of the agreement the *coup d'état* of September 1898 had taken place, and a violently anti-foreign sentiment had developed in the capital. Prudence would then require any provincial official to encourage, and even organize, resistance against foreign occupation of Chinese territory. Eventually it was decided that, even if outstanding points remained at issue, the take-over would be on 17 April 1899. When a company of Hong Kong Volunteers (the local militia) and some police went on the fourteenth to make arrangements, they found uniformed men in prepared positions, supported by artillery. An extra three companies, each with a Maxim gun, were dispatched, and given covering fire by the gunboat *Fame*. This enabled the Union flag to be raised a day early, on 16 April. Some Chinese were killed and wounded, but there were no British fatalities, and the Volunteers enjoyed the exercise. Their commander, Captain Berger, wrote: 'After the basely material life one continuously sees in Hong Kong, it was certainly a treat to find oneself among purely natural people where . . . a man would not actually die if he had forgotten to put a flower in his coat, or to curl the ends of his moustache.' Another scuffle took place on the seventeenth, with a number of attacks by some three thousand Chinese being easily repulsed. All in all, though several hundred Chinese casualties were taken, 'while the gravest injury to the British forces was caused by an enraged and patriotic buffalo', resistance was neither fierce nor protracted, but served to indicate the difficulties that might have been encountered sixty years previously, had prosperous Chusan been selected as a place for settlement rather than the sparsely populated island of Hong Kong.

Although in 1841 the island of Hong Kong contained only a small fishing community, the population of the New Territories was considerable and well-established. While the island had little recorded history before the arrival of the British, the mainland county of San-on (Xin'an) was, although small and distant, a recognized part of the administrative structure of Kwantung.[12] The earliest inhabitants seem to have concentrated around the littoral, where there was abundant food, and left permanent traces of their occupation in the form of rock carvings. A number of these have been found around the shores, and even at their early date – probably first millennium B.C. – have a distinctly 'Chinese' look about them, quite different from the contemporary cup-and-wheel engraving found in northern England, although the autochthonous people were not of the Han.

At what time the coastal area came under Imperial rule is not clear, since there are few recorded references before the eleventh century A.D. Long before that date the Han had colonized, if not settled, here, but it is only with the Sung Dynasty that any records are to be found. Of these the most prominent is on a boulder in Joss House Bay (Tai Miu Wan): a rock inscription dated 1274 A.D. records the generosity of a saltworks official, Yen I-chang, who built a pagoda on Tung Lung island and renovated the Tai Miu Tin Hau temple which stood near the site of its modern successor. For some time before Yen's visit Han Chinese settlers, who called themselves 'Punti' (natives, which they were not), had been moving in. The supplanted aboriginals are said to have formed the present 'Tanka' boat-dwellers, who accounted for a substantial proportion of the original population of Hong Kong island. Those edifices constructed by the five great clans of Punti settlers – the Tang, Hau, Pang, Liu and Man families – are the oldest existing buildings in Hong Kong, although it is doubtful if any now remaining date before the end of the seventeenth century.

It was then that the inhabitants of San-on county were devastated by the ruthless action of the new Ch'ing governors, in their drastic forced evacuation of 1662, when the populace were moved away from the coast, as the East India Company factor at Surat had reported (p. 26):

> The boundary was marked straight with a rope . . . A deep ditch was dug . . . One step beyond the ditch, and the punishment was death . . . Fathers abandoned their sons, and husbands their wives . . . sons were sold for a peck of rice, daughters for 100 cash . . . Some families took poison en masse, others jumped in the river . . . The authorities treated the people as no more than ants and made no provision for relief . . . It is recorded that several hundred thousand people from the eight departments affected died.

Since the evacuation had been preceded by a ferocious campaign against the Ch'ing, during which 'for three years the country presented the appearance of a battlefield . . . The ground was covered with bones, in the day time nothing could be heard but the humming of flies, and at night the voice of weeping,' the population was much depleted. From over thirty thousand in the sixteenth century it had declined to 17,871 before the evacuation, after which it slumped to just over two thousand. It took nearly a century to return to its former level.

The increase was in large measure due to an influx of newcomers from the coastal provinces further north, the Hakka, who reinvigorated the local agriculture. The Tankas were joined by another fishing community, the Hoklos, from the coast of Fukien. The different peoples lived uneasily together. E.J.M. Rhoads comments:

> contention and at time outright warfare have characterized relations among the three groups. One of the causes has been the contempt of the Puntis toward both Hoklos and Hakkas, whom they consider not as Han Chinese at all but as uncultivated aborigines. Another has been the aggressiveness of the Hakkas. Born to adversity, the Hakkas developed a reputation for hard work, frugality, and studiousness.[13]

Since 1573 the San-on district gazetteer has recorded the more important events, and Sung Hok P'ang's collection gives some interesting biographies.[14] The two best-remembered worthies are the Viceroy of Canton, Cho Yau-tak, and the Governor, Wong Lai-yam, who in 1669 successfully petitioned the Emperor K'ang-hsi to rescind the order for evacuation and are commemorated in the study-library named after them in Kam Tin, to the east of Yuen Long. Ancestral halls, study-libraries, temples, forts and walled villages remain scattered about the New Territories, often overshadowed by new developments and difficult to discover. Also in Kam Tin are the Tang clan walled villages of Kat Hing Wai, Wing Lung Wai, and Tai Hong Wai, and the Hakka folk museum of Sam Tung Uk in Tsuen Wan, all of which give an indication of life in the New Territories before 1898.[15] The Tung Chung fort on Lantau is a fair representation of a fortified military headquarters rather than a serious defensive work; the walled city of Kowloon was a larger version of a similar installation.

The lack of co-operation from Canton and the abortive insurrection provided an excellent excuse for the British to clarify the walled city question to their own advantage. The quickest and most attractive option was to withdraw the concession on the continued Chinese jurisdiction over the walled city; it was therefore discovered that the military defence of the colony was imperilled by this, and British rule was unilaterally imposed on 27 December 1899. As far as the British were concerned the walled city was from that time integrated with the colony; the Chinese reserved their views, but from time to time made it clear that they did not agree. Many of the Hong Kong British would have pressed for absolute cession of the territory, but the British government was consistent in its policy of not encouraging other powers to make further demands on China. That did not stop succeeding Governors from agitating for advantage to be taken of any opportunity to convert the lease into permanent possession – May in 1905, Lugard in 1909, Stubbs in 1921 and Clementi in 1927.

One reason for the delay in taking possession of the New Territories had been the desirability of waiting until a new Governor was in post. Sir Henry Blake, who arrived in the colony in November 1898, was a large, cordial Irishman with all the qualities of humanity that his predecessor John Pope Hennessy possessed, and a great many others beside. By 1898 he had fifteen years' experience of colonial governorships, in the Bahamas, Newfoundland and Jamaica. Since he had served eight years in his last post, a long home leave had delayed his arrival in Hong Kong. He enjoyed stable relations with staff and community alike, although some comments were heard when his wife, Edith, invited the first Chinese ladies to Government House. The fact that Edith's sister was a Duchess (of St Albans) made that rash act more acceptable to the Englishwomen. Blake had gone into the Colonial Service from the Irish police where he had been a resident magistrate – an excellent school for the art of administration – and he showed a policeman's skills in an emergency, personally attending to plague victims and turning out to assist in typhoon rescues. His appreciation of the Chinese case appears in the book he later wrote:

> The Chinese who have come into contact with the foreign Powers regard them as bullies, who have by their destructive prowess forced themselves upon the Middle Kingdom. No definite complaint has been formulated in this matter so far; but it must not be assumed that there is no feeling of irritation on the subject . . . and we do not know how soon the demand for reconsideration of foreign relations may become inconveniently pressing.[16]

Responsibility for the New Territories – 365 square miles, rather than the two hundred mentioned by Lord Salisbury, was given from the beginning to James Haldane Stewart Lockhart, who combined the offices of Colonial Secretary and Registrar-General.[17] Lockhart was in a different mould to his chief; short, aggressive, competent and Scottish, with little capacity for suffering fools gladly or otherwise. He had been in Hong Kong for eighteen years, since his arrival as a cadet, and combined an intimate practical knowledge of Chinese customs with considerable scholarship. This modified the characteristics of brisk and sometimes unsympathetic efficiency that were often displayed by competent colonial officials, but Lockhart had all the professional's disdain for box-wallahs whose 'object in coming to the Colony is to acquire wealth and return to Great Britain as soon as they possibly can'. These sentiments restricted his usefulness in a colony like Hong Kong, populated by Chinese and English whose great object was 'to acquire wealth', and that as soon as may be. It was only to be expected that Lockhart and Blake would not see eye to eye on a number of matters. Although on leave in London at the time the agreement with China was signed, Lockhart was promptly returned to Hong Kong to provide a preliminary assessment: it was later he who agreed the boundaries, hoisted the flag, and accompanied the troops on their brief sweep through the New Territories.

Differences in approach between Blake and Lockhart quickly became apparent. On the same night that the British took over the New Territories, three Chinese villagers were murdered. Lockhart dealt with the crime by burning the suspects' houses and fining the village, actions which Blake criticized: 'we have come to introduce British jurisprudence, not to adopt Chinese ways'. Lockhart was 'disappointed to say the least ... British jurisprudence is excellent in theory, but in practice was quite inapplicable.' But Blake's policy of offering a reward was effective; the murderers were caught, tried and sentenced, one to death. Since two of the culprits were gentry members they would, under Chinese law, have been able to escape severe punishment.

Lockhart was also angered to discover that some of the gentry had petitioned the Imperial Magistrate at San-On to prevent the British occupation. He wanted them immediately banished and their property confiscated, but Blake refused, considering the petitioners were perfectly entitled to take the action they had, and that the Chinese population were more likely to be won over by encouragement and fair

measures than by bullying. Blake and Lockhart were in better agreement over the need to preserve as much of Chinese law and customs
as was compatible with British notions.

The task of administering this newly-acquired slice of China was
approached with suitable delicacy. The Order in Council dealing with
the administration of the New Territories had specified that they were
'part and parcel of Her Majesty's Colony of Hong Kong in like manner
and to all intents and purposes as if they had originally formed part
of the said Colony' (20 October 1898). Blake, realizing that conditions
in the New Territories were totally different from those in urban and
developed Hong Kong, where the population had adjusted to British
methods, wanted to manage things with a single British Resident, and
for the administration to function through committees of elders – the
system of indirect rule that had been pioneered in Africa. An exception
had to be made for New Kowloon, the part of the peninsula that had
not already been ceded, and Lantau, both of which areas were considered to be capable of assimilation into the adjacent Hong Kong
territory. Assisted by a handful of young cadets, including the brilliant
Cecil Clementi, later to become Governor, Lockhart was given scope
gently to bring the eighty thousand inhabitants of the rest of the area
under Queen Victoria's aegis, without undue offence to settled habits.

Land tenure, in a community of farmers, was a sensitive topic.
Unlike the existing colony, in which, being British Crown property,
long leases could be granted, in the New Territories the ninety-nine-
year Crown tenure limited freedom of movement. The Governor's
proclamation that 'commercial and landed interests will be safeguarded
and their usages and good customs will not in any way be interfered
with'[18] was little more than an acknowledgement of the restrictions
imposed by the tenure. But discovering what the landed interests were
was a complex matter: there were different classes of land, graded
according to value, varying types of tenure (individual, ancestral, temple
and registered associations), and no fixed measurement of area.
Reports were made in terms of 'maus' – about 0.15 acres, but rents
were calculated on the amount of grain needed to sow a field. In the
absence of any plans it was impossible to be precise as to which fields
were described, and often the putative owners were unable to identify
their own property. Many were reluctant to do so: 'as is well known,
the Chinese are a suspicious race and it is not easy to allay their
suspicions once aroused . . . Long experience of their own Government methods has made the inhabitants distrustful of all officials gener-

ally.' But many who had experience of the reliability of the British administration hastened to buy lands for less than they were worth from the unduly suspicious. MacDonald, second to none in his distrust of the Hong Kong community, claimed that for years past some colonists, while agitating for the expansion on patriotic grounds, had surreptitiously been buying up land on the cheap in what they hoped would become British territory – 'and a thundering good thing they will make of it'.

In due course things were clarified, and the first survey of the territory was made by Indian surveyors between 1899 and 1903. Roads were built, telephone lines installed, and effective policing introduced, the previous situation having been chaotic: attacks by pirates and bandits were frequent; one walled village in Lung Leuk T'au was besieged for three months by robbers. Although it remained too easy for bad characters to roam the area, crime rapidly declined with the establishment of regular policing. Since there was to be no immediate attempt to impose British standards and customs, the New Territories were exempted from many regulations, and administered in a different way from Hong Kong. Every village, or unit of one hundred people, was entitled to nominate members of sub-district committees to consult with the government – although in a discreetly paternalistic way. The system of indirect rule was not over-successful; Dr Baker comments: 'the former viability of the unofficial system rested on the unwillingness and inefficiency of the official one',[19] but given an incorrupt and accessible British magistrate, confidence in the courts developed so rapidly that few requests for help in settling disputes were ever referred to the committees. For the first time the farmers saw an opportunity to escape from the gentry's hold on the land, and of escaping the various clan taxes and payments in kind which had previously been levied. At least one district, Ch'eung Chau, 'voluntarily offered to pay increased Crown Rent, or such increased land tax as I may recommend to be fair'.

All this striving after justice did not come cheap, and the New Territories were an expensive acquisition. In the first eight months $233,034 was spent, and only $7,273 received from all sources. Far from being fertile farmland, 90 per cent was scrub and rock:

> Of the 1,060 km² of land in Hong Kong about 67km² can be considered as arable land, out of which some 6,943 ha. are farmed. The rest of the land consists largely of steep and unproductive

hillsides where the soils are generally acidic and low in nutrients
. . . From the time of the leasing of the New Territories . . . until
the Second World War . . . farmers produced vegetables on a
limited scale only and mainly for home production.[20]

The crops grown were not of good quality, and required scientific
improvement. The Governor seemed to be scraping the bottom of the
barrel in his cautious first report, on 19 February 1900:

> It remains to be seen to what extent the New Territory can be
> developed. Much depends upon the possibility of producing suc-
> culent grasses or trees of commercial value upon the hill slopes. If
> the former, there is no reason why a very valuable cattle-breeding
> industry should not develop. Mr Ford [the Government Forestry
> Officer] is about to try some experiments with camphor trees and
> vines. Either could be a valuable addition to the resources of the
> colony.

Although in time the acquisition of the New Territories was to change
the whole character of the colony, it was some years before any effect
was felt. The territory was large and its population was widely dispersed, totalling only about one quarter of the colony's total; their
habits and independence from the pattern of life in Victoria tended to
keep them apart, as it still does in such spots as Tai O on Lantau.

Scoundrelly leaders of secret societies

The 1890s were a time of considerable financial stress for Hong Kong,
caused largely by the fall in the value of silver, which made even the
Hongkong and Shanghai Bank look shaky. A rumour that the Bank
might have to close its doors circulated in January 1890, and caused
Sir Robert Hart to transfer £50,000 of the Customs monies held there
to the Bank of England. Two years later he continued to be worried,
and wrote on 19 June 1892: 'I have gradually sent most of the H'kong
Bank money to the B. of E: the outlook is not reassuring.' Hart became
quite snappy about the Bank: ' What with its constant cricket matches
. . . and the careless way of doing things generally . . . Its new idea
[of appropriating interest] is monstrous.'[21]
  A good deal more monstrous, in the opinion of Sir Robert's Chinese

employers, was the Hong Kong government's practice of harbouring rebellious Chinese dedicated to overthrowing the Ch'ing Dynasty. The opportunities provided in Hong Kong for young people to absorb Western ideas of constitutional government and to learn the English language were unparalleled elsewhere in China. Some of the first proposals to emerge at the beginning of the 1890s were hardly revolutionary. Yang Ch'ü-yün and Hsieh Tsuan-t'ai had both studied in Hong Kong, where they had been brought up to speak English (Yang to the extent of having very little Chinese), and had discovered in the methods of British government what they conceived to be a workable alternative to the shaky Ch'ing regime. By virtue of their education they were also conscious of how limited were their own opportunities in a rigidly racially restricted British administration. Their society, the Fu-jen wen-se (the Literary Society for the Promotion of Benevolence),[22] was a mild enough affair, and much less serious than the secret meetings held by the 'four bandits' – Yang Ho-ling, Ch'en Shao-pai, Yu Lieh and Sun Yat-sen – at the Red House (Hung Lau), in Tuen Mun, then still part of Kwantung province. For the next twenty years the Red House served as refuge, hospital, and bomb factory for hundreds of revolutionaries.

The 'four bandits' had all become familiar with Western concepts and habits in Hong Kong. Sun Yat-sen, the future founder of the Kuomintang and President of the Chinese Republic, was in 1892 the newly qualified, and most distinguished, graduate of Dr Manson's Hong Kong College of Medicine. He had been exposed to British influences for most of his formative years, having been at a Church of England school in Hawaii and Queen's College, Hong Kong except for two short periods at Oahu College and a Canton hospital.

It is possible that the young revolutionaries would not have passed from discussion to action had they not engaged the sympathy of some prosperous backers, including none other than Sir Ch'i Ho Ch'i, that anomalous member of the Legislative Council who had strongly opposed the imposition of Western sanitary and medical methods at the same time as funding the new College of Medicine and the Alice Memorial Hospital. Ho had been one of Sun's supervisors at the College of Medicine, and might almost be regarded as standing in the same relation to him as Engels did to Marx, but he went further in providing support for armed intervention, and himself contributed to the organized thinking about a new society for China. Like other leaders of the Hong Kong Chinese, Ho's command of the Chinese language was shaky, and he engaged the services of a collaborator to assist with the publication of his political ideas. His collected works were written with the assistance of Hu Li-yan, who had also been educated in Hong Kong. The essays published as *Hsin-cheng Chen-ch'üan* (A Collection of Essays on Reform) started appearing in 1887; they have not been translated into English, but are described by Dr Kit-ching Chan Lau: 'Ho maintained that to remove China's accumulated weakness, Western learning and the Western system must be understood and adopted in their totality, both in terms of spirit and methodology. In doing so, however, a clear order of priorities must be followed. Civil reforms must precede military ones, and the solution of internal problems must come before that of external ones.'

Ho's experience of China was limited, and his models were Britain, of which he had intimate knowledge, and even more Hong Kong, where he played an active part in the government for over twenty years. How far Ho's solutions could ever have been applied to so enormous a country as China, with no experience of formal democracy, is questionable, but many of his priorities were in fact followed by twentieth-century Chinese governments. Ho wanted 'a government manned with like-minded people' (which has, usually by drastic means, been the case in China) and democratically elected (unfortunately still to be attempted), together with the abolition of corruption and the whole-hearted encouragement of all forms of Western education. Only when these reforms had been achieved might radical economic reforms and defence improvements be attempted, instead of the half-hearted and piecemeal efforts which were at that time being made, and which proved ineffectual.

This programme was to be carried out with the help of foreign investment, rather than by adopting an intolerant anti-foreign stance and insisting China could 'go it alone'. Foreigners had already proved what vital help could be given to China through the establishment of the Maritime Customs, and Ho suggested that their powers should be extended to the control of internal revenue duties. By foreigners Ho meant British, for he was a thorough Anglophile, who 'had a clear bias for Britain, the Western power for which he had the highest esteem. To him Britain was unquestionably the power of powers whose political institutions should be modelled upon.' Moreover,

Ho Ch'i held great pride in and an unswerving loyalty towards his place of origin – British Hong Kong. To him it was the crown jewel on the diadem of British power and prestige. It epitomized the very government system he admired and advocated. The Hong Kong education and examination systems were far superior to the Chinese ones. In the colony too commerce thrived and the merchant class occupied an important position in society. Ho, above all, held that the Chinese in Hong Kong received fair treatment from the British, and were given every opportunity to rise in society so long as they had the ability to do so.

Events moved from theory to action in February 1895 when Sun Yat-sen, who had left Hong Kong on taking his degree, returned to establish a local branch of the Hsing Chung Hui – the Association for the Regeneration of China – which he had founded in Honolulu. Hong Kong, owing to its geographical position and relative freedom from official interference, rapidly became the most important centre of the organization's work. Its members included Sun's old friends from the Red House, but one important new member was the rich businessman Huang Yung-shang, son of Wong Shing (Huang Shen), who had succeeded Ng Choy on the Legislative Council. A locally financed coup was immediately planned, its aim being to overthrow the government in Canton. The coup was well publicized by a not-unsympathetic English-language press in Hong Kong, Ho Ch'i having ensured its sympathy: the Reform Party, as Sun's organization was called, was described as intending to secure 'judicial reforms, diffusion of modern education, religious toleration, economic development, and improvement of local government'; it promised to open more trading centres and ports and the 'repeal of all laws that have a retarding effect upon trade'; all of which was eminently soothing and gratifying to the mercantile community.

Advance publicity is not the best of strategies for conspirators, and hardly helped these plotters, whose planning was hopelessly ineffective. In October 1895, four hundred coolies were hired in Hong Kong at $10 a head, and shipped off to Canton, where they were immediately apprehended, their arms being found concealed in barrels of cement. Three of the conspirators were executed, but most managed to escape back to Hong Kong, where the Red House is said to have sheltered two to three hundred dejected revolutionaries.

The government of Hong Kong was placed in a difficult position; whatever private sympathies with the aims of the revolutionaries might exist, they did not want to be seen to be encouraging those bent on the downfall of a friendly power; and the Governor at that time, Sir William Robinson, was no friend of revolution. No arrangements existed for extradition to China on political grounds, but Robinson was willing to consider altering this in return for some tangible benefit – by which he meant the Kowloon extension. Lord Salisbury, even more antipathetic to those disturbing the established order, thought it a 'capital bargain' that Britain should be rewarded while at the same time disposing of 'a few of the scoundrelly leaders of secret societies who harbour in Hong Kong'.[23] This cynical piece of *realpolitik* was nipped in the bud at the Colonial Office by Joseph Chamberlain, who, as his involvement in the Jameson raid in the Transvaal in 1895 showed, was not averse to *realpolitik* when it suited him, but found this suggestion 'monstrous', and blankly refused to consider it.

Robinson was able to deal with the problem of Sun Yat-sen by issuing an order refusing him permission to return to the colony. In spite of some protests, this worked, until Sun made the British newspaper headlines in 1896 by being kidnapped in London and spirited off to the Chinese Embassy, whence he was only rescued by the efforts of his old teacher at the Hong Kong School of Medicine, James Cantlie. Michael Davitt, the former Fenian revolutionary – now a little more respectable, having served two terms in jail and at last taken his seat in Parliament after being four times elected – raised in the House of Commons the question of why Sun should be denied the privileges of political refuge in Hong Kong that he was allowed in Britain. Davitt, a man of great integrity and powers of oratory, succeeded in embarrassing the government but not in getting the ban lifted. Sun thereafter avoided Hong Kong, although it continued to serve as an important headquarters for his revolutionary cells.

Ho Ch'i, being a realist, decided that he had backed a loser, and withdrew from public support of the revolutionaries until a more appropriate time, contenting himself with financing publicity for revolutionary causes. Events in China were hardly promising. In 1898 the Emperor Kuang-hsu made his bid for freedom and reform, which ended after a hundred days with his abduction and imprisonment by the Dowager Empress. Reformers were executed, but one of the most prominent, K'ang Yu-wei, managed to make his escape to Hong Kong. From that time it appeared that there was little realistic hope that the Manchu Court would permit constitutional reform, and that a successful revolution was therefore almost inevitable.

Then, after the Court gave its support to the absurd Boxer revolt, and forced an issue with the Western powers that could have only one result, there was no hope at all. When the violently anti-foreign Boxers besieged the Western legations in Peking, an expeditionary force was dispatched, and the rising, which had been for the most part restricted to north-west China, was speedily suppressed. Reparations for the damage done and the two hundred or so Westerners murdered were enormous – nearly a thousand million taels, to be paid in instalments over thirty-nine years. Peking was occupied by foreign troops and the dynasty humiliated beyond recovery. In Hong Kong the Boxers were viewed with shocked distaste. With only one exception the Chinese press stigmatized the rebels as 'bandits'. The conversion of the Empress to measures of reform was too late to do anything more than stimulate the pressure for revolution.

Conditions for revolutionary refugees in Hong Kong improved with the arrival of Sir Henry Blake in November 1898 and the emergence of an extraordinary tripartite alliance between the new Governor, Ho Ch'i, and that great survivor, Li Hung-chang, who had been exiled to be Viceroy of the two Kwangs. When the Boxer rising began Li, in common with many of the more sensible provincial Governors, could foresee the inevitable outcome, and endeavoured to dissociate himself from it. He went so far as to consider declaring his provinces independent of Peking, and asked Sun, then in Japan, to meet him in Canton. Sun, also convinced that the revolt would be speedily suppressed and of the wrath that would follow it, agreed. At the time the approach was made to Sun, Blake was absent from the colony, but on the day of his return Ho Ch'i hurried to enlist his support. The Governor was informed of the potential agreement between Li and Sun and shown a proclamation drafted by Ho and agreed by Sun which announced the establishment of an independent southern government 'headed by Li with Sun Yat-sen's co-operation and Britain's protection'.

Blake was sufficiently in favour to telegraph the Colonial Office the same day to the effect that some 'Chinese gentlemen' had told him of rebellions planned against the dynasty, but that these were in no sense intended to be anti-foreign, and their leaders were indeed hoping for British support. Ten days later this was followed by another telegram which proposed 'that to safeguard British interests, Sun should be allowed to enter an agreement with Li Hung-chang who, according to Blake's sources, offered to arm the "reformers". The Governor believed that the proposed pact was the best guarantee to avert great disturbance which might develop into an anti-foreign movement in the south.'

Surprisingly enough, the government of Lord Salisbury, hardly a friend to revolutions, was willing to consider support for Sun, but only if Li approved; and Li had changed his mind. When Sun reached Hong Kong, on 17 July 1900, Li had been summoned to Peking. The invitation was not accepted immediately, Li being in no hurry to commit himself. But he was conscious that his presence in Peking, as the single figure of international eminence, might, as the dynasty crumbled, result in the greatest of prizes – the establishment of Li himself 'either as king or president', as Blake put it. Relying on the support of the Powers, Li decided to take the risk, and left Canton on the same day that Sun arrived in Hong Kong.

Blake had heard in advance of Li's intentions, by which time he was so committed to the concept of a Li—Sun alliance that he not only asked the British Consul in Canton to dissuade Li from going to Peking, but telegraphed the Colonial Office for permission to detain him in Hong Kong. This peculiar and quite inadmissible request was peremptorily denied by Chamberlain, who replied 'categorically forbidding him to detain Li or in any way forcibly interfere with his movements'. The Governor and Viceroy did meet, on 18 July, but without Sun Yat-sen, who was kept cooling his heels on board a ship in the harbour. In his conversation with Blake, Li not only made no reference to the previous plan, but urged Blake not to allow the colony to be used by rebellious characters. If he was successful in his bid for power, Li wanted no more truck with revolutionaries. He attempted rather to persuade Blake of the wisdom of this policy, and dwelt largely on 'entering his bid as the "most suitable person of Chinese nationality" to become the ruler of China should the powers be in the position to make the choice if all the foreign ministers had indeed been butchered by the Boxers, as it was widely rumoured'.

Blake had not abandoned his position of support for the revolutionaries, and Ho renewed his efforts on Sun's behalf to obtain British backing for yet another venture, a planned rising in Hui-chou, to the north of Kowloon. This was too much; the Governor suggested instead that a petition should be submitted to the Powers, specifying the reforms Sun and his supporters wanted; he then telegraphed Chamberlain in an endeavour to persuade the Colonial Secretary that the British government should press for these demands to be included in any peace settlement. Ho Ch'i summarized the reformers' programme, which was drawn from his own writings on the subject; there was to be a temporary arrangement whereby a head of government would be 'responsive to the people's wishes and subject to constitutional restraints', with active support from foreign representatives, followed by the steady introduction of democracy, modernization and economic improvements, with unrestricted access to trade and industry. It was a programme calculated to appeal to any liberally-minded foreign government, but Chamberlain was having nothing to do with such ideas. Blake was unequivocally ordered to desist and to suppress all types of revolutionary activity in the colony.

The planned revolt went ahead, and, in spite of Blake's unwillingness to cooperate with the Ch'ing authorities in Canton to suppress it – he had again to be ordered to do so by Chamberlain – was quickly and bloodily put down. Once again Ho Ch'i withdrew into the background as far as support for revolution was concerned, and the next, again abortive, plot planned in Hong Kong went ahead without his participating.

The Canton government did not rest content with quelling these revolts, but attempted to punish the originators, even when they had been accorded asylum in Hong Kong. On 10 January 1901 Yang Ch'ü-yün, one of Sun's original collaborators in Hong Kong, was teaching an evening class when four men burst in; one 'whipped out a revolver and fired four shots in rapid succession . . . Every one of the shots had taken effect, one entering the head and the others penetrating the left shoulder, chest and abdomen . . . not a word was spoken on either side, the whole affair occupying just a few seconds.' It was suspected, and subsequently proved, that the assassins had been employed by the Canton government.

The whole of Hong Kong opinion was outraged, and pressed for vigorous actions against the Canton authorities, but the affair was smoothed over by a variety of methods; Canton, after having rewarded the perpetrators, executed first the actual killer, and later one of the others; a third was arrested in Hong Kong and similarly dealt with. The Viceroy who had instigated the murder died, and although Blake pressed for compensation and further punishments the Foreign Office decided that enough was enough. Blake also managed a moral victory on behalf of the revolutionaries: when the Canton authorities sent him a list of those suspected of revolutionary activities in Hong Kong – among whom was Ho Tung, later Sir Robert Hotung – the Governor responded only by indignantly protesting that none of those named

had been implicated in any way. The real leader, Li Chi-t'ang, was
even given extensive police protection against any further attempts at
revenge on the part of the Canton government.

Sir Matthew's railway

In November 1903 Blake left Hong Kong to take over the Governorship of Ceylon, leaving the colony in the hands of the Colonial Secretary Frank May[24] until the arrival of the next Governor in July the
following year. May, who had come to Hong Kong in 1881 after
Harrow and Trinity College, Dublin, was a reserved authoritarian of
understated efficiency. Twenty years younger than Blake, he did not
share his departing master's enthusiasm for radical changes in China,
was deeply antipathetic to revolutionaries, and suspicious – often with
good reason – of their approaches to the Governor. Later, when he
had himself attained that post, the first cadet officer to do so, he was
strongly critical of Ho Ch'i, whom he found 'treacherous'.

May immediately took advantage of his new position to undo some
of the late Governor's work by pushing through the Peak Reservation
Ordinance, which was designed to exclude non-Europeans from that
favoured area. The ordinance was, in deference to liberal opinion at
home, put a little less baldly than that, since it included the sop: 'It
shall be lawful for the Governor-General in Council to exempt any
Chinese from this Ordinance.' In fact the Governor-General in Council thought fit to do so on only one occasion, when the Anglo-Chinese
knight Sir Robert Hotung (who, unlike Ho Ch'i, always adopted
Chinese dress) applied. Lethbridge described the Peak as 'Surbiton
or Wimbledon, in an atmosphere as truly British as roast beef or
muffins.' Chinese, even if they managed to convince the Governor that
they were fit to live there, would have been automatically excluded
from the Peak Club, 'a centre for tea dances and bridge parties before
dinner'. It is reasonable to add that the Chinese, sensible people,
showed no sign of wishing to join in such pursuits. Ho Ch'i felt that
the Ordinance had 'a decided savour of the nature of class legislation,
but having consulted members of the Chinese community he found
that they had no strong feelings or objections'; the 'change of phras-
eology so as to make it less blatantly obvious that the Chinese were
excluded' would suffice.

The move infuriated Blake, who wrote from Ceylon to the Colonial

Office complaining about this discrimination. He was even more dismayed when May deported the editors of a number of Chinese-language newspapers who had been attacking the Ch'ing government. Strictly speaking May did not possess the powers to do this, although the orders of banishment were retrospectively confirmed. The Colonial Office hesitated, but Blake's defence of the citizen's right to 'think and speak what he likes and to act as well so long as he obeys the laws' was not effectual. When the next Governor, Sir Matthew Nathan arrived in July 1904, he backed May's restrictive laws with growing enthusiasm; one Colonial Office clerk commented: 'Punch would get short shrift in Hong Kong if he was of Chinese nationality.'[25]

It might have been expected that when Francis May found himself subordinate to a man with as little knowledge of China as Nathan, and two years younger than he was, he might well have felt himself aggrieved; but he exhibited no sign of it. Nathan's prejudices coincided with May's, and their areas of expertise were gratifyingly complementary. Nathan had a number of disadvantages, of which he was strongly conscious. He was young – forty-two – a Jew, from a modest background, with an equally modest rank (Major in the Royal Engineers), and inept in personal relationships. He was also, and so remained, a bachelor, which rather helped matters since Mrs May then became the 'burra mem', senior lady in the colony and entitled to take the lead in social matters.

Although anti-Semitism in England was never as strong as in France, it was not easy for a Jew to become a colonial Governor as young as Nathan had been on his first appointment, which was to Sierra Leone at the age of thirty-seven – and to do so from an army career.[26] Such an advance was only possible with considerable talent, which Nathan certainly possessed, and energetic political backing, which he had from Joseph Chamberlain himself, on whose Colonial Defence Committee Nathan had served as Secretary. These assets were combined with a steady ambition and a suppression of emotional ties which might have interfered with his career (as his successor Lugard's marriage so nearly did with his). Nathan had no intimate male friends, and his wide circle of talented and interesting female acquaintances (which included Mary Kingsley) was kept at a certain distance. Not being a pushy individual, although conscious of the importance of maintaining the dignity of his position, Sir Matthew rarely adopted autocratic attitudes; May, with twenty-five years' experience of Hong Kong, was left a free hand in all matters where Nathan did not wish to play a personal role.

It is probable that, in appointing Nathan, the Colonial Office had in mind that the New Territories needed a man with some experience of the District Officer type of government which was normal in Africa. Certainly Nathan showed much interest in the development of the New Territories, and was instrumental in building Nathan Road – 'Nathan's Folly', as it was known at the time – in order to link the Kowloon settlement with the hinterland. The project for which he was best fitted, and which became of consuming importance to him, was the Kowloon–Canton railway. A concession had already been granted to the British and Chinese Corporation, a company linked with Jardine Matheson, but between the Corporation and the Canton government – Nathan blamed both for dilatoriness, suspecting that the Corporation's directors were more interested in holding out for a profitable sale of the concession than in seeing the project through – nothing tangible had been done for six years. In 1905 it was discovered that the concession to build a line from Canton to Hankow, which in conjunction with that from Kowloon would bring Hong Kong into direct connection with the heartland of China, was up for sale. Nathan believed that if Britain cooperated with China in buying back the concession it would not only prevent it from falling into the hands of France and Russia, but also stimulate the progress of the Kowloon–Canton line. Using his considerable influence at the Colonial Office, Nathan persuaded them to offer through the Crown Agents a favourable loan to Canton – 4.5 per cent at par, a far better rate than any previous loan, and one that failed to tempt the market, leaving most of the issue with the underwriters.

Sir Matthew was very pleased with what he called 'his financial coup', but it really was a very muddled affair. It took another year of difficult negotiations with the Viceroy in Canton before final agreement on the finance, building and operation of the railway was reached, which tried Nathan's patience so sorely that he decided to start the line from Kowloon at least as far as the Chinese border. As a professional engineer he was in his element, but his anxiety to participate in the detailed work caused constant friction both with the contractors and the Colonial Office; Sir Matthew's biographer writes of an 'almost obsessional interest in the railway together with his peevish and overbearing manner', which had the effect of causing the Colonial Office's initial enthusiasm for the Governor to show signs of waning.

When the railway was eventually opened, to the border in 1910, and all the way to Canton two years later, long after Nathan had left,

Kowloon developed rapidly. In the fifty years of British occupation prior to the completion of the terminus, building in Kowloon had not proceeded much beyond the line of Jordan Road. Some pleasant residential property had been built behind St Andrew's church, in the area of Kimberley and Granville Roads, but the lion's share of the land was still occupied by the services, who had Whitfield Barracks in what is now Kowloon Park as well as a number of smaller installations. Nathan Road, commemorating the Governor, was little more than a track in his own time, and it took the impetus given by the railway for Kowloon to begin emerging as a considerable community.

Nathan showed his abilities to more effect in coping with the problems caused by the Russian war with Japan in 1904–5. The Russian fleet, which had already demonstrated its incompetence by firing on British fishing boats in the North Sea in mistake for the Japanese navy, found its way to the South China Sea, causing the British Admiralty to be nervous lest the Russians should attack Hong Kong, whether intentionally or in error. This resulted in a six-week alert for both the colony's garrison and the China squadron of the Royal Navy. The island became crowded with Russian refugees, who were promptly interned; smuggling of arms to Russia necessitated vigilance, and the Chinese in Hong Kong began to demonstrate their solidarity with the motherland.

The demonstrations took the form of protest, not against Russia, but against American laws designed, according to President Benjamin Harrison, to 'defend our civilization by excluding alien races' – by which he meant the Chinese, described by his Secretary of State, the 'morally obtuse' James Blair, as 'bringing the seeds of moral and physical disease, of destitution, and of death'.[27] These laws had been roughly enforced, and when extended to the newly-conquered territories of the Philippines and Hawaii they generated great resentment. Sparked off by a student's protest suicide in Shanghai, a wave of protest erupted all over China. Coolies went on strike, a general boycott of American goods was observed, and American cigarettes were publicly destroyed. The Chinese Chamber of Commerce planned a public meeting in support, which Nathan quickly banned as 'an attack on the commerce of a friendly power'. He also expelled the editor of a newspaper for publishing anti-American cartoons. Nathan was thanked by William Howard Taft, then the United States Secretary of War, but the Colonial Office, now under Alfred Lyttelton, was less enthusiastic, and dubious about the legality of the Governor's actions. Lyttelton was right to be worried about the subject, since he was responsible in 1904 for the decision to admit Chinese indentured labourers to South Africa under conditions which looked to the British public very much like slavery, and which was to lead to the downfall of his government.

This affair may have contributed to Nathan's early removal from Hong Kong in 1906, after only three years in office. It was not that Nathan had made himself actively unpopular either in Whitehall or Hong Kong, although the new Liberal government did not see any reason to favour one of Chamberlain's protégés, especially one who had opposed the Liberal defence cuts to the point of threatening resignation, as Nathan did in 1905. His brother W.S. Nathan was also attracting some attention for his involvement in the Kaiping mines administration; there was more than a hint of anti-Semitism in that, since G.E. Morrison of *The Times*, at the same time as criticizing Nathan, described the mines' chairman as 'a Jew who would cheat his blind grandmother at cards'.[28]

The real reason for Nathan's premature removal was the redoubtable Flora Shaw, now Lady Lugard, who wanted her husband transferred to a climate she found more congenial, and the Lugards were hard to resist. Flora Shaw was a rare phenomenon, a successful career woman, an influential journalist and an expert on colonial matters, 'a woman of remarkable ability and enterprise', according to L.S. Amery. She had married Frederick Lugard four years previously when he became High Commissioner in Northern Nigeria. In order to make room for Lugard in Hong Kong, a colonial musical chairs took place. Blake, then sixty-five, was retired from Ceylon, being replaced there by Sir Henry MacCallum from Natal, whither Nathan was unwillingly dispatched, at a reduced salary. Once again Francis May was left holding the baby in Hong Kong pending the arrival of a new Governor.

12

HONG KONG AND THE
CHINESE REVOLUTION

Pernicious parliamentarians

When, after succeeding Lord Salisbury, Arthur Balfour's ministry split
in December 1905, eleven years of Conservative government were
superseded by a Liberal administration under Sir Henry Campbell-
Bannerman, which was subsequently strengthened by a decisive election victory. The new Liberal Cabinet was every bit as virtuous and
talented as any of Gladstone's: the Grand Old Man's youngest son,
Herbert, was Home Secretary, his biographer, John Morley, had the
India Office, Sir Edward Grey was Foreign Secretary, and James
Bryce, the historian, was given Ireland; the only note of raffishness
might be said to be struck by Lloyd George at the Board of Trade.
Among the juniors, at the Colonial Office under the 9th Earl of Elgin,
son of the former Plenipotentiary, was the thirty-one-year-old Winston
Churchill, a recent recruit to the Liberal Party.

In colonial affairs the new government took a tone strongly critical
of its Imperialist predecessor, and one that reflected the moral concerns of its Non-conformist supporters. One issue on which the election victory had been gained was that of 'Chinese slavery', a convenient
if hardly correct description of the Chinese indentured labour in South
Africa. The worst aspects of the 'pig trade' that had so maltreated
previous Chinese emigrants had been reformed, but reports from
South Africa disturbed liberal consciences. Coolies had been imported
on three-year contracts for labour on the Rand mines, where they
were kept in compounds under harsh and restrictive conditions, with
frequent use of corporal punishment, a system which the Liberals

had promised to end. Public opinion was moving from chauvinistic certainties and was ready to redress such offences against Liberal morality, of which the old question of opium was not the least important.

On 30 May 1906 Theodore Taylor, a Lancashire Liberal, raised in the House of Commons the motion that 'the Indo–Chinese opium trade was morally indefensible', and asked that 'such steps as might be necessary for bringing it speedily to a close' should be taken. Morley was placed in a difficult situation, for he did not wish to defend what he described in the debate as 'a horrible drug . . . a pestilential evil', but it was an evil that produced 7 per cent of the total income of the government of India, some £2,250,000 per annum. If the Chancellor of the Exchequer were to be asked to replace that revenue he would doubtless be willing to discuss it, but John Morley 'did not think the discussion would take long'. If, however, 'China wanted seriously and in good faith to restrict the consumption of the drug in China, the British Government would not close the door . . . even though it might cost us some sacrifice'. Since this guarded pledge bound nobody to any specific action, it was little more than a formality for the House to pass the motion unanimously.

Somewhat to the surprise of many, the Chinese seemed anxious to make real progress. The Dowager Empress, still at the helm after half a century, issued an edict closing the smoking dens and extinguishing opium production over a period of ten years. In reciprocation the British and Indian governments agreed to restrict the export of opium to China *pari passu* over the same period.

Some consternation was felt at the news in Hong Kong, since the income derived from the opium monopoly was a good deal more significant to the colony than to India. Bowring, as part of his pragmatic legislation, had created an opium monopoly which gave the right to prepare opium in the colony, whether for sale or re-export, up to a specified quantity. This valuable privilege was sold to the highest bidder, and in the course of time had brought in a substantial sum. In the previous year, although it showed signs of declining, it had comprised, at $2,040,000, no less than 29 per cent of the colony's income. May, holding the fort after Nathan's recall, shot off an acerbic memorandum to the Colonial Office, but it was left to the incoming Governor to deal with this potentially damaging issue.

Sir Frederick Lugard arrived in July 1907, a reluctant appointee; he wrote to his brother Edward that he had never been faced with an assignment 'for which I feel less aptitude, and from which I shrink more'. Lugard was a romantic figure; campaigns in Afghanistan, the Sudan and Burma, interrupted by big-game hunting (he bought his favourite rifle with his reward for shooting a man-eating tiger), explorations and fights against slavers in Africa had led him to work for Sir George Goldie, the founder of the United Africa Company, in opening up Nigeria.[1] For six years from 1900 he had fought and negotiated with the emirs of Northern Nigeria to pacify and unite that vast territory. During much of this time he was undergoing an unhappy love affair with a London society lady, and was in a state of emotional tension.

Flora Shaw, colonial editor of *The Times*, had been in love with George Goldie, but when he was free to marry he jilted her, and Flora married Lugard. They were both in their forties, and made a powerful couple. It might be that Lugard's appointment to Hong Kong owed much to his wife (Susanna Hoe quotes a note from the Perham Papers in Rhodes House that Lugard's biographer believed 'It seems that a good woman was wanted in H'Kong and that the appt was as much of *her* as of him'[2]), but he came to Hong Kong with the most impressive record of any Governor, as the most distinguished figure in the Colonial Service of the day. As well as bringing vast tracts of Africa under British rule, Lugard had very nearly succeeded in the perhaps more difficult task of persuading the Colonial Office to change its whole system of working. His proposal was that Governors should spend only half the year in post, the other half being passed in Whitehall occupying themselves with the other aspects of their responsibilities and relations with other departments. Churchill had frowned on that, in early Churchillian style: 'We will not simplify the labours of the Colonial Office by converting it into a Pantheon for proconsuls on leave.'[3]

Sir Frederick himself was furiously energetic and decisive, but not autocratic and indeed personally rather retiring – 'really too retiring', one Hong Kong lady observed. He enjoyed pottering in Government House gardens, and was once taken for the gardener by a young man anxious to sign the visitors' book. Neither Lugard nor his wife had any taste for gossip or frivolous parties, or for protocol and precedence. Flora's attempts to raise their intellectual level by organizing reading parties was not appreciated by the colony's ladies. But the quality of the Lugards' opposition can be gauged by a letter from Murray Stewart, a bullion dealer, former correspondent to *The Times* and member of the

Legislative Council: 'I could not honestly say nice things about the joint occupants of the throne . . . they don't attract me, that is all.' He went on to write: 'some of our "Indian" fellow-subjects – Bagdadis, Parsees, Bengali Baboos et hoc genes – would have been naturally wounded in their precious feelings by being differentiated from Englishmen. Do not some of them belong to the Carlton and others boast friendship with the King?'[4] Lugard would have regarded such racial gibes as 'pernicious', one of his favourite adjectives.

Any chance of a well-thought-out solution to the opium problem disappeared in the following May when one Mr William Johnston, the backbench Liberal Member for Nuneaton, succeeded in the draw for a Private Member's Bill and chose to resuscitate the opium debate. He claimed that although the Indian and Chinese governments had moved forward, the Colonial Office had done 'next to nothing', and the Hong Kong authorities nothing at all. The motion he put forward was specific: 'to take steps to bring to a speedy close the system of licensing opium dens now prevailing in some of our Crown Colonies, more particularly Hong-Kong, the Straits Settlements, and Ceylon'. Theodore Taylor took up where he had left off two years previously, having visited China in the interim, and was equally hard on Hong Kong, 'our own corner of China', where we were 'raising millions of dollars from this opium traffic', and where 'nothing had been attempted, nothing done'.

The unenviable task of replying for the government was given to Colonel Jack Seely, the newly-appointed Under-Secretary for the Colonies. Seely was a man more noted for courage and dash than prudence, and his answer was the first speech that he was called upon to make in his new role. It proved, as Hilaire Belloc put it, that 'Decisive action in the hour of need, Denotes the hero, but does not succeed.' Without any consultation, he announced that he had sent the previous day a telegram to Lugard: 'His Majesty's Government have decided that steps must be taken to close opium-dens in Hong Kong.' Although some cautions were issued during the debate on the effect that any acceleration in the agreed programme of eliminating opium production would have in India, no one was able to point out the much more serious consequences for Hong Kong, and the motion was accordingly once more passed unanimously.

In Hong Kong the news was received with indignation and incredulity, much exacerbated when it was learned that Seely, having been criticized in Parliament on 28 July 1908 for his lack of consultation, had replied that, 'Although they did their best to ascertain the views of the people, it was quite impossible to get anything like a reasoned opinion from the inhabitants of Hong Kong.' To those inhabitants that sounded like a lie, and an offensive one at that. A vote of censure on Seely was moved in the Legislative Council, supported by all the unofficial members, but automatically defeated by the official majority. Lugard was obliged to defend as best he could his masters in London, but did so without enthusiasm. His own researches failed to convince him of the deleterious effects of the drug; visiting a large number of 'divans', a term he preferred to the emotive 'dens', he found them 'very different from what I imagine Colonel Seely's conception of a "Den" is . . . All were animated and intelligent, and there were none besotted or stupid . . . the net impression conveyed to one's mind was that the so-called "vice" was really a most extraordinarily temperate and satisfactory substitute for alcohol etc. . . . You could not find such scenes in English public houses.'[5]

The episode was typical of the misunderstandings between a London government whose policy, for better or worse, was subjected to political pressures, and a Hong Kong impotent to defend what it conceived, rightly or wrongly, to be its own domestic interests. Members of Parliament, backbenchers in particular, have as their most important audience not the House of Commons, but their own constituents, and Mr Bennett, Liberal Member for Woodstock, probably thought it well worth taking a rap over the knuckles from Sir Edward Grey to be able to attack 'That imperialistic fetish called the "man on the spot" whose superior intelligence and experience was held to be paramount in deciding great questions of policy and morality' (6 May 1908). Bennett met Lugard's arguments with a violent attack (27 July 1909) on 'Imperial officials who thwart the action of their own government . . . an intolerable state of things, and I think that some very sharp reprimand should be administered to officials of this type.'

Lugard was hardly the man to whom sharp reprimands could be addressed with impunity, and the matter was sorted out by a grant being made by the Colonial Office to help Hong Kong overcome its potential loss of income. This proved to be only an interim solution, since the whole question was raised again after Lugard's departure. His denunciation of 'the Faddists' was made privately in a letter to his wife of 26 July 1909: 'These pernicious parliamentarians who . . . have swollen heads because they are M.P.'s for some villa settlement . . . do a great deal of harm and make the Colonies hate the Mother country. Nor is it entirely useful for the Chinese to read these censures on their Governor.'[6]

An act of high patriotism to fornicate

Lugard was an ideal man to have at the head of affairs during the difficult times of the Chinese Revolution. He was able to rely upon Francis May's assistance – he described his second in command as 'a living dictionary of knowledge' – and shared May's conservative distrust of revolutionaries. Given this official disapproval at the top it is remarkable that throughout Lugard's period of office the revolutionary movement should have been allowed so free a hand in Hong Kong, where it had by far its strongest base.

The T'ung-meng Hui – the Revolutionary Alliance – which in the course of time developed into the Kuomintang, was founded in Tokyo in August 1905 by the exiled Sun Yat-sen, and rapidly established its branch in Hong Kong, which was to be for the next six years the centre of revolutionary activity in China.[7] Bomb factories were established, arms collected, recruits assembled and risings and assassinations planned. No fewer than six attempted coups were launched in Canton and Kwangsi, all planned from Hong Kong, and all failures. Ho Ch'i and his fellow member of the Legislative Council, Wei Yuk (an alumnus of the Dollar Academy in Perthshire and later also knighted), although retaining their sympathy for the aims of the revolts, steered clear of these incompetent conspirators. Ho acted in a professional capacity as solicitor for one Yü Chi-ch'eng, a known revolutionary, when the Canton authorities attempted to extradite him on a trumped-up charged of robbery. The court was convinced by Yü's counsel, Sir Henry Berkeley, K.C., that his client was in truth wanted for a political offence, for which he enjoyed the protection of the Hong Kong laws and could not therefore be extradited to China.

The last effort of the Hong Kong revolutionary cells took place in April 1911 and ended in another complete fiasco, although one attended with considerable bloodshed, in the city of Canton, after which the movement in Hong Kong lost much of its enthusiasm. When the successful rising that eventually brought down the Ch'ing came later that year, it was in the Hupei city of Wuchang, and had little to do with the inept efforts of the T'ung-meng Hui. Huang Hsing, the revolutionary leader in Hunan-Hopei, had distanced himself from

Sun's policy and followed his own strategy. It was not a civilian plot but an army mutiny that sparked the outbreak, which was quickly followed by similar outbreaks in the other provinces which declared their independence from the central government. The Ch'ing administration in Peking by then depended entirely on the support of that skilled trimmer Yüan Shi-kai, and when he decided to support the revolution the outcome was inevitable. On 11 February 1912 the five-year-old Pu-Yi, the Emperor Hsuan-t'ung, formally abdicated. By that time all the provinces except one were controlled either by Yüan or by local notables: only in Kwantung had the T'ung-meng Hui–Kuomintang proved successful. The Ch'ing Viceroy at Canton, the last to hold that post, was Chang Ming-ch'i, a young man of considerable ability, who managed to avert a military revolution in the city, and the Kuomintang was able to take over peaceably in November 1911, Hu Han-min, a moderate, becoming head of the government.

The attempts to overturn the Manchu rule, which had cost so many millions of lives in the previous century, had finally been successful. The new order, however, was no very clear improvement. Sun Yat-sen resigned his claims to leadership in favour of Yüan, who was accepted as the only potential head of government. An election in December 1912, held with a limited franchise, but still the only legitimate election ever to be attempted in China, resulted in the Kuomintang being returned as the largest single party. This was too much like democracy for Yüan, who then had the Kuomintang declared a 'seditious organization' and banned. Thereafter Yüan imposed an increasingly personal and neo-imperial rule which became so unpopular that many provinces renounced allegiance to the central government.

The news of events in November 1911 in Canton, which was taken, a little prematurely, to signify the end of the Empire, was received in Hong Kong, Lugard wrote, with 'the most amazing outburst which has ever been seen and heard in the history of the Colony ... The entire Chinese populace appeared to become temporarily demented with joy. The din of crackers ... was deafening and accompanied by perpetual cheering and flag-waving – a method of madness most unusual to the Chinese.'[8] The Governor also wrote to his brother that 'Even the Prostitutes have announced in posters and in the press that they are paying half their earnings to "the Cause", and inviting extra custom from patriotic motives. Where but in China would you find it an act of high patriotism to fornicate!'[9] Wisely, Lugard chose to turn a blind eye to these manifestations, and on 13 November sought the advice of Ho Ch'i and Wei Yuk. A compromise was reached, and it was agreed that another demonstration could be held, not to sanction a revolution which was still its early stage and the success of which was by no means guaranteed, but to 'signify joy at the absence of bloodshed in Canton'. Ho and Wei, tongues firmly in cheeks, assured the Governor that the demonstration was without political significance, which Lugard found it prudent to believe.

A few days later, on 19 November, Lugard had a meeting with the leading Chinese members of community at which he explained that while they were at liberty to entertain their own views on Chinese politics, and that he 'would sympathize with their legitimate aspirations', there were certain rules of conduct that must be observed within the colony. Public enthusiasm had spilled over into a certain amount of the old anti-foreign conduct, looting and obstructing the police, mostly originating among Cantonese 'min-Chuen' – bluntly, bandits – who had arrived in considerable numbers. This was exactly the sort of situation which Lugard had met often before in Nigeria, and he took some pleasure in dealing with it, sending army patrols through the worst affected areas and proclaiming an emergency Peace Preservation ordinance enabling magistrates to impose summary floggings, 'so that a very considerable proportion of the disaffected riff-raff [were] engaged in scratching their sterns in public, and prefer standing to sitting'. In all some fifty 'riff-raff' were flogged before the emergency legislation was lifted in the following February. Although considerable alarm was felt at what seemed to be a return to the bad old days of street violence and attempted poisonings, this was trivial compared to what was taking place just over the border. Dr Chan Lau concludes that 'the governor ensured that Hong Kong behaved appropriately in terms of its external relations during the revolution. By adopting stern and severe policies in dealing with the so-called lawless elements, he succeeded in restoring law and order within the colony.'[10]

Lugard, like all Governors after him, was constrained in his action by more than the Colonial Office restrictions. The Chinese Empire was obviously crumbling, and British policies remained to prop it up for as long as reasonably possible – and even for longer, as the determined British effort to back Yüan Shi-kai's attempt to restore a monarchy in 1915 proved. Hong Kong's external interests, which were much more closely concerned with what was happening in Canton than with who held the reins of power in Peking, had to take second place. It was a frustrating state of affairs for Lugard, the last of the

empire-builders, habituated to being able to call up a punitive expedition to reinforce diplomatic efforts, but he showed more awareness
of the delicacy of his situation than did his immediate successors,
and exerted himself to establish good relations with the authorities at
Canton. He was so successful in this as to annoy the Colonial and
Foreign Offices, who felt that he was poaching on preserves that should
have been the responsibility of the British Consul-General at Canton.

But the support of the Canton Viceroy was critical to the success
of what proved to be Lord Lugard's most important contribution to
Hong Kong, the central part he played in founding the University.[11]
There had been talk of such a project since the 1880s, when the
College of Medicine was founded, and W.H. Donald, the editor of
the *China Mail*, 'a congenial and unendingly cheerful man', had been
enthusiastically backing the idea for some time before Lugard threw
out the suggestion that a new university could be combined with the
existing College of Medicine and with the Technical Institute, which
had just been established to provide evening classes.

Manson's college, although successful in producing a small number
of competent doctors, had always been a scratch affair, relying on
local medical men providing free tuition, and having only $2,500 of
government assistance per annum. It was essential that any new institution should be properly funded, and this seemed likely to prove a
difficult task. H.N. Mody, a successful Parsee, immensely sympathetic,
and a great admirer of Lady Lugard ('dear old Mody – he almost
worships you, the dear old man', Lugard wrote to Flora[12]) offered a
generous opening contribution. The speed at which events subsequently moved is an object lesson in how a colonial administration
could get things done. Mody confided to A.H. Rennie, the promoter
of the Hong Kong Flour Mills, about the initial approach ('I cannot
see the use of meeting HE on this subject, as I leave everything to you
. . . I have every confidence in you, my good friend, and you may have
a lakh and a half of dollars for the building of a University if you are
satisfied with the site and all other arrangements'[13]). On 17 February
1908 Rennie met Lugard, and produced a one-page feasibility study,
which envisaged departments of Medicine, Commerce, and Engineering. Lugard consulted Sir Paul Chater, and decided to proceed:
another meeting was held, with May – no enthusiast – and Rennie on
13 March, and, three days later, a Committee was invited which held
its first meeting on the eighteenth. Advice was sought from the Universities of Tokyo, Birmingham, Manchester and Glasgow and a detailed

feasibility study with capital and revenue costs prepared. (Shortly after-wards the Flour Mills failed, and Rennie committed suicide.) The selection of a site presented some problems; Mody thought the pro-jected Tai-ping-shan location 'a hotbed of plague and shunned by the Chinese'; the College of Medicine believed Pokfulam too inaccessible.

By October the decisions were made, and Lugard launched the campaign with an appeal to the more conservative Chinese. A university was needed in Hong Kong, since ten years, which was the time needed to complete a secondary and university education abroad, was too long for young men to be separated from their parents, and 'I have heard, too, that Chinese parents find by experience that their sons return from a course of study in a foreign country with revolutionary ideas and become a danger to the state. It should be the special care of Hong Kong University to see that no such pernicious doctrines are encouraged or tolerated here.' Chinese reactions were cautious; were the Chinese only to have the privilege of paying for the University, or were they going to be given a share in its management; were the fees not high in relation to those charged in London; and, after all, might it turn out to be no better than an *Indian* university? Lugard assured them that they would indeed be expected to serve on the controlling board, and that their contributions would be recorded on a suitable plaque, 'In order of the amount donated and not according to the social standing of the donors.' A list of suggested names was sent to Edward Irving, the Registrar-General, for vetting: he found the suggestions acceptable – 'They are all quite private individuals and their sole recommendation is that they are wealthy. I do not think that there is any reason to object to any of them.' But it seemed that Taotai Wu of Canton had been instructed by the Viceroy to say that two of them 'had the reputation of being active participants in the revolution-ary party led by Dr Sun Yat-sen'. May, the expert, investigated the suggestion and reported on 13 March 1909: 'Chan is the editor of a Chinese newspaper ... dresses in European style ... but not a revolutionary. If he really were dangerous like Dr Sun he would have been finished long ago.'

The European community proved initially even more suspicious than the Chinese, and large donations were slow in coming in. It proved fortunate that one of the most important Hongs, Butterfield and Swire, was having trouble with the Chinese: one of their ticket collectors had been accused of kicking an elderly Chinese to death, and a retaliatory boycott was imposed. Their handsome donation of £40,000 was enough to have the boycott called off and was matched by an equal gift from the China Association.

Some actual obstruction had to be coped with; after the Legislative Council had, with some encouragement, been persuaded to vote $50,000 to the project, the Colonial Office stepped in to veto the grant. To some extent they had been influenced by a rival concern, backed by the Revd. Lord William Cecil, later Bishop of Exeter, who was seeking backers for a specifically Christian university, and expressed his distaste for Lugard's project in pious terms: 'We Christians put before them [young men] the higher moral tone. A merely Utilitarian University leaves to a great extent the enthusiasm of youth unoccupied and therefore it becomes a hotbed of revolutionary intrigue.' All that was eventually forthcoming from the Imperial government was the miserable sum of £300 a year to fund the King Edward VII Scholarships. The Peking government did much better, with £25,000 in addition to the similar sum given by Canton. The rest of the money, a total of one and a quarter million dollars, was scraped together, and the foundation stone was laid on 16 March 1910. At the ceremony, Lugard made a speech remarkable for its lack of prescience: 'Let us exercise our imperial imagination . . . we are forging a link in the chain which binds us in friendship and goodwill with the great Empire on whose confines this Colony is situated' – this in the year before that Empire finally collapsed.

In one of its aims, to avoid having students enthused by revolutionary doctrines, the University of Hong Kong has been quite remarkably successful – in spite of Lord William Cecil's gloomy prognostication. In the other, to attract Chinese from the mainland, it has not done so well. Japan, where the language difficulties were not great and where Chinese were not met with that bland condescension that was the best they could expect from the British, was much more popular among Chinese youth, and the American universities in China were funded with a generosity that placed them in a different rank from that of Hong Kong. Nor was the University conceived on a large enough scale; when, duly built, staffed and incorporated, it opened its doors in 1912, it was to only seventy-seven undergraduates, mainly from China, to begin their studies in the Faculties of Medicine, Engineering and the Arts. Lord William Cecil, far removed from the real world, noted disapprovingly: 'Most unfortunately the English started the Hong Kong University on a secular basis . . . if the Hong Kong University had been established on a thoroughly Christian basis and had, as we wished, also taught reverence for the Confucian philosophy, probably there would have been no trouble in Canton.'[14]

The first Vice-Chancellor was an odd choice. Sir Charles Eliot had been among Benjamin Jowett of Balliol's star pupils, 'one of the chief academic wonders of Oxford', a slim willowy youth, bright-eyed, mobile lipped', who spoke twenty-seven languages fluently, but 'had great difficulty in adding up a column of £, s and d' and 'disliked the work of engineers, which he said made cities filthy with smoke and made primitive people discontented':[15] neither of these last attributes was likely to be helpful to the head of what was essentially a technical university, with the largest faculty that of engineering, and one urgently seeking to improve its finances. Eliot had been in the Diplomatic and Foreign Service and served from 1901 to 1904 as Commissioner for British East Africa, where his white-supremacist attitudes and policies had proved too much for even that not excessively sensitive institution. Some quotations from *The East African Protectorate*, which he published in justification, give a flavour of the first Vice-Chancellor's quality: 'American negroes are not fit for the suffrage'; 'the absence of any feeling for art in the African is remarkable'; 'Fusion between Europeans and negroes is of course out of the question'. The 'lower races of mankind', he agreed, 'must be protected from unjust aggression, and be secured sufficient lands for their wants; but with this proviso, I think, we should recognize that European interests are paramount.'[16] On his dismissal from British East Africa Eliot had become Vice-Chancellor of the University of Sheffield, and from there he went to Hong Kong in 1912. He was not a great success, and in 1920 the University had to be rescued by a grant of $1,700,000 from the colonial government, which paid off debts of over half a million dollars and provided an endowment fund. This windfall came from the old prop and stay of the colony's finances, opium; the new Chinese republican government was energetically suppressing the drug (recidivism was reduced to almost nil by the simple practice of shooting those who re-offended), which had the effect of making the Hong Kong government monopoly extremely profitable, and the University one of the few to be financed by the drug trade. A typical Hong Kong row followed Eliot's resignation in 1918 to become British High Commissioner in Siberia; the Council had asked Reginald Johnson, administrator of Weihaiwei, to take the Vice-Chancellorship but the Senate of the University – it is said because Johnson had a 'pronounced anti-missionary bias' – refused to confirm this. It was believed that Cecil Clementi of the Colonial Office was willing to take the post, but this proved not to be so.[17] The outcome was that Johnson went to Peking to become tutor to the boy Emperor, now confined in the Forbidden City and Clementi, six years later, came to Hong Kong as Governor.

In its effort to provide leadership for the new China the University was not successful. A review in 1937 correctly, if slightly cynically, assessed its intentions:

China in 1911 was beginning to awake; her educational system was still woefully inadequate; and there was a vast field for development of railways and roads, waterworks, power plants and factories. What could be more fitting than that Great Britain, always in the forefront of engineering matters, should provide in its outpost in China the means by which the engineers required for this awakening could be trained? There would be prestige; there would be something like benevolence; and there might be the indirect advantage of making China's pioneers think in terms of British standards and material when it came to purchase of plant.

This had not happened; most of the Chinese graduates had not returned to China, and of these 'the majority are filling posts which are not at all commensurate with the cost of their education'. Medical graduates, having obtained degrees that entitled them to international recognition, had been even more reluctant to return to China, and the Faculty of Arts had 'attached itself like some half-unwanted stepbrother to those two scientific Faculties which, to the founders at least, gave such promise of a sturdy manhood'.[18]

When Lugard left to resume his interrupted career in Africa in March 1912, Francis May at last got the job for which – at least in his own opinion – his experience had so well qualified him. In fact it is doubtful whether May, that superb assistant, ever had possessed the qualities of a Governor. He may well have reached his level as Captain-Superintendent of Police between 1893 and 1902, when he had effected a complete reform, and a severe cull, of the force. His actions as Officer Administering the government had often been rash and ill-considered, and he lacked the public presence which might have enabled him to face down criticism. Only to some extent were his deficiencies compensated by the qualities of his wife, the Helena May of the eponymous Institute.[19] Almost as much a Hong Kong veteran as her husband – being the daughter of General Digby Barker, who had advocated the Kowloon extension – Helena was for twenty-five years at the forefront of energetic good works in the colony.

Hong Kong was May's second and last governorship, thirty-one years after he had first come to the colony. In 1910 he had been promoted away to Fiji, as Governor, and on his return in 1912 he found China a very different country from the one he had first known under Pope Hennessy, and even from that he had left only two years previously. In that brief time the Manchu Empire had disappeared and been replaced by a shaky republic under the presidency of Yüan Shi-kai.

A demonstration of the new state of affairs was offered on the first day of his term of office, when, as Sir Francis was actually proceeding in state from the quay to City Hall for the inauguration ceremony, he was shot at from the crowd. Violence against officials was unknown in Hong Kong, in stark contrast to Canton, where in 1910 two military governors had been assassinated in the space of a few months. Nor was the attempt on May politically inspired, but the result of a misunderstanding. In a letter to the *Times* correspondent in Peking, G.E. Morrison, May wrote on 11 August 1912 that 'The attack on me has no political significance at all. The man was I am sure crazy although the doctors who examined him at my instance pronounced him sane. Curiously enough he mixed up Fiji with South Africa (Feichau in Cantonese) and thought that I was governor of the Transvaal and had turned his compatriots out of that country.'[20] The Liberal government's ban on indentured Chinese labour in the Transvaal had clearly not been popular among those it was meant to protect. But however little political violence was directed against the British authorities in Hong Kong, any unrest in Canton inevitably affected the colony, especially in the New Territories, where bands of min-Chuen roamed across the borders. In August 1912 the little island of Ch'eung Chau, off Lantau, was raided by pirates, the police station destroyed and the constables killed.

Altogether more typical of Hong Kong was the trouble on the tramways. As a matter of convenience Canton coins, of the same size and denomination as those of Hong Kong, had been widely accepted in the colony, but in the autumn of 1912 the Canton currency had depreciated to such an extent that the Hong Kong government attempted a currency reform which would have the effect of banning Canton coinage from circulation. The tramways and the Star Ferry Company had to insist on payment being made only in Hong Kong currency, a move which was widely resented. As well as being an inconvenience it was seen as an insult to the new Republic of China, and a boycott of the trams followed. May's authoritarian habits prompted him to issue an extraordinary coercive measure, the Boycott Prevention Ordinance, which gave wide powers to punish incitement to boycott and provided for penal taxation on areas which submitted to a boycott.

This 'most objectionable' law aroused considerable suspicion in Whitehall, and May was in fact instructed to repeal it, an instruction which he was successfully able to disregard.[21] The Governor also angrily berated any Chinese he thought was not pulling his weight in fighting the boycott. In fact the local press and almost all the prominent Chinese sided with the government, but this was not enough to save them from May's wrath. In particular he pursued his old adversary Ho Ch'i, whom he accused of 'not having made two speeches helpful to the government'. May seemed unable to adapt himself to the thought that Chinese should form part of the apparatus of government, and Ho Ch'i's knighthood that year may well have irked him: he reported to the Colonial Office: 'While Mr Wei Yuk [the other Chinese member of the Legislative Council] still retains as much of my confidence as experience proves that it is safe to repose in any Chinese, I regret that I cannot say the same of Sir K'ai Ho Kai.'[22] The Secretary of State, Sir Lewis Harcourt, a Liberal of liberal tendencies, was no admirer of Sir Francis, whom he believed had 'mismanaged' the tramways affair and on whose behaviour he commented ironically, 'This man is so efficient I shall have to promote him to St Helena.' As a compromise it was agreed that no Legislative Council member should serve for more than two terms, which barred Ho Ch'i, a member since 1890, from reappointment. Only one month later May put forward Wei Yuk's name for a third term of office, making nonsense of the previous decision.

The financial difficulties of the Republican government in Canton grew steadily worse, much to the concern of the merchants there and in Hong Kong, but things began to look brighter in the spring of 1913, when President Yüan offered a loan from Peking to bail out the Canton government. The suggestion was warmly received by the Chinese population of Hong Kong, who had lost most of their enthusiasm for Sun Yat-sen and his followers, to the extent that when Sun passed through Hong Kong in June 1913 he was met only with neglect; and rumours even circulated that photographs of the father of the revolution had been stoned. The 'Second Revolution' of July 1913, when Yüan moved against those provinces held by the Kuomintang, was generally welcomed in Hong Kong, and especially by the colonial authorities, who saw in a provincial government supported by Peking the possibility of stability in Kwantung. They were therefore prepared to tolerate the 'acts of gross corruption, inefficiency, excess and brutality'[23] that took place over the border so long as they did not affect the tranquillity and prosperity of Hong Kong.

After August 1914 events in China ceased to occupy the attention of Europe, and Hong Kong became of even more peripheral interest to the British government than previously. Life in Hong Kong was not much interrupted by the First World War. The Hongkong and Shanghai Bank was the object of some nervousness – suspected, because of the number of German nationals on the board and its links with German banks, of being subject to German influence. German nationals were interned and German businesses closed down, and Hong Kong's Britons volunteered in great numbers, but the prosperity of the colony waxed, in part due to that old standby, opium.

In spite of the reservations of the British government, it seemed that the Chinese were more seriously intent on suppressing the drug than they had been given credit for. Sometimes, perhaps, the enthusiasm was more apparent than real. Dr Chan Lau notes that: 'Under the guise of banning opium in the province [of Kwantung] a so-called opium inspection office . . . was set up . . . in Canton, which in reality attempted to amass supplies, centralize sales, and channel profits to Peking.'[24] But in other provinces vigorous action was taken, especially after the 1911 revolution, when in Hunan alone forty-seven people, including five women, were shot for producing or smoking opium. So dangerous an addiction rapidly lost much of its attraction, and the demand for imported opium slumped. An interesting situation then arose. Opium stocks in Hong Kong amounted to as much as £12 million, funded by British banks operating in the Far East. China's action to end consumption of the drug rendered these stocks, in the immediate future, almost unsaleable; and the Indian producers were still turning out more opium in the quantities permitted by the ten-year agreement. Merchants and banks frantically attempted to pressure the British government into forcing upon the Chinese authorities an observance of the ten-year agreement, which would allow opium to be imported once more.

It looked very much like a re-run of 1839–40, and similar arguments

were again advanced in the House of Commons. On 7 May 1913 the
Revd. Josiah Towyn Jones, a Welsh Nationalist, moved that China
should be released from her treaty obligation to admit opium, and that
'she should be set free to prohibit the importation of the stocks of
Opium now accumulated at the treaty ports and Hong Kong'. If successful, the motion would have led to enormous, perhaps crippling
losses. Jones apologized for any defects in his maiden speech, since
English was to him a foreign language, but he did remarkably well:

> In Britain we label opium a poison . . . as far as its effects are
> concerned, they are disease, debauchery, and death everywhere,
> irrespective of colour and creed, country and clime . . . the fact
> that the British Government are enforcing this immoral trade
> against the will and conscience of China by unrighteous treaties,
> consequent upon most unjust wars, adds immeasurably to our
> guilt and shame.

Henry Keswick, the Jardine Taipan who had retired from Hong Kong
to become Member of Parliament for Epsom, attempted to stem the
flow: 'If you believe all that has been said in this House tonight, you
would imagine that the smoking of opium was necessarily a most horrible evil. It is no more an evil than the taking of a glass of beer or a
glass of wine.' When Taylor asked if he would like his own son to
smoke opium, Keswick agreed that he would not: 'I have tried it myself,
and it made me very ill indeed,' but went on to suggest that what port
and whisky were to the British, opium was to the Chinese constitution, and as for his three sons, he would look forward to their partak-
ing of such beverages 'in due course . . . with discretion'.

It would have been impossible for a Liberal government in 1913 to
adopt the strong line Palmerston might have taken, and equally impossible to force the banks into such large losses. The only conceivable
solution was put forward with a suitable rhetorical flourish by Edwin
Montagu, the Under-Secretary of State for India:

> I am glad to be able to tell the House that . . . notwithstanding
> the Treaty which China made with us, notwithstanding that we
> may get from these chests of opium [those allowed under the
> Treaty for the unexpired period] roughly speaking something like
> eleven millions sterling revenue . . . we are prepared not to sell

any more opium to China not only this year, not only while the stocks are being absorbed, but never again.

The motion was withdrawn, and the debate ended in mutual congratulations at having done the right thing at the least expense.

On the international front enough progress had been made to enable a Hague Convention to be agreed, in 1912, providing for 'gradual and effective measures' aimed at the complete suppression of the trade. Taken in conjunction with the ban on Indian sales to China, commercial difficulties were inevitable in renegotiating the contract between the Hong Kong government and its opium sub-contractor. In an endeavour to circumvent these the Colonial Office took the initiative in suggesting that the system be ended and that the Hong Kong government should take the opium monopoly into their own hands. Since, in an effort to substitute a tax on alcohol and tobacco for the revenues lost in closing the divan-dens, a preventative force had already been formed, this could be done without extra expense: the customs men could control all the addictive drugs at the same time. May and his councils agreed, and the House of Commons was satisfied with the explanation that the change was all part of a long-term project to ban the trade. (This turned out to be very long-term indeed, since it was another thirty-two years before opium became illegal in Hong Kong. It was finally prohibited by the post-war military government on 20 September 1945 – and was only made possible by the absence of a colonial authority which would doubtless have continued to defend this source of government income as stoutly as had its predecessors. But Theodore Taylor was alive to celebrate it, since he lived until 1950, having reached the age of 102.)

The change was immediately, even embarrassingly, successful. Under the previous system, hampered by the effort of the abolitionists, opium revenue had fallen to $1,183,200 by 1912. The first year of the government monopoly saw this shoot up to $2,680,617, to peak in 1918 at nearly $8 million, at which level the income from the drug amounted to no less than 46.5 per cent of all Hong Kong government revenue. While highly satisfactory, this needed to be kept decently quiet lest earnest reformers should complain, and the opium monopoly proceeds were therefore camouflaged in the official returns as 'Licences and Internal Revenue not otherwise specified'. It is typical, and wryly amusing, that G.R. Sayer, who was involved as Secretary to the Governor during the establishment of the monopoly, omits any mention of the subject in his history of Hong Kong, and attributes the wartime prosperity of the colony to more respectable sources, which enabled $5 million to be 'placed forthwith at the disposal of His Majesty's Government'.[25] The total net income from opium during the five war years amounted to just over $25 million.

The First World War, in spite of its frightful casualties among fighting men, had less permanent effect upon Britain than is sometimes assumed. The Edwardian upper classes were able to resume their comfortable lives in a post-war world where unemployment ensured that servants – perhaps a trifle less polished than before – were still plentiful. Imperial expectations had been handsomely fulfilled: not only the white British dominions, Australia, New Zealand and Canada, flocked to the banner of the Mother Country, but South Africa, Ireland and the USA sent volunteers in hundreds of thousands. Indian troops had served loyally (apart from one or two mutinies), and it seemed as if the pieces of the Empire could be retrieved and reassembled, to be set slowly on the road to self-government.

Given such a background, it would have been too much to expect that the rulers of Hong Kong would be sensitive to new developments, especially those that related to Chinese nationalism and to Communism. The effort to establish first a viable republic, and then a monarchical form of government in Peking, foundered with Yüan Shi-kai's death in 1916, and it appeared as though China was splitting into regions where control rested with whichever local commander could muster the most effective body of troops. Sun Yat-sen attempted once again to use Canton as a base for establishing power, but a government he founded there in 1917 was short-lived. The incessant shifts of power in warlord-dominated China led to his return in February 1923, as 'Grand Marshal', head of a military government.

Popular support in the colony for any mainland leader continued to be limited and less than enthusiastic, but the government was denied a period of post-war tranquillity. May reluctantly left in September 1918, after a mild stroke, to be succeeded in September 1919 by Sir Reginald Stubbs, the interim being administered by the Colonial Secretary, Claud Severn – 'a clever, humorous old stoutie', ' a kindly man, if somewhat pompous', who once, detailed to give away a bride, fell asleep in church while waiting.[26] Severn came from a modest colonial background, was fond of cricket, given to composing light verse, and devoted to his newly wedded wife Nan, but his new chief was cast in a sterner mould.

The son of the famous Bishop Stubbs of Oxford, the foremost historian of his generation and a man of overpowering personality, Sir Reginald 'inherited all his father's academic ability and more than his share of his father's directness of speech'.[27] With a double first in classics and greats he was able to pass easily into the Colonial Office, but chose to transfer after thirteen years in Whitehall to the Colonial Service. As a young man Stubbs had, like all the other Whitehall clerks, been highly critical of the 'men on the spot', and especially those in Hong Kong, where 'even the cadets were prepared to advance claims to act on behalf of the Almighty'.[28] After only six years in the service, as Colonial Secretary in the well-ordered colony of Ceylon – an unprecedentedly short apprenticeship – he was appointed to Hong Kong at the age of forty-three. The rarefied atmosphere of Oxford and Whitehall, hardly dispersed by spending the war years in the relative tranquillity of Ceylon, had equipped Stubbs but inadequately to cope with the rapid changes taking place in China. In addition, he had a short fuse which, combined with a firm conviction of the rectitude of his own rather conventional views, often got him into trouble, sometimes seriously.

The post-war Hong Kong government found itself in a permanent dilemma. Its own dealings, as a matter of practical necessity, had to be with whatever administration was in power in Canton, three hours away along the railroad. But the British government's ambassador was, with the rest of the Diplomatic Corps, accredited to Peking, where a quite different set of politicians and generals, usually at loggerheads with those in the south, were in charge. Sir John Jordan in the capital had never thought much to Hong Kong, and the post-war settlement seemed a useful opportunity to improve Anglo–Chinese relations by returning the New Territories to China. It would be, he conceded, 'a considerable sacrifice ... But without sacrifices on the part of all Powers who acquired or inherited leased territories of 1898 no solution of the [China] problem seems possible.' Lord Curzon, then Foreign Secretary, brushed this 'idealistic and impracticable' notion aside: 'We cannot begin to dig up by the roots all previous cessions, perpetual leases etc. To give back the Kowloon extension is in my view out of the question.' The Chinese desk of the Foreign Office remained unconvinced.

What transpired in the north often had little effect on events in Hong Kong. When it was revealed during the negotiations for the Versailles Treaty that rights in Shantung province had been granted extensively to the Japanese by the previous Peking government, with the backing of the Western allies, all China seemed to react with anger and dismay; but the May Fourth movement of 1919, when students demonstrating in Tiananmen Square fired the rest of China with excitement, caused few ripples in the colony. The Chinese community in Hong Kong, whatever their political preferences, tended, for reasons of profitability, to favour whichever group seemed to offer the prospect of reasonable stability in Canton. From 1913 to 1916 the Yunnanese warlord General Lung Chi-kuang's brutal and corrupt regime had at least survived and been supported by Peking. Opposition by Kuomintang supporters in Hong Kong was suppressed by May, who stated to the Colonial Office on 4 May 1916: 'My endeavour has been and is to support the existing authority, which has shown itself alone able to maintain order in the province, by preventing the Chinese in Hong Kong from rendering assistance to the rebels either actively or by revolutionary propaganda.'

But after Yüan's death in June 1916 General Lung withdrew from Canton, and an old colleague of Sun's, Ch'en Chiung-ming, previously a member of the Hong Kong T'ung-meng Hui, took charge. Attitudes in Hong Kong began to differ: Ch'en's single-minded commitment to the welfare of Kwantung and his pragmatic avoidance of revolutionary rhetoric appealed to the more conservative, while the younger and more enthusiastic supported Sun Yat-sen. May, who believed Sun to be a 'closet Bolshevik', had no doubts on the matter, but by the time of Stubbs's arrival Sun's flirtation with Communism was cooling. The label of the Revolutionary Party, which had been adopted after Yüan's coup, was quietly dropped and the Kuomintang resurrected.

Sun would probably always have preferred to obtain the support of Britain, a country he knew well and for whose institutions he had a high regard. When, immediately after gaining power in Canton, he paid an official visit to Hong Kong in February 1923 he was cordially received and entertained by Stubbs at Government House. In a speech to the University Sun described the island as his 'intellectual birth-place' where he had learned his 'revolutionary and modern ideas'. In the midst of 'deafening cheers' he lauded the British Parliamentary system, and urged his audience 'to carry the example of good government to all parts of China'.[29] Such acceptable sentiments stimulated Stubbs's anxiety to assist Sun, but this got him into difficulties at home and very nearly cost him his job.

The need to live on amicable terms with the powers in Canton had been made painfully obvious to Stubbs in the previous year. The provincial government was in constant financial difficulties, largely because it was cut off from access to the most reliable source of income, the revenue from the Maritime Customs, which was paid direct to Peking, where it stayed. If a due portion of this, after deduction of the agreed repayments on foreign obligations, could come direct to Canton, the provincial government could use this as security for a much-needed loan to be raised in Hong Kong. The Peking authorities, who wanted the money themselves, very naturally took a poor view of this, and urged their case on the foreign diplomats still stationed there. Stubbs was accordingly approached to deploy his good offices on behalf of Canton. This he proved remarkably willing to do, writing to the Colonial Office to ask that Sun's claims on the customs income should not be opposed: 'I urge most strongly that His Majesty's Government should not intervene further than is absolutely necessary to secure payment of foreign loans. This would be provided for by adoption of Sun's latest proposals.'

This intervention by a mere colonial Governor in matters of state was too much for the Foreign Office, then headed by Lord Curzon, a man acutely conscious both of the proprieties and of his own importance. Stubbs must be made an example of: either he must be sacked, or at the very least a 'sharp reproof' must be administered. Reproval and promised amendment duly followed, and in the next crisis Stubbs behaved in a correctly circumspect fashion.[30]

The Canton Merchant Volunteer Corps affair of 1924 has never been satisfactorily explained, since the chief participant died shortly after this extraordinary adventure, in which a respectable bank engaged in gun-running. A.G. Stephen, Chief Manager of the Hongkong and Shanghai Bank, had been a creative banker, ready to take chances at which a more conventional lender might have hesitated. The Merchant Corps was a private army – a common enough thing in China at the time – raised by contributions from the merchants and intended to defend Cantonese business interests against revolutionary outsiders. Connecting Canton and Hong Kong was Ch'en Lien-po, Compradore of the Bank in Canton, Commandant of the Corps, and an extremely rich man. Stephen gave his enthusiastic backing to Ch'en's scheme of importing a large quantity of small arms, at least ten thousand rifles and pistols together with several million rounds, contrary both to British policy and to existing agreements. The plot was exposed and the arms confiscated, but the suggestion was made by Stephen that

Stubbs had given at least tacit consent. This potentially extremely damaging insinuation Stubbs denied indignantly: 'Mr Stephen had certainly never discussed it with me . . . I do not understand the observation in Mr Stephen's letter . . . that he thought that "the Hong Kong Government would preserve a benevolent blindness" . . . I find it difficult to believe that anybody who knew me as intimately as Mr Stephen did could have formed this opinion.'[31]

Within two months the merchant force and the Kuomintang had come into collision, which rapidly resulted in the complete victory of the latter. The news was not well received in Hong Kong: 'Sun Must Go' was the headline in the *Hong Kong Telegraph*, and the Chinese press were equally scathing. By this time it had become clear that Sun had decided, for want of any alternative, to rely on Russian support. Borodin, the Russian 'special adviser', had arrived in Canton in October 1923 and engineered a rapprochement between the new Chinese Communist Party and the Kuomintang, while Blücher, the veteran Civil War cavalry leader, instructed the cadets at the new military academy at Whampoa. Both were quickly effective and by March 1925, when Sun died at the age of fifty-nine, the left wing of the Kuomintang and the Communists were jointly in control of Canton, and bent on causing trouble in the imperialist outpost to the south.

Organized strikes and boycotts had been used before by Hong Kong's Chinese population in order to protest against what they believed to be injustices, but Stubbs was faced with these techniques brought to perfection. The first occurred in April 1920, shortly after his arrival, when engineers, represented by the Hong Kong Engineering Institute, demanded a 40 per cent pay rise in compensation for the increased cost of living. This trade union had been formed ten years previously, and was well prepared to take action when post-war price rises, especially of the staple food, rice, made it nearly impossible to earn a living wage. Their polite request was turned down by the employers, whereon the mechanics, some nine thousand of them, simply took themselves off to Canton. By this time Hong Kong had become, at least in part, a modern industrial society, with telecommunications, tramways, electricity and gas industries serving the growing industrial base, and the sudden withdrawal of all skilled engineering labour quickly brought life to a standstill. It took only a fortnight for the employers to agree a 32.5 per cent increase. Unlike previous strikes, no chance was given to such traditional institutions as the Tung Wah

Committee to intervene; this was a straightforward example of well-organized workers confronting their employers.

More serious trouble broke out the following year when the Chinese Seamen's Union demanded similar increases.[32] Seafarers were notoriously the least well-organized and most put-upon of workers, and the Chinese seamen had more than most to complain about. They were paid only a fraction of European wages for the same work, and had to pay a high proportion of these to the shipmasters who found berths for them and provided board and lodging between voyages. Fortunately for them, the very system that gathered seamen together in squalid lodgings made it easier for them to organize. Representatives from each lodging house elected an effective Committee for Raising Wages, with both English and Chinese secretaries, and requested an increased scale of pay. With a compound of folly and incivility the employers did not even acknowledge the request, and on 13 January 1922 the seamen followed the example set by the mechanics, and departed for Canton. They were joined by increasing numbers of other workers, including domestic servants, engineers and coolies, some 120,000 workers in all, the majority of the colony's labour force. The coolies' employers wisely offered an immediate increase, but the men, in a demonstration of solidarity, insisted on staying on strike until the seamen's demands were met. Faced with resistance on this scale the employers, government and traditional Chinese leaders went into a nervous and ineffectual huddle. Those who had previously defended Chinese interests on the Tung Wah Committee were now, in defence of their own pockets, wholly on the side of the employers and government. They denounced the strikers as selfish simpletons: Sir Shouson Chou, who in 1926 became the first Chinese member of the Executive Council, insisted the government must not in any circumstances 'retreat one inch', and wanted all labour unions officially suppressed. Encouraged by 'responsible Chinese opinion', the government issued an Emergency Regulations Bill giving themselves extraordinary powers, proscribed the Seamen's Union and raided its headquarters. The worst moment came when, Chinese having been forbidden to leave the colony, Indian troops supporting the police fired on a large crowd attempting to cross the border and killed five of their number.

Such repressive measures did not go uncriticized in London; Colonel Josiah Wedgwood, a Labour Member, complained on 6 March 1922 that by preventing labourers from leaving the Hong Kong government was in effect forcing them 'to take work with the alternative of

RIGHT: Sikh policemen with a Chinese culprit in the stocks.

BELOW: An Assistant Superintendent of Police gives instructions to a Sikh Constable (*China Punch*, June 1867).

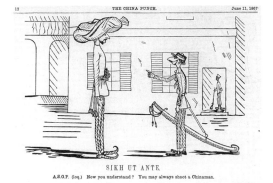

BELOW: A performance of Gilbert and Sullivan's *H.M.S. Pinafore*, c.1880.

The personage in the sedan chair was probably a draper's assistant, but his lordly bearing might be taken as typical of those superior British attitudes that so annoyed the Chinese.

The Jardine Matheson Taipan's house, c.1860.

Dent's Fountain and Beaconsfield Arcade, c.1860. Such colonial elegance has disappeared from Hong Kong, but is still to be found in Macao.

This view of Taipingshan, from the present site of Hospital Road, shows the Tung Wah Hospital in the left foreground, with the roof and belfry of the German mission church beyond it. Facing the church across Po Yan Street is the Chinese Theatre.

The meeting between the veteran Li Hung-chang and Sir Henry Blake, 18 July 1900. Li was then Viceroy at Canton, and considering whether to support or oppose the Ch'ing government. J.S. Lockhart stands between them, in full uniform. Blake was usually photographed in civilian clothes.

The typhoon of 1906. This French torpedo boat was one of the many vessels wrecked. Deaths, estimated at more than ten thousand, included that of the Bishop of Victoria, Dr C.J. Hoare.

Chinese and British middle classes in Stella Benson's Hong Kong.

starvation'. As well as being discreditable, the Hong Kong government's attempts at repression were useless. In an ignominious retreat government and employers, complaining bitterly of Communist support for the strikers, were forced to concede a famous victory for the seamen. Stubbs was thrown into despondency, and prophesied to the Colonial Office on 16 September 1922 that 'we should hold Hong Kong for twenty years at the most'.[33] This might be regarded as an unusually accurate estimate, for just over nineteen years later, in December 1941, Japanese troops occupied the colony. In the same letter Stubbs forecast, equally accurately, 'a boycott, more or less open': this duly occurred three years later, and developed into a test of wills between the new left-wing administration in Canton and the Hong Kong government.

It was sparked off in 1925 by the 30 May incident, when eleven demonstrators were killed in the Shanghai International Settlement by Chinese and Indian police under British command. There was tremendous indignation all over China, and general strikes were called in Shanghai and Hong Kong. A good deal of stirring-up on the part of the Canton Communist labour leaders active in the colony was needed before the strike call was heeded, but when three weeks later another crowd was fired upon in Canton by British-led troops, killing fifty-two, there was no need for agitation. Protracted investigation subsequently failed to establish which side began the clash, but this was hardly relevant in view of the relative casualty figures (only one foreigner was killed) and Chinese bitterness at having such an armed foreign enclave in the heart of a Chinese city. Cantonese fury was almost ungovernable, many clamouring for war. For the first time a violent and specifically anti-British feeling swept Hong Kong, and the strike rapidly became general: within just over a month a quarter of a million strikers and their families had left for Canton, where they were fed and housed by a highly-organized and well-funded strike committee. In addition to the central committee there were bureaux for reception, transport, recreation, correspondence, propaganda and finance, a strikers' court, and a staff of two thousand uniformed pickets, amounting to something very like an alternative government. For perhaps the first time it seemed that a Chinese city administration had developed its own effective and responsible institutions of government.

But the authorities in Hong Kong were capable of responding. A run on the Chinese banks was halted by a government guaranteed loan; volunteers staffed hospitals and essential services; temporary departments were set up to control food supplies, labour and transport; the directors of the Tung Wah gave their backing to the government, taking for the first time an active part in politics, and the usual emergency regulations were proclaimed. Intimidation, of which there were many examples, was met by counter-intimidation, and strikers' propaganda by anti-Communist attacks. By the end of July the back of the strike was broken, and the workers were flowing back to the colony. But the Canton committee had a more powerful weapon to employ: the complete boycott of all British goods and a ban on all ships using Hong Kong. This continued until October the following year, after Stubbs had left, and was savagely damaging to Hong Kong.

Stubbs had asked to be allowed to stay on in an effort to see out the crisis, but it became apparent that, unlike the strike, the problem of the boycott was incapable of being solved from Hong Kong. The Canton strike committee's actions were clear breaches of treaty agreements, but there was nothing the Peking government could do about it. The only alternative open to Britain was a reversion to gunboat diplomacy, compelling those in power at Canton to adhere to treaty terms by the use of armed force. This the Foreign Office, in spite of much urging from Stubbs to the Colonial Office, whose responsibility it was, did not feel justified in attempting. The Governor grew increasingly agitated and determined to bring down the Bolshevik regime in Canton. A glimmer of light seemed to appear in August 1925; Severn wrote to his wife, Nan, 'We are hoping that some action will be taken regarding Canton and the flagrant breach of the treaties. Yesterday the leading labour leader and communist was assassinated and this may have some effect.'[34] The victim was Liao Chung-k'ai, who had been a prominent Kuomintang man since before the revolution, but his removal did nothing to discourage the vigorous prosecution of the boycott.

Stubbs turned again to the possibility of funding the 'Anti-Red' opposition, and pressed upon the Colonial Office a proposal from the unofficial members of the Legislative Council that a million dollars should either be given from public funds or be collected from private sources. When the Foreign Office once more turned down the suggestion the increasingly desperate Stubbs suggested bribing the Peking authorities to intervene 'to compel Canton to put an end to anti-British actions and should be offered assistance by His Majesty's Government for this purpose both in money and material' (12 November 1925). The sum of $3 million was suggested as a suitable gratuity, but when this plan too was rejected in Whitehall Stubbs had recourse to a sadly minor piece of chicanery which implicated the Tung Wah Hospital in secretly (but it was very much an open secret) advancing $50,000 to finance a coup. When this fizzled out miserably the hospital was left with a deficit in its accounts, which eventually had to be paid by an expostulating Colonial Office protesting about a 'scandalous and possibly criminal misappropriation of trust funds', while the left-wing Chinese accused the hospital committee of being 'English dogs', caring only to keep their property and disregarding 'the loss of national prestige'.

By the time this came into the open Stubbs had departed (in October 1925), leaving the boycott in full swing.

13

A COLONIAL BACKWATER

Faces shut like doors

Governor Stubbs's agitated quest for an end to the boycott either by bribery or by force was followed by the quieter policy of his successor, Sir Cecil Clementi. An oddity in the Colonial Service, Clementi, after a brilliant Oxford career, had passed out high enough in the Civil Service examinations to have been able to take his pick of departments. He might have chosen the Indian Civil Service, the Foreign Office or the Treasury, but elected instead the Eastern Colonial Service, thought of as something of a haven for intellectual also-rans. A man of wide interests – his edition of the *Pervigilium Veneris*, a fourth-century erotic Latin poem, is one of the few scholarly works ever attempted by a colonial Governor – and considerable personal charm, Clementi was posted to Hong Kong in 1900 and worked on land registration in the New Territories. His chiefs spoke of his abilities with enthusiasm; Blake thought him 'one of the ablest men in the Eastern Service – a scholar and a thinker, and will go far one day',[1] and Lugard found him not only brilliant but sympathetic and agreeable. Before coming to Hong Kong as its Governor Clementi's name had been seriously canvassed as Vice-Chancellor of the University. He travelled extensively in China, learning many of the languages, and in 1907 embarked on a three-thousand-mile walk from Central Asia to Kowloon. Thereafter, for reasons best known to the Colonial Office, Clementi spent twelve years in British Guiana and Ceylon, where an intimate knowledge of China was not particularly relevant.

Poor Claud Severn, the Colonial Secretary, had hoped for the

Governor's job: 'The appointment of Clementi as Governor has been rather startling,' he wrote to his wife Nan on 22 August 1925. 'I think he should do well and that the appointment is a good one, but hardly while I am here, and that's felt I gather pretty generally.'[2] On his arrival in Hong Kong, in November 1925, Clementi immediately straightened out the tangled communications left by Stubbs and established relations not only with the Canton government but also with the British Foreign Office and its representatives in Peking and Canton. A sigh of relief was breathed by James Jamieson, the Consul-General at Canton, who had found both Stubbs and Severn incurably ignorant of the Chinese: 'Even more than in mainland China foreigners in Hong Kong ... had failed to grasp the nature and the extent of changes'. What Jamieson correctly identified as 'the growth of an exceedingly sensitive spirit of nationalism' was received in Hong Kong with 'apathy and abysmal ignorance'.[3]

The new Governor also attempted to enlist public opinion on his side. In this he was helped by Robert Kotewall, later a member of the Executive Council, and Shouson Chou, who, with the help of a government subsidy, began an anti-Communist newspaper which was widely circulated both in the colony and among the Chinese diaspora. Clementi later attempted to consolidate this success but complained to London that he had been banned from attempting any 'defensive counter propaganda ... I hope the experiences of the last general strike have created a body of opinion in local labour circles sufficiently convinced that the whips of capitalist exploitation are lenient beside the scorpions of union tyranny.'[4] Some counterblast to Communist propaganda was essential; the government's alleged practice of burying very small children under bridges to ensure their stability might only be believed by the more credulous, but the claim that 'In 1919 more than 10,000 of the On Chat Lai[?] tribe had a meeting in a public garden, and the British soldiers swept them with machine gun fire, leaving none of them un-killed,' was not without plausibility at the time of the notorious Amritsar massacre in the Punjab. The Colonial Office was not unduly concerned about morale within the colony: Walter Ellis, an Assistant Secretary, minuted on 21 February 1927: 'I think the talk about "strain on the loyalty" of the Hong Kong Chinese can be discounted. Surely any Chinaman who has anything to lose must thank his gods that he is living in Hong Kong under British justice and not at the mercy of [?] warlords and Reds.'[5]

It soon became apparent that while the Canton government lent general support to the strikers, it was not in control of their activities. The strikers demanded a complete climb-down, reinstatement, strike pay and compensation, amounting to over $20 million. This loss of face the Hong Kong government was not willing to tolerate, and after inconclusive discussions Clementi's thoughts turned to the possibility of coercion. Although this was strongly opposed by the British Consul-General in Canton, now Sir John Brenan, Clementi had the general support of the Colonial Office, which had from November the previous year been under Leo Amery, who was at that time always ready to assume an ultra-imperialist attitude. Amery wrote in his autobiography of his concern that 'the growth of an aggressive anti-European national-ism in China . . . led to much controversy between the Foreign Office, out for appeasement, and those of us who were more concerned to defend the interests built up by British enterprise in a prosperous colony like Hong Kong . . . But,' he added regretfully, 'little could be done to protect Hong Kong from the consequences of Chinese boycott.'[6]

These included such intolerable inconveniences as the demise of the chit. Paul Morand, a French diplomat, happily reported:

> Hong Kong is falling asleep . . . Little by little, revolutionary China endeavours to bring the city to its knees by commercial ruin . . . As a rule, everything is paid for with a signature in these countries, and even cocktails can be paid for on credit. Now, however, and this is quite unprecedented, signs put up in hotels and stores warn people that 'You will greatly help us by paying in cash'.[7]

But events were moving in the colony's favour. On Sun Yat-sen's death Chiang Kai-shek succeeded to the leadership of the Kuomin-tang. Chiang, who had been trained by the Japanese army, and had spent some time in Moscow examining the organization of the Red Army, had been appointed Commander of the military academy in Whampoa. From this base he had developed a powerful army, which was thereafter used to re-establish a central authority. As a first step, Chiang was preparing a northern expedition towards Shanghai and Nanking, and needed therefore to secure his position in Canton. In March 1926 a coup was engineered by Chiang's supporters which drew the Communists' teeth, and the atmosphere lightened considerably; Brenan spoke of 'a total volte-face', and in June Chiang issued an eight-point programme, of which one requirement was the end of the boycott. From thenceforward a settlement was merely a matter of time, encouraged by a little muscle-flexing by the Royal Navy in clearing pickets from the docks and a stubborn refusal by Hong Kong to pay any ransom money to the strikers. In October 1926 the boycott quietly ended without any payment being made. The conclusion was aptly put by Chan Lau: 'It was evident that the strike-boycott came to an end because the Canton government saw to it that it did . . . The lesson was difficult to forget. For the rest of Clementi's term of office in Hong Kong, he acted with the conviction that, for the sake of the colony's well being, the goodwill of Canton had to be cultivated and maintained at all cost.'[8]

The cumulative effect of the strike-boycott was severely damaging to Hong Kong. Chan Lau believes an estimated cost of £5 million a week 'quite conservative', and gives a figure of a total decrease in property value of £500 million. *The Times* estimate on 6 April 1927 was much lower, at £100 million, and it has to be appreciated that both these figures included notional losses due to the decline of property values. In the nature of things these would, and did, recover, any losses being realized only if property were sold under distress conditions. Current losses should have been reflected in the accounts of the banks, but the largest of these, the Hongkong and Shanghai Bank, showed record dollar, and only slightly reduced sterling, earnings in the critical year of 1926. Even with these limitations, however, there can be no doubt that the harm done to Hong Kong trade was considerable and protracted.

Chiang Kai-shek's northern expedition was eventually successful. By 1928 most of China was held either by the Kuomintang or by local potentates associated with the movement. The major exceptions were in Manchuria, where a provincial general, Marshal Zhang Zuolin, had established a quasi-independent state, and a nucleus of committed Communists remained in Jianxi, under the leadership of Mao Tsetung. A new capital was established at Nanking, well away from the dangerously exposed Peking (now renamed Peiping). Local disputes continued: a small civil war occurred between Kwangsi and Kwantung in 1929, and when this was settled the two provinces jointly fell out with Nanking. Even after their squabble with the central government was resolved the two Kwangs remained at least semi-autonomous, and enjoyed an unprecedented prosperity. This was shared to some extent by other Chinese cities, although not by the countryfolk, and the

Nanking decade, from 1928 to 1937, seemed as though it might be the start of a newly permanent Chinese state under the Kuomintang. The regime was recognized by the Powers, and the embassies moved from Peking to Nanking (Nanjing). Western encroachments were recovered; Tsingtao and Weihaiwei were returned by the Japanese and the British. International sympathy for China took on some practical forms; defaulting bonds were written down and renegotiated and new lendings arranged. These, interestingly enough, agreed with an aggressively independent nationalist state, were on almost identical terms to those negotiated up to half a century earlier and presumed to be imperialistically exploitative.

At the height of the strike Severn had written to his wife, on 21 August 1925: 'I feel sure that a great change is coming and that there will be a fearful retribution for the Russians in Canton when the people realize how they have been duped.'[9] Retribution was a little delayed, but came savagely in December 1927. Stalin had issued instructions to his agents in Canton to stage an uprising, instructions which were faithfully followed, with the usual amount of atrocities, mayhem and bloodshed. There was little support for the brief commune that followed, which was speedily crushed by the Kuomintang forces, to the accompaniment of even more of the usual atrocities, in the course of which five of the six remaining Russians in the Consulate were killed. Thereafter Canton had some stable interludes under the control of one or other of the Kuomintang factions and managed to enjoy its share of increasing prosperity.[10] Past asperities were forgotten, and when Clementi visited the city he was received with 'an almost effusive display of pro-British sentiments'.

Compared with such violent happenings Hong Kong remained a relative haven of tranquillity, and life resumed its normal pattern. It was not, from many points of view, an attractive one. The racial segregation begun with the creation of the Peak reservation was continued with an ordinance in 1902 setting aside twenty thousand acres of Kowloon for European occupation, on specious grounds of health (the Chinese could not be trusted to keep down mosquitoes). Attitudes had undergone a change since the earliest days, comparable to that which had occurred in India. The first colonists had seen the Chinese they met as exotic, fascinating, often difficult, sometimes admirable characters, but at least as individual fellow-humans. In 1842 the Chief Justice danced with the Emperor's uncle; Pottinger and Ch'i-ing were on the friendliest terms; Richard Woosnam, a surgeon who became a member of Pottinger's team, shed a tear over the death of 'poor old Elepoo'. But these Chinese were high officers of the Empire, men of great power, which always exercises considerable attraction. Once the colony was settled, the only Chinese coming into contact with the Westerners were in very subordinate positions – servants, shopkeepers, at best a compradore or merchant. Social discrimination was added to racial attitudes. Nor were the Westerners from the top drawer; the Civil Service, with few exceptions, was shuffled together from third-raters; the great taipans, who had commanded fleets and influenced governments, had retired, leaving commercial gentlemen to run their businesses, often extremely successfully, but rarely with the same panache.

For some time there was limited flexibility; in the 1850s Mrs Daniel Caldwell, a Chinese, was acknowledged as a member of Hong Kong society, had her children christened in the cathedral, and entertained the impresario Albert Smith, who passed with her family 'one of the most agreeable evenings of his visit'. The Caldwells were pillars of the cathedral, and also employed a private chaplain in their twenty-four-strong household. Church society, which should have been more egalitarian, ossified, at least as far as the Anglicans, firmly attached to notions of social status, were concerned. The Non-conformists were more liberal: in 1877 Miss Rowe, of the London Missionary Society, described a service attended by Chinese families:

> they made it a social function; babies were brought, and old women to nurse them, little children and girls to play with them . . . and even the family dogs to please the little folk . . . a kind of subdued picnic . . . the singing was dreadful . . . Everyone who could read the characters felt it was his or her duty to shout them aloud, as if like the priests of Baal, they thought God was sleeping.[11]

As well as being an assiduous Anglican, Daniel Caldwell was also a Freemason, and it was many years before the Hong Kong lodges of that society could bring themselves to admit Chinese. As late as 1895 it was recorded that 'Grand Lodge is strongly opposed to the admission of Chinese into Freemasonry, and though we have the misfortune to have one or two of such nationality attached to one of our lodges, their numbers are not likely to increase.'[12]

1869, the year of Affie's visit, might be taken as a watershed, when Hong Kong British society began to set in its mould, with the Governor and the permanent cadet officers at the centre, flanked by the Commander in Chief, the Bishop (Anglican, of course) and taipans forming the apex; a very small group, perhaps thirty in all, with their wives. The respectable persons, Justices of the Peace, special jurors, proprietors of businesses, were perhaps another three hundred; the remainder were 'pong pans' – subordinates, clerks, shopkeepers. Within this society, but knowing their place, were a handful of Jews, Armenians, Portuguese and Parsees who knew which fork was which and who were admissibly rich. Outside were a number of other Portuguese and Eurasians who quietly fulfilled essential clerical and minor administrative roles. Stations in society were evident from membership of the clubs; the elite belonged to the Jockey Club and the Hong Kong Club, while the Victoria Club admitted the others; Germans had their own club, the Germania, and Portuguese the Lusitania. The Cricket Club and Amateur Dramatic Corps cast their nets wider in search of talent, as presumably did Lord Saltoun's Madrigal Club.

Only later did one or two Chinese infiltrate British society, without ever being thoroughly accepted. The first of these, Sir Ch'i Ho Ch'i, a man of both worlds, insisted that Chinese were different; some Europeans appeared 'to forget that there are wide cultural differences between a native of China and one who hails from Europe. They do not allow for differences of habits, usage, mode of living and a host of other things.'[13] Spitting, Ho convinced Lugard, was doubtless objectionable, but the Chinese should not – indeed could not – be prevented from doing it. Ho believed that Chinese did not object to segregation, but among the second generation of Chinese knights Sir Man-Kam Lo, speaking on the occasion of abolition of residential segregation (which did not take place until 1946), insisted: 'There was very strong and bitter opposition to the measure on the part of the Chinese community . . . solely on the grounds of racial discrimination.'[14]

It took as long for the Matilda Hospital to change its policy. Under the terms of the businessman Granville Sharp's will, the Matilda, named after his wife, and opened in 1906, was to be 'for the benefit, care and happiness of patients primarily who are helpless . . . and emphatically . . . for the poor, the helpless, the forsaken and for him who is alone and desolate'. As long, that is, as he was white. (Although, as it was made clear in 1940 when an American woman married to a Chinese was refused admission, it was nationality, rather than colour, that was the officially advanced reason. Once again 'no Chinese' was universally understood without having to be embarrassingly specified.)

Sharp, a universally respected businessman, displayed crudely supremacist attitudes: 'We have been too lenient in the past,' he said in 1896. 'When first I came to Hongkong every Chinese coolie doffed his cap and stood on one side to allow you to pass. When do you see a coolie do that now? We do not exercise our undoubted superiority. We must rule by power . . .'[15]

Sharp was complaining about the decay of the Europeans' previous casual brutality, which had been replaced by irritating assumptions of superiority which were deeply resented by the Chinese: in the 1870s a Chinese gentleman had protested that he was not given the courtesy title 'esquire', which his British colleagues were accorded; on public property there could be no official segregation, but this did not prevent squabbles about sharing access to the city museum or sitting on the same park benches. In 1908 there was even a proposal to reserve some park areas and parts of public transport for foreigners. 'Of course,' Dr Chan commented, 'no such legislation so manifestly discriminatory materialized,'[16] but the attitude of mind that it represented was both unconcealed and widespread. Institutionalized discrimination did in fact exist: there was no question, for example, of Chinese being admitted to the higher ranks of the Eastern Colonial Service. It was not until 1942 that the Colonial Office dropped its demand that all candidates should be 'of pure European descent', and even as late as 1992 the most senior posts were all held by British officers.[17] This was in contrast with the practice in the Indian Civil Service, a more highly-regarded service, which had encouraged Indian applicants to qualify for the most senior positions since the 1920s. In Ceylon one-third of all appointments in the highest grades were reserved for Singhalese. Even junior posts, which in other parts of the empire would have been filled by locals, were reserved in Hong Kong for expatriate, white, staff. It was alleged that Cantonese police could not be relied upon to control their fellow countrymen in times of stress, and were unable or unwilling to counter intimidation by strikers. Europeans, Indians, and Chinese from Weihaiwei were recruited instead. Not until just before the Second World War were Chinese admitted to the police force at the rank of sub-inspector, and even then they were placed under the orders of British ranks junior to them. As late as 1946 this inexcusable policy was defended by the reactionary Chief of Police Colonel Sansom, who wanted also to ban inter-racial marriages. No excuse was offered when in other parts of the service Europeans, often not expatriate but locally recruited, were paid more than Chinese for the same work purely on grounds of race. At all ranks, from probationary clerks to medical officers, Chinese were treated differentially.

This practice did not create as much obvious discontent as might have been thought; even Sir Man-Kam Lo, in 1936, maintained that Chinese did not expect to receive the same salaries as Europeans.[18] Allowance has to be made for the racial attitudes of the Chinese themselves, which went far to mitigate the worst effects of discrimination. Few Chinese particularly wanted to spend their time with Europeans; unlike Indians they did not play cricket, or polo, or ride to hounds, or earnestly emulate British middle-class mores. To be Han has always been, to the Han, to be almost different in kind to the rest of humanity; and, observing the progress of Chinese communities, the rest of the humanity must often wonder whether there isn't something in that belief. If the unpleasantly sweaty, cheese-eating, Westerners wanted to keep their objectionable habits to themselves, the Chinese were not complaining. In so far as the British mandarins were worthy, the respect accorded to authority in traditional Chinese society would be forthcoming; the more so since these great men were, to all practical purposes, incorruptible. There was no undue resentment at the fact that opportunities for modest corruption were taken by the lower ranks, irrespective of race. It had always been accepted that official underlings, the yamen runners, would benefit from their position, and no hard feelings were necessarily aroused when their modern equivalents acted similarly, nor much annoyance provoked by the common practice of offering appropriate gifts to smooth any small difficulties that might arise between the citizen and the police, or other officials.

Other sections of the population might well have felt injured by the attitudes of some of the British. The Portuguese were habitually slighted, and confined to the lower ranks of the service. Although there had been proposals to have Portuguese representation on the Legislative Council before, it was not until 1927 that a Portuguese, Jose Pedro Braga, was appointed. At least the insults to them were not quite as blatant as those made by Sir Henry Norman, M.P., to the Jews – 'that peculiar contingent known as the black brigade, recognizable by the physiognomy of Palestine and the accent of Spitalfields' – who were to be found in the lobby of the Hong Kong Club.[19] Braga himself had some success in combating institutionalized racism, when in 1921 he persuaded the newly-formed League of Fellowship to seek 'the elimination of racial disabilities . . . irrespective of race, class or creed'.

Henry Pollock, the Chairman, attempted to argue that no racial discrimination existed, but Braga, supported by Man-Kam Lo, carried the day. But nothing much subsequently happened.[20]

The European, and more specifically the British community, was divided within itself by stultifying snobbishness and a nervous adhesion to proprieties. A remorselessly accurate picture of the colony in the early thirties is given in the diaries of the novelist Stella Benson. As a successful writer and wife to James O'Gorman Anderson, Commissioner of the Chinese Maritime Customs, Stella had a recognized position in Hong Kong society, which her decided and unconventional views sometimes jeopardized. She did not think much to Hong Kong – 'this dreary place' – although she enjoyed the sailing and the bathing. It was the narrowness of the society she found tedious: 'There is nobody here who reads, nobody who is interested in European politics . . . Really nobody likes even the mildest honesty here . . . Faces shut like doors unless we talk about games or the weather.'[21] Gossip was the prime recreation, and Claud Severn dutifully relayed the best examples to his wife: 'As regards Captain Bloxham's marriage. In the spring a Vaudeville Company visited here twice and one of the features were six young ladies who danced called "Lee White's Peaches". Your friend Harriman admired one and bought a ring, which she is said to have pawned in Manila. To our amazement Captain Bloxham got engaged to another, Audrey Jones.'[22]

Stella Benson found some useful employment when her assistance was sought by another writer, Bella Woolf, Lady Southorn, who was Virginia Woolf's sister-in-law, although little clue to the relationship can be found in Bella's own undistinguished works. As wife of the Colonial Secretary Mrs (as she then was) Southorn was responsible for entertaining the second rank of British residents: 'By a clever ruse she managed to include both the Kowloon Decayed Gentlewomen and the Peak Flourishing Gentlewomen' in her tea parties by inviting the latter 'to polish off the rabble'. Stella enlivened one tea party on 18 August 1931 by 'roguishly' teaching 'Mrs Southorn and two rather nice Chinese men, Chow and T'ang, to play poker'. The Southorns were not among Stella's favourites, as her diary indicates: 'Mr Southorn is a somehow under-baked person – he is rather handsome yet flabby somehow, not enough crust on . . . just a little doughy. Mrs S. is very sharp and plain, a very flattering manner with which makes you feel, somehow, that she makes it her business to be very pleasant to everybody in order to Help Her Husband's Career – It is very curious she should be Leonard Woolf's sister, and yet have no subtlety at all.'

Stella herself had a sharp eye for social distinctions: 'Hong Kong girls seem all to belong to the type of girls one sits behind on the top of buses in London talking with sibilant imbecility,' and dedicated to 'slavish self-offering to men'. When Dame Rachel Crowdy, a most distinguished lady, who had been in charge of the Voluntary Aid Detachments of nurses in France during the war and was Chief of the League of Nations Bureau on Social Questions and the Opium Traffic arrived in Hong Kong, she met Stella before going to Government House. Only when confronted by the Governor's aide 'with a wholly frosty face' was Stella made aware of 'the enormity of what I had done in entertaining a Governor's guest before the Governor had time even to offer her a biscuit. I became at once sick with fear lest I had injured James' career.' The aide confirmed that since the Governor had kept lunch waiting for half an hour while Dame Rachel had been illicitly seeing Stella, he was indeed much annoyed, and that a profound apology would be in order. This was duly proffered, and Stella was forgiven, but James was made to suffer at dinner where he was placed below the salt: 'it seems very odd that pork butchers, men who mend the electric light, insurance touts etc, should be placed above the representative of the Chinese government.'

A fretful concern with precedence had always been a characteristic of Hong Kong society. On formal occasions a list of acknowledged degrees of social status was observed; it included such arcane information as, for example, the fact that wives of Members of the Royal Victorian Order (5th class) ranked ahead of daughters of Knights Bachelor, who in turn were senior to wives of the younger sons of peers' younger sons. While this might be helpful to the ladies concerned – who were usually very well aware of their precise grade – it was of little practical use in Hong Kong. Of the 178 ranks listed, Hong Kong society was almost exclusively composed of the 173rd, immediately after Subaltern Officers of the Army: 'Professional Gentlemen, as solicitors, attorneys, proctors, engineers, architects, medical practitioners, artists, literary men, merchants, master manufacturers, scientific professors and others.' Among this heterogeneous class it was observed that while they were 'considered to possess some station in society', there was no legal order of precedence between them.[23]

The ritual of the 'book' divided the classes. It was, and still in some circles is, considered polite when visiting a foreign capital, and especially a colonial possession, to make one's presence known by signing the visitors' book in the embassy, high commission or Government House. In Hong Kong this was an essential part of protocol; Sir Alexander Caldecott, Governor from 1935 to 1937, explained tongue in cheek how it worked in an imaginary colony: 'Heads of Department *must*, their deputies *should*, other officers of more than ten years seniority *might* ... Members of the Legislature *must*, Town Councillors *should*, heads of mercantile houses and persons authorized to sign for them "per pro", *might* ... All others *might not*.'[24] The book was then used as the guide as to whom should be invited to what, from intimate dinners to the *omnium gatherum* garden party on the Queen's Birthday.

'Pomposity,' recorded Sir Alexander Grantham (Governor 1947–57), 'seemed inseparable from important persons such as the Colonial Secretary and heads of firms. The machinery of the Hong Kong government was ponderous in the extreme with great attention to detail.' He was 'amazed and shocked at the amount of time the Governor, the Colonial Secretary and other senior officials spent on matters of minor importance that should have been left to junior officers'.[25] Judgements were made simpler by recognizing wealth as a very important criterion, while the poorer, in Hong Kong as in England, found some satisfaction in gentility. The jokes in *Punch* of the period depend on the knowledge that certain phrases were just never uttered, nor some clothes ever worn.

The parochial and restricting snobbery that made life in Hong Kong so difficult for the more enlightened was aggravated by the practices of the large firms. Employees of the Hongkong and Shanghai Bank agreed to spend the first ten years of their career in the East in a state of respectable celibacy, except by permission of the Chief Manager. This post was held in the 1930s by Vandeleur Grayson, a man of great energy, but described as 'coarse, arrogant, headstrong and tactless'. Coarseness was certainly displayed in his letters on the subject of staff marriages: 'I look with disfavour on marriages to non-British women', and 'Foreign, native, half-caste are definitely taboo.'[26] (This discrimination would, as it happened, have banned Lady Pope Hennessy, who was of mixed race, and Lady Bowen, who was Italian, from Corfu.) But Grayson was only one example of such crassness, and the Hongkong and Shanghai Bank, in its policy of having no Chinese on the board, was more obviously racist than some other Eastern exchange banks. Other Hong Kong firms were happy to have their staff marry Europeans, but would draw the line at Chinese – and in fact many

Hong Kong bank officers did marry foreigners, but never a Chinese. Captain Hardy, a junior officer on the China station before the Second World War, told me that he was warned by his Captain after evincing too great an enthusiasm for dancing with a young Chinese lady, a graduate of an American university and from an extremely rich family.[27]

When Sir Alexander Grantham, who had been a Cadet Officer in Hong Kong between 1932 and 1935, returned after the war as Governor, he noticed a change for the better:

> A marked decline in social snobbishness was one of the first things I noticed after my return. The 'taipan' and the senior government official were no longer regarded, nor did they so regard themselves, as demi-gods . . . I observed, too, a greater mixing of the races . . . It is the mental arrogance of some Europeans towards Asians that has created as much, if not more resentment than the physical aggressions like the establishment of colonies and extraterritoriality. The basis of the arrogance is the assumption that the European is inherently superior to the Asian, taking such forms as the exclusion of Asians from clubs, downright rudeness or a patronizing manner.[28]

Any such assumptions had been cruelly shattered between 1941 and 1945.

A war with Japan! But why should there be a war with Japan?

On 16 September 1922, while on leave in England, Governor Stubbs wrote gloomily to the Colonial Office: 'This is the beginning of the end. I told you the other day that I believed we should hold Hong Kong for another fifty years. I put it now at twenty at the most.'[29] Even while Stubbs was writing the British government was drifting into taking up a position which led, in an even shorter time than Sir Reginald had prophesied, to the loss of Hong Kong.

At the end of the Great War the question had arisen of the Anglo—Japanese Treaty, due for renewal in 1922. This treaty had been negotiated before the war, when Japanese naval strength in the Pacific was sought by Britain as a counter to the threat posed by the German navy. Japanese participation in the war had indeed been useful, if not particularly active; what had been vital, the security of communications in the Pacific and Indian Oceans, might have equally been gained by Japanese neutrality. By 1922 it was clear that the only powers likely to clash with Japan were China and the USA, with both of whom Britain was on friendly terms (Russia was considered too involved with internal problems to present much of a threat). Chinese interests could be, as they usually were, relegated to an inferior position, but friendship with the USA was judged to be of paramount importance. Australia and New Zealand, who had benefited most from the Japanese alliance, were realistic about the unwillingness of America – at that time embarked upon a decade of inglorious isolation – to defend its former allies' interests. An effort to clarify matters was made in 1921–22 at the Washington Conference, a long-drawn-out and complex affair, with three simultaneous conferences, each having a different grouping of members, intended to settle future policies in the Far East and the Pacific Basin and to agree on limitations of naval forces. It resulted in an agreement between the USA, Britain and Japan to limit their naval tonnages to the ratio of 5:5:3 respectively, a maximum size of capital ships restricted to thirty-five thousand tons, a moratorium on capital ship-building for ten years – and the non-fortification of Hong Kong. In a move which was to have profound consequences, the Anglo–Japanese alliance was not renewed. Correlli Barnett regards the Washington Naval Treaty as 'one of the great catastrophes of English history',[30] but it is doubtful if the Treaty itself had any dramatic effect. Given the reluctance of Britain between the wars to spend more than the inescapable minimum on armaments, it is difficult to believe that, even had no treaty limitations existed, enough would have been spent on the Royal Navy to enable it to make more than a show of fulfilling the role that it was asked to play.

The failure to renew the Anglo–Japanese Treaty was a cause of grave concern to the Joint Chiefs of Staff, who correctly identified the Far East as the most dangerous potential trouble spot. Their view was not shared by the then Chancellor of the Exchequer, Winston Churchill: 'A war with Japan! But why should there be a war with Japan? I do not believe there is the slightest chance of it in our lifetime . . . suppose we had a dispute with Japan about something in China and we declared war on her, what would happen? We should have to move the best part of our Fleet to Singapore. Hong Kong would of course be taken by Japan in the early days.' Even so dedicated a supporter of the Navy as Churchill, a 'former naval person', as he called himself in the Second World War, was therefore ready briskly to cut Admiralty spending: 'They should be made to recast all their plans and scales and standards on the basis that no naval war against a first class Navy is likely to take place in the next twenty years.' There were also electoral considerations: 'We should come up to the Election with these enormous Navy Estimates and nothing else to show . . . I cannot conceive of any course more certain to result in a Socialist victory'. A Labour government would, Churchill argued, cut spending even more, so the Navy would end up even worse off.[31]

Good strategic reasons existed for choosing Singapore rather than Hong Kong as the British Far Eastern base. A cruiser squadron operating from there could within two days be either in the Indian Ocean or off the southern coast of China. Singapore lay at the end of a peninsula which was also British territory, and was protected by a solid bloc of British, Dutch and French possessions, with only the independent kingdom of Siam identified as a likely jumping-off ground for Japanese aggression. Hong Kong, on the other hand, although well situated for action in the China Sea, was uncomfortably close to Japan, and even closer to the Japanese-held territory of Formosa. There was little disagreement with Churchill's view that Hong Kong was virtually indefensible – at least with any force likely to be allocated for that purpose – from any attack coming from the mainland. The Washington Treaty provisions stipulated that Hong Kong's fortifications should not be developed; Sir Samuel Hoare wanted to go even further and dismantle some of the existing works, which were slight enough (the island's total armament consisted of two 9.2-inch and two 6-inch guns), but, Foreign Secretary Lord Curzon opposing, the suggestion was dropped.[32] In these circumstances Hong Kong's safety lay in China's remaining either in tolerably friendly hands, or at least in those without much power for mischief. Active defence, it had always been assumed, would be dependent on the swift arrival of the Royal Navy. Two factors were to alter this: the Japanese war with China and the development of air power.

Throughout the twenties it seemed that the policy established at Washington was likely to succeed. Japan showed no signs of giving trouble, joined the League of Nations, and behaved as a model member. No hint was given of Japanese resentment at what appeared, by the failure to renew the Anglo—Japanese Treaty, to be their desertion by Great Britain, their old friend and mentor, who had made Admiral Togo, vanquisher of the Russian navy, a national hero and in whose shipyards the first victorious Japanese fleet had been constructed. There was also a damagingly racist factor. In 1924 the USA passed an immigration act blatantly designed to limit the number of non-northern-European immigrants. It was particularly restrictive to the Japanese, superseding a 'gentleman's agreement' that had previously been applied, and fixing an absurdly low quota of two hundred immigrants a year, at a time when there were already a hundred thousand Japanese settled in California alone.[33]

The decision to concentrate forces on Singapore, although the development of the installation there took very much longer than originally expected, limited the strategic importance of Hong Kong. The colony's commercial importance was also declining as that of Shanghai advanced. By 1911 tonnage entering and clearing Shanghai (18,179,472) was already approaching that of Hong Kong (20,490,520), but since much of the Hong Kong figure consisted of ships in transit, liners and cargo vessels on their way to other Oriental ports, the truly international trade of Shanghai was already greater. Between 1911 and 1915, 28.3 per cent of China's total foreign trade passed through Hong Kong; in the five years after the strike-boycott it had dropped to 16.4 per cent. Although all British trade suffered from the Chinese anti-British sentiments of the 1920s, Hong Kong bore the brunt. The remainder of the British Empire trade to China, most of which went through Shanghai, rose to almost exactly the same share as Hong Kong's – 16.7 per cent in 1930 compared to Hong Kong's 16.8 per cent. The benefits of British decline accrued to the Japanese and Americans. By 1918 Japan had nearly 40 per cent of China's trade, after which this declined, while the American share steadily increased, to reach the same proportion as that of the other main competitors.

The International Settlement and the French Concession at Shanghai were considerably more entertaining places than the British colony of Hong Kong, as W.H. Auden recorded:

> the tired or lustful business man will find here everything to gratify his desires ... You can attend race meetings baseball games football matches. You can see the latest American films. If you want boys or girls, you can have them, at all prices, at the bathhouses and brothels. If you want opium you can smoke it in the best company, served on a tray, like afternoon tea. Good wine is difficult in this climate, but there is whisky and gin to float a fleet

of battleships . . . Finally, if you ever repent, there are churches
and chapels of all denominations.[34]

All these delights were certainly, one way or another, available also at
Hong Kong, but were much more hedged about with legal and social
prohibitions. Half a century earlier Kipling had observed in *From Sea
to Sea*: 'Vice must be pretty much the same all the world over, but if
a man wants to get out of pleasure with it, let him go to Hong Kong.'
Things had not much changed in the interim.

When coupled with the continued advance of trade at Shanghai, this
resulted in Hong Kong becoming even more of a colonial backwater, a
status reflected in the appointments of Clementi's successors as Governor. Colonial Governors, as the men on the spot, are traditionally
given considerable latitude by the home government. When the Governor is a man of acknowledged talent – and fully conscious of his own
merits – this can result in his assuming an unwelcome independence.
Clementi sometimes had the Colonial Office worried: 'He thinks that
in his capacity as Governor of Hong Kong he is responsible for the
control of all the naval, military and air forces in south China as well
as shaping our policy there.'[35]

Clementi's sudden departure in 1930 was caused by a crisis arising
in the Straits Settlements which demanded a senior replacement as
Governor there. Disappointed at what he took to be an unsympathetic
Colonial Office, both Clementi and his wife Penelope left Hong Kong
reluctantly and with personal sadness: 'It will be a great wrench to
both of us to leave Hong Kong where we have been very happy . . . I
would gladly have stayed here rather than anywhere else in the world.'[36]

Sir William Peel, hurriedly found to replace Sir Cecil, had never
expected to be given so important a job, and was somewhat alarmed
at the prospect. Much less gifted than Clementi, Peel was a dignified
personage unlikely to cause nervousness at Whitehall. 'A handsome
stolid old man,' was Stella Benson's first impression, 'almost exactly
like any other amiable orthodox old man controlling any tassel of the
fringe of empire,' although she later found the Governor 'a rather
charming and sapient old man'. Sir William had worked his way for
thirty-two years through the Colonial Service to this, his first appointment as Governor. His prior post had been as Colonial Secretary in
the Federated Malay States, so he had therefore a fair knowledge of
the Chinese people, which was immediately put to the test over the
by now well-aired questions of the *mui-tsai* and prostitution.

The result of the previous confrontation between the Colonial Office and the government of Hong Kong on the control of prostitution had been a stand-off (see Chapter 9). The Contagious Diseases Act, which had aroused the reformers' indignation, had been abolished, but at the same time the Hong Kong government had retained powers to close brothels. Since any brothel of which the government disapproved could therefore be shut down, this gave the authorities the right to specify precisely which brothels they were prepared to tolerate: in fact to introduce whatever systems of control seemed to them best. The opportunity was eagerly embraced:

> Brothels were classified into those catering for Europeans (with sub classes of those with European, Japanese, or Chinese prostitutes), brothels for Indians, and brothels for Chinese (subdivided into first-class, second-class, and third-class houses). The Secretariat fixed the charges which the mistresses might levy on their girls for board and lodging. All those wishing to practise the profession had to attend before the Secretary for Chinese Affairs, bringing three photographs with them, and they were closely questioned to ensure that they were entering the profession of their own free will. When the authority was satisfied on this point, and that the girl was over nineteen years of age, she was given a card showing her number, name, and address, to which one photograph was attached. One photograph was retained by the Secretariat and the third by the brothel mistress, who pasted it in a record book kept in the brothel.[37]

A more complete and efficient system for institutionalizing prostitution could hardly be conceived, and it worked extremely well, to the satisfaction of all concerned and to the avoidance of venereal disease. But the forces of international morality demanded change, which was signalled to Hong Kong by the visit, in 1921, of a Commission from the National Council for Combating Venereal Disease consisting of Mrs Olive Neville-Rolfe and Dr Hallam, who recommended measures which, when eventually implemented, had the effect of promptly tripling the incidence of venereal disease. Governor Stubbs, who had already been castigated by the moral campaigner Mrs Clara Haslewood on the subject of *mui-tsai*, refused to co-operate with them.

It was not difficult for the Committee to find objects for criticism, since the Hong Kong government had, since the 1890s, followed their established practice of leaving things Chinese to the Chinese, and enforcing only the minimum of public health standards. As a result child mortality and morbidity were high, and Chinese brothels more laxly supervised than those used by Europeans. A logical answer might have been to insist upon the same standards being observed in both communities, and indeed the arguments for not so doing were wearing patently weak as more Chinese flocked to Hong Kong in order to escape the violence developing in China, but this would be tantamount to encouraging vice (a word which signified only one of the seven deadly sins to British moralists). Brothels must be abolished.

Singapore was the first to fall victim to the new wave of morality. Brothels had indeed been suppressed there in 1916, with effects so dire that a medical committee urged the full reinstatement of the Contagious Diseases Act. This was dead against the feeling of the times, and Singapore was sternly instructed by Whitehall to close its brothels. Hong Kong's Governors practised some more masterly inactivity. Stubbs had other things to contend with, and Clementi found ways of avoiding an issue which the Conservative government was not keen to press. Peel, who had been able to see things at first hand in Singapore, followed the same line, and did his best, assisted by the Colonial Office, to retain the existing system. He urged in vain the argument about retaining Chinese 'loyalty', and pointed out that 'the Chinese do not view prostitution as we do . . . Prostitutes are not social outcasts to the same extent as in "Western" countries. A prostitute often becomes a highly respectable concubine.'[38] This was hardly an argument calculated to convince such opponents as Lady Astor, to whom concubines were quite as undesirable as prostitutes. Nor did it, and Peel's hand was forced. In 1932 the European brothels were closed, the Chinese ones following three years later.

The consequences were precisely those that had been predicted by everyone with experience of the subject. Street walkers flourished, 'sly' brothels proliferated under the guise of massage parlours or dancing academies, and venereal disease among servicemen increased from 7 per cent to 24 per cent. Figures for the population at large were unknown, but almost certainly higher. Yet another committee was appointed in 1938, and concluded 'The results of abolition, namely the increase in venereal disease with its appalling effect upon the defence forces of the colony, and the unpleasant conditions of the streets are much more of a disgrace than the tolerated houses ever were.'[39] As conditions on the mainland worsened, new recruits to the oldest profession poured across the border. Wanchai was established as the new centre for organized prostitution; when the Japanese came in 1941 the Nam-ping and Sun Wah hotel-brothels formed what were considered suitable temporary quarters for the Hong Kong bankers.

Stella Benson was shocked by the procrastination over closing the brothels, and wrote on 1 November 1930: 'With great slickness and disingenuousness it is now quite clear that the government (the present existing members of the government, amongst them Mr Hallifax [the Secretary for Chinese Affairs] – Mr Wood – Sir Cecil Clementi) deliberately switched the limelight to the *mui-tsai* or domestic slaves – and abolished that system because it was a Chinese one and did not affect the Europeans.'

Little sisters

British external policy during the hundred years between 1850 and 1950 was overshadowed by the importance of India. The responsibility for this enormous and complex territory, with a diverse population comprising something like one-fifth of the human race, brought with it large-scale problems which were met with appropriately imperial solutions. Aggressive, and sometimes defensive, actions in Burma, Tibet, Afghanistan, Nepal, Egypt, Sudan and China were thrust upon usually reluctant British governments by what were perceived to be Indian necessities. In other colonial territories a full-blown imperialism never emerged, except for the brief and controversial episode in South Africa, where British attempts to force imperial rule on Boers and blacks alike ended in the fiasco of the Jameson Raid and the Boer War. By 1906 the supporters of imperialism were discredited; Lord Milner, its chief proponent in South Africa, had been sacked and censured in the House of Commons, Joseph Chamberlain had been defeated and terminally incapacitated, and colonial policy was finally set in its twentieth-century mould, defined by the Duke of Devonshire, Colonial Secretary in 1922, as 'based on the fundamental principle that the interests of the local people are paramount'. The principle of what became known as the 'Devonshire Declaration' may have been somewhat patchily applied, but it was often closely followed, and no more so than in anything that bore the taint of slavery.

It had long been felt that Hong Kong's Chinese population were not free from suspicion on this issue, and the question of *mui-tsai* –

little sisters – had been raised long before. The custom of adoption, of both boys and girls, by which poor families transferred their rights in their children for a cash payment, was long established, and the forms clearly defined in the Confucian volumes of Domestic Rites. There was more than a suspicion however that girl *mui-tsai* were treated as 'pocket daughters' and trained as prostitutes. 'At an early age they are the victims of debauchees [who] deflower them in "sly brothels", paying the "pocket mother" a large price, and the girl is thus launched on a brothel career.'[40] At the same time there is no doubt that many perfectly respectable arrangements were made for the adoption of poor children who would otherwise have been very badly off indeed. The subject of the *mui-tsai* was first raised by the pugnacious Chief Justice Sir John Smale in 1878, who asserted that there were from ten to twenty thousand female slaves in the colony. Some respectable Chinese led by Fung Ming-shan, a rich and well-known compradore and a director of the Tung Wah, attempted to explain the difference between the venerable custom and its abuses. As a practical step Fung obtained permission to form a Society for the Protection of Women and Girls, the Po Leung Kuk, which had as its object the prevention of kidnapping, and incidentally thereby the preservation of the *mui-tsai* system. In time the Po Leung Kuk became closely associated with the Tung Wah and accepted by the government as reliably representative of the best Chinese opinion. When a debate on the subject in the House of Lords on 21 June 1880 led to an investigation by the Colonial Office, this resulted in the legal guardianship of *mui-tsai* being vested in the Secretary for Chinese Affairs, who worked closely with the Po Leung Kuk.

There the matter rested until Colonel John Ward had it brought to his notice while passing through Hong Kong in 1917. Ward was a colourful and powerful figure, who started work as a navvy at the age of twelve, founded the Navvies' Union and became Liberal Member of Parliament for Stoke on Trent. He commanded a battalion of the Middlesex Regiment on the Western Front, and after the war fought against the Bolsheviks in Russia, being created a Cossack Ataman. These activities prevented him from doing more than drawing the attention of the Colonial Ofice and the Trades Union Congress to the question, until Clara Haslewood and her husband, a retired naval officer, took a hand late in 1919.

How far the Haslewoods' campaign against the *mui-tsai* system was justified in view of the many other more scandalous injustices then being perpetrated is perhaps open to question, but it is certain that the efforts of the Hong Kong government, and Stubbs in particular, to silence them by what Susan Hoe describes as 'lies and distortion' were scandalous. Haslewood was forced to resign his Admiralty post – he was Superintendent of the Chart Department in Hong Kong – and Mrs Haslewood was subjected to angry and condescending criticism from the Governor. But Ward, back in Britain, raised the matter in the House on 26 April 1920, asking that action should be taken 'to remove this stain upon the British name in the Far East'. The Colonial Secretary at the time being the reinstated Lord Milner, sympathetic reactions could hardly be expected, but in February 1921 he was succeeded by Winston Churchill. It took some time, and the good offices of such influential supporters as Colonel Wedgwood and Eddie Marsh, Churchill's Secretary, to get Churchill, then absorbed with the problems of the Middle East, to focus on what by comparison was a minor issue.

When Churchill acted, it was in typically forthright fashion. On 22 February 1922 a telegram went out to Stubbs: '*Mui-tsai*. I am not at all satisfied. Unless I am able to state that this institution does not involve the slightest element of compulsory employment (which is the essence of slavery) and that every *mui-tsai* of a certain age is in law and in practice free if she wishes to leave her adopted parents or employers, I cannot defend its continued existence in a British Colony.'[41] Churchill went on to instruct Stubbs that a proclamation must be issued immediately making it clear that the status of *mui-tsai*, as understood in China, would not be recognized in Hong Kong. Stubbs found himself in the old predicament of Hong Kong Governors – caught between fits of morality in Britain and the dogged determination of the Chinese to defend their ancient customs, reinforced by a British community in the colony resentful of any Whitehall dictation. He telegraphed back to Churchill that the Hong Kong government and its Chinese advisers considered 'that the issue of a proclamation would be dangerous, especially as exposing a large number of girls to the wiles of procuresses; and they deprecate it'. Churchill was having none of this, and on 21 March he sharply ordered Stubbs to 'issue without delay a Proclamation as directed'.

The well-oiled machinery of Hong Kong governmental procrastination was put into gear. A report would be required before taking precipitate action. This was inconveniently promptly forthcoming, but recommended a comprehensive and extremely expensive scheme for rescuing and training the *mui-tsai* in a new industrial school. The potential cost of this proposal aroused the indignation of the taxpayers of Hong Kong, and the Governor took the opportunity of suggesting a compromise. This arrived in London on 24 July, not a propitious season for government action. A month later Churchill instructed that the Governor's plans 'should be brought into operation without delay'. This succeeded only in producing a telegram, not from Stubbs, who had gone on leave, but from Claud Severn, the Colonial Secretary, explaining why even this action was inadvisable in view of the strong objections of the Chinese community. By this time Churchill was out of office, and it was his successor, the Duke of Devonshire, a decent but baffled man, who had to cope with the problem. Another delay was allowed while the subject was once more discussed.

In Hong Kong the debate that took place in the Legislative Council on 28 December 1922 was unusually heated. Sir Shouson Chou was concerned that if *mui-tsai* were legally liberated at eighteen, an age 'when control is more than ever desirable', they might misuse their freedom in all sorts of ways. P.H. Holyoak, a member of both the Executive and Legislative Councils, complained of 'base insinuations, positive misrepresentations and exaggerated absurdities in the British Press'. Governor Stubbs, while being obliged to use the official majority in order to enforce his instructions from Whitehall, assured the Councillors that he disassociated himself 'entirely from the venomous attacks which have been made on the Chinese population by ignorant persons at Home'.

In due course, nothing in Chinese affairs ever being quite as simple as Churchill might have wished, an ordinance was promulgated in March 1923, a year after he had first commanded it 'without delay'. The new law made it clear that no rights in the person of the *mui-tsai* could be transferred for payment, provided for the registration of existing girls, and banned new contracts being made. But the registration clause merely empowered the Governor to demand registration, without specifically requiring him to do so. Since the opposition to such action by the Legislative Council and the Chinese institutions was unanimous, that part of the ordinance was suspended, no registration was effected and the matter kept as quiet as possible.

In 1928 another energetic lady became interested in Hong Kong. 'Little Red Ellen' Wilkinson, the Labour Member for Middlesbrough, raised the question of Yeung Ping Wong, a houseboy who had been flogged and imprisoned for having in his possession two copies of a publication called the *Red Flag*. Leo Amery, the unrepentantly imperialist Colonial Secretary, gave her short shrift on that occasion, but was forced to reopen the question of *mui-tsai*, and asked Sir Cecil Clementi, who had succeeded Stubbs, for his advice. The new Governor transmitted exactly the same views, those of the 'respectable' Chinese, to Whitehall. There was one embarrassing complication in that the Chinese government had, two years previously, published a law for the 'Emancipation of Slaves and *Mui-tsai*', an unhappy pairing.

Clementi began his dispatch of 16 May 1929 by stating 'very definitely that the abolition of the *mui-tsai* system is the settled and declared policy of this Government', but then went on for ten pages plus addenda to prove that the Chinese government had not been successful in liberating *mui-tsai*, except by the wily ruse of renaming them 'adopted daughters'. Since he was entirely opposed to 'any schemes of legislative "eyewash"', Clementi concluded that 'effective abolition seems impossible except by gradual education of the Chinese community on this subject and by slow, but constant, pressure and by discouragement of the system in every possible way ... It would be as hard to free Hong Kong from it as to keep a place clear of mud at the mouth of the Canton River.' He made the point that whatever might have happened in the previous century there was no evidence that the *mui-tsai* were now recruited as prostitutes: '*Mui-tsai* are by training not suited for use as prostitutes. The sale of a girl to be a *mui-tsai* has indeed the effect of protecting her from prostitution.' Even child prostitution was much jollier than might be thought: 'children acquired for training as prostitutes are not employed as domestic servants. They are generally taught to sing and play Mah Jong and to act as entertainers at restaurants; and in China large numbers of these girls, who are known as "guitar girls", may be seen frequenting restaurants, where they are called to amuse customers at dinner.'[42]

This bland account might have satisfied Amery, but Clementi's dispatch was never received by him. In May 1929 the Conservatives were defeated in a general election and a Labour government formed with Liberal support. The new Colonial Secretary was Sidney Webb, the Fabian scholar, now Lord Passfield, who required more positive action. On 22 August a dispatch went out to Clementi, instructing him in the clearest terms:

> After making all allowance for the difficulties in bringing the system to an end which are described at length in your dispatches,

it is my duty to inform you that public opinion in this country and in the House of Commons will not accept such a result with equanimity . . . I must therefore direct that the third part of the Domestic Service Ordinance should be brought into force forthwith . . . and that it will not be allowed to be a dead letter . . . I fully realize that time will be required to make the Law effective, but I am not prepared to acquiesce in a merely nominal enforcement of the law.

This ought to have been, as Stella Benson believed it had been, the end of the affair, but that was to underestimate Hong Kong's powers of resistance to change.

The registration programme on which Sir Cecil Clementi had reluctantly been made to embark had trawled out something over four thousand *mui-tsai*, and, after more pressure, inspectors were appointed to superintend their welfare. This was not enough for the reformers. The League of Nations Permanent Advisory Committee of Experts on Slavery,[43] the Anti-Slavery and Aborigines Protection Society, the National Council of Women, the Society of Friends, and the Archbishops of Canterbury and of York wanted more. Many free trips to the East followed. The League of Nations' expert report of 1934 was reviewed by a Hong Kong Committee and heavily amended in 1935. A subsequent British government Committee of Inquiry toured Hong Kong and Singapore and reported in turn in 1937; its recommendations were at first accepted, and then shelved in favour of a minority report.

The upshot of it all was that in 1938 arrangements were made for all adopted daughters to be registered, which would, it was felt, unearth the missing *mui-tsai*: this registration found precisely one girl who had slipped through the net. Nor did the eventual Act of May 1938 lead to the discovery of a single child who had been procured for the purpose of prostitution. Nor, it should be said, did any adverse Chinese reaction to the invasion of privacy the registration and inspection necessitated appear. As before, reports of ill-treatment were followed up and prosecutions initiated without any assistance from the registration system.

Stumbling towards the twentieth century

Both these dissensions – on the registration of prostitutes and of *mui-tsai* – between Hong Kong and London arose from a similar cause, which was that Hong Kong was becoming the only Crown Colony with so severely limited a form of self-government. During the First World War the question of establishing some element of democratic representation was once more raised, with the proposal that unofficial members of both Councils should be elected rather than nominated. A petition was sent in January 1916 to the Secretary of State asking that a government 'more representative of the wishes of the business men of this colony' should be created. This should be done, it was suggested, by increasing the number of unofficial members of the Legislative Council by four, which would have given them a majority, and in the Executive Council by two.[44] The petition was bluntly rejected, but pressure for change continued after the war. All suggestions advanced were characterized by an extremely restricted and indirect form of election, which would entirely exclude the Chinese population (then some 96 per cent of the total). They would have to rest content with their two, or perhaps three, representatives appointed by the Governor.

Even if the British government had wished to alter the Hong Kong constitution, such a move, in the post-war climate of decolonialization and the rights of subject people, would have been politically unthinkable. Clementi summed the situation up correctly in October 1928: 'The European desire for constitutional reform has been more or less killed by the realization that any changes would have to be in a Sinophile direction.'[45] (The unconscious loading in the word 'Sinophile' is instructive: it was not love for the Chinese, but a recognition of political realities that inspired the British government.)

In practice it was impossible to move far along that road. The unstable internal condition of China made it difficult enough to run Hong Kong safely even when full powers remained at Westminster. Many examples could be given by an aggrieved Colonial Office of how limited their theoretically absolute power could be: reluctant Governors with the support of their councils could delay action on instructions, sometimes for a very long time indeed. A democratically elected Council, however limited its power, would have tremendous moral authority, which would be almost impossible for a British government to resist. And such councils would inevitably be swayed by Chinese nationalist passions, although it might be remarked that even so conservative an administration as Peel's afforded considerable protection to dissidents and revolutionaries. Ho Chi Minh founded the Vietnam Cong-San Dan in Hong Kong in 1930; in due course it became the Vietminh, dedicated to liberating Vietnam from the French, and later known as the Vietcong. When Ho was arrested the following year his extradition was demanded by the French authorities. His case was taken up by a British lawyer, Frank Loseby, and fought through to the Privy Council. An out of court settlement was reached whereby Ho was allowed to leave for a destination of his own choice, the Hong Kong government contributing to the costs of his appeal. There have often been discreditable shifts and shabby subterfuges resorted to by Hong Kong governments, but the rule of law has almost always prevailed.

What the Colonial Office did agree to do was to accept in 1928 Clementi's suggestion of an enlarged Legislative Council, with two more of both official and unofficial members. The selection of these was left to the Governor, and Clementi's choice of one Chinese and one Portuguese served as an indication of how completely out-of-date were hopes for an increase in the representation of the – British – 'businessmen of this colony'. The appointment of the first Chinese to the Executive Council was a straw in the wind. Sir Shouson Chou, although born in Hong Kong, had made a career first in the Imperial and then the Republican Chinese governments before returning to the colony. Clementi's request to appoint Sir Shouson caused a flurry in Whitehall, where neither the Foreign Secretary, Austen Chamberlain, nor the Colonial Secretary, Leo Amery, were men of advanced views. Concern was expressed that Chou could not be trusted to observe the confidentiality of proceedings in the Council; Clementi replied that neither could the European members. He might have added that so little of moment was discussed at their meetings that confidentiality was not of the highest importance. Clementi gained his point, but the Foreign Office insisted that no secret documents should in future be shown to Council members. The irony that a Chinese could be a member of the highest administrative body of the colony while no one of the same race could rise above the rank of Constable in the police force passed without comment.[46]

For their part there was no discernible pressure from the Chinese for increased representation; all the agitation had come from the British community, and only a section of that. At least one method of canvassing public opinion might have been used, but in the elections to the Sanitary Board, the only public body tinged with democracy, enthusiasm was minimal. Elections were usually uncontested, and in only one, in 1932, was any attempt made at electioneering.

A reconstruction in 1908 had perpetuated the unofficial majority on the Board of six to four. Of the six, two Chinese and two others were nominated by the Governor. This left two who underwent a form of election by those on, or exempt from, the jury list, which included many Chinese. This system resulted not only in there being an unofficial majority on the Board, but in the possibility of the majority of unofficials being Chinese.

Not that there was much that the Board could do, since administrative control was firmly held by the government. The President of the Sanitary Board was not medically qualified, but a cadet officer, appointed on the traditional grounds that it needed one trained in Chinese language and customs to ensure that tranquillity should be preserved, rather than efficiency attained. Powerful support for this attitude, and energetic opposition to change, came from the Chinese unofficial members, determined 'to have some kind of buffer interposed between them and the demands of a professional hygienist who might intrude upon the privacy of their homes and family life, interfere with their freedom to overcrowd tenements for maximum profit, and infringe upon their liberty to live under insanitary conditions and spread diseases to their neighbours'.[47]

It took seven years for the first Director of Medical and Sanitary Services, Dr A.R. Wellington, appointed in 1929, to convince the government of the necessity to have a more modern system of sanitation. Clementi had been sympathetic, but Peel persistently obstructed any change. In 1935 much sewage disposal was still being carried out in the time-honoured bucket method that had shocked Mrs Gordon Cumming in 1878. When reform did come, it was effected in the most economic way, satisfying all those who resisted change, by altering almost nothing except the name. The Sanitary Board, still under the direction of a cadet officer, with the same membership, elected from the same voters' roll and with substantially similar powers, became the Urban Council. This neatly removed the objection that while some relevant qualifications might be desirable for the head of a public health organization, quite clearly none were needed for the Chairman of an Urban Council. It was not until 1939 that the new Director of Medical Services was given a real measure of control.

Precisely similar objections were raised concerning the Department of Education. Again, this was run not by a qualified teacher, but by a cadet officer, without any suitable training. The dangers of this had been pointed out in 1927 by W.G.A. Ormsby-Gore, later Lord Harlech and at that time Under-Secretary of State to Amery; it lowered the prestige of the service and by cutting off promotion prospects made recruitment difficult. The system should, he wrote, be amended when the next vacancy arose. But the whole theory of British administration was, and to a considerable extent still is, based on the presumption that the generalist can turn his hand to any task. A facility in Latin verses is no longer absolutely requisite for admission to the higher grades of the Civil Service, but any analysis of the most senior posts will still indicate the predominance of Oxbridge degrees in the liberal arts. The post of Director of Education in the thirties was held by G.R. Sayer (Classics, Queen's College, Oxford), author of a history of Hong Kong, translations from the Chinese and an edition of Horace. Not only was this unsatisfactory in principle, but Sayers was obviously not competent to be in charge of education. His only previous experience in charge of a department had been the Sanitary Board, for which he was equally unqualified.

The matter was picked up again in 1934 by Sir Philip Cunliffe-Lister, Secretary of State, who wrote to Peel uncompromisingly that, if Hong Kong's education was to be brought up to the standards available to Chinese elsewhere, 'This must necessarily mean that the Director of Education in the Colony shall be equipped with professional experience and technique to advise how best to apply in Hong Kong the continual improvements which have been made and are being made in School organization, methods of teaching, etc. It cannot be expected that a Cadet officer can equal a professional educationalist in up-to-date knowledge of this specialist character.'[48]

Sayer was less equal than most. His lack of capacity was noted by the Advisory Committee on Education in the Colonies in August 1937, after a report on Hong Kong had been submitted to them: 'we saw no reason to question the recommendations contained in the Burney Report, and we thought it impossible for effect to be given to these recommendations if the education policy of the Government of Hong Kong continued in accordance with the views expressed by Mr Sayer'.[49] Soon after this conclusion was reached, in August 1937, Sayer was retired early, but modernization of the structure of education in Hong Kong had to wait for the end of the war.

Health and education might be left in the control of a less-than-competent generalist without too great danger, but finance is a more sensitive subject. Hong Kong did not suffer as badly in the thirties as did much of Europe or the USA, but it did not escape all the effects of the Depression. Silver rose steadily in price throughout the first years of the decade under American buying pressure, to the extent that in 1935 China renounced the silver standard, forcing the colony to follow suit. For the first time the government was able to manage the colony's own currency, which it did to some purpose, devaluing the Hong Kong dollar to a competitive level and thereby giving a sharp impetus to the colony's trade. In spite of the disadvantage this caused to the colonial finances – since much of the expense had to be funded in now revalued sterling, which led to a cut being levied on Civil Service salaries – between 1935 and 1939 the total revenue rose steadily from $28.4 million to $41.5 million.

In order to manage financial affairs more professionally the post of Colonial Treasurer, in all colonies, was upgraded in 1937 to that of Financial Secretary, who became the third most senior officer in the administrative hierarchy, and in Hong Kong often the most influential. Cadet officers had already proved unsatisfactory in this function, the last, C.M. Messer, having been replaced in 1931 by a specialist financial controller. This was Edwin Taylor, who had already spent thirty years in the Board of Trade and in African financial administration, and who prepared the ground for the first Financial Secretary, Sydney Caine. A young (thirty-five) graduate of the London School of Economics, of which he was later Director, Caine soon provided for the colony a modern financial planning system which included, for the first time, a comprehensive system of taxation. The opium monopoly, which had previously been so reliable a contributor to revenue, then represented a mere 1 per cent of the total.

These reforms were negotiated through a not always receptive Legislative Council by Sir William Peel's successors. Sir Alexander Caldecott, who was appointed in 1935, was in office for less than eighteen months before being succeeded by Sir Geoffry Northcote, who lasted only a year longer. Caldecott was a personable and popular man who had spent thirty years in Malaya and was speedily promoted from Hong Kong to be Governor of Ceylon, where he did much to prepare for self-government. Northcote was amiable and conscientious but suffered persistent ill health, which might account for one embarrassing incident when, having sent a dispatch to the Colonial Office, he found that he had forgotten signing it, and could not remember whose recommendations were incorporated; but knew that he disagreed with them.

Many of the less competent cadet officers, promoted beyond their ability, had been disposed of, but Northcote was left with one of the most unsatisfactory. R.A.D. Forrest was allotted the admittedly difficult task of running the Immigration Department at a time when thousands of refugees were pouring over the frontier in flight from the Japanese armies. By 1920 the population had risen steadily to about 600,000. The uncertainties in China had pushed this up to over a million by 1938, but in the next two years over half a million Chinese fled to Hong Kong, sometimes at the rate of five thousand a day, and all required documentation. The opportunities for corruption were considerable, and appear to have been taken with alacrity. A government commission of inquiry found that Forrest was 'an irresponsible incompetent, unfit to run a government department'. He became only the second cadet officer in the history of the service to be asked to resign.

14

THE GREATER EAST ASIA
CO-PROSPERITY SPHERE

A passive and shameful acquiescence

The wars between China and Japan that spluttered in 1932 and finally ignited in 1937 were due to something more complex than unprovoked Japanese aggression. Not that there was any doubt about Japan's often violent expansionary tactics since the Meiji restoration in 1868, which had included war with China in 1895, resulting in the annexation of Formosa (Taiwan) with the Pescadores; war with Russia in 1905, which brought cession of Russian gains in Manchuria; and the annexation of Korea in 1910. During the First World War Japan succeeded in extorting from the government of Yüan Shi-kai an agreement (the Twenty-One Demands) which strengthened Japan's commanding position in northern China, a position even further developed by a 1918 deal with Yüan's successor Tuan Ch'i-jui (Duan Qirai). Much to the disgust of politically aware Chinese, these agreements were, for the most part, consolidated into the post-war settlements.

Since 1919 there had been a distinct softening of Japanese attitudes, as it seemed that a democratic system was beginning to take root (adult male suffrage was granted in 1925, and a government of generally liberal tendencies held office). There could also be some element of self-satisfaction in contrasting the orderly situation in Japan, and indeed in the territories it had come by, with that of China, still divided among warring factions. The earnest co-operation of Japan with the League of Nations indicated a desire to turn over a new leaf internationally, but by the end of the 1920s Japan was torn with internal dissension as a rapidly increasing population, export markets ruined by the Depression, discriminatory American legislation and Chinese boycotts led to near-revolutionary levels of discontent. In the first two years of the thirties two Prime Ministers and a Finance Minister were assassinated. Democratic government became increasingly impossible as frustrated army commanders, who could rely on backing from the discontented younger men, struck out on their own.

It was an on-the-spot army decision, enforced literally at swordpoint over the protests of their own Consul, that led to the Japanese annexation of Manchuria in 1932 and the establishment of the puppet state of Manchukuo under the *fainéant* Emperor Pu-Yi. Some excuses could be advanced; Manchuria, under the personal rule of the older and younger Marshal Zhangs, had become something of a wild card, almost independent of China. But this action by one of its few reliable supporters had to be viewed with dismay by the League of Nations. The affair might even then have been smoothed over had not – and again this was a decision by a local commander, taken without reference to Tokyo – Japanese forces attacked Shanghai. Manchuria was remote, with few Westerners watching what happened there, but Shanghai was thoroughly internationalized and in the full glare of world attention, which was aroused to indignation at the violent deaths of several hundred civilians. The subsequent League investigation, although tactfully conducted, could not avoid some criticism of Japan, resulting in that country indignantly withdrawing from the League in 1933. From that time on Japan gave numerous signals that the plan of a 'Greater East Asia Co-Prosperity Sphere' – Japanese rule from the Russian border south as far as might be managed – was now operational. Using Manchuria as a base the neighbouring Chinese provinces of Jehol and Hopei were invaded, and by May 1933 Japan controlled the whole of north-east China, with Japanese troops stationed in Peking itself.

The Kuomintang government resisted these encroachments as best they could, which was not very well. The corruption of the Nanking government nullified Chiang Kai-shek's efforts to establish an effective dictatorship, along the lines of Fascist Italy. But if Chiang could not emulate Mussolini's economic reforms, the Chinese army was able, in the next three years, to demonstrate a courage that the Italian forces signally failed to show a little later.

The undeclared war that began just south of Peking, at the Marco Polo bridge, in July 1937 developed to form a savage and brutal conflict that continued for eight years and was followed by another four years of civil war between the Kuomintang and the Communists. The incident at the bridge, however, was not planned, being once again the result of a local clash which both countries then decided to make a *casus belli*. Chiang Kai-shek opened the real fighting by a bombing raid on Shanghai; the attack was meant to destroy the Japanese fleet, but was badly mishandled and succeeded only in killing more civilians. The ferocious battle around Shanghai that followed eventually cost China a quarter of a million casualties. It was followed by a Japanese advance on Nanking, the Kuomintang capital, and the withdrawal of Chiang's government to a refuge in Chungking. Atrocities equal to the 'Rape of Nanking' had occurred before in China – less than a century ago, in the same place, in fact, during the Taiping rebellion – but Japanese brutality there was recorded in such shocking detail on newsreels and in newspapers that the world shuddered. From that time on Japan was, somewhat piously, considered a pariah state with which no civilized accommodation was possible. Inevitably this uncompromising attitude led to the rebuff of advances from the more liberal and pacific sections of Japanese opinion and ensured the triumph of the militarists.

Before this stage had been reached it might have been possible for Britain to have re-established relations with Japan by recognizing that country's position in China. However distasteful, such an action would have made admirable sense in strategic terms. A weakened Britain, which had – encouraged by economically-minded governments – faithfully observed all the treaty limitations on armaments, was facing the growing likelihood of a major European conflict. It would have been impossible at the same time to resist an attack in the Pacific by Japan, which after withdrawing from the naval treaties had made manifest her intention of pressing ahead with large-scale naval building. Correlli Barnett believes that British failure to reach an accommodation with Japan was due to electoral pressures from 'an urban, rootless and emotional middle class, always ready to get in the fidgets of moral indignation'.[1] If this was true in 1935, when the subject was discussed internationally, Japanese actions two years later would have made it all but impossible for any self-respecting government to compromise.

Once full-scale, although still undeclared, war with China had begun, Japan endeavoured to cut off supplies to the mainland by a blockade of the whole of the Chinese coastline, excluding only the foreign ports, of which Hong Kong was incomparably the most important. Enormous quantities of arms – estimated at sixty thousand tons per month – poured from the colony into China, in spite of Japanese demands, energetically backed by Sir Robert Craigie, the British Ambassador in Tokyo, to prohibit military goods crossing the border. The Japanese blockade was speedily reinforced, both by bombing Canton and the Chinese section of the Canton—Kowloon railway and by increased diplomatic pressure on the British government. This pressure public feeling, the Foreign Office and the Colonial Office, for once in agreement, resisted, although both France and Portugal caved in under Japanese threats to their regional possessions.

British readiness to stand up to the Japanese was however becoming more and more restricted as war with Germany began to look increasingly inevitable, and the necessity of conciliating Japan, so avoiding the impossible situation of a war on two fronts, became clearer. Only if the United States had been willing to offer some support would a British stand against Japan have been possible, but this was not forthcoming. It had always been understood, at least by the British, that Britain and the USA would work together in order to secure an Anglo—American predominance in the Pacific. Under the terms of the Washington Conference, confirmed by the London Agreements of 1933, the British and American fleets available in the Pacific, even allowing for the two-ocean strategy (the need to keep naval superiority in both Atlantic and Pacific) imposed upon them, could match the Japanese. But Japan had denounced the agreements in 1934, and initiated an extensive naval building programme, while America had consistently refused to become embroiled in foreign concerns, declining to join the League of Nations – which condemned that worthy initiative to ultimate failure – or to attempt any resistance to the emerging totalitarian regimes. The American public, shocked by pictures of burnt and abandoned babies, might be emotionally committed to China, but was still nervously isolationist and reluctant to resist aggression: 'A passive and shameful acquiescence in the wrong that is being done,' as the former Secretary of State Henry Stimson put it. Since it was also clear that Hong Kong was likely to be the centre of any Anglo—Japanese conflict, the more furiously pacific of American isolationists would have seized on the excuse of not abetting British imperialism in order to withhold their support.

So Britain, left on her own, could do little but sit on the fence, not restricting exports of war material to China while at the same time attempting to soothe Japan, until the problem was solved on 12 October 1938 by the Japanese capture of Canton. Sir Archibald Clark Kerr, the British Ambassador in Chungking, saw this as the beginning of the end: 'Canton had felt safe in its proximity to Hong Kong, an unreasonable feeling if you will, but one which has been none the less deep. The occupation of Canton and our puzzling acquiescence in it had shaken the hundred-year-old Chinese belief in the prestige of Great Britain which would now shift to Japan.'[2]

Hong Kong was thereby immediately brought into the front line. The issue now became whether Hong Kong, the stream of arms from which had been so useful to the Chinese cause, would be opened to the Japanese to supply their own military needs. To their credit (although the probability of strikes by Chinese in the colony had they succumbed was not unnoticed) the British government stood firm against this, but did agree in January 1939, again in the absence of any US support, to suspend arms shipments across the land frontier.

In September 1939 the long-expected war in Europe finally broke out. Just as British strategy in the Far East had assumed American co-operation, in Europe it depended on France holding off an attack for long enough to enable British forces to be raised, trained and equipped. The unexpectedly sudden collapse of France in June 1940 left Britain alone facing Germany and her allies. In these circumstances a war with Japan was unthinkable, and further concessions inevitable. Supplies to China through Hong Kong were beginning to be replaced by those passing over the newly constructed Burma Road, and the Japanese insisted that this source be cut off. Lord Lothian, the Ambassador in Washington, attempted to enlist American support in resisting the demand, but was informed that the USA 'could do nothing effective'. Cordell Hull, the Secretary of State, advised Lord Lothian that 'It would be better to retreat, while refusing irrevocable concessions.' How the two parts of this policy were to be reconciled he did not vouchsafe. Hull also blandly suggested that 'perhaps the British Government might care to explore on their own initiative the possibility of a settlement with Japan'. In spite of this extraordinary suggestion, Hull felt justified in complaining, when the British government agreed to close the road for a three-month period in November 1938, that their action was 'unwarranted'.[3]

Such British concessions were greatly resented by the Chinese, much more concerned with their own fight against the Japanese invader than with the British war in Europe, a concern which the Hong Kong government shared. At this point the Cantonese spirit of enterprise reasserted itself, and a considerable smuggling trade in petrol and spare parts burgeoned, with the benevolent neglect of the Hong Kong authorities. More robust support seemed to be forthcoming when Northcote pressed for this activity to be legalized and the British undertaking not to pass military supplies through the port withdrawn. Since at the time the Japanese forces were staging frequent provocative incidents aimed at Hong Kong, such a move might well have led to a full-scale Japanese attack on the colony, independent of any more general Pacific action. Whether this would have been an immediate *casus belli* or not would have been open to question, but the British Ambassador in Tokyo, Sir Robert Craigie, desperately attempting to avoid 'an incident provoked by the local Japanese military . . . at so exposed a point', convinced the British government that things were best left as they were. (Craigie was also attempting to patch up an agreement with the Japanese for the resumption of supplies in return for their withdrawal from Indo-China, but even had this succeeded it would only have exacerbated the situation in China.) One prescient official, the Permanent Under-Secretary at the Foreign Office Sir David Scott, commented on 8 August 1941: 'I think we might leave it at that for the time being. The question will probably solve itself one way or the other very shortly.'[4]

Essentially a blockade

Sir David was proved right in December of that year when the Japanese finally struck. The speed and power of their attack took their victims completely by surprise. The raid on Pearl Harbor (7 December) was followed the next day by landings in Malaya and air raids on Hong Kong and the Philippines; twenty-four hours later the British battleship *Prince of Wales* and the battle cruiser *Repulse* were sunk. In his memoirs Churchill recorded his shock at the news: 'In all the war I have never received a more direct shock. The readers of these pages will realize how many efforts, hopes, and plans foundered with these ships. As I turned over and twisted in bed the full horror of the news sank in upon me . . . Over all this vast expanse of waters, Japan was supreme, and we everywhere were weak and naked.'[5] Nowhere was this more true than in Hong Kong.

On 7 January 1941 Churchill, now Prime Minister, had written to General Ismay, Commander-in-Chief, Far East, who had been urging that reinforcements be sent to Hong Kong:

if Japan goes to war with us there is not the slightest chance of holding Hong Kong or relieving it. It is most unwise to increase the loss we shall suffer there. Instead of increasing the garrison it ought to be reduced to a symbolical scale. Any trouble arising there must be dealt with at the Peace Conference after the war. We must avoid frittering away our resources on untenable positions ... I wish we had fewer troops there, but to move any would be noticeable and dangerous.[6]

Hong Kong became, in September 1941, the responsibility of a new Governor, Sir Mark Young. Northcote had been ill for some time, and was obliged to leave in May 1940 for treatment; on his return it was clear that he was still not fit for duty. Sir Mark Young had no experience of the East, apart from his time as a cadet in Ceylon. Since 1928 his postings to East and West Africa, Palestine and Barbados, had given him little training useful for leading a Chinese community under attack.

The position of Hong Kong, should war with Japan break out, had been the object of some discussion by the British government. Its loss would be a terrible blow to British prestige – a point the Foreign Office found particularly sensitive – but there was not much that could be done to defend the colony. Of the three defensive standards discussed – A, B and C, which ranged downwards from the defence required by a main naval base – the lowest, providing for the minimum needed to support a delaying action, was unanimously agreed upon. The only task required of the colony was to hold the Japanese for long enough to allow Singapore to be reinforced. Ironically, when hostilities began Admiral Sir Tom Phillips pressed for Hong Kong's defences to be upgraded to the highest standard as a deterrent to Japan, 'that hidebound nation', who would be 'nervous of being cut off by the British Fleet'. When the time came Phillips and his battleships were at the bottom of the sea, sunk by the hide-bound nation's mastery of the new weapon, carrier-borne aircraft. The Defence Committee would not agree with Phillips, and held to their previous policy that 'Hong Kong must be regarded as an outpost and held as long as possible. We should resist the inevitably strong pressure to reinforce Hong Kong and should certainly be unable to relieve it.'[7]

In spite of this accurate assessment reinforcements of a sort were sent to Hong Kong. Two regiments of Canadian infantry had reached the colony in mid-November 1941, although without their heavier equipment. On 1 December the Joint Chiefs of Staff decided to ask the Canadian government for the balance of an infantry brigade (essentially one more infantry battalion together with brigade artillery and engineers), but fortunately this could not be done in time. In spite of the ultimately disastrous outcome, the strategic thinking was not at the time unsound. Anglo–American co-operation, sedulously nurtured by Churchill, had strengthened to the point where a joint embargo on strategic materials going to Japan, and clear threats of war if further aggression was attempted, were issued. (It is possible that Japan might have been willing to compromise in order to have this embargo lifted; Sir Robert Craigie certainly believed that he had such an agreement within his grasp.) But there was still no American undertaking to respond to a Japanese attack on British territory, nor any real likelihood of any such undertaking being given. British planners could only assume that sooner or later the Americans would join in, and that a holding operation until this occurred was the best that could be managed.

The staggering success of the Japanese attacks in early December 1941 overturned these assumptions. America was in the war with a vengeance, but with her naval power in the Pacific almost wiped out, along with the British battleships. Singapore, into which troops had been poured, was still considered capable of holding out for at least six months, but there was no hope for Hong Kong. 'The garrison,' Churchill acknowledged, 'were faced with a task that from the outset was beyond their powers.' After the arrival of the Canadians in November there were six infantry battalions – one each of the Royal Scots, the Middlesex, Punjabis, Rajputs, Winnipeg Grenadiers and Royal Rifles of Canada – from three separate armies, supplemented by the Hong Kong Volunteers, who were to prove by no means less effective than the regulars. A reasonable standard of all-round fixed coastal defence was provided against a naval attack that never materialized. As a result many of the bigger guns – eight of the 1893 pattern 9.2-inch and fifteen later six-inch pieces – were pointing in the wrong direction for much of the time. Close infantry support was left to the Hong Kong Regiment of Royal Artillery, partly equipped with Kipling's 'screw guns' – mule-borne light guns – and its usefulness further limited by the complete absence of air spotting or, after the first Japanese strike, any forward observation posts. By contrast the Japanese counter-battery fire was unfailingly accurate, based upon careful observations and map references prepared before the attack by the Japanese fifth-column within the colony. It had always been intended that the defence of the colony would be the task of the Royal Navy, but when the invasion came the Navy could muster only one destroyer, four small gunboats and some motor launches. From the beginning the Japanese had total control of the air, having destroyed the few obsolete RAF planes on the ground.

There was, as the Prime Minister had previously acknowledged, no possibility of reinforcement. In spite of this, the beleaguered Sir Mark Young was to cable the Secretary of State in London on 20 December: 'Forces of General Yu han mou now within a very short distance.'[8] This was strictly true in that a few units of the Chinese army were not very far behind the Japanese, but evincing only the most peaceable of intentions. Chiang Kai-shek had however previously claimed that two Chinese divisions were rushing to the aid of the colony and fiercely engaging Japanese forces; this was the purest eyewash. In the absence of any prospect of relief a successful defence could not be thought of, and the only question was when a surrender would be made.

It came about more quickly than expected owing to a combination of bad luck, poor planning and tactical incompetence on the British part and fine fighting by the Japanese.[9] The military commander, Major General C.M. Maltby, had taken post only in August, and had therefore had limited opportunities for training, a serious disadvantage since not only were the ground troops insufficient in numbers, but they were inadequately trained and badly equipped. The greater part of their mortars and mortar bombs were missing, and the 9.2-inch coastal defence guns had only fifteen shells apiece. The infantry were required to man an incompetently constructed line of defences – the Gin-drinkers line – extending right across the New Territories, which was incapable of being held by the forces committed to it. Three battalions, some three thousand rifles, were expected to hold the eleven-mile line for at least a week. It was a wildly optimistic estimate, and the fighting lasted for only forty-eight hours before a withdrawal from the mainland, including the city of Kowloon, was decided upon.

In his signal to the Commander-in-Chief, Far East, Maltby put the best construction on the situation. On the previous day, 11 December, he had reported that enemy progress had been confined, and that they had been 'beaten off'; in a classic military meiosis he continued: 'Position, however, called for re-adjustment of the line.'[10] Fortified by this misleading assessment, the Commander-in-Chief, in a cable to the War Office that showed the miserable qualities of British military

intelligence, referred to the Japanese operation as 'essentially a blockade'.[11] The truth must have dawned the following day when they
received Maltby's next cable: 'The position was unsuitable for a protracted resistance, and by noon the decision was made [to abandon
the only defensive line that existed and to evacuate the mainland]
... Morale of civil population considerably shaken by unexpected
evacuation of Kowloon. Fifth column active.'

The island of Hong Kong itself now became the target for concentrated artillery fire and bombing raids. Fixed batteries were put out of
action and deserted by their Chinese gunners, but the army command
maintained, either from ignorance or habit, a stiff upper lip in its
reports to the Commander-in-Chief. The casualties suffered on 16
December were 'remarkably light' – nine officers and 102 other ranks
killed or missing. A Chinese merchant, Chau Lim Pak, had been
arrested for 'defeatist talk', and the morale of the civil population
'continues to improve'. The Japanese offer to accept a surrender was
rejected: General Maltby considered 'all is not well in their camp,
although it is difficult to say whether this is due to the Chinese threat
to their communications or to the loss we have inflicted'. Accordingly
the War Office were given to understand by the Commander-in-Chief
on 18 December that the Japanese had been surprised by 'the robust
attitude of the defence', and the request for air support to relieve
pressure on Hong Kong made three days previously to C-i-C India
was not pressed. Far from being disconcerted, the Japanese had been
agreeably surprised by the ease of their victory, which came 'much
faster than anticipated'.[12]

In his own mind Churchill had written off Hong Kong, and he was
depending on Singapore to hold the Far Eastern front while arrangements were made with the Americans. Within four days of the news
of Pearl Harbor he had left to meet Roosevelt in Washington, and
sent his message of support to Hong Kong en route: 'We are all
watching day by day and hour by hour your stubborn defence of the
port and fortress of Hong Kong. You guard a link between the Far
East and Europe long famous in world civilization. We are sure that
the defence of Hong Kong against barbarous and unprovoked attack
will add a glorious page to British annals.'[13]

On the same day that the Commander-in-Chief reported the 'robust
attitude of the defence', the Japanese landed on the island itself. Maltby
signalled that he was 'using all resources to evict them', and Governor
Sir Mark Young issued a message to H.M. Forces: 'The time has

come to advance against the enemy. The eyes of the Empire are upon you. Be strong, be resolute, and do your duty.' Talk of advancing against the enemy was by then sadly inapposite, for after an initial vigorous resistance, communications had collapsed to an extent that both Governor and General Officer Commanding were out of touch with the action. In his cable to London of 20 December Sir Mark claimed: 'we launched a successful counter attack in neighbourhood of Wong Nei Chong Gap. Japanese were thrown back . . . There have been no further enemy advances . . . Parties of enemy mopped up in Repulse Bay area.' In fact the action resulted in the defeat of the British at all points and with heavy losses; the truth was that the British forces had been so cut up as to be separated both from central command and supply points, as described by the Naval Officer Commanding in a signal to the Admiralty of 21 December: 'little of Hong Kong still in our hands, unable to reach food and ammunition store as position surrounded'.

That day the Governor cabled to London asking for authority to surrender at discretion, only to be answered by more Churchillian verbiage: 'The eyes of the word are upon you. We expect you to resist to the end. The honour of the Empire is in your hands.' Although this cable had in fact been sent before Young's message was received, the Prime Minister then being in mid-Atlantic, the Governor was specifically told that 'H.M.G's desire is that you should fight it out as in Prime Minister's message.' This was confirmed by another cable of 21 December from Churchill, which started on a critical note: 'We were greatly concerned to hear of the landings on Hong Kong . . . We cannot judge from here the conditions which rendered these landings possible or prevented effective counter-attacks upon the intruders,' and went on: 'There must however be no thought of surrender. Every part of the island must be fought and the enemy resisted with the utmost stubbornness. There must be vigorous fighting in the inner defences, and, if the need be, from house to house,' and concluded: 'by a prolonged resistance you and your men can win the lasting honour which we are sure will be your due.'[14]

Many criticisms have been made of Churchill's order to resist, reinforced as it was by rhetoric that in the cold light of hindsight sounds overstuffed and meaningless. Allowance needs to be made for the fact that the Prime Minister, on his way to a critical meeting, had many more important concerns than the future of Hong Kong and its defenders, a future certain to be short and unpleasant: as so often,

Hong Kong was low on the list of British priorities. And a resistance had to be offered, the only question being when the surrender should be made. Years after the event, it seems obvious that, lacking any coherent plans for the defence of the island, or the means to do so, and with no realistic hope of relief, the wisest course would have been to take the up the first Japanese offer, made on 13 December. But the Governor and the General Officer Commanding obeyed their instructions, and passed on the order to their troops. General Maltby sent a message: 'Let this day be historical in the annals of our Empire. The Order of the Day is to hold fast.' Fight it out and hold fast they did, with heavy losses, subjected to intense bombardment by the units of heavy and siege artillery that the Japanese had brought up, together with some squadrons of tanks, until Christmas Day. The Hong Kong Volunteers attracted well-deserved admiration, as their Scottish, Chinese and Portuguese companies fought alongside the regular troops; one company, the 'Methusiliers', composed entirely of over-age volunteers, held their position for twenty-four hours against a fierce assault, with many casualties.

There was some baffled criticism of their commanders on the part of those who were being asked to write the Annals of Empire. One of the volunteers, Captain Potts, was disappointed to find GHQ 'safely below ground', largely unaware of what was happening, and dependent on the telephone for communications. Another, Private Remedios, had taken Churchill's words to heart: 'I was perhaps very naive at the time. I thought that Hong Kong would be fought for until the last soldier died.' So did Captain Boletho: 'I had believed and had been told to tell my troops that we would fight to the last man, to the last bullet. So to be told to capitulate was a serious blow to me.'[15] When the pugnacious Potts did get some Japanese in his sights, and opened up, he was reprimanded by a regular officer for having fired without proper military permission. Such adherence to protocol did not prevent the Matilda Hospital being used as an ammunition store, nor St Stephen's Hospital being made to serve – by the Canadians – as a firing point, with tragic results.

British accounts of the fall of Hong Kong have highlighted the atrocities committed by the Japanese. The rape of nurses and slaughter of doctors and patients certainly took place, together with all the usual accompaniments of the violent capture of a city. One account may be allowed to stand for a catalogue of shameful brutality, that of Second Lieutenant Osler Thomas, who was at the Advanced Dressing Station at the Salesian Mission: 'After the wounded were murdered, the doctors and orderlies other than Banfill (Commanding, Captain RCAMC) were taken out, stripped to the waist, lined up alongside a storm drain and, amid shouts of laughter, were bayonetted or hacked to death.'[16] But much of the horror was due to the fact that the British were unaccustomed to being on the receiving end of such acts. Every European country had experience of death and pillage at the hands of an invader, and a great number of countries all over the world have felt the after-effects of a British army, even if these were often, at least in more recent times, comparatively innocuous. The blame for the worst of the atrocities has to be shared with lax British command that permitted the improper use of medical premises for combat, as at St Stephen's. There is some evidence that Japanese commanders themselves attempted to restrain the troops, and one witness relates that the some of those responsible were subsequently shot.

It was the Chinese population who suffered most in the taking of Hong Kong. Dr Li Shu-fan, who was attempting to run a hospital in Kowloon, estimated that he had to treat at least ten thousand victims of rape: many were bayonetted in the streets. Others were disposed of with greater originality: some had their hands threaded together through bayonet holes before being thrown into the harbour; John Stericker saw on the trees by the Peak tram station 'three strings, like beads, of Chinese ... as one dropped from exhaustion he pulled another down and there they were left to die'.[17]

Thanks to Japan, we are now a free people

After the Japanese invasion, a small group of civilians of all ages and many nationalities, although chiefly British, was bundled together in a prison camp on the Stanley peninsula and subjected for three years to malign neglect, near-starvation, harsh discipline and the permanent possibility of torture and death, punctuated by occasional acts of kindness and humanity. Organization was left to the inmates themselves, under the official guidance of the senior British administrator. This was Franklin Gimson, formerly the Colonial Secretary, Sir Mark Young having been separated from the others by the Japanese. Although later most brutally handled the Governor was, to begin with, treated well enough. He was lodged in the Peninsula Hotel, from whence he wrote to Gimson on 30 December, saying that the Japanese were 'very polite' and asking for warm clothes, together with a long list of requisites for a Governor-in-captivity, which included sock-suspenders and copies of Jane Austen and *Stalky and Co.*[18]

Gimson, with a splendidly unfortunate sense of timing, had arrived in Hong Kong on 7 December. Then fifty-one, he had spent his whole career in the Ceylon Civil Service, where the pleasant and privileged life was not an ideal preparation for a Japanese prison camp, but he was a true-blue colonial administrator, not blessed with a lively sense of humour but completely reliable and capable of bringing some order into the most tumultuous of conditions. He was only allowed to join the other prisoners in March 1942, by which time they had organized themselves into a British Communal Council. This body was directly elected by all the prisoners, and it is significant that they declined to vote for any government official, with the exception of the Commissioner of Police, John Pennefather-Evans. The Executive Committee consisted of a newspaper editor and three taipans, with the Defence Secretary as an ex-officio member.

To the embittered prisoners the Hong Kong government had been thoroughly discredited. Dissatisfaction had begun long before the Japanese invasion. A compulsory evacuation in 1940 of British-national women and children had aroused great controversy, since those with white skins were sorted out by a pair of British ladies to be sent on to Australia, while those with brown or yellow complexions were dropped off at Manila. This 'disgraceful discrimination' was attacked in the Legislative Council, where it was claimed that 'Government . . . has forfeited to a great extent the respect and confidence of the community.' The emergency services, even after more than two years of preparation, were 'inefficient beyond description'. Accusations of fraud and incompetence in the preparation of air-raid defences and in the Immigration Department had led to a full-scale Commission of Inquiry into corruption in the public service. This had been aborted by the Japanese attack, but the retiring Governor, Sir Geoffry Northcote, had been seriously concerned, reporting to the Colonial Office that 'Several Government officers are under the gravest suspicion of having taken bribes . . . I fear that the other disturbing outcome is going to be the revelation of serious laxity in the control of Government expenditure . . . All this leaves me with a nasty taste in my mouth on my departure hence, and I feel somewhat culpable myself.'[19]

No suspicion of course attached to the newly arrived Gimson, who was clearly entirely honourable and incorruptible, but his personal prickliness, amounting to arrogance, did little to mollify the malcontents. He was insistent that the legitimate government of Hong Kong, embodied in his person, continued to exist, an attitude that did much to ensure that at the end of the war Hong Kong did in fact remain British: but he had little use for democracy within the camp, which he did his effective best to reduce to a purely advisory capacity. In particular he distrusted, and indeed despised, the businessmen, going to the extraordinary lengths of recording in his diary: 'It is impossible for businessmen to discuss political questions, [which] must be borne in mind in considering any proposals for the future of Hong Kong,' and that the elected Council was 'a revolutionary body . . . a subversive organization'.[20]

Under Gimson as Camp Commandant the Camp Committee, in which the official element gradually predominated, took what decisions they could on domestic matters, and a Camp Court, presided over by the Chief Justice, Sir Athol MacGregor, settled disputes. John Stericker described the proceedings of the Committee, of which he was Secretary: 'It was most extraordinary because the British love committees and if you have committees they have to be serious. Everything has to be done properly and you sit solemnly and take notes.' With a vision firmly fixed on the end of the war, Gimson resisted proposals that British prisoners should be repatriated, as the Americans were, in order that an Imperial presence in Hong Kong would visibly be continuous. In this aim the Japanese unconsciously helped, since they preserved the separate identity of the colony as a Japanese territory with its own Governor, rather than incorporating it in the occupied area of Kwantung.

Under the stress of life in the camp some unpleasant characteristics came to the surface. Sir Robert Hotung's daughter, Jean Gittins, who was among the internees, reported:

There were some Britishers who felt that if it was not for the many Eurasians in the camp, there would be sufficient food for them. Racial discrimination had by no means moderated in the face of general adversity and that type of person was too bigoted in outlook to understand that the food was provided, not in a lump quantity, but rationed by the Japanese, according to the number of mouths to be fed.[21]

The near-starvation of the prisoners was not a matter of deliberate policy by the Japanese, but rather one of inefficiency and lack of resources. In principle, and sometimes in practice, both Red Cross and outside relief was available. An important factor in this was the presence outside the camp of the senior members of the Hongkong and Shanghai Bank staff, headed by Sir Vandeleur Grayson. This group had been retained by the Japanese to liquidate the resources of the Bank and to issue countersigned bank notes which were then used by the Japanese Yokohama Specie Bank. Being lodged in Victoria they were able to develop a network which went far beyond their permitted tasks to include systematic intelligence links with the British Army Aid Group operating in China. Through these connections escapes were planned and substantial sums smuggled in to the civilian and military camps. Their activities were eventually betrayed by an Indian informer and one member, C.F. Hyde, was executed, while two others, including Grayson himself, died in the prison hospital, basically from gross neglect.[22]

Another outstation existed at St Paul's French Hospital, where Dr Selwyn Selwyn-Clarke and his wife Hilda had been allowed to stay to control sanitary services. Selwyn-Clarke specialized in smuggling medical supplies into the camps; drugs were not too difficult, but 'To amateur smugglers a dentist's chair was quite a challenge.' By careful observation the Clarkes had timed the movements of Japanese patrols, and calculated that they had a window of opportunity of thirty minutes to break into the stores, remove the chair, and reseal the entrance. The penalty for such behaviour was death, and although the smugglers were successful on that occasion Clarke was eventually betrayed and arrested by the Kempeitai, the Japanese military police.[23]

These internal resisters were supported by a network operating through occupied China, the British Army Aid Group. One of those peculiarly British private enterprises, the BAAG had been started by some escapees from Hong Kong, of whom the most prominent was Lindsay Ride, Colonel in the Volunteers and Professor of Physiology at Hong Kong University. He gathered about him an eclectic selection, some hundreds of students, doctors, nurses and soldiers, who became officially part of the Indian Army. Based in Kweilin, with forward stations including one at Weichow on the East River, the BAAG collected intelligence in south China and kept up constant communication with the prisoners, civilian and military, in Hong Kong.[24]

The great achievement of Japanese rule in Hong Kong was to convince the Chinese population that, by comparison with that of the Greater East Asia Co-Prosperity Sphere, British rule was both benign and competent. It might have been otherwise, since the Japanese had some strong cards to play, especially in the matter of race. Half a century of aggression, culminating in the deaths of millions of Chinese, might not have endeared the Japanese to their prospective partners, but Chinese resentment against often unconscious British attitudes of racial superiority, although usually subdued, had always been strongly felt. The *Hong Kong News*, edited during the occupation by the Japanese, hammered this point home. A regime which gave power to 'callow British youths' and 'half-witted Englishmen' had been replaced: 'Thanks to Japan, we are now a free people, and the shapers of our own destiny. The question of colour is dead.'[25] And to some extent at least the Japanese did go further than the British ever had in extending Chinese participation in the decision-making process. District and area bureaux and central councils were established which exposed a much larger number to some nominal share in government.

If the influence of these councils was largely illusory, it was not much more so than that of the previous Municipal Council, but any goodwill the Japanese might have won in this direction was eliminated a thousand-fold in others. Corruption, which under the British had been confined to the lower levels of police and other officials, and usually kept within modest bounds, became vicious and endemic. A mass of petty regulations gave innumerable opportunities for every branch of the Japanese administration to exercise squeeze. Li Shu-fan described how 'Japanese orders could not work because of the almost impossible and cumbersome red tape . . . [There was] a great deal of quarrelling and personal sabotage among the Japanese officers over private plunder and jockeying for position.' It is estimated that over ten thousand Hong Kong civilians were executed by the Japanese, but the form of persecution that aroused most resentment, according to Dr Li, was the constant face-slapping that any Japanese indulged in on the slightest provocation.[26]

An effort was made to teach Japanese in lieu of English, but education, in common with every other public service, collapsed almost completely. Before the occupation there were some 120,000 children in Hong Kong's schools; under the Japanese the number never rose above one-tenth of this figure, and towards the end was as low as three thousand.

It is not surprising that with very few exceptions there was no enthusiastic collaboration with the invaders, and a fair amount of resistance, especially in the New Territories, which were constantly infiltrated by Chinese guerrillas. Such staunch action was not shown by many prominent Chinese, since it was with somewhat disappointing unanimity that the non-European members of the Legislative and Executive Councils transferred their allegiance to the Japanese. Sir Robert Kotewall, Sir Shouson Chou and Sir Man-Kam Lo all joined the Rehabilitation Committee, and the first two later became members of the Chinese Representative Council and the Chinese Co-operative Council. It was true that both Sir Robert (who became Lo Kuk-wo during the occupation) and Sir Shouson had been specifically asked, by a deputation for the British Hong Kong administration, which included the Attorney-General and the Defence Secretary, 'to promote friendly relations between Chinese and Japanese to the extent necessary to restore public order, protect life and property and preserve internal security', but at least one of Sir Robert's statements, that 'All Chinese must try their best to support China and Japan to work for the early victory of the sacred war and for the establishment of the Greater East Asia Co-Prosperity Sphere,'[27] seems to have gone beyond the bounds of decent co-operation. As soon as the British Civil government took over after liberation Sir Robert was told that he must absent himself from public life pending investigation, but he was later reinstated. Fortunately for future good relations the two most enthusiastic collaborators, Ch'en Lien-po, the old instigator of the Merchant Volunteer Corps Plot, and Lau Tit-shing, a Japanese-educated merchant, both died before the British returned. Some were tried, but it was recognized that most Chinese who had worked with the Japanese could not be blamed for submitting to another, equally foreign, rule.

The British Empire has been entirely written off

Whether Hong Kong would indeed revert to British rule at the end of the war was hardly a question that bothered any of the prisoners at Stanley, with the exception of Franklin Gimson, steadfastly pursuing his colonial role. China certainly did not intend that this should happen, and saw its participation in the war as a lever for settling such old scores as extra-territoriality together with the foreign concessions and leases. These grievances were made the subject of a draft treaty presented by China to Britain in October 1942, which also included a clause providing for the surrender of the New Territories lease. This the British government was not prepared to consider, but under pressure conceded that the matter could be discussed after the war. This conclusion enabled the surrender of extra-territoriality and the concessions to be agreed, leaving the way open to concentrate on the future of Hong Kong.

A conference had been sponsored by the Americans to take place at Mont Tremblant, near Quebec, between 4 and 14 December 1942 to discuss post-war policy in the Far East. At such discussions China could reasonably look to the United States for support in persuading Britain to modify its position on sovereignty. When Pearl Harbor forced America into the war the sympathy which prudence had hitherto held in check overflowed. Chiang Kai-shek's government, which by then was doing little actively for the allied cause – other than engaging some Japanese attention (and, by January 1941, turning its attention to fighting Communists rather than Japanese) – contributions more than counterbalanced by the huge amount of material that was being absorbed, unused, and which would have been much better employed in Europe – was given a generous loan and China acclaimed as a 'great power'. Roosevelt's draft of the initial United Nations declaration placed China second after the United States, before the USSR and Britain, which gives an idea of the workings of the President's mind; the draft was later amended.[28]

Roosevelt was personally committed to the Chinese cause, and many visitors were reminded that his maternal grandfather, Warren Delano, had been a partner in Russell's and that his mother had spent part of her childhood in Hong Kong. The fact that Russell's had been active in the opium trade, and that the happy family memories were of life in a British colony, did not seem to cross the President's mind. Oliver Stanley, Secretary of State for the Colonies and son of the 17th Lord Derby, was told by the President when visiting Washington in January 1945, 'I do not wish to be unkind or rude to the British . . . but in 1841 when you acquired Hong Kong, you did not do so by purchase.' To which Stanley, thinking on his feet, replied, 'Let me see, Mr President, that was about the time of the Mexican War, wasn't it?'[29]

The President had an active bee in his bonnet on the subject of colonialism in Asia, and was particularly down on the French. Although quite specific commitments had been made by the United States, on more than one occasion, that 'all territories, continental and colonial, over which the French flag flew' would be restored to French sovereignty at the end of hostilities, Roosevelt privately told anyone who happened to be about, including for example the Egyptian Minister at Washington, that 'He did not think his pledges about the French Empire were of importance.' Attempting to explain this somewhat cavalier attitude, Secretary of State Cordell Hull told the British Ambassador, Lord Halifax, that the President believed 'France has milked it [Indo-China] for a hundred years. The people of Indo China are entitled to something better than that.' An excuse for Roosevelt might be his alarming ignorance of Asian affairs. He actually told Chiang Kai-shek that he should take over French Indo-China after the war, which might be compared to Churchill instructing de Gaulle to recover Louisiana, and which would certainly have been most violently resisted by the Vietnamese.[30]

Hull attempted to pacify the most 'vociferous persons in the United States, including Vice-President Wallace, who wanted immediate independence for all colonies [and] a certain Texan [who] particularly urged that Britain should return Hong Kong to China. I retorted that Hong Kong had been British longer than Texas had belonged to the United States, and I did not think anyone would welcome a move to turn Texas back to Mexico.' The British government was uncomfortably aware of such American feelings. Sir Ashley Clarke, of the Foreign Office's Far Eastern Department reported on 11 June 1942 after a visit to America that China was not only considered of equal importance to Britain as a war partner, but that the 'underlying relationship was much warmer and more confident'. The Foreign Secretary, Anthony Eden, agreed: 'The British Empire has been entirely written off by the American opinion.'

And by some, at least, in Britain: almost all the Foreign Office staff, for example, were content that Hong Kong, which had always been something of a thorn in the side, interfering with their own much more important and dignified work, should be returned to a Chinese government. They had attempted to do so at the end of the First World War when Sir John Jordan, the British Ambassador at Peking, had suggested at least the return of the New Territories. It would be, he conceded, a sacrifice, but without such sacrifices 'no solution of the problem seems possible'. Curzon dismissed such sentiments as 'idealistic and impractical', and refused 'to dig up by the roots all previous cessions, leases etc.' Now, once more, some Foreign Office mandarins attempted to disembarrass themselves of the unwanted colony: Gladwyn Jebb was all for giving it up; Sir Neville Butler, of the North American Department, felt it essential because of 'America's passion for the Chinese'; Ashley Clarke and Sir John Brenan (formerly the Canton Consul-General, who had always despised the 'abysmal ignorance' of the Hong Kong government) of the Far Eastern Department concurred. Only Sir Maurice Peterson, head of that department, considered many of the arguments fallacious, and firmly stated that 'In view of the ignominious circumstances in which we have been bundled out of Hong Kong, we owe it to ourselves to return there and I personally do not believe that we will ever regain the respect of the East unless we do.'[31]

In the Colonial Office a rather more robust view was taken. It was suggested only that 'the maintenance of British sovereignty in the Colony is [not] a matter beyond the scope of such discussions', but only Leo Amery, the tough old right-winger, then at the India Office, considered the welfare of the inhabitants of Hong Kong. They were British subjects, and they should not be surrendered[32](this is not a view that would necessarily have attracted his successors in future Conservative governments).

The consensus of opinion was that Britain should be prepared to negotiate on giving up Hong Kong only if this was part of a general settlement in South-East Asia; there were too many unknown factors, including the increasingly likely possibility that the Kuomintang would not be in control of China after the war, to make any hard and fast decisions on the future. Lord Cranborne, Colonial Secretary at the time, gave the considered official view in a minute of 14 July 1942 which was to become a foundation of government policy on Hong Kong. Resentment of America was evident:

> ... we should not allow ourselves to be manoeuvred into the position of having been alone responsible for what has happened in the Far East. In fact, I feel that the responsibility of the United States is far heavier than ours. If they had been willing to collaborate with the League of Nations in the early days of the China incident, all that has happened since might, and probably would, have been averted. In fact, they hung back not only until it was too late to save the situation, but until they were actually attacked.

The return of sovereignty to China could be agreed only as part of a general settlement in Asia, which might include both Singapore and Hong Kong being 'managed, both as to their defence and administration, by international bodies' – but only if the Chinese and Dutch entered into similar arrangements and the Americans agreed to include Honolulu and Manila. In the absence of such a settlement Hong Kong would remain British.[33]

The Colonial Office representative whose memorandum had inspired Lord Cranborne's declaration, and who attended the Mont Tremblant conference, was David MacDougall, who had been Chief Information Officer of the Hong Kong government before the invasion. He had made his escape from the colony just before the capitulation in a particularly bold venture headed by the Chinese Admiral Sir Chan Chak. MacDougall wrote an ironic letter from Mont Tremblant to Noel Sabine back at the Foreign Office: there was much 'choplicking of Americans ... by profession anti-British', and two predominant feelings at the conference: 'The Chinese are a nation of saints and heroes, above and beyond approach', and 'a distrust of Britain and in particular her intentions re colonies'. The critical tone was too much for Arthur Creech Jones, Minister for Labour and National Service, Ernest Bevin's Parliamentary aide and post-war Colonial Secretary, sent to toughen up the delegation, who 'got rather red in the face – like a labour leader and not in the least like a "sahib". Hands on hips, he rounded on the whole lot of them . . . and barked and bit in a very forthright fashion. It was a wonderful scene . . . .[he] brushed aside with contempt the adolescent questioning of concepts which . . . had been settled years ago in England.'[34]

Creech Jones's spirited attack was, as far as Hong Kong was concerned, vitiated by the Foreign Office representative, Sir John Pratt, who quite on his own initiative assured the conference that 'when the time came to deal with Hong Kong, the Chinese would be completely satisfied'. Even the Foreign Office was disturbed at that; the obvious pun was made, and Sir Maurice Peterson indignantly minuted of Pratt: 'The best thing we can do is to bring him home and keep him here.'

At least the Mont Tremblant Conference took Hong Kong's future off the immediate agenda, since China was satisfied that the Americans would force Britain to disgorge. This impression was reinforced at the Allies' Cairo Conference in November 1943, when it became known that Roosevelt offered to support Chiang in preventing Britain from staying in Hong Kong if Chiang would co-operate with the Chinese Communists in fighting the Japanese. This was done in personal meetings between the President, Marshal Chiang and his wife, of which no records were kept, a circumstance not likely to allay British suspicions. But it was also the first time that Roosevelt and Chiang had met, and the President's romantic attachment to the Chinese cause took a considerable battering when he was exposed to the ineptitude of its representative. In a discussion with Lord Louis Mountbatten, head of the South-East Asia Command, about the plan of campaign in Burma, in which the monsoon was, as ever, the limiting factor, Madame Chiang admitted of her husband: 'Believe it or not, he does not know about the monsoon.'[35]

Roosevelt can hardly have imagined that he would find it easy to persuade his British allies to agree to this one-sided bargain, for Churchill had always made his own position abundantly clear. Stanley Hornbeck, of the State Department, had faithfully reported Churchill's view that Hong Kong was 'British territory and he saw no good reason why it should cease to be such ... He referred to public utterances of his own to the effect that he was not Prime Minister for the purpose of being a party to the liquidation of the British Empire.'[36]

As the war progressed it became more difficult for America to exert an influence on British colonial policy. The Allied landings in Italy and, in June 1944, in Normandy, had shifted the decisive land battles from the Pacific to those waged there and by Anglo—American forces. It was therefore of the utmost importance not to disturb that accord, but in the other theatre of war Chiang was increasingly showing himself not to be in control of more than a section of China, and the unpleasant facts of the Kuomintang administration were beginning to impinge on the American consciousness.

Although American rhetoric on behalf of Chiang did not falter, his regime was increasingly sliding into disrepute, its corruption and inefficiency becoming a byword. 'The leaders in Chungking had no intention of expending their forces in China against the Japanese; their plan was to harbour them, such as they were, for employment ... particularly against the Communists in the north, after the war.' Their value was to hold down a large number of Japanese troops, but the very fact of the occupation of China, even had there been no fighting (and for most of the time there was not a great deal) would have had the same effect. When the Japanese made an attack, in the summer of 1944, they were able to roll back Chiang's dispirited conscripts hundreds of miles with little effort, helped by the Chinese peasants who turned against what was nominally their own army. Only in Burma, fighting alongside British troops and under the command of General Stilwell, were properly trained Chinese soldiers effectively deployed.

Powerful voices were also raised in defending British interests: General Douglas MacArthur, Commander of Allied Forces in the South-West Pacific, 'expressed on several occasions his support for the cause of the British Empire in the Far East. In October 1944 he told General Lumsden that he fully appreciated the need for British forces to recapture Hong Kong.' Indian politicians were beginning to show nervousness about the possible threat of a revived post-war China; Mountbatten had an old Hong Kong hand, John Keswick, as his adviser, who succeeded in putting the colony's case forcefully.

It should have been possible to soft-pedal the question, but Roosevelt continued to press what he believed to be the Chinese cause, although it was becoming increasingly evident that the Communists under Mao Tse-tung were a much more capable force than the irremediably decayed Kuomintang. In August 1944 he sent Patrick J. Hurley as an emissary to Chiang. Hurley, who has been described as both 'a rather old-fashioned American' and as 'insensitive and blustering, a braggart and a liar',[37] was of Irish descent, and irreconcilably anti-British. His view of British colonial policy, which by then had been committed to decolonialization for the better part of twenty years, was a caricature: 'British imperialism seems to have acquired a new life. This appearance, however, is illusory. What appears to be a new life of British imperialism is the result of the infusion, into its emaciated form, of the blood of productivity and liberty from a free nation through lend-lease ... Britain ... must accept the principles of liberty and democracy and discard the principles of oppressive imperialism.'[38]

In spite of Hurley's enthusiastic espousal of Chiang's claims – which attitude was later developed by his fellow Irish-American, Senator Joseph McCarthy – by the time of the crucial Yalta Conference, in February 1945, it was clear that the Chungking regime could offer nothing more to the war, and that Russia must be brought into the fight against the Japanese. Roosevelt could not continue his opposition when Churchill spelt out his view of how the future of Hong Kong would be dealt with in the forum of the new United Nations: 'If His Majesty's Government agreed to the President's proposals [on the future structures of the United Nations] China might ask His Majesty's Government to return Hong Kong.' His Majesty's Government would have the right to state their case fully against the Chinese. It would be open to China 'to make her full case' and it would be open to the UN Security Council to 'decide on any of those questions without His Majesty's Government being allowed to vote'. The British government 'accepted' this position. There should be no Great Power veto on matters concerning itself. Of course, Churchill added, 'there was no question of their being compelled by the Security Council to give Hong Kong back to China if they did not think that this was the right step for them to take'.[39]

Some more of the heat went out of the matter in April 1945 when, on the death of Roosevelt, Harry S. Truman became President. Although he accepted the State Department's recommendation that 'we would welcome and assist when appropriate, amicable arrangements, including . . . restoration of Hong Kong to China',[40] the new President did not share Roosevelt's passionate support of China. Which of the Allies laid hands on Hong Kong was, he considered, 'primarily a military matter of an operational character',[41] and depended on whose forces got there first. Singapore, with the British in Rangoon and no Chinese troops in the region, could quickly be retrieved into the imperial fold, and was officially part of South-East Asia Command under Mountbatten, but Hong Kong was in the Chinese sector, with Chinese irregulars somewhere at hand.

When at the Potsdam Conference in July 1945 the British were told of a proposed joint American—Chinese thrust towards Canton and Hong Kong, the danger of Hong Kong being liberated by the Chinese regular army became greater. While this could be forestalled by the Royal Navy dispatching a squadron, all British forces in the Far East had been put under American command as part of the planned final offensive on Japan, and formal approval for such a move had to be sought. Churchill, who had just been defeated in a general election, had been replaced by his erstwhile colleague Clement Attlee, at the head of a Labour government in which the Foreign Secretary was the redoubtable Ernest Bevin, a man quite as devoted to the Empire as any Tory. Some sharp exchanges followed as the British pressed the point that they, and not the Chinese, would accept the surrender of their colony. Truman believed the Chinese proposals for a compromise reasonable, and sent Chiang a 'personal message of appreciation for his considerate action': but Bevin was adamant, and Hurley reported that the Generalissmo considered 'the British attitude imperialistic, domineering, and unbecoming a member of the United Nations'. In spite of considerable agitation in the American press an agreement between the British and Americans was reached, and General Mac-Arthur was instructed to arrange that the British commander should take the surrender of the Japanese at Hong Kong. After some reluctance Chiang agreed to this, having been assured by President Truman that this concession to the British did not necessarily reflect subsequent American policy on the future of Hong Kong.

When the Japanese surrender became inevitable – it was finally announced on 14 August – negotiations on this ticklish subject had to be speedily concluded. Admiral Sir Cecil Harcourt had been sent with his squadron from Sydney at the shortest of notices, with the stores still unpacked on the decks. They had to wait at Leyte in the Philippines until clearance to enter Hong Kong Harbour was received, and it was not until 30 August that Harcourt reached Victoria. He was received, not by the defeated Japanese, but by the redoubtable Gimson. The gap had been filled by the Colonial Secretary, who at the moment of high drama when the Japanese surrender was announced, took the decisive steps expected of a good civil servant, and called a committee. He recorded: 'Doubts were expressed . . . as to whether it would be politic for me to take the oath as officer administering the government, as I was certainly entitled to do, and a decision on this was deferred.' But he did not let this stop him: 'Perhaps, rather elated from the altered relationship of captor and captive, I felt it was an occasion to assert my authority by saying "As senior official of the Hong Kong government I will take charge of the administration." ' When the Japanese demurred, pointing out that Hong Kong might not be restored to the British, Gimson was having none of it: 'I replied that this view was merely their expression of opinion with which I was not concerned. I intended to carry out those duties to which I had been appointed by His Majesty's Government.' Gimson was then contacted by a Chinese member of the BAAG, who confirmed the Japanese surrender, on which he 'immediately summoned a few of the leading personnel in Stanley and the Chief Justice of the Colony, Sir Athol MacGregor, administered to me the oath of office'.[42]

For the next two weeks Gimson took charge, working from the French Mission building, and keeping control of the Japanese, who were still the only force in the colony, by exerting his impressive personality. When the Japanese were about to refuse permission for a British plane to land at Kai Tak to begin making arrangements for the surrender, Gimson decided: 'I felt I must assert my authority.' He instructed the unhappy Japanese liaison officer: 'Details of this refusal must be inserted in your message. Omission to do so, as well as your attitude with regard to the landing of the plane at Kai Tak, will be treated as offences triable by a criminal court.' Gimson got his way, and in due course and proper form was able to welcome the Royal Navy as the Officer administering the colony.

Gimson's nearly single-handed period of rule ended when he was relieved by Admiral Harcourt on 30 August. Some opposition from the Japanese suicide squads had been expected, but only one craft, which might have been a suicide boat but was otherwise described, was encountered. As *Swiftsure*, on which Admiral Harcourt had hoisted his flag, came into the harbour a signal was received that a 'pirate' junk had been spotted in Mirs Bay. *Swiftsure* radioed back to the aircraft carrier *Indefatigable*, which was following, and soon after received the laconic reply 'Junk sunk.'[43] Some desultory firing greeted them on shore, partly from Japanese in plain clothes, who were summarily dealt with, guilty or not: 'The Chinese take the opportunity to beat a few Japanese to death, hauling them off the trams and smacking at their heads with hammers.' The landing party was horrified by the state of the dockyard, described by Lieutenant John Gibson in authentically nautical terms of disgust: 'Untidiness and filth was the general rule. Bottles of apple wine and beer lie around, some half full. The paintwork is shabby . . . the ropes are fifth-rate.'[44]

The takeover from Gimson's interim government was a delicate matter, since the liberated prisoners who were holding affairs together were mostly in poor physical condition and extremely fatigued, but jealous of their responsibilities and inclined to look upon the newcomers as interlopers. They had also to adjust to a changed world; a news-sheet put out by BAAG attempted to describe it – Britain was now no longer the power it had been, but a debtor nation, with income tax at ten shillings in the pound, although there were some compensations, in that people were friendlier and less reserved, and the beer was getting stronger. Mr Attlee helped by sending a personal message to Gimson on 8 September in which he said: 'My admiration has been aroused by the vigour and courage with which you, in spite of the ordeal of internment, yourself took the first steps . . . in re-establishing British rule in Hong Kong.'[45]

The new administration was entrusted to David MacDougall, who had been working with a small staff in Whitehall to prepare for the restoration of British rule.[46] Although officially a military administration, under the command of Admiral Harcourt as Commander-in-Chief, with military ranks being given to its civilian members – MacDougall was a Brigadier – the new government was composed of colonial civil servants. Their task was alarming, since the collapse of Japanese administration had left the colony's economy destroyed and its inhabitants starving and ill. Did, indeed, the Chinese population want British rule restored? Only a scattering of Union flags were seen among the thousands of Chinese flags that greeted Admiral Harcourt's arrival. The deaths of a Chinese girl, murdered by a British seaman, and a hawker, accidentally killed by an Indian policeman, provoked angry disturbances. But for the moment this question could be shelved, since practical difficulties were urgently pressing.

Besides their own abilities, aided by MacDougall's splendid wry humour, the staff had little immediately to offer by way of relief. Mac-Dougall reported: 'By shifts and evasions we have carried on for nine weeks to conceal the essential weakness of our position, which is that the larder is bare . . . and that the liberators brought nothing that fills stomachs or furnishes houses.' But somehow they managed to progress the considerable task of clearing up the chaos that Japanese rule had left. Between thirty and forty thousand coolies were immediately employed in clearing up the mess, supplemented on 4 September by three thousand RAF technicians.

Admiral Harcourt later said that the great thing was that the British government did not give him any orders, but 'completely dictatorial powers', which he was able to pass on to MacDougall as required. To begin with the only policing force available was formed from 'some seven hundred Chinese gangsters, who had been allowed by the Japanese to run gambling dens in return for maintaining law and order, [and] were used as police in the hope that they would keep themselves out of mischief and the rest of the Chinese underworld under control. They were denied the lucrative perquisite of gambling dens, but were compensated by the receipt of pay and the promise that they would be allowed to make their escape when it became possible to form a more orthodox force.'[47]

Civil administration was restored on the return of Sir Mark Young on 1 May 1946, and the intervening eight months of the Military Administration may be taken as a turning point in Hong Kong's development, personified in the differences between Franklin Gimson and David MacDougall. Gimson, like Maltby and Young, was a product of Victorian and Edwardian imperial certitudes, his attitudes formed by a pre-First World War (in which Young and Maltby both served) education. MacDougall, born in 1904, was a post-war man, of the Devonshire Declaration era of colonial administrators, brought up to assume that colonial rule was an interim stage – hence his annoyance that the Americans at Mont Tremblant had not recognized this fact. Gimson served admirably as an upright pillar of rectitude in the most difficult of circumstances, but MacDougall had the flexibility to control a community precariously balanced on the brink of chaos. It was a community too from which the previous leaders had been summarily expelled. British prestige, which had held together an empire without any real force of arms to bolster it, was irredeemably shattered; henceforward it would have to rest upon performance, and not myth.

That performance MacDougall and his team provided. With the brave co-operation of the Hongkong and Shanghai Bank the colony's currency was restored. The Bank agreed to honour those 'duress notes' which had been issued by their officers under Japanese occupation, and to freeze all wartime debts. Funds were immediately provided to enable public utilities to function. Price controls, and a minimum wage, were introduced; emergency food supplies were rushed in and free meals provided. Jack Cater, who was later to be Colonial Secretary and a prominent figure in Hong Kong affairs, helped Dr Geoffrey Herklots, a biologist just emerged from the Stanley internment camp, to restore the fishing industry, a vital source of food. This vigorous and constructive effort was so quickly successful that by November 1945 it was possible to lift government controls and restore a free-enterprise system, a post-war adjustment unparalleled elsewhere. Confidence in British rule, shattered by the experiences of 1941, was regained. The local Chinese 'were impressed by the speed with which the rehabilitation of the economy was achieved, by the establishment of law and order and of a milieu favourable to the acquisition of wealth ... Its post-occupation record was admirable – it believed in business first.' The near-complete departure of the pre-war British had another important effect, in that many posts previously reserved for British expatriates had to be filled by Portuguese and Chinese. It was a change almost entirely for the better, but some time was needed before the full implications were realized.

The electorate of Britain didn't care a brass farthing about Hong Kong

Sir Mark Young was not restored to Government House without opposition from the Foreign Office, where his appointment was seen as a determination to assert the pre-war status quo. In reality there was no question of this being so. Admiral Harcourt had recognized the existence of a '1946 outlook' which demanded more just and equitable treatment for the Hong Kong Chinese. Sir Man-Kam Lo, at the first session of the restored Legislative Council, made it clear that 'the interests of the Colony as a whole and not those of any particular section of the community' must be advanced.

Young, convinced of the benefits of representative rule, needed no such warnings. His first act was to announce proposals for a change in the Hong Kong Constitution by which 'the inhabitants of the Territory can be given a fuller and more responsible share in the management of their own affairs'.

It was significant that Sir Mark described Hong Kong as a territory, rather than a colony, as indicating the British Labour government's commitment to decolonialization that was to result the following year in the grant of independence to India, Pakistan and Burma. The suggestions for Hong Kong were not so dramatic: Sir Mark specified the transfer of 'important functions of government' to 'a Municipal council constituted on a fully representative basis'. This proposal became known as the 'Young Plan', although in fact Sir Mark was transmitting a version of ideas drafted by a committee of the Colonial Office during the war. With the support of the Hong Kong taipans in the China Association the committee had suggested a complete reorganization of the Municipal Council as a democratic institution, accompanied by an expansion of representation on the Legislative Council.[48]

Before any conclusion was reached, the Governor asked for a full discussion among the community which might enable the proposals to be finalized before the end of the year. Comments were forthcoming in some quantity, enabling Sir Mark to sketch on 26 August what appeared to be a satisfactory consensus. This was to introduce direct elections for two-thirds of the Municipal Council seats, split equally between Chinese and non-Chinese constituencies, the remainder being appointed by representative bodies. Equal representation between officials and non-officials on the Legislative Council would leave the Governor holding the casting vote. The merit of concentrating on the Municipal Council as a representative institution was that the franchise could be extended to all adults, British subjects or not, while voting for the Legislative Council must, it was considered, be restricted to British subjects, only a minority of the whole.

These proposals were promptly dispatched to London, where they ran into a sandbank of discussion and delay. There was little dissension in the House of Commons: Walter Fletcher, Conservative M.P. for Bury, in a debate on 16 May 1947, asked for the government to make 'quite certain that the status of Hong Kong and the leased territories remains quite openly and clearly where it is now, with no foreshadowing of change for a long time to come'. This was followed on 29 July by a rather confused discussion. Colonel David Rees-Williams, later Lord Ogmore, believed that 'the democratic element in China (however that might be defined) does not want to see Hong Kong handed over to the Kuomintang government', and Ivor Bulmer-Thomas for the government announced that 'considerable progress has been made in introducing a stable regime in Hong Kong ... We have shaped a more democratic constitution, including a municipality ... prepared a ten-year programme for economic growth, and taken all the necessary steps to obtain stability and economic growth.' 'Shaped' was a well-chosen word, giving the impression that constitutional reform was much further advanced than in reality it was. Walter Fletcher, for the opposition, agreed that 'we all now give a great deal of adherence' to the principle of 'a greater degree of native representation' (whatever 'native' might mean in the Hong Kong context), but pointed out that 'it is an extremely dangerous moment in Hong Kong to do such a thing', adding that there had been an influx of more than a million refugees.

Although the House of Commons was left with the impression that great things had been done in Hong Kong, it took nearly three years before detailed Bills could be produced. Woodrow Wyatt, then a Labour Member, asked on 30 November 1949, 'Why has it taken so incredibly long?' An embarrassed Arthur Creech Jones, now Colonial Secretary, had to admit that 'it was not possible, for a variety of reasons, to make much progress', and when pressed the following month by another Labour Member: 'Does he not think it really necessary to have some form of democratic legislature, municipal or otherwise, in Hong Kong?' could only agree, but added that 'Making constitutions is not too easy or fast a procedure.'

One contributor to the delay had been the new Governor, Sir Alexander Grantham, who succeeded Sir Mark Young in July 1947. Sir Mark's health had been broken as a result of his treatment by the Japanese, but his personal qualities were to be missed. David MacDougall considered Grantham to be 'a competent enough civil servant', less inclined than Young to be 'adventurous or innovative', and lacking his predecessor's 'qualities of imagination and personality'. But Grantham, 'a shrewd and deceptively dandyish figure', was something of a high-flyer – Sandhurst and Cambridge, a commission in the Hussars, the Imperial Defence College and the Colonial Service. Governor for ten years, the self-contained – and perhaps self-satisfied – Grantham ran Hong Kong without much interference from Whitehall during a difficult period. Having served as a cadet officer in the colony for thirteen years before the war, he had developed his own ideas of its future, which did not include the Young Plan; a benevolent autocracy, he considered, was needed, and this he provided.[49]

The proposals that eventually appeared before the Legislative Council dealt only with the Municipal Council and provided for a highly complex system of election, with the franchise being dependent on nationality, length of residence and literacy, resulting in a list of some ten thousand voters. No mention was made of any changes in the Legislative Council itself, a fact which immediately produced opposition from those who thought that this must logically come first. The Legislative Council then produced suggestions for its own reform, which were debated in June 1949. These were introduced by Sir Man-Kam Lo, who had become once again a leading figure in Hong Kong affairs. Sir Alexander Grantham described 'M.K.' as having 'a first-class brain, great moral courage and a capacity for digging down into details without getting lost in them . . . when a complex but dull matter was being dealt with by the circulation of papers, on which members would write their opinions, I would look to see what "M.K." had written and, as often as not, save myself the tedium of reading all the other minutes. He was invariably right to the point.'[50]

In the debate 'M.K.' isolated the prime difficulty of all constitutional reform in Hong Kong, which was that of race. The last available census of British subjects had been taken in 1931, and had identified their racial backgrounds as follows:

Chinese	61,640
Europeans	6,636
Eurasians	717
Portuguese[51]	1,089
Indians	3,331
Others	453
Total	73,866

But this was a mere fraction, less than one-tenth, of the total population of Hong Kong, and therefore hopelessly unrepresentative. 'M.K.' concluded: 'To suggest that members elected by a fractional electorate can and will more adequately represent the Colony as a whole than nominated members is a proposition with which I profoundly disagree.' The Legislative Council agreed that its own reorganization should take priority, and another set of proposals was dispatched to London for prolonged and lengthy consideration.

By 1949 events in China had moved so far that the population imbalance in Hong Kong was becoming even greater. Once the war with Japan was ended, Chiang set about the unfinished business left over from the 1920s, that of destroying the Communists. Driven by its belief in an evil Moscow-led Communist conspiracy, America continued to send massive aid to the Nationalists, and to fret about Hong Kong as a potential source of further conflict. The US Ambassador in London had suggested in March 1947 that the colony should be 'graciously and generously' returned to China 'at a given date', and when a mob burnt the British Consulate in Canton in 1948, in retaliation for civilians being fired upon in Kowloon, there was little American sympathy. In Chungking American Ambassador Clark told the British representative, Sir Ralph Stevenson, that 'He could expect that Hong Kong would remain a constant irritant in Anglo-Chinese relations . . . and I thought the British Government would wish to take into consideration whether the best interests of Britain lay in continuing the irritant or in removing it at some appropriate time.'[52] Although Clark went on to say that Stevenson expressed his agreement, he can hardly have thought it likely that Britain would seriously consider negotiating with the discredited Nationalists, who were failing to make any headway against the Communists, and were about to be driven relentlessly from all their strongholds. Peking fell to the Communists in January 1949, Nanking in April, Shanghai the following month and Canton in October.

Hong Kong had already become a refuge for opponents of Chiang, as it was once more the only place in China where personal liberties were secured. Now a different set of refugees began to pour into the colony, swelling the population to an estimated 2,360,000 by March 1950.[53] They came not only from Canton, but from further afield, and in particular the refugees from Shanghai brought valuable new talents to the colony. Abruptly Shanghai ceased to be the commercial centre of China, as those who had made it so left, businesses closed, and an exodus to Hong Kong ensued. Such an influx, at a time when the colony was still hard put to replace the housing destroyed during the occupation, placed intolerable strains on the administration. With nowhere else to live many of the incomers made their homes in corridors, lofts and roadways, erecting shacks out of any available material. Previous refugees had tended to be anti-Kuomintang; the newcomers were usually, if not pro-Nationalist, firmly anti-Communist, which soon caused considerable friction. It was something of a relief to the colonial authorities, who wished to maintain the traditional policy of free access, when the Communists took the initiative by closing the border in November 1949.

The Communist triumph aroused only moderate consternation in Whitehall; the Kuomintang had elicited no confidence at all, and the Communists were generally accepted to be much more effective. The new regime did however present a potential threat to British interests. Particular patriotic emotions were aroused by the attack on the gunboat *Amethyst*, which was trapped by the People's Liberation Army on the Yangtse in April 1949, and her subsequent dramatic escape. Speaking in the House of Commons on 5 May 1949 Harold Macmillan, then a member of the Conservative opposition, insisted that Hong Kong was the 'Gibraltar of the East', and must be held. It would have been difficult for him to explain why. Gibraltar was a strategically significant station on the route to the Suez Canal, which could still, even after Indian independence, be regarded as a vital waterway. Hong Kong led nowhere and defended nothing. The Labour Minister of Defence, A.V. Alexander, replied that 'Hong Kong has long had a tradition of neutrality and non-interference with the politics of China ... steps have been taken ... to deal with any breach of the conditions under which Chinese nationals, either Kuomintang or communist, are allowed to reside there.' Police forces had been doubled in strength since 1941, and two brigade groups had been dispatched to reinforce the garrison. This last was meant as a warning gesture to China's new regime that Britain took the future of Hong Kong seriously; as Grantham later explained, the policy was that sufficient forces could be deployed to delay any advance for long enough to enable diplomatic pressures to be employed. The later experience of the Korean war exemplified both how valuable such a delaying action might be and that a small British force could defend a position against a much larger Chinese attack.

It was left to John Paton, M.P. for Norwich, a labour pioneer and one of the old Independent Labour Party, to enunciate the principle which was to guide all subsequent British governments: 'Do not any honourable Member imagine for a moment that we can maintain our position in Hong Kong indefinitely against an actively hostile Communist China. If we begin to think in those terms we shall inevitably lose Hong Kong.' Paton was supported by Woodrow Wyatt (somewhat ironically, in view of Lord Wyatt's later move to the right), who pointed out that Mao Tse-tung, who would certainly win the civil war, was of a different calibre from the Russians and no Stalinist, bent on territorial expansion. Some creative suggestions were made that the leased territories could be extended or – last example of that nineteenth-century yearning for something better than the 'barren island' – that Hong Kong might be exchanged for Formosa.

The following year the post-war Labour landslide was nearly overturned in a general election, leaving Attlee's government with a majority of only six. When in October 1951 Labour was replaced by the Conservatives under Churchill, enthusiasm for decolonization noticeably subsided. Nevertheless, the newly appointed Colonial Secretary, Oliver Lyttelton, put the modified Young Plan to the Cabinet on 16 May 1952, with Grantham's backing, minuting that:

> Constitutional reform in Hong Kong was promised after the war and has been under discussion since 1946. When I visited Hong Kong in December the Governor represented to me . . . the fact that there had been no progress towards reform was beginning to lead to agitation, that he would find it increasingly difficult to hold the position much longer.

He blamed the Foreign Office for the delay:

> These proposals were agreed on as long ago as the end of 1950, but were postponed at the request of the Foreign Office, on the grounds that, since they did not provide for a wide Chinese franchise, they might provoke a propaganda campaign.

But now all the Departments of State were agreed:

> The matter was taken up with the Foreign Office, the Commonwealth Relations Office, the Ministry of Defence . . . all agreed that the time had come.[54]

But before the new arrangements were made public, the Governor was visited by a delegation of the most prominent members of both Councils with a plea that he should 'stop this madness which will be the ruination of Hong Kong'. They argued that there was 'no real demand whatever' for extended representation, which had been pressed by 'a doctrinaire Colonial Office'. In spite of having told the Colonial Secretary only a few months before that the 'agitation' for reform was such that he would find it 'increasingly difficult to hold the position', Grantham accepted their proposals that the project should be dropped. When this was put to the Colonial Office the officials were aghast: 'They held up their hands in horror and said "But Grantham, your proposals have already been approved by the Cabinet."' Lyttelton, however, had no objection to telling his colleagues that he had changed his mind, and minuted: 'I regret having to trouble the Cabinet again . . . (having discussed with the Governor) I do not propose to proceed with these reforms until conditions are more settled.'

In his autobiography Sir Alexander wrote only that the Secretary of State agreed to drop constitutional reform because 'the matter did not interest the British electorate'. In an unpublished radio interview in 1968 he was more direct and much more revealing: Lyttelton was 'quite willing to turn down the proposals because all any British government was interested in was getting back into power, and the electorate of Britain didn't care a brass farthing about Hong Kong'.[55] That was true in 1951, and has continued to be so.

It has often been suggested that the quiet burial of the Young Plan marked the last chance to implement a measure of democracy in Hong Kong's government without risking Chinese intervention. On the other hand, it is possible that the restricted franchise proposed, which isolated so much of the population from any political power, would have become an entrenched and powerful force operating against any further reform.

15

BETWEEN FOUR STOOLS

Anglo-Saxon attitudes

Post-war Governors of Hong Kong and their colleagues found themselves surrounded and embattled. The governments of the People's
Republic of China (Beijing) and the Republic of China (Taiwan) both
considered Hong Kong rightfully part of their own territory, but set
their claims aside while using the colony as a convenient location
for espionage, agitation and propaganda one against the other. The
government of the USA, wrath against the People's Republic of China
and wholly supporting the Republic of China, made free use of the
espionage facilities, while gravely damaging the colony's economy in
the interests of its crusade against Communism. The government of
Great Britain, nominal masters of Hong Kong, were content to let
things take their course as long as neither the People's Republic of
China (too important politically), nor the USA (essential economically),
was offended. The interests of the people of Hong Kong were not
much considered by any of these powers, but were reasonably well
looked after, according to its own lights, by the colonial administration.

Both Britain and the USA showed themselves to be slow learners
in post-war Asia. On 15 August 1947 India and Pakistan became
independent; the strategic consequences of this hardly began to be
reflected in British foreign policy for another twenty years, and even
today have not been fully appreciated, in that British governments still
cling to the concept of Great Britain as a world power. In January
1949 the People's Republic under Mao Tse-tung was established in
Peking – henceforward Beijing – and the Nationalists were shortly

afterwards confined to the island of Formosa – now to be known as Taiwan, where they ruthlessly established an authoritarian regime. It also took twenty years for American policy to accept that this did not constitute the government of China. Both these long-continued misconceptions had their effects on Hong Kong.

The emotional American support that had sustained Chiang Kai-shek's Nationalists during the civil war was reinforced by their defeat. It seemed that nothing could persuade American opinion that Chiang, assisted by his wife and her predatory family, was the corrupt and incompetent leader of a faction that had miserably failed the Chinese people, and filched hundreds of millions of dollars' worth of American public money. Taiwan, and the offshore islands of Quemoy and Matsu, became in American mythology beleaguered outposts of democratic decency in a wicked, Communist-dominated East. Even with evidence of massive misappropriation before it, the Truman administration was reluctant to criticize what was well known to be, in Taipei as it had been in Chungking and Shanghai, a corrupt and dictatorial regime. This is even more astonishing in view of the open support given to the Republican Party by Chiang's representatives: Truman's opponent in the 1948 presidential election, Thomas Dewey, was awarded the Special Cravat of the Order of the Auspicious Star in anticipation of his victory.

The rising tide of McCarthyite hysteria made it impossible for saner minds to question the Chiang myth; when the 'China hands' in and around the State Department came to the conclusion that 'Chiang Kai-shek and his evanescent, predatory and combat-resistant armies were not on the wave of the future', they were 'called severely to account by John Foster Dulles and McCarthyites on Capitol Hill'. Barbara Tuchman concluded that the 'attacks and savagery of that "tawdry reign of terror" [that] raged over America's China policy . . . cowed the future exercise of independent judgement in the Foreign Service'.[1]

For some time, it must be allowed, the issues were blurred. The People's Republic had to establish what might be generally admitted as the legitimate boundaries of its interests. The United Nations action in Korea, the British operations in Malaya, the *de facto* acceptance of the territorial integrity of Taiwan, the scuffle with India on the Ladakh borders, the definition of relations with the USSR and the re-establishment (to put it civilly) of suzerainty over Tibet were all necessary preliminaries. After these had been settled, which they were by

1962, whatever grievances remained – although they were many – hardly affected strategic decisions in any but the longer terms. China had regained what could be regarded as her historic boundaries, with the major exceptions of Taiwan and Hong Kong, and was willing to allow negotiations for the restoration of these to take their course without more pressure.

It took some years before the dust settled. As the People's Liberation Army moved south to Canton in October 1949 – encountering little resistance, it being accepted that the mandate of heaven had descended to the new regime – the British Labour government signalled its determination to hold Hong Kong by reinforcing the garrison to a strength sufficient to make the issue of a forcible take-over highly doubtful. Ernest Bevin, the rugged Labour Foreign Secretary, as hostile to Communism as few outside the right wing of his Party can be, promised to make Hong Kong 'the Berlin of the Middle East'. Thirty thousand troops, with armour and air support, including that of a carrier group, should have been sufficient to stop dead any advance by the People's Liberation Army.

Britain had already indicated a firm intention to protect the new Federation of Malaysia from aggressive infiltration, and would have been even more unyielding in the protection of Hong Kong. The Cabinet agreed that 'Until conditions change, we intend to remain in Hong Kong,' although when appropriate 'we should be prepared to discuss the future of Hong Kong with a friendly [the word 'democratic' was in the draft, but was wisely deleted] and stable Government of a unified China'. Not that the new government in Beijing had any wish to invade; as Peng Zhen, who later attempted to halt the madness of the Cultural Revolution, but was then very much a hard-liner, wrote at the time, 'It is unwise of us to deal with the problem of Hong Kong rashly and without preparation.'[2] With only a few gestures of defiance from units of the People's Liberation Army, the existing boundaries were confirmed.

Relations between Hong Kong and Beijing were tolerably polite (those with Canton were more acerbic), apart from a short time in 1952 when something of a mutual propaganda war ensued. Two serious incidents occurred, a navy patrol boat being shelled and a civilian airliner shot down by Chinese forces, both with loss of life, but these were hardly more than might have been expected as the penalties for having as a neighbour a great, newly revolutionary and powerful state. A *modus vivendi* was established, for Hong Kong was too valuable to

China, earning nearly half the country's total foreign income, and trade with China was essential to the colony.

Before this happened the refugee population had swollen to something like three million. (The preferred term was 'squatter','refugee' implying that the people in question were fleeing an unpleasant condition, and were a responsibility of the host; this was both insulting to the People's Republic of China and expensively inconvenient for Hong Kong.) The inrush of newcomers, which quadrupled Hong Kong's population in a few years, swamped all available facilities and posed huge problems for a colonial administration fully engaged in post-war reconstruction and harassed by external pressures. 'Squatters', it was understood, were there on sufferance, and little obligation to provide anything more than the essential minimum for them was accepted by the Hong Kong authorities. Denis Bray, one of the last cadet officers, who joined the Hong Kong government in 1950, related his experience in the 1991 Hong Kong Annual Report: 'I had to manage the screening of squatters cleared for development when all they were offered as resettlement was four pegs in the ground marking a plot where they could build. Gradually a little government money was found to do some site formation, to provide stand pipes, to pave paths, to do a good deal but not to provide housing.'[3] Most of the newcomers were apolitical, relieved to be alive and anxious only to be left alone; insofar as they manifested an interest in politics it was likely to be unsympathetic to the Communists they were attempting to avoid. Leftists, as Communist sympathizers were generally termed, were usually restrained; it was the extreme Nationalist supporters who presented a more acute threat to the tranquillity of the colony.

Very soon after liberation in 1945, Nationalist agitators had started coming to the colony, and cautious support was offered to them by T.W. Kwok, an official of the Kuomintang government seconded as 'Special Commissioner for Hong Kong', a title that reflected the Nationalist claim to sovereignty. Nationalist papers in Hong Kong consistently reinforced this by calling for speedy restoration of the colony to the Taiwan government. At least one nasty incident had taken place in 1948 when the Chinese magistrate over the border declared the Walled City of Kowloon to be Chinese territory, precipitating demonstrations. The police sent in to the area opened fire, killing one man and wounding a number of other residents; in the wave of retaliations the British Consulate in Canton was burnt down.

After the Communist success forced a change of tack, the Hong

Kong supporters of Chiang Kai-shek turned their energies towards attacking the Beijing government and coercing the British by terrorism within the colony. Within the British community there were differences of opinion as to which of the opposing parties was more dangerous. Bishop Ronald Hall, a moderately left-wing prelate, clashed with the conservative Grantham and his 'comic opera government' more than once over the Bishop's Workers' Schools – 'completely communist-dominated and centres of communist and anti-British indoctrination', according to the Governor.[4] It took American pressure on behalf of the other side, exerted in the clumsiest of fashions, to prove that it was the Nationalist element in Hong Kong that stood more in need of government vigilance than Bishop Hall's schools.

While the Hong Kong administration did not share the American admiration for Chiang Kai-shek, although at the same time not being enthusiastic about the Communists, most people in Hong Kong had not initially been averse to the new government in China, believing that almost any change from the Kuomintang would be for the better. London agreed; after some hesitation, and following the established pragmatic principle of recognizing any government in obvious control of its territory, Britain was among the first, in January 1950, to offer recognition to the new regime in Beijing. Since Britain continued also to acknowledge the legitimacy of Taiwan, it was many years before relations were formalized by an exchange of ambassadors, but the China Hong Kong had to deal with was now the People's Republic. Since Beijing refused to agree that Hong Kong was anything other than an integral part of China, temporarily under foreign administration, it was impossible to have direct diplomatic links between the two; the dilemma was solved by entrusting Chinese interests to Xinhua (Hsin Hua), the New China News Agency, which operated from the Bank of China building, ostensibly as a news agency but in fact, and quite openly, as the representative of the People's Republic.

None of this was at all to the liking of the United States, still committed to the support of the Kuomintang, and bitter criticisms of British weakness towards Communism were forthcoming. American subjects were advised to leave the colony, and some American companies closed shop. A rapprochement between the wartime allies was achieved in June 1950 when the Labour government, enthusiastically supported by Churchill, followed the United States' lead in opposing the North Korean invasion of the south, but British and American attitudes to the Chinese participation, on the side of the North, in the war that followed were markedly different. Prime Minister Attlee may not have needed to rush to Washington in December 1950 in order to dissuade President Truman from attacking China, but General MacArthur, and a considerable section of American opinion, was willing, even eager, to do so. The use of atomic weapons was much canvassed, and the unlikely theory of a Communist plot led by China and Russia working together to subdue the 'free world' was unquestioningly accepted by many Americans. British governments, Conservative or Labour, worked on the differing assumption that Chinese Communism had to be distinguished from Russian imperialism, and that China must not be driven into the arms of Russia.

In such conditions the advantage to the USA of having a co-operative listening post on the borders of China was manifest, and was taken full advantage of. The staff of the US Consulate in Hong Kong suddenly, and not at all mysteriously, multiplied, to the embarrassment of the colonial government. In 1938 there had been a Consul-General, two Consuls, and two Vice-Consuls: in 1953 there were 115 in all, including four Consuls and twenty Vice-Consuls, to administer the affairs of an American community of 1,262 – including themselves. Sir Alexander Grantham was, once more, less discreet in his 1968 radio interview than in his autobiography: 'I took a poor view of it [the consulate] – the largest anywhere in the world', with a staff 'at enmity with the lawful government of mainland China'. The CIA especially were 'extremely ham-handed at one time until we had to take a very strong line to stop them being so stupid'.[5]

Thomas Dewey, who visited Hong Kong at that time, had trouble understanding how liberal a British colonial government's 'strict adherence to the rules of free speech' could be: 'The British are a serious handicap to our intelligence . . . [they] thwart efforts hostile to Red China, which include American efforts at espionage.' Dewey was also shocked to find that Reuters news agency, unimpeded by US pressure, sent out items that had been suppressed by Associated Press, their American counterpart, who 'never sent out that kind of news' (race riots, in this instance) 'to countries where it would do us such damage'. Was such an injudicious attachment to personal freedom, Dewey wondered, 'playing cricket or Russian roulette?' But Dewey was comforted to hear that the battle against Communism was being waged by more reliable allies than Britain when the French General de Lattre de Tassigny assured him that 'We are winning in Indo-China against Ho Chi-minh.'[6]

Another cause of Anglo–American friction at this time was the great aeroplane affair.[7] Most of the assets of the two government-owned Chinese airlines, including eighty-three passenger planes, had been transferred to Hong Kong away from the civil war on the mainland. These were without doubt the legal property of the Chinese government: but which government? Britain had not at that time – the end of 1949 – yet recognized the Communist regime in Beijing, but was appearing likely to do so. Claire Chennault and Whiting Willauer, the founders of China Air Transport (CAT), an American-owned company closely associated with the CIA, believed it essential to keep the planes from Communist China, since they might be used for an air attack on the Nationalists in Formosa. In an effort to do this a series of companies was formed, beginning in Panama and ending in Delaware with Civil Air Transport Inc. (CATI). CATI, it was planned, would purchase the aircraft from the Nationalist government, thus creating a *fait accompli*. This scheme was put into effect, but the Hong Kong government had to be persuaded of its legitimacy before it would prohibit the transfer of the planes to the People's Republic. This was indeed already happening, since twelve of the aircraft, and the general managers of the airlines, had already taken off for Beijing. Grantham was accordingly visited on 4 January 1950 by two hard men, 'Big Bill' Donovan, formerly chief of the Office of Strategic Services, and Richard Heppner, his former man in China. Donovan metaphorically thumped the table and demanded that the aircraft be handed over to him without further ado, adding that if it had not been for the United States Britain would have lost the war, and threatening adverse consequences for Sir Alexander personally if he did not co-operate. This was not the wisest of approaches; the Governor naturally refused to concede anything, and also denied the American inspectors accompanying Donovan access to the planes.

When, the very next morning, it was announced that Britain had decided to recognize the Communist government, the feathers began to fly. The case was brought before the Hong Kong courts, where it was decided that the aircraft were indeed the lawful property of the People's Republic of China. Washington threatened economic action against Britain, Beijing refused to re-establish full diplomatic relations with Britain, and Nationalist agents in Hong Kong bombed seven of the remaining planes. American pressure proved the more successful, and the British government, while refusing to overturn the verdict of the Hong Kong court (as indeed it could not lawfully do), instructed Grantham to hold the aircraft until 'the full processes of the law' had been exhausted. The Governor was dismayed: 'Who was I, a mere Governor of a colonial dependency, to complain, and what good would it have done if I had? Nonetheless I felt unhappy: altogether a sorry business.' Grantham had become a skilled fence-sitter, however, and the US Consul-General in Hong Kong was able to tell the State Department that the Governor had assured him that the aircraft 'would not be permitted to leave Hong Kong for the mainland regardless of the outcome of the case'.[8]

It took more than two years for the outcome to emerge, in July 1952, when the Judicial Committee of the Privy Council agreed that the aircraft were the rightful property of Chennault's company. Legally the decision was dubious, but the former Attorney-General, Sir Hartley Shawcross, put the case brutally plainly. It was a question of 'whether the Government's action should be directed to placating the United States or the Chinese People's government'. For Chennault it was a Pyrrhic victory, since not only were the aircraft by that time unflyable, but the British government insisted that they must under no circumstances be transferred to Formosa. CATI was therefore left with some expensive aircraft to remove from Hong Kong, and had to appeal to the United States Navy to lend them an aircraft carrier to do so. Sir Alexander had to suffer another rebuff from his own side the following year, when he was ordered by London, over his unavailing protests, to allow a Chinese tanker to be requisitioned by the Taiwanese government; as he said, the British government 'was more scared of what the United States might do to Britain than of what China might do to Hong Kong'.[9]

This was not the last of Grantham's difficulties with aeroplanes. Under mysterious circumstances – all trace has been removed from the records available to the public – a Chinese Nationalist warplane landed in Hong Kong in 1955. It took a year for the British government to decide what to do about it. It seems that Grantham, in the interests of a quiet life, had agreed with the Colonial Secretary, Alan Lennox-Boyd, with whom he was on friendly terms, to hand plane and pilot back to Taiwan, with suitable complaints about 'this abuse of Hong Kong's facilities'. This decision was queried on 13 March 1956 by the Prime Minister, Anthony Eden, who was 'doubtful whether it was necessary that special steps be taken to return this aircraft, which would certainly annoy the communists', but Lennox-Boyd managed to convince the Cabinet that 'The Governor would prefer to be finally rid of this embarrassment.'[10]

Something peculiar was certainly going on between Britain and the United States at that time. The Republican General Eisenhower had become the President in 1953, thereby ensuring that the anti-Communist China lobby's influence would continue undiminished. John Foster Dulles, the Secretary of State, was implacably opposed to Communist China and angry with what he believed to be British unhelpfulness in South-East Asia, while his successor, Dean Rusk, is said to have believed that the People's Republic of China hardly existed; 'China was not a separate entity; it was, he asserted, "a Soviet Manchukuo" without any of the effective attributes of sovereignty':[11] a view appropriate only to that world of fantasy in which American foreign policy wandered for many years. In December 1953 Eisenhower was seriously considering the use of atomic weapons should the Korean truce be broken, since he did not recognize a distinction between atomic and conventional weapons. Churchill, who in 1951 had returned as Prime Minister, took some pains to dissuade the President from this course, and to withdraw his draft statement that the USA was 'free to use the atomic bomb'.[12]

But Britain was poorly placed to change American political attitudes; Churchill's Conservative government had followed much of its Labour predecessor's foreign policy, but not without internal dissent. Considerable heat had been generated by the then Foreign Secretary Anthony Eden's desire to see the People's Republic take up the China seat in the United Nations. Churchill objected violently to this, to the extent of a 'blood row' between the two men (on 4 July 1954).[13] The dispute between the Prime Minister and the Foreign Secretary was resolved, and it was agreed that 'A way ought certainly to be found of bringing Red China into the United Nations on terms tolerable to the USA.' This could not happen quickly, since Britain urgently needed American assistance in the Middle East, particularly after the Suez débâcle of 1956, a piece of international policy described even by Churchill, who had by then stood down as Prime Minister, as 'the most ill-conceived and ill-executed imaginable', and 'a great error'.[14] From the sidelines, Churchill did his best to assist a reconciliation with America, but the subsequent fence-mending operations were the responsibility of the new Prime Minister, Harold Macmillan, and the Foreign Secretary, Selwyn Lloyd, who met Eisenhower in October 1957. In the course of their discussions the President offered to assume some responsibility for the security of Hong Kong in return for Britain withdrawing support for China. This proposal was immediately agreed in a letter of 25 October 1957 from Selwyn Lloyd: 'The present government of the United Kingdom will not seek or support, without prior agreement with the US government, any change in regard to the representation of China in the United Nations, its dependent agencies and other international organizations in which this question may arise.'

Macmillan made the *quid pro quo* clear in the draft of his memoirs, recording that 'as part of the deal' he had agreed 'not to press for admission of the Communist Chinese to the United Nations . . . In return, the US agreed to regard Hong Kong as a joint defence problem.' This major abdication of responsibility for an important piece of foreign policy was wisely kept secret: when the Cabinet Secretary saw Macmillan's draft he asked for the information to be removed, and Selwyn Lloyd's letter is only available by virtue of the US Freedom of Information Act.[15]

While its future was being thus subsumed under greater international issues, Hong Kong was being seriously embarrassed by the embargoes on its trade with the People's Republic, imposed during the Korean war, which were pinching the colony's economy badly. The government review of 1951 described the year as one of difficulty and depression, in which events had 'put Hong Kong in an economically impossible position'. There were two embargoes, one on strategic goods imposed by the United Nations, and a total embargo by the United States on trade of any kind with China. Since the Communist take-over had led to the ejection of foreign firms from the old treaty ports, the greater part of international trade had passed through Hong Kong. These embargoes, which cut this trade down to 'a mere trickle', in Grantham's phrase, were gravely damaging. It was, as Lord Elibank, a veteran of the punitive expedition against the Boxers, put it, as though 'you were to give [a man] a knife and tell him that it was in his interests to go and cut his own throat'.

A corps of American inspectors was added to the already swollen Consular staff in order to ensure that nothing of Chinese origin found its way, even indirectly, onto the free soil of the United States. The colonial authorities had to attempt to prove the ideological purity of their exports to the satisfaction of the American embargo inspectors; shrimps, for example, might be caught in the admissible waters of Hong Kong, but had the crustaceans begun their lives there, or were they Communist infiltrators? In the absence of unequivocal evidence all shrimps, therefore, were banned. Ducks presented a similar difficulty. They might well be hatched, live and meet their ends in the colony, but were the eggs they came from true-blue?

General MacArthur himself intervened to complain that, under the other embargo, militarily important goods were finding their way to China, as was shown in Hong Kong's returns of trade. For the British government the Attorney-General, Sir Hartley Shawcross, pointed out that the quantity of such items listed was 'nil', and that the only thing that might be objected to was hardly of strategic importance – a single camera. He added that while Hong Kong's trade with China was being sharply reduced, Japanese trade with that country had increased from half a million dollars a month in the first half of 1950 to $3 million in the final quarter; and that Japan was at the time being governed by General MacArthur. Smugglers too responded to the challenge posed by the restrictions, doubtless fortified, as during the period before the war, by the thought of combining patriotism with profit. Their profits had to be shared with the Revenue Department, in order that unseemly brawls should be avoided; Sir Alexander explained that one popular method was for smuggler and Revenue officer to agree that the latter 'at a certain time . . . should be at point B. The smuggler would then slip through somewhere near point A.'[16]

Although post-war recovery was rendered more difficult by the restrictions on trade, the embargoes did have one significant beneficial effect in that as the entrepôt trade dwindled, manufacturing industries developed. Leading this movement were those Shanghai entrepreneurs either discouraged by the inefficiency and corruption of the Kuomintang, or later driven from the city by the Communist advance. They had a high opinion of themselves as 'more intelligent, efficient, flexible and generous than the Cantonese', whom they regarded as 'uncouth provincials'. Shanghai business had always been more international than that of Hong Kong, which was tied more closely to British apron strings, and Dick Wilson, editor of the *Far Eastern Economic Review*, considers that 'the economic impact of the Shanghai industrialists was decisive', and that the Hong Kong government conceded that the colony had a ten- to fifteen-year start over the rest of Asia, due to the 'injection of Shanghai experience and capital'.[17]

The newcomers' interests included film-making (Sir Run-Run Shaw), the great textile families of Tang, Lee and Wong, and the shipping concerns of Y.K. Pao, C.Y. Tung and T.Y. Chao. Shanghainese also became prominent in the civil service and politics; Lydia, Lady Dunn, is the senior Hong Kong politician, a member of both

Legislative and Executive Councils and of the House of Lords. Although many of this community had been forced to quit Shanghai with very little of their wealth intact, others, especially those with machinery ordered and paid for but not yet delivered – including both C.C. Lee and P.Y. Tang – were able to divert their resources to the colony. As a result, by 1955 the government could speak of 'the rapid emergence of Hong Kong as an industrial producer'. At first activity was heavily concentrated in the textile sector, which by 1962 had reached over £100 million, or 52 per cent of all exports. Diversification into other industries, including artificial flowers, but also basic electronics, began thenceforward to increase.

One result of the embargoes had been considerable capital losses as large stocks of goods became virtually unsaleable, and had to be disposed of at great loss. Traders were assisted in surviving this blow by the policy of the Hongkong and Shanghai Bank. G.M. Sayer, Chief manager between 1972 and 1977, described the changing attitudes of the Bank: until 1950 there had been little direct contact between Bank officials – almost all Europeans – and their Chinese customers. All such business went through the compradore; only in Shanghai, where 'people were generally more sophisticated and better educated and so on, and certainly more commercially knowledgeable', had there been dealings between the Bank and its customers without the compradore acting as intermediary. This personal knowledge, combined with their experience of Hong Kong conditions, enabled the management to cover shortfalls, and to make further advances for new buildings and equipment. It was not lost on Hong Kong businessmen that, in spite of manifold difficulties, recovery in the colony moved more rapidly than in the mother country, where all forms of credit continued to be bureaucratically regulated for many years. Hong Kong also enjoyed the valuable freedom of being able to make purchases in US dollars, while in the UK currency restrictions continued for as long as thirty-five years after the end of the war.[18]

The Korean war ended in 1953, and when Malayan independence was established in 1957, British strategic interests in the Far East were almost at an end. Some help was given to repel Indonesian infiltration in Borneo, but Britain steered clear of the major trouble centre in Asia, Indo-China. This withdrawal was signalled in Hong Kong first by the reduction of the garrison to a level compatible only with the maintenance of internal security, and later, in 1958, by the closure of the naval dockyard. From that date Hong Kong was an appendage, one without any strategic significance, and from which decreasing commercial advantage was to be expected. British Parliamentary interest was minimal, and British public interest in Hong Kong, except as an exotic spot for expensive holidays, somewhat less.

From 1951 to 1964 Conservative governments were in office in Britain, and following the established policy towards Hong Kong, one of benign neglect. When Oliver Lyttelton visited the colony, the first Colonial Secretary to do so while in office, he knew what to avoid noticing, and therefore found life there very agreeable. Grantham was 'one of the ablest and most successful of all colonial governors . . . Lady Grantham, a charming American, had lavished exquisite taste upon Government House . . . the scarlet liveries of the Chinese servants, curtains, carpets, furniture, flowers and food all showed what discernment and discrimination can do.'[19] There was mild admiration for the colonial authorities' handling of economic problems, which did not go so far as to stimulate much in the way of assistance. On the contrary, inessential expenditure, as on the 4,700 jobs in the dockyard, was to be rigorously pruned. Nor did the Labour opposition offer much challenge on behalf of the colony. When Lancashire Members, whose constituencies included textile producers, complained about the increasing competition from Hong Kong industries, they were told by the Conservative government that 'Hong Kong wages are nearer to West European standards than the latter are to American' – implying, with some justification, that British manufacturers should stop moaning and step up their own exports to the USA. Questions on the progress of democratization in Hong Kong – which, following the quiet funeral of the Young Plan, was non-existent – were pressed only by the tenacious John Rankin, one of the Glasgow Labour Members.

Members showed immediate interest only when the larger question of relations with China appeared to be involved. The first of these occasions was the aftermath of a fire in the Tung Tau squatter camp, when some ten thousand people were made homeless. The only remedy the Hong Kong administration could provide was to move them to another makeshift collection of huts, thereby contributing a propaganda opportunity to the new Canton government. A 'comfort mission' from Canton was proposed, 'the outcome of which', Sir Alexander believed, 'was not difficult to foresee . . . fiery speeches would have been made against the "imperialists", aid would have been promised from "Mother China" . . . Rioting would have broken out.'[20] Although the mission was banned from coming, the riots duly ensued in March

1952, and one person was killed. This fact was not revealed to the House of Commons, who were told that only one round had been fired from a shotgun, and that twelve people had sustained minor injuries.

The colonial authorities' attitude towards refugees was likened to that of a railway station's employees towards the passengers; their responsibility was to look after the permanent staff, and not 'to shower benefits on passengers merely passing through'. They were prepared to let the 'squatters' in, but thereafter they had to look after themselves. This attitude only began to change after an even more disastrous fire in the squatter camp at Shek Kip Mei, on Christmas Day 1953, when more than fifty thousand people lost what primitive shelter they had. A momentous decision was then forced upon the Hong Kong government; Denis Bray described what happened:

> It was not until a meeting at six o'clock in the morning of Boxing Day in 1953 that Sir Alexander Grantham took the decision to put the government into housing . . .
> The resettlement programme of the fifties was not a housing programme for the poor. It was a means to clear land for development. You could not apply for a resettlement flat. You were offered one if your hut was about to be pulled down. What you were offered was a concrete box allowing twenty-four square feet a head, in a seven-storey structure with no lifts, no windows but wooden shutters, no water, but access to communal kitchens and bathrooms. If this sounds dreadful, it was, but such was the alternative that people fought to get into the new blocks where you had your own place legally – and it would not burn down.[21]

By the end of 1956, 630 acres had been developed for resettlement, and 23,300 tenement rooms and 13,800 cottages built which would have – somehow – to accommodate two hundred thousand people, allowing each a space equivalent to less than that occupied by a double bed. It was the beginning of a creditable effort, the more remarkable since it was initiated from the colony's own resources, supplemented by some help from America and China. From the Mother Country Hong Kong received 'lots of nice verbal comment, praise from HMG, but nothing in the way of cash, nothing at all'. Only when the United States provided a grant was the Colonial Office shamed into matching it. Previously Grantham's appeals for help with rehousing had received even shorter shrift from Whitehall: 'I requested financial assistance from H.M.G. I begged, I pleaded, I wrote despatches, I wrote letters, I spoke to officials, I spoke to ministers. But all in vain, we got nothing.'[22] Hong Kong was, as it always had been, only deemed worthy of attention when some disaster had occurred or when one of Britain's own interests was concerned.

It was extraordinary that for more than ten years after the war, there was no serious trouble in Hong Kong apart from sporadic terrorism from Nationalist agents. More than two million refugees from China had poured into the colony, and received only the most basic support. Some were given temporary accommodation, and all were given access to food and water, but apart from that they were left, until the Shek Kip Mei fire, largely to their own devices. Many of the refugees were profoundly uninterested in politics, but active Nationalist supporters were a small minority, as were active Communists. The government had to avoid causes of tension between these two passionately antagonistic communities, and succeeded tolerably well in doing so. There was a strike on the tramways at Christmas 1949, encouraged by Canton, which looked as if it might have turned into a replay of 1922. The strikers left for Canton, where they were given a big reception; but that was all. No funds were offered, and the strikers were left stuck in Canton, unable to return to Hong Kong. Grantham considered that the strike was 'an eye-opener for potential trouble makers. It showed that the government was master in its own house.'

One of the few occasions on which Hong Kong was mentioned in the House of Commons was by the Prime Minister, Winston Churchill, on 24 March 1955, in one of his last Parliamentary statements before his resignation on 5 April. An account of the conversations held at Yalta in 1945 had just been published, which recorded President Roosevelt's desire that Hong Kong should be returned speedily to China. Sir Ian Horobin, Conservative M.P. for Oldham, the constituency which had given Churchill his first seat in the House fifty-five years before, asked if 'Her Majesty's Government are resolved to maintain their position in Hong Kong?' He received the Churchillian assurance that this was so, and that 'According to the record President Roosevelt said he knew I would have strong objections to this. That is certainly correct and even an understatement.'

Sir Alexander Grantham conducted Hong Kong affairs with smooth aplomb and the minimum of interference from London, and it was not until 1956 that real trouble erupted, on 10 October, the 'double ten', the anniversary of the 1911 October revolution which brought about the downfall of the Ch'ing. This was the most important Nationalist festival, and the disturbances started when an officious resettlement officer ordered some Nationalist flags to be removed. Mobs spread from the settlements to Kowloon, looting shops and attacking property known to belong to Communist sympathizers. Hoping that the disorder would die out with the festival, the authorities refrained from firm intervention, but by the next day a full-scale riot had developed. The Communist areas were the main targets of Nationalist attack, the most violent incidents taking place in the satellite town of Tsuen Wan, five miles away from central Kowloon on the other side of the container port. A mob stormed a clinic and welfare centre, killing four and ransacking the premises. Prisoners were taken to the Nationalist headquarters and badly knocked about. Communist-owned factories were attacked, the workers forced to kowtow and shout Nationalist slogans, and some were brutally killed. Foreigners were not especially singled out for attack, but a number inevitably became involved, the worst case being in Kowloon when a car was fired and a passenger, the Swiss Consul's wife, burnt to death. Most casualties, however, were incurred in the battles in Tsuen Wan between Nationalists and Communists.[23]

Decisive action was then taken, the armoured cars of the 7th Hussars being brought in to reinforce the police, who were instructed to fire 'without hesitation'. Communists were given sanctuary in the police compounds, and by the twelfth the riots had subsided, leaving fifty-nine dead – forty-four as a result of police action, and fifteen killed by the rioters. Of those rioters killed, thirteen had police records, and there is no doubt that under cover of the disturbance a lot of old scores were settled and opportunities for looting made the most of. In the subsequent trials four people were convicted of murder and sentenced to death.

The short adjournment debate on the riots on 8 November 1956 was opened by John Rankin M.P. This inquiry into an extremely serious and violent episode in a British colony lasted for thirty minutes, and its conduct accurately reflected the very low priority accorded to Hong Kong. Rankin gave a reasonably accurate account of the riots, pointing out that poor conditions and low wages were conducive to unrest, that Triad members had taken advantage of the uproar for their own nefarious ends, and that the elections to the Urban Council, the only elected body in the colony, continued to be a sham. He might have added, although it was not evident from the information given to the House, that while the suburban actions were clearly aimed at the Communists, the disturbances in central Kowloon were at least in part due to the boredom and desperation resulting from severe deprivation. It was left to the Minister of State for Colonial Affairs, John Maclay, later Viscount Muirshiel, to answer: Maclay had newly been appointed to the Colonial Office from the Ministry of Transport, and was to stay there for only three months before being promoted to the Scottish Office; his brisk peregrination through these departments illustrates how the Colonial Office was still viewed as a convenient waiting room for able young Ministers who needed temporary accommodation on their way to better things. It was Maclay's first appearance in his new role, and he betrayed his ignorance of the colony, contradicting Rankin flatly when the Labour Member attempted to draw a distinction between the clearly political riots that had broken out in the suburban areas and those in Kowloon: Tsuen Wan, the Minister insisted, was in Kowloon.

After that flurry, British interest in Hong Kong subsided to its usual level. The labour adviser to the Secretary of State paid an official visit to the colony in 1958, and new regulations placing some restrictions on working hours and regulating conditions of employment came into force. The industrious Rankin kept on eye on things, occasionally prodding on the question of electoral reform and criticizing 'dictatorships, however benevolent', only to be stonewalled by the Colonial Secretary, Lennox-Boyd, announcing that he was 'satisfied that there was no general demand or need for the introduction of an elected element into the Legislative Council'. Rankin managed to score one point on 16 December 1955 when the patrician Oliver Lyttelton dismissed a petition for constitutional change since 'a large number of people who have signed are hawkers and other workers unlikely to have any real understanding of the issues involved'. Rankin was able to snap back: 'Does the honourable gentleman mean that an individual who is a hawker has no place in the British Commonwealth?'

The only matters given serious attention were those briefly considered by an almost empty House on 23 May 1958. The standards of employment in Hong Kong were generally accepted as disgraceful by European standards and even, according to Ernest Thornton, Labour Member for Farnsworth in Lancashire,[24] by Asian standards. Thornton had a natural reason to be concerned, since his own constituents in cotton mills were being put out of work by cheap imports of textiles, frequently from Hong Kong. Having visited India, Pakistan, Japan and South Korea, he found that only Hong Kong mills worked seven days a week, and that only in Hong Kong and South Korea were women working twelve-hour shifts. Many mills only allowed two, or even one and a half days off per month, although even these could be worked 'in very exceptional circumstances'. No one disputed the accuracy of Thornton's facts, and the Minister, Mr Profumo, announced that a draft Employment Bill to control working conditions was being prepared by the Hong Kong government. The conclusion assented to was that 'The House of Commons is seriously disturbed and worried to learn of these bad conditions and feels that they ought not to be tolerated.' What was not pointed out was that an additional factor was the modern machinery employed in Hong Kong, at a time when many British manufacturers were refusing to invest in plant and equipment and British banks were reluctant to lend for redevelopment. Hong Kong's prosperity might have owed much to exploited workers, but competent banking practices, and a reluctance of government to intervene in business more than absolutely necessary, were at least as significant.

Sir Alexander Grantham retired in December 1957, after the better part of ten arduous years, loaded with appreciative tributes. His tenure of office was remarkable chiefly because of the difficulties that he had so neatly side-stepped. No open ruptures had occurred with China, Taiwan or the United States, in spite of many potentially dangerous episodes. British rule had been restored with a light hand, and at a time when so much of the British Empire was disintegrating under nationalist pressures, Hong Kong was politically quiet, and evincing remarkable powers of absorption.

For better and for worse, Grantham personally did much to define the colony's future. The democratic proposals advanced by Sir Mark Young were politely buried, interred by an alliance between Hong Kong business interests, the colonial administration and the British government, all united by an understandable, even laudable, anxiety not to rock a precariously stable boat. This was a policy Grantham's successors were to continue for more than twenty years.

The next Governor, Sir Robert Black, was a quieter personality, well attuned to the comparative calm that Hong Kong experienced during his period of office.

Autodecolonization

It was not until 11 April 1963 that the House of Commons had an opportunity of reviewing post-war Hong Kong in any detail, and the debate then held summarizes British views about the colony. Even after so long an interval since the return of Hong Kong to British rule, there were those who wanted to continue to avoid the issue, and the debate very nearly did not take place. Dr Jeremy Bray, an erudite and serious Labour Member, Denis Bray's younger brother, who had been born in Hong Kong, was due to open the debate when he received a call to the Labour leader's office. There he found not only Harold Wilson but the Lord Privy Seal, the future Conservative Prime Minister Edward Heath. He was told that the Foreign Office and the Governor of Hong Kong were worried about debating the future of Hong Kong publicly, and asked him to call off the debate. Bray was able to convince Heath that an open discussion would not imperil the future of the colony. He said nothing about the incident at the time, but the near-paranoia of the colonial authorities and their close political links with the Conservative Party were neatly exemplified.[25]

It was also typical that the reply on behalf of the government was given not by the Colonial Secretary, Duncan Sandys, but by Nigel Fisher, the Under-Secretary, who had to admit that he had not even visited the colony. It was also typical that this was the highest post that Fisher, an inconveniently independent-minded politician, was ever to achieve; high-flyers were not put in that particular slot. In the course of the short – only an hour and a half was allowed – proceedings the by-now familiar points were raised. The continuing US embargo on trade with China was deplored, and the Nationalist attempts at subversion, supported by the USA, strongly criticized (from the Conservative benches); the lack of progress on popular representation was again regretted, and heads gravely shaken over the wretched conditions of factory workers (although it was noted that these were slowly improving). Sir Robert Black had taken over from Grantham in 1958, and his administration had quietly gone about its business and kept out of trouble, while relations with China had stabilized. There was little controversy between the two sides of the House and general agreement that Hong Kong was doing well; hospital beds had been increased to ten thousand, education for all between the ages of seven and fourteen was being introduced, and the industry and enterprise of the population were commended. Hong Kong might not be the 'showcase of democracy in the East', as it had once been hopefully described, but Britain could be proud of her 'remarkable colony. Its story is a success story if ever there was one,' Fisher enthused, but he went on to make the revealing point: 'I find that even Treasury Ministers smile when I mention Hong Kong, because it is one of the few colonies that does not make large demands on the British taxpayer.'

The continuation of this happy state of affairs was in large measure due to the work of Sir John Cowperthwaite, Financial Secretary from 1961 to 1971. During most of this time Sir John was able to exercise virtually complete control of the colony's finances. An anonymous colleague reported that 'Apart from Burgess [Claude Burgess, Colonial Secretary 1958–63], no one could keep Sir John Cowperthwaite in line. His brilliance and argumentation prevailed and he thus made policy by ruling on all items of expenditure.'[26] Both Governors he served under, Sir Robert Black (1958–64) and Sir David Trench (1964–71) were sympathetic to the Financial Secretary's policies, which were also enthusiastically supported by the business community. Professor Alvin Rabushka, who made a study of the Hong Kong economy, described Cowperthwaite as 'brilliant, well-trained in economics, suffered no fools, and was highly principled. He wouldn't last five minutes in a similar post in Britain, since he was not predisposed to compromise any of his principles – only the constitutional structure of Hong Kong allowed him that power.'[27] A political economist in the tradition of Gladstone or John Stuart Mill, Sir John personified what might be called the Hong Kong school of economists, unreconstructed Manchester-school free-traders, or, as it was described, 'positive non-intervention'. Politicians and civil servants did not necessarily know more about business than did businessmen (a heretical thought in Britain at that time); nor did politicians have to suffer the consequence of business failures. They should therefore keep their noses to their own grindstones. Market mechanisms should be left to adjust fluctuations in the economy, and the government should concern itself only with sharply focused and minimal intervention on behalf of the most needy.

The success of Cowperthwaite's policies was undoubted. With the most minimal restraints on maximizing profits, continued low taxation and rigid control of public expenditure, Hong Kong, in spite of the continuing embargo on trade between China and the USA, became 'a Gladstonian Paradise' and 'a living laboratory in which to observe market place competition'. In the Cowperthwaite decade real wages rose by 50 per cent after allowance for inflation, and the percentage of households with incomes of less than $400 per month (which could be regarded as fairly acute poverty) fell from well over 50 per cent to 16 per cent. In spite of a scare in 1965, when a number of small banks failed, with consequent frustrations and disappointments, it could be said that, from an impoverished colony struggling to cope with the influx of refugees, Hong Kong had become 'a stable and increasingly affluent society comparable with the developed world in nearly every way'.[28]

It was also during the 1960s that Hong Kong acquired what have become its typical modern attitudes; that single-minded dedication to money-making which powered the engine of expansion, and an impatience with anything that smacked of the 'Welfare State'. Britain was regarded with something approaching contempt for its comparative economic sluggishness, attributed to the lack of enterprise generated by government support for lame ducks. Professor Rabushka enthusiastically praised 'The pure form of *homo economicus*. His given name is homo Hongkongus,' and claimed that 'Hong Kong = Happy Kingdom, while UK = Unhappy Kingdom'.[29] Cowperthwaite himself was not so brash. Like Gladstone, he had a sense of obligation towards the most unfortunate, which was combined with what he described as a traditionally Scotch reluctance to spend money without seeing a corresponding advantage. He objected to governmental borrowing, which Hong Kong could easily have effected, citing reasons that might have sounded out-of-date to Adam Smith. At the same time he rejected that sacred cow of British governments, mortgage interest tax relief, on the unassailable grounds that it benefited the better-off, and that 'whatever we do for the middle-income groups must not be such as to prejudice, by diversion of resources or energy, the continuation of our maximum housing effort at the lower end of the scale'.[30]

However gratifying to free-market economists was Hong Kong's undoubted success, criticisms can be made of the Cowperthwaite philosophy, and it may be asserted that a rather more sophisticated view of cost-benefit was needed in assessing public expenditure. Money spent on education, for example, has potent, if indirect effects upon the prosperity of a community: expenditure on health care can have many complex economic consequences, even if not all of them are fiscally beneficial. If government loans had been raised in the sixties in order to fund some of these desirable aims they would have been at rates that would, within a very short time, have looked attractive, and could have been easily repaid from the colony's economic growth.

Furthermore, the practice of turning the screw tightly on departmental expenditure and rewarding the managers who spend least is a primitive form of budgetary control. It is implicit in a realistic system of financial management that cost-centre proposals are not plucked out of thin air but are the fruit of methodical planning. A department is charged with producing specified services and prepares properly costed plans to enable this to be done. Deviations from the budget at the end of the period need to be explained, and failure to use those resources which have been allocated demands just as much explanation as does overspending.

But, under the Hong Kong system, departments consistently reported large surpluses without incurring any criticism.

		1967–8	1968–9	1969–70	1970–1
Education	Budget	288,603	327,811	383,451	471,258
	Actual	254,052	279,315	326,816	397,996
University	Budget	68,084	77,728	93,615	131,413
	Actual	35,235	65,888	63,406	93,588
Social spending	Budget	15,858	19,881	22,498	40,324
subvention	Actual	12,965	16,914	19,205	23,206
Medical	Budget	54,609	62,085	64,023	88,882
	Actual	46,341	52,458	57,732	63,147
Social welfare	Budget	9,888	11,625	12,741	16,167
	Actual	7,814	9,350	11,069	12,425

(,000 Hong Kong Dollars)

No explanation was demanded as to why, for example, the University funds were so wildly underspent – by nearly a half in 1967–8 and by a third in 1969–70 (in spite of restrictions a second university had been founded, supported almost wholly by public funds; the Chinese University of Hong Kong quickly developed into a highly-regarded institution). More seriously, at a time when tuberculosis was still a major source of concern, the minuscule medical budget was underspent every year. In the last of the Cowperthwaite years the medical budget of about $89 million was underspent by well over 25 per cent. Not much over one pound a head went towards the people of Hong Kong's medical needs. Yet substantial progress had taken place; by 1963 refugees were being rehoused in permanent quarters at the rate of five hundred per day, and mortality and morbidity statistics both showed steady improvement.

The ability of Hong Kong to manage its own financial affairs without interference or control from Whitehall, which evolved during Sir John's period in office, materially assisted him in striking out on an independent policy. It had previously always been expected that government purchases would, wherever possible, be made in Britain through the Crown Agents. This system took a blow when substantial irregularities were discovered in the Crown Agents' organization, sharply reducing their standing as commercial partners. As previous Imperial tariffs and restrictions were removed the Hong Kong market was opened to foreign competitors, and any restraint on the Hong Kong authorities' ability to buy in the most favourable market vanished. Similarly, in the immediate aftermath of the war the devastated economy had received considerable financial help from the not-much-less devastated British government, and direct Treasury control was consequently imposed. The speed with which Hong Kong recovered took everyone by surprise; by 1947 no further grants were needed from London, although Colonial Office approval for the larger supplementary provisions was still required. By 1958 this restriction was removed, and the Financial Secretary given extensive powers, including loan-raising, which could be exercised without seeking Whitehall approval; all that Sir John was required to do was occasionally to consult with London and to hold the colony's credit balances in sterling.

In November 1967 the British Labour government, which had not been pursuing such pure *laissez-faire* policies, found themselves in severe economic trouble, and were forced to devalue the pound. This resulted in a loss of some HK$450 million of Hong Kong's hard-earned savings; to put this in context, the colony was spending at the time about HK$46 million a year on medical care, and the loss therefore represented therefore some ten years' expenditure on this vital item. In an effort to persuade independent countries within the sterling area, who had suffered similarly, not to withdraw their balances to some safer haven, the British government negotiated the Basle Agreement with the major central banks, which provided a guarantee of the pound/US dollar exchange rate. In spite of the fact that Britain could have insisted on Hong Kong, as a Crown Colony, retaining its colonial funds in sterling – the Hong Kong funds represented 23 per cent of all external sterling balances – the same guarantee was extended to Hong Kong. Five years later the Hong Kong administration was freed from any restrictions and promptly – and wisely – diversified out of sterling into a wide range of currencies. From that time on Hong Kong was able to conduct its financial affairs in very much the same way as would have been done had it been an independent state. It chose to exercise its freedom in a fashion which, at the time when a Labour government was in power, was very much contrary to the ideas of the British administration.

When a Labour government under Harold Wilson was returned in 1964, it might have been expected that the criticisms levied against the Conservatives, especially of their failure to encourage the development of democratic institutions in Hong Kong, would be remedied. This did not prove to be so. The bipartisan feeling evident in the 1963 debate continued in 1965. Once again Mr Rankin asked what plans there were for 'some form of popular representation' in Hong Kong. The question was taken by a Junior Minister, Mrs Eirene White. (Labour followed Conservative practice of making Hong Kong the concern of the second division, but in the Colonial Office this was represented at that time by two talented women, Eirene White and Judith Hart, relegated only because of their sex, then an inevitable handicap in the Labour Party.) Mrs White cautiously replied that 'proposals for an extension of the franchise are now being studied', and confirmed that 'another four unofficial members would be admitted to the Urban Council, two of whom would be elected . . . there are no plans for internal self-government'. Once again it had been a Governor, this time Sir David Trench, who succeeded Sir Robert Black in 1964, who had taken the initiative in proposing some advances in democratic representation by setting up a committee to study what might be done in the machinery of local government 'as distinct from the needs of the population as a whole'. Although in economic matters Sir David encouraged cautious policies, he was one of the more reformist Governors; but like Sir Mark Young before him he found political advances difficult to achieve.

There the matter was allowed to rest until the next debate, in February 1967. It was an adjournment debate, filling in an odd half-hour of the House's time, but it gave the Minister of State, Judith Hart (who, as so often with those given responsibility for Hong Kong in the British government, 'had not been able to visit the colony'), an opportunity to restate, quite clearly, the policy that had been followed by all British governments since the 'Young Plan' was shelved in 1951. Mrs Hart did not hide behind the excuse of there being no demand in the colony for change, but came out openly with the real reasons why there was to be no move towards democracy, then or later:

Hong Kong is in a completely different position from any other of our Colonies. For international reasons alone, there are problems in planning for the usual orderly progress towards self-government. Because of Hong Kong's particular relationship with China, it would not be possible to think of the normal self-government and not possible, therefore, to consider an elected Legislative Council.

There remained, however, one field where some progress might be made. The Working Party on Local Administration, appointed by Trench, to which Mrs White had referred two years previously, had just published its recommendations. These suggested a comprehensive reorganization of all local administration based on a majority of elected members, leaving the existing colonial government unaltered. With the dignified lack of haste that characterized reform in Hong Kong, it was not until 1973, after the production of a White Paper, that any changes were made in the Urban Council; even as late as 1992 there was still no majority of directly elected members of the Urban Council.

Stiff upper lips

Both great Communist empires, the Russian and the Chinese, assumed many of the characteristics of the autocracies that had preceded their revolutions. Mao Tse-tung thought, and was able to act, very much as a reforming Emperor might have done two centuries before. Under the guidance of heaven he could propose great schemes of change which the inspired Chinese people would obediently execute. This was duly done: the Hundred Flowers Blooming Campaign of 1956 was succeeded in 1958 by the Great Leap Forward, followed in turn by the Great Proletarian Cultural Revolution, which began in 1966. In the course of these some twenty million Chinese died, a great part of Chinese heritage was destroyed, and the legend of Mao's divine infallibility shattered. It was also made clear that China had drifted far apart from Soviet Russia, both philosophically and strategically. Chinese foreign policy has since moved from the aggressive mode in which Mao had contemplated an invasion of Taiwan, thereby frightening off his Soviet allies, to one in which accommodation with the West is sought. But this took a decade of lost opportunities, and caused suffering that is still felt.

The Great Leap Forward was an insane plan of Mao's which deployed a massive and wasteful effort in order to create a 'technological revolution to overtake Britain in fifteen or more years'. Huge irrigation works were carried out, and nearly all the peasant population merged into twenty-six thousand communes. Rhetoric was substituted for sound management, with the result that grain production dropped, and at least twenty million people starved to death: by 1963 more than half of all deaths were of children under ten. Five years of relative sanity, allied to Chinese ingenuity and industry, allowed a recovery from the Great Leap Forward before Mao plunged the country into even greater turmoil with the Great Proletarian Cultural Revolution, a period of persecution, terrorism and wholesale wanton destruction of China's past, far more effective than anything ever managed by the Western barbarians. Ten million fanatic young Red Guards marched through Beijing, shouting the praises of Emperor Mao, and were let loose to destroy the four 'olds' – old ideas, old customs, old culture, old habits – all the things that had made China a great civilization. After 1971 there was a relaxation in the more atrocious aspects of the Cultural Revolution, but in all ten years were wasted before Mao's death in 1976 made it possible for reconstruction to begin.

The first effects of the Cultural Revolution outside China were seen in Macao in 1966, when rioting Red Guards were fired upon by Portuguese troops. The Hong Kong equivalent was less serious, and was handled less drastically. In April 1966 a protest against a rise in Star Ferry fares (illogical, since it was only the first-class fares that were to be increased) became focused on the hunger strike of a deranged young man and led to riots in Kowloon. These started as spontaneous demonstrations by young people. Henry Lethbridge described them as 'reminiscent of a children's crusade . . . a procession, twisting and turning like lion dancers . . . boys, laughing, grimacing and showing off'. The playfulness turned more destructive as looting and arson spread. One adult rioter was killed by police fire.[31]

The root cause of the disturbances was certainly not the ferry fares, but more probably relative deprivation and endemic boredom. With very few communal facilities available, street life was the centre of social intercourse. A young man who lived in a shared cubicle in an overcrowded tenement would find it very difficult to stay out of any excitement on the streets, and the criminally minded would find the cover irresistibly useful. The privileged and comfortable colonial authorities showed a deplorable lack of imagination in failing to appreciate these factors. They were not alone in this failure, for compared to the urban riots taking place in the United States at that time the Star Ferry disturbances were inconsiderable; but in the atmosphere of Hong Kong, traditionally peaceable but always edgily conscious of the proximity of a potentially revolutionary China, civilian unrest was a cause of much worry.

Elsie Elliott (now Mrs Elsie Tu), a member of the Legislative and the Urban Councils, did her best to draw attention to the very real causes for distress. Mrs Tu has been a shining light of liberal opinion in Hong Kong for thirty years. A working-class Tyneside girl, she had come to China in 1948 and to Hong Kong in 1951 as an unsalaried 'faith missionary'. In her school work she had first-hand experience of official corruption ('everything in those days was done by simple corruption'[32]), negligence, and brutal indifference. She wrote to an Assistant Director of Education complaining of underfunding, and received the retort: 'We have built housing for the underprivileged. Do you expect us to give them education too?' Mrs Elliott was able to produce dozens of examples of corruption, especially among the police, although she found it an unprofitable exercise so to do. The Colonial Secretary (at that time Michael Gass) 'was not willing to listen to anything that might lead him to the truth. His own reign in Hong Kong was short.' Her complaints led to Mrs Elliott being attacked by both the Chairman of the inquiry held into the riots, Sir Michael Hogan (Chief Justice of Hong Kong) and the Police Counsel, D.J.R. Wilcox (Crown Counsel, Hong Kong in 1965). The officials accused Mrs Elliott of 'inciting' the demonstrators, and of making 'unsubstantiated' allegations against the police. Nigel Cameron described the outcome of the inquiry as 'appalling flummery':

> The Enquiry censured Mrs Elliott, Sir Michael sentencing her (because there was nothing to which he could legally send her for trial) 'to the bar of public opinion where she must meet the censure and repudiation of all those right-minded people who believe in the freedom of the innocent from the taint of unwarranted suspicion and in the principles of frankness and fair dealing in the affairs of men.[33]

The next year's violence was more organized, more prolonged, and much more serious. Red Guards burnt down the British Legation in Beijing, and in London 'diplomats' from the Chinese Embassy attacked the police with axes. In Hong Kong young followers of Mao, clutching the Chairman's great works to their bosoms, besieged Government House, although in the most orderly fashion, guarded by a handful of British soldiers; all Communist-owned buildings were placarded with anti-British slogans; the Bank of China's loudspeakers poured out more of the same. David Bonavia described the situation:

> The worlds of Somerset Maugham and Mao Tse-tung met face to face in Hong Kong today. Both were baffled. Long before sundown the tumult and the shouting died, and on balance it was a draw with points in favour of Maugham. The gates of Government House were chained but ajar. Just inside was a wooden desk for the reception of petitions. Parking meters nearby were hooded and new police signboards proclaimed 'Parking space reserved for petitioners' . . . The demonstrators sang vigorous songs of the Cultural Revolution and chanted slogans. At times different groups were singing different songs, with cacophonous results which ill accorded with the sentiments of the most popular number, 'Unity is Strength' . . . A police cordon kept further comrades from joining the fun. The cheerleaders became still hoarser until some of them were barely squeaking. In the black cars, the anti-persecution committee sweltered . . . Eventually the cordon moved off, with demonstrators pushing the leading car, which had overheated . . . As it was already lunch time, the demonstrators knocked off and returned an hour later to resume chanting until five o'clock, when they all went home. The only casualty was the Governor's pet poodle, which went frantic with indignation and had to be removed from the scene. The posters were scraped off the gate and thrown away.[34]

More seriously, as the disturbances continued through the summer, thousands of bombs were planted, which killed fifteen people, including some children, and wounded many more. The colonial government handled the situation authoritatively. Their reaction was measured and firm. Demonstrations were dispersed and the noise from the Bank of China loudspeakers drowned out by light music. Except to quell a disturbance on the frontier, in which some police were killed by Red Guards, the army was not called upon. The police showed great courage and determination, losing ten killed and many wounded, while continuing to act with disciplined restraint: 'Hong Kong neither bent nor broke before the storm. The Governor, Sir David Trench, who had been awarded the Military Cross for his courageous activities behind enemy lines during the war, continued, with aplomb, to play golf at Fanling, and cricketers continued with their ritual in Central.'[35]

Sir David was a personage of substantial presence, which helped to reassure the nervous, and very much the right man to have at the head of the colony in times of crisis. He was also the first Governor to have had no real exposure to the pre-war Empire. Sir Robert Black had joined the Colonial Service in 1930, but Sir David only came down from Cambridge in 1938, and was posted to the Solomon Islands, out of the Imperial mainstream. A combination of a bluff – even gruff – manner and considerable sensitivity was exactly what the difficult times demanded. However well-directed were the Hong Kong government's reactions, they could not have been effective if the great majority of the population had not been willing to support the authorities; nor indeed if China had chosen to give substantial backing to the demonstrations. But the majority of the population were distressed by the interruption to the even tenor of their ways, and kept their heads down. The Kaifong Association leaders, who had been silent during the previous year's disturbances, hastened to assure the Governor of their support, and were rewarded by being asked to a garden party. Nor did the Chinese authorities offer much more than vocal, and discreet financial, support.

Active support for the rioters came from the Red Guards who had seized power in Canton; the government in Beijing, with only shaky control over the monster Mao had unleashed, were more cautious. The most decisive measures available to the Chinese authorities, simply cutting off Hong Kong's supplies of food and water, were not used. The water weapon alone would have been decisive, for since 1963 the colony's water supply had become critical, as the demand soared above anything that could be provided from its own resources. Domestic taps received water only once every four days for one period of four hours, while stand-pipes in the streets, at which huge queues formed, were only open for an hour or two each day. A major new reservoir scheme at Plover Cove was under construction, but it was clear that water would have to be piped from China to meet the colony's needs. The very considerable figure of ten thousand million gallons a year had been negotiated, and if this were discontinued for any length of time Hong Kong would come to a halt. China's reluctance to do this suggests that the Hong Kong and Macao demonstrations were local and spontaneous, part of the near-collapse of central authority at the time, rather than a policy originated by Beijing. Certainly when the Portuguese offered to evacuate Macao completely this was refused by China, signifying an intention to retain the existing status there as in Hong Kong.

The response of the Labour government to these dramatic events was exactly what might have been expected from the Conservatives: yes, there was involvement by the Chinese officials in the colony; no, the United Nations would not be asked to intervene, the police and the Governor were doing splendidly. Both Jeremy Thorpe, the leader of the Liberal Party, and Robert Maxwell, then a Labour Member, raised the question of electoral reform, to receive the by-now established negative.

1971 was the next critical year for Hong Kong, and might be taken as marking the beginning of its modern history as a city-state. Sir David Trench was replaced by Sir Murray Maclehose, Sir John Cowperthwaite by Philip Haddon-Cave, and the United States finally abandoned its support of Taiwan and agreed to the succession of the People's Republic to the China seat on the Security Council of the United Nations. The full story of that most interesting period, when China called a halt to the self-destruction of the Great Proletarian Cultural Revolution and began to take her rightful place in the world, has never been fully told. It could be said to begin with the election of President Nixon, who took office in January 1969, with a policy of disengagement from Vietnam, which was duly announced one year later. At about the same time coded signs appeared that China was seeking a change: Harold Wilson recorded that 'we noted with interest from the diplomatic telegrams an improvement in relations between China and Britain. It was, at this point, only at the level of gestures; but in Peking gestures are not accidental.'[36] Other 'gestures' included a message, passed to US Secretary of State Henry Kissinger via Pakistan, suggesting that talks might be profitable, which was followed by an invitation in April 1971 to the USA table-tennis team to visit Beijing. This hint was correctly interpreted, and in July Kissinger paid a private visit to Zhou Enlai, then Premier of the State Council, preparing the way for more formal talks. The same month American trade sanctions against China were lifted, and President Nixon's visit was announced for the following February.

Bit by bit, American support for Taiwan, which had been a cornerstone of foreign policy for so long, was seen to diminish: a move in October

1971, sponsored by the USA, to allow Taiwan to keep its place in the United Nations was rejected, and the People's Republic of China, twenty years after the event, was admitted to the United Nations and to China's seat on the Security Council, without demur from the American government. Nixon's triumphant visit culminated in the famous Shanghai Communiqué of 28 February 1972. It was, announced the President, 'the week that changed the world'.

It certainly changed the face of Hong Kong, since in reference to Taiwan the communiqué announced: 'The United States acknowledges that all Chinese on either side of the Taiwan Strait maintain there is but one China and that Taiwan is a part of China. The United States does not challenge that position.' If the United States agreed that Taiwan, their own protectorate, was to be part of China, there was not much hope that Hong Kong, always looked upon askance as a 'colony', and thus anachronistic and deplorable, should be treated differently. It should therefore have been no surprise when, only five days later, the United Nations Committee on Decolonization was asked by the Chinese representative in Lake Success, Huang Hua, to remove Hong Kong from the list of colonial territories. He explained China's view that:

> The question of Hong Kong and Macao belong to the category of questions resulting from the series of unequal treaties which the imperialists imposed on China. Hong Kong and Macao are part of Chinese territory occupied by the British and Portuguese authorities. The settlement of the questions of Hong Kong and Macao is entirely within China's sovereign right and does not at all fall under the ordinary category of 'Colonial Territories' covered by the declaration on the granting of independence to colonial countries and people ... the Chinese government has consistently held that they should be settled in an appropriate way when conditions are ripe.[37]

Had Britain wished it would have been entirely open for the Foreign Office to have objected, and put the alternative view, which Britain had constantly maintained, that Hong Kong was a Crown Colony, a British Possession, ceded by a 130-year-old treaty, while the New Territories were the subject of a subsequent agreement which would expire in the course of time and which would need further discussion. But the Prime Minister, Edward Heath, and the Foreign Secretary,

Sir Alec Douglas-Home, took no action, and the Chinese case was accepted by default. The reasons for doing nothing were manifest. Only a few days later – on 13 March – a joint Anglo—Chinese communiqué was issued establishing embassies in London and Beijing, and agreeing 'principles of mutual respect for sovereignty and territorial integrity'. This was the culmination of twenty years' negotiations, and, taken in conjunction with Britain's tacit acquiescence in the removal of Hong Kong from the list of colonies, made it clear that the die had been cast. Both Mr Heath and Sir Alec had been members of the government in 1957 and would have known of the secret agreement then made by Selwyn Lloyd and Macmillan. It is difficult to believe that similar conversations were not held between Britain and America in the spring of 1972. Although Heath did not regain office after the defeat of the Conservatives in 1974, he continued to enjoy excellent relations with the Chinese leadership, and was often able to speak more authoritatively than British Ministers. When in 1974, visiting Hong Kong as Leader of the Opposition, Heath confirmed that Hong Kong would indeed be handed back to the Chinese in 1997, his statement should have been taken as definitive; it also strongly suggested the existence of a previously arranged understanding.[38]

The British government had reason to be satisfied with whatever settlement had been reached, for they were in an indifferent position to negotiate. No longer could Britain send a division of troops to defend Hong Kong's borders, and indeed such a move would have been pointless. The 1967 disturbances had proved how easily China could take back the territory by cutting off supplies. Even more simply, the border could be opened. An anonymous civil servant put it succinctly: 'All they have to do is to send in two million of the buggers . . . and we can kiss it all goodbye.'[39] More damaging criticisms would be that, in agreeing the retrocession of Hong Kong at some future date, the British government were paying little attention to the welfare of its inhabitants. Trade with China was the first objective, and was actively pursued. Civil and military aircraft, machine tools and computers were eagerly presented to the Chinese; a major machine tools and scientific instruments exhibition was staged in Shanghai; trade missions were exchanged and export restrictions relaxed. 'Clearly,' wrote Peter Walker, then Secretary of State for Trade and Industry, 'the world's most populous country must be a trading partner of great significance for this country and indeed the whole Western world.' This has proved an illusory objective: some sales were made – thirty-five Hawker Siddeley Trident airliners being the most important, but China remained, as it had done in the previous century, a disappointment to British exporters. By 1977, after five years of effort, China still imported a lower value of British goods than did Korea or Pakistan, and only 3 per cent of that taken by that old benchmark, Holland.

In pursuit of this elusive aim the interests of Hong Kong were relegated to a subordinate position. If doubts lingered that Britain had any intention of accepting more than a strictly confined responsibility for the future of its colony, they should have been dispelled by the Immigration Act of 1971, which conferred the right of abode in the United Kingdom only on 'citizens of the United Kingdom and Colonies who are connected with Britain by birth, adoption, naturalization or registration or are children or grandchildren of such persons . . . or who have been resident in Britain for a continuous period of five years . . . Those having this right of abode are known as "patrials".'[40] Although more than three million Hong Kong Chinese were British citizens (the remainder, never having so registered, were presumed to be citizens of China residing in Hong Kong – although in the People's Republic's view all, without exception, were Chinese citizens), very, very few Hong Kong Chinese qualified as patrials. Those who did not so qualify were thereby warned that they could not look for refuge in Britain. From then on Hong Kong was not to be referred to as a colony, but as a territory, and the stage was set for the eventual, and inevitable, British abdication.

16

THE GOLDEN YEARS

The judicious application of cash

If the sixties might be termed the Cowperthwaite years, a period of stern abandonment of the economy to the free play of market forces, the seventies might be the Maclehose years, when central planning was accompanied by rapidly-increasing public expenditure. Like most convenient generalizations these need qualification, but it cannot be denied that a new Hong Kong has emerged since 1972, changed to a degree that makes the colony of that time almost unrecognizable. The community had prospered under the Cowperthwaite policy, but the prosperity had not been spread sufficiently wide. Londoners in the 1980s became inured to the sight of young people begging in the Underground and sleeping in cardboard boxes, but such concomitants of a *laissez-faire* economy were considered objectionable in the seventies. Hong Kong in 1971 was described as 'a cruel society, in which very little assistance is given to the poor. The Government has consciously pursued policies designed to foster economic growth, in the conviction that the economic prosperity of the whole colony would inevitably, in due course, filter down even to the poorest.'[1] But the filtering down was taking far too long, especially since colonial rule was approaching the end of its scheduled life. Sir David Trench had been a colonial Governor in the great tradition, with the virtues and limitations that implied. Sir Murray Maclehose, coming from another milieu, was given different tasks; those of moving towards a less unequal society and away from colonial traditions. He had also to bear in mind the ever-approaching retrocession, due in 1997, and the sensitive negotiations that this would entail: if Hong

Kong was to be handed back it must not be as a colony, but as near to an independent state as might conveniently be contrived, and in a condition that did credit to its previous owners.

Foreign Service and Colonial Service officers tended still, as they had done in the nineteenth century, to come from different stables. The popular conception of the Foreign Service as being composed of elegant young Etonians decorating the salons of Europe, while Colonial Services were khaki-clad pipe-puffing district officers secluded in the bush was exaggerated, but held a grain of truth. The two services inculcated different attitudes: the Foreign Service was responsible for representing British government views abroad (an Ambassador, as one seventeenth-century cynic put it, is one sent to lie abroad for the good of his country); the Colonial Service officer grew to feel himself more a representative of his territory, defending its interests, sometimes passionately, even against (or perhaps especially against) the Imperial government. The merging of the Foreign Office with the Colonial Office (by then renamed the Commonwealth Relations Office) in 1968 had not changed the attitudes of the existing staff. In selecting Maclehose, his successor Sir Edward Youde, and later Sir David Wilson, all from the Foreign Service, successive British governments were indicating that the most important task facing Governors was not that of looking after Hong Kong, but of dealing with Beijing. Anyone who might 'go native' and manifest undue enthusiasm for Hong Kong interests would be dangerous.

Murray Maclehose took over in November 1971. Although the extensive powers theoretically possessed by colonial Governors are in practice considerably restricted, an able and persistent Governor can exercise great influence, especially when his most senior colleagues are of like mind, and when he has the support of the British government. Murray Maclehose had all the qualities needed to influence events; he had previous experience of China as a Consul in Hankow after the war, and as Political Adviser to Sir Robert Black in Hong Kong in 1963; in the critical years of 1967–69 he had been British Ambassador in Saigon, and had held a number of posts in the Foreign Office and Colonial Office. Of these the most important was as Principal Private Secretary to the Foreign Secretary from 1965 to 1967, at a time when the post was held by Michael Stewart and George Brown. Coping with the often brilliant but unpredictable and unsober Brown must have been a useful preparation for the stresses of Saigon and Hong Kong.

Continuity of government, in spite of the changing direction of policy, was ensured by a succession of able Financial Secretaries. This post had only four incumbents, all highly competent, in the thirty years to 1991, a period in which the post of Colonial Secretary changed hands eight times; two Financial Secretaries, John Cowperthwaite and Philip Haddon-Cave, put in twenty years between them, and as Sir Philip went on to become Chief Secretary – the old post of Colonial Secretary renamed to suit the times – Maclehose had all the support he needed for new policies. Support too was offered from Whitehall by a succession of governments with generally liberal social policies – the administrations of Edward Heath, Harold Wilson and James Callaghan.

The new order was to reflect social, rather than political, changes, for British governments continued to shy away from any moves towards more representative government in Hong Kong; nor were there many signs in Hong Kong of a desire for such changes. What alterations did take place, which are described in the next chapter, were however accompanied by so many public-relations efforts as to alter the public perception of Hong Kong quite radically. Hong Kong moved quickly from being a Crown Colony to a Dependent Territory, in accordance with the wishes of the governments of Britain and China, if not necessarily with those of Hong Kong's people. Change was made easier as improved relations were established between China and the United States. Hong Kong was freed from the embargo on its trade and could reasonably expect an even more prosperous future.

It was quickly apparent that the new Governor intended changes:

> Maclehose immediately began to dismantle much of the pomp associated with the post. He dispensed with the use of the governor's limousine for the short journey from Government House to Legco [Legislative Council] Chambers, preferring to walk there for meetings. A common touch quickly became apparent as the new governor took regular walks, in short-sleeved, open-necked shirts, through densely populated residential areas. All indications were that here, at last was a governor of the people. This in itself came as quite a shock to the colonial system.[2]

Right-wing politicians, impressed by the arguments of monetarist economists, maintain that problems cannot be solved by 'throwing money' at them; such an emotive term can hardly be allowed to obscure the fact that many serious problems of society can only be solved by the application – preferably judicious – of a great deal of money indeed. This the Hong Kong government under Sir Murray's leadership proceeded to do. Social expenditure (hitherto restricted partly for ideological reasons, but also out of the impossibility of establishing satisfactory standards for the continued influx of refugees – the population had grown from 3,133,131 to 4,064,400 in the decade before 1971) could now reasonably be increased, and the budgetary stringencies of the preceding period had left resources to enable this to be done. The 1971 Hong Kong Annual Review, the first to be issued under the influence of Maclehose, was a bold document, amounting to nothing less than a manifesto for change, and foreshadowing the policies of the 1970s, which made that decade a 'golden age' for Hong Kong. A usually bland and formal official publication was charged with new energy. After appropriate acknowledgements to the previous incumbent the areas for expansion were identified – water and power supply, education, health care, and, above all, housing: 'housing is the one major social service that remains to be reviewed. It is a key to so much – health, standards of behaviour, family solidarity, community spirit, distribution of labour, communications needs, to name a few factors only.'[3]

(The standard of much of Hong Kong's housing was dreadful. Many of the squatters had been rehoused, but only in the most basic way: the standard unit of 120 square feet of concrete box, without any facilities, was intended to house five adults, but often accommodated many more. Each floor, which housed up to five hundred people, had 'one, and only one sanitation unit with taps but no basins and with separate latrines for males and females'.[4] It is hardly surprising that life in the squatter camps was reported to be healthier, which was just as well, as half a million people still lived in such matshed and biscuit-box shacks. The 1971 report claimed, without much evidence, that these resettlement units were 'by the standards of the time, regarded by the occupants as entirely acceptable', but admitted that the time had come when something a great deal better was needed.)

The whole review section of the report indicated that radical changes were intended. An entirely new concern was manifested for the 'rapidly deteriorating state of the environment': 'The Urban Council was faced with a general public, certain industries, agriculturalists and others who seem blinded by selfishness or obstinacy to the fact that pollution is unhealthy and expensive, avoidable and invariably at least as much one's own fault as anybody else's.'

Fresh attitudes were highlighted by welcoming, albeit with some reserve, the sort of criticism that had previously been so bitingly attacked by such civil servants as Sir Michael Hogan:

Young people who have the time spare to help other people in their complaints to authority ... may at times be affected by hubris and give encouragement to violent protest, but often they are sincere. It is gratifying, if the word does not smack too much of patronage, to note signs of a wider sense of involvement in the community among so many young men and women who are poles apart from the juvenile criminals. This encouraging trend has, not surprisingly, been paralleled by an increasing interest in – and criticism of – the machinery of government. The younger generation, as in all urbanized society, has moved away from the traditional view that life is centred on the family, still more the clan, and that 'government' is a remote and impersonal entity whose ways are inherently incomprehensible.

This was indeed stirring talk from a Hong Kong government publication.

Implementation of the new order was swift. A more effective budgetary system was immediately established, with department heads making more realistic assessments of their requirements, and no longer being patted on the back for underspending. In 1972–73, the first year of Maclehose's period of office, the education and social services departments succeeded, for the first time in many years, in spending the whole – and slightly more – of their entitlement, a much healthier state of things.

Item	Estimate	Actual
General Services	636.6	637
Social Services	1327.3	1357.2
Education	683.2	694.0
($million)		

Total government expenditure was increased by over 50 per cent between 1970 and 1972, and has continued to increase steadily since then – more than doubling in the five years previous to 1992, for example, and showing an average growth in real terms of nearly 6 per cent in each of those years. In the year 1992 public expenditure on all items, excluding the security services and economic expenditure – social welfare, health, housing, environment, education, infrastructure and community affairs – amounted to the equivalent of over £1,000 a head, a far cry from the austerity of the Cowperthwaite years.

Such a programme is bound to attract objectors: 'Philip (Haddon-Cave) just let things go to his head . . . Revenues from land sales were booming, and he just spent, spent, spent. There was no one with authority to check him,' one disgruntled official complained.[5] Some criticisms were doubtless valid – the cost overruns of the University of Science and Technology, the funding of the underground Mass Transit Railway and the aesthetic qualities of the new cultural centre may be cited as evidence – but the spending was no panic response to an unacceptable situation. The planning effort involved was huge, perhaps without parallel, involving as it did the reconstruction of a transport system, rehousing half the population, and providing acceptable levels of education and health care, all in short order. New skills needed to be introduced into the civil service, and the existing methods employed there sharply improved.

Even though rebuilding in Hong Kong proceeded at an uncomfortably rapid pace, the complexity of the reconstruction necessitated protracted planning studies. These were put in hand during the Maclehose years, but results often did not appear until much later, the new-town programme being a case in point. In 1972 the total population of the suburban communities was about half a million, gathered mainly in the older, and rapidly deteriorating, areas of Tsuen Wan and Kwai Chung, where the riots of 1957 had started. The new development programme provided for a network of satellite towns stretching around the coast from Tai Po and Sha Tin in the east to Sheung Shui and Fanling adjacent to the border with China. By 1991 over two million people had been housed in these new communities; to put the achievement in perspective, it took Britain, with a population ten times as numerous, the same length of time to rehouse three million people in the post-war slum-clearance programme. Some of the new towns are huge, far bigger than anything contemplated in Britain – Sha Tin's population is planned to rise from 570,000 in 1991 to 700,000. Since Sha Tin is only five miles from downtown Kowloon, it hardly requires all the facilities that might be expected of an independent city, but a community with two universities, a racecourse, a fine museum and a large concert hall is rather more than a dormitory suburb. Tsuen Wan is at present even larger, with a population of over 700,000, but this is decreasing as moves are made to the more modern locations.

The diversification of population means that Hong Kong people need to move about a lot, and the detailed planning of the new towns was integrated with a careful survey of transport, begun in 1973. Natural disadvantages – the steep terrain and the division of the territory into mainland and islands – present peculiar difficulties to movement. The road network is the most intensively used in the world: on average some seven million journeys are made on it every day by public transport, to say nothing of those made by the over two hundred thousand private cars. Movement would be impossible without the links between the two city-centres and the new towns provided by the Canton–Kowloon electrified line and the Mass Transit Railway, the busiest underground railway in the world (many statistics about Hong Kong tend to be records of this sort). When the MTR was opened in 1980, connecting Central with Kowloon, it was as a result of a compromise between the Hong Kong preference for private enterprise and the impossibility of running such a system without public funding. It is proving not inexpensive for the public purse, with equity injections of nearly $10,000 million from that source demanded in the last three years, but to anyone who has experienced the New York or London systems the Hong Kong metro is a vision of a different world – clean, quiet and reliable.

'Throwing money about' in other areas has produced dramatic effects in Hong Kong. To most of the world it may seem like a Utopia, and not only to the developing countries. Millions of Americans might wish to live under a system where no one is deprived of adequate medical treatment through lack of funds. Medical charges remain low, reflecting a substantial subsidy from public funds. Patients in the general wards of government hospitals are charged $4.37 a day (the figures have been converted to US dollars, and should be interpreted in the context of the average daily wage in Hong Kong being about US$25), which covers everything from meals, medicines and investigative tests, to surgery or any other treatment required. 'The charge may be reduced or waived in cases of hardship . . . The charge for consultation at general out-patient clinics is $2.30, while that for specialist clinics is $3.56 . . . Attendance at geriatric or psychiatric day centres and home visits cost $3.43. These fees may also be waived if warranted. The charge for injections and dressings in general out-patient clinics is 90 cents, while charges for visits to family planning clinics and methadone clinics remain at 13 cents . . . Free medical services continued to be offered at maternal and child health centres, tuberculosis and chest clinics, social hygiene clinics, and accident and emergency departments.[6]

Like any health-care system, that of Hong Kong is not immune from criticism, and criticism is readily forthcoming from 'The Other Hong Kong Report'. This valuable corrective to official self-satisfaction offers an alternative view by distinguished contributors who are not connected with the government. In the 1989 edition Antony Ng found that 'The medical and health service has essentially remained in the colonial era . . . by emphasizing public health measures,' that 'the rigid government and bureaucratic system has been slow to adapt', and that 'a lack of a clear policy direction' had led to a 'dismal state'. In the following year he reported that 'After years of procrastination and bureaucratic bungling . . . the system . . . has been creaking along from crisis to crisis.'[7] Although Dr Ng's grievances are probably justified, any review of British health services would be at least equally critical. Health care does not lend itself to careful design, even when this is seriously attempted, in the way that town planning does. In Hong Kong it has 'just growed', and the quality of care is spotty. Specialist high-technology medicine is not as widely available as in the United States or the United Kingdom, but the generally satisfactory standards are reflected in the statistics for mortality and most morbidity, which are generally better than in either of those other two countries. And no statistics can adequately reflect the mental security given by freely – and quickly – available medical care.

However impressive Hong Kong's health care system, the most surprising advance has been in education. Only as late as 1971, that critical year, did the government succeed in providing even comprehensive primary education. Twenty years later there were over 1,300,000 students at all levels, with more than $20 thousand million being spent on education by the government, a sum which represents 84 per cent of recurrent annual expenditure. From 5 per cent of the relevant age group studying in universities or polytechnics in 1981, 18 per cent have places in 1991, and it is planned to accommodate 25 per cent by 1994–5. This ambitious plan can hardly be fulfilled without some alteration in standards, especially since teaching staff are leaving in worrying numbers. But Hong Kong tertiary institutions have never been as research-orientated as the best of those in Britain, concentrating, except for some specialized fields, on undergraduate teaching. Graduates have then often gone abroad for postgraduate work. It is much easier to expand only undergraduate teaching than at the same time to extend research facilities to what would elsewhere be considered a balanced level.

Parallels may be found in the veritable passion with which Hong Kong approaches examinations to the prestige attached to learning in classical China. The system is highly competitive and demanding, with the inevitable result that high standards are achieved, but at the expense of throttling back more creative and discursive approaches. Hong Kong students are often respectful and deferential, and less critically enquiring than might be wished. Once through the system many graduates do in fact seek further training abroad, with the great advantage that their instruction has usually been (with the exception of the Chinese University) in English. Graduates therefore find it easier to find places in universities in English-speaking countries with more facilities for research – and not only there, since English is now, as even the Institut Pasteur has acknowledged, the language of all scientific research. In 1991 18,425 students left Hong Kong for courses in the USA, Canada, the UK and Australia (many of those going to American universities were pursuing undergraduate courses, the requirements of admission there being often lower than in Commonwealth countries). Chinese-speaking students preferred to go to Taiwan rather than China, and that in considerable numbers. Some five thousand were in residence in Taiwan in 1989, but only eighty-two chose Chinese universities in that year.

That the best of the Hong Kong youth have easy access to the English-speaking world is a great actual, and even greater potential, asset to the community. Concern is expressed at the reluctance of some students to return, and the fact that a command of Putonghua (Mandarin) will be necessary for advancement in the civil service may damage the international character of Hong Kong; but this must surely be counterbalanced by the stimulating effect of overseas experience on Hong Kong young people – some of the liveliest anywhere in the world once freed from the tyranny of examinations.

Providing adequate affordable housing for most of the population has been the third unquestioned achievement of the Hong Kong government. After the initial effort to provide basic accommodation for the wave of post-war refugees a plan for creating and maintaining public housing of a tolerable standard evolved. The outlines of a new policy had emerged in Trench's day, and were described in the Hong Kong White Papers of 1964 and 1965, but the pace of building accelerated after the recognition dawned that the deplorable conditions in which people lived might have something to do with the discontent that erupted in the 1966 riots. A beginning was made with the replacement of the most grossly inadequate blocks built after 1954. Because of Hong Kong's peculiar topography, and its acute shortage of suitable building land, construction has been difficult, necessitating much land reclamation. The first programme was succeeded by another, begun in 1986, which provides for 1,150,000 new flats, of which 500,000 have been completed. Of the remainder 400,000 will be in the public sector, which already accommodates nearly three million people. Heavily subsidized housing is available for both sale and rent, the target being to provide accommodation for a sum equivalent to 7 per cent of the average family's income. New flats rent from about US 35 cents per square foot per month, and are available for sale at US$25,000 upwards. This is very creditable, but as Denis Bray has said, 'We often produce statistics to show how prosperous we are, but we do not often point out that most of us live in a one-room flat':[8] and there are still some 288,000 people living in grossly unsatisfactory temporary quarters.

Among these the most wretched are not perhaps the inhabitants of cardboard boxes by the Star Ferry terminal, but the 'caged men' of Mongkok, the pensioners without a family, whose home is a bed space surrounded by wire mesh to keep their few belongings safe, with a one-twentieth share of a lavatory and bathroom. The social security system in Hong Kong does not claim to be anything except a safety net, to prevent absolute destitution and starvation, and is targeted very narrowly. A minimum income of about US$2,500 a year is provided for the over seventies, with a supplement for disability. If the old people are part of a family unit this is adequate, but with a rapidly-ageing population, thanks in part to rising standards of health care, the old and lonely have a poor time of it.[9] They would have a worse time were it not for help from a wide variety of non-governmental sources, many of which are organized by the Community Chest to produce about US$15 million a year for charitable purposes. It has long been a Chinese tradition that good works are meritorious; and equally that they deserve formal recognition – a scroll, a plaque, a dedicated room, or, for the most generous, a building commemorating the donor. It is very like Britain a century before, when Peabody housing and Carnegie Libraries, (both funded by Americans) supplemented more spartan local authority provisions.

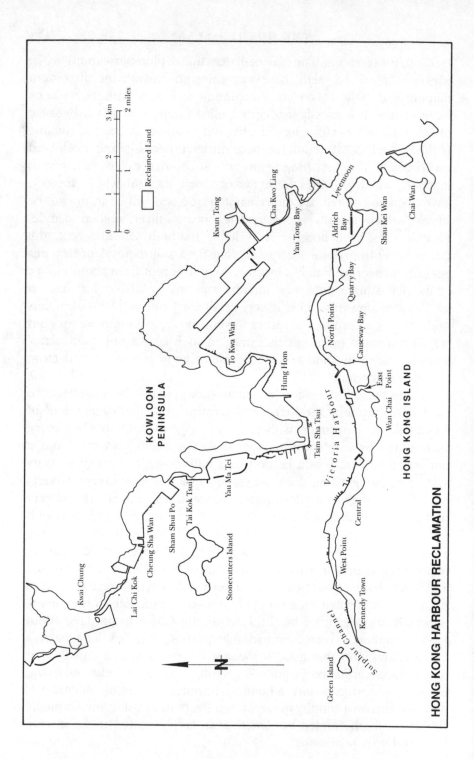

HONG KONG HARBOUR RECLAMATION

Heading the list of all charitable donors is the Royal Hong Kong Jockey Club. Since betting on horseracing is the only legal form of gambling in Hong Kong (although illegal mah jong flourishes fairly openly), and since the pursuit of good fortune amounts to a passion among Cantonese, and is not despised by the British, the 'nice little 7 furlong race course' that Kipling admired generates, with its associated facilities for gambling, thousands of millions of dollars every year. A substantial slice goes to government: in 1991 the Jockey Club contributed some £500 million (the larger part of the £1,200 million of the Hong Kong government's 'internal revenue', which amounts to about 15 per cent of total government income from all sources, comes from betting). After tax and transfers to reserves all the Jockey Club's profits are distributed to charity. These are very substantial, in 1991 totalling some £80 million (HK$1,104 million).[10] To put this in perspective, such a sum would have been sufficient to cover, with a generous overlap, the whole of the public social security in the previous year (HK$984 million). The distribution of these funds is officially part of the patronage of the Club Stewards; an unelected and – in the strictest sense of the word – unaccountable body, responsible only to the members of the institution. In practice these very responsible and serious-minded gentlemen, in close co-operation with the government, make honourable and effective use of their patronage. The Royal Hong Kong Jockey Club is, for example, not only funding the Hong Kong University of Science and Technology, but is managing its construction. It is questionable, however, whether this is the best way to fund so large a proportion of public spending, and it is significant that the government is coy about drawing attention to the Jockey Club's contribution. There is no entry for the Club in the index to the 1992 Annual Review, nor is their contribution to tertiary education even mentioned in the relevant section, although it was much greater than the *whole* of the government's capital expenditure ($437 million) on *all* educational institutions.

Solid progress under Sir Murray Maclehose's administration was supplemented by some more cosmetic adjustments. It was modish during the 1970s and 1980s to engage McKinsey & Co., the eminent management consultants, to suggest corporate re-organizations; and the considerable expense of their studies usually meant that many of their recommendations were accepted. In Hong Kong this was quickly done. The Colonial Secretary was renamed Chief Secretary, and the Secretary for Chinese Affairs banished to the history books, to be replaced by the Secretary for Home Affairs. (It is a measure of the inertia of old colonial attitudes that it had taken until 1973 for this to be done; in a community 98 per cent Chinese the total inappositeness of the title might have been spotted before.) The triumvirate of Governor, Chief Secretary and Financial Secretary had full executive power to act within the general policies of the home government and the loose restraints of the Hong Kong Constitution. Reporting directly to them were a number of Secretaries, each in charge of one or more executive branches, acting very much as managers of subsidiary companies reporting to a main board executive committee. In this analogy members of the Councils might be considered as shareholders, sometimes helpful, sometimes bothersome, but irrelevant to most decisions.

A more official explanation, advanced in successive Government Annual Reviews, is that the Executive Council 'plays a role somewhat similar to that fulfilled by the Cabinet in a Westminster-style system'. This needs so much qualification as to render it almost a convenient fiction. Of the fifteen members of the Executive Council, five are there by virtue of their contracts of employment – Governor, Chief Secretary, Financial Secretary, Attorney General and Officer Commanding British Armed Forces. The remaining members – all appointed by the Governor – are eminent and busy people, who in 1992 included the Chairman of the Hongkong and Shanghai Bank, the Vice-Chancellor of Hong Kong University, and Baroness Dunn, a member of the House of Lords and director of the Swire Group. Only one member has any departmental responsibility – at the time of writing Mr E.B. Wiggnam, Secretary for the Civil Service.[11] It would be quite impossible for members to have the sort of detailed discussion that takes place between British Ministers, not only in Cabinet itself, but in the many Cabinet committees. Executive Councillors' powers, too, are much more restricted than the almost dictatorial authority of a British Cabinet. Allocation of finance is decided by the ex-officio members themselves in consultation with Secretaries, and presented as a *fait accompli* to the Council. On other items the Council has limited opportunity to intervene:

> Usually the Council is presented with an agreed recommendation, backed by a detailed explanation of the rationale behind it. The Executive Council may question, vary, amend, or refer back for further study ... But outright rejections are unusual, and the

Council very rarely takes up a general discussion of a problem, and attempts to formulate its own solutions.[12]

Nor has the Governor anything like the powers of a Prime Minister. A Prime Minister may dismiss the whole of his Cabinet, and replace it overnight, but a Governor is stuck with the members he inherits or appoints until their time in post has run out. The limited time available to Executive Council members to fulfil their functions is reflected in the changed wording of the government's annual review; until 1990 they were accustomed to meeting 'at least once a week', but they now meet 'normally once a week'. On these days, between the meetings of the Legislative Council in the morning and the Executive Council in the afternoon, the Governor was accustomed to lunch with his officials; this was known as the 'Tripe Club', since tripe was served in the morning and afternoon sessions and might also be available in between. The mores of government have perhaps changed since then, but the ultimate executive power in Hong Kong rests much more firmly with the officials rather than with the Council members.

Nevertheless, although nothing was done to extend democratic participation in the Hong Kong government, some constitutional changes took place during the 1970s which increased the effectiveness of the Councils. From 1976 Sir Murray Maclehose, simply by not appointing the full complement of official members to the Legislative Council, gave the unofficials a majority, which rose from two to ten in 1984, although the hypothetical possibility of immediately appointing enough officials to carry a contested motion remained. Not that the unofficial majority showed any sign of kicking over the traces; the debates, which had been described as 'like an antiphonal chant by Government and Opposition members on "the voice that breathes o'er Eden"' retained their 'calm . . . with the absence of overt opposition [that] is mirrored across the world, from Budapest to Beijing, from Havana to Moscow'.[13]

Another long-overdue move was the recognition in 1974 of Chinese as an official language jointly with English, providing that 'both languages possess equal status and enjoy equality of use for the purposes of communication between the government and members of the public'. This sounds more impressive than in fact it was, since the new law did not require Chinese versions of even current legislation to be issued. Only in 1989 did laws begin to be issued in both languages, and the existing corpus of law is still being translated. English remained the only language that could be used in the higher courts, Chinese being accepted only in magistrates' hearings. Even there the change seems to have been largely cosmetic; Jan Morris describes a magistrate who, 'sitting as he does alone upon his bench, hearing cases involving simple Chinese in a language he does not understand . . . bullies defendants mercilessly . . . bludgeons witnesses . . . testily proclaims his own importance – "This is a court of Law . . . Do you understand that? Do you hear me? I am not speaking German or Greek to you." '[14]

It is instructive to contrast the situation with that pertaining in Wales, where, according to the 1981 census, about half a million people (from a total of 2,791,851) were able to speak Welsh. Very few of them, if any, could not also command English. But Welsh enjoys fully equal status with English in all aspects of government, while in Hong Kong, where more than 90 per cent of the population speak Cantonese, and only a moderate proportion also have English, they have to put up with the sort of insulting behaviour Jan Morris describes; but the Welsh, of course, have votes.

Whatever the deficiencies of Hong Kong policy, its people seem reasonably well-satisfied with the results. Criticisms are very similar to those made in any advanced country, where taxes providing for public expenditure are much higher. Hong Kong has been able to achieve its level of provision without blunting the edge of its competitive efficiency by increased taxation. And, which worries liberally-minded observers exceedingly, without more than the vestiges of democratic representation. Governments in the colony have maintained that their peculiar system of consultation through osmosis works, and that, since they do not have to placate special interests in order to obtain votes, they can take a cool and unprejudiced view of the community's needs. On the question of social policy at least it must be admitted that the theory remains to be disproved. When complaints are voiced the most widespread desire, and one frequently expressed, is not for greater provision of public benefits, but for a more stringent level of policing, and severer penalties for law-breakers. Hong Kongers are more worried about personal than social security.

'Corruption, the most infallible symptom of constitutional liberty'
Edward Gibbon

Nothing initiated by Sir Murray proved more rapidly effective than his vigorous action against corruption. Institutionalized in Hong Kong since the earliest days, corruption had been an indispensable mechanism to smooth the functioning of a society where the only unifying factor was the hope of profit. In an established society like that of Britain, corruption could take less blatant forms. The award of honours and the allocation of offices could serve instead of cash, and stimulate the innate – and real enough – loyalty of the community to the state. In the twentieth century the system was greatly expanded: a whole new order, that of the British Empire, was invented to spread the previously restricted honours downward throughout the community. For a short time, these were more or less openly for sale while David Lloyd George was Prime Minister – he himself ended his days as Earl Lloyd-George and Viscount Gwynneth of Dwyfor – but today these affairs are managed more discreetly (yet only the very innocent believe that the Chairman of a public company that gives large sums of other people's money to a political party will not, when that party is in power, be offered some reward). In Hong Kong the system was slightly adapted. Prominent citizens, for public service (which can mean either the expenditure of time and energy, or cash), are rewarded with the appropriate button of the modern mandarinate – Member, Order, or Commander of the Order of the British Empire, or even with the rare peacock feather of a K (Knight) for outstanding contributions. At higher levels this works well enough, but on the streets there is no substitute for cash.

Unease about police corruption had been expressed since the inception of the colony, but after the Second World War the practice settled into a generally accepted and comfortable pattern. Apart from the official hierarchy of the force, the organization of the police on the beat was in the hands of staff sergeants, equivalent to senior warrant officers in the army, and to the station sergeants working under them. With very few exceptions these Chinese officers were all profitably engaged in a highly-organized system of corruption. They acted as 'caterers', arranging liaisons between their subordinates and the criminals and collecting payment for their services. These considerable sums were then distributed in agreed proportions among their subordinates and superiors. In return the heads of criminal fraternities and gangs undertook to settle their own differences and to allow the

ordinary citizen to go about his business. This system sometimes
aroused horror among newcomers – the first new post-war Commissioner exclaimed that he had 'never seen such wide-spread corruption anywhere' – but its convenience prevented any drastic action from
being taken. An anti-corruption office was established, but since this
itself was part of the police force organization its members were not
encouraged to manifest too indiscreet an enthusiasm for their task.[15]

Westminster first showed interest in the subject on 10 March 1960,
when Ernest Thornton asked whether the Colonial Secretary would
consider appointing an independent inquiry to investigate bribery in
Hong Kong, only to receive the shortest answer: 'No, sir.' Thornton
kept at it, and elicited the information that the Standing Committee
on Corruption, which was said to assist the Governor, had only met
eleven times since 1957. He also produced evidence from a number of
sources that the problem existed. Mr Justice Charles had said: 'Corruption is all too prevalent in the colony'; Mr Brooke Bernacchi, speaking
for the Hong Kong Reform Club, that 'Corruption is bad in every big
city, but Hong Kong is one of the worst in the world'; the *China Mail*
that 'corruption is the millstone around our neck'.

Thornton did not get far in his crusade. Edward du Cann, Conservative Member for Taunton, assured the House: 'It is plain . . . that all
the leading businessmen and Civil Servants are scrupulously honest
and above suspicion.' Iain MacLeod, the Colonial Secretary, agreed,
adding that the Governor, 'a man of very wide experience in these
matters . . . does not feel that there should be such an inquiry'. There
must have been many in Hong Kong who were delighted with that
news.

It was not until the official Committee of Inquiry into the 1966 riots
began to take evidence that the subject was forced into the limelight.
Very uncomfortably, the Commissioner, Henry Heath, was obliged to
admit the police to be corrupt, but not more corrupt than other parts
of the government; in any case police were different, since detectives
needed to take bribes if they were to be able to pay their informers.
The Committee was not meant to discover such inconvenient facts,
especially when the police force behaved so well during the following
year's disturbances. They were the colony's heroes, now the Royal Hong
Kong Police Force, and such distinguished sleeping dogs should be
left to gnaw their illegal bones in peace. Criticisms were rejected
with a note of hysteria, since to criticize the colony's defenders was
to jeopardize the security of the community. The Colonial Secretary,

Sir Michael Gass, who had spent his career in West Africa, remote from even such democratic institutions as obtained in Hong Kong, made his unprecedented public attack on Mrs Elliott of the Urban Council. It was assumed too that only the lower ranks, all Chinese, were corrupt, while the more senior, expatriate policemen were honest; they were, after all, British.

The view from the Palace of Westminster was more accurate. No one cared to contradict James Johnson, the reliable Labour Member for Rugby, when he stated on 27 February 1967: 'only last week the Honourable Member for Wanstead and Woodford [Patrick Jenkin] and I joined forces in referring to the widespread allegations of corruption of the police. These allegations have been made by too many people for my comfort – people in all levels of society, of all colours, and in all positions. I, and others, have discussed the matter with the Governor, who was most helpful. I am aware of his difficult position . . . but I ask my Honourable Friend seriously to consider setting up a commission of inquiry into the affairs of this most unusual Colony.'

Johnson may have been thought of by some cynical Conservatives as making party points, but Patrick Jenkin, a Conservative M.P. himself, and one of acknowledged integrity, who later became Secretary of State for Social Services and for Industry, was a man whose apprehensions should have been taken seriously.

The colony managed to avoid its commission for a few years yet. Bribery was taken a good deal less seriously there than in Britain – this was before the great exposures of 1972, which claimed among many other casualties the career of the Home Secretary, Reginald Maudling – and it was assumed that corruption existed only at the lowest of levels. It might often even serve a laudable purpose, for complaints about junior staff (hospital employees and receptionists being frequently complained of) were often of mere incivility, which could be remedied by a dollar or so of tea money.

Colonial complacency was shattered only when in 1973 it was discovered that one of the most distinguished veterans of the riots, Chief Superintendent Peter Godber, had been on the take to the extent of several million dollars. The discovery was made as a result of a cleaning-up operation begun by Commissioner Charles Sutcliff, who arrived in 1969 and rapidly begun weeding out the staff sergeants, virtually all of whom left in some precipitation to a comfortable retirement. Two years later, Sir David Trench, who had shown little sympathy for crusaders against corruption – when questioned on British television on the subject he 'sat before the cameras as rigid as a totem-pole, brusque and non-committal' – was replaced by Sir Murray Maclehose, with a brief for making changes in the colony. The inquiry into the Godber case led Sir Murray to conclude that the police could not be relied upon to be sufficiently energetic and impartial in investigating allegations made about their own colleagues, and that an independent anti-corruption unit was therefore needed.

The Independent Commission Against Corruption (ICAC), established by Sir Murray under the leadership of Sir Jack Cater, quickly proved embarrassingly successful. Cater, a quietly impressive and independent officer, was reinforced by Sir John Prendergast, who had a remarkable record of colonial policing in Palestine and Africa, where he won a George Medal for his work in Kenya during the Mau Mau troubles of the 1950s. Having served previously in Hong Kong as Director of the Special Branch, Prendergast brought valuable police experience to supplement Cater's determination.

The team was, if anything, too effective. Policemen were arrested in veritable droves – fifty-nine sergeants from a single division, one Senior Superintendent dead by his own hand, and three British Superintendents in custody – as investigations revealed highly-organized corruption on an enormous scale. This was too threatening, and the police took matters into their own hands, staging a mass meeting which resulted in the offices of ICAC being stormed and members of staff assaulted.

Faced with the fact that corruption was endemic, and that investigations could not be pushed further without risking the collapse of the whole system of public order, the Governor had to retreat, and allowed an amnesty for all but the most serious offences. At the same time he made it clear that any future misdemeanours would be severely dealt with. It took some years for the dust to settle, but the results were not unsatisfactory. Nigel Cameron commented:

> It would appear from the statistics that corruption in the police force has greatly diminished. To what degree the figures reflect a general lessening in the scope of corruption is an open question. Certainly large-scale syndicated corruption has been vanquished, but just as surely small-scale activities have not.[16]

The report of the Committee seems to bear this out: prosecutions of police officers now form an insignificant proportion of the whole.

	1986	1987	1988	1989	1990	1991
Total prosecutions:	251	485	382	333	284	314
Of which police:	19	14	12	16	10	8

There remains the possibility that much underhand activity continues to be associated with the drug world. At a time when drug use has not noticeably declined the number of serious offences reported and of persons prosecuted has steadily dropped, while the seizures of narcotic drugs have plummeted:

	Narcotics Seized (kg)	Serious Offences	Persons Prosecuted
1987	737	4,143	5,231
1988	942	5,527	6,579
1989	1,154	5,040	6,050
1990	265	3,604	4,390
1991	184	2,998	3,631

Prudently enough, the government annual review does not attempt to explain this tendency, but the figures must be taken to indicate either an increase of effectiveness unparalleled elsewhere in the world, or a degree of collusion with Triad dealers. That it may well be the latter is instanced by the trial of the senior narcotics officer in the Customs and Excise Department, Senior Inspector Cheung Ying-lun, in 1990, on charges of smuggling fifty kilos of heroin into Australia.

Losing nerve

The most visible sign that Hong Kong was ceasing to be a British colony and becoming a Chinese society was not a result of government action but of spontaneous commercial change. By the time of Murray Maclehose's appointment the energetic Shanghainese who had fled from their city in 1949 had rebuilt their fortunes and begun to emerge as leading players in the financial world, often supplanting some of the older Chinese magnates. Of these newcomers the most prominent and successful was Sir Yue-kong Pao, who began his shipping enterprise in 1955 with a single small vessel, and within twenty years had built it into a twenty-million-ton fleet, before diversifying into a wide variety of quoted investments. The other great entrepreneur, Li Ka-shing, was not from Shanghai, but was a native of Chiu Chow, in Guangdong. He had begun his plastic-flower manufacturing business in 1950 at the age of twenty-two, and was also in a position to make himself felt by the 1970s.

These 'new men' were cast in a different mould from previous Chinese magnates such as Sir Robert Ho Tung or Sir Kenneth Fung, who had made a point of being closely associated with the colonial government. If Li or Pao needed government action they could, and did, go direct to the heads of the British or Chinese governments. Sir Yue-kong gave an example of this during the meetings between Margaret Thatcher and Deng Xiaoping in Beijing in September 1982. Kevin Rafferty reported: 'Pao seemed to go everywhere ... "He behaved as if it was the Y.K. Pao benefit show, with Thatcher and Deng reduced to supporting rôles," chuntered a still aggrieved British official.'[17]

Parallel to the expansion of Hong Kong Chinese businesses came a notable increase in mainland investments as, encouraged by Deng's economic reforms begun in 1978, Communists (nominal Communists, at least) took advantage of the opportunities offered by capitalism. One of these groups, the China Merchants' Steam Navigation Co., now owning some forty different Hong Kong enterprises, is something of a curiosity. The company dates from 1872, when it was founded as one of Li Hung-chang's initiatives in order to provide Chinese competition for the foreign-owned companies – at that time mainly Russell's, Jardine's and Swire's. Li's venture, funded by compradores and merchants, was immediately successful; Russell's was bought out, and even Jardine's considered selling their interests, as the CMSN became the biggest operation of its kind in China. Only modestly less venerable was the Bank of China, established in Shanghai in 1912, which survived the Japanese invasion and the civil war only to have its entire gold stock clandestinely removed to Taipei by Chiang Kai-shek in 1949. The Bank of China, professionally managed from its splendid new Hong Kong building, is second only to the Hongkong and Shanghai Bank, with over three hundred branches, and probably accounts for over a quarter of all banking deposits in Hong Kong.

More recently the China Resources Company, which acts as representative of China's exporters, and the China International Trust and Investment Corporation (CITIC) have rapidly expanded. CITIC's most prominent investments include minority holdings in Cathay Pacific Airlines, the Eastern Harbour Tunnel and Hong Kong Telecom. Even the Chinese government – perhaps especially the Chinese government – cannot keep track as enterprising mainland Chinese have set up a proliferation of companies in the colony, without wishing to report their activities to their own regulating authorities. According to Kevin Rafferty, neither the China Resources Company nor the New China News Agency have been able to compile a list of such businesses, but the US State Department has identified more than 750 Chinese companies, and the total Chinese investment in the colony is thought to be over US$10,000 million, which would represent some 10 per cent of all capital investment in Hong Kong.[18] Other statistics tend to confirm this: in 1989, for example, Chinese-owned firms won 18 per cent of all engineering contracts awarded. It was almost a repetition of events a century previously; enterprising and capitalist-oriented Chinese from the mainland joined the foreigners in Hong Kong at their own game, and were bitterly criticized for their enterprise by traditionally-minded supporters of the established order in Peking.

As the new Chinese enterprises from both within and without the colony expanded and began to show their readiness to muscle in, some of the old-established Hongs suffered what appeared to be a collective failure of nerve. The British had concentrated their commercial power within a small group of taipans; the Hongkong and Shanghai Bank, Hutchison's, Jardine Matheson, Butterfield and Swire, Dairy Farm and Wheelock Marden, all had interlocking directorships: Sir Douglas Clague, Taipan of Hutchison's, was on the board of the Hongkong and Shanghai Bank, Dairy Farm, Wheelock Marden, the Cross-Harbour Tunnel and a Steward of the Jockey Club; J.L. Marden, of Wheelock Marden, was on the board of Dairy Farm and Hutchison's as well as leading his own company; Michael Herries, when Taipan of Jardine's, was also a member of both the Executive and Legislative Councils, as well as being on the board of Dairy Farm and the Hongkong and Shanghai Bank. From very similar social backgrounds – Herries, like the Keswicks and Swires, was an Etonian, and almost every Taipan had, as a matter of course, been to either Oxford or Cambridge – meeting at the Hong Kong Club, the Yacht Club and the Jockey Club, such men formed a closely-knit circle who could co-operate easily, both together and with the senior government officials.

The first sign that this group might be threatened came in 1980, when Li Ka-shing made a move on Hutchison-Whampoa. Hutchison's had been established in docks and shipping since the 1860s, and expanded under the vigorous leadership of Douglas Clague, 'a natural wheeler-dealer',[19] into one of the biggest of the hongs. Clague financed the Cross-Harbour Motor Tunnel, which when opened in 1972 changed the whole balance of Hong Kong life by providing road access between Central and Kowloon. But the 'random and opportunistic'[20] expansion proved too rapid to sustain, and the Hongkong and Shanghai Bank was forced to arrange a reconstruction of the company, which included a merger with the Whampoa Dock Co. (the Hong Kong and Whampoa Dock Company was a merger of Lamont's Aberdeen dock and Cowper's of Whampoa, a survivor of the original Canton trade), an even more venerable institution. As part of the reorganization the Bank had taken a large shareholding, and on completion offered their stake, on advantageous terms, to Li, one of their rising customers. 'Hutchison was sold far too cheaply. It was a steal,' its former Chief Executive W.R.A Wyllie complained, but the Bank wanted to see a 'long term and constructive holder'.[21] With Li, this was exactly what they got. Hutchison's was restructured under the effective command of Simon Murray, previously with Jardine's. It is very much a sign of the times that this company, now the largest on the Hong Kong Stock Exchange, is run by a combination of Chinese enterprise and owner-ship, working together with a formal and responsive management struc-ture. Li's holdings are now widely spread, with powerful Hong Kong property interests, a controlling minority of the Hong Kong Electric Company and extensive Canadian investments, capable of producing annual profits of US$1,000 million. Although the most successful and powerful capitalist in Hong Kong, Li has maintained close and ami-cable relationships with the Chinese authorities; he is generous to mainland Chinese universities to a degree that would make impover-ished Oxford and Cambridge senates lick their corporate lips – his donations totalled some $94 million by 1990.

Another pillar of the British establishment, Wheelock Marden, fell to Sir Yue-kong Pao in 1985. As part of the transaction 'Sir Y.K.', as he was generally known, inherited part of Hong Kong's imperial past, the Lane Crawford department store, more ancient than Harrods, founded by one Mr Lane, formerly a butler in the East India Company factory at Canton, who migrated to Hong Kong in the 1840s to found the business with Mr Norman Crawford. Marden's was a much more recent arrival, founded in 1946 by George Marden, 'one of the toughest characters on the China coast', previously an employee of the Chinese Maritime Customs.

Even the greatest of the Hongs seemed in danger after control of the Hong Kong and Kowloon Wharf and Godown Co. was seized unexpectedly by Sir Y.K. in 1979. The Wharf Company had been founded by William Keswick in 1889, with a constitution designed to secure permanent board control to Jardine's, and carried with it a highly visible part of Hong Kong's history, in the shape of the Star Ferry and tramway systems. That it should be taken by a newcomer, and a Chinese newcomer at that, was bad enough, but Jardine's found it particularly injuring that Pao's coup had been backed by the Hongkong and Shanghai Bank, their ancient ally. When the following year it became clear that substantial inroads into both Jardine's and their quoted associate Hong Kong Land had also been made by Li Ka-shing, bringing Li's holding to nearly as much as that of the Keswick family, decisive action seemed necessary. A truce was arranged, shares were repurchased and an ingeniously defensive corporate structure devised which made it difficult for an unwelcome bid to succeed.

As a reinforcement of their defensive strategy Jardine's attempted a diversification of their interests from Hong Kong. The most important was intended to be the acquisition of a minority stake in the New York investment firm Bear Stearns: this was an odd decision for such an exclusively Anglo-Scottish firm as Jardine's, since Bear Sterns was not one of the traditional East Coast 'Wasp' investment houses (although it had the magnificent address of 'One Wall Street'), its partners being almost all Jewish or Irish. Unhappily the project proved a major miscalculation and shareholders received a nasty shock. In 1989, after it had proved necessary to cancel the deal, they were informed that HK$50 million would be needed to terminate the transaction. The following year they learned that the sum had risen to US$57 million – or about eightfold, a significant loss even to a firm of the size of Jardine's. As happens at such times a rapid turnaround of managing directors, and even chairmen, ensued. The Taipan, David Newbigging, was succeeded by Brian Powers (an American, which tells one something about Jardine's anxieties to branch out into new territories), who lasted for less than six months. Henry Keswick, earlier replaced by his brother Simon as Chairman, resumed that office and things settled down.

In spite of these attempts at diversification, the bulk of Jardine's assets remained in Hong Kong – 66 per cent of shareholders' funds and 58 per cent of profits after tax in 1990. These figures are smudged by the fact that much of the Hong Kong assets is in property, and is therefore subject to adjustment as the swings of the property market affect valuations. The Hong Kong results also include the very modest investments in China, Jardine's having remained wary of too close an involvement with the People's Republic (run by a Marxist-Leninist thuggish government, according to Henry Keswick[22]), and taken the view that Japan, Korea, Singapore, Taiwan and even Indonesia offer better prospects. To date these policies have been proved successful; after four nervous years of uncovered dividends between 1982 and 1985 profits have risen steadily, helped by asset sales and releases from reserves.

Although Jardine's management was anxious to play down the change, insisting that their presence in Hong Kong would continue to be of the greatest importance (their shares and those of their associated companies represented some 12 per cent of the total value of securities quoted on the Hong Kong Stock Exchange), the decision to move the registered office to Bermuda, taken in 1984, was only the beginning of a corporate disengagement: in the 1990 Report and Accounts, for the first time, the head office of Jardine Matheson ceased to be shown as being in Hong Kong. No reference to this change was made in the Chairman's report, the address of the head office simply being omitted from the front page, and the auditors shown not as the Hong Kong branch of Price Waterhouse, but the London office of that firm; similarly, the company registry was moved from Hong Kong to Bermuda. The Chairman, Henry Keswick, explained only that: 'Your Board has concluded that it is not in the Company's or its Shareholders' interests that its principal regulatory centre should remain in Hong Kong when constitutional change is impending and when it is vital to maintain the confidence of trading partners and others on whom the Company's success depends.' This would result in 'the Company's quotation on the London Stock Exchange becoming its primary listing for regulatory purposes'. The Managing Director, Nigel Rich, was perhaps more forthright when he wrote that 'freedom from politically influenced regulation' was 'the crux of the matter'.

Such concern about the commercial future of Hong Kong has not been shown by the other remaining great British Hong, John Swire and Sons. Well protected by restricted voting shares, Swire's had no reason to fear a contested bid even if their trading record had been less successful that it has proved. As one of Jardine Matheson's earliest

The mounts of the Fanling hunt would have met with a cool reception in the Shires.

LEFT: A dejected group of Japanese officers about to surrender to the Royal Navy in August 1945.

BELOW: Survivors of the Stanley camp, August 1945.

ABOVE: Communist – 'Leftist', as they were generally known – workers under arrest during the disturbances of 1967.

RIGHT: Bamboo scaffolding is used for high-rise building. This intricate network has the Mandarin Hotel as a background.

ABOVE: Imperial Hong Kong remained intact in 1950. The magnificently four-square Hongkong and Shanghai Bank building forms a backcloth to the Law Courts, the Hong Kong Club and the cricket ground. Sir Alexander Grantham still had an uninterrupted view of the harbour from the first floor of the 'Japanned' Government House.

BELOW: Forty years later, only one of the buildings in the previous photograph can still be seen. The Law Courts, now the Legislative Council, are now several hundred yards from the sea-front. Behind them the new Hongkong Bank building is easily topped by its neighbour, the Bank of China. Between them part of the gardens around the cathedral is visible. On the right the Mandarin Hotel is on the 1950 waterfront. The City Hall, nearer the centre, is on reclaimed land.

ABOVE: 1970, and the Hilton Hotel is bigger than the Hongkong Bank. The Mandarin Hotel and City Hall are seen left centre. The extent of the reclamation, seawards of Connaught Road, can clearly be seen. Queen's Road, the original main thoroughfare, runs in front of the Bank building.

BELOW: Only twenty years later, the same view is almost unrecognizable. The cylindrical Hopewell block dominates Wanchai, and the bare foreshore in the centre distance has been replaced by the new town of Tseung Kwan O. The dark spire is the Bank of China building, and to the left Government House is now entirely hemmed in.

competitors in the China trade, Swire's had always shown a positive attitude towards China, exemplified by their actions in 1926. When Sir Cecil Clementi developed his plan for provoking the Canton pickets in order to enable the Royal Navy to stage an intervention, Jardine's, with some reluctance, agreed to co-operate, but Swire's declined, expressing themselves 'unwilling to take the risk of any action in Canton that might reflect to prejudice its interests at other ports in China'.[23] In the years after the Second World War John Kidston Swire, the grandson of the founder and then Chairman, took the considerable risk of backing the embryonic airline that developed into Cathay Pacific, one of the larger, and certainly one of the best, international airlines.

One Hong Kong institution that has shown little indication of losing its nerve, in spite of some worrying moments, is the Hongkong and Shanghai Banking Corporation. London bankers were apt to regard 'Honkers and Shaggers' with patrician scorn as a stolid bank, staffed by irreproachably honest and industrious Scots, but unsophisticated and inept in the world of international finance. Those who did so have had to eat their words. As the nearest thing Hong Kong has to a central bank, 'the Bank' has had to assume much of the responsibility taken in Britain by the Bank of England in corporate rescues and restructurings, and acts as clearing bank and a lender of last resort. These activities have assisted the management to develop skills in crisis control and clearing-up operations, skills which proved useful after the takeover of Marine Midland Bank of New York. This Buffalo-based bank had undertaken a rash expansion in the 1970s which brought it to the edge of collapse. The Hongkong and Shanghai Bank's initial 51 per cent stake, taken in 1980, had later to be increased to full ownership, as further bad debts were accumulated. The unravelling of these, and of a disappointing venture in Australia, proved a costly exercise for the Bank, but have been brought under control, Marine Midland's losses being reduced to under US$200 million and those of the Hongkong Bank of Australia to the equivalent of under US$30 million. The management experience thus gained will come in useful in sorting out the Bank's latest acquisition, that of the Midland Bank in Britain.

This undertaking represents a massive diversification from Hong Kong. The Midland is a British clearing bank, one of the 'Big Four' with branches in every High Street in the country – 1,600 of them, staffed by fifty-seven thousand employees serving four million customers. The Hongkong Bank had previously dipped its toes in London waters by the purchase of Anthony Gibbs, a venerable but dull merchant bank, and James Capel, a noted firm of stockbrokers, but the purchase of the Midland Bank is a much more significant investment, and one which will test the management skills of the Hongkong Bank executives. Until recently considerably bigger than the Hongkong Bank – in 1972 its assets were three times as large – the Midland has since declined sadly. Extravagant loans and investments were made both in developing countries and in the United States with the monstrously ill-judged purchase of the Crocker National Bank. Attempting to recover from these misfortunes, Midland changed to a policy of making domestic loans, which only compounded previous errors by creating exposures on a declining property market. Combined with the losses caused by the succession of business failures that characterized the British economy in the 1980s, a takeover became inevitable.

Although the prize was disputed with another British clearing bank, Lloyds, the Hongkong Bank had established a lead by the purchase, four years previously and at a generous price in the circumstances, of just under 15 per cent of Midland's equity, and set in motion a limited rationalization of the two banks' businesses. It is a tribute to the Hongkong Bank's reputation that a feeling of relief was noticeable in the City of London when the full takeover was announced; Midland would be, it was reasonably assumed, in safer hands.

Inevitably, so very large a diversification will drastically change the nature of the Hongkong Bank's business. Before the takeover the Bank held £53,390 million in Asia and the Middle East, and only £20,200 million in America. These figures rose only slightly after the Midland was absorbed, but the assets in Europe shot up from £15,610 million to £71,927 million.[24]

From being predominantly an Asian, and supremely a Hong Kong bank, the new Hongkong and Shanghai Bank Holdings will initially have perhaps only one-third of its assets in Hong Kong. Even if there is no intention to decrease the Bank's Hong Kong activities, this will have profound effects. Even before the acquisition the Bank had reorganized itself under a new holding company, HSBC Holdings plc., incorporated in England and quoted on the London Stock Exchange. The intention now is that the new bank will be 'a UK-based international banking group with major banking franchises in Europe, Asia and North America'. As a British bank, more stringent reporting requirements would be enforced, which might reduce the Bank's activities in corporate affairs – a straw in the wind has been the reduction of the Bank's holding in Cathay Pacific as part of a policy of 'slowly reducing non-financial investments'. But the colony will benefit from having a major international bank with weighty financial power, if not resident, then as very substantial presence.

All these developments, constitutional, social and financial, begun in the seventies and continuing into the nineties, succeeded in moving Hong Kong a considerable way from being a colonially administered society to an independent city-state, developing its own policies and something resembling a genuinely national identity.

17

RECESSIONAL

'Now, when you say that, you don't have to go into, to say, well now, precisely what is the nature of this link and the nature of the law and so on.' Margaret Thatcher, BBC World Service interview, 1 November 1983

When politicians, especially those rarely stumped for an answer, are reduced to incoherence, it may be assumed that they are deeply embarrassed. Mrs Thatcher, when invited to say whether she hoped to keep a British presence in Hong Kong after 1997, found herself in such a situation.

Secrecy still clouds the events of 1972, when the future of Hong Kong was defined between Britain and China. Suggestions have been made that if no approach to China had subsequently been initiated the whole question might have been allowed to remain unasked, with nothing being done to disturb the existing order. Hong Kong, it was said, was too valuable to China for her to risk an upheaval there. William Rodgers, then Labour Minister of Defence, spoke of an 'unarticulated understanding . . . that the status quo should remain'. Some optimists thought that an extension of the New Territories lease might be negotiated, subject to a recognition of Chinese sovereignty over the whole territory; after all, something similar was being allowed in Macao. Dr Peter Wesley-Smith, an authority on Hong Kong's Constitution, pointed out how this might be elegantly achieved simply by accepting China's contention that the previous treaties were invalid, in which case the lease otherwise due to expire in 1997 did not legally exist.[1]

But Hong Kong bankers – both domestic and American – were concerned about the security of mortgages on what were leases now of less than twenty years' duration, granted under the head Crown lease of the New Territories negotiated in 1898 and due to expire in 1997. At their request a meeting with the Governor was convened, as a result of which it was decided that the Chinese government should be approached on the matter. Some experienced men in the civil service argued that, since opening the subject indicated concern – a poor negotiating tactic according to well-understood Chinese tradition – it would have been wiser to wait for Beijing to make the first move. This opinion is supported by Dr T.L. Tsim in his introduction to 'The Other Hong Kong Report 1989':

> If Britain did not raise the question of the ninety-nine-year lease with China, so far as Beijing was concerned, it would have been all right to carry on as if nothing would happen. If foreign banks were apprehensive about granting fifteen-year mortgages to property developments in the New Territories after 1982, the Bank of China could take the lead in offering mortgage loans to properties north of Boundary Street and that would be that. The Chinese leaders have the ability to live with a problem without trying to seek a solution before conditions are ripe . . .
>
> As late as April 1981, in response to constant and persistent probing by the British and Hong Kong Governments, the Chinese line on Hong Kong had been something like this. 'You think there is a problem. We don't think there is a problem. If you still think there is a problem, it is your problem.' The Chinese leaders refused to be drawn and complained, in private, about British officials 'trying to force their hand'.[2]

Sir Murray Maclehose, however, had been invited to Beijing at the end of 1978 – and by the Foreign Trade Minister, which in view of Britain's continuous struggle to increase the still unsatisfactory sales to China was an opportunity not to be missed. The ensuing talks, in March and April 1979, 'opened a Pandora's box of misunderstanding, forced hands and allegations of bad faith', but did, after much travail, lead to an agreement on the future of Hong Kong. Sir Murray was affably received; this was in itself, as the first visit from a Governor of Hong Kong while still in post, an historic occasion, and was made during a year of great importance in the development of China's international relations. On 1 January 1979 full diplomatic relations were established between the United States and the People's Republic. This entailed renunciation of the American defence agreement with Taiwan and the termination of diplomatic relations between Washington and Taipei; the United States formally recognized 'the Government of the People's Republic of China as the sole legal government of China'. By that time Taiwan could manage quite satisfactorily without American patronage. Chiang Kai-shek's son, Chiang Ching-kuo, who had succeeded in 1975, had begun to convert Taiwan into a more reputable democracy, as well as an economic success, enjoying a growth rate of 20 per cent per annum: but a residual feeling of responsibility for helping Taiwan in the future remained a powerful force in American policy.

For his part Deng Xiaoping had disposed of those last relics of the Cultural Revolution, the 'Gang of Four', including Mao's widow, and was able to initiate more reasonable economic policies. Among these was the establishment of Special Economic Zones, in emulation of a Taiwanese original. These were in the maritime provinces of Guangdong and Fujien – two in the old treaty ports of Swatow and Amoy, and one each just outside Macao and Hong Kong; the most important of these, Shenzhen, is immediately over the border from the New Territories and has developed into the provincial powerhouse, exporting goods to a value of some US$500 million annually. The intention was that the Special Economic Zones, as had the more successful of the treaty ports, would develop as centres of foreign investment.

In these circumstances the Chinese leaders did not wish to damage their prospects by upsetting investors or by interrupting Hong Kong's valuable contribution to China's improving prosperity. They preferred instead to shelve the issue of Hong Kong's future. Mao's successor as Chairman, Hua Guofeng, announced that 'A reasonable solution can be found through consultations.' When the suggestion was floated by Sir Murray that something should be done to remedy the concern being manifested about the shortening terms of leases, 1997 being only eighteen years away, Deng advised the Governor to assure investors that they could 'put their hearts at ease', but privately made it clear that China intended to resume sovereignty at the expiry of the lease. Given the unmistakable signals sent out in 1972 that China did not recognize the validity of the British claims, reinforced by Mr Heath two years later, and formalized in the Sino–American declarations, it is surprising that this intention was ever in doubt; but there was optimism that the resumption of sovereignty might not necessarily involve the end of British administration.[3]

It was sometimes suggested – but rarely seriously – that Britain might simply refuse to budge, resting her case to have absolute sovereignty over Hong Kong Island and Kowloon town, and demanding a re-negotiation of the lease. Some right-wingers even advocated building a 'Berlin Wall' along the line of Boundary Street, separating British Kowloon from the New Territories. The impossibility of doing this was evident, and only slightly less clear was the impracticability of retaining the New Territories in the face of Chinese opposition – the water problem being only one of the more obvious difficulties. Outright defiance, however, might just have been possible. International law would probably have conceded Britain's sovereignty over the island and Kowloon, and internationalist sentiment might well have agreed to a 'grant of independence' by Britain to Hong Kong. It would not have been easy for China to have defied both international law and goodwill, and forcibly to have resisted; and had the Chinese authorities, at the time of the negotiations, shown the brutality they demonstrated in June 1989 at Tiananmen Square, the outcry at any Chinese intervention would have been immense.

But in 1982 such a policy was too risky. The USSR was still a world power, embroiled in Afghanistan and hanging on with increasing difficulty to its European satellites. Although Sino–Soviet relations were strained (they began to improve only in 1985), Russia would have vetoed any United Nations move to secure the independence of Hong Kong against the determined opposition of China. Had the USA been involved, something might have been done, but at that time, with President Reagan in the White House, US rhetoric was much more concerned with Iran, Nicaragua, Vietnam and the USSR; military and civilian sales to China were improving, and human rights within that country were not the subject of anxiety that they later became.

And, at bottom, Britain was not prepared to fight it out. The days when Hong Kong had been an asset, either strategically or commercially, had long passed. Independence for Hong Kong would doubtless be desirable, but trade and good relations with the largest country in the world were very much more so.

This inglorious but realistic attitude was appreciated by prudent businessmen in Hong Kong, who were growing more concerned with the passage of time. A nervous Simon Keswick attempted to win support from the liberals: 'We must *all* work to stop Communists from taking this place . . . At all costs.'[4]

Towards the end of 1982, with Rhodesian independence settled and the Argentinians ejected from the Falkland Islands, the Conservative government headed by Margaret Thatcher was ready to begin discussions. Cynics – and it is difficult not to be at least sceptical about the purity of British motives – noted that one essential preliminary to disposing of the Hong Kong problem had been hastened out of the way. The British Nationality Act of 1981 allowed a loophole in the definition of 'patrialism' (the test by which the right of abode in Britain was granted) in order to favour Falkland Islanders and Gibraltarians, but at the same time excluded those Hong Kongers who, as British subjects, had constitutionally been in exactly the same category. Should negotiations with China fail and conditions in Hong Kong become intolerable, at least Britain would not be plagued by some 3.3 million Chinese demanding to live there.

The start of formal discussions was marked in September 1982 by a visit from the Prime Minister to Beijing. It was not a success. The opening British position which Mrs Thatcher, fresh from her triumph over Argentina's General Galtieri, advanced with some energy was based on an assertion of British rights under the existing treaties, the validity of which, China had made abundantly clear for many years, was not accepted by them. Felix Patrikeeff reported that Mrs Thatcher 'apparently behaved with extraordinary naivety: during her audience with Deng Xiaoping she referred to the importance of the nineteenth-century treaties governing Hong Kong, treaties which had been weighted heavily in Britain's favour. When her words were translated for Deng his response was said to be so violent and filled with expletives that the interpreter could not translate it for her.' The conservative *Daily Telegraph* quoted Deng as muttering to an aide: 'I can't talk to that woman, she is utterly unreasonable.' A mystery surrounds this visit, since at a press conference held in December 1984 Mrs Thatcher claimed that she did not know 'the content of any talks which Lord Maclehose may have had' during his 1979 visit to Beijing.[5] Such a statement does not ring true: Sir Percy Cradock, the Ambassador at Beijing, had been present at the talks between Murray Maclehose and Deng in 1979 and those in 1982 with Mrs Thatcher. It is hardly conceivable that the Prime Minister was left in ignorance of what had passed at the previous meeting.

After Beijing, the Prime Minister called at Hong Kong. Her stay was reported by David Bonavia of *The Times*: 'Mrs Thatcher left the next day, somewhat like one of those typhoons which run in from the Western Pacific, leaving a trail of destruction behind them. Seldom in British Colonial history was so much damage done to the interests of so many people in such a short space of time by a single person.' Felix Patrikeeff suggests that the Prime Minister's 'hatred' of Hong Kong's 'second-class' businessmen was manifested, but it is doubtful whether, apart from making the task of the British negotiators more difficult, Mrs Thatcher's intervention had any disastrous long-term effects. The fact is that China was determined, and that Britain had few cards to play.

Militarily, Britain could do nothing to resist a Chinese move; the success of the Falklands expedition had been a very near thing indeed – and China was not Argentina, nor Hong Kong any longer a barren island. China had absolute certainty of the rights of her own case, which had effectually been acknowledged by the United Nations in removing Hong Kong from the list of colonies. Even in Hong Kong itself, although the great majority of the population would prefer that things continued under the British administration they had become accustomed to (85 per cent according to one survey made in 1982, as against only 4 per cent who wanted a return to China[6]), there was a highly vocal minority, particularly among students, who were emotionally critical of the 'unequal treaties' and had a strong sense of Chinese nationalism.

One key factor that did materially assist the British negotiators was the backing of the United States. Post-war British governments accepted that a foreign policy independent of America was, if not impossible, at least extremely difficult. Churchill had put his finger on it on 5 July 1954:

> Speaking very earnestly, he implored [Anthony Eden] not to quarrel with America, whether China was or was not a member of the United Nations . . . 'Up to July 1944 England had a considerable say in things; after that I was conscious that it was America who made the big decisions. She will make the big decisions now.'
> Winston said this with an air of finality.
> 'We do not yet realize her immeasurable power.'[7]

Anglo–American relations at the time of the talks with China were particularly good, assisted by the personal friendship that had developed between President Reagan and Mrs Thatcher. It was American support that had enabled the Falklands expedition to proceed unhampered by the United Nations, in the face of considerable opposition – a support that was later repaid by British acquiescence in the American invasion of a Commonwealth country, Grenada. There were sound reasons for the United States to want a peaceful handover in Hong Kong. Not only was China an essential ally in what was still at the time viewed as a life-and-death struggle against the 'evil empire' of Soviet Russia, but there was no prospect of Taiwan reaching an accommodation with China if this could not first be satisfactorily arranged with Hong Kong. This need to keep on the right side of the Chinese led to such perversions of foreign policy as the support, both British and American, for the despicable Pol Pot regime in Cambodia; it was enough that Pol Pot was opposed by Vietnam, the current American villain, and Vietnam was at odds with China (odds that had led to a border campaign in which the deficiencies of the People's Liberation Army were pitilessly exposed). More practically, American investment in Hong Kong, amounting to hundreds of millions of dollars, was worth safeguarding.

But nothing much could be done in the aftermath of Mrs Thatcher's démarche in Beijing, and the talks that began in the autumn of 1982 stalled over the British reluctance to admit the restoration of Chinese sovereignty. At bottom, this may have been due to a barrier in communications between the Prime Minister and the Foreign Office. It is difficult to believe that the Foreign Office was not aware of the Chinese feelings on the subject of 'unequal treaties'. This had been demonstrated in a practical fashion in 1975 when those treaties had been quietly dropped from the official British register of international agreements, a move not followed by the French, who continued to regard their agreements, reached at the same time, as continuing in force. The orthodox way of proceeding according to the best Chinese usages would have been for the British gracefully to acknowledge the treaties' non-existence and start with a clean sheet. The urgency of 1997 would have disappeared, face been restored all round, and an arrangement which might even have included the continuity of British administration been worked out. But Mrs Thatcher was not on easy terms with either the Foreign Office or with Mr Heath, who was equally well briefed on the Chinese viewpoint, and who could have offered valuable guidance. The Foreign Office had let her down over the Falklands, the Foreign Secretary Lord Carrington having resigned on the issue, and

Mr Heath had not hidden his dislike of his successor – a feeling which she heartily reciprocated. Mrs Thatcher had been trained as a lawyer, and chose to stick to the letter of the law.

There were political as well as personal reasons for this initial intransigence. After the Prime Minister's Falklands triumph the opportunity for a general election beckoned, and until that was safely out of the way it would be imprudent to show any signs of yielding on Hong Kong. The parallels between the two cases made comparisons uncomfortable; there was the question of allowing British subjects to pass under the rule of an unacceptable regime, and the even more embarrassing one of the Nationality Act. Although it had been apparent in December 1972 that the Chinese simply were not going to accept any continuation of British sovereignty, over any portion of the colony, it was not until the June 1983 election was safely won that negotiations were resumed (or, in fact, really started). These were confided by the British to a team led by the Ambassador to China, initially Sir Percy Cradock, later Sir Richard Evans, together with the new Governor of Hong Kong, Sir Edward Youde, who had replaced Maclehose just before the 1982 meeting in Beijing. Like Maclehose, Youde had a Foreign Office, rather than a Colonial Office background. He was an excellent choice, having begun his service in Nanking and Peking immediately after the war when he had been responsible for negotiating with the People's Liberation Army over the release of HMS *Amethyst*. Subsequently Sir Edward spent much time in China, culminating in the Ambassadorship between 1974 and 1978. While in London he had put in some time as Private Secretary to the Prime Minister, and was therefore both experienced in Chinese affairs and well-known in Downing Street. He was a dedicated and much-admired man, whose tireless activity contributed to his early death in 1986.

Between them the team, under the guidance of the Foreign Secretary, the long-suffering and patient Sir Geoffrey Howe, spent more than a year attempting to negotiate a settlement for the future of Hong Kong. They did not have an easy time of it, starting off as they had on the wrong foot: as one of them admitted, the Chinese were able to 'hammer the shit' out of them.[8] When presenting the eventual agreement to the House of Commons on 5 December 1984, Sir Geoffrey Howe was only able to explain the year's delay by saying: 'The people of Hong Kong certainly expected that we would, as a first step, see if [the retention of sovereignty] was possible.'

The negotiations that took place were only between Britain and

China, Hong Kong not being represented. (When Sir Edward Youde suggested that he, as Governor, represented the people of Hong Kong, he was sternly contradicted by the Chinese; the people of Hong Kong were Chinese, and their interests were the concern of China. Sir Edward was only present as part of the British delegation.) Apart from secret briefings of the Executive Council there was no consultation with the people of Hong Kong, and reports of progress were vague and unspecific. When Fenner Brockway, the veteran left-winger and opponent of privilege, later Lord Brockway, asked in the House of Lords on 14 November 1983 if 'anything might be done to relieve the frustration among the people in Hong Kong – 98 per cent Chinese – because the talks are conducted by a non-elected governor of a non-elected Legislative Council?', he was answered by Lord Trefgarne, the Minister responsible for Hong Kong: 'Those who are representing the United Kingdom are taking very fully into account the views of the people of Hong Kong.' Lord Trefgarne would not, of course, have been able to explain quite how these views had been conveyed to the negotiators, in the absence of any communication between them and the people. (It is worth recording, as typical of the slight importance accorded to Hong Kong by the British government, that Lord Trefgarne's previous government experience had been four years as a Whip, followed by a few months as Parliamentary Under-Secretary at the Department of Trade: he spent a similarly short time at the Foreign and Commonwealth Office before pressing on to the Department of Health and Social Services.) The resultant confusion and uncertainty in Hong Kong led to a rapid erosion of confidence, a financial crisis, and pressure on the Hong Kong dollar, so that when the news was broken (by the *Sunday Times* on 22 January 1984, but by Sir Geoffrey Howe only four months later) that in 1997 Britain would turn over Hong Kong to China, absolutely, both as to sovereignty and administration, a certain amount of relief that the worst was known tempered the anxiety felt for an unknown future.

Under great pressure from the Chinese, and with the dedicated personal support of Sir Geoffrey, who concluded 'most of the major issues' during a visit to Beijing in July, a final agreement emerged in September 1984. The Sino–British Joint Declaration on the Future of Hong Kong was presented as a *fait accompli*; there was 'no possibility of an amended agreement. The alternative to acceptance of the present agreement is to have no agreement . . . This is a choice . . . imposed by the facts of Hong Kong's history.'

The Joint Declaration of the British and Chinese Governments initialled on 26 September 1984 is a remarkable document.[9] Lord Maclehose, as the former Governor had become on his retirement, believed: 'For a Communist government to commit itself to maintaining this capitalist enclave may seem to sound so bizarre as to be incredible.'[10] It was certainly the result of much patient negotiation, which reflected great credit on all those concerned. Nothing quite like it had ever been done before; an agreement to transfer a territory with a population greater than that of Norway, Israel or Ireland, not as the result of war, and without the people concerned having any direct say in the matter; an agreement in which China undertook to retain laws, customs and a social system quite alien to her own, and to allow freedoms denied to her own people to those living in Hong Kong.

On sovereignty, the Chinese view unequivocally prevailed:

> The Government of the People's Republic of China declares that to recover the Hong Kong area (including Hong Kong Island, Kowloon and the New Territories, hereinafter referred to as Hong Kong) is the common aspiration of the entire Chinese people, and that it has decided to resume the exercise of sovereignty over Hong Kong with effect from 1 July 1997.

The phrase 'decided to resume the exercise of sovereignty' indicates a clear and firm one-sided decision by China, rather than a mutual agreement. The possibility of any British involvement in administration after sovereignty had been transferred was not mentioned. After 1997, what went on in Hong Kong would be an internal Chinese affair, and no concern of Britain's. A polite gloss had to be put on it from the British side:

> The Government of the United Kingdom declares that it will restore Hong Kong to the People's Republic of China with effect from 1 July 1997.

With the sovereignty question disposed of, a century and a half of events viewed by China as humiliations were brought to a close with some elegance. The Chinese authorities could afford – indeed, face demanded it – to be generous and accommodating. Annex 1, in which the Chinese undertakings were detailed, included pledges to maintain all existing Hong Kong laws, the judicial system, the capitalist

economic and trade systems, and educational policies; the Hong Kong
Special Administrative Region (HKSAR), as it was to be known, would
have its own form of government, with the existing institutions, including a Governor, and a 'high degree of autonomy'. It was to be allowed
to levy its own taxes, all of which were to be retained, to decide its
own monetary and financial policies, and to continue issuing its own
convertible currency. Any People's Liberation Army units stationed in
Hong Kong would not interfere in the internal affairs of the HKSAR;
Hong Kong would be free to participate in international organizations
and trade agreements, and to establish official missions abroad; it
would even have its own flag. Individual rights were detailed:

> The Hong Kong Special Administrative Region Government shall
> maintain the rights and freedoms as provided for by the laws
> previously in force in Hong Kong, including freedom of the
> person, of speech, of the press, of assembly, of association, to
> form and join trade unions, of correspondence, of travel, of move-
> ment, of strike, of demonstration, of choice of occupation, of
> academic research, of belief, inviolability of the home, the freedom
> to marry and the right to raise a family freely . . .
>
> Every person shall have the right to confidential legal advice,
> access to the courts, representation in the courts by lawyers of
> his choice, and to obtain judicial remedies. Every person shall
> have the right to challenge the actions of the executive in the
> courts . . .
>
> Religious organizations and believers may maintain their
> relations with religious organizations and believers elsewhere, and
> schools, hospitals, and welfare institutions run by religious organ-
> izations may be continued.

On the face of it this was a remarkable list of concessions, which would
result in Hong Kong remaining a much pleasanter place than any other
part of China. What had been done was, for all practical purposes, to
create of Hong Kong a treaty port, much after the pattern of those
established by the Treaty of Nanking. Like, say, Shanghai then, Hong
Kong would be an enclave in China controlled by its own inhabitants,
not subject to Chinese law but obeying its own regulations enforced
by its own judicial system – something very closely resembling that
extra-territoriality so fiercely denounced by previous Chinese governments! Independent in many ways, the HKSAR had privileges

unknown in the old treaty ports – no taxes paid to China and an elected legislature.

The Joint Declaration was subject, especially in Hong Kong, to the minutest scrutiny, and many possible weaknesses were indeed exposed. A common suspicion was that pledges were indiscriminately loaded into the Declaration, without any intention on the Chinese government's behalf of keeping them. It was also noted that preparation of the 'Basic Law', which was to be the HKSAR's constitution, would be the responsibility of the National People's Congress, albeit with Hong Kong representation on the drafting committee. Whatever reservations might be expressed, however, the Joint Declaration remained a hopeful achievement, and the only agreement on offer.

The draft agreement was duly submitted to such representative institutions as existed in Hong Kong. There being no question of a referendum, and no democratically elected body in Hong Kong which might ratify the terms more authoritatively, the proposals were put to the Hong Kong people indirectly, through a series of polls and opinion surveys, made after a mass distribution of the explanatory White Paper. These generally indicated wide, if not enthusiastic, support: the most reliable poll, carried out in October, indicated that, out of a random sample of 6,124 people, 79 per cent of those answering agreed that sovereignty should be returned to China, and 77 per cent believed the agreement to be the best obtainable under the circumstances; but 71 per cent were only willing to credit the agreement as 'quite good'.[11] There was a considerable question over how many actually understood what was happening; in another poll, of 4,614 respondents 27 per cent admitted to not understanding the agreement. Younger people were especially insistent on the need for more democracy and for active participation by Hong Kong people in drafting the Basic Law.

An Assessment Office and Independent Monitoring Team, led by Sir Patrick Nairne, a civil servant of great experience and integrity, and Mr Justice Simon Li, reported on the result of these soundings. They concluded that 'most of the people of Hong Kong find the draft agreement acceptable', and found 'a general feeling of relief and a wish to build Hong Kong's future on the foundation provided by the draft agreement', but noted that of the one thousand or so written views received, more than two-thirds expressed dissatisfaction with the agreement. The business community had few reservations: the worrying uncertainty had been replaced by some strong assurances. Even if these were not cast-iron guarantees, businessmen do not expect certainties: 'What guarantees are there that there will be a democratic capitalist market in West Germany in 1997?' asked Sir Michael Sandberg, the Chairman of the Hongkong Bank, somewhat rhetorically.[12] Simon Keswick spoke of 'unqualified support'; but neither Sir Michael nor Mr Keswick, like other senior Hong Kong businessmen, will have to stay there if it happens not to suit them. Those who had no choice in their future were less happy, and pointed out that a due performance of the guarantees depended on the continuance of a like-minded government in Beijing; and that while, since 1949, West Germany had a steady record of elected democratic governments, China had suffered an unhappy succession of wars and coups, changes of course, the Hundred Flowers Blooming, the Cultural Revolution, and had only recently, under Deng Xiaoping, settled into what seemed to be a reasonably stable economic policy. But what would happen after Deng was still very much an open question.

Indications of future trouble could therefore understandably be discerned. One member of both the Executive and Legislative Councils, Mr T.S. Lo, resigned, and two Legislative Councillors abstained from voting on the acceptability of the draft agreement – one, Mr J.J. Swaine, on the grounds that British policies on immigration had shut out from Britain those Hong Kong people who had regarded themselves as British subjects. They now found their future was being arranged for them by Britain, in negotiations in which they had no say, and the results of which they had perforce to accept. This question of moral responsibility was given an 'offhand dismissal' by Mrs Thatcher, who 'fudged ... bullied ... and blustered'[13] when she called briefly at Hong Kong after signing the agreement in Beijing.

For their part, the British negotiators had agreed to some clauses in the Joint Declaration which were likely to present difficulties:

1. To allow China the final voice in determining the Basic Law of the new Hong Kong, albeit in accordance with the principles established in the Joint Declaration. Some Hong Kong citizens were to be asked to contribute their thoughts, and reflections that 'democracy' and 'representative institutions' might imply very different things in Beijing and London were suppressed.

2. To form a Joint Liaison Group with China 'to ensure a smooth transfer of government in 1997'. The group, which was to continue in being until 2000, was consultative only and 'would play no part in the administration of Hong Kong or the HKSAR.

Nor shall it have any supervisory role over the administration.'
Mrs Thatcher, in the course of her unfortunate visit to Hong
Kong, had declared that the Governor, Sir Edward Youde, would
be a member of this group. This was never the intention, and
indeed never happened, but once more indicated how the Prime
Minister was either fudging issues or paying very little attention
to what was being decided about Hong Kong.[14]

3. Although this was not part of the Joint Declaration, to consult, in some unspecified fashion, the people of Hong Kong.

*'Democracy substitutes election by the incompetent many
for appointment by the corrupt few.' George Bernard Shaw*

Such consultation was rendered difficult by the absence of directly
elected representative bodies. One interesting undertaking in the Joint
Declaration was that 'the legislature of HKSAR shall be constituted
by elections. The executive authority shall abide by the law and shall
be accountable to the legislature.' There are, of course, elections and
elections, and those current in the People's Republic of China were
not identical with those in Western countries. Under British rule in
Hong Kong, there had been no elections to the legislature at all, and
it was felt that some progress towards establishing a Western-style
representative government ought to be ventured, however unwelcome
this might be to China. As a first step the Hong Kong Green Paper
of July 1984 recorded the government's intention 'to develop progressively . . . a system of government . . . which is able to represent authoritatively the people of Hong Kong, and which is more directly
accountable to the people of Hong Kong'.

The Green Paper proposed that twelve of the fifty-seven Legislative
Council seats be open to election; this was amended by Parliament to
twenty-four. Elections were not to be directly democratic, as is usual
in Western societies, but by a system described by Dr Miners as 'hid-
eously complicated',[15] with twelve functional constituencies representing business and the professions, including two seats for 'labour',
together with an electoral college comprising members of the Urban
and Regional Councils and geographic constituencies based on the
District Boards. The principle of functional constituencies is a classic

oligarchic device to ensure that acceptably 'responsible' people get elected.

Functional seats were allocated to bodies representing the professions and corporate bodies – businesses, banks, trades unions and social service organizations. So closely knit were many of these 'constituencies' that no election was needed, since candidates were often unopposed – in the first election, in October 1985, five of the twelve representatives were returned without the need for a vote. Some constituencies were narrowly confined; the medical function, for example, excluded nurses. The electoral college was similarly restricted, the number of electors in each constituency varying from twenty-seven to sixty-three. Such a system enabled, in 1985, twenty-four members of the Legislative Council to be elected by a total of 25,206 voters, or rather more than half of 1 per cent of those who in a normal system might have had the franchise: hardly a great extension of democracy. Apart from the Labour Party in Britain, which retains a similar system for trades union representation, such undemocratic practices have long since ceased to have any place in British politics.

Since 1985 the mechanics of selecting members of the Legislative Council have been somewhat simplified and made more democratic. By 1992 the Council comprised only three ex-officio members, eighteen appointed members, twenty-one members elected by functional constituencies, and eighteen directly elected – in 1991 for the first time – by geographical constituencies. Each directly elected member was therefore responsible to some 225,000 constituents (or would be, if those qualified chose to register). On the other hand a functional constituency member could be elected with only 216 votes, and twelve of the functional constituency members underwent no election at all, being returned unopposed. The most understandable of these unquestioned elections was that of Mrs Elsie Tu, sent to the Legislative Council on behalf of the Urban Council which she had served so well for so long.

Few people could have thought after the first elections in 1985 that they would have to wait until 1991 for further progress. In 1984 vague statements had been made by members of the British government implying that direct elections would begin reasonably soon. There was a good deal of talk about 'the determination of the British people and their government to fulfil our moral obligations to the people in Hong Kong' (Lord Fanshawe, House of Lords, 21 May 1984).[16] Mrs Thatcher referred, while in Hong Kong on 27 September 1982, to

Britain's 'moral responsibility and duty to the people of Hong Kong'. Sir Geoffrey Howe had promised that 'during the years immediately ahead, the government of Hong Kong will be developed on increasingly democratic lines', and it was not easy to argue, in 1984, that 1991 was a year which could reasonably be regarded as 'immediately ahead'. On 5 December 1984 Sir Geoffrey's Junior Minister, Richard Luce, said in the House of Commons: 'We all fully accept that we should build up a firmly-based, democratic administration in Hong Kong in the years between now and 1997.' On 21 January the following year Mr Luce spoke of 'a progressive strengthening of representative government in the territory during the next ten years'; a progression that began only in the sixth of those years. When closely examined, all these and similar statements did not amount to a firm promise quickly to implement at least some elements of democratic practice, but they were, not unreasonably, taken as such by those who very much wanted to believe them.

The Hong Kong government had also produced, at the time of the first reform of electoral procedures in 1985, a White Paper, developing the proposals put forward the previous year and suggesting that the Hong Kong people would be consulted in 1987 over the question of direct elections. In that year there would be ten years remaining before the handover, and it was therefore reasonable to assume that some action would be forthcoming soon after the consultation, since elections in 1988 would leave only nine years for the practice of democracy to begin to take root. This proposal however had immediately been severely criticized by the Chinese government as contrary to the Joint Declaration. Beijing felt that a system of government in Hong Kong which had suited London for the best part of 150 years without any change, and which contained no hint of democracy, would also suit them very well indeed. What was sauce for the goose should also be offered with the gander, and not adulterated with democratic flavours to make digestion more difficult. This severely embarrassed the Hong Kong government, but it was felt that a commitment of some sort had been made, and a Green Paper was therefore produced in May 1987 setting out proposals for discussion. Again, in the absence of credible representative institutions, these proposals had to be canvassed colony-wide, and arrangements were duly made for this to be done.

It has long been acknowledged that questions can be put in such a way as to elicit the required answer, and the suspicion is that the Hong Kong government conducted its 1987 enquiries into the question of direct elections in a similar spirit. The 1987 White Paper, possibly with intent, was a complex and confused document, which a great number of Hong Kongers found difficult to understand. Indignant denials were made that this was an attempt to fudge the issue, but suspicions were not allayed by the Managing Director of A.G.B. McNair and Co., the company engaged by the Hong Kong government to assess the reactions to their proposals. When asked her view on the effectiveness of the survey she was quoted in the House of Commons as saying that 'given a free hand to ask a wider sample more direct questions, the questions on the survey were not the ones that would have been asked'.[17]

But they were the questions that produced the answer the government wanted, which was that no widespread enthusiasm for direct elections existed, and that those who would favour them at some future date felt that 'the time was not yet ripe'. There is some evidence that the response in favour of direct elections was played down; the assessors refused to accept one petition with 230,000 authenticated signatures, and other polls showed results contrary to those found by McNairs. Dr Miners found the conclusion of the assessors 'extraordinary' in view of the fact that of a total of 368,431 written submissions or petitions, 265,078 were in favour of direct elections being held in the next year.[18]

The business community agreed among themselves, and with Beijing, in finding little virtue in constitutional change. They had almost a monopoly of representation on the Executive Council, and were secure in the Legislative Council. Even after the 1991 elections the business interest was assured of twelve out of twenty-one of the functional elected seats, and since the eighteen appointed members chosen by the government were unlikely to be radically at odds with government policy, undue pressure for democracy could be contained. Dr Helmut Sohmen, a prominent businessman who was also an appointed member of the Legislative Council, went further than most in rejecting democracy, giving the classic view of all oligarchs since Plato; elections would 'denigrate the role and the remarkable work of past and present councillors who were appointed or indirectly elected, and in the public mind will be relegated in future to second or third rank behind their directly elected colleagues'[19] – which is, after all, precisely what democracy is about. A democratically elected representative possesses a moral authority much superior to that of an appointee; but morality is a tricky business.

When the question was debated in the House of Commons on 20 January 1988 some powerful voices were raised in support of elections being held that year. The most weighty was that of Edward Heath, who urged that 'there is much greater danger of our dragging our feet than of being over-hasty', and warned that 'unless action is taken quickly now we shall be unable to hand over any form of experienced representative government'. None could speak with greater authority than the former Prime Minister, who had in 1972 taken the first critical decision to end the colonial status of Hong Kong, and who had thereafter correctly interpreted the Chinese views at times when his colleagues were badly off course. The Labour Shadow Foreign Secretary, Gerald Kaufman, agreed that direct elections should begin immediately, but the majority preferred a more gradual approach, and the decision was taken not to take a decision.

The motion was not put to a vote, but the conclusion of the debate is not without a sad relevance. Sir Geoffrey Howe was speaking:

There can be no cast-iron guarantees about the future of Hong Kong, but that is true of any country or territory. I believe that Hong Kong is well equipped to face the future and –

It being Seven o'clock and there being private business set down by direction of THE CHAIRMAN OF WAYS AND MEANS under Standing Order No. 16 [time for taking private business], further proceedings stood postponed.

Threads from the Imperial knapsack[20]

Making the best of things appeared to be the general mood in Hong Kong after 1984. The popular Governor, Sir Edward Youde, died in 1986 and was replaced by Sir David Wilson, another appointment from the Foreign Office. Sir David's background was unconventional in that after having served in Hong Kong (as a Foreign Service language student) and Beijing (as First Secretary) he resigned to prepare a Ph.D thesis at the School of Oriental and African Studies in London and afterwards to edit the *China Quarterly*. On rejoining the service he served in the Cabinet Office during Harold Wilson's premiership and as political adviser in Hong Kong to Sir Murray Maclehose. This varied and useful experience, combined with personal toughness and charm, was to be very much called upon in his difficult task.

For the first years after the publication of the Joint Declaration the economy continued to expand. Growth rates in 1986 and 1987 were high, with the economy operating at near full capacity. Hong Kong was affected, as were all other markets, by the Stock Exchange crash of October 1987, and 1988 did bring warning signs of rising inflation and slower rates of growth.

	GDP Year on Year Percentage Increase	Inflation
1986	12	
1987	14	5.5
1988	7.9	7.5
1989	2.8	10.1
1990	3.0	9.8
1991	3.9	12.0

A crop of questionable financial incidents implicating the then Chairman of the Stock Exchange (one of which, the collapse of the Carrian Group, bringing allegations of extensive fraud against the Bumiputra Bank of Malaysia, still remains to be cleared up) confirmed the continuing ability of Hong Kong to produce material for scandal. Economic co-operation with China flourished: in 1985 China became, and has since remained, Hong Kong's largest trading partner, and by 1987 Hong Kong had in turn overtaken Japan to become China's largest trading partner. By 1988 China accounted for 29 per cent of Hong Kong's overall external trade, and Hong Kong for a similar proportion of China's. Financial links developed to the extent that by the end of 1988 Hong Kong claims on Chinese banks reached $100,000 million, and Hong Kong's share of foreign investment in China was somewhere between 50 and 70 per cent. Personal contacts increased, nearly eighteen million visits to China by Hong Kong residents and tourists being made in the course of 1988.[21]

After 4 June 1989 such progress came to a sudden halt, as confidence was shattered by events in Tiananmen Square, in the centre of Beijing, when unarmed students demonstrating in favour of democratic rights were shot down by the People's Liberation Army. The pictures shown on the world's television screens horrified Hong Kong; the thought that a regime capable of slaughtering their own people in hundreds, or thousands (Beijing insists the figure was much lower, but that belief is not general), was going to be responsible for the colony's future in a few years' time was terrifying. Even most Communist institutions in Hong Kong protested against the Chinese government's action, and banners appeared even on the Bank of China building. Beijing's defiant response did nothing to help matters. Deng congratulated the army on their massacre of 'counter-revolutionaries', and asked for a moment's silence in memory of the soldiers who had died (some were, it is said, torn to pieces by the enraged populace).

Students who had previously cried 'Down with the unequal treaties! The treaties forced upon China should not be recognized!'[22] and called for reunification presumably had second thoughts, as the question was incessantly and anxiously asked whether Britain would still consent, in these circumstances, to hand over the colony. One possible strategy would indeed have been, if not to tear up, at least to shelve indefinitely the Joint Declaration. The British government could have declared it humanly impossible to cede the people of Hong Kong to a government capable of such atrocities. World opinion would have supported such a move, and China could have done little immediately to counter it. But the arguments against it were overpowering. The future of the Hong Kong would once more be thrown into the melting-pot, with resultant great uncertainty and confusion. Relations with China would be shattered, and Deng, who had held to a policy of economic liberalization, and was a predictable and reliable factor, would quite possibly be replaced by a more aggressive hard-liner. Moreover, Britain by now lacked the moral authority to take such drastic action in the name of the Hong Kong people. After painfully negotiating the Joint Declaration, and assuring its acceptance, and that of the Basic Law, only a representative Hong Kong government would be capable of taking such a stand; and such a government was far away. Nor was Britain herself irreproachable; she may have had little to be ashamed of in her governance of Hong Kong, but it was only seventeen years since the Parachute Regiment had fired on unarmed demonstrators in Londonderry, an action comparable with, if smaller in scale than, that of the People's Liberation Army in Beijing.[23] It would have been more logical for the British to have objected much earlier to the tens of thousands of executions then – and apparently still – carried out every year in China for offences which in other countries would be regarded as comparatively trivial. But if this readily defensible attitude had been adopted negotiations would never have started.

Other drastic measures were considered. The moral guarantees given earlier were recalled: did not these oblige Britain to provide a refuge if the future for Hong Kong under Chinese rule should prove intolerable? This opinion was reinforced by the Governor, who spoke of Britain's moral obligation to give Hong Kong British citizens right of entry. There were those in Britain who would have agreed, and welcomed the prospect of an influx of Hong Kong energy and enterprise into an economy tottering on the brink of protracted recession. *The Times* spoke of duty and honour, which demanded that Britain should welcome those who held British passports, even if those passports had been neutered under the 1981 Nationality Act; both Sir David Wilson and Lady Dunn, the senior member of the Executive Council, supported this. In spite of these praiseworthy sentiments, it was vain to expect much of a response: there was no prospect of a British government agreeing to extend the right of abode even to those in Hong Kong who had British citizenship – some 3.3 million from a total of 5.6 million. With unemployment in Britain having risen to a true total of at least three million, such an influx would never be acceptable at the constituency level, always distrustful of immigration. This would be true either of the Conservative government or the Labour opposition (the Liberal Democrats, secure in the knowledge that, having only a handful of seats in the House of Commons, they would never be called to decide, were more favourably inclined on the issue of passports).

Gerald Kaufman, the Labour spokesman, made this clear in the House of Commons on 5 July 1989: 'The Opposition believe that it would not be right to offer any commitment to Hong Kong British Dependent Territory passport holders on the right of entry into the United Kingdom.'

Support to those who thought differently, and believed that moral obligations should override political expediency, could not be offered by the Foreign Office. China had made it clear that any large-scale grant of the right of abode would be considered by them as a grave affront, showing a complete lack of confidence in Chinese guarantees, given in the Joint Declaration and elaborated in the Basic Law. Sir Geoffrey Howe, still Foreign Secretary, had placed much stress on the agreement which his department had negotiated, and was deeply embarrassed in April 1984 when he honourably attempted to explain these facts in Hong Kong, to be greeted by cries of 'Bullshit!' Sir Geoffrey left the Foreign Office shortly afterwards.[24]

A compromise which offered some comfort was advanced by the British government's agreement in July 1990 to issue full British passports to fifty thousand heads of families who had, it was considered, some special claim to consideration by virtue of their importance to the satisfactory running of Hong Kong. This concession followed a vigorous campaign begun in July 1989 to get British passports for as many people as possible. It was supported by pillars of the establishment including the Hongkong Bank, Jardine's, Swire's, Hutchison's, the Stock Exchange, the General Chamber of Commerce and others. Simon Keswick, the Chairman of Jardine's, complained that the Foreign Office had 'the vision of a bat', and both Keswick and Simon Murray of Hutchison's compared Howe's assurances over the agreement to Neville Chamberlain waving his piece of paper after meeting Hitler in Munich in 1938.[25] It was also said that 'encouragement' was given tangible form by large donations from some Hong Kong businessmen to the Conservative Party. While this is not admitted, the party of free enterprise being remarkably shy about disclosing the sources of its income, it is certainly true that some Hong Kong business leaders enjoyed free access to 10 Downing Street, both before and after the fall of Mrs Thatcher in November 1990, to an extent that surprised the Hong Kong Office in London. Approval for this concession was not unanimous among the Hong Kong leadership, Lady Dunn believing that it would be divisive and indefensible.

The eventual allocation of passports was seven thousand to the 'disciplined services' (police and customs), six thousand to the 'sensitive services' (senior civil servants and the media), and 36,500 to others considered to be key workers (professionals and businessmen), with five hundred reserved for important investors. Eventually, after a good deal of pressure, passports were also offered to the Portuguese and Chinese survivors of the Hong Kong Volunteers. Applications for passports were not as numerous as might have been expected; there were 65,700 applicants for the first tranche of 43,250 places. The offer did have the political bonus of putting the Labour opposition in an unhappy dilemma. While wishing to appear liberal, the leadership knew that the rank and file of the party would never allow them even to advocate the admission of so many immigrants, so they had to content themselves with opposing the limited grant of passports as 'élitist'. From the government side Norman Tebbit, former Chairman of the

Conservative Party, and noted for the bluntness of his comments, exemplified this sentiment. In an interview in January 1990, he claimed that: 'Coming to Britain in such large numbers the immigrants from Hong Kong would not integrate . . . They would maintain themselves as Hong Kong Chinese, with their own values and customs . . . There is a very nasty smouldering resentment which is concealed when life is reasonably good. But ties of blood and history and religion are far stronger than government directives.' In what amounted to an attack on his former Cabinet colleagues, Mr Tebbit said that it was part of Britain's democratic system that governments should not reverse manifesto commitments without good reason. The Tory pledge to oppose further large-scale immigration had been unequivocal: 'I get a bit huffy when people who campaigned and were elected on that manifesto now accuse me of neo-racist populism for wanting to adhere to it.'[26] He believed that at least 100 Conservative backbenchers thought government policy wrong, but only managed to persuade forty-three other Tory M.P.s, 'those legislators who would see Hong Kong tear itself to shreds rather than vote to vary the Nationality Act to help non-Caucasians',[27] to vote against the Bill, which secured a substantial majority.

The government of China naturally saw the decision to issue British passports in this way as a serious violation of the Joint Declaration, and as being unnecessary, insulting and provocative. It was made clear that anyone holding these passports would have doubtful prospects of public office in the HKSAR, and that the documents might not even be regarded as valid there or in China; but they did not carry their objections to the sticking point. Beijing did however hold the trump card of being able to decide the form of the new Basic Law. Discussions on successive drafts of this law were protracted and serious, with representatives of most sections of Hong Kong opinion on both the drafting committee, which had a majority of Beijing nominees, and the consultative committee, composed of Hong Kong residents. Points of principle were cogently argued, most evidently by Martin Lee, Q.C., the prominent advocate of democratic rights, and substantial amendments were agreed by Beijing.

Constitutional lawyers and those equipped to understand the issues followed the discussions closely, but the great majority of Hong Kong residents did not. Some suspicion existed that, whatever the provisions of the Basic Law, their observance by a future government in Beijing was doubtful. In spite of the good faith that had been demonstrated during the drafting process, a number of questions remained unanswered. The vocabulary of constitutional thought differed widely between Beijing and London. It was only since 1982 that China had enjoyed a recognizable constitution, under which the rule of law had any meaning, and there had been no opportunity for constitutional debate to emerge – indeed, one of the interesting features of the Basic Law drafting process was the opportunity provided for Chinese lawyers and officials to define their own constitutional ideas. With so many potential misunderstandings, could even a sincere agreement hold up?

In many respects the Basic Law provided for a considerably more advanced democratic constitution than that of colonial Hong Kong. The Chief Executive was not to be appointed, but elected. He had extensive powers, but less than those of a British Governor. The Legislative Council over which he was to preside had powers to initiate legislation and even to impeach the Chief Executive himself. But Britain had rarely exercised its wide-ranging imperial powers, and it had become accepted that Hong Kong would be left to deal with its own affairs, as matters of little importance to Whitehall.

To China Hong Kong was of very great importance indeed – its largest trading partner, the biggest source of foreign funds, its leading investor, and the sample of Chinese flexibility which was intended to attract Taiwan back to the fold. A Chinese government was more likely than a British one to wish to take advantage of its constitutional powers (and perhaps less likely to interpret them liberally). This impression was reinforced by the shock waves emanating from Tiananmen Square. The first 'Other Hong Kong Report', produced in 1989, carried a fiercely indignant article by John Walden, who had served for thirty years in the Colonial Administration, retiring in 1981 as Director of Home Affairs, on the 'sad saga of poor political judgement, wishful thinking, broken promises, lack of determination and deliberate misrepresentation'[28] that had characterized the British government's handling of Hong Kong's future.

When the Basic Law was finally promulgated on 4 April 1990, the tone was quieter. Where the published drafts had been amended, it was in the interests of the Hong Kong people. Although the production had been the undivided responsibility of the Chinese government, real notice had been taken of points raised by the Hong Kong representatives on the drafting committee. Particular attention was paid to the responsibilities of the Chief Executive of the new autonomous region – the replacement Governor – and to the method of his appointment, which was to be by a form of election. The more suspicious might point out that many of the freedoms guaranteed in China's own constitution were hardly detectable in practice, and that any document that mentioned elections, without defining the role that the Communist Party might be expected to play in them, was perilously near fantasy. But, bearing in mind that political practice in China looked to be evolving in a less oppressive direction, and that previous authoritarian excesses were at least less common, the Basic Law was accepted without much demur. There seemed little point in raising objections to individual articles when no one could forecast what sort of government there might be in China by 1997, and few were confident that any conceivable government in Beijing would not be prepared to take whatever action it thought necessary, however unconstitutional. Television cameras in the streets were a better guarantee of human rights than any constitutional document.

The Basic Law was not received with much enthusiasm: 'there was hardly any interest in the document. It was felt that the freedoms that Hong Kong people will continue to enjoy will be those restricted to dancing and horse racing . . . their freedoms, human rights and the rule of law will probably be considerably eroded.'[29] Dick Wilson, an experienced journalist, agreed: 'The people who continue to live here are not going to have the same sort of freedom. They will, I think, have the same freedom to make money and to live as Chinese. That's going to be less of a problem for the lower half of society. The people to whom it will be a problem are the Westernized Chinese. And they are the people who are likely to leave anyway.'[30] But Wilson, also a former editorial adviser to Singapore's *Straits Times* group, does not believe Hong Kong will end up quite like that island state with its 'one man, one-party' system and what he calls its 'arid politics'.

The British and Hong Kong governments gave a cautious welcome to the Basic Law. Sir David Wilson commented: 'The really important point is that most people in Hong Kong now accept that the Basic Law is there, that it has been passed whether they agree with every single paragraph of it or not, that it is now the framework for the present.'[31]

Presenting the Basic Law to the British Parliament as part of his first report on Hong Kong was the task of the new Foreign Secretary, Douglas Hurd. Mr Hurd's appointment suggested that Hong Kong might be treated more expertly by the British government during his tenure of office. He was the first Foreign Secretary to have personal experience of China – two years at the Beijing Embassy in the 1950s – and he had also written a good book on the *Arrow* war (as well as a novel, *The Smile on the Face of the Tiger*, which is set in Hong Kong). But it was also probable that his experience in China and his Foreign Office background would incline the new Foreign Secretary more to reach an accommodation with Beijing than aggressively to represent the views of Hong Kong. On 26 April 1991, in his annual report to the House of Commons on Hong Kong, he stated that the 'concern throughout the drafting process was to ensure consistency between the Basic Law and the provisions of the Joint Declaration. On the whole [the Hong Kong government] are satisfied that this has been achieved and that the Basic Law provides a firm foundation for Hong Kong's future as a Special Administrative Region of China. But there are some provisions that they would have preferred to have seen omitted or drafted differently.'[32] The extent of the Hong Kong government's enthusiasm for the Basic Law may be judged from the space devoted to it in their annual reviews. It was given the same attention as that accorded to the Outward Bound School, and much less than the Urban Council Parks. As some protection to those who would, willy nilly, have to remain in Hong Kong, a Bill of Rights was prepared which gave legal effect in the territory to the International Agreement on Civil and Political Rights, which should therefore govern Hong Kong legislation before and after 1997.

Drastic though the effect of the Tiananmen Square massacre was on confidence in Hong Kong, economic ties with China continued to flourish. In 1990 the total visible trade between Hong Kong and China was $395 thousand million, up approximately 15 per cent from the previous year, although that increase was significantly lower than the ten-year average of 35 per cent per annum. The government review laconically commented that this 'was at least partly related to China's austerity programme'.[33] Since then trade has probably picked up, and certainly the performance of the stock market, which has risen to record highs, indicates a returning confidence in at least the financial future.

This was not supported by the sharp increase in the numbers of those deciding to leave Hong Kong. Before 1989 the annual review published by the Hong Kong government had not found it necessary to mention emigration, but after Tiananmen it was quickly discovered that 'Emigration has been a feature of life in Hong Kong for over 100 years,' as numbers leaving rose steeply – sixty-two thousand in 1990 and a similar forecast for 1991.[34] The true figure was certainly higher, as persons not defined as emigrants managed to acquire resident status abroad and as young people studying abroad failed to return. Optimistic statements are sometimes made by officials that many emigrants are returning, but this is generally taken with a pinch of salt. Since half the forty-odd thousand recent 'economically active' emigrants were from the professional and managerial classes, and a majority of the remainder were students, the brain drain is becoming a source of increasing concern. Writing in 'The Other Hong Kong Report', Dr Tsim reported that 'Hong Kong is operating at a level below what it was capable of several years ago. The tell-tale signs are beginning to show. Many staff in the best hotels do not understand English; many salesmen cannot operate the office equipment they are selling; mistakes have crept into the utilities bills; some senior civil servants cannot express themselves in either English or Chinese. Standards are going down across the board.'[35]

At the time the Basic Law appeared, Sir David Wilson had suggested that 'Quite rightly, people's attention is now focused on the more immediate things in Hong Kong – like how to make a success of the 1991 elections.' As part of the fence-mending between British and Chinese governments that took place after Tiananmen the rate of progress towards direct elections for the Legislative Council had been agreed. It was to be at a much slower place than that indicated by the British government in 1984, and that recommended by such knowledgeable figures as Edward Heath. Far from having 'the firmly-based, democratic administration' by 1997 that Mr Luce had spoken of in 1984, there were to be only eighteen directly-elected seats (out of sixty) in the Legislative Council by 1991; in the ensuing elections, to be held at four-yearly intervals, these would rise to twenty, twenty-four, and thirty in 2003, by which date parity would be achieved with the thirty members elected by functional constituencies. It was not entirely the fault of the British government that the rate of progress was so slow, since the recommendations of the Hong Kong Councils were more hesitant than those of the House of Commons; but the Councils were hardly representative of the Hong Kong people. Their own position was safeguarded since membership of the Executive Council, 'the most important executive authority', would continue to be entirely nominated or ex officio – although the possibility did exist that it might be advisable, as at least a nod in the direction of democracy, to nominate some of the directly elected members of the Legislative Council to the Executive.

When the first election took place, in September 1991, the democratic candidates did better than expected. The United Democrats – described as 'experienced pressure group politicians with close grass-roots ties'[36] – were forecast to capture at least half the Legislative Council seats; on the day they won twelve of eighteen, with another three going to other liberal candidates. Martin Lee, the party's highly visible leader, had a personal triumph in gaining 76,831 votes, more than a tenth of all those cast. To put this figure in perspective, the lowest-polling successful candidate received only 21,702 votes. What might be termed the conservative candidates were unable to mount much of a challenge, only three 'independent' candidates being elected, while the pro-Beijingers did predictably badly. The real structure of power within the colony remained little affected by all this democratic activity.

When the results of the elections were announced the opportunity was indeed taken to appoint a directly elected member to the Executive Council. Four new councillors were appointed; one, Mrs Selina Chow Liang Shuk-yee, was an appointed member of the Legislative Council; two, Edward Ho Sing-tin and Hui Yin-fat, were members of the Legislative Council elected by functional constituencies. Hui had been elected unopposed for the Social Services Constituency, and Ho returned by the 552 votes of the Architectural, Surveying and Planning Constituency. But one of the new Executive Councillors had been democratically elected, so it seemed that, for the first time, at least one member of the Executive Council was there with a valid claim to represent the people's will. It was, however, not quite as simple as that. Mr Andrew Wong was not a member of the United Democrats, who had so convincingly won the popular vote, but one of the three independents. Nor was he even the preferred choice of the electorate of the New Territories East, who had given Miss Emily Lau of the United Democrats 46,515 votes, and Mr Wong 39,806. Nor, for that matter – and it is not clear whether this is relevant or not – is Mr Wong a British subject.

The result of this was that the more than 600,000 voters (representing some 85 per cent of those who cast their votes) who had elected 'so-called' liberals[37] had no representation whatsoever on the Executive Council. This was certainly a very moderate progression towards the principles of a democratic government for Hong Kong.

Although the Legislative Council elections were more politically significant, other elections manifested a similar new interest. The

Urban Council had also undergone a measure of reform and expansion of the voting base. In the 1981 elections the miserable total of 6,195 votes was cast – from a potential electorate of some 3 million – for the twelve seats. That year the existing restricted franchise was altered to simple adult suffrage. Registration increased considerably, to over 700,000, of whom some 160,000 actually cast votes, which did indicate a perceptible improvement in political participation. In 1985 the Regional Council took over the Urban Council's New Territory responsibilities, and was given a similar mixture of appointed and elected members – thirty-six, of whom twelve are elected directly, on a similar franchise. Many of the appointed and elected members have come through the Heung Yee Kuk, an advisory body, originally of village elders, founded in 1926.

Whether the inarticulate masses could be considered to have spoken in these free and democratic elections was another question. The number of those qualified to vote in Hong Kong elections is estimated at 3,690,000 (1992 Review): of these 1,916,925 – 51.9 per cent – have registered, thus signifying some interest in political affairs, but less than half of these commonly proceed to vote. In 1991 215,869 votes were cast in the Urban Council elections – 21 per cent of those registered but only about 10 per cent of those who could have done so qualified. In the Regional Council election 177,895 voted – 23.6 per cent of the registration. Taken together these amounted to 393,764, or less than 11 per cent of the total number of potential voters. At the District Board elections 423,923 voted from 1,305,714 registered; since in the 1985 election 477,000 voted, this shows an actual decline in interest.

Those elections were held in May 1991; in September the Legislative Council elections saw, from the same electorate, 750,467 votes cast. This was 39 per cent of the registration, and just over 20 per cent of the estimated potential – considerably better than in the other Councils' elections, but not perhaps quite as the 1992 Review described it: 'Election fever gripped Hong Kong in the autumn when 39 per cent of electors turned out to vote in Hong Kong's first direct elections to the Legislative Council.'[38] The nearly 80 per cent who could have voted but didn't seem to have been remarkably immune to this fever, and the political lethargy of Hong Kong would seem to be not entirely a fiction. A brave face was put on it by the authorities, but the sceptics felt themselves to have been vindicated.

Those who had, like Edward Heath and Sir Mark Young before

him, argued for an earlier introduction of democratic elections, had been proved right. Not enough time has been left to develop the habits of democracy in Hong Kong. The traditional reluctance to be involved too closely with government (except when wanting some specific action from an official still often regarded in the ancient light of a father-mother mandarin, a solver of individual problems) had been sustained by the variety of complaints channels available. A worried citizen could appeal to a Mutual Aid Committee, Area Committee, District Officer, the Heung Yee Kuk, the Regional or Urban Councils, the Office of the Members of the Legislative Council (OMELCO), the Police Complaints body, ICAC or the Commissioner for Administrative Complaints, all government or government-sponsored bodies. This long-established attitude had by 1991 straddled over to a new concern. With 1997 bringing a new sovereign power, and one not famous for tolerating political opponents, it would not be prudent to appear publicly, even to the extent of being seen to vote (party workers are able, in Hong Kong elections, to muster outside ballot stations), and certainly not to have one's name and address appearing on any political list.

But merely bringing forward direct elections to 1988 would have affected events in 1991 only marginally; the killings in Tiananmen Square in 1989 provoked such universal indignation that a newly elected minority of members could not have added much weight to the protests of the Legislative Council. Fewer liberals would, in all probability, have been elected in 1988 than were successful in 1991, and the pressure on the British government to increase its ration of passports might have been more effective. Jobbing backwards, it seems that the real opportunity was lost when the Young Plan, or one of its derivatives, was rejected. China was in no position to object to democratic reforms in 1947, and America would have welcomed them. Even in 1950, with the Labour government's determination to preserve British rule manifested by the show of military strength, the new People's Republic could not have intervened. After that date the received wisdom, that no demand for democratic advance existed, was only called seriously into question by the Star Ferry riots of 1966. The colonial government was thereafter too nervous that liberalization would lead to disorder to initiate any but the most subdued moves towards reform, and the negotiations between the West and China which began soon afterwards served to stop any progress. Thirty-five years had to elapse after Sir Mark Young's proposals before the first democratically elected legislator was returned.

Two cheers for colonialism

British enthusiasm for their Chinese colony has almost always been muted. Palmerston, Churchill and Bevin may from time to time have growled in Hong Kong's defence; and General Sargent, assisted by an outbreak of endemic francophobia, succeeded in getting his guns – although losing his job for his pains – but when faced with stark choices in 1940 and 1941, Hong Kong was judged 'not really important'. After the war, although a certain vicarious pride was taken in the colony's achievements, Hong Kong was primarily a source of embarrassment, an obstacle to Britain's relations with China and the USA, and in its success a reproach to Britain's economic decline. In some quarters the advent of 1997 was awaited with relief, and efforts to slide out of responsibility for the last great Crown Colony began many years previously.

The current Government Annual Review tactfully suppresses any direct reference to the Crown Colony or Dependent Territory status of Hong Kong, blandly stating that 'Hong Kong is administered by the Hong Kong Government, and its administration has developed from the basic pattern applied in all British-governed Territories overseas'[39] – a formula which cleverly does not suggest that Hong Kong is in any way the responsibility of the British government, or that Britain is the sovereign power. This contrived impression was hardly sustained by the fact that at that time *all* the most senior posts – Governor, Colonial Secretary, Financial Secretary, Attorney-General and Commander British Forces, all ex-officio members of the Executive Council, together with 40 per cent (in 1990) of the 1,220 directorate officers – were held by expatriates. Of the locally-appointed officers, a growing proportion, it is very likely that the majority will be among those who are awarded full British passports, giving them the right of abode in Britain. A complex situation will emerge in a few years' time when the great majority of senior officials will be able to leave Hong Kong when they so wish, while the junior ranks will, whatever the situation, be obliged to stay.

But if still constitutionally a colony – and events in 1992 were to show how a firm assertion of Imperial authority might still be made – Hong Kong is now neither economically nor socially a British territory. The power of the great British Hongs has been firmly displaced by that of Chinese enterprise; even Jardine's and the Hongkong Bank have signalled their intention to diversify much of their business outside the colony. The Taipans of the future will be in the pattern of Li Ka-shing and Gordon Wu, Chairman of Hopewell Holdings. The end of an era was signalled when in 1991 the Hong Kong Club was succeeded by the China Club as the community's most eminent social institution. This splendidly equipped new club, on the top floors of the old Bank of China building, was opened by Zhou Nan, the head of the New China News Agency, accompanied by Michael Heseltine, British Cabinet Minister and successful entrepreneur, and T.T. Tsui, representing Hong Kong business, with the daughter of Deng Xiaoping looking on. Even as foreign investors the British are on the way to being replaced by Japanese and Americans; over US$1,000 million of Japanese capital was invested in Hong Kong by 1991. There had never, as Ng Choy had pointed out in 1914, been much economic advantage to Britain in holding Hong Kong, although the colonial taxpayers grumbled about the sum expected as a contribution towards defence costs. The originally British-owned firms in the colony have become, with the exception of Swire's, public companies with a wide shareholding. The great personal fortunes once made by Jardines and Mathesons are now those of first-generation Hong Kong Chinese. Those British remaining are less conventional and sharper than their immediate predecessors. Many are very able indeed, judged by stringent international standards. Some, like Simon Murray, Managing Director of Hutchison, have the same brisk competence that characterized James Matheson himself. They compare favourably with British exporters, who after the liberation of Hong Kong from sterling area constraints had no advantage over others, and had to compete on equal terms – which they have signally failed to do. From their once commanding position the British share of the Hong Kong market had fallen by 1986 to just 3.9 per cent, and in the following six years declined to 2.1 per cent – less than one-quarter the share of Taiwan. China had become unquestionably Hong Kong's largest trading partner, with the USA, Japan and Germany all powerful participants.[40]

That part of the Chinese economy that loomed largest in Hong Kong was naturally and unquestionably the province of Guangdong. The Bocca Tigris, where once *Hyacinth* and *Imogene* tacked under the guns of the Ch'ing forts, is to be crossed by a massive road bridge, the east–west link in a superhighway system that will join Canton to Shenzhen and Hong Kong on the east of the Pearl River delta and to Zhuhai and Macao on the West. The first phase of this, 123 kilometres between the Hong Kong border and Canton, is due to open in June

1993. Taken in conjunction with the new Hong Kong airport on Lantau island the project will confirm Guangdong as the centre of Chinese
international trade. The superhighway is mainly due to the energy of
Gordon Wu, who is in some ways typical of the newer generation of
Chinese taipans. Wu's grandfather came to Hong Kong as a gardener
and pig farmer; his son saved to buy a taxi, and by the time he retired
had built up a fleet of 378. Gordon Wu is an engineer with great faith
in engineering principles rather than a property developer making a
quick killing (though few true Hong Kongers can resist a clever deal).
If some of the new British businessmen in Hong Kong are in the
mould of Matheson or Dent, Wu does not resemble earlier Chinese
entrepreneurs. He does not seem to be anxious for imperial honours
or rank, but follows his own sometimes unpopular line.

The new airport on Lantau has been the centre of much dispute
between Britain and China. Beijing expressed serious concern that the
expense of construction would exhaust Hong Kong's financial reserves.
It was claimed that cost-overruns might be considerable, and that
Beijing was accurately representing Hong Kong feeling by questioning
the need for so enormous an investment (estimated in the government's
1992 Review at some £9,500 million – $127,000 million – at 1989
prices). British officials were reported as 'accusing China of withhold-
ing its approval for the airport in order to force Britain to limit democracy in Hong Kong' (*The Times*, 7 July 1992). Certainly every time
relations between Britain and China become strained the future of the
airport is threatened, but domestic Chinese interests are also objecting.
When completed, it will be by far the most modern airport in China,
and will act as the international gateway, thus fortifying the economic
pre-eminence of Guangdong over the rest of the country.

Guangdong is already showing, from Beijing's point of view, somewhat alarming success. Guangdong Enterprises, owned by the provin-
cial government, is a major international company with an income of
US$3,200 million from holdings in Guangdong, Hong Kong, the
USA, Canada, Australia and Thailand. Two-thirds of households in
Canton are said to have an annual disposable income of about
US$1,400; the *Far Eastern Economic Review* (16 May 1991) believes
this 'grossly under-report[s] the real level of affluence. Perhaps more
telling are official figures showing that 90 per cent of households in
Canton owned a colour television last year ... and that 76 per cent
of families in the city owned refrigerators.' Guangdong is at least as
essential to the future of Hong Kong as vice versa. The competitive

edge of Hong Kong industry relies on three million Cantonese 'working for Hong Kong companies either through joint ventures or in tasks commissioned by Hong Kong companies'.[41] In this way the design, marketing and managerial skills of Hong Kong are supplemented by the relatively low wages in Guangdong, although these are considerably higher than those in the rest of China. Such a situation cannot be static; internal immigration into Guangdong is rising, as 100,000 workers per day arrived at Canton station in February 1992 in search of jobs that would bring the chance of refrigerators and colour televisions. It is probable that Guangdong will not be content with merely providing a pool of labour for Hong Kong businesses.

Whether Beijing will continue to allow a widening gap to appear between the standard of living in different parts of the country is also an open question. 'The mountains are high, and the Emperor is far away' is a Cantonese phrase often quoted to suggest that existing manifestations of independence in the coastal provinces may increase to an actual separation from the north. After what has happened in the former Union of Soviet Socialist Republics it would be rash to suggest that this is impossible, but there are different factors at work. China, including Hong Kong and Taiwan, is ethnically and culturally far more homogeneous than the USSR, and the sense of national pride and identity has survived all the catastrophes of the last fifty years. But Tiananmen proved that a dictatorial central control can never be exercised from Beijing once that unity of purpose is shattered.

It is doubtful whether anything as crude as Tiananmen could be repeated in Canton – and much less in Hong Kong. A demonstration in the capital city, with a million people assembled outside the historic heart of China, the Imperial Palace, was a challenge to a dictatorial authority that was impossible for it to ignore. The same thing, far away in the provinces, is both less threatening and more difficult to deal with decisively. Indications of this appeared at the time of Tiananmen; there was a delay in finding troops willing to crush the demonstrators, and in Shanghai a similar movement was defused without bloodshed by the local authorities. However unco-operative and unruly the citizens of Hong Kong and Guangdong turn out to be, Beijing will undergo much provocation before getting the tanks on the streets.

Hong Kong remained safely insulated from all earlier turbulences in China. Only during the Japanese occupation of the Second World War were its people left unprotected by their colonial masters. Their recovery from the devastation this caused was largely self-generated, neither much helped nor hindered by Britain. A whole post-war generation did without anything but the most basic social provisions and worked with astonishing energy in often wretched conditions. Left to their own devices they have created a society of which they can be properly proud.

It is hardly surprising therefore that Hong Kong looks on both Britain and China with a jaundiced view. Since the war Britain has, it seems, lurched from one economic crisis to another, drifting inexorably down the table of developed countries. The lack of candour and firmness with which the retrocession of Hong Kong to China has been handled has aroused disillusion sometimes amounting to disgust. By 1992 the real desire in the colony for democracy conflicted with an equally pressing anxiety not to provoke confrontation and so endanger a peaceful transfer of sovereignty. China, on the other hand, after twenty-five years of governments often slipping into disorganized lunacy, has settled into a rather more effective society, although disorder and discontent are checked by bloody repression.

From the British point of view there is this to be said: it may be that British troops have never had to defend the colony against China, but this is at least in part because the determination not to run from responsibilities was shown in Malaysia, Korea and Borneo. It is certainly true that the British as colonialists have been usually condescending, often exploitative, and sometimes devious; but they have established a rule of law which defines and protects individual rights. Hong Kong has certainly never become 'a showplace of democracy', although its citizens have hardly manifested any overwhelming desire that it should be; but this is perhaps an omission for which Britain may be forgiven. Corrupt dictatorships everywhere stridently proclaim their undying attachment to democratic principles; but there is no society in Asia that has enjoyed for so long as Hong Kong the freedom that democracy is commonly supposed to guarantee.

EPILOGUE

Times change; but political life in Britain follows a consistent pattern. In 1833 the Whigs, obliged to find a decent job for their stalwart supporter Lord Napier, who had lost his seat in Parliament, sent him off to the Pearl River estuary at a most generous salary. One hundred and fifty-nine years later the Tories, needing to find a suitably dignified position for their energetic Party Chairman Chris Patten, who had lost his seat in Parliament, sent him off to the Pearl River estuary at a most generous salary; and, to prove that colonies continued to serve the same purpose, also found a comfortable berth for another election casualty, former Home Secretary David Waddington, as Governor of Bermuda.

Like Lord Napier, Mr Patten had no diplomatic experience, although he did have the advantage of three previous short visits to Hong Kong; air travel has some merits. But there the similarity ends. Mr Patten had proved himself to be a cultivated, humorous, able and subtle politician, none of which useful qualities was possessed by Lord Napier; he was also, unlike Lord Napier, who had been nothing more than a respectable name to Lord Palmerston, a close political ally of the Conservative leadership, with immediate access to Downing Street.[1] While Sir David Wilson had to go 'through channels', consulting with Lord Glenarthur, Lord Caithness, or whichever very junior Minister was responsible for Hong Kong, Mr Patten is able to settle things directly with the Foreign Secretary or the Prime Minister, rather than following the Foreign Office officials' guidance.

This independence was demonstrated only a short time after his arrival, when on 7 October 1992 Mr Patten gave a long address to the Legislative Council on his intentions for the future. It was phrased boldly, even arbitrarily: 'The policies of the government I lead will be based on four key principles' – which, while hardly in the spirit of consensus politics, gave a clear lead.

It was the fourth of these principles that caused the uproar: '. . . We must make possible the widest democratic participation by the people of Hong Kong in the running of their own affairs, while reinforcing certainty about Hong Kong's future.' Mr Patten summarized his personal political convictions: 'I owe it to the community to make my own position plain. I have spent my entire career engaged in a political system based on representative democracy. It would be surprising if that had not marked me.'

The new Governor admitted he was 'constrained' in progressing towards a democratic system, but progress was *only* constrained, 'and not stopped in its tracks'. It had previously been assumed that with the introduction of some directly elected members to the Legislative Council, democratization had gone as far as permitted under the Joint Declaration and the Basic Law. Mr Patten did not agree: 'Standing still,' he insisted, 'is not an available option.' Those who drafted the Basic Law, he argued, doubtless recognized that the community wanted a greater measure of democracy. This was, to say the least, open to question. Drafting the Basic Law was the responsibility of the Chinese government, although the views of the Hong Kong representatives were taken into account; and what the Chinese government meant by 'democracy' was unlikely to be the same as Mr Patten's interpretation.

The Governor's proposals divided into two sections, the first of which was presented as a *fait accompli*. Radical alterations to the Constitution were to be immediately effected:

> I have concluded that, at the present stage of our political development, there should not be any overlapping membership between the Executive and Legislative Councils. I intend, for the time being, to separate the non-official membership of the two bodies.

Those members of the Executive Council who were also members of the Legislative Council had to resign – only a year after some of them had been appointed – and were replaced by appointed members, both officials and nominated outsiders.

The Legislative Council, shorn of its links with the Executive Council, would be 'left free to run its own affairs, and, in the process, to develop further its relationship with the government'. A wary observer might conclude that this meant that the Council would be allowed to bombinate in a vacuum, without any real power. Such an interpretation would be fortified by the Governor's statement that he would be 'answerable as the head of the Executive to this Council [the Legislative Council]'. Being 'answerable' Mr Patten defined as: 'to make myself available to answer members' questions and to discuss government policies and proposals, on at least one Thursday every month that you are in session'. This is an idiosyncratic definition of a word for which the *Oxford English Dictionary* gives as its first meaning: 'Liable to be called to account; responsible . . . e.g. 1. He was answerable with his head.'

Mr Patten's head is unlikely to be sacrificed to the Legislative Council, but the second part of his constitutional alterations provoked violent reactions from the Chinese government. Unlike the first section, which had been implemented by government decision, the proposals that aroused most controversy were only those of an 'understanding' which Mr Patten hoped might be reached. They were: 1) That the voting age be reduced from twenty-one to eighteen; 2) Single-seat constituencies for direct elections; 3) An extensive revision of the functional constituencies. This last suggestion involved the franchise in each constituency being extended to individuals rather than corporations, and the creation of nine new constituencies to cover all industrial and commercial activities. The result would be for the franchise of the thirty functional constituencies to be extended to all eligible voters – nearly all the working population.

China's reaction to this was nothing less than explosive. Patten's proposals, it was claimed, flouted the Basic Law, and if persisted with would ruin any prospect of a peaceful handover. China would cease to co-operate, cancel all commercial agreements previously signed by the Hong Kong government, and even abrogate the Joint Agreement.

There was also vocal opposition from within the colony, as many businessmen sympathized with the Chinese response. Never over-keen on democracy, many in the business community deplored any action that threatened commercial stability. Robert Fell, a former Chairman of the Hong Kong Stock Exchange, wrote to *The Times* complaining that Mr Patten had 'chosen to begin his stint as Governor with the wrong agenda and has compounded his error by the manner of its initiation' (9 December 1992). Others spoke of 'disruptive ventures' and 'one of the many mistakes the Conservative government has made'.

Another voice raised in protest was that of Sir Percy Cradock, the former British Ambassador to Beijing, who had been the most prominent among the original negotiators of the Joint Declaration. He too believed that Mr Patten's initiative was ill-advised, and in another letter to *The Times* (1 December 1992) warned against 'open breaches and threats of strength for which Hong Kong will have to pay'.

It was Mr Patten's proposals for changes in the franchise that were the main cause of the angry Chinese reaction. They were, however, merely proposals, and could be altered or withdrawn if pressure proved too great. More interesting was the way in which the Governor had been able to alter the entire framework of government by a simple directive, in the first of his constitutional changes. This was an example of the wide-ranging powers possessed by a Colonial Governor who could count on the support not only of his own Minister, but of the whole British Cabinet. Mr Patten's actions were literally unprecedented; Sir John Bowring had been able to bring his country to the brink of war with China, but he was Plenipotentiary as well as Governor, and had the advantage of poor communications, while his successor in 1992 was able to put his cat among the diplomatic pigeons while remaining a mere Governor, commonly regarded as little more than a decorative figurehead. To the Chinese authorities, this seemed an impudent usurpation of powers, which fuelled their wrath. Negotiations were possible, they insisted, only with the British Government.

How successful this bold enterprise may prove remains to be seen. As the terminal date of 1997 draws near both China and Britain have, in 1993, weak and unpopular governments, with an uncertain future. By 1997 there should have been an election in Britain and a resolution of the Chinese succession. To any British government Hong Kong will remain a peripheral concern, as it always has been. To Beijing Hong Kong's future is a matter of greater moment, but the people of Hong Kong will be unhappily aware that their existing freedoms will depend much more on events in the rest of China than on any constitutional arrangements.

APPENDICES

APPENDIX A British Governments and Prominent Chinese

	PRIME MINISTER	FOREIGN SECRETARY	COLONIAL SECRETARY	PLENIPOTENTIARY GOVERNOR	EMPERORS AND PROMINENT CHINESE
1830	Lord Grey (Whig)	Lord Palmerston	Lord Goderich		Emperor Tao-kuang Mu-chang-a
1833			Lord Stanley		
1834	Lord Melbourne (Whig) (December) R. Peel (Conservative)	Duke of Wellington	T. Spring Rice Lord Aberdeen	Lord Napier J. Davis	
1835	Lord Melbourne (Whig)	Lord Palmerston	C. Grant (Lord Glenelg)	G. Robinson	
1836				C. Elliot	Lin Tse-hsü
1839			Lord Normanby		Ch'i-shan
1840			Lord Russell		I-li-pu
1841	R. Peel (Con)	Lord Aberdeen	Lord Stanley (later 14th Lord Derby)	H. Pottinger	
1844				J. Davis	Ch'i-ing
1845			W. E. Gladstone		
1846	Lord John Russell (Whig)	Lord Palmerston	Lord Grey	G. Bonham	
1848					Hsu Huang-chin
1849					Emperor Hsien-feng
1850					
1851		(Dec.) Lord Granville			Yeh Ming-ch'en

Year	Prime Minister	Foreign Secretary	Colonial Secretary	Governor of Hong Kong	China
1852	(Feb.) 14th Lord Derby (Con) (Dec.) Lord Aberdeen (coalition)	Lord Malmesbury Lord John Russell	J. Pakington Duke of Newcastle		
1853		Lord Clarendon			
1854				J. Bowring	
1855	Lord Palmerston (Liberal)	(Feb.) S. Herbert (Feb.) Lord Russell (July) W. Molesworth (Oct.) H. Labouchere	G. Grey		
1858	14th Lord Derby (Con)	Lord Malmesbury	Lord Stanley (later 15th Lord Derby)		
1859	Lord Palmerston (Lib)	Lord John Russell	Duke of Newcastle	H. Robinson	
1862					Emperor T'ung-chi Prince Kung Tseng Kuo-fan Chang Ch'i-tung Wo-jen Li Hung-chang
1863					
1864					
1865	Lord John Russell (Lib)	Lord Clarendon	E. Cardwell		
1866	14th Lord Derby (Con)	Lord Stanley	Lord Carnarvon	R. MacDonnell	
1867			Duke of Buckingham		
1868	B. Disraeli (Con) (Dec.) W. E. Gladstone (Lib)	Lord Clarendon	Lord Granville		
1870		Lord Granville	Lord Kimberley		
1872				A. Kennedy	
1874	B. Disraeli (Con)	15th Lord Derby	Lord Carnarvon		Emperor Kuang-hsu Ascendancy of Dowager Empress

APPENDIX A – *Contd.*

	PRIME MINISTER	FOREIGN SECRETARY	COLONIAL SECRETARY	PLENIPOTENTIARY GOVERNOR	EMPERORS AND PROMINENT CHINESE
1877				J. Pope Hennessy	
1878		Lord Salisbury	M. Hicks-Beach		
1880	W. E. Gladstone (Lib)	Lord Granville	Lord Kimberley		
1882			15th Lord Derby		
1883				G. Bowen	
1885	Lord Salisbury (Con)	Lord Salisbury	F. A. Stanley (16th Lord Derby)		
1886	(Feb.) W. E. Gladstone (Lib) (Aug.) Lord Salisbury (Con)	Lord Rosebery Lord Iddesleigh	Lord Granville E. Stanhope		
1887		Lord Salisbury	Lord Knutsford	W. Des Voeux	
1891				W. Robinson	Sun Yat-sen
1892	W. E. Gladstone (Lib)	Lord Rosebery	Lord Ripon		
1894	Lord Rosebery (Lib)	Lord Kimberley			
1895	Lord Salisbury (Con)	Lord Salisbury	J. Chamberlain		
1898				H. Blake	K'ang Yu-wei Liang Ch'i-ch'ao Emperor Hsuan-t'ung
1900		Lord Lansdowne			
1901					Ascendancy of Yüan Shi-kai

Year	Prime Minister	Foreign Secretary	Colonial Secretary	Governor of Hong Kong	China
1902	A.J. Balfour (Con)				Emperor Pu-Yi
1903			A. Lyttelton	M. Nathan	
1904					
1906	H. Campbell-Bannerman (Lib)	E. Grey	Lord Elgin		
1907				F. Lugard	
1908	H.J. Asquith (Lib)		Lord Crewe		
1911			L. Harcourt	F. H. May	
1912					
1915	(coalition)		Bonar Law		
1916	D. Lloyd George (War Cabinet)				
1919	(coalition)	A. Balfour / Lord Curzon	Lord Milner	R. Stubbs	
1921			W. S. Churchill		
1922	Bonar Law (Con)		Duke of Devonshire		
1923	S. Baldwin (Con)				
1924	J. R. MacDonald (Labour) / (Nov.) S. Baldwin (Con)	J. R. MacDonald / A. Chamberlain	J. H. Thomas / L. S. Amery		Chiang Kai-shek
1925				C. Clementi	
1929	J. R. MacDonald (Lab)	A. Henderson	Lord Passfield		
1930				W. Peel	
1931	(Nov.) (coalition)	Lord Reading / J. Simon	J. H. Thomas / P. Cunliffe-Lister		
1935	(June) S. Baldwin (coalition) / (Nov.)	S. Hoare / A. Eden	M. MacDonald / J. H. Thomas	A. Caldecott	

APPENDIX A – *Contd.*

	PRIME MINISTER	FOREIGN SECRETARY	COLONIAL SECRETARY	PLENIPOTENTIARY/ GOVERNOR	EMPERORS AND PROMINENT CHINESE
1936	N. Chamberlain (Con) (coalition)		W. Ormsby-Gore		
1937				G. Northcote	
1938		Lord Halifax	M. MacDonald		
1940	W. S. Churchill (War Cabinet)	A. Eden	Lord Lloyd		
1941			Lord Moyne	M. Young	
1942			O. Stanley		
1945	C. Attlee (Lab)	E. Bevin	G. H. Hall		
1946			A. Creech Jones		
1947				A. Grantham	
1950			J. Griffiths		Mao Tse-tung
1951	(Oct.) W. S. Churchill (Con)	H. Morrison A. Eden (Lord Avon)	O. Lyttelton (Lord Chandos)		
1954			A. T. Lennox-Boyd (Lord Boyd)		
1955	A. Eden (Con.)	H. Macmillan S. Lloyd			
1957	H. Macmillan (Con)				
1958				R. Black	

1959			I. McLeod		
1960		A. Douglas-Home			
1961			R. Maudling		
1962			D. Sandys		
1963	A. Douglas-Home (Con)	R. Butler			
1964	H. Wilson (Lab)	P. Gordon Walker		D. Trench	
1965		M. Stewart			
1966		G. Brown			
1968		M. Stewart (FOREIGN AND COMMONWEALTH OFFICES NOW AMALGAMATED)			
1970	E. Heath (Con)	A. Douglas-Home			
1971				M. Maclehose	
1974	H. Wilson (Lab)	J. Callaghan			
1976	J. Callaghan (Lab)	A. Crosland			
1977		D. Owen			
1978					Ascendancy of Deng Xiaoping
1979	M. Thatcher (Con)	Lord Carrington			
1982		F. Pym		E. Youde	
1983		G. Howe			
1987		J. Major		D. Wilson	
1990	(Nov.) J. Major (Con.)	D. Hurd			
1992				C. Patten	

APPENDIX B

Governors of the Colony of Hong Kong

January – August 1841	Captain Charles Elliot (Administrator)
August 1841 – May 1844	Sir Henry Pottinger (Administrator August 1841 – June 1843); (Governor June 1843 – May 1844)
May 1844 – March 1848	Sir John F. Davis
March 1848 – April 1854	Sir George Bonham
April 1854 – May 1859	Sir John Bowring
September 1859 – March 1865	Sir Hercules Robinson
March 1865 – March 1866	(administered) William T. Mercer
March 1866 – April 1872	Sir Richard Graves MacDonnell
April 1872 – March 1877	Sir Arthur E. Kennedy
April 1877 – March 1882	Sir John Pope Hennessy
March 1882 – March 1883	(administered) Sir William H. Marsh
March 1883 – December 1885	Sir George F. Bowen
December 1885 – April 1887	(administered) Sir William H. Marsh
April – October 1887	(administered) Major-General N. G. Cameron
October 1887 – May 1891	Sir William Des Voeux
May – December 1891	(administered) Major-General Digby Barker
December 1891 – January 1898	Sir William Robinson
February – November 1898	(administered) Major-General W. Black
November 1898 – July 1903	Sir Henry A. Blake
November 1903 – July 1904	(administered) Sir Francis H. May
July 1904 – April 1907	Sir Matthew Nathan
July 1907 – March 1912	Sir Frederick Lugard
July 1912 – February 1919	Sir Francis H. May
September 1919 – October 1925	Sir Reginald E. Stubbs
November 1925 – February 1930	Sir Cecil Clementi
May 1930 – May 1935	Sir William Peel
December 1935 – April 1937	Sir Alexander Caldecott
November 1937 – May 1940	Sir Geoffry Northcote
September 1941 – May 1947	Sir Mark Young
July 1947 – December 1957	Sir Alexander Grantham
January 1958 – March 1964	Sir Robert Black
April 1964 – October 1971	Sir David Trench
November 1971 – May 1982	Sir Murray Maclehose
May 1982 – April 1987	Sir Edward Youde
April 1987 – July 1992	Sir David Wilson
July 1992 –	Christopher Patten

NOTES

INTRODUCTION

1. Palmerston, private letter to Charles Elliot 21 April 1841. Queen Victoria, letter of 13 April 1841, Queen Victoria, *Letters*, vol. i, pp. 261ff. Tao-kuang Emperor; R. Pelissier, *The Awakening of China 1793–1949*, p. 90.
2. United Nations Demographic Analyses; US Government reports; Hong Kong Government Information Department.
3. A remarkable analysis of the difficulties Chinese writers have had, and continue to have, in deciding whether they are 'first a Chinese or first a scholar' is given in Jia Qing-guo's essay 'Between Sentiment and Reason' in Roberts, *Sino-American Relations Since 1900*.
4. See Appendix A, which lists British governments from 1830 to 1993.
5. Colonial Office (CO) 129/3, 3 June 1843
6. Peyrefitte, *The Collision of Two Civilisations: The British Expedition to China 1792–4* (published in the United States as *The Immobile Empire: The First Great Collision of East and West*), pp.xx-xxi

7. Teng and Fairbank, *China's Response to the West*, p. 2
8. Wakeman, *The Fall of Imperial China*, p. 67
9. Matheson, *The Present Position and Prospects of the British Trade with China*, p. 3

CHAPTER I

It is not easy to find a satisfactory short history of China. Those published in Beijing (e.g. Bai Shouyi and Jian Bozan) have inescapably Marxist views, complicated by an only slight acquaintance with British history. Rodzinski, in two volumes and a one-volume version, has to be taken with a similar pinch of pro-colonial salt, but if this is applied it is a good deal better than the Chinese histories. For the period from the eighteenth century to recent times two larger works, Hsü's *The Rise of Modern China* and Jonathan Spence's *The Search for Modern China* are excellent, as is one shorter book, F. Wakeman's *Fall of Imperial China*. Wakeman's *The Great Enterprise* is the best work on the Ch'ing Empire as a whole. Needham's first volume of *Science and Civilization in China* has a

good precis, and for an understanding of
Chinese history and civilization the
whole of that massive work is
unparalleled. On a similar scale is the
Cambridge History of China, with the
relevant volumes edited by John King
Fairbank and Roderick MacFarquhar.
The Canton trade is well documented,
with Michael Greenberg's *British Trade
and the Opening of China* covering the
subject succinctly and authoritatively to
1842, and extended to 1852 by John
King Fairbank's *Trade and Diplomacy on
the China Coast*. The two great names
are Fairbank, one of the finest modern
historians, and Morse, on whom all
subsequent writers rely. There are also
good and entertaining accounts of
Canton in Maurice Collis's *Foreign
Mud*, Peter Fay's *Opium War*, and
Christopher Hibbert's *The Dragon
Wakes*. C.H. Philips' standard work on
the East India Company has been
supplemented by John Keay's *The
Honourable Company*, but this does not
extend to the Canton trade. Jack Gray,
in *Rebellions and Revolutions*, is
knowledgeable about British attitudes
towards China.

1. See Blue Book, 1840, vol. viii, Select
   Committee of the House of
   Commons Minutes, 23 November
   1829
2. *Receuil des Lettres Edifantes des
   Missionaires Jesuites*, 1702. Early
   European visitors mistook the name
   of the province for that of the town,
   and the error has survived, Canton
   only recently being given its proper
   transliteration – Guangzhou.
3. H.D. Talbot, in *Journal of the Hong
   Kong Branch of the Royal Asiatic
   Society* (JHKBRAS), vol. 10, 1970:
   'Hong Kong is to be known
   officially as Xianggang; this is
   putonghua, or Mandarin, and will
   have a stiff fight with the Cantonese.'

4. Although Ch'ien-lung abdicated in
   1796, he actually retained power until
   his death in 1799.
5. Quoted in Michael, *Origins of
   Manchu Rule*, p. 106. On accession
   to the throne Chinese Emperors
   abandoned their personal name for
   names by which their reigns should
   be known; thus Abahai became either
   Emperor T'ai-tsung or the
   T'ai-tsung Emperor, and all events
   were dated from the year of his
   accession.
6. John Nievhoff, quoted in Collis, *The
   Great Within*, pp. 110, 119
7. Cranmer-Byng, *Embassy to China*,
   p. 237
8. Journal entry, 10 July 1637. *Peter
   Mundy's Journal*, edited by R.C.
   Temple (Hakluyt Society), is a
   fascinating account of
   seventeenth-century travel. An
   interesting account of the tea trade is
   found in Hobhouse, *Seeds of Change*.
9. Philips, *The East India Company*,
   p. 73
10. ibid., p. 308
11. Peter Mundy gives a lively account
    of the expedition, complaining of
    'having been for these 6 Months
    variously Crosed in our Designe, our
    lives, shipping, goodes etts.,
    Molested, endaungered, Dammified,
    Our Principalls with Much Meanes
    Deteyned att Canton' (p. 300).
12. Morse, *Chronicles of the East India
    Company Trading to China*
    (*Chronicles*), vol. i, p. 32
13. *Brice's Topographical Dictionary*,
    'Macao'
14. Cranmer-Byng, op. cit., p. 211
15. Morse, *International Relations of the
    Chinese Empire* (*Int. Rel.*), vol. i,
    p. 34. All provinces of the Chinese
    Empire were headed by officials
    known to the British as 'Governors';
    some 'twin' provinces, such as

Kwantung/Kwangsi, came under the administration of more senior mandarins, commonly referred to as either 'Governor-General' or 'Viceroy'.

16. Morse, *Guilds of China*, p. 17
17. Fairbank, *Trade and Diplomacy on the China Coast*, p. 51
18. Morse, *Chronicles*, vol. ii, p. 104
19. Greenberg, *British Trade and the Opening of China*, pp. 60–1
20. Hunter, *The Fan-kwae in Canton*, pp. 40, 26

CHAPTER 2

Apart from the essential Morse, the debate leading up to the end of the East India Company's commercial activities, which cleared the way for the private traders, the real founders of Hong Kong, has not been well covered. Much reliance is here placed on primary sources, of which the most important are the Jardine Matheson archives in the Cambridge University Library, and the Parliamentary Papers – Blue Books – issued for each session. These collate papers often several years after their original issue: thus the 1829 Select Committee Minutes only surface in 1840. *China's Response to the West*, a collection of Chinese documents translated and edited by S.Y. Teng and J.K. Fairbank, is invaluable to monoglots.

1. For Macartney's embassy see Cranmer-Byng, op. cit., and Alain Peyrefitte, *The Collision of Two Civilisations* (US title *The Immobile Empire*). Collis, *The Great Within* and Nigel Cameron, *Barbarians and Mandarins* are good on early contacts between China and the West. Jonathan Spence in *The China Helpers* (US title *To Change China*) continues the subject into the twentieth century.

2. Working through the relevant boxes in the First Historical Archives in Beijing the Deputy Director, Mr Wu, discovered a note which turned out to have been made by George Thomas Staunton, later Sir George, who became President of the Select Committee at Canton, a member of the Amherst embassy, and a founder of the Royal Asiatic Society.
3. Teng and Fairbank, *China's Response to the West*, p. 19
4. For opium see D. Latimer and J. Goldberg, *Flowers in the Blood*
5. *Caledonian Society Journal*, 1820
6. Morse, *Chronicles*, vol. ii, p. 316
7. Spence, in Wakeman et al., *Conflict and Control*, p. 149
8. Morse, *Chronicles*, vol. ii, p. 325
9. Macartney's instructions are quoted in Morse, *Chronicles*, vol. ii, p. 239: '. . . if it [the importation of opium] shall be made a positive requisition, or any article of any proposed Commercial Treaty . . . you must accede to it . . . in which case the sale of our opium in Bengal must be left to take its chance in an open market, or to find a consumption in the dispersed & circuitous traffic of the Eastern Seas'.
10. Ingram, *Two Views of British India*, p. 237
11. Source: East India Company consolidated returns. The Company's annual returns and accounts were published with the Proceedings of the House of Commons.
12. Greenberg, op. cit., points out (pp. 67–9) that the effect of the squeezes was exacerbated by the fact that legal trading was increasingly unprofitable, and that losses were almost always incurred by the Hong merchants when payment was taken

in kind, by way of imports, rather than in cash.

13. Colonel Sweny Toone, quoted in Philips, op. cit., p. 190

14. Morse, *Chronicles*, vol. ii, p. 158

15. Amherst was known to be something of a bumbler, 'as good a barren choice as could be made' according to Canning at a later date (Philips, op. cit., p. 239).

16. For biographies of Chinese see A.W. Hummel, *Eminent Chinese of the Chi'ing Period*, and for Juan Yuan see Weh Peh-t'i in JHKBRAS, vol. 21, 1981

17. C.T. Downing, *The Fan-Qui in China*, pp. 54–5

18. See Blue Book 1840, vol. vii, Select Committee of the House of Commons 1829 minute 442

19. W.S. Davidson took over the opium business of George Baring in 1807, selling out to Thomas Dent in 1824. He was regarded as the spokesman of the older generation of 'private English' as opposed to the 'next and more agressive generation' (Greenberg, op. cit., p. 71). The Dents were originally modest 'statesmen' – yeomen farmers – of Westmorland. Lancelot (born 1799) and Wilkinson (1801) were sons of William Dent of Trainlands, Crosby Ravensworth, and brothers of Thomas. They were succeeded in Hong Kong by their nephew John, whose notoriously lavish expenditure contrasted with Lancelot's more careful approach. Wilkinson did not enjoy the same high reputation as his elder brother. One of their ships' officers wrote: 'WD is trying to assume the power of Lancelot Dent but it is quite useless. The jackdaw with the peacock's feathers did not pass current among the birds' (T.C.

Leslie, quoted Jones, *Chief Officer in China 1840–53*, p. 88).

20. For the Canton and Hong Kong press see F.H. King, ed., *Research Guide to China Coast Newspapers*. It is an indication of the wide interest in Canton that of the print run of the *Chinese Repository* – one thousand – two hundred copies were sold locally, 154 in the USA, the balance going mainly to India and Britain.

21. This is, of course, Longfellow's 'Excelsior':

A youth who bore through
  snow and ice
A banner with a strange device:
  'Excelsior'.

22. *Chinese Repository*, vol. iv, p. 429

23. Morse, *Chronicles*, vol. iv, 23 November 1829

24. For the Baynes episode see Morse, *Chronicles*, vol. iv; Hunter, op. cit., pp. 120–1; Downing, op. cit., p. 135

25. See *Saturday Magazine*, June 1838. Hing-tai's fine contributed to his bankruptcy in 1837, which inspired another episode in the Matheson–Dent feud: see p. 146

26. Lord W.C. Bentinck, *Correspondence*, pp. 513–14

27. *Chinese Repository*, vol. i, pp. 142–3

28. Prominent Europeans were given nicknames by the Chinese: Jardine won his by remaining imperturbable after being hit on the head during a scuffle; Gutzlaff was known as 'Windy Bowels'

29. Downing, op. cit., p. 135

30. William Jardine, Private Letter Book (WJPLB), Jardine Matheson Archives, Cambridge. Jardine's bold hand contrasts with his partner's more sophisticated style.

31. e.g. Collis, *Foreign Mud*, p. 79

32. The account of Matheson's early career is taken from J.W.E. Cheong,

Mandarins and Merchants, Chapter II. This is the only detailed review of the earliest days of Jardine Matheson based upon the firm's archives.

33. James Matheson, Private Letter Book (JMPLB), 25 August 1831
34. In Rhodes House, uncatalogued
35. Morse, *Chronicles*, vol. iv, p. 356
36. See Cheong, op. cit., pp. 81–4 and Select Committee House of Commons 1829 minute no. 87
37. JMPLB, 11 March 1832
38. For Parry's escapade see ibid., 30 May 1839. For the condemnation of Grant see Blue Book 1840, vol. xxx, 'Correspondence Relating to China' (CRC)
39. Morse, *Chronicles*, vol. iv, p. 333
40. JMPLB, 31 January 1831 and see Blue Book 1833, vol. xxv 'Papers relating to the ship *Amherst*'
41. *Asiatic Journal*, vol. xii, p. 212
42. *Quarterly Review*, vol. l, p. 431
43. J. Crawford, *China Monopoly Examined*
44. For the debate in the East India House, an instructive example of contemporary views, see *Asiatic Journal*, vol. xi, Annex
45. J. Slater, *Notices on the British Trade to the Port of Canton*, p. 8
46. Blue Book 1833, vol. xxv, 12 February 1833
47. WJPLB, 29 February 1832
48. ibid., 16 March 1832

CHAPTER 3

1. JMPLB, 16 June 1833. For the brawl and the demon see Morse, *Chronicles*, vol. iv, p. 268
2. For all extracts from official British documents in this chapter see Blue Book 1840, vol. xxxvi, CRC
3. *Asiatic Journal*, 1833 Annex;

Hansard, Commons, 26 March 1833, Lords, 5 October 1833
4. CRC 25 January 1834. When the Orders in Council were published J.G. Ravenshaw, a director of the Company, wrote to Bentinck forecasting 'a pretty confusion' (Bentinck, op. cit., pp. 1155–6)
5. See, e.g. Bell, *Dictionary and Digest of the Law of Scotland*
6. Downing, op. cit, vol. iii, p. 92
7. It was not the first time Napier had suggested himself for a post. In two of his few previous contributions to the Lords (30 November and 10 December 1830) Napier suggested that he should be appointed to a committee to superintend the abolition of slavery; the proposal was not well-received.
8. Hardinge, *Letters*, p. 171; *Palmerston —Sulivan Letters*, p. 141
9. Blue Book 1840, Minutes of Select Committee. nos. 385–420
10. Although an illuminating justification of the founder of Hong Kong appears in Henry Taylor's *Autobiography*, the only biography of Charles Elliot is Clagette Blake's. Elliot's correspondence and that of his wife, Clara, with her sister, Lady Hislop, in the Minto Collection of the National Library of Scotland, Accs. 5534, 7287, has been made excellent use of by Susan Hoe in *The Private Life of Old Hong Kong*, but neglected by other historians. Although Elliot made Hong Kong possible, he was not an empire-builder like Raffles at Singapore, but a conscientious naval officer almost accidentally placed in a situation of great complexity, in which he exercised remarkable initiative.
11. *Dictionary of National Biography* (DNB)

12. Hugh Elliot was given his first diplomatic posting at the age of twenty-one. Over the next twenty years he contrived to insult Frederick the Great, fight a duel with a German nobleman, stop a war between Denmark and Sweden, and engage in a secret mission to revolutionary Paris.

13. Elliot Correspondence

14. *Asiatic Journal*, 1837, p. 4

15. WJPLB, 10 June 1834

16. Hsin-pao Chang, *Commissioner Lin and the Opium War*, p. 53 – the best book on the confrontation, but does not use Elliot sources

17. For a review of the Chinese reactions see Morse, *Int. Rel.*, vol. i, pp. 123–36. British comments from CRC under appropriate dates.

18. Robert Morrison, *Memoirs*, vol. ii, p. 524

19. C.C.F. Greville, *Memoirs*

20. ibid., 8 February 1835

21. See Spence, *The Search for Modern China*, pp. 162–3. Professor Spence also suggests that the officials and generals – such as Lu K'un – who had distinguished themselves in Sinkiang were then posted to the south-east coast, in order that the same policies might be pursued there.

22. See Chang, op. cit., pp. 81–4 for the 'Forward' party – Jardine Matheson, Innes, etc. and the 'Moderates' – Dent, Whiteman and Brightman

23. Elliot Correspondence

24. CRC

25. ibid.

26. See n.22 above

27. CRC, 21 February 1837

28. JMPLB, to Captain Rees

29. WJPLB

30. JMPLB

31. Jardine Matheson Day Book, Canton, 13 August 1837

32. Hansard, Commons, 7 June 1840

33. Quoted in the *Friend of China*, 28 April 1842. The first issue appeared on 17 March 1842, and the often controversial but always lively publication survived until 1859.

34. *Chinese Repository*, 1842, pp. 275–89

35. Bai Shouyi, *Outline History of China*, p. 131

36. Jian Bozan et al, *A Concise History of China*, p. 86

37. Philips, op. cit., pp. 167, 178

38. Hibbert, *The Dragon Wakes*, p. 110, echoing Chang (see n.41, below)

39. Fairbank, *The Great Chinese Revolution*, pp. 92ff.

40. Hsü, *The Rise of Modern China*, p. 246

41. Chang, op. cit., p. 15

42. ibid., p. 92. Part IV is the best short account of the Chinese debate on the opium trade. Lin's proposal is reproduced in full in Kuo, *A Critical Study of the First Anglo—Chinese War* – an excellent source – Doc. 6.

43. Bingham, *Narrative*, pp. 403ff., and *Canton Press*, 20 July 1839. According to Matheson (JMPLB, 1 May 1839), Lin had a vocabulary of foreign words and used to astonish listeners by dropping the odd English or Portuguese expression into his conversation. For Lin see also G. Chen, *Lin Tse-hsü*

44. Teng and Fairbank, op. cit., p. 25

45. Jardine Matheson Day Book, Canton

46. WJPLB, 16 December 1838

47. ibid.

48. JMPLB, 3 May 1839: Dent had been reluctant to arrange insurance cover

49. Morse, *Int. Rel.*, vol. i, p. 216

50. JMPLB, 24 March 1839
51. CRC, Select Committee Minutes, 7 May 1840
52. Nye, *The Rationale of the Chinese Question*, p. 37
53. JMPLB, 24 March 1839
54. ibid., 25 March 1839
55. ibid., 3 May 1839
56. Queen Victoria, *Letters*, vol. i, p. 156, 8 May 1839
57. Published in CRC
58. H.T. Easton, *History of a Banking House*, p. 29
59. Cranbrook, *Diary*, p. 588
60. *Chinese Repository*, vol. viii, pp. 854, 327, quoted Chang, op. cit., p. 181
61. Lin to Emperor, 6 October 1839, quoted Chang, op. cit., p. 185
62. JMPLB, 24 August 1839
63. The sailors were from Jardine Matheson and Dent ships. Elliot paid the compensation himself, and was refunded readily by Jardine's but not by Dent's, whose captain, Airey of the *Mangalore*, refused to pay. Matheson wrote indignantly on 2 August 1839: 'My dear Captain Elliot, there is not a member of our community who would not blush at the very idea of your being left to pay the piper out of your private purse': except, of course, those deplorable Dents.
64. A. Waley, *The Opium War through Chinese Eyes*, p. 64. This account, from Chinese sources, is an entertaining corrective to the British versions.
65. J.A. Whitbeck, *Historical Vision*, p. 129
66. Some analogies exist today. It is, for example, against the laws of Saudi Arabia to allow the import and sale of whisky, which in the United Kingdom is freely on sale. Some people in Britain consider alcohol deplorable, but this is not a generally held opinion, and many more people think Saudi justice barbaric. The Saudi authorities would doubtless, unlike the Chinese, take vigorous action, but the British government could not prevent some enterprising salesman setting up a depot convenient for, but outside the jurisdiction of, Saudi Arabia and selling as much Scotch as he could persuade the inhabitants to buy. It is even possible that many people would wish him well, but whether the Foreign Office would want to discourage such activities depends on how anxious it was to keep on the right side of the Saudi Arabian government. So it was in the nineteenth century. Opium was freely admitted into Britain and freely on sale: certain sections of the population disapproved, but this objection was by no means general; and Chinese justice was considered barbaric. The Chinese authorities showed only intermittent and feeble opposition to the traffic; the best solution, it was thought, would surely be that China should drop its unreasonable ban and allow the importation and sale of opium.
67. Quoted in Morley, *The Life of Gladstone*, vol. ii, p. 225. There was, to be sure, an element that objected to the opium trade on moral grounds: but the Tory opposition, while ready to take advantage of these sentiments (which, on the whole they did not share, but Gladstone had a problem of addiction in his family), were out, first and last, to lever the Whigs from power.

CHAPTER 4

Admiral William Parker's papers (still largely untapped) in the National

Maritime Museum, Greenwich, indicate the difficulties of working with Pottinger. Parker, who had been one of Nelson's frigate captains, was a disciplinarian with a great capacity for detail: 'No officer of Parker's day made so deep an impression on the navy, by reason, not of extraordinary talent, but of exceptional fixity of purpose' (DNB). It was to be expected that he would find Pottinger's high-handed and violent methods unpalatable, but even Gough, the most aggressive – in a military sense – of commanders (and like Pottinger, very 'Irish'), thought the Plenipotentiary went too far.

Not all the relevant documents on Hong Kong are to be found in the First Historical Archives in Beijing, since some were removed to Taiwan in 1949. But the practice of making copies of all zouzhe memorials, together with the Imperial comments thereon, has ensured that a rich and informative collection remains, preserved under modern conditions. The exchange between Ch'i-ing and the Emperor, translated here by Charles Aylmer, Head of the Chinese Section of the Cambridge University Library, indicates how it was the preservation of revenue, and not the relatively minor point of allowing the British to take Hong Kong, that preoccupied Tao-kuang.

1. Chang, op. cit., p. 212
2. JMPLB, 13 January 1841.
   Matheson had mixed feelings about Elliot; he understood the Superintendent's aversion to needless slaughter, and applauded his honesty, but was frequently exasperated by what seemed his indecisivess.
3. CRC. Jardine to Palmerston, 'A Paper of Hints', 14 December 1839
4. Vol. ii, no. 8, p. 369
5. Foreign Office (FO) 17/4, 27

December 1833; and see Captain Maxwell's log, quoted Sayer, *Hong Kong: Birth, Adolescence and Coming of Age*, p. 28. The account is of the East Lamma Channel; the Amherst embassy did not approach Victoria Harbour.
6. FO 17/36, 17 November 1839
7. Hansard, Lords, 7 May 1841
8. Queen Victoria, *Letters*, vol. i, 1 April 1841. The Princess Royal was the Queen's first child, later Empress of Germany and mother of Kaiser Wilhelm II.
9. The text is printed in Morse, *Int. Rel.*, vol. i, Appendix G
10. Elliot Correspondence, R1 (56) 83
11. ibid.
12. Fay's *The Opium War 1840–42* gives the best account of the fighting. Gough was a difficult man to stop. He had similar problems with Henry Hardinge during the first Sikh war, perhaps the hardest-fought campaign of the nineteenth century.
13. Even Professor Wakeman has been affected by the Chinese view of San-yuan-li, stating (*The Fall of Imperial China*, p. 137) that 'English' troops had been attacked. It was precisely because they were Indian that they were especially commended by Wellington himself (House of Lords, 14 February 1843).
14. Emily Eden, *Letters*, 1 August 1841. Emily was one of her cousin Charles's sternest critics.
15. Elliot Correspondence, 24 August 1841
16. ibid., 20 October 1841
17. Greville, op. cit., 19 November 1841
18. All from Elliot Correspondence
19. See e.g. Houston's letters of 7 May and 15 June 1843, in the Houston Collection, University of Texas.

20. Abbé Huc, *A Journey through Tartary and Thibet*, vol. ii, p. 285
21. Parker Papers, National Maritime Museum, Greenwich
22. Queen Victoria, *Letters*, vol. i, p. 265
23. Bentinck, op. cit., pp. 1209–10
24. Emily Eden, op. cit., to Lady Buckingham, 8 October 1841
25. Moneypenny and Buckle, *The Life of Disraeli*
26. FO 17/56, 13 April 1842
27. Parker Papers
28. First Historical Archives, Beijing
29. Ouchterlony, *The Chinese War*, p. 232
30. Fairbank, *Trade and Diplomacy*, p. 92
31. Kuo, op. cit., p. 163
32. H. Knollys, *The Life of General Sir Hope Grant*, vol. i, p. 36. Grant, an amiable man and effective soldier, owed his staff appointment to his skill with the 'cello, since Lord Saltoun, his commander, was putting together an ensemble.
33. *Canton Register*, 1 September 1842
34. A Chinese view of the negotiations is given in the diary of Chang Hsi (trans. S.Y. Teng). Chang writes of himself in the third person: 'When the barbarian chieftains . . . poured a cup of foreign wine and presented it to him, he drank it in one gulp without leaving a drop. As lucid and straightforward as a heap of pebbles falling down, he had not the slightest sense of suspicion or fear. The barbarians respected his frankness and especially esteemed his great capacity for drinking.'
35. Knollys, op. cit., p. 34. The 'naval observer's' impressions are recorded in the *Nautical Magazine*, vol. xii, p. 748, 1843.
36. S. Lane-Poole, *Sir Harry Parkes in China*, pp. 28, 33
37. E.H. Cree, *Journals*, p. 113. Cree's journals, edited by Michael Levien, and illustrated with Cree's own sketches, give an incomparable impression of early Hong Kong.
38. Queen Victoria, *Letters*, vol. i, p. 441, 23 November 1842
39. *Punch*, vol. iii, p. 238
40. The 'most-favoured nation' concept is viewed by Marxists as a capitalist plot. It was meant as a method of ensuring 'free trade' but became an excuse to extract concessions from China: it is now of great importance to China that she remains a 'most-favoured nation'.
41. CRC, Pottinger to Aberdeen, 29 August 1842
42. J.B. Urmston, 'Chusan and Hong Kong'
43. Wang Tseng-Tsai, *Tradition and Change in China's Management of Foreign Affairs*
44. Hansard, Lords, 11 February 1843
45. FO 705/54, 11 December 1841
46. For a discussion of the treaty ports system see Fairbank, *Trade and Diplomacy*
47. First Historical Archives, Beijing, trans. Charles Aylmer
48. ibid.
49. ibid., Emperor to Ch'i-ing, in Ch'i-ing to Emperor, 13 December 1843
50. ibid., Ch'i-ing to Emperor, 31 December 1843
51. Little Frederick Keying became in due course Inspector Sir Frederick Pottinger of the New South Wales Police, and features in the history of that state and in Rolf Boldrewood's novel *Robbery Under Arms*
52. Fairbank, *Trade and Diplomacy*, p. 114

CHAPTER 5

1. Johnston mss. in Hong Kong Public Records Office

2. See CRC. As Governor-General, Lord Auckland was directly in charge of the British expedition to China, but both he and Elliot were also very conscious of their family connexion.

3. *Hong Kong Gazette* (the official journal of the colony, later published with the *Friend of China*), 7 June 1841; and see Eitel, *Europe in China*, pp. 172ff

4. Johnston mss.

5. *Canton Register*, 25 April 1836

6. *Friend of China*, 4 May 1844

7. For a description of the China Coast journals see F.H.H. King (ed.), *A Research Guide to China Coast Newspapers 1822–1911*

8. FO 17/56, 3 May 1842

9. FO 705/49, November 1841

10. Ashburton was a convenient pocket borough for the China trade. Even after the Reform Act it had only 262 electors (in 1846), who could be purchased reasonably inexpensively. Jardine was succeeded by James Matheson, and James by his nephew Alexander.

11. A. Reid, in M. Keswick (ed.), *The Thistle and the Jade: 150 Years of Jardine Matheson*, a handsome account of the Princely Hong.

12. C. Sedgewick, *Letters from Abroad*

13. Thackeray, *Mr Brown's Letters*

14. FO 705/42 and /49; and see Cheong, op. cit., on the Hong debts

15. FO 705/54, from a private letter to Morrison, 3 March 1842

16. ibid., 22 February 1843

17. *Canton Register*, 18 December 1842

18. Hoe, *The Private Life of Old Hong Kong*, pp. 58–9

19. G. Pottinger, *The War of the Axe*, p. 273

20. G.M. Theal, *History of South Africa*, p. 51

21. In *Chinese Review*, vol. i, pp. 163–76

22. See W.K. Chan, *The Making of Hong Kong Society*, pp. 75ff. This book, which draws upon the Jardine Matheson and the Tung Wah Hospital records, as well as official sources, is essential to an understanding of the evolution of Chinese leadership in Hong Kong.

23. J.F. Davis, in CO 129/23, quoted in Chan, op. cit., p. 72

24. Spence, *The Search for Modern China*, pp. 197–8

25. As with many Chinese who have become prominent in Hong Kong, Ho-Ch'i's name is rendered in many ways. The most usual alternative is Ho Kai.

CHAPTER 6

1. *Friend of China*, 5 August 1846

2. Alexander Matheson Hong Kong Private Letter Book (AMPLB), 19 June 1844

3. ibid., 27 March 1844

4. Lord Fitzmaurice, *Life of the Second Earl Granville*, vol. i, p. 148

5. FO 17/85, 28 April 1844

6. Martin's allegations eventually resulted in the publication of the voluminous collection, 'Papers Relating to the Colony of Hong Kong' (PRCHK), of which this is No. 1, 20/8/44. The extracts which follow on the Martin affair are from the same source under the appropriate date.

7. Chamberlain, *Lord Aberdeen*, p. 367

8. The statistics are taken from Morse, *Int. Rel.*, vol. i

9. 'Statements and Suggestions Regarding Hong Kong Addressed to the Hon. Francis Scott M.P.'

10. Legge, 'The Colony of Hong Kong', in *Chinese Review*, vol. i, 1872

11. Blue Book 1847, vol. v, Select Committee, para. 2175
12. Hoe, op. cit., p. 52
13. PRCHK No. 1
14. Blue Book 1847, vol. v, Select Committee, para. 2882
15. Notary Public, Coroner, Clerk of the Court and Interpreter at twenty-two, Registrar-General four years later, Samuel Fearon was the son of Charles and Eliza Fearon, residents of Macao since 1820.
16. CO 129/12, 24 June 1845
17. Affaires Diverses Consulaires, Quai d'Orsay. The French Département des Affaires Etrangères collection has limited information on Hong Kong, since there was no consulate in the colony for some time, but what does exist is informative and entertaining.
18. CO 129/11, 8 March 1845
19. *Friend of China*, 5 July 1845. For the activities of the Hong Kong courts see J.W. Norton-Kyshe, *History of the Laws and Courts of Hong Kong.*
20. Quoted Fairbank, *Trade and Diplomacy*, p. 245
21. CO 129/3 77, 24 August 1843
22. ibid.
23. The extracts in this paragraph are from AMPLB 27 March 1844, 6 May 1844 and 28 April 1845 respectively
24. The unpublished letters of Lieutenant Collinson (Collinson mss.) in Hong Kong Public Records Office. These letters are one of the best sources of information on early Hong Kong.
25. Conynghame, *The Opium War*, pp. 203ff
26. Collinson mss.
27. AMPLB by A. Reid in Keswick, op. cit. Jardine's Bazaar and Jardine's Crescent (which it isn't)

do exist in Wanchai, but there is still nothing named after their rivals.
28. Collinson mss., 26 January 1845
29. Eitel, op. cit., p. 222
30. W. Leslie etc., 6 December 1844. Eitel, op. cit., p. 226
31. G.B. Endacott, *The Government and People of Hong Kong 1841–1962*, pp. 75–6
32. FO 288/34
33. Fairbank, *Trade and Diplomacy*, p. 242
34. Quoted in ibid., p. 135. The Chinese original document has not (I think) been published, and I did not find a copy in the Beijing Archives: but there were good reasons for Ch'i-ing not wishing to publicize this concession. Pottinger sent a translation in his despatch of 3 November 1842, which is published in the Opium Papers 1857, and the British certainly believed (they had good reasons for wishing to believe) these encouraging sentiments: see also n.36 below.
35. Whitbeck, 'The Historical Vision of Kung Tzu-chen', pp. 205–6
36. The Hope case is discussed in Fairbank, *Trade and Diplomacy*, pp. 138–43, but see n.37
37. In the Parker Papers, which do not seem to have been consulted by Fairbank
38. Mitchell Report, 28 December 1850, PRCHK
39. First Historical Archives, Beijing
40. Fairbank, *Trade and Diplomacy*, p. 281
41. First Historical Archives, Beijing, November 1844
42. ibid., July 1844
43. ibid., reporting on Davis's visit to Liantong
44. G. Smith, *Narrative of an Exploratory Visit to Each of the Consular Cities of*

China, p. 495, and Morse, *Int. Rel.*, vol. i, p. 371

45. For a review of the Compton case see W.C. Costin, *Great Britain and China*, pp. 120–34

46. 'Pencillings on the Rock', D'Aguilar ms. in Royal Commonwealth Society

47. ibid. D'Aguilar had seen trouble coming, writing in March 1847: 'worse and worse, an Englishman cannot shew himself now without insult and even the risk of his life'.

48. Nye, op. cit. For the reaction of the British in Canton, see Eitel, op. cit., pp. 216–17

49. Norton-Kyshe, op. cit., p. 96

50. Cree, op. cit., p. 175

51. Eitel, op. cit., p. 249

52. Legge, op. cit., p. 163

CHAPTER 7

1. Select Committee of the House of Commons to Enquire into the Present State of the Commercial Relations between Great Britain and China, March 1847, Items 1940—

2. Lord Grey, *The Colonial Policy of Lord John Russell's Administration*, pp. 263–5

3. Wakeman gives an excellent précis of the period in *The Fall of Imperial China*

4. Bai Shouyi, op. cit., p. 43

5. An account of Bowring's dubious transactions in the Greek Committee is given in W. St Clair, *That Greece Might Still be Free*, Chapter 22. For Bowring's personal history see his *Autobiographical Recollections*.

6. George Villiers, Earl of Clarendon, *Life and Letters*, p. 80

7. See P.C. Coates, *China Consuls*, for an interesting account of the early selection policy – and much else

8. Quoted in Fairbank, *Trade and Diplomacy*, p. 380

9. Affaires Diverses Consulaires, Quai d'Orsay

10. The relevant documents, from which the following extracts are taken, are published in the Parliamentary Papers as Correspondence Relative to Entrance into Canton (CREC)

11. See J.Y. Wong, *Anglo–Chinese Relations 1839–60*, for a thorough discussion

12. Grey, op. cit., p. 265

13. 'Statements to Francis Scott M.P.', op. cit.

14. From Lane-Poole, op. cit., vol. i p. 194

15. Alcock's report to Bowring of 15 June 1854, in FO 97/100, quoted in Fairbank, *Trade and Diplomacy*, Part 5, p. 456, n.K

16. Fairbank, *Trade and Diplomacy*, p. 462

17. ibid., p. 277

18. The correspondence between Parkes and Bowring, from which these extracts are taken, is – understandably, since it gives far too much away of the collusion between the two – not reproduced in CREC, but is found, still unpublished, in the Parkes Papers, Cambridge University Library

19. Malmesbury, *Memoirs*, vol. ii, 6 February 1857

20. Queen Victoria, *Letters*, vol. iii, p. 231

21. Fitzmaurice, op. cit., vol. ii, p. 245

22. Lord Blachford, *Letters*, p. 162

23. Queen Victoria, *Letters*, vol. iii, p. 300, 4 September 1858

24. J. Morley, *The Life of Gladstone*, vol. i, p. 565

25. See Hibbert, *The Dragon Wakes*, Chapter 14, passim

26. Lane-Poole, op. cit., vol. i, p. 284

27. FO 17/287, 31 March 1858

CHAPTER 8

1. *Punch*, vol. xv, 1848, p. 125
2. The Anstey saga is published, in tedious detail, in Papers Relating to Abuses in the Colony of Hong Kong (Blue Book), from which subsequent extracts are taken
3. But Julian Pauncefote, Hong Kong Attorney-General and later a distinguished diplomat, took a more pragmatic view of Caldwell: 'Some think that he is an ill-used, but respectable man, while others do not share this opinion, but so long as he comes and says "I can get the murderers" we can give no other answer than "we are glad if you can".' Mowat, *The Life of Lord Pauncefote*, p. 17
4. Hibbert, op. cit., Chapter 13, n.1
5. Eitel, op. cit., pp. 310ff
6. ibid., p. 311
7. Quoted Hao, *The Commercial Revolution in Nineteenth-Century China*, p. 200
8. *Hong Kong Gazette*, no. 35, 14 February 1857
9. ibid., no. 95, 25 June 1857
10. Ellis, *Hong Kong to Manila*, pp. 5-7
11. Printed in Correspondence Relative to the Reconstruction of the Legislative Council of Hong Kong (Blue Book), 1855, 1856
12. For an account of the conditions in the trade see W.K. Chan, op. cit., Chapter 5
13. See Keppel's own, unapologetic, version of the story in his autobiography. For missions see G. Smith, *Narrative*; C.T. Smith, *Chinese Christians*; Endacott and She, *Diocese of Victoria*
14. Hoe, op. cit., p. 121
15. CO 129/22, 16 January 1847, quoted in Sweeting, *Education in Hong Kong*, p. 177. This useful commentary includes a wide range of primary material.
16. Even bishops could not be replaced without scandal in Hong Kong. Bishop Alford, who succeeded Smith, was appointed as a result of a political 'job'.
17. For the Keenan episodes see US State Department Archives, Hong Kong Consular Papers
18. 'A Memorandum on the Kowloon Peninsula', 6 June 1859
19. J. Bodell, *A Soldier's View of Empire*, p. 64
20. Knollys, op. cit., vol. ii, p. 49
21. See Parkes Papers, Cambridge University Library, and Lane-Poole, op. cit.
22. Professor Wakeman (*The Fall of Imperial China*, pp. 157-8) minimizes the gravity of the offence when he writes that the negotiators were 'imprisoned'. Torturing and killing the correspondent of *The Times*, to say nothing of the others, was as shocking then as it would have been today: and the reprisals today might well be more brutal.
23. Knollys, op. cit., vol. ii, pp. 164ff.
24. Eitel, op. cit., p. 362
25. To Sir George Arthur, 6 April 1844. Quoted J.W. Cell, *British Colonial Administration in the Mid Nineteenth Century*, p. 15
26. See G.O. Trevelyan, *Macaulay's Life and Letters*, Chapter 17
27. For cadets see H.J. Lethbridge, *Hong Kong: Stability and Change*, Chapter 2
28. Professor Frank King's monumental four-volume *History of the Hongkong and Shanghai Banking Corporation* relieves the researcher of a great deal of trouble, and is here much drawn upon
29. Kendall letters, National Maritime Museum, P.& O. collection

30. For the National Bank of India see G. Tyson, *One Hundred Years of Banking in Asia and Africa*
31. John Dent's extravagance – he spent £10,000 on a racehorse for the Hong Kong track – may have been in part to blame. Young Alfred Dent, a clerk in the Shanghai office at the time, was determined to resurrect the family Hong, which he did by creating the firm which became the British National Borneo Company.
32. B. Lubbock, *The Opium Clippers*, pp. 371–3
33. King, op. cit., vol. i, p. 160
34. 33 Henry VIII c.9
35. These and subsequent extracts are from Correspondence Relating to Gambling Houses in Hong Kong, 1868 (Blue Book)
36. ibid. Memorandum of the Attorney General, 29 November 1870
37. Eitel, op. cit., pp. 440ff.
38. See monograph, 'Seals and Flags', in Hong Kong Collection, Hong Kong University.
39. A. Smith, *To China and Back*, pp. 23–35
40. A. Weatherhead mss., Hong Kong Collection, Hong Kong University
41. Bodell, op. cit., pp. 61–71. Bodell enjoyed himself more than

Lieutenant Orlando Bridgeman of the 98th, who tetchily recorded: 'I am going this afternoon to see the thoughtless part of the garrison play cricket. I call them thoughtless because I conceive it to be perfect madness . . . to play cricket under a vertical sun . . . I have no desire to leave my body in this horrid place.' Robin Maclachlan in JHKBRAS, vol. 14, 1974.
42. For Masonic activities see Haffner, *The Craft in the East*
43. Many histories of Hong Kong have ignored or glossed over the emergence of Chinese organizations within the colony. After the publication of Dr Elizabeth Sinn's monograph on the Tung Wah Hospital, 'Power and Charity' in 1989, and Dr W.K. Chan's *The Making of Hong Kong Society* in 1991, an entirely fresh look must be taken at the development of such extra-governmental bodies, which are likely to be of importance in the future.
44. Y.P. Hao, *The Comprador in Nineteenth-Century China*, pp. 201–6. For the importance of compradore finance in the early industrialization of China see the following table, compiled from Hao:

Source of Capital of Chinese Enterprises (percentage)

Enterprise	Government	Merchants	Gentry/ official	Compradores	Total ($,000)
Chinese Steamship Co	6.94	25.79	12.77	54.5	1,958
Coal Mines				62.7	3,645
Cotton mills	20.98	21.9	33.89	23.23	18,047
Machinery	17.36	27.36	27.64	27.68	2,887

CHAPTER 9

1. Papers Relating to Restrictions upon Chinese at Hong Kong (PRRC), Ayres, 8 July 1880
2. Eitel, op. cit., p. 514
3. Pope Hennessy is the subject of a biography by his grandson, James Pope-Hennessy, *Verandah*, from

which the information is derived. The suggestion is made that Hennessy was the prototype for Trollope's hero Phineas Finn.

4. Rhodes House: Pope Hennessy Collection (Box 8). The exasperated officials' comments run to many pages. It was not only the Governor's personal acerbities but such other disadvantages as his inability to distinguish between Capital and Revenue income that infuriated the permanent civil servants.

5. Kimberley journal: John Wodehouse, Earl Kimberley, succeeded as Colonial Secretary when the Liberals came to power in 1880. But by then Hennessy had exhausted whatever sympathy he might have had from his own party.

6. PRRC, Hennessy, 19 April 1880 and 29 April 1881, and Price, 15 August 1881

7. PRRC, 20 August 1881

8. PRRC, Chadwick para 248, 18 July 1882

9. Blue Book 1866, vol. l, 25 July 1865

10. Papers Relating to the Flogging of Prisoners in Hong Kong: Hennessy to Hicks Beach 28 September 1878, Blue Book 1878–9, vol. li

11. ibid., 13 May 1879

12. Labouchere to Bowring, 29 July 1856; see also Chapter 8

13. See Endacott, *The Government and People of Hong Kong 1841–1962*, p. 95. Ng Choy is known in Chinese history as Wu Ting-fang.

14. Source: *Encyclopaedia Britannica*, 9th edition

15. For the regulation of prostitution see Papers Relating to the Contagious Diseases Ordinance, Hong Kong (PRCDO), and N. Miners, *Hong Kong Under Imperial Rule 1912–1941*, Chapter 10

16. Labouchere to Bowring, 27 August 1856, printed in PRCDO, p. 207

17. Colonial Surgeon's report for 1869 printed in China Association's submission to the Colonial Office, enclosed in Robinson to Chamberlain, 30 June 1897, PRCDO

18. J. Pope-Hennessy, *Verandah*. For the illegitimate children see p. 52, and for Hennessy in Hong Kong see Book vi.

19. Carnarvon to Hennessy, 25 January 1878, PRCDO

20. Enclosed in Admiralty to Colonial Office, 13 November 1879, PRCDO

21. Kipling, *From Sea to Sea*

22. Minute, 10 February 1863, on Shanghai British Chamber of Commerce memorial of 4 September 1862 to Lord John Russell. BT Gen Dept 114/1863

23. Coates, op. cit., p. 198

24. JM Letter Book, 30 March 1861

25. Circular No. 8, 1864, quoted Morse, *Int. Rel.*, vol. iii, Appendix D

26. For the above, and a detailed discussion of relations between British traders and investors in China, represented by the China Association and the British authorities – relations rarely cordial, and always tinged with the suspicion of which Mallet's outburst is only one example – see N. Pelcovits' erudite and witty *Old China Hands and the Foreign Office*

27. For details of the Revenue dispute see the prolix and tedious 'Correspondence relating to the Complaints of the Mercantile Community in Hong Kong against the Action of Chinese Revenue Cruizers and the neighbourhood of the Colony', initiated by Kennedy on 10 July 1874, and the 'Further

Correspondence relating to &c.'
continued by Acting Governor
Gardiner Austin on 9 June 1875.

28. Morse, *Int. Rel.*, vol. ii, p. 382

29. Quoted in Spence, *The Search for
    Modern China*, p. 204. Wen Hse-ang
    (Wenxiang) was Prince Kung's
    right-hand man at the Tsungli
    Yamen until his death in 1876. For
    the British government's views see
    Blue Book 1870, China, No. 11, 7

30. Blue Book, 'Correspondence re
    Cruizers' and 'Further
    Correspondence' for this and
    subsequent extracts

31. Coates, op. cit., p. 198

32. Hart, *Letters: The I.G. in Peking*,
    letters 577 (11 July 1886) and 595
    (8 April 1887)

33. Morse, *Int. Rel.*, vol. ii, p. 389

34. Pope-Hennessy, op. cit., Book vi

35. Mosby, in his *Memoirs*, gives an
    account of Consular existence,
    which he seems to have enjoyed

36. I. Bird, *The Golden Chersonese*,
    p. 125, and letter in Rhodes House
    CH Box 8, 8 January 1879, in which
    she says the Bishop's wife is 'perhaps
    a little like Mrs Proudie'. Some
    more unpublished comments of
    Isabella Bird are found in Susanna
    Hoe's excellent book, pp. 125–6

37. Mrs G. Cumming, *Wanderings*. For
    the theatre see C.T. Smith, in
    JHKBRAS, vol. 22, 1982

38. Lady Brassey, *A Voyage in the
    'Sunbeam'*, p. 373

39. J. Thomson, *The Straits of Malacca*,
    pp. 203–8

40. Quoted Pope-Hennessy, op. cit.,
    p. 193

41. R. Hart, *Journals: Entering China's
    Service*, p. 15; for racial
    discrimination see Chan, op. cit.,
    pp. 117ff

42. Kipling, *From Sea to Sea*

CHAPTER 10

1. So protracted a political career is
   almost unparalleled. In American
   terms, this might be compared to
   Lincoln having started his career in
   a Jefferson administration.

2. G. St Aubyn, *The Royal George: The
   Life of the Duke of Cambridge*, p. 144

3. Source: *Encyclopaedia Britannica*, 9th
   edition

4. Moneypenny and Buckle, op. cit.,
   vol. v, pp. 194–6

5. In the Suez crisis of 1956, which
   forced Anthony Eden from office

6. Colomb's brother, Admiral Philip,
   was equally as tireless an advocate of
   Imperial defence

7. V. Duruy, *Histoire du France*, vol. v,
   p. 899

8. Mallet de Bassilan, Quai d' Orsai

9. Fairbank, *Trade and Diplomacy*,
   pp. 197–8 and notes for French
   sources

10. First Historical Archives, Beijing,
    394 for Ch'i-ing correspondence
    with Cécille

11. Mallet de Bassilan

12. Quoted in C. Dilke, *Problems of
    Greater Britain*, vol. ii, pp. 536–7

13. For the '*mission civilisatrice*' and
    French colonial policy see S.M.
    Persell, *The French Colonial Lobby
    1889–1938*

14. There is an excellent account of the
    strike by Dr Sinn in JHKBRAS,
    vol. 22, 1982

15. In the nineteenth century, honours
    were given much less lavishly than
    after the inauguration of the Order
    of the British Empire in 1916. The
    order of St Michael and St George
    was originally introduced in 1818
    to reward natives of Malta and the
    Ionian Islands, and extended in 1868
    to include any colonial or foreign
    service member. The grades were:

Companion (CMG, vulg. 'Call me God'); Knight Commander (KCMG, 'Kindly Call me God'); and Knight Grand Cross (GCMG, 'God calls me God').

16. Irving Carlyle, in DNB

17. See Bowen's autobiography and letters, *Thirty Years of Colonial Government*

18. B.L. Blakely, *The Colonial Office*, p. 118

19. W. Des Voeux, *My Colonial Service* (an unintentionally revealing autobiography), vol. i, p. 263

20. The *Telegraph* was biased, it should be said, its founder and editor, Robert Fraser-Smith, being strongly anti-Bowen, and given to violence of language; he went to prison for libel more than once.

21. *A Soldier's Correspondence*, from which the account of the Sargent story is taken

22. For Bowen's account of his time in office – a rose-tinted one – see *Thirty Years of Colonial Government*. Des Voeux (vol. ii, pp. 275–6) recounts his 'total disagreement' with his predecessor's constitutional reforms.

23. See Choa, *The Life and Times of Sir Kai Ho Kai*. Like Presidents Kennedy and de Gaulle, Ho's name is perpetuated in that of an airport – Kai-tak, Hong Kong's international airport.

24. Cumming, op. cit., p. 25

25. Chan, op. cit., p. 118

26. 1889 Hong Kong Annual Report

27. ibid.

28. 1894 Hong Kong Annual Report, from which the following extracts are also taken: for a more balanced appreciation see E. Sinn, 'Power and Charity'

29. Quoted Chan, op. cit., p. 88

30. Coates, op. cit., p. 204

31. See D.E.E. Evans in JHKBRAS, vol. 10, 1970

32. See *Life of Sir Patrick Manson*, Chapter 7

33. Hong Kong Hansard, 23 January 1930

34. For a discussion of the constitutional issues see Miners, *Hong Kong Under Imperial Rule 1912–1941*

CHAPTER 11

1. Jonathan Spence, in his excellent work *The Search for Modern China* (p. 231), starts the relevant section: 'During 1898 and 1899, as part of their general wave of imperialist expansion, the foreign powers intensified their pressures and outrages on China. The Germans used the pretext of an attack on their missionaries to occupy the Shandong port city of Quingdao . . . The British took over the harbour at Weihaiwei . . . and forced the Qing to yield a ninety-nine-year lease on a large area of fertile farmland on the Kowloon peninsula north of Hong Kong, which the British henceforth called "The New Territories".' Fertile farmland there was, but it represented a very small proportion of the rugged and inhospitable countryside.

2. The article was published in the *China Mail* on 9 February 1887, and immediately prompted a critical review by Dr Ho Ch'i. Tseng Chi-tse was the son of Tseng Kuo-fan, the mentor of both Li Hung-chang and Yung Wing. Tseng followed the first Chinese representative at the Court of St James, Kwo Tsing-tao, appointed in 1876.

3. Hart letters, Nos. 947, 942

4. Quoted Teng and Fairbank, op. cit., p. 35
5. Khlemet, 28 November 1896, quoted P. Joseph, *Foreign Diplomacy in China 1894–1900*, p. 195
6. Morse, *Int. Rel.*, vol. iii, p. 108
7. Pelcovits, op. cit., pp. 250–6
8. Joseph, op. cit., pp. 234–54; and see Lipson, *Standing Guard*, p. 43, for more recent opinion: '[British] policies [in China] were rigorous, but they were carefully limited. They proved harder to sustain as France and Germany moved abroad more aggressively ... Even so, departures from earlier practice were generally reluctant, and when possible, temporary.' It is worth recording that Hicks Beach's 'Monroe Doctrine' preceded John Hay's 'Open Door' by nearly two years.
9. Joseph, op. cit., pp. 286, 306
10. For dispatches see Parliamentary Papers Session 1898: for a comprehensive study see Wesley-Smith, *Unequal Treaty 1898–1997*, which is relied upon for much of this account of the occupation of the New Territories.
11. According to Joseph Walton, M.P., in *China and the Present Crisis*
12. Much work has been done on the history and culture of the New Territories, especially since in recent years it has beeen one of the few parts of China where traditional forms of society have been allowed to continue. Perhaps the best introductions are P.Y.L. Ng and H.D.R. Baker, *New Peace County* and J. Hayes, *The Hong Kong Region 1850–1911*, both with good bibliographies.
13. E.J.M. Rhoads, *China's Republican Revolution*, p. 13
14. See JHKBRAS, vols. 13, 14

15. For a description of Hong Kong antiquities see S. Bard, *In Search of the Past: A Guide to the Antiquities of Hong Kong* and S. Rodwell, *Historic Hong Kong*
16. H. Blake, *China* (1909). Although basically a picture book, Blake's text is interesting as revealing his personal opinions.
17. For Lockhart see Airlie, *The Thistle and the Bamboo*, and Lethbridge, *Stability and Change*, Chapter 6
18. This and subsequent extracts from 'Report on the New Territory at Hong Kong', November 1900, cd. 403
19. H.D.R. Baker, *A Chinese Lineage Village*, pp. 12ff
20. C.T. Wong in Chiu and So, *A Geography of Hong Kong*, pp. 161, 164
21. Hart letters, Nos. 736, 843 (19 June 1896), 1039 (18 October 1890)
22. The Fu-jen wen-se's motto was *Ducit Amor Patriae*, which gives a flavour of the movement. For the revolutionaries in Hong Kong see Dr Kit-ching Chan Lau, *China, Britain and Hong Kong 1895–1945*, from which the subsequent extracts are taken. For events in Canton see Spence, *The China Helpers*.
23. Chan Lau, op. cit., p. 36
24. Francis Henry May. References to him are to be found under both his Christian names: in his personal correspondence he is 'Frank'.
25. For Nathan see A.P. Haydon, *Sir Matthew Nathan*; Nathan is one of the few Hong Kong Governors to have a biography, although his Hong Kong period of office formed only a modest part of his career; see also Hyam, *Empire and Sexuality*
26. Sir Frederick Guggisberg, the only other Jew to be a colonial Governor,

was also a Sapper, but was fifty when appointed to the Gold Coast

27. Quoted Spence, *The Search for Modern China*, p. 215. For the character of Blair see Morison, *Oxford History of the United States*, vol. iii, p. 44.
28. Morrison, *Letters* (8 September 1906, to V. Chirol)

CHAPTER 12

1. Dame Marjorie Perham's authoritative biography of Lugard remains the standard work; but see also Hyam, *Empire and Sexuality*. The Lugard papers in Rhodes House have been well researched by Dr Chan Lau.
2. Hoe, op. cit., p. 209
3. Perham, *Lugard*, vol. ii, p. 242
4. Letters to Morrison, 6 June 1908: Morrison, *Letters*
5. Perham, op. cit., vol. ii, p. 329
6. ibid., p. 335
7. See Chan Lau, op. cit., Chapters 1 and 2, and A. Ng in JHKBRAS, vol. 21, 1981
8. Chan Lau, op. cit., p. 103
9. Perham, op. cit., vol. i, p. 361
10. Chan Lau, op. cit., p. 105
11. For the University see B. Mellor, *The University of Hong Kong*, and Misc. Documents, 'The Conception and Foundation of the University of Hong Kong' (CFUHK), in Hung On-to Memorial Collection
12. Perham, op. cit., vol. ii, p. 351
13. For this and subsequent extracts see CFUHK
14. Mellor, op. cit., p 73
15. H. Parlett, memoir, in Eliot, *Japanese Buddhism*
16. Eliot, *The East African Protectorate* (1905)
17. For the story of this typical Hong Kong squabble, see Severn mss., Rhodes House Ind. Oc. S176
18. Report of the University Committee, 1937
19. The Helena May Institute is described by Susanna Hoe as a 'successful women's club in charming and historical premise. Sally Howell reveals that it is also known as the 'Virgin's Retreat'
20. Morrison, *Correspondence*
21. N. Miners, *Hong Kong Under Imperial Rule*, p. 75
22. Chan Lau, op. cit., p. 117
23. ibid., p. 131
24. ibid., p. 134
25. G.R. Sayer, *Hong Kong 1862–1919*, pp. 120–1
26. Stella Benson, quoted in Hoe, op. cit., p. 184
27. Sir Harry Luke in DNB entry; see also Severn mss., Rhodes House
28. Perham, op. cit., vol. ii, p. 368
29. Chan Lau, op. cit., p. 154
30. ibid., p. 158
31. For the Merchant Corps affair see King, op. cit., vol. iii, pp. 156–7 and Chan Lau, pp. 159–68
32. The best account of the strikes and boycott is given in W.K. Chan, op. cit., Chapter 5. For the Communists in Canton see J. Spence, *The China Helpers*
33. Quoted Sweeting, op. cit., p. 393
34. Severn mss., Rhodes House

CHAPTER 13

1. Letter to G.E. Morrison, 8 May 1903 (Morrison Letters)
2. Severn mss., Rhodes House
3. Coates, op. cit., p. 456
4. CO 129/499, 4 February 1927
5. ibid., 21 February 1927. The 'On Chat Lai' tribe are unknown and presumably fictitious, and the

adjective qualifying 'warlords' is illegible.

6. L. Amery, *Life*, vol. ii, p. 305
7. R. Pelissier, *The Awakening of China 1793–1949*, p. 282
8. Chan Lau, op. cit., pp. 218–19
9. Severn mss., Rhodes House
10. Needless to say, a very different interpretation of events is provided by Communist writers. Jian Bozan et al, in *A Concise History of China*, claim that 'erroneous' policies took the place of the 'valuable opinions of Stalin and Maozedong'.
11. C.T. Smith, *Chinese Christians*, pp. 173ff
12. Haffner, *The Craft in the East*, p. 73
13. Memo of objections to Sanitary Board, 2 December 1886, quoted in Choa, *The Life and Times of Sir Kai Ho Kai*, p. 105, and Perham, op. cit., vol. ii, p. 315
14. H.J. Lethbridge, in I.C. Jarvie and J. Agassi, *Hong Kong: A Society in Transition*, p. 95; see Grantham, *Via Ports*, p. 110 for view of Man-Kam Lo
15. See J.S. Smith, *Matilda*, p. 89 and W.K. Chan, op. cit., p. 120
16. Chan, op. cit., p. 119
17. At the time of writing (1992), all ex-officio members of the Executive Council – Governor, Chief Secretary, Financial Secretary, Attorney General and Commander, British Forces – are British
18. Miners, op. cit., p. 85. Man-Kam Lo was making the point that Sinification of the Civil Service could go faster.
19. H. Norman, *The Peoples and Politics of the Far East*, Chapter 1
20. Chan, op. cit., pp. 135–6
21. Stella Benson's unpublished diaries (add. mss. 6762–6802 in the Cambridge Univerity Library) are a rich source of material, used to much effect by Susanna Hoe
22. Severn mss., Rhodes House
23. See eg. Dod's *Peerage, Baronetcy and Knightage &c.*, and see J.W. Ferris, Rhodes House mss. Brit. Emp. S.281: 'The government published annually a "blue book" (universally known as the "Studbook") . . . it was invaluable to hostesses because of course a non-gazetted officer could not move in higher circles.'
24. A. Caldecott, *Fires Burn Blue*, p. 181; J.W. Ferris adds of the Government House Visitors' Book: 'You could not sign it if you were divorced – or rather if any one knew you were divorced.' The use of Christian and surname was also rigidly prescribed.
25. Grantham, op. cit., p. 13: and in a radio interview (Rhodes House mss. Brit. Emp. S.288), Grantham described his pre-war seniors as 'on a plane by themselves . . . we almost had to walk out backwards in front of them'.
26. King, op. cit., vol. iii, p. 286
27. Private information
28. Grantham, op. cit., p. 104
29. Quoted Sweeting, op. cit., p. 395
30. C. Barnett, *The Collapse of British Power*, p. 272
31. M. Gilbert, *Winston Churchill*, vol. v, pp. 75ff
32. 5 January 1925, Cabinet Documents (CAB) 2.5. Quoted M. Beloff, *Imperial Sunset*, vol. ii
33. Japanese liberals had taken America and Britain as models; the double betrayal gravely damaged their cause and did much to ensure the militarists' subsequent success.
34. W.H. Auden, *Journey to a War*, pp. 237–8
35. FN Sir Samuel Wilson P US, 20 December 1926. Quoted Miners, op. cit., p. 291.

36. Letter to Nathan, 31 December 1929. Quoted Chan Lau, op. cit., p. 253.
37. Miners, op. cit., p. 197. For a good description of the prostitution control system see Miners, Chapter 10; Dick Hughes, (*Hong Kong: Borrowed Place, Borrowed Time*, p. 76) found the same 'Blue card' system working effectively in the 1970s. In *Yellow Slave Trade* (published in 1968), Sean O'Callaghan described Hong Kong as 'the centre of the traffic in women and children in the Far East'.
38. Miners, op. cit., p. 202
39. ibid., p. 204
40. See Hong Kong Contagious Diseases Commission Report, 1879 and Report on Child Adoption, 18 July 1886
41. Hong Kong: Papers relative to the *Mui-Tsai* question, Cmd 5363
42. No. 20 in above
43. An entertaining fictitious account of the League's activities in such matters is given in A.G. Macdonell's *England, Their England*
44. For the 1916 petition see Endacott, *The Government and People of Hong Kong*, Chapter 7
45. Quoted Miners, op. cit., p. 141
46. ibid., p. 139
47. ibid., p. 149
48. CO 129, quoted Sweeting, op. cit., p. 404
49. ibid.

CHAPTER 14

1. For an analysis of the British pre-war psyche see Barnett, *The Audit of War*, Chapter 1
2. To Lord Halifax, 11 November 1938, Documents on British Foreign Policy III, vii, p. 233
3. A. Cadogan, *Diaries*, p. 310 4.vi.40

4. Quoted Chan Lau, op. cit., p. 289. Craigie's efforts to avoid war are only now becoming clear as new material is uncovered. Sir Robert was convinced that most of the Japanese Cabinet, and Admiral Yamamoto, were opposed to war with the USA, and would have accepted a negotiated settlement. The subject has been explored in Henry Clausen's *Pearl Harbor: Final Judgement*, and James Rusbridger and Eric Nave's *Betrayal at Pearl Harbor*.
5. Churchill, *The Second World War*, vol. iii, p. 551
6. ibid., p. 157
7. Admiralty (ADM) 116/4271 81 1940
8. Cabinet (CAB) 80/51
9. The best published account of the Japanese attack and occupation is Endacott and Birch, *Hong Kong Eclipse*. See p. 327, n.16, quoting B.A. Lee. A clear narrative of the Indian forces' role is found in Bhargava and Sastri, *Official History of the Indian Armed Forces in the Second World War*.
10. This and the following signals concerning the fighting are to be found in Cabinet History Series, PRO
11. C-in-C Far East to War Office, 11 December 1941
12. Endacott and Birch, op. cit., Appendix 6, quoting post-war US report
13. Churchill, op. cit., vol. iii, p. 562
14. ibid., p. 563
15. Potts, 'War Diary', ms. in Hong Kong Collection, HKU. H. Boletho, 'Hong Kong Defence Force' ms. in Rhodes House Ind. Oc. c.108
16. Quoted in E. Ride, *The British Army Aid Group: Hong Kong Resistance*, p. 3
17. Li Shu-fan, *Hong Kong Surgeon*;

J. Stericker in Birch and Cole, *Captive Years*

18. Gimson, Unclass. WM/194, Rhodes House

19. H.J. Lethbridge, *Hard Graft in Hong Kong*, p. 47

20. Endacott and Birch, Appendix 5, citing Gimson Diary, Rhodes House, Ind. Oc. Mss. 222. Holding the views he did, it must have been annoying for Gimson to find the taipans more trusted than the officials.

21. See J. Gittins, *Eastern Windows, Western Skies*, and W.K. Chan, op. cit., pp. 118ff.

22. For Hongkong and Shanghai Bank staff see King, op. cit., vol. iii, Chapter 12

23. Selwyn-Clarke, *Footprints in the Sands of Time*

24. For the extraordinary story of the British Army Aid Group see E. Ride, op. cit.

25. Quoted Endacott and Birch, pp. 98ff

26. Li Shu-fan, op. cit.

27. 10 January 1943. Lethbridge in Jarvie and Agassi, op. cit., p. 112

28. B.W. Tuchman, *Stilwell and the American Experience in China 1911–1945*, p. 300

29. C. Thorne, *Allies of a Kind*, p. 25

30. For Roosevelt's views see Woodward, *British Foreign Policy in the Second World War*, vol. v, p. 533, C. Hull, *Memoirs*, vol. ii, p. 1596, and Tuchman, op. cit. The Vichy French had given strategic control of Indo-China to the Japanese in July 1941.

31. See Hull, op. cit., p. 1599 and Woodward, op. cit., Chapters 59 and 60

32. Amery, op. cit., vol. ii, p. 955

33. CO 825/35/55 104/1942

34. MacDougall's account is in Rhodes House, Ind. Oc. 300, 22 December 1942

35. Tuchman, op. cit., p. 518

36. Woodward, op. cit., p. 519

37. Thorne, op. cit., p. 640

38. See Thorne, op. cit., p. 573, and Hurley to Roosevelt, 2 December 1943

39. Gilbert, op. cit., vol. v, p. 1183

40. H.S. Truman, *Memoirs*, p. 106

41. ibid., pp. 380, 383

42. Gimson Diary, Endacott and Birch, op. cit.

43. Private information from Lieutenant Commander Hardy

44. J. Gibson, 'Sweet Waters', *Blackwood's Magazine*, January 1946

45. Hill, 'The Fall of Hong Kong', Rhodes House, Ind. Oc. S73

46. For MacDougall's part in Hong Kong see F.S.V. Donnison, *British Military Administration in the Far East 1943–46*, pp. 203ff, and S. Tsang, *Democracy Shelved*

47. Lethbridge, in Jarvie and Agassi, op. cit., p. 127

48. For a detailed discussion of the Young Plan see Tsang, op. cit., essential to the understanding of post-war attempts to design some system of representative government; and see Donnison, op. cit., p. 138

49. For opinions of Grantham, see Tsang, op. cit., pp.viii and 186ff., and D. Wilson, *Hong Kong! Hong Kong!*

50. Grantham, op. cit., p. 110

51. In Hong Kong, the term 'Portuguese' is also used to describe Chinese with Portuguese names

52. Foreign Relations of the United States, 1947, vol. vii, 4 March 1947; 1948, vol. vii, 29 January 1948

53. ibid., 1947, vol. vii: Hong Kong is described as 'the best refuge for politically dissident elements . . . a

refuge for Chinese capital ... the only point in South China where there is any freedom of publication'

54. C(52) 165

55. See Grantham, op. cit., p. 112 and Grantham radio interview with D. Crozier, 2 August 1968, Rhodes House, Br. Emp. 288

CHAPTER 15

1. J.K. Galbraith, *A Life in Our Times*, p. 258; Tuchman, op. cit., pp. 671ff; and see Miles, *The Odyssey of the American Right.* The State Department men did have an unduly benign image of the Chinese Communist Party, which they saw as 'seeking orderly democratic growth towards socialism, as in England', a view hardly warranted by the circumstances.

2. CAB 128/16, 29 August 1949, quoted Tsang, op. cit., p. 105.

3. 1991 Hong Kong Annual Review, p. 9.

4. Grantham, op. cit., p. 115, and D.M. Paton, *The Life and Times of Bishop Ronald Hall of Hong Kong*, p. 188

5. Radio interview, Rhodes House, op. cit. Grantham told an American audience that the US Consular staff in Hong Kong was more numerous than that in any other city – not excluding London (H.F. Armstrong Papers, Princeton).

6. T. Dewey, *Journey to the Far Pacific*, pp. 147–59. Since Ho Chi-Minh had, in 1931, obtained refuge in Hong Kong and successfully fought off a French extradition order, Dewey had even more reason to be annoyed with British ideas of freedom under the law. Another American, Gene Gleason, was more impressed: 'How do 15,000 British

run this place – it is evident from the most perfunctory glance around the streets that the British do run Hong Kong; autocratically, efficiently, firmly, sometimes unimaginatively, never with any pretence of popular rule, but always with strict justice.' But, he added sadly, 'if only they were a little more lovable'. (Gleason, *Hong Kong*)

7. See Grantham, op. cit., pp. 162–3; also W.M. Leary, 'Aircraft and Anti-Communists', in *China Quarterly*, No. 52, December 1972

8. Foreign Relations of the United States, 1952–54, vol. xiv, p. 70 n.2

9. Radio interview, Rhodes House, op. cit.

10. CAB 13 March 1956 22 (11) and CM 41 (55), Item 3

11. Galbraith, *A Life in Our Times*, p. 419

12. J. Colville, *The Fringes of Power*, vol. ii, pp. 350–1

13. See Gilbert, op. cit., vol. vii, pp. 1015–16

14. ibid., p. 1224

15. This information is from an interesting article in the *South China Morning Post*, 12 April 1992, by Mark Roberti; and see A. Horne, *Macmillan*, vol. ii, p. 56

16. For Shawcross see B. Porter, *Britain and the Rise of Communist China*, pp. 120ff: for smugglers see Grantham, op. cit., p. 166 and Rhodes House radio interview

17. D. Wilson, op. cit.

18. Quoted in King, op. cit., vol. iv, p. 352

19. Lord Chandos (Oliver Lyttelton), *Memoirs*, p. 375

20. Grantham, op. cit., p. 159

21. 1991 Hong Kong Annual Review, p. 9

22. Grantham, op. cit., p. 158

23. Grantham, 'Report on the Riots in Kowloon', 23 December 1956
24. Thornton, who died in 1992, was a Labour Member of the old school, who had started work at the age of thirteen and was indefatigable in his efforts to improve workers' conditions
25. Dr Bray only told this story a quarter of a century later, during the debate in the House of Commons on 24 January 1988
26. See A. Rabushka, *Value for Money*, p. 55
27. A. Rabushka, *Hong Kong: A Study in Economic Freedom*, p. 42
28. 1971 Hong Kong Annual Review, p. 2
29. Rabushka, *Hong Kong: A Study in Economic Freedom*, p. 83
30. Rabushka, *Value for Money*, pp. 88–91
31. H.J. Lethbridge, *Hard Graft in Hong Kong*, p. 57
32. E. Elliott, *Crusade for Justice*, from which the following account and extracts are taken
33. N. Cameron, *An Illustrated History of Hong Kong*, p. 310
34. D. Bonavia, *Hong Kong: The Final Settlement*
35. ibid.
36. H. Wilson, *The Labour Government 1964–70*, p. 989
37. Quoted e.g. K. Rafferty, *City on the Rocks*, p. 382
38. See F. Patrikeeff, *Mouldering Pearl*, p. 127
39. D. Wilson, op. cit., p. 197
40. HMSO Britain 1976, pp. 11, 12

CHAPTER 16

Two good, indignant books by journalists resident in Hong Kong for much of the time are Kevin Rafferty's *City on the Rocks* and Felix Patrikeeff's *Mouldering Pearl. Hong Kong! Hong Kong!*, by Dick Wilson, is written with the inside knowledge of the founding editor of the *Far Eastern Economic Review*. Lau Siu-kai's *Society and Politics in Hong Kong* is a valuable sociological analysis of the evolution of Hong Kong attitudes. The two volumes of 'The Other Hong Kong Report' are a valuable corrective to the sometimes bland official view.

1. Keith Hopkins, in *Hong Kong: The Industrial Colony*, p. 277
2. Patrikeeff, op. cit., pp. 66–7
3. 1971 Hong Kong Annual Review
4. J. Agassi, in Jarvie and Agassi, op. cit., p. 248.
5. K. Rafferty, op. cit., p. 156
6. 1992 Hong Kong Annual Review
7. The Other Hong Kong Report 1990 (TOHKR)
8. 1991 Hong Kong Annual Review
9. In October 1992 the new Governor, Chris Patten, outlined a programme of social reforms which should go a long way towards meeting criticisms of inadequate public spending. It was admitted that the colony had its 'darker side'. The proposals to lighten this were extensive, including a commitment to spend $7,300 million within five years on a 'sewerage strategy programme', improvements in social security payments, increased spending on health, education and research, and training. These, Mr Patten suggested, could well be afforded by an economy in which by 1997 the per capita GDP would have reached US$30,500 – comparable with that of Italy and the Netherlands in 1992. Tactfully, he did not mention that in 1992 the GDP of the United Kingdom was already lower than that of the two countries he had chosen as illustrations. He had, after all, been a member of the Cabinet at

the time the UK slipped into that undistinguished position.

10. 1991 Royal Hong Kong Jockey Club Annual Report

11. The situation described in this section was that pertaining at the beginning of 1992. In October of that year the new Governor, Chris Patten, radically changed the whole balance of power on the Councils (see pp. 536–40).

12. Secretary for Home Affairs, August 1976, quoted Miners, *The Government and Politics of Hong Kong*, p. 206n.; and see Lau Siu-kai, op. cit., pp. 145–8

13. R. Adley, *All Change Hong Kong*, p. 29

14. J. Morris, *Hong Kong*, p. 243

15. See Lethbridge, *Hard Graft in Hong Kong*, the standard work on the Independent Commission Against Corruption

16. Cameron, op. cit., p. 319

17. Rafferty, op. cit., p. 313

18. ibid., pp. 332–3

19. D. Wilson, op. cit., p. 185

20. King, op. cit. vol. iv, p. 708

21. Rafferty, op. cit., p. 297

22. D. Wilson, op. cit., p. 182

23. Chan Lau, op. cit., p. 216

24. From both banks' annual reports, and Hongkong Bank Final Offer. The exchange rate is calculated at £1:HK$14

CHAPTER 17

1. For Rogers see Patrikeeff, op. cit., p. 117; for Wesley-Smith see Chen, pp. 203ff. Chen prints a valuable collection of documentary evidence.

2. TOHKR 1989, p.xxiv

3. Chen, op. cit., Introduction and Chapter 1

4. Patrikeeff, op. cit., p. 115

5. ibid., pp. 1123, 1136; and Hansard, Commons, 21 January 1985

6. Chen, op. cit., p. 85

7. Gilbert, op. cit., vol. vii, p. 1016

8. Patrikeeff, op. cit., p. 128

9. Published as a British White Paper on the same date, from which the text is taken

10. Hansard, Lords, 10 December 1984

11. Report of Assessment Office, Chapter 3

12. Rafferty, op. cit., pp. 441–2

13. Patrikeeff, op. cit., pp. 135–6

14. Denis Healey enjoyed pressing this point (Hansard, Commons, 21 January 1985), but did not succeed in getting an explanation

15. Miners, op. cit., p. 119

16. As Anthony Royle, Lord Fanshawe had been the Minister responsible for Hong Kong from 1970 to 1974

17. Hansard, Commons, 20 January 1988

18. TOHKR 1989, p. 3

19. Quoted Rafferty, op. cit., pp. 446–7; and see H. Sohmen, *Legislative Interludes*

20. '[Hong Kong is] one of certain residual responsibilities. Some loose ends which a previous historical epoch had left hanging untidily from the threadbare Imperial knapsack.' Lord Carrington, *Reflecting on Things Past*, p. 220

21. 1989 Hong Kong Annual Review, pp. 60–1

22. Chen, op. cit., p. 30. The students' opposition to the treaty settlements was not based on much knowledge. Chen records (p. 16) that in an entrance examination for the Chinese University in 1983 less than 5 per cent could even give the names and dates of the treaties.

23. 'Bloody Sunday', 30 January 1972,

when thirteen unarmed
demonstrators were shot dead
24. Patrikeeff, op. cit., p. 227
25. Rafferty, op. cit., p. 483
26. *Independent*, 25 January 1990
27. ibid., 8 June 1989
28. TOHKR 1989, p. 55
29. TOHKR 1990, p. 33
30. *South China Morning Post*, 17 April 1990
31. *Independent*, 26 September 1990
32. 1991 Hong Kong Annual Review
33. ibid., p. 58: and the number of Hong

Kong residents visiting China
continued to increase
34. ibid., p. 375
35. TOHKR 1989, p.xxxii
36. Lee Ming-kwan in TOHKR 1990, Chapter 5
37. So described in *Dateline*, the Hong Kong government's London newspaper
38. 1992 Hong Kong Annual Review: caption to photograph pp. 28–9
39. ibid., p. 17

40.   *Exports, Imports and Re-exports*

	(Percentages shown underneath)					
	1986	1987	1988	1989	1990	1991
Imports						
China	81,633 (29.6)	117,357 (31.1)	155,634 (31.2)	196,676 (34.9)	236,134 (36.8)	293,356 (37.7)
Japan	56,398 (20.1)	71,905 (19.0)	93,008 (18.6)	93,202 (16.6)	103,632 (16.1)	127,402 (16.4)
Taiwan	23,977 (8.1)	33,377 (8.8)	44,357 (8.9)	51,587 (9.2)	58,084 (9.0)	74,591 (9.6)
UK	9,347 (3.5)	11,713 (3.1)	12,292 (2.6)	12,965 (2.3)	14,118 (2.2)	16,545 (2.1)
Exports						
USA	64,219 (41.7)	72,817 (37.3)	72,884 (33.5)	72,162 (32.2)	66,370 (29.4)	62,870 (27.2)
China	18,022 (11.7)	27,871 (14.3)	38,043 (17.5)	43,272 (19.3)	47,470 (21.0)	54,404 (23.5)
Germany	11,003 (7.1)	14,855 (7.6)	16,157 (7.4)	15,757 (7.0)	17,991 (8.0)	19,318 (8.4)
UK	9,918 (6.4)	12,908 (6.6)	15,524 (7.1)	14,638 (6.5)	13,496 (6.0)	13,706 (5.9)

Re-exports

USA	22,362 (18.2)	32,454 (17.8)	49,483 (18.0)	72,033 (20.8)	87,752 (21.2)	110,802 (20.7)
China	40,894 (33.4)	60,170 (32.9)	94,895 (34.5)	103,492 (29.9)	110,908 (26.8)	153,318 (28.7)
Germany	2,688 (2.2)	5,533 (3.0)	6,420 (2.3)	13,502 (3.9)	23,406 (5.7)	32,073 (6.0)
UK	2,489 (2.0)	4,271 (2.3)	4,459 (1.6)	8,918 (2.6)	12,107 (2.9)	14,663 (2.7)

41. Hong Kong Annual Review, p. 54

EPILOGUE

1. Mr Patten was only forty-eight in 1992. He had gone straight from Oxford to join the Conservative Research Department, becoming its Director in 1974. M.P. for Bath from 1979, he lost his seat in the 1992 election. Although not too popular with his own party's right wing, Mr Patten was highly regarded in most other quarters.

BIBLIOGRAPHY

UNPUBLISHED PRIMARY SOURCES

Public Records Office, Kew
For the period prior to Hong Kong's acceptance as a colony the relevant documents are in FO 17, concerning diplomacy, and FO 228, concerning the Superintendency of Trade; subsequently the most important source is CO 129, original correspondence. There is also much material relating to Sir Henry Pottinger in FO 705, of which the correspondence with John Morrison and Admiral Parker is particularly interesting. CAB Series are Cabinet Documents and CM Cabinet Minutes.

Cambridge University Library
1. Jardine Matheson Archives. The main sources are the Canton and Hong Kong Letter Books, copies of the partners' outgoing correspondence, and the Canton Day Book, an annotated record of each day's transactions.
2. Stella Benson, Diaries 1929–32 (add. mss. 6762–6802)
3. Sir Harry Parkes Papers (with Jardine Matheson Archives, not catalogued)

Rhodes House, Oxford
1. Sir Alexander Grantham, 'Recollections' (Interview, Brit. Emp. S288)
2. H. Boletho, 'The Hong Kong Defence Force' (Brit. Emp. S85)
3. Lugard Papers (Brit. Emp. S67)
4. D.M. MacDougall, Letters (Ind. Oc. 300)
5. J. Hill, 'The Fall of Hong Kong' (Ind. Oc. S73)
6. Nathan Papers
7. Pope Hennessy Papers (Brit. Emp. 409)
8. J.W. Ferris, 'Nothing to Declare' (Ind. Oc. S281)
9. Nan Severn, Letters (Ind. Oc. S176(2))

National Maritime Museum, Greenwich
1. Admiral Sir William Parker, Correspondence
2. F.R. Kendall, Lettters (P&O 374.792)

Royal Commonwealth Society, London
Sir G. D'Aguilar, 'Pencillings on the Rock' and letters, which include a long account of the 'buccaneering expedition'.

Département des Affaires Etrangères, Paris
Affaires Diverses Consulaires. Unclassified papers relating to British activities in Canton and Hong Kong between 1830 and 1860.

First Historical Archives of China, Beijing
Memorials relating to Hong Kong, Series 3/166 and 167, divisions 9257, 9224, 9226

Hung On-to Memorial Collection, Hong Kong University
1. Alfred Weatherhead, 'Life in Hong Kong, 1856–59'
2. The Conception and Foundation of the University of Hong Kong 1908–1913 (typescript collection)
3. E.S. Taylor, 'Hong Kong as a Factor in British Relations with China 1834–60' (M.A. Thesis, School of African and Oriental Studies, London University, 1967)
4. A.P. Potts, War Diary

Public Records Office, Hong Kong
1. A. Johnston, ms. letter 26 March 1852
2. Lt. Bernard Collinson, letters

National Archives, Washington
State Department Records, Hong Kong Consular

Princeton University Library
Hamilton Fish Armstrong Papers, S.G. Mudd Collection

PRINTED PRIMARY SOURCES

Blue Books – Parliamentary Papers: 1831 vi, 1840 vii and xxxvi, 1847 v, 1860 lxviii, 1866 l, 1878–9 li. The Irish University Press has a useful series of reprints of British Parliamentary Papers (1971).
Britain 1976, HMSO
Foreign Policy Documents USA
Hansard (House of Commons and House of Lords)
Hong Kong Hansard

PERIODICALS: CURRENT

China Quarterly
Economist
Far Eastern Economic Review
Harvard Journal of Asian Studies
Hong Kong Branch of the Royal Asiatic Society Journal (JHKBRAS)
Illustrated London News
South China Morning Post
The Times
Weekly digests issued by the New China News Agency

PERIODICALS: NON-CURRENT

Asiatic Journal
Blackwood's Magazine
Canton Press
Canton Register
China Magazine
China Mail
China Punch
Chinese Repository

Chinese Review
Friend of China
Hong Kong Daily Press
Nautical Magazine
Punch

SECONDARY SOURCES

Adams, E.D., *British Interests and Activities in Texas 1838–46* (Gloucester, Mass., 1963)

Adley, R., *All Change Hong Kong* (Poole, 1984)

Aimer, G. (ed.), *Leadership on the Chinese Coast* (London, 1988)

Airlie, S., *The Thistle and the Bamboo: The Life and Times of Sir J.S. Lockhart* (Hong Kong, 1989)

Ambekar, G.E. and Divekar, V.D., *Documents of China's Relations with South and South-East Asia* (Bombay, 1964)

American Diplomatic and Public Papers, Series 1, vol. 18

Amery, L., *Life* (London, 1953)

Andrew, K., *Hong Kong Detective* (London, 1962)

Annan, N., *Leslie Stephen* (London, 1984)

Anon ('A Resident'), 'A Letter from Hong Kong' (London, 1845)

Anon, 'Statements and Suggestions Regarding Hong Kong Addressed to the Hon. Francis Scott MP' (London, 1850)

Anon ('JFL'), 'A Few Observations on the Canton Outrage' (London, 1857)

Anon, 'Our Policy in China' (London, 1858)

Anon ('A Resident'), 'A Letter from Hong Kong' (London, 1859)

Anon, 'Jardine Matheson & Co.: An Historical Sketch' (Hong Kong, n.d.)

Anon, 'The May Upheaval in Hong Kong' (Hong Kong, 1967)

Anon, 'Sir Edward Youde: In Memoriam' (Hong Kong, 1986)

Anstey, T.C., *Crime and Government at Hong Kong* (London, 1859)

The Association for Radical East Asian Studies, *Hong Kong: Britain's Last Colonial Stronghold* (London, 1972)

Attlee, Lord, *Empire into Commonwealth* (London, 1961)

Atwell, P., *British Mandarins and Chinese Reformers* (London, 1985)

Auber, P., *China* (London, 1834)

Auden, W.H., *Journey to a War* (London, 1939)

Bai Shouyi, *Outline History of China* (Beijing, 1982)

Baker, H.D.R., *A Chinese Lineage Village* (London, 1968)

Baker, J.F., *Race* (London, 1974)

Bard, S., *In Search of the Past: A Guide to the Antiquities of Hong Kong* (Hong Kong, 1988)

Barnett, C., *The Audit of War* (London, 1968)

– *Britain and Her Army 1509–1970* (London, 1970)

– *The Collapse of British Power* (London, 1971)

Belcher, E., *A Voyage Round the World* (London, 1843)

Bell, W., *Dictionary and Digest of the Law of Scotland* (Edinburgh, 1845)

Beloff, M., *Imperial Sunset* (London, 1969, 1987)

Bentinck, Lord W.C., *Correspondence* (ed. Philips, C.H.) (Oxford, 1927)

Benton, G., *The Hong Kong Crisis* (London, 1983)

Bernard, W.D., *Narrative of the Voyage &c. of the 'Nemesis'* (London, 1844)

Berridge, V. and Edwards, G., *Opium and the People* (London, 1981)

Bhargava, K.D. and Sastri, K.N.V., *Official History of the Indian Armed Forces in the Second World War: Campaigns in South-East Asia 1941–42* (New Delhi, 1960)

Bingham, J.E., *Narrative of the Expedition to China* (London, 1843)

Birch, A., *Hong Kong: The Colony that Never Was* (Hong Kong, 1991)
- and Cole, M., *Captive Years* (Hong Kong, 1982)
-, Jao, J.C. and Sinn, E., 'Research Materials for Hong Kong Studies' (Hong Kong, 1990)
Bird, I., *The Golden Chersonese* (London, 1883)
Blachford, Lord, *Letters* (ed. Marindin, G.) (London, 1896)
Blake, C., *Charles Elliot* (London, 1960)
Blake, C.F., *Ethnic Groups and Social Change in a Chinese Market Town* (Hawaii, 1981)
Blake, H., *China* (London, 1909)
Blakeley, B.L., *The Colonial Office* (Durham, North Carolina, 1972)
Boardman, R., *Britain and the People's Republic of China 1949–74* (London, 1976)
Bodell, J., *A Soldier's View of Empire* (ed. Sinclair, K.) (London, 1989)
Bodelsen, C.A., *Studies in Mid-Victorian Imperialism* (London, 1960)
Bonavia, D., *Hong Kong: The Final Settlement* (Hong Kong, 1985)
Borg, D., *The US and the Far Eastern Crisis of 1933–35* (Cambridge, Mass., 1964)
Bourne, K., *Palmerston: The Early Years* (London, 1982)
- (ed.), *The Palmerston—Sulivan Letters*, Camden 4th Series vol 23 (London, 1979)
Bowen, G., *Thirty Years of Colonial Government* (ed. Lane-Poole, S.) (London, 1889)
Bowring, J., *Autobiographical Recollections* (London, 1877)
- and Villiers, G., *First Report on the Commercial Relations Between France and Great Britain* (London, 1834)
Boyden, S., *The Ecology of a City and its People* (Canberra, 1981)
Bozan, J. et al, *A Concise History of China* (Beijing, 1981)

Brassey, Lady, *A Voyage in the 'Sunbeam'* (London, 1878)
Braudel, F., *Capitalism and Material Life 1400–1800* (London, 1974)
Brereton, W.H., *The Truth About Opium* (London, 1882)
Brice, R., *Topographical Dictionary* (Exeter, 1757)
Bristow, E.J., *Vice and Vigilance* (Dublin, 1977)
Broomfield, F., *Scandals and Disasters of Hong Kong* (Hong Kong, 1985)
Bruce, P., *Second to None: The Story of the Hong Kong Volunteers* (Hong Kong, 1990)
Bueno de Mesquita, B., *Forecasting Political Events: The Future of Hong Kong* (New Haven, 1985)
Buhite, R.D., *Patrick Hurley and American Foreign Policy* (Ithaca, 1973)
- *Decision at Yalta* (Washington, 1986)
Bullock, A., *Ernest Bevin* (London, 1983)
Burgess, C.M., *A Problem of People* (Hong Kong, 1966)
Cadogan, A., *Diaries* (ed. Dicks, D.) (London, 1971)
Caldecott, A., *Fires Burn Blue* (London, 1948)
Cameron, N., *Barbarians and Mandarins* (New York, 1970)
- *Hong Kong: The Cultured Pearl* (Hong Kong, 1978)
- *The Milky Way: The History of Dairy Farm* (Hong Kong, 1980)
- *An Illustrated History of Hong Kong* (Hong Kong, 1991)
Cantlie, J., *Sun Yat-sen* (London, 1899)
Carey, W.H., *The Good Old Days of Honourable John Company* (Calcutta, 1907)
Carrington, Lord, *Reflecting on Things Past* (London, 1989)
Cecil, Lord, *Changing China* (London, 1911)
Cell, J.W., *British Colonial Administration in the Mid Nineteenth Century* (New Haven, 1970)

Chailley-Bert, J., *The Colonisation of Indo-China* (London, 1894)

Chamberlain, M.E., *Lord Aberdeen* (London, 1983)

Chan, W.K., *The Making of Hong Kong Society* (Oxford, 1991)

Chandos, Lord, *Memoirs* (London, 1967)

Chang, C.S. (ed.), *The Making of China* (Englewood Cliffs, 1975)

Chang, H.P., *Commissioner Lin and the Opium War* (Cambridge, Mass., 1964)

Chan Lau, K.C., *Anglo—Chinese Diplomacy 1906–1920* (Hong Kong, 1978)

– *China, Britain and Hong Kong 1895–1945* (Hong Kong, 1990)

Chen, G., *Lin Tse-hsü* (Yenching, 1934)

Ch'en, J., *State Economic Policies of the Ch'ing Government 1840–1895* (New York, 1980)

Chen, J.Y.S., *Hong Kong in Transition* (New York, 1986)

Chen, V., *Sino—Russian Relations in the Seventeenth Century* (The Hague, 1966)

Cheng, I., *Clara Ho Tung* (Hong Kong, 1986)

Cheong, J.W.E., *Mandarins and Merchants: Jardine Matheson and Co.* (London, 1978)

Chesneaux, J., *The Chinese Labor Movement 1917–27* (Stanford, 1968)

– *Secret Societies in China* (London, 1971)

Chiu, H. et al, *Symposium: Hong Kong 1997* (Baltimore, 1985)

– *The Future of Hong Kong* (New York, 1987)

Chiu, T.N., *The Port of Hong Kong* (Hong Kong, 1973)

– and So, C.L. (eds.), *A Geography of Hong Kong* (Hong Kong, 1983)

Choa, G.H., *The Life and Times of Sir Kai Ho Kai* (Hong Kong, 1981)

Chou, E., *A Man Must Choose* (London, 1963)

Ch'ü, T.T., *The Gentry* (New Jersey, 1975)

Chung, T., *China and the Brave New World* (Durham, North Carolina, 1978)

Churchill, W., *The Second World War* (6 vols, London, 1948–53)

Clark, G., *Economic Rivalries in China* (New Haven, 1932)

– *The Later Stuarts* (Oxford, 1972)

Clarke, P. and Gregory, J.S., *Western Reports on the Taiping* (London, 1982)

Clausen, H.C. and Lee, B., *Pearl Harbor: Final Judgement* (New York, 1992)

Clayton, A., *The British Empire as a Superpower* (London, 1986)

Coates, A., *Prelude to Hong Kong* (London, 1966)

– *Myself a Mandarin* (London, 1968)

– *Macao Narrative* (Hong Kong, 1978)

Coates, P.C., *China Consuls* (Hong Kong, 1988)

Cochran, S., *Big Business in China* (Cambridge, Mass., 1980)

Cole, B.D., *Gunboats and Marines* (Delaware, 1983)

Collins, C., *Public Administration in Hong Kong* (London, 1952)

Collis, M., *The Great Within* (London, 1941)

– *Foreign Mud* (London, 1946)

– *Wayfoong* (London, 1965)

Colomb, J.C.R., *Colonial Defence* (Dublin, 1897)

Colville, J., *The Fringes of Power* (2 vols, London, 1985, 1987)

Conacher, J.P., *The Aberdeen Coalition* (Cambridge, 1968)

Conynghame, A., *The Opium War* (Philadelphia, 1845)

Cooke, J.J., *New French Imperialism 1880–1910* (Newton Abbot, 1973)

Costin, W.C., *Great Britain and China* (Oxford, 1937)

Cranbrook, Lord, *Diary* (ed. Johnson, N.E.) (Oxford, 1981)

Cranmer-Byng, J.L., *Embassy to China* (London, 1962)

Crawford, J., *China Monopoly Examined* (London, 1830)

Cree, E.H., *Journals* (ed. Levien, M.) (Exeter, 1981)

Criswell, C.H. and Watson, M., *The Royal Hong Kong Police* (Hong Kong, 1982)

– *The Taipans* (Hong Kong, 1981)

Crocombe, L., *Slow Ship to Hong Kong* (London, 1952)

Cumming, Mrs G., *Wanderings in China* (London, 1888)

Curtis, W.E., *Egypt, Burma and British Malaysia* (New York, 1905)

Curzon, Lord, *Problems of the Far East* (London, 1896)

Dally, P., *Hong Kong: Time Bomb* (Cheltenham, 1984)

Davies, S., *Political Dictionary of Hong Kong* (Hong Kong, 1991)

Davis, J.F., *China During the War and Since the Peace* (London, 1852)

Davis, L., *Hong Kong and the Asylum Seekers from Vietnam* (Hong Kong, 1988)

Davis, M.C., *Constitutional Confrontation in Hong Kong* (London, 1989)

Deacon, R., *History of the Chinese Secret Service* (London, 1974)

Dean, B., *China and Great Britain: The Diplomacy of Commercial Relations* (Cambridge, Mass., 1974)

Des Voeux, W., *My Colonial Service* (London, 1903)

Dewey, T., *Journey to the Far Pacific* (New York, 1952)

Dilke C., *Problems of Greater Britain* (London, 1890)

Dod's Parliamentary Companion (London, annually)

Donnison, F.S.V., *British Military Administration in the Far East 1943–46* (London, 1956)

Dowes, J. and Shaw, Y., *Hong Kong: A Chinese and International Concern* (London, 1988)

Downing, C.T., *The Fan-Qui in China* (London, 1838)

Drage, C., *Taikoo: Butterfield and Swire* (London, 1970)

Duruy, V., *Histoire de France* (Paris, 1892)

Eames J.B., *The English in China* (London, 1909)

Easton, H.T., *History of a Banking House: Smith, Payne and Smith* (London, 1903)

Edelstein, M., *Overseas Investment in the Age of High Imperialism* (New York, 1982)

Eden, E., *Letters* (ed. Dickinson, V.) (London, 1919)

Eitel, E.J., *Europe in China* (London and Hong Kong, 1895)

Eliot, C., *The East African Protectorate* (London, 1905)

– *Japanese Buddhism* (memoir by Sir H. Parlett) (London, 1935)

Elliot, C., 'A Plan for the Formation of a Maritime Militia' (London, 1852)

Elliott, E., *Crusade for Justice* (republished as *Elsie Tu: An Autobiography*, Hong Kong, 1988)

Ellis, H.T., *Hong Kong to Manila* (London, 1859)

Endacott, G.B., *Government and People in Hong Kong 1841–1962* (Hong Kong, 1964)

– *An Eastern Entrepôt* (London, 1964)

– *A History of Hong Kong* (Oxford, 1977)

– and Birch, A., *Hong Kong Eclipse* (Hong Kong, 1978)

– and She, B.E., *The Diocese of Victoria* (Hong Kong, 1949)

Endicott, S.L., *Diplomacy and Enterprise: British Chinese Policy 1933–37* (British Columbia, 1975)

Evans, D.M.E., *Constancy of Purpose* (Hong Kong, 1987)

Evans, E.W., *The British Yoke* (London, 1949)

Fairbank, J.K., *Trade and Diplomacy on the China Coast* (Stanford, 1964)

– *The United States and China* (Cambridge, Mass., 1971)
– *The Great Chinese Revolution* (Cambridge, Mass., 1986)
–, Teng, S.Y. et al, *China's Response to the West* (Cambridge, Mass., 1954)
– (ed.), *The Chinese World Order* (Cambridge, Mass., 1968)
– (ed.), *The Missionary Enterprise in China and America* (Cambridge, Mass., 1974)
– (ed.), *Cambridge History of China*, vols 11–13 (Cambridge, 1978–86)
Farnie, D.A., *The English Cotton Industry and the World Market* (Oxford, 1979)
Farrell, B., *Queen Victoria's Little Wars* (London, 1973)
Fauré, D., *The Structure of Chinese Rural Society* (Hong Kong, 1986)
Fay, P.W., *The Opium War 1840–42* (Chapel Hill, 1975)
Ferguson, T., *Desperate Siege: The Battle of Hong Kong* (Toronto, 1980)
Fiddes, G.V., *The Dominions and Colonial Offices* (London, 1926)
Field, E., *Twilight in Hong Kong* (London, 1960)
Fieldhouse, D.K., *Economics and Empire 1830–1914* (London, 1973)
Fingarette, H., *Confucius: The Secular as Sacred* (New York, 1972)
Fitzgerald, C.P., *China: A Short Cultural History* (London, 1935)
– *The Chinese View of their Place in the World* (Oxford, 1964)
Fitzgerald, S., *China and the Overseas Chinese* (Cambridge, 1972)
Fitzmaurice, Lord, *Life of the Second Earl Granville* (London, 1905)
Fitzsimmons, R., *The Baron of Piccadilly* (London, 1967)
Fok, K.C., *Lectures in Hong Kong History* (Hong Kong, 1990)
Foster, J.W., *American Diplomacy in the Orient* (Boston, 1904)
Fox, G., *British Admirals and Chinese Pirates* (London, 1940)

Franke, W., *China and the West* (Oxford, 1967)
Fry, W.S., *The Opium Trade* (London, 1840)
Fung, E.S.K., *The Diplomacy of Imperial Retreat* (Hong Kong, 1991)
Furber, H., *John Company at Work* (Cambridge, Mass., 1948)
Galbraith, J.K., *Ambassador's Journal* (New York, 1970)
– *A Life in Our Times* (London, 1983)
Gambrell, H., *Anson Jones* (Austin, 1964)
Garner, J., *The Commonwealth Office 1925–68* (London, 1978)
Geddes, P., *In the Mouth of the Dragon* (London, 1982)
Gérard, A., *Ma Mission en Chine* (Paris, 1918)
Gerson, J.J., *Horatio Nelson Lay and Sino—British Relations 1854–64* (Harvard, 1972)
Gibson, J., 'Sweet Waters', in *Blackwood's Magazine*, January 1946
Gilbert, M., *Winston Churchill*, vols iii–viii (London, 1971–88)
Giles, H.A., *China and the Manchus* (Cambridge, 1912)
– *China and the Chinese* (New York, 1902)
– *Adversaria Sinica* (Shanghai, 1914)
Gill, G.H., *The Royal Australian Navy, 1942–45* (Canberra, 1968)
Gittins, J., *Eastern Windows, Western Skies* (Hong Kong, 1969)
Gladstone, W.E. (ed. Foot, M.R.C.), *Diaries* (Oxford, 1968)
Gleason, G., *Hong Kong* (London, 1964)
– *Tales of Hong Kong* (London, 1967)
Goldsmith, M., *The Trail of Opium* (London, 1939)
Goldsworth, D., *Colonial Issues in British Politics 1945–61* (Oxford, 1971)
Graham, G.S., *Great Britain in the Indian Ocean* (Oxford, 1967)
– *The China Station: War and Diplomacy 1830–60* (Oxford, 1978)
Grant, J., *Stella Benson* (London, 1987)

Grantham, A., 'Report on the Riots in Kowloon' (Hong Kong, 1956)

– *Via Ports* (London, 1965)

Gray, J., *Rebellions and Revolutions* (Oxford, 1990)

Greenberg, M., *British Trade and the Opening of China* (Cambridge, 1951)

Greville, C.C.F., *Memoirs (George IV and William IV)* (ed. Reeve, H.) (London, 1875)

– *Memoirs (Victoria)* (ed. Wilson, P.W.) (London, 1927)

Grey, Earl, *The Colonial Policy of Lord John Russell's Administration* (London, 1853)

Griffin, E., *Clippers and Consuls* (Ann Arbor, 1938)

Guillermaz, J., *The Chinese Communist Party in Power 1949–76* (Folkestone, 1976)

Haffner, C., *The Craft in the East* (Hong Kong, 1977)

Halpern, A.M. (ed.), *Policies Toward China* (New York, 1965)

Hao, Y.P., *The Comprador in Nineteenth-Century China* (Cambridge, Mass., 1970)

– *The Commercial Revolution in Nineteenth-Century China* (Berkeley, 1986)

Harding, A., *A Social History of English Law* (London, 1966)

Hardinge, H., *Letters 1844–47* (ed. Singh, B.S.), Camden 4th Series, vol. 32 (London, 1986)

Harland, K., *The Royal Navy in Hong Kong Since 1841* (Liskeard, 1985)

Harrison, B., *Waiting for China* (Hong Kong, 1979)

– (ed.), *The University of Hong Kong: The First Fifty Years* (Hong Kong, 1962)

Harrop, P., *Hong Kong Incident* (London, 1943)

Hart, R., *Letters: The I.G. in Peking* (ed. Fairbank, J.K. et al) (Cambridge, Mass., 1975)

– *Journals: Entering China's Service* (ed. Bruner, K.F. et al) (Cambridge, Mass., 1986)

Haydon, A.P., *Sir Matthew Nathan* (Queensland, 1976)

Hayes, J., *The Hong Kong Region 1850–1911* (Hamden, 1977)

– *The Rural Communities of Hong Kong* (Hong Kong, 1983)

Hedetoft, U., *British Colonialism and Modern Identity* (Aarlborg, 1985)

Henson, C.T., *Commissioners and Commodores: The East India Squadron and American Diplomacy in China* (Alabama, 1982)

Hertslet, E., *China Treaties* (London, 1908)

Hess, G.R., *The United States' Emergence as a South-Eastern Asian Power* (New York, 1987)

Hibbert, C., *The Dragon Wakes* (London, 1970)

Hobhouse, H., *Seeds of Change* (London, 1985)

Hodson, H.V., *Twentieth Century Empire* (London, 1948)

Hoe, S., *The Private Life of Old Hong Kong* (Hong Kong, 1991)

Hong Kong Government Information Services Annual Review 1946–1992

Hopkins, K. (ed.), *Hong Kong: The Industrial Colony* (Hong Kong, 1971)

Horne, A., *Macmillan* (London, 1988)

Hsü, I.C.Y., *The Rise of Modern China* (New York, 3rd edition 1983)

Hsüeh, C.T., *Hsuang Hsing and the Chinese Revolution* (Stamford, 1961)

Huang, R., *China: A Macro History* (Armonk, 1988)

Huc, Abbé R.E., *A Journey through Tartary and Thibet* (London, 1855)

Hughes, R., *Hong Kong: Borrowed Place, Borrowed Time* (London, 1968)

Hugill, S., *Sailortown* (London, 1967)

Hull, C., *Memoirs* (London, 1948)

Hummel, A.W. (ed.), *Eminent Chinese of the Chi'ing Period* (Washington, 1943–4)

Hunt, M.A., *The Making of a Special Relationship* (New York, 1989)

Hunt, R.S. and Randal, J.F., *New Guide to Texas* (New York, 1845)

Hunter, W.C., *The Fan-kwae at Canton* (London, 1882)

– 'Journal of Occurrences at Canton', JHKBRAS, vol. iv, pp. 64ff

– *Bits of Old China* (London, 1885)

Hurd, D., *The 'Arrow' War* (London, 1967)

Hutcheon, R., *Wharf: The First Hundred Years* (Hong Kong, 1986)

Hwang, Y.C., *Overseas Chinese and the Chinese Revolution* (Kuala Lumpur, 1976)

Hyam, R., *Elgin and Churchill at the Colonial Office 1905–8* (London, 1968)

– *Empire and Sexuality* (Manchester, 1990)

Hyde, F.E., *John Swire* (Liverpool, 1957)

Ingram, E. (ed.), *Two Views of British India* (Bath, 1970)

Ingrams, H., *Hong Kong* (HMSO, 1952)

Ireland, A., *The Far Eastern Tropics* (Hong Kong, 1900)

Iremonger, L., *Lord Aberdeen* (London, 1978)

Iriye, A., *Pacific Estrangement* (Cambridge, Mass., 1972)

– (ed.), *After Imperialism* (Cambridge, Mass., 1965)

Jao, Y.C., *Banking and Currency in Hong Kong* (London, 1974)

– *Hong Kong* (Hong Kong, 1985)

Jarvie, I.C. and Agassi, J. (eds.), *Hong Kong: A Society in Transition* (London, 1969)

Jaschok, M., *Concubines and Bondservants* (Hong Kong, 1988)

Jeffries, C., *The Colonial Police* (London, 1952)

Johnson, D. (ed.), *Popular Culture in Late Imperial China* (Berkeley, 1985)

Johnson, N.E., *The Diary of G. Gathorne-Hardy* (Oxford, 1981)

Johnston, H.J.M., *British Immigration Policy 1815–30* (Oxford, 1972)

Jones, C., *Chief Officer in China 1840–53* (Liverpool, 1955)

Jones, C., *Promoting Prosperity* (Hong Kong, 1990)

Joseph, P., *Foreign Diplomacy in China 1894–1900* (London, 1928)

Joyce, R.B. (ed.), *Australian Dictionary of Biography* (Melbourne, 1969)

Keay, J., *The Honourable Company: A History of the English East India Company* (London, 1991)

Keeton, G.W., *The Development of Extra-Territoriality in China* (London, 1928)

Kelly, I., *Hong Kong: Political and Geographic Analysis* (London, 1987)

Kent, P.H., *The Passing of the Manchus* (London, 1912)

Keppel, H., *A Sailor's Life* (London, 1899)

Keswick, M. (ed.), *The Thistle and the Jade: 150 Years of Jardine Matheson* (London, 1982)

Kiernan, F.A. and Fairbank, J.K., *Chinese Ways in Warfare* (Cambridge, Mass., 1974)

Kiernan, V.G., *British Diplomacy in China 1880–1885* (Cambridge, 1939)

– *The Lords of Human Kind* (London, 1969)

– *European Empires from Conquest to Collapse* (Leicester, 1982)

Kimball, W.F. (ed.), *Churchill and Roosevelt: The Complete Correspondence* (Princeton, 1984)

Kimberley, J. (Earl), *Journal* (London, 1958)

King, A.Y.C. and Lee, R., *Social Life and Development in Hong Kong* (Hong Kong, 1981)

King, D., *St John's Cathedral* (Hong Kong, 1987)

King, F.H.H., *The History of the Hongkong and Shanghai Banking*

Corporation (4 vols, London, 1988–91)

– (ed.), *A Research Guide to China Coast Newspapers 1822–1911* (Harvard, 1965)

– (ed.), *Eastern Banking* (London, 1983)

Kipling, R., *From Sea to Sea* (London, 1890)

Kirkup, J., *Hong Kong and Macau* (London, 1970)

Knollys, H., *The Life of General Sir Hope Grant* (London, 1894)

Kuan, H.C. and Lin, T.B., *Hong Kong: Economic, Social and Political Studies in Development* (White Plains, 1979)

Kuo, P.C., *A Critical Study of the First Anglo—Chinese War, with Documents* (Shanghai, 1935)

Kwan, A.Y.H., *Hong Kong Society* (Hong Kong, 1989)

Lamour, C. and Lamberti, M.R., *The Second Opium War* (London, 1974)

Lane, K.P., *Sovereignty and the Status Quo* (Boulder, 1990)

Lane-Poole, S., *Sir Harry Parkes in China* (London, 1901)

Lasater, M.L., *Hong Kong's Role in US—China Policy* (Washington, 1978)

Latimer, D. and Goldberg, J., *Flowers in the Blood* (New York, 1981)

Lau Siu-kai, *Society and Politics in Hong Kong* (Hong Kong, 1982)

– and Kuan, H.C., *The Ethos of the Hong Kong Chinese* (Hong Kong, 1988)

Leary, W.M., 'Aircraft and Anti-Communists', in *China Quarterly*, No. 52, December 1972

Leavermouth, C.S., *The Arrow War with China* (London, 1901)

LeCordeur, B. and Saunders, C., *The War of the Axe 1841* (Johannesburg, 1981)

Lee, B.A., *Britain and the Sino—Japanese War* (Stanford, 1973)

Lee, J.M., *Colonial Office War and Development Policy* (London, 1982)

Lee, R., *France and the Exploitation of China* (Hong Kong, 1989)

Le Fevour, E., *Western Enterprise in Late Ch'ing China* (Cambridge, Mass., 1968)

Legge, J., 'The Colony of Hong Kong', in *China Review*, vol. 1, pp. 163–76 (Hong Kong, 1872)

Lethbridge, H.J., *Hong Kong: Stability and Change* (Hong Kong, 1978)

– *Hard Graft in Hong Kong* (Hong Kong, 1985)

Leung, C.K. (ed.) et al, *Hong Kong Dilemmas* (Hong Kong, 1980)

Li Chien-hung, *History of China* (Princeton, 1950)

Lin, T.B. and C. (eds.), *Hong Kong Economic, Social and Political Studies in Development* (Folkestone, 1979)

Lindsay, H., *British Relations with China* (London, 1836)

Lindsay, O., *The Lasting Honour* (London, 1978)

– *At the Going Down of the Sun* (London, 1981)

Lipson, C., *Standing Guard* (Berkeley and London, 1985)

Li Shu-fan, *Hong Kong Surgeon* (London, 1964)

Lloyd, C., *Mr Barrow of the Admiralty* (London, 1970)

Lo, H.L., *The Role of Hong Kong in the Cultural Interchange Between East and West* (Tokyo, 1967)

Lovis, W.R., *British Strategy in the Far East* (Oxford, 1971)

Low, C.R., *History of the Indian Navy* (London, 1877)

Lubbock, P., *The Opium Clippers* (Glasgow, 1933)

MacFarquhar, R. (ed.), *Cambridge History of China*, vols 14, 15 (Cambridge, 1987, 1991)

Macgowan, J., *The Imperial History of China* (London, 1897)

Mackenzie, A., *A History and Genealogy of the Mathesons* (Edinburgh, 1880)

Mackenzie, C., *Realms of Silver* (London, 1954)

McLintock, A.H. (ed.), *Encyclopedia of New Zealand* (Wellington, 1966)

Malmesbury, Lord, *Memoirs of an Ex-Minister* (London, 1884)

Manson-Bahr, P.H. and Alcock, A., *The Life of Sir Patrick Manson* (London, 1927)

Marder, A.J., *Old Friends, New Enemies* (Oxford, 1981)

Marriner, S., *Rathbones of Liverpool 1845–73* (Liverpool, 1961)

Martin, W.A.P., *A Cycle of Cathay* (New York, 1896)

– *The Awakening of China* (London, 1907)

Matheson, J., *The Present Position and Prospects of the British Trade with China* (London, 1836)

Mellor, B., *The University of Hong Kong* (Hong Kong, 1980)

Michael, F., *The Origin of Manchu Rule in China* (Baltimore, 1942)

Michie, A., *The Englishman in China* (London, 1900)

Miles, M.W., *The Odyssey of the American Right* (Oxford, 1980)

Mills, L.A., *British Rule in Eastern Asia* (Oxford, 1942)

Miners, N., *The Government and Politics of Hong Kong* (Hong Kong, 1986)

– *Hong Kong under Imperial Rule 1912– 1941* (Hong Kong, 1987)

Moneypenny, W.F. and Buckle, G.E., *The Life of Disraeli* (London, 1910–20)

Montalto de Jesus, C.A., *Historic Macao* (Macao, 1926)

Morgan, D.J., *The Official History of Colonial Development* (London, 1982)

Morgan, H., *The Peoples and Politics of the Far East* (London, 1895)

Morison, S.E., *Oxford History of the United States* (3 vols, New York, to 1972)

Morley, J., *The Life of Gladstone* (London, 1903)

Morrell, W.P., *British Colonial Policy in the Mid-Victorian Age* (Oxford, 1969)

Morris, J., *Farewell the Trumpets* (London, 1981)

– *Hong Kong* (London, 1988)

Morrison, G.E., *An Australian in China* (London, 1895)

– *Correspondence* (ed. Lo, H.M.) (Cambridge, 1976)

Morrison, R., *Memoirs* (ed. Morrison, Mrs R.) (London, 1839)

Morse, H.B., *The Guilds of China* (London, 1909)

– *The International Relations of the Chinese Empire* (3 vols, London, 1910–18)

– *The Trade and Administration of China* (London, 1921)

– *Chronicles of the East India Company Trading to China* (3 vols, London, 1926–29)

– and McNair, H.F., *Far Eastern International Relations* (Boston, 1931)

Mosby, J.S., *Memoirs* (Indiana, 1959)

Mowat, R.B., *The Life of Lord Pauncefote* (London, 1929)

Mushkat, M., *The Making of the Hong Kong Administrative Class* (Hong Kong, 1982)

– *The Economic Future of Hong Kong* (Hong Kong, 1990)

Nelson, M., *Hong Kong, Macao and Taiwan* (London, 1984)

Ng, P.Y.L. and Baker, H.D.R., *New Peace County: A Chinese Gazetteer of the Hong Kong Region* (Hong Kong, 1983)

Ng Lun, N.H., *Interactions of East and West* (Hong Kong, 1984)

Nicol, J., *Life and Adventures* (ed. Grant, G.) (London, 1822, 1937)

Norman, F.H., *Martello Tower in China* (London, 1902)

Norman, H., *The Peoples and Politics of the Far East* (London, 1895)

Norton-Kyshe, J.W., *History of the Laws and Courts of Hong Kong* (London, 1898)

Nye, G., *The Morning of My Life in China* (Macao, 1873)
– *The Rationale of the Chinese Question* (Macao, 1887)
O'Callaghan, S., *Yellow Slave Trade* (London, 1968)
Oliphant, L., *Lord Elgin's Mission to China and Japan* (New York, 1860)
Oliphant, O., *China, A Popular History* (London, 1857)
Osgood, C., *The Chinese* (Tucson, 1975)
Ouchterlony, J., *The Chinese War* (London, 1844)
Owen, D.E., *British Opium Policy in China and India* (Yale, 1934)
Owen, E.P. and N.C, and Tinghay, F.J.F., *Public Affairs for Hong Kong* (Hong Kong, 1969)
Parkinson, C., *The Colonial Office from Within 1909–45* (London, 1947)
Pascoe, C.F., *Two Hundred Years of the Society for the Propagation of the Gospel* (London, 1900)
Paton, D.M., *The Life and Times of Bishop Ronald Hall of Hong Kong* (Gloucester, 1985)
Patrikeeff, F., *Mouldering Pearl* (London, 1989)
Pearson, J.D. (ed.), *Guide to Manuscripts Relating to the Far East* (Oxford, 1977)
Pearson, L.M., *The Colonial Background of British Foreign Policy* (London, 1930)
Pelcovits, N., *Old China Hands and the Foreign Office* (New York, 1948)
Pelissier, R., *The Awakening of China 1793–1949* (London, 1967)
Perham, M., *Lugard* (London, 1960)
Persell, S.M., *The French Colonial Lobby 1889–1938* (Stanford, 1983)
Peyrefitte, A., *The Collision of Two Civilisations: The British Expedition to China 1792–4* (London, 1993. Published in the US as *The Immobile Empire: The First Great Collision of East and West*)

Philips, C.H., *The East India Company 1784–1834* (Manchester, 1940)
Phillips, R.J., *The Kowloon—Canton Railway* (Hong Kong, 1990)
Platt, D.C.M., *Finance, Trade and Politics in British Foreign Policy 1815–1914* (Oxford, 1968)
Pope-Hennessy, J., *Verandah* (London, 1964)
– *Half Crown Colony* (London, 1969)
Porter, A.N. and Stockwell, A.J., *British Imperial Policy and Decolonization 1938–1964*, vol. i (Basingstoke, 1987)
Porter, B., *Britain and the Rise of Communist China* (London, 1967)
Pottinger, G., *The War of the Axe* (Johannesburg, 1981)
– *The Afghan Connection* (Belfast, 1983)
Preston, A. and Major, J., *Send a Gunboat!* (London, 1967)
Pullinger, J., *Crack in the Wall, Chasing the Dragon* (London, 1989)
Pusey, J.R., *China and Charles Darwin* (Cambridge, Mass., 1983)
Pu Yi, A.G. (trans. Jenner), *From Emperor to Citizen* (Oxford, 1987)
Rabushka, A., *Value for Money* (Stanford, 1976)
– *Hong Kong: A Study in Economic Freedom* (Chicago, 1979)
Rafferty, K., *City on the Rocks* (London, 1989)
Ramm, A., *The Political Correspondence of Mr Gladstone and Lord Granville* (Oxford, 1962)
Rand, C., *Hongkong: The Island Between* (New York, 1952)
'Ranger', *Up and Down the China Coast* (London, 1936)
Reston, G.W., *The Development of Extraterritoriality in China* (London, 1928)
Rhoads, E.J.M., *Nationalism and Xenophobia in Canton* (Cambridge, Mass., 1962)
– *China's Republican Revolution* (Cambridge, Mass., 1975)

Ride, E., *The British Army Aid Group: Hong Kong Resistance* (Hong Kong, 1981)

Ride, L., *Robert Morrison* (Hong Kong, 1957)

Roberts, P.M. (ed.), *Sino—American Relations Since 1900* (Hong Kong, 1991)

Rodwell, S., *Historic Hong Kong* (Hong Kong, 1991)

Rodzinski, W., *A History of China* (Oxford, 1979)

– *The Walled Kingdom* (London, 1984)

Ross S., *The Manchus* (London, 1880)

Royal Commission on Historical Manuscripts, *Private Papers of Colonial Governors* (London, 1986)

Royal Hong Kong Jockey Club, Annual Report and Accounts

Rozman, G. (ed.), *Soviet Studies of Pre-Modern China* (Ann Arbor, 1984)

Rusbridger, J. and Nave, E., *Betrayal at Pearl Harbor* (London, 1991)

Ryan, T.F., *Jesuits Under Fire* (London, 1944)

St Aubyn, G., *The Royal George: The Life of the Duke of Cambridge* (London, 1963)

St Clair, W., *That Greece Might Still be Free* (London, 1972)

Sargent, J.N., *A Soldier's Correspondence* (London, 1893)

Saw, S.H. and Cheng, S.H., *Bibliography of the Demography of Hong Kong* (Singapore, 1976)

Sayer, G.R., *Hong Kong: Birth, Adolescence and Coming of Age* (London, 1937)

– *Hong Kong 1862–1919* (Hong Kong, 1975)

Scott, G.L., *Chinese Treaties* (Dobbs Ferry, 1975)

Scott, I., *Political Change and the Crisis of Legitimacy in Hong Kong* (Honolulu, 1989)

– *Hong Kong*, World Bibliographical Series vol. 115, 1991

– and Burns, J.P., *The Hong Kong Civil Service: Personnel, Policies and Practices* (Hong Kong, 1984)

– and Burns, J.P., *The Hong Kong Civil Service and its Future* (Hong Kong, 1985)

Seaburg, C. and Paterson, S., *Merchant Prince of Boston: T.H. Perkins, 1754–1859* (Cambridge, Mass., 1971)

Seagrave, S., *The Soong Dynasty* (New York, 1985)

Sedgewick, C., *Letters from Abroad* (New York, 1841)

Selwyn-Clarke, S., *Footprints in the Sands of Time* (Hong Kong, 1975)

Sewell, W.G., *Strange Harmony*, (London, 1946)

Shai Shao, A., *Britain and China 1941–47* (Oxford, 1984)

Shao, W., *China, Britain, and Businessmen* (Oxford, 1991)

Shepherd, B., *The Hong Kong Guide* (Hong Kong, 1893)

Simpson, C., *Asia's Bright Balconies* (Sydney, 1962)

Singer, A., *The Lion and the Dragon* (London, 1992)

Singh, N.P., *The East India Company's Monopoly Industries in Bihar 1773–1833* (Bihar, 1980)

Singh, S.B., *European Agency Houses in Bengal 1783–1833* (Calcutta, 1966)

Sinn, E., 'Power and Charity: The Early History of the Tung Wah Hospital' (Hong Kong, 1989)

Sitwell, O., *Escape with Me* (London, 1935)

Slater, J., *Notices on the British Trade to the Port of Canton* (London, 1830)

Smith, A., *To China and Back* (London, 1859)

Smith, C.T., *Chinese Christians* (Oxford and Hong Kong, 1985)

Smith, G., *Narrative of an Exploratory Visit to Each of the Consular Cities of China* (London, 1847)

Smith, J.S., *Matilda* (Hong Kong, 1988)

Smith, S.R., *The Manchurian Crisis* (New York, 1945)

Smith, W.D., *The German Colonial Empire* (Chapel Hill, 1978)

So, F., *The Asian Dragons* (Cambridge, 1987)

Sohmen, H., *Legislative Interludes*, (Hong Kong, n.d.)

Soothill, W.E., *China and the West* (Oxford, 1925)

Spence, J.D., *The China Helpers* (London, 1969. Published in the US as *To Change China: Western Advisors in China 1620–1960*)

– *The Search for Modern China* (London, 1990)

– and Wills, J.E. (eds.), *From Ming to Ching* (New Haven and London, 1979)

Spencer, I.D., *The Victor and the Spoils* (Providence, 1959)

Staunton, G.T., 'Observations on our China Commerce' (London, 1850)

Steele, E.D., *Palmerston and Liberalism 1855–65* (Cambridge, 1991)

Stericker, J., *A Tear for the Dragon* (London, 1958)

Stock, E., *The History of the Church Missionary Society* (London, 1899)

Stokes, G.G., *Queen's College* (Hong Kong, 1962)

Sutton, J., *Lords of the East: The Honourable East India Company and its Ships* (London, 1981)

Swanson B., *The Eighth Voyage of the Dragon* (Annapolis, 1982)

Sweeting, A., *Education in Hong Kong* (Hong Kong, 1990)

Swisher, E., *China's Management of the American Barbarians* (New Haven, 1951)

Szczepanik, E., *The Economic Growth of Hong Kong* (London, 1958)

T'ang Leang-li, *The Foundations of Modern China* (London, 1928)

Taylor, H., *Autobiography* (London, 1874)

Temple, R.C., *Peter Mundy: Travels*, Hakluyt Society Series ii, vols xlv and xlvi

Teng, S.Y., *Chang Hsi and the Treaty of Nanking* (Chicago, 1944)

Theal, G.M., *History of South Africa* (London, 1908)

Thompson, E.M.L., *English Landed Society in the Nineteenth Century* (London, 1963)

Thomson, J., *The Straits of Malacca* (London, 1875)

Thorne, C., *Allies of a Kind* (Oxford, 1978)

– *The Far Eastern War* (London, 1985)

Tikhvinsky, S.L. (ed.), *The Modern History of China* (Moscow, 1972)

Tolley, K., *Yangtse Patrol* (Annapolis, 1971)

Trevelyan, G.O., *Macaulay's Life and Letters* (London, 1876)

Truman, H.S., *Memoirs* (New York, 1965)

Tsang, S., *Democracy Shelved* (Hong Kong, 1988)

Tsim, T.L. and Luk, B.H.K., 'The Other Hong Kong Report 1989' (Hong Kong, 1989); see also Wong, R.Y.C. and Cheng, J.Y.S.

Tuchman, B.W., *Stilwell and the American Experience in China 1911–1945* (New York, 1971)

Tung, W.L., *Wellington Koo and China's Wartime Diplomacy* (New York, 1977)

Turner, H.A., *The Last Colony, But Whose?* (Cambridge, 1980)

Turner, J.A., *Kwang Tung, or Five Years in South China* (Oxford, 1982)

Tyson, G., *One Hundred Years of Banking in Asia and Africa* (London, 1963)

Urmston, J.B., 'Chusan and Hong Kong' (London, 1847)

Victoria, Queen, *Letters* (ed. Benson, A.C. and Esher, Lord) (London, 1908)

Villiers, G., Earl of Clarendon, *Life and Letters* (ed. Maxwell, H.) (London, 1913)

Vogel, E.F., *Canton Under Communism* (Cambridge, Mass., 1969)

Wacks, R. (ed.), *The Future of the Law in Hong Kong* (Hong Kong, 1989)

Wainwright, M.D. and Matthews, N., *A Guide to Western Manuscripts and Documents in the British Isles Relating to South and South-East Asia* (London, 1965)

Wakeman, F., *The Fall of Imperial China* (New York, 1975)

– *The Great Enterprise: The Manchu Reconstruction of Imperial Order* (Berkeley, 1985)

– and Grant, C. (eds.), *Conflict and Control in Late Imperial China* (Berkeley, 1975)

Walden, J., *Excellency, Your Gap is Showing* (Hong Kong, 1983)

Waley, A., *The Opium War through Chinese Eyes: Extracts from 'Ya-p'ien Chen-cheng Tan-liao Ts'ung-k'an'* (Shanghai, 1955)

Walker, A. and Rawlinson, S.M., *The Building of Hong Kong* (Hong Kong, 1990)

Walker, P.G., *The Cabinet* (London, 1970)

Walter, R., *A Voyage Round the World* (London, 1745)

Walton, J.A.S., *China and the Present Crisis* (London, 1900)

Wang Tseng-Tsai, *Tradition and Change in China's Management of Foreign Affairs* (Taipei, 1972)

Ward, B.E., *Through Other Eyes* (Hong Kong, 1985)

Warner, J., *Fragrant Harbour* (Hong Kong, 1976)

Webster, C.K., *The Foreign Policy of Palmerston, 1830–41* (London, 1951)

Wesley-Smith, P., *Unequal Treaty 1898–1997* (Hong Kong, 1980)

– and Chen, A.H.Y., 'The Basic Law and Hong Kong's Future' (Hong Kong, 1988)

Whitbeck, J.A., 'The Historical Vision of Kung Tzu-chen' (unpublished thesis, U. Cal., Berkeley, 1980)

Wieger, L.S.J., *Textes Historiques* (Hopei, 1929)

Wight, M., *The Development of the Legislative Council* (London, 1946)

Williams, A.R., *Eastern Traders* (London, 1975)

Willmott, H.P., *Empires in the Balance* (London, 1982)

Wilson, D., *Hong Kong! Hong Kong!* (London, 1990)

Wilson, H., *The Labour Government 1964–70* (London, 1971)

Wilson, H.W., *Ironclads in Action* (London, 1895)

Wilson, K.M. (ed.), *British Foreign Secretaries and Foreign Policy* (Beckenham, 1987)

Wong, A.K., *The Kaifong Associations and the Society of Hong Kong* (Taipei, 1972)

Wong, J.Y., *Anglo—Chinese Relations 1839–60* (Oxford, 1983)

Wong, R.Y.C. and Cheng, J.Y.S., 'The Other Hong Kong Report 1990' (Hong Kong, 1990); see also Tsim, T.L. and Luk, B.H.K.

Wong, S.T., *The Margary Affair and the Chefoo Agreement* (London, 1940)

Wood, W.A., *A Brief History of Hong Kong* (Hong Kong, 1940)

Woodward, L., *British Foreign Policy in the Second World War*, vol. v (London, 1970)

Woolf, B.S. (Lady Southorn), *Under the Mosquito Curtain* (Hong Kong, 1935)

– *Chips of Old China* (Hong Kong, 1935)

Wright, S.F., *Hong Kong and the Chinese Customs* (Shanghai, 1930)

Young, G., *Beyond Lion Rock* (London, 1988)

Young, L.K., *British Policy in China 1895–1902* (Oxford, 1970)

Young, M.B., *The Rhetoric of Empire:
American China Policy 1895–1901*
(Cambridge, Mass., 1968)

Youngson, A.J., *Hong Kong Economic
Growth and Policy* (Hong Kong, 1982)

– *China and Hong Kong: The Economic
Nexus* (Hong Kong, 1983)

Zhang, Y., *China and the International
System 1918–20* (Oxford, 1991)

ILLUSTRATIONS

The French were in no doubt of the malevolent intentions of the Royal Navy in forcing opium upon the Chinese. *Bibliothèque Nationale, Paris*

The Dent schooner-rigged clipper *Eamont*.

Section of a scroll depicting Pottinger's first expedition. *Author's collection*

Chief Justice Hulme dancing a hornpipe, sketched by Edward Cree. *National Maritime Museum, Greenwich. Reproduced by permission of Brigadier G.H. Cree*

Jardine Matheson's establishment at East Point, c.1845. *Martyn Gregory*

Ch'i-ing's formal reception in Hong Kong, November 1845. *Hong Kong Government Information Service (GIS)*

Colonel Caine. *GIS*

A satirical comment on the loans raised to fund the Greek War of Independence, 1826. *Reproduced by courtesy of the Trustees of the British Museum*

Chinese merchants' lorchas.

Thomas Chisholm Anstey, M.P.

The original façade of Government House. *GIS*

The interior of Government House in the 1860s. *GIS*

The saloon of Flass, the Dent family house in Westmorland. *Author's collection*

'The Parade at Hong-Kong', 1857.

The Sepoy barracks in 1857.

Punch cartoon referring to the destruction of the Summer Palace.

Kowloon Peninsula in the 1860s.

A Chinese tea-room, c.1860. *GIS*

Opium smokers, c.1860. *Author's collection*

Sikh policemen with a Chinese culprit in the stocks. *GIS*

An Assistant Superintendent of Police gives instructions to a Sikh Constable.

A performance of *H.M.S. Pinafore*, c.1880. *GIS*

Superior British attitudes greatly annoyed the Chinese. *GIS*

The Jardine Matheson Taipan's house, c.1860. *GIS*

Dent's Fountain and Beaconsfield Arcade, c.1860. *GIS*

View of Taipingshan. *Wellcome Institute Library, London*

The meeting between Li Hung-chang and Sir Henry Blake, 18 July 1900. *GIS*

The typhoon of 1906. *GIS*

Chinese and British middle classes in Stella Benson's Hong Kong. *GIS*

INDEX

ABOUT THE AUTHOR

Frank Welsh was born in Britain and was educated at Magdalene College, Cambridge University. He has had a varied career in international business and banking, and has contributed to several British government studies. He was a visiting lecturer at the University of Tennessee from 1979 to 1985. He is the author of books on business, travel and history, including an account of building the trireme, an ancient Greek man-of-war vessel. Frank Welsh lives in England and France.